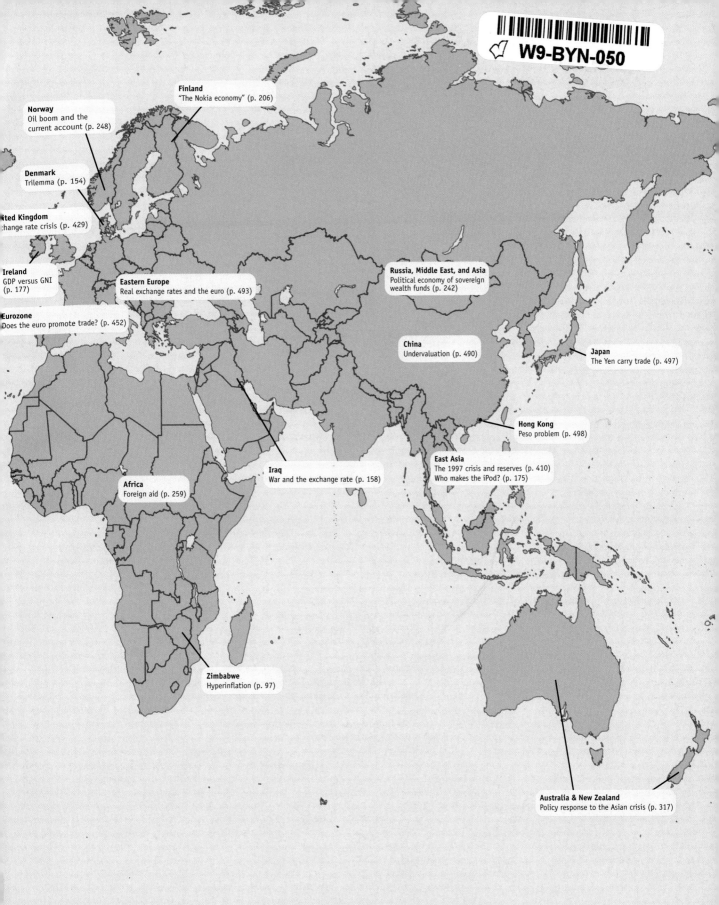

W9-BYN-050

Finland
"The Nokia economy" (p. 206)

Norway
Oil boom and the
current account (p. 248)

Denmark
Trilemma (p. 154)

ited Kingdom
change rate crisis (p. 429)

Ireland
GDP versus GNI
(p. 177)

Eastern Europe
Real exchange rates and the euro (p. 493)

Eurozone
Does the euro promote trade? (p. 452)

Russia, Middle East, and Asia
Political economy of sovereign
wealth funds (p. 242)

China
Undervaluation (p. 490)

Japan
The Yen carry trade (p. 497)

Hong Kong
Peso problem (p. 498)

Iraq
War and the exchange rate (p. 158)

East Asia
The 1997 crisis and reserves (p. 410)
Who makes the iPod? (p. 175)

Africa
Foreign aid (p. 259)

Zimbabwe
Hyperinflation (p. 97)

Australia & New Zealand
Policy response to the Asian crisis (p. 317)

To our parents

international macroeconomics

ROBERT C. FEENSTRA
University of California, Davis

ALAN M. TAYLOR
University of California, Davis

WORTH PUBLISHERS

Senior Publisher: Craig Bleyer
Acquisitions Editor: Sarah Dorger
Development Editor: Jane Tufts
Development Editor, Media and Supplements: Marie McHale
Senior Marketing Manager: Scott Guile
Associate Managing Editor: Tracey Kuehn
Project Editor: Mike Ederer, Graphic World Inc.
Art Director: Babs Reingold
Senior Designer: Kevin Kall
Photo Editor: Cecilia Varas
Photo Researcher: Elyse Rieder
Production Manager: Barbara Anne Seixas
Composition: TSI Graphics
Printing and Binding: RR Donnelley

Cover Photos: *Eye:* Indexstock/© Peter Griffith/Masterfile
Globe: © George Diebold Photography/Getty Images

ISBN-13: 978-1-4292-0691-4
ISBN-10: 1-4292-0691-8

Printed in the United States of America

First printing 2008

Worth Publishers
41 Madison Avenue
New York, NY 10010
www.worthpublishers.com

About the Authors

Robert C. Feenstra and **Alan M. Taylor** are Professors of Economics at the University of California, Davis. They each began their studies abroad: Feenstra received his B.A. in 1977 from the University of British Columbia, Canada, and Taylor received his B.A. in 1987 from King's College, Cambridge, U.K. They completed graduate school in the United States, where Feenstra earned his Ph.D. in economics from MIT in 1981 and Taylor earned his Ph.D. in economics from Harvard University in 1992. Feenstra has been teaching international trade at the undergraduate and graduate levels at UC Davis since 1986, where he holds the C. Bryan Cameron Distinguished Chair in International Economics. Taylor has been teaching international macroeconomics, growth, and economic history at UC Davis since 1999, where he directs the Center for the Evolution of the Global Economy.

Both Feenstra and Taylor are active in research and policy discussions in international economics. They are research associates of the National Bureau of Economic Research, where Feenstra directs the International Trade and Investment research program. They have both published graduate level books in international economics: *Advanced International Trade* (Princeton University Press, 2004), by Robert Feenstra, and *Global Capital Markets: Integration, Crisis and Growth* (Cambridge University Press, 2004), by Maurice Obstfeld and Alan Taylor. Recently, Feenstra received the Bernhard Harms Prize from the Institute for World Economics, Kiel, Germany, in 2006, and delivered the Zeuthen Lectures at the University of Copenhagen in 2007. Taylor was awarded a Guggenheim Fellowship in 2004 and was a visiting professor at the American University in Paris and London Business School in 2005–06.

Feenstra lives in Davis, California, with his wife Gail, and has two grown children: Heather, who is pursuing a master's degree in genetic counseling; and Evan, who is studying at Pitzer College. Taylor also lives in Davis, with his wife Claire, and has two young children, Olivia and Sebastian.

Brief Contents

Contents

PART 4
Applications and
Policy Issues

Preface

The twenty-first century is an age of unprecedented globalization. In looking at existing texts, we saw that the dramatic economic developments of recent years had not been incorporated into a newly written undergraduate text, and felt the time was ripe to incorporate fresh perspectives, current topics, and up-to-date approaches into the study of international economics. With this book, we have expanded the vision of international economics to encompass the latest theory and events in the world today.

In decades past, international economics was taught differently. There was a much greater emphasis on theory and a strong focus on the advanced countries. Policy analysis reflected the concerns of the time, whether strategic trade policy or the Bretton Woods system. Today, the concerns are not the same. In addition to new theoretical developments, there is a much greater emphasis on empirical studies. A wave of applied research in recent years has proved (or refuted) existing theories and taught us important new lessons about the determinants of trade, factor flows, exchange rates, and crises. Trade and capital flows have been liberalized and allowed to grow, and more attention is now devoted to emerging markets and developing countries, regions that now carry substantial weight in the global economy.

Covering new and expanding ground is part of the challenge and excitement of teaching and learning the international economics of the twenty-first century. Our goal is to provide new material that is rigorous enough to meet the challenge yet approachable enough to nurture the excitement. Many of the new topics stand apart from conventional textbook treatments and in the past have been bypassed in lectures or taught through supplementary readings. In our view they deserve a more prominent place in today's curriculum.

We have taught the chapters of this book ourselves several times, and have benefited from the feedback of professors at colleges and universities in the United States and throughout the world. Like us, they have been enthusiastic about the response from students to our fresh approach, and we hope that you will also enjoy the book.

New Features

Each chapter includes several new features that bring the material alive for the students, and include:

- **Applications,** which are integrated into the main text and use material that has been covered to illuminate real-world policies, events, and evidence;

- **Headlines,** which show how topics in the main text relate directly to media coverage of the global economy;

- **Side Bars,** which include topics that, while not essential, are still of interest;

- **Net Work** boxes, which provide an opportunity for the students to explore chapter concepts on the Internet.

In addition, the book is issued in a combined edition *(International Economics)* and in two split editions *(International Trade* and *International Macroeconomics),* allowing greater flexibility for instructors to assign their preferred text and keep costs down for students.

New Topics and Approaches

Reviewers and class testers have been enthusiastically supportive of the many new topics we have included in our presentation. New topics covered in the international trade portion of *International Economics* or *International Trade* include the foreign outsourcing of goods and services (Chapter 6); tariffs and quotas under imperfect competition (Chapter 9); and international agreements on trade, labor, and the environment (Chapter 11). These topics are in addition to core chapters on the Ricardian model (Chapter 2), the specific-factors model (Chapter 3), the Heckscher-Ohlin model (Chapter 4), trade with increasing returns to scale and imperfect competition (Chapter 6), import tariffs and quotas under perfect competition (Chapter 8), and export subsidies (Chapter 10).

New chapters in international economics in this book or the combined edition, *International Economics,* include the gains from financial globalization (Chapter 6 or Chapter 17 in *International Economics*), fixed versus floating regimes (Chapter 8 or Chapter 19), and exchange-rate crises and the operation of pegs (Chapter 9 or Chapter 20). These topics are in addition to core chapters on foreign exchange markets and exchange rates in the short run and the long run (Chapters 2–4 or Chapters 13–15), the national and international accounts (Chapter 5 or Chapter 16), the open economy IS-LM model (Chapter 7 or Chapter 18), the euro (Chapter 10 or Chapter 21), and a chapter on current important issues (Chapter 11 or Chapter 22).

In writing our chapters we have made every effort to link them analytically to other chapters. For example, while immigration and foreign direct investment are sometimes treated as an afterthought in international economics books, in *International Economics* and *International Trade* we integrate these topics into the discussion of the trade models by covering the movement of labor and capital between countries in Chapter 5. Specifically, we analyze the movement of labor and capital between countries in the short run using the specific-factors model, and explore the long-run implications using the Heckscher-Ohlin model. Chapter 5 therefore builds on the models that the student has learned in Chapters 3 and 4, and applies them to issues at the forefront of policy discussion.

In the macroeconomics section from this book or *International Economics,* this analytical linking is seen in the parallel development of fixed and floating exchange rate regimes from the opening introductory tour in Chapter 1 (Chapter 12 in the combined edition), through the workings of exchange rates in Chapters 2–4 (Chapters 13–15), the discussion of policy in the IS-LM model of Chapter 7 (Chapter 18), to the discussion of regime choice in Chapter 8 (Chapter 19). Many textbooks treat fixed and floating regimes separately, with fixed regimes often treated as an afterthought. But given the widespread use of fixed rates in many countries, the rising macro weight of fixed regimes, and the collapse of fixed rates during crises, we think it is more helpful for the student to grapple with the different workings and cost-benefit tradeoffs of the two regimes by studying them side by side. This approach also allows us to address numerous contemporary policy applications.

In addition to expanding our coverage to include up-to-date theory and policy applications, our other major goal is to present all the material—both new and old—in the most teachable way. To do this, we ensure all of the material presented rests on firm and up-to-the-minute empirical evidence. We believe this approach is the right way to study economics, and it is our experience, shared with many instructors, that teaching is more effective and more enlivened when students can see not just an elegant derivation in theory but, right next to it, some persuasive evidence of the economic mechanisms under investigation.

The fact that international issues are in the headlines nearly every day has made our job easier, and you will find many recent and historical applications in the book. These applications are part of the main text and apply the theory that the student has just learned. For example, in Chapter 5 (in both *International Economics* and *International Trade*) we discuss the historical effects of immigration on wages in the "old world" and "new world" and in the United States in recent years. Chapter 6 looks at NAFTA's effects on Canada, Mexico, and the United States, and discusses the gravity equation. The steel tariff applied by President Bush in 2001 and the end of the Multifibre Agreement in textiles and apparel are covered in Chapter 8, and the discussion of international agreements (Chapter 11) includes a discussion of the Kyoto Accord as well as many examples of how WTO rulings potentially affect the environment.

In macroeconomics from this book or *International Economics,* under exchange rates, we look at the fall of the U.S. dollar and, in another application, we study wartime currency fluctuations in Iraq in Chapter 4 (Chapter 15 in the combined edition); when studying the balance of payments we study Ireland's extraordinary deficit on factor income in Chapter 5 (Chapter 16); we also have applications that explore why capital doesn't flow to poor countries in Chapter 6 (Chapter 17), how policies in Australia and New Zealand responded successfully to the Asian Crisis in Chapter 7 (Chapter 18), and how exchange-rate crises have unfolded in countries as different as Peru and the United Kingdom in Chapter 9 (Chapter 20).

The Arrangement of Topics: International Trade (from International Economics and International Trade)

Part 1: Introduction to International Trade

The opening chapter sets the stage by discussing global flows of goods and services through international trade, of people through migration, and of capital through foreign direct investment. The chapter includes maps depicting these flows, so the student can get a feel for which countries have the greatest flows in each case. Historical examples of trade and barriers to trade are also provided. This chapter can serve as a full introductory lecture.

Part 2: Patterns of International Trade

The core models of international trade are presented here: the Ricardian model (Chapter 2), specific-factors model (Chapter 3), and Heckscher-Ohlin model (Chapter 4). Some of the topics conventionally included in the specific-factors and Heckscher-Ohlin model, like the effects of changing the endowments of labor or capital, are not covered in those chapters but are instead examined in Chapter 5, which deals with the movement of labor and capital between countries. For example, the "factor price insensitivity" result is deferred to Chapter 5, as is the Rybczynski Theorem. By discussing those two results to Chapter 5, we keep the discussion of the Heckscher-Ohlin model more manageable in Chapter 4, focusing there on the Heckscher-Ohlin theorem, the Stolper-Samuelson theorem, and empirical testing of the model. In summary, the ordering of topics among Chapters 3, 4 and 5 as well as many of the applications are new, and these chapters are linked together tightly in their pedagogical approach.

Part 3: New Explanations for International Trade

In the next section we cover two new explanations for international trade: increasing returns to scale (Chapter 6), and foreign outsourcing (Chapter 7).

Formal models of trade with increasing returns to scale and monopolistic competition have been popular since the early 1980s, but there is no standardized method for presenting this topic in undergraduate textbooks. In Chapter 6, we fall back on the original, graphical discussion from Edward Chamberlin, who introduced the *DD* and *dd* curves (what we label in Chapter 6 as simply *D* and *d*). The *D* curve represents the share of the market going to each firm, and traces out demand if all firms charge the same prices. In contrast, the *d* curve is the demand facing a firm when other firms keep their prices constant. The distinction between these two demands is crucial when analyzing the impact of trade liberalization: the *d* curve clearly shows the incentive for each individual firm to lower its price after trade liberalization, but the steeper *D* curve shows that when all firms lower prices, then losses occur and some firms must exit.

Chapter 7 is devoted to foreign outsourcing, and we have found that students readily understand this new material. The model used illustrates a piece of intuition that students enjoy: the movement of one student from, say, a physics class to an economics class can raise the average grade in *both* classes. Likewise, foreign outsourcing can raise the relative wage of skilled workers in both countries. The chapter deals with the recent critique by Paul Samuelson, who suggested that outsourcing to China or India might be harmful to the United States. That argument is shown to depend on how outsourcing affects the U.S. terms of trade: if the terms of trade fall, the United States is worse off, though it is still gaining overall from international trade. In fact, we argue that the U.S. terms of trade has been rising in recent years, not falling, so the argument by Samuelson is hypothetical so far.

Part 4: International Trade Policies

The concluding part of the book dealing with international trade is devoted to trade policy: tariffs and quotas under perfect competition (Chapter 8), under imperfect competition (Chapter 9), export subsidies (Chapter 10), and a discussion of international agreements on trade, labor, and the environment (Chapter 11). Our goal is to present this material in a more systematic fashion than found elsewhere, with both very recent and historical applications.

Chapter 8, dealing with tariffs and quotas under perfect competition, is the "bread and butter" of trade policy. We adopt the partial-equilibrium approach, using import demand and export supply curves, along with consumer and producer surplus. Our experience is that students feel very comfortable with this approach from their microeconomics training (so they can usually label the consumer surplus region, for example, in each diagram before the labels are shown). The chapter uses the tariff applied by President George W. Bush on U.S. steel imports as a motivating case, which we analyze from both a "small country" and a "large country" perspective.

Chapters 9 and 10 bring in some of the insights from the literature on the "strategic" role of trade policy, which was developed in the later 1980s and 1990s. While that literature focused on oligopoly interactions between firms, to simplify the analysis in Chapter 9 we focus on monopoly cases, either home monopoly or foreign monopoly, deferring discussion of a duopoly case to the analysis of export subsidies in Chapter 10. Most of the theory in these chapters is familiar, but the organization is new as are many of the applications, including infant industry protection in Chapter 9 and a detailed discussion of agricultural subsidies in Chapter 10.

Chapter 11 begins by drawing upon tariffs under perfect competition (from Chapter 8), and showing that large countries have a natural incentive to apply tariffs to move the terms of trade to their advantage. That creates a prisoner's dilemma situation that is overcome by rules in the WTO. The chapter then moves on to discuss international rules governing labor issues and the environment. Students are especially interested in the environmental applications.

The Arrangement of Topics: International Macroeconomics (from this book and *International Economics*)

Part 1 (or Part 5 in *International Economics*): Introduction to International Macroeconomics

This part consists of just Chapter 1 (Chapter 12 in the combined edition), which sets the stage by explaining the field and major items of interest, with an elementary survey of the three main parts of the book: money and exchange rates, the balance of payments, and the role of policy.

Part 2 (or Part 6): Exchange Rates

We depart from the traditional presentation by presenting exchange rates before balance of payments, an approach that we and our students find more logical and appealing. We begin the core macro material with exchange rates because (for macroeconomics) the exchange rate is the key difference between a closed economy and a world of open economies. In addition, starting a course off with balance of payments accounting often engenders boredom, and if this material is followed by a long detour into exchange rates, the balance of payments concepts are often long forgotten by the time they are brought up in later chapters. Our approach, supported by our own experience and that of our reviewers and class testers, first treats all price topics together in one part, and then moves on to quantity topics.

Chapter 2 (Chapter 13) introduces the basics about exchange rates and the foreign exchange (forex) market (including the principles of arbitrage) and exposes students to real-world data on exchange rate behavior. It describes how the forex market is structured and explains the principles of arbitrage in forex markets. It ends with interest parity conditions, which is then repeated for better understanding in Chapter 4 (Chapter 15).

Chapter 3 (Chapter 14) presents the monetary approach to the determination of exchange rates in the long run. We cover the long run before the short run because long-run expectations are assumed to be known in the short-run model. Topics include goods market arbitrage, the Law of One Price, and purchasing power parity. We first develop a simple monetary model (the quantity theory) and then look at the standard monetary model, the Fisher effect, and real interest parity. The chapter ends with discussion of nominal anchors and their relationship to monetary and exchange rate regimes.

Chapter 4 (Chapter 15) presents the asset approach to the determination of exchange rates in the short run. Uncovered interest parity, first introduced in Chapter 2 (Chapter 13), is the centerpiece of the asset approach, and the expected future exchange rate is assumed to be given by the long-run model. Short-run interest rates are explained using a money market model. We show how all the building blocks from the monetary and asset approaches fit together for a complete theory of exchange rate determination. Finally, we explain how the complete theory works for fixed as well as floating regimes, and demonstrate the trilemma.

Part 3 (Part 7): The Balance of Payments

Chapter 5 (Chapter 16 in the combined edition) introduces the key macroeconomic quantities: the national and international accounts and the balance of payments (BOP). The BOP is explained as the need for balancing trade on goods, services, and assets (with allowances for transfers). We also introduce external wealth and valuation effects, which are of increasing importance in the world economy.

Chapter 6 (Chapter 17) links the balance of payments to the key question of the costs and benefits of financial globalization, an increasingly important topic to which students should be exposed. The chapter begins by explaining the significance of the long-run budget constraint and then examines the three key potential benefits of financial globalization: consumptions smoothing, efficient investment, and risk sharing.

Chapter 7 (Chapter 18) links the balance of payments to output, exchange rates, and macroeconomic policies. This is the standard chapter on the short-run open economy Keynesian model. The approach is as simple and clear as possible. We use IS-LM and forex market diagrams, with the interest rate on a common axis. This means we are using tools (IS-LM) that many students have already seen, rather then inventing new ways to present the same model with new and challenging notation. In this chapter we also discuss fixed and floating rate regimes side by side, not in different chapters. We think it helpful throughout the book to study these regimes in parallel and at this point it also helps to set up the next chapter.

The ordering of Part 3 (Part 7) echoes that of Part 2 (Part 6): start with definitions, then cover long-run topics (the gains from financial globalization), then move to short-run topics (IS-LM). This ordering of topics allows a smooth transition from some key definitions in Chapter 5 (Chapter 16) to their application at the start of Chapter 6 (Chapter 17), a link that would be impossible if the balance of payments chapter were placed before the coverage of exchange rates.

Part 4 (Part 8) Applications and Policy Issues

Chapter 8 (Chapter 19 in the combined edition) confronts one of the major policy issues in international macroeconomics, the choice of fixed versus floating exchange rates. Motivation is supplied by a case study of a country caught in two minds: Britain during the 1992 ERM crisis. The analysis begins with the two classic criteria for two regions to adopt a fixed exchange rate—high levels of integration and symmetry of economic shocks. The chapter then goes on to consider other factors that could make a fixed exchange rate desirable, especially in developing countries—a need for a credible nominal anchor and the "fear of floating" that results from significant liability dollarization. Empirical evidence is provided for all of these influences. A brief section summarizes the debate over the desirability and possibility of coordination in larger exchange rate systems. Finally, a historical survey uses the uses the tools at hand to understand the evolution of international monetary arrangements since the nineteenth century.

Chapter 9 (Chapter 20) studies exchange rate crises. Before explaining how pegs break, the chapter spends some time studying how pegs work. The focus here is on reserve management and the central bank balance sheet, when an economy faces shocks to output, interest rates, and risk premiums. The framework is a simple world without banks, but an extension to consider Lender of Last Resort actions allows for more realism. The setup can be used to discuss recent controversies over reserve accumulation in China and other emerging markets, and also suggests how pegs can fail. To conclude, two models of crises are presented: a first-generation model with ongoing monetized deficits with fixed output and flexible prices (applying the logic of the flexible-price model of Chapter 3 (Chapter 14)); and a second-generation model featuring an adverse shock with fixed prices and flexible output (applying the IS-LM-FX model of Chapter 7 (Chapter 18)).

Chapter 10 (Chapter 21) discusses common currencies, with particular focus on the euro. The basic Optimal Currency Area (OCA) criteria are developed as an extension of the fixed versus floating analysis of Chapter 8 (Chapter 19), and this framework allows us to consider additional economic and political reasons why countries might join a common currency area. Empirical evidence is then presented to show the differences between the U.S. and the Eurozone with respect to the OCA criteria, to explain why so many economists believe that the Eurozone currently is not an OCA. To explain the euro project therefore requires an appeal to other forces, which are considered in the remainder of the chapter: the possible endogeniety of the OCA criteria and the role of noneconomic factors. The latter takes us on a discussion of history and politics, which helps illuminate the institutional details of the Eurozone, especially the key monetary and fiscal issues.

Chapter 11 (Chapter 22) is a collection of four "mini chapters" that tackle important topics in macroeconomics. In this edition, these topics are: the failure of UIP and exchange rate puzzles in the short run (including the carry trade and limits to arbitrage); the failure of PPP and exchange rates in the long run (including transaction costs and the Balassa-Samuelson effect); the debate over global imbalances (including the savings glut hypothesis and the role of exchange rate adjustments); the problem of default (including a simple model of default as insurance and a discussion of triple crises). Each of these topics is presented in a self-contained block. They can be taught as is, or in conjunction with earlier material. The UIP material could be added on to Chapter 2 or 4 (Chapter 13 or 15). The PPP material would nicely augment Chapter 3 (Chapter 14). The global imbalances material could be presented with Chapter 5, 6, or 7 (Chapter 10, 17, or 18). The default topic could be paired with the discussion of currency crises in Chapter 9 (Chapter 20).

Alternative Routes through the Text

Because this book is available as a combined edition and split volumes, it can be used for several types of courses, as summarized below and in the accompanying table.

A semester-length course in international trade (say, 15 weeks) would start at Chapter 1 (from *International Economics* or *International Trade*), but for a shorter, quarter-length course (say, 10 weeks), we suggest skipping Chapter 1 and going straight to the Ricardian model (Chapter 2), which has a self-contained introduction. Chapters 2, 3 (the specific-factors model), and 4 (the Heckscher-Ohlin model) form the core of trade theory. The movement of labor and capital between countries (Chapter 5) builds on these chapters theoretically, and summarizes the empirical evidence on immigration and foreign direct investment.

The new approaches to international trade covered in Chapters 6 (economies of scale and imperfect competition) and 7 (foreign outsourcing) can be taught independently of each other. (A quarter course in international trade may not have time for both these chapters.) The final four chapters in international trade deal with trade policy. Chapter 8 (tariffs and quotas under

SUGGESTED COURSE OUTLINES

	International Trade		International Macro		Combined
	10 week	13–15 week	10 week	13–15 week	
Chapters 1–11 of *International Economics*, or **Chapters 1–11 of *International Trade***					
1 Trade in the Global Economy		X			
2 Trade and Technology: The Ricardian Model	X	X			X
3 Gains and Losses from Trade in the Specific-Factors Model	X	X			X
4 Trade and Resources: The Heckscher-Ohlin Model	X	X			X
5 Movement of Labor and Capital between Countries	Choose two from 5, 6, 7	X			
6 Increasing Returns to Scale and Imperfect Competition		Choose one from 6, 7			
7 Foreign Outsourcing of Goods and Services					
8 Import Tariffs and Quotas under Perfect Competition	X	X			X
9 Import Tariffs and Quotas under Imperfect Competition	X	X			
10 Export Subsidies in Agriculture and High-Technology Industries	X	X			
11 International Agreements: Trade, Labor and the Environment		X			X
Chapters 1–11 of *International Macroeconomics*, or **Chapters 12–22 of *International Economics***					
1 (12) The Global Macroeconomy				X	
2 (13) Introduction to Exchange Rates and the Foreign Exchange Market			X	X	X
3 (14) Exchange Rates I: The Monetary Approach in the Long Run			X	X	X
4 (15) Exchange Rates II: The Asset Approach in the Short Run			X	X	X
5 (16) National and International Accounts: Income, Wealth, and the Balance of Payments			X	X	X
6 (17) Balance of Payments I: The Gains from Financial Globalization			X	X	
7 (18) Balance of Payments II: Output, Exchange Rates, and Macroeconomic Policies in the Short Run			X	X	X
8 (19) Fixed Versus Floating: International Monetary Experience			Combine with 10 (21)	X	
9 (20) Exchange Rate Crises: How Pegs Work and How They Break			X	X	
10 (21) The Euro			Combine with 8 (19)	X	
11 (22) Topics in International Macroeconomics			1 or 2 (as time permits)	3 or 4 (as time permits)	

perfect competition) should be discussed in any course regardless of its length. Tariffs and quotas under imperfect competition (Chapter 9) digs more deeply into the effects of trade policy, followed by a discussion of export subsidies (Chapter 10). Some or all topics in the final chapter on international agreements can be covered as time permits.

A semester course in international macroeconomics (say, 15 weeks) would start at Chapter 1 in this book (Chapter 12 in *International Economics*), but for a shorter quarter course (say, 10 weeks), one might skip Chapter 1 (Chapter 12) or assign it as a reading and go straight to the foreign exchange market presented in Chapter 2 (Chapter 13). Core material on exchange rate theory then follows, with the long run in Chapter 3 (Chapter 14) followed by the short run in Chapter 4 (Chapter 15). Next come the core definitions of the national and international accounts and the balance of payments, presented in Chapter 5 (Chapter 16). After this point choices would be required if time is short. A course with a macro emphasis would want to cover the costs and benefits of globalization in Chapter 6 (Chapter 17) and IS-LM in Chapter 7 (Chapter 18). To still allow time for crises from Chapter 9 (Chapter 20), given the similar apparatus in the two chapters, treatment of regime choice in Chapter 8 (Chapter 19) might be combined with a discussion of the euro in Chapter 10 (Chapter 21). Topics from Chapter 11 (Chapter 22) could be selected as time permits: a more finance-oriented course might focus on the first two exchange rate topics; a more macro-oriented course might focus on global imbalances and default. In a semester-length course, there should be time for almost all the topics to be covered.

We recognize that many schools also offer a *combined* course in international trade and macroeconomics, sometimes to students outside the economics major. Because of its wealth of applications, this book will serve those students very well. For international trade (in both *International Economics* and *International Trade*), we recommend that the combined course cover Chapters 2–4 as the basic trade chapters, followed by Chapter 8 on tariffs and quotas under perfect competition and then Chapter 11 on trade agreements and the environment. Those five chapters will offer the students a solid perspective on international trade and trade policy. They can be followed by Chapters 2–4 in *International Macroeconomics* (Chapters 13–15 in *International Economics*) on exchange rates and Chapters 5 (Chapter 16) and 7 (Chapter 18) on macroeconomics for a basic grounding in international macroeconomics. This coverage will give students a grasp of the key differences between fixed and floating even without the later chapters. Other material can be added as time permits, and the topic format of Chapter 11 (Chapter 22) would allow considerable flexibility.

Supplements and Media Package

In addition to all its pedagogical innovations, our book brings to the market an innovative supplement and media package. These supplements were given the same careful thought, time, and preparation as the text. We are happy to provide a full suite of teaching materials for instructors along with a complete set of resources to aid students in reviewing the key concepts presented in the text.

Instructor Supplements

Instructor's Manual with Solutions Manual

The Instructor's Manuals for each portion of the book, prepared by UC Davis graduates Alyson Ma (University of San Diego) and Kristin Van Gaasbeck (California State University, Sacramento) are available. For each chapter in the textbook, the Instructor's Resource Manuals provide:

- *Notes to the instructor:* notes that include a chapter summary with additional comments.

- *Lecture notes:* a complete set of notes, including a detailed outline of the chapter for aid in preparing class lectures.

- *In-class problems:* 10 to 15 problems per chapter, including in-depth suggested answers.

- *Solutions to textbook problems:* including detailed solutions to all end-of-chapter problems.

Printed Test Bank

The test bank provides a wide range of creative and versatile questions ranging in levels of difficulty and format to assess students' comprehension, interpretation, analysis, and synthesis skills. Containing over 125 questions per chapter, the test bank offers a variety of multiple-choice, true/false, and short-answer questions. All questions have been checked for continuity with the text content and reviewed extensively for accuracy. The test bank was coordinated by Ron Davies (University of Oregon), with the help of contributing authors Terry Monson (Michigan Technological University), Jaishankar Raman (Valparaiso University), and Millicent Sites (Carson-Newman College).

Computerized Test Bank

The test bank is also available in CD-ROM format, powered by Brownstone, for both Windows and Macintosh users. With this Diploma software, instructors can easily create and print tests as well as write and edit questions.

Instructor's Resource CD-ROM

Using the Instructor's Resource CD-ROM, instructors can easily build classroom presentations or enhance online courses. This CD-ROM contains all text figures (in .JPEG and .GIF formats), PowerPoint Lecture Presentations, and detailed solutions to all end-of-chapter problems in the textbook.

Student and Instructor Supplements

Study Guide with Worked Examples

Students' economic thinking will be challenged and extended by a creative new Study Guide with Worked Examples prepared by Stephen Yeaple of the University of Colorado, Boulder. This study guide complements the textbook by providing students with additional opportunities to develop their knowledge of international economics through active learning. This innovative resource reinforces the topics and key concepts covered in the text. For each key section of each chapter, the Study Guide with Worked Examples provides:

- *Key themes:* detailed discussions of key concepts.

- *Key terms:* a summary of important vocabulary within the chapter, including space for students to record their own notes.

- *Review questions with tips:* detailed, thorough problems for students to test their comprehension, along with tips to help students work through the problems. To identify common mistakes and to demonstrate common features of different types of economic problems, *tips* are provided immediately following questions that delve into particularly important or difficult topics.

- *Worked-out solutions:* including solutions to all Study Guide review questions.

Companion Web Site for Students and Instructors

The companion site http://www.worthpublishers.com/feenstrataylor is a virtual study guide for students and an excellent resource for instructors. For each chapter in the textbook, the tools on the site include:

Student Tools

- Detailed learning objectives

- Practice quizzes: A set of questions with feedback and page references to the textbook. Student answers are saved in an online database that can be accessed by instructors.

- Key-term flashcards: Students can test themselves on key vocabulary with these pop-up electronic flashcards.

- Web exercises

- Web links to relevant research and demonstrations

Instructor Resources

- Quiz gradebook: The site gives instructors the ability to track students' interaction with the practice quizzes via an online gradebook. Instructors may choose to have student results emailed directly to them.

- PowerPoint lecture presentations: These customizable PowerPoint slides, prepared by Marie Truesdell (Marian College) and Kristin Van Gaasbeck (California State University, Sacramento) are designed to assist instructors with lecture preparation and presentation by providing original animations, graphs from the textbook, data tables, key concepts, and bulleted lecture outlines.

- Image gallery: A complete set of figures and tables from the textbook in JPEG and PowerPoint formats.

eBooks

All three editions (*International Economics, International Trade,* and *International Macroeconomics*) are available as eBooks. Students who purchase the Feenstra/Taylor eBooks have access to interactive textbooks featuring:

- Quick, intuitive navigation

- Customizable note-taking

- Highlighting

- Searchable glossary

- Access to a dynamic array of online resources.

With the Feenstra/Taylor eBooks, instructors can

- Focus on only the chapters they want. You can assign the entire text or a custom version with only the chapters that correspond to your syllabus. Students see your customized version, with your selected chapters only.

- Annotate any page of the text. Your notes can include your own text or graphs, Web links, and even photos and images from the book's media or other sources. Your students can get an eBook annotated just for them, customized for your course.

- Access online quizzing. The eBook integrates the online quizzing from the book's Companion Web Site.

Web-CT E-pack

WebCT The Feenstra/Taylor WebCT e-packs enable you to create a thorough, interactive, and pedagogically sound online course or course website. The e-pack provides you with online materials that facilitate critical thinking and learning, including preprogrammed quizzes, tests, activities, and an array of other materials. This material is preprogrammed and fully functional in the WebCT environment.

BlackBoard

 The Feenstra/Taylor BlackBoard Course Cartridge allows you to combine BlackBoard's popular tools and easy-to-use interface with the Feenstra/Taylor text-specific, rich Web content, including preprogrammed quizzes, tests, activities, and an array of other materials. The result is an interactive, comprehensive online course that allows for effortless implementation, management, and use. The files are organized and pre-built to work within the BlackBoard software. They can be easily downloaded from the BlackBoard content showcases directly onto your department server.

Acknowledgments

A book like this would not be possible without the assistance of many people, which we gratefully acknowledge.

First, the renowned team at Worth has spared no effort to help us; their experience and skill in publishing economics textbooks were invaluable. Numerous individuals have been involved with this project, but we must give special mention to three: the project was initiated by acquisitions editor Charlie van Wagner and guided to completion by acquisitions editor Sarah Dorger. Through it all, the manuscript was improved endlessly by our development editor Jane Tufts. We are greatly in their debt.

We have also relied on the assistance of a number of graduate students in collecting data for applications, preparing problems, and proofreading material. We would like to thank Leticia Arroyo Abad, Chang Hong, David Jacks, Alyson Ma, Ahmed Rahman, Seema Sangita, Radek Szulga, and Yingying Xu for their assistance. We are especially grateful to Benjamin Mandel, who has worked on many of the international trade chapters from their earliest stages through to their completion. Thanks also to Christian Broda, Colin Carter, Michele Cavallo, Menzie Chinn, Sebastian Edwards, Ann Harrison, Mervyn King, Philip Lane, Karen Lewis, Christopher Meissner, Gian Maria Milesi-Ferretti, Michael Pakko, Ugo Panizza, Giovanni Peri, Eswar Prasad, Andrés Rodríguez-Clare, Jay Shambaugh, and Martin Wolf for providing data used in the applications.

We have taught the chapters of this book ourselves several times, and have benefitted from the feedback of colleagues. The book has also been class-tested by a number of individuals.

We would like to thank these instructors for giving us comments on early drafts. These colleagues have been enthusiastic about the reception of their students to our fresh approach. They include:

Joshua Aizenman, *University of California, Santa Cruz*

Scott Baier, *Clemson University*

Paul Bergin, *University of California, Davis*

Matilde Bombardini, *University of British Columbia*

Drusilla Brown, *Tufts University*

Avik Chakraborty, *University of Tennessee, Knoxville*

Gordon Hanson, *University of California, San Diego*

James Harrigan, *Federal Reserve Bank of New York*

Takeo Hoshi, *University of California, San Diego*

David Hummels, *Purdue University*

Samuel Kortum, *University of Chicago*

John McLaren, *University of Virginia*

Robert Murphy, *Boston College*

Constantin Ogloblin, *Georgia Southern University*

Kevin O'Rourke, *Trinity College, Dublin*

Sanjay Paul, *Elizabethtown College*

Priya Ranjan, *University of California, Irvine*

Andrés Rodriguez-Clare, *Pennsylvania State University*

Katheryn Russ, *University of California, Davis*

Stephen Stageberg, *University of Mary Washington*

Bruce Wydick, *University of San Francisco*

Stephen Yeaple, *University of Colorado, Boulder*

A huge number of colleagues were very helpful in providing their reviews of the texts. We wish to thank the following reviewers:

Joshua Aizenman, *University of California, Santa Cruz*

Mohsen Bahmani-Oskooee, *University of Wisconsin-Milwaukee*

Scott Baier, *Clemson University*

Richard Baillie, *Michigan State University*

Joe Bell, *Missouri State University*

Paul Bergin, *University of California, Davis*

Robert Blecker, *American University*

Roger Butters, *University of Nebraska, Lincoln*

Francisco Carrada-Bravo, *Arizona State University*

Menzie Chinn, *University of Wisconsin, Madison*

Richard Chisik, *Florida International University*

Ann Davis, *Marist College*

Robert Driskill, *Vanderbilt University*

James Fain, *Oklahoma State University*

David H. Feldman, *College of William & Mary*

Diane Flaherty, *University of Massachusetts, Amherst*

Jean-Ellen Giblin, *Fashion Institute of Technology*

Bill Gibson, *University of Vermont*

Thomas Grennes, *North Carolina State University*

Gordon Hanson, *University of California, San Diego*

Mehdi Haririan, *Bloomsburg University*

James Harrigan, *Federal Reserve Bank of New York*

Takeo Hoshi, *University of California, San Diego*

Douglas Irwin, *Dartmouth College*

Hiro Ito, *Portland State University*

Michael Klein, *Tufts University*

Kala Krishna, *Pennsylvania State University*

Maria Kula, *Roger Williams University*

Ricardo Lopez, *Indiana University*

Mary Lovely, *Syracuse University*

Barbara Lowrey, *University of Maryland*

Steven Matusz, *Michigan State University*

Jose Mendez, *Arizona State University*

Shannon Mitchell, *Virginia Commonwealth University*

Farshid Mojaver Hosseini, *University of California, Davis*

Marc A. Muendler, *University of California, San Diego*

Maria Muniagurria, *University of Wisconsin, Madison*

Robert Murphy, *Boston College*

Ranganath Murthy, *Bucknell University*

Kanda Naknoi, *Purdue University*

Constantin Ogloblin, *Georgia Southern University*

Kevin O'Rourke, *Trinity College, Dublin*

Kerry Pannell, *DePauw University*

Jaishankar Raman, *Valparaiso University*

Raymond Robertson, *Macalester College*

Andrés Rodriguez-Clare, *Pennsylvania State University*

Hadi Salehi-Esfahani, *University of Illinois at Urbana-Champaign*

Andreas Savvides, *Oklahoma State University*

Till Schreiber, *College of William and Mary*

Gunjan Sharma, *University of Missouri, Columbia*

John Subrick, *George Mason University*

Mark P. Taylor, *University of Warwick*

Linda Tesar, *University of Michigan, Ann Arbor*

Geetha Vaidyanathan, *University of North Carolina, Greensboro*

Kristin Van Gaasbeck, *California State University, Sacramento*

Gary Wells, *Clemson University*

Mark Wohar, *University of Nebraska, Omaha*

Susan Wolcott, *SUNY Binghamton*

Bin Xu, *China Europe International Business School*

Stephen Yeaple, *University of Colorado, Boulder*

We received useful feedback from focus group participants. We would like to thank the following individuals:

Mohsen Bahmani-Oskooee, *University of Wisconsin, Milwaukee*

Roger Butters, *University of Nebraska, Lincoln*

Francisco Carrada-Bravo, *Arizona State University*

Mitchell Charkiewicz, *Central Connecticut State University*

Menzie Chinn, *University of Wisconsin, Madison*

Carl Davidson, *Michigan State University*

Ann Davis, *Marist College*

Robert Driskill, *Vanderbilt University*

Eric Fisher, *California Polytechnic State University, San Luis Obispo*

Diane Flaherty, *University of Massachusetts, Amherst*

Bill Gibson, *University of Vermont*

Thomas Grennes, *North Carolina State University*

Mehdi Haririan, *Bloomsburg University*

Andreas Hauskrecht, *Indiana University*

Andrew Hughes-Hallett, *Vanderbilt University*

Eckhard Janeba, *University of Mannheim*

Mary Lovely, *Syracuse University*

Marc Melitz, *Princeton University*

Norman Miller, *Miami University of Ohio*

Shannon Mitchell, *Virginia Commonwealth University*

Ranganath Murthy, *Bucknell University*

Rebecca Neumann, *University of Wisconsin, Milwaukee*

Constantin Ogloblin, *Georgia Southern University*

Lucjan Orlowski, *Sacred Heart University*

Jeff Pliskin, *Hamilton College*

Francisca Richter, *Cleveland State University*

Hadi Salehi-Esfahani, *University of Illinois, Urbana-Champaign*

Bin Xu, *China Europe International Business School*

We would like to thank the following individuals who have provided feedback on the initial preliminary version of the text:

Scott Baier, *Clemson University*

Paul Bergin, *University of California, Davis*

Luisa Blanco Raynal, *Pepperdine University*

James Cassing, *University of Pittsburgh*

Ted Fu, *Stanford University*

James Harrigan, *Federal Reserve Bank of New York*

David Hummels, *Purdue University*

Farshid Mojaver Hosseini, *University of California, Davis*

Maria Muniagurria, *University of Wisconsin, Madison*

Kanda Naknoi, *Purdue University*

Raymond Robertson, *Macalester College*

Andrés Rodriguez-Clare, *Pennsylvania State University*

Jeffrey Rosensweig, *Emory University*

Jennifer Steele, *University of Texas, Austin*

Asha Sundaram, *Syracuse University*

Kristin Van Gaasbeck, *California State University, Sacramento*

Wolfgang Keller, *University of Colorado, Boulder*

We would like to thank the following instructors who have aided us in the preparation and extensive review of the ancillary package. They include the following:

Francis Ahking, *University of Connecticut*
Ron Davies, *University of Oregon*
Alyson Ma, *University of San Diego*
Terry Monson, *Michigan Technological University*

Robert Murphy, *Boston College*
Sanjay Paul, *Elizabethtown College*
Jaishankar Raman, *Valparaiso University*
Millicent Sites, *Carson-Newman College*
Marie Truesdell, *Marian College*

Kristin Van Gaasbeck, *California State University, Sacramento*
Stephen Yeaple, *University of Colorado, Boulder*

We would also like to thank our families, especially Claire and Gail, for their sustained support during the several years we have devoted to writing this book.

Finally, you will see an accompanying picture of children in La Primavera, El Salvador, with their teachers, on the future site of a small schoolhouse that will be built for them by Seeds of Learning (www.seedsoflearning.org), a nonprofit organization dedicated to improving educational opportunities in rural Latin America. A portion of the royalties from this book go toward supporting the work of Seeds of Learning.

Robert C. Feenstra

Alan M. Taylor

Davis, California, August 2007

Courtesy Seeds of Learning

Students in La Primavera, El Salvador, are excited to help build three new classrooms on this land, through the activities of Seeds of Learning.

The Global Macroeconomy

So much of barbarism, however, still remains in the transactions of most civilized nations, that almost all independent countries choose to assert their nationality by having, to their inconvenience and that of their neighbors, a peculiar currency of their own.

John Stuart Mill

Neither a borrower nor a lender be; / For loan oft loseth both itself and friend. / And borrowing dulls the edge of husbandry.

Polonius, in William Shakespeare's *Hamlet*

History, in general, only informs us of what bad government is.

Thomas Jefferson

International macroeconomics is devoted to the study of large-scale economic problems in interdependent economies. It is macroeconomic because it focuses on the study of key economy-wide variables such as exchange rates, prices, interest rates, income, wealth, and the current account. It is international because a deeper understanding of the global economy emerges only when the interconnections among nations are explored in greater depth. In the chapters that follow, we build on some familiar macroeconomic ideas while at the same time examining the particular features of the global macroeconomy that define and distinguish the field of international macroeconomics.

Drawing on the wisdom encapsulated in the preceding epigraphs, the essential and unique features of international macroeconomics can be reduced to three key elements: the world has many monies (not one), countries are financially integrated (not isolated), and in this context economic policy choices are made (but not always very well).

■ **Money** John Stuart Mill echoes the complaints of many exasperated travelers and traders when he bemoans the profusion of different monies around the world. But Mill's vision of a world with a single

NET WORK

Visit one of the many websites that lists all of the current exchange rates between different currencies around the world. Try a financial newspaper site such as ft.com (follow the links to "Market Data," and then "Currencies"), or try websites devoted to foreign exchange market data such as oanda.com or xe.com (dig down; don't just look at the major currency tables). According to these lists, how many distinct currencies exist around the world today? Are some currencies used in more than one country?

currency is now an even more distant prospect: in his day, the number of currencies was far smaller than the more than 150 currencies in use today (see the **Net Work** exercise). Why do all these monies exist, and what purposes do they serve? What are their implications for the working of our global economy? What are the causes and consequences of the changing value of one currency against another? Aside from national pride, does a country enjoy benefits from having its own money? Or does it suffer costs?

■ **Finance** William Shakespeare's Polonius would surely be distressed by the sight of today's mounting debts owed by the United States to the rest of world. For Polonius, happiness means financial isolation, with income exactly equal to expenditure. But ever since finance has existed, the Poloniuses have tended to be in the minority among individuals and among nations, and in today's global economy the scale of international financial transactions has risen to record levels as capital has become ever more mobile internationally. Why do all these transactions occur, and what purposes do they serve? Who lends to whom, and why? Why are some debts paid but not others? Is the free flow of finance a source of economic benefits? What about potential economic costs?

■ **Policy** Thomas Jefferson's blunt assessment of government may be extreme, but looking at economic outcomes around the world today, it surely contains a germ of truth. If government policies were always optimal, recessions never happened, currencies never crashed, debts were always paid . . . well, that would be a nice world to inhabit. The flawed reality is that policy making is not on optimal autopilot, even at the best of times in the best-run countries. In the worst-run countries, poverty, underinvestment, hyperinflation, crises, and debt problems are common events. How can such devastating economic failures be understood? And even when problems are not so glaring, what can be said about the more mundane choices governments make about monetary and fiscal policies, or about exchange rates and capital mobility? Are the right choices being made? What are the trade-offs? Is there a single "right" answer?

The chapters that follow address all of these issues and combine relevant economic theory with compelling empirical evidence to explain the workings of today's global macroeconomy. This introductory chapter briefly explains the road ahead.

1 Foreign Exchange: Of Currencies and Crises

In most branches of economics, and even when studying international trade, it is common to ignore the role of money by assuming that all goods are priced in a common currency. The relative prices of different goods can then be studied, but the *exchange rate*—the price of foreign currency—is ignored. Despite this departure from reality, these approaches deliver important insights into the workings of the global economy.

However, for a country that has transactions with other countries—that is to say, virtually any country in the world—a complete understanding of how its economy works requires that we study the exchange rate. As products and investments move across borders, they also usually move between currencies. Fluctuations in exchange rates have important economic implications through their effects on the relative prices of home and foreign goods, services, and investments. By starting our analysis of the global economy with the theory of exchange rates, we see how and why these fluctuations occur. Later, this knowledge helps us see why exchange rates matter for economic outcomes and why they are an important focus of economic policy making.

How Exchange Rates Behave

In studying exchange rates, it is important to understand the types of behavior that any theory of exchange rate determination must explain. Figure 1-1, which displays two of the most noteworthy exchange rates in recent years, illustrates some basic facts about exchange rates. Panel (a) shows the exchange rate of China with the United States, in yuan per U.S. dollar ($).[1] Panel (b) shows

FIGURE 1-1

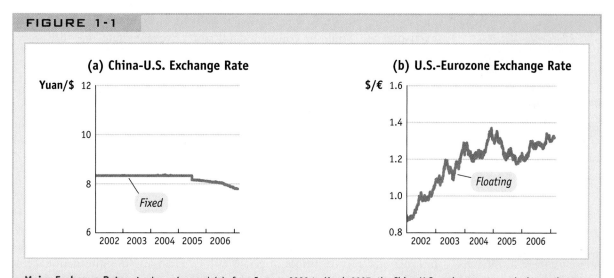

Major Exchange Rates As shown in panel (a), from January 2002 to March 2007, the China-U.S. exchange rate reached a maximum of 8.32 yuan/$, a minimum of 7.73 yuan/$, and the average daily change was only 0.01% (in absolute value). It would be considered a fixed exchange rate. In panel (b) over the same period, the U.S.-Eurozone exchange rate reached a maximum of 1.36 $/€, a minimum of 0.86 $/€, and the average daily change was 0.33% (in absolute value). It would be considered a floating exchange rate.

Note: For comparative purposes, the two vertical scales have the same proportions: the maximum is twice the minimum.

Source: oanda.com.

---

[1] The Chinese yuan is also known as the renminbi ("people's currency").

the exchange rate of the United States with the Eurozone, in U.S. dollars per euro (€). (Note that the choice of units is arbitrary; the same exchange rates could have been expressed in U.S. dollars per yuan, or euros per U.S. dollar.)

The behavior of the two exchange rates is very different. The yuan-dollar rate is almost flat. In fact, for many years it was literally unchanged, day after day, at 8.28 yuan/$. Finally, on July 23, 2005, it dropped exactly 2%. Since then, it has changed—but only slightly and along a fairly smooth trend: by September 2006, it had fallen by 4% in total; by March 2007, it had fallen 6%. On a *daily* basis, in this period, the average absolute change in the exchange rate was just one-hundredth of a percent (0.01%).

In contrast, the euro-dollar exchange rate experienced wide fluctuations over the same period. It saw increases, and decreases, in excess of 5% over the span of a month or two. In the course of some days, it even changed by 1% or more. On a *daily* basis, the average absolute change in this exchange rate was one-third of a percent (0.33%), more than 30 times as large as the average change in the yuan-dollar rate.

Based on such observable differences in exchange rate behavior, economists can divide the world into two groups of countries: those with **fixed** (or *pegged*) exchange rates and those with **floating** (or *flexible*) exchange rates. In Figure 1-1, China's exchange rate with the United States would be considered fixed; it was literally so up until July 2005, but even since then the very mechanical and predictable path of the exchange rate, and its very limited range of movement, would be judged as fixed.[2] In contrast, the euro-dollar exchange rate would be considered a floating exchange rate, one that moves up and down over a much wider range.

Key Topics How are exchange rates determined? Why do some exchange rates fluctuate sharply in the short run, while others are almost constant? What explains why exchange rates rise, fall, or stay flat in the long run?

Why Exchange Rates Matter

Having studied exchange rate fluctuations, we have to consider how and why such fluctuations might matter. We highlight two channels through which changes in exchange rates can affect the economy: by changing the international relative prices of goods and by changing the international relative prices of assets. Both can be illustrated with reference to recent changes in the U.S. dollar-euro exchange rate in Figure 1-1.

100 Chinese yuan, U.S. dollars, Eurozone euros

---

[2] As of early 2007, it appeared that China's de facto policy was to control its exchange rate in such a way that it followed a fixed trend against the U.S. dollar. See Jeffrey A. Frankel and Shang-Jin Wei, 2007, "Assessing China's Exchange Rate Regime," National Bureau of Economic Research (NBER) Working Paper No. 13100. The Chinese exchange rate's behavior may remain in flux; for example, in May 2007, the People's Bank of China announced that the yuan would be allowed to fluctuate more widely against the dollar, although what this might mean for the trend was not immediately clear.

In the goods market, the figure tells us that, in late 2002, when the exchange rate was 0.9 \$/€, something worth €10 in Europe had a U.S. dollar value of \$9. But in 2007, when the exchange rate was 1.3, a similar €10 item had a U.S. dollar value of \$13. This example shows how changes in an exchange rate can cause one country's goods and services to become more or less expensive relative to another's when expressed in a common unit of currency. It is easy to imagine why such price changes might have important macroeconomic implications: when European products become more expensive for Americans, exporting European products to the United States is likely to get more troublesome.

For example, in 2003 to 2004, German automaker Volkswagen blamed the rise in the dollar–euro exchange rate for some of its business problems. Volkswagen's manufacturing costs were largely in euros, but its U.S. sales were in U.S. dollars. Imagine Volkswagen paid, say, €10 an hour in labor costs. In dollar terms, those costs were pushed up by exchange rate changes from \$9 to \$13, as we just noted. What could Volkswagen do? Charging more to U.S. customers would hurt sales and dent profits, but leaving U.S. dollar prices fixed would also hurt profits. This was a problem for all European firms trying to export to the United States. But U.S. firms exporting to Europe faced an opposite and less troubling trend: their manufacturing costs were looking cheaper compared with those of their European rivals.[3] Figure 1-2 shows how short-run exchange rate movements can dramatically affect relative manufacturing costs in different countries.

Exchange rate movements change not only the domestic value of foreign goods but also the domestic value of foreign assets. These fluctuations in wealth can then have important implications for the overall prosperity of the firms, governments, and individuals in an economy. For example, the Eurozone countries held about \$200 billion in U.S. dollar assets at the end of 2002. These assets were worth approximately €200 billion, since €1 was then worth about \$1, as we saw in Figure 1-1. A year later, at the end of 2003, those same assets were worth the equivalent of only €160 billion. Why? The dollar was then worth only €0.80, and 0.8 times 200 equals 160. Hence, *simply as a result of a change in the exchange rate,* the inhabitants of the Eurozone suffered a €40 billion loss in their total wealth.[4]

Key Topics How do exchange rates affect the real economy? How do changes in exchange rates affect international prices, the demand for goods from different countries, and hence the levels of national output? How do changes in exchange rates affect the values of foreign assets, and hence change national wealth?

---

[3] Peter Gumbel, "Don't Blame It on the Euro," Time.com, May 11, 2003. Jack Ewing and Laura Cohn, "Beware the Brawny Euro: As It Strengthens, Europe's Currency Threatens to Snuff Out a Tenuous Recovery," BusinessWeek.com, November 29, 2004.
[4] Data for this example are based on U.S. Treasury reports.

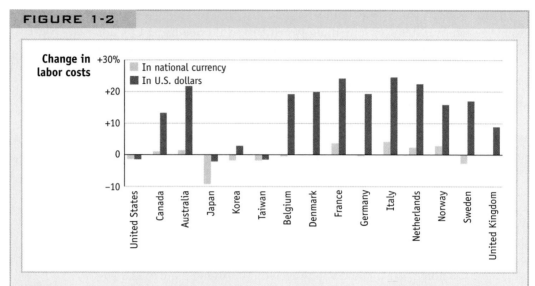

FIGURE 1-2

Exchange Rates and Manufacturing Costs The U.S. Bureau of Labor Statistics collects data on the changes in unit labor costs of manufacturing industries in different countries. This chart shows the changes from 2002 to 2003. Changes measured in local currency are small, but changes in U.S. dollar terms can be much larger due to the effect of exchange rate changes. In this period, the dollar depreciated against most floating currencies, so labor costs in those countries rose dramatically when measured in U.S.-dollar terms.

Source: U.S. Bureau of Labor Statistics, News, *October 27, 2005.*

When Exchange Rates Misbehave

Even after studying fixed and floating exchange rates, and after considering the economic impacts of each, we face the challenge of explaining the one type of event that is almost guaranteed to put exchange rates front and center in the news: the **exchange rate crisis.** In such a crisis, a currency experiences a sudden and pronounced loss of value against another currency, following a period in which the exchange rate had been fixed or relatively stable.

One of the most dramatic currency crises in recent times occurred in Argentina from December 2001 to January 2002. For a decade, the Argentine peso had been fixed to the U.S. dollar at a one-to-one rate of exchange. But in January 2002, the fixed exchange rate became a floating exchange rate. A few months later, one Argentine peso, which had been worth one U.S. dollar, had fallen in value to just $0.25 (equivalently, the price of a U.S. dollar rose from one peso to almost four pesos).

The drama was not confined to the foreign exchange market. The Argentine government declared a world-record **default** (i.e., a suspension of payments) on its $155 billion of debt; the financial system was in a state of near closure for months; inflation climbed; output collapsed and unemployment soared in the midst of an existing recession; and more than 50% of Argentine households fell below the poverty line. At the height of the crisis, violence flared and the country had five presidents in the space of two weeks (see **Headlines: Economic Crisis in Argentina**).

Argentina's experience was extreme but hardly unique. Exchange rate crises are fairly common. Figure 1-3 lists 19 exchange rate crises in the six-year period from 1997 to 2002. In almost all cases, a fairly stable exchange rate experienced a large and sudden change. The year 1997 was especially eventful, with seven crises, five of them in East Asia. The Indonesian rupiah lost 49% of its U.S. dollar value, after losing only 4% per year on average during the previous two years. Similar exchange rate movements were seen in Thailand, Korea, Malaysia, and the Philippines in 1997. Other notable exchange rate crises in this period included Liberia in 1998, Russia in 1998, Brazil in 1999, as well as Argentina in 2002.

Crisis episodes display some regular patterns in poorer countries. Output typically falls, banking and debt problems emerge, households and firms suffer. In addition, political turmoil often ensues. Government finances worsen, and embarrassed authorities may appeal for external help from international development organizations, such as the **International Monetary Fund (IMF)** or **World Bank,** or other countries. Although we could confine our study of exchange rates to normal times, the frequent and damaging occurrence of crises obliges us to pay attention to these abnormal episodes, too.

FIGURE 1-3

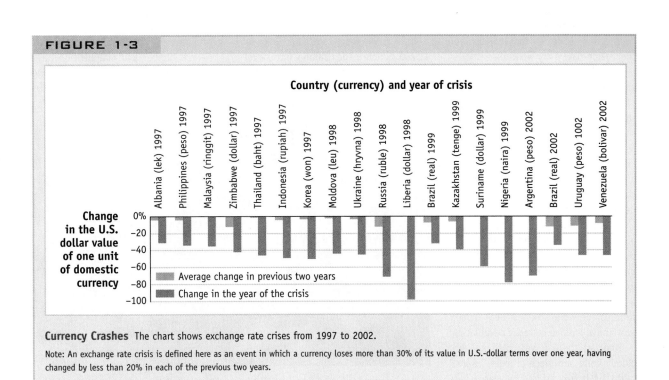

Currency Crashes The chart shows exchange rate crises from 1997 to 2002.

Note: An exchange rate crisis is defined here as an event in which a currency loses more than 30% of its value in U.S.-dollar terms over one year, having changed by less than 20% in each of the previous two years.

Source: IMF, International Financial Statistics.

HEADLINES

Economic Crisis in Argentina

This article was written just after the start of the severe economic crisis that engulfed Argentina in 2002, following the collapse of the fixed exchange rate. Real output shrank by 15% in 2002 and took two years to bounce back. Even as late as 2006, the official unemployment rate was still above 10%. The country sank into the most acute economic depression it had ever recorded, in terms of depth and length, worse even than the painful crises of the 1930s, 1910s, and 1890s.

ROSARIO, Argentina—Word spread fast through the vast urban slums ringing Rosario. There was food on the freeway—and it was still alive.

A cattle truck had overturned near this rusting industrial city, spilling 22 head of prime Angus beef across the wind-swept highway. Some were dead. Most were injured. A few were fine.

A mob moved out from Las Flores, a shantytown of trash heaps and metal shacks boiling over with refugees from the financial collapse of what was once Latin America's wealthiest nation. Within minutes, 600 hungry residents arrived on the scene, wielding machetes and carving knives. Suddenly, according to accounts from some of those present on that March day, a cry went up.

"Kill the cows!" someone yelled. "Take what you can!"

Cattle company workers attempting a salvage operation backed off. And the slaughter began. The scent of blood, death and fresh meat filled the highway. Cows bellowed as they were sloppily diced by groups of men, women and children. Fights broke out for pieces of flesh in bloody tugs of war.

"I looked around at people dragging off cow legs, heads and organs, and I couldn't believe my eyes," said Alberto Banrel, 43, who worked on construction jobs until last January, when the bottom fell out of the economy after Argentina suffered the world's largest debt default ever and a massive currency devaluation.

"And yet there I was, with my own bloody knife and piece of meat," Banrel said. "I felt like we had become a pack of wild animals . . . like piranhas on the Discovery Channel. Our situation has turned us into this."

The desolation of that day, neighbor vs. neighbor over hunks of meat, suggested how profoundly the collapse has altered Argentina. Traditionally proud, Argentines have begun to despair. Talk today is of vanished dignity, of a nation diminished in ways not previously imaginable. . . .

Until last year, Argentines were part of the richest, best-educated and most cultured nation in Latin America. . . . The poor here lived with more dignity than their equals anywhere else in the region. Argentina was, as the Argentines liked to say, very civilized.

Not anymore. . . .

With government statistics showing 11,200 people a day falling into poverty—earning less than $3 daily—Buenos Aires, a city once compared to Paris, has become the dominion of scavengers and thieves at night. Newly impoverished homeless people emerge from abandoned buildings and rail cars, rummaging through trash in declining middle- and upper-class neighborhoods. People from the disappearing middle class, such as Vicente Pitasi, 60 and jobless, have turned to pawn shops to sell their wedding rings.

"I have seen a lot happen in Argentina in my day, but I never lost hope until now," Pitasi said. "There is nothing left here, not even our pride.". . .

Food manufacturers and grocery stores are raising prices even as earning power has taken a historic tumble. A large factor in both the price rises and the slump in real wages is a 70 percent devaluation of the peso over the last six months. . . .

Severe hunger and malnutrition have emerged in the rural interior—something almost never seen in a country famous for great slabs of beef and undulating

Beatriz Orresta, 20, holds her malnourished son in Rio Chico. She had been feeding her children soup made with the dried bones of a dead cow her husband had found.

Silvina Frydlewsky for The Washington Post, August 5, 2002

Continued on next page.

fields of wheat. In search of someone to blame, Argentines have attacked the homes of local politicians and foreign banks. Many of the banks have installed steel walls and armed guards around branch offices, and replaced glass windows decorated with ads portraying happy clients from another era.

Economists and politicians differ on the causes of the brutal crisis. Some experts blame globalization and faulty policies imposed by the International Monetary Fund. But just as many blame the Argentine government for runaway spending and systematic corruption. The one thing everyone agrees on, however, is that there is no easy fix. . . .

What had been a snowball of poverty and unemployment has turned into an avalanche since January's default and devaluation. A record number of Argentines, more than half, live below the official poverty line. More than one in five no longer have jobs.

"We've had our highs and lows, but in statistical and human terms, this nation has never faced anything like this," said Artemio Lopez, an economist with Equis Research. "Our economic problems of the past pale to what we're going through now. It's like the nation is dissolving.". . .

For some rural families, the crisis has gone further. It has generated something rarely seen in Argentina: hunger.

In the province of Tucuman, an agricultural zone of 1.3 million people, health workers say cases of malnutrition have risen 20 percent to 30 percent over the previous year.

"I wish they would cry," whispered Beatriz Orresta, 20, looking at her two young sons in a depressed Tucuman sugar cane town in the shadow of the Andes. "I would feel much better if they cried."

Jonatan, 2, resting on the dirt floor behind the family's wooden shack, and Santiago, the 7-month-old she cradled in her arms, lay listlessly.

"They don't act it, but they're hungry. I know they are," she said.

Source: Excerpted from Anthony Faiola, "Despair in Once-Proud Argentina: After Economic Collapse, Deep Poverty Makes Dignity a Casualty," Washington Post, August 6, 2002.

Key Topics Why do exchange rate crises occur? What explains the precise timing of their occurrence? Are they an inevitable symptom of deeper problems in the economy, or are they an avoidable result of manias, panics, or other irrational forces in financial markets? Why are these crises so economically and politically costly? What steps might be taken to prevent crises, and at what cost?

Summary

International macroeconomists frequently refer to the exchange rate as "the single most important price in an open economy." If we treat this statement as more than self-promotion, we should endeavor to see why it might be true. In our course of study we will encounter fixed and floating exchange rates, as well as the catastrophic changes seen during exchange rate crises. We will explore what determines the exchange rate, how the exchange rate affects the economy, and how crises occur.

Signing away: In January 1998, President Suharto of Indonesia signed an agreement for assistance watched by IMF Managing Director Michel Camdessus. Suharto's authoritarian government endured for decades but could not survive the humiliations of the 1997 crisis. Suharto resigned in May 1998.

Plan of Study Foreign currencies trade in markets, the structure and operation of which we explore in Chapter 2. The theory of exchange rates is laid out in Chapters 3 and 4. We then develop the tools necessary to understand international transactions in goods and assets in Chapter 5, including an understanding of how exchange rate changes affect wealth. We examine the impact of exchange rates on demand and output in the short run in Chapter 7. We can then understand some of the trade-offs facing governments as they choose between fixed and floating exchange rates, a topic covered in Chapter 8. Crises are the subject of Chapter 9. After examining their characteristics, we explore two models of crises that shed light on controversial policy debates—crises may emerge from inept macroeconomic policies or from shifts in beliefs of financial markets. Chapter 10 covers the euro, a common currency used in many countries. Chapter 11 further explores exchange rate topics.

2   Globalization of Finance: Of Debts and Deficits

Financial development is a defining characteristic of modern economies. Households' day-to-day use of financial instruments such as credit cards, savings accounts, and mortgages is taken for granted, as is the ability of firms and governments to use the products and services offered in financial markets. Remarkably, only just a few years ago, very little of this financial activity spilled across international borders. Countries were very nearly closed from a financial standpoint. In contrast, today many countries have become more open: financial globalization is now taking hold around the world, starting in the rich, economically advanced countries and increasingly spreading to many so-called emerging market countries.

How can we understand financial transactions between countries? By appealing to familiar accounting concepts that we apply at the household level, such as income, expenditure, and wealth. We develop these concepts at the national level to understand how flows of goods, services, income, and capital make the global macroeconomy work. We can then see how the smooth functioning of international finance can make countries better off by allowing them to lend and borrow. Along the way, we also recognize that financial interactions are not always so smooth. Defaults cause frequent and notable disruptions in international financial markets, so we explore how defaults occur and what effects they can have.

Deficits and Surpluses: The Balance of Payments

Do you keep track of your finances? If so, you probably follow two important figures: your income and expenditure. The difference between the two is an important number: if it is positive you have a surplus; if it is negative you have a deficit. The number tells you if you are living within or beyond your means. What would you do with a surplus? The extra money could be added to savings or used to pay down debt. How would you handle a deficit? You could run down your savings or borrow and run up your debt. Thus, imbalances between income and expenditure require you to engage in financial transactions with the world outside your household.

The same ideas apply when we move to the national level: we can make the same kinds of economic measurements, of **income, expenditure, deficit,** and **surplus,** many of which are important barometers of economic performance and the subject of heated policy debate. For example, Table 1-1 shows

TABLE 1-1

Income, Expenditure, and the Current Account The table shows data for the United States from 1991 to 2006 in billions of U.S. dollars. During this period, in all but one year U.S. expenditure exceeded income, with the U.S. current account in deficit. The last (small) surplus was in 1991.

	Income *Gross National Disposable Income*	Expenditure *Gross National Expenditure*	Difference *Current Account*
1990	$5,811	$5,881	$-70
1991	6,037	6,023	+14
1992	6,334	6,371	-37
1993	6,652	6,723	-70
1994	7,061	7,166	-105
1995	7,398	7,489	-91
1996	7,813	7,913	-100
1997	8,296	8,406	-110
1998	8,720	8,907	-187
1999	9,255	9,529	-274
2000	9,800	10,197	-397
2001	10,125	10,495	-370
2002	10,436	10,894	-458
2003	10,948	11,460	-512
2004	11,677	12,326	-649
2005	12,401	13,173	-771
2006	13,197	14,009	-812

Source: U.S. National Income and Product Accounts, Tables 1.1.5 and 4.1, April 2007, bea.gov.

measures of U.S. national income and expenditure since 1990 in billions of U.S. dollars. At the national level, these concepts get special names. The income measure is called *gross national disposable income;* the expenditure measure is called *gross national expenditure.* The difference between the two is a key macro-economic aggregate in the open economy: the *current account,* which reflects income–expenditure imbalances.

Since posting a small surplus in 1991, the U.S. deficit on the current account (a negative number) grew steadily to $812 billion by 2006, or about 6% of U.S. national income. Income, from all sources, was not enough to cover expenditure in these years. How was this shortfall in resources bridged? By financial transactions with the outside world, just as in the case of a house-hold; that is, the United States borrowed the difference.

However, it is impossible for the world to run a deficit: the world *as a whole* is a closed economy (we can't borrow from outer space, as yet). Thus, if the United States is a net borrower, running a current account deficit with income less than expenditure, then the rest of the world must be a net lender to the United States, running surpluses with expenditure less than income. Globally, the world's finances must balance in this way, but individ-ual countries and regions can exhibit pronounced imbalances one way or the other. Figure 1-4 shows the massive scale of some of these recent imbalances, dramatically illustrating the impact of financial globalization in today's global macroeconomy.

Key Topics How do different international economic transactions contribute to current account imbalances? How are these imbalances financed? What causes the imbalances? How long can they persist? Why are some countries in surplus and others in deficit? What role do current account imbalances perform in a well-functioning economy in the long run? And in the short run? Why are these imbalances the focus of so much policy debate?

FIGURE 1-4

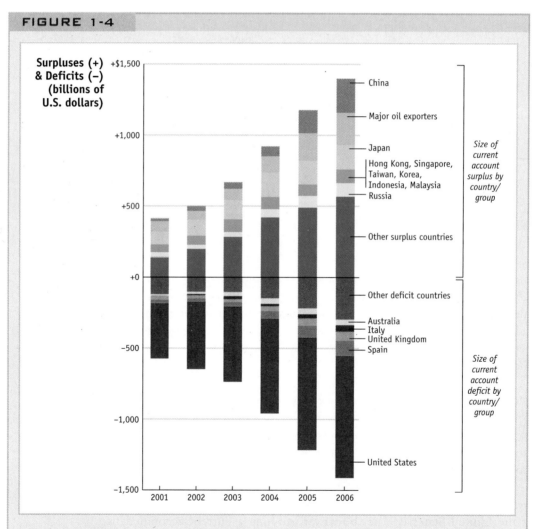

Global Imbalances In recent years the United States has run a record current account deficit, accounting for over half of all deficits globally. Major offsetting surpluses have been seen in Asia (e.g., China and Japan) and in oil-exporting countries.

Source: IMF, International Financial Statistics.

Debtors and Creditors: External Wealth

To discuss **wealth,** we can again invoke the household analogy. Your total wealth or net worth is equal to your assets (what others owe you) minus your liabilities (what you owe others). When you run a surplus and save money (buying assets or paying down debt), your total wealth, or net worth, tends to rise. Similarly, when you have a deficit and borrow (taking on debt or running down savings), your wealth tends to fall. Again, the household logic can be adapted to the national level. From an international perspective, a country's measured net worth is called *external wealth* and is equal to the difference between its foreign assets (what it is owed by the rest of the world) and its foreign liabilities (what it owes to the rest of the world). Positive external wealth makes a country a creditor nation; negative external wealth makes it a debtor nation.

Changes in external wealth can result from imbalances in the nation's current account: a surplus leads external wealth to rise, and a deficit leads to a fall, all else equal. For example, a string of U.S. current account deficits, going back to the 1980s, has been a major factor in the steady decline in U.S. external wealth, as shown in Figure 1-5, panel (a). The United States had been a creditor nation for decades until the mid-1980s; now it is the world's largest debtor, with external wealth equal to –$2,500 billion in 2005.[5] In Figure 1-5, a year with a current account surplus such as 1991

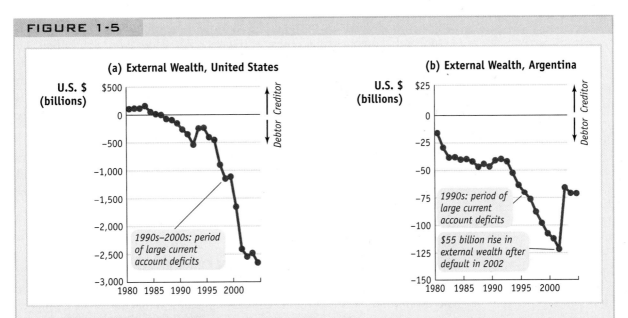

FIGURE 1-5

(a) External Wealth, United States

(b) External Wealth, Argentina

External Wealth A country's net credit position with the rest of the world is called external wealth. The time series charts show levels of external wealth from 1980 to 2004 for the United States in panel (a) and Argentina in panel (b). All else equal, deficits cause external wealth to fall; surpluses (and defaults) cause it to rise.

Source: Gian Maria Milesi-Ferretti and Philip R. Lane, 2006, "The External Wealth of Nations Mark II: Revised and Extended Estimates of Foreign Assets and Liabilities, 1970–2004," IMF Working Papers 06/69.

---

[5] Only provisional 2005 data from bea.gov were available at the time of this writing.

stands out as a rare moment when U.S. external wealth briefly halted its decline. Another country with persistent current account deficits in the 1990s, Argentina, also saw its external wealth decline, as panel (b) shows.

But a closer look at these figures shows that there must be other factors that affect a country's external wealth. For example, even after 1991, when the United States ran deficits every year, external wealth sometimes went up, not down. How can this be? Let us return to the household analogy. If you have ever invested in the stock market, you may know that even in a year when your expenditure exceeds your income (you run a deficit of $1,000, say), you may still end up wealthier if the value of your stocks went up (by $10,000, say, leaving you, on net, $9,000 wealthier overall). Again, what is true for households is true for countries: their external wealth can be affected by **capital gains** on investments, so we need to give quite careful thought to the complex causes and consequences of external wealth.

We also have to remember that, with investments, what goes up can also go down. When the infamous U.S. energy company Enron went bankrupt in 2001, for example, the wiping out of Enron's debt liabilities (a gain for Enron) simultaneously wiped out its creditors' assets (a loss for them). The same applies internationally: a country can gain not only by having the value of its assets rise but also by having the value of its liabilities fall. In 2002 Argentina announced a record default on its government debt. Debt to organizations such as the World Bank and IMF was paid in full, but the Argentine government offered to pay on average only about 30¢ for each dollar of debt in private hands. Foreigners held most of this debt. They lost about $55 billion at a stroke. But at the very same moment, Argentina simultaneously and symmetrically gained about $55 billion in external wealth, as shown by the sudden jump in Figure 1-5, panel (b). So you don't have to necessarily run a surplus to increase external wealth—external wealth rises not only when creditors are paid off but also when they are blown off.

Key Topics What explains the level of a nation's external wealth, and how does it change over time? How does it relate to the country's present and future economic welfare? How important is the current account as a determinant of external wealth? What forms can external wealth take, and does the composition of wealth matter?

Darlings and Deadbeats: Defaults and Other Risks

As an illustration of government debt default, the recent Argentine case is by no means unusual. Here is a recently compiled list of defaults since 1980:

Argentina 1982, 2001	Pakistan 1997–1998
Chile 1983	Peru 1980, 1983
Dominican Republic 1982, 1999	Philippines 1983
Ecuador 1999	Russia 1991, 1998
Indonesia 1998	South Africa 1985, 1989
Mexico 1982	Ukraine 1998
Nigeria 1983, 1986	Uruguay 1990, 2003

These episodes highlight some peculiar risks of international finance: creditors may be poorly protected in foreign jurisdictions. Sovereign governments can repudiate debt without legal penalty. And aside from default, there are many other ways for debtors to hurt creditors, including the wholesale expropriation of assets as well as opportunistic changes in the regulatory environment once investments have been put in place.[6]

Risk carries a price, and markets are very interested in trying to get that price right. How do they do that? By careful assessments and monitoring. For example, any financial misbehavior will end up on your credit report: a grade-A credit score means easy access to low-interest loans; a grade-C score means more limited credit and possibly punitive interest rates. Credit markets apply similar ratings to corporations. For example, on October 15, 2001, Enron was rated a very high BBB+ by the Standard & Poor's (S&P) agency; by November 9, news of its hidden losses had emerged and it dropped to a grade of BBB−; by November 30, it was downgraded to a CC; and when the company filed for bankruptcy on December 3, it was rated a D.

But it's not just individuals and firms whose risks are graded this way; so, too, are countries. Advanced countries, for whom country risk is essentially zero, usually have good credit ratings. But emerging markets often find themselves subject to lower grades. Bonds rated BBB− or higher are considered high-grade or *investment-grade bonds;* bonds rated BB+ and lower are called *junk bonds.* Poorer ratings tend to go hand in hand with higher interest rates, commonly measured by **country risk,** which is the additional annual interest paid by a government on its bonds compared with the interest paid on a safe "benchmark" U.S. Treasury bond. For example, if U.S. bonds pay 3% and the country pays 5% per annum on its bonds, the country risk is +2%.

Figure 1-6 shows country risk (and S&P ratings) for 16 emerging-market countries in June 2005. The top four countries were judged investment grade (BBB±), but the others were given junk bond ratings (BB± or B±). The BBB± bonds paid between 0.49% and 1.69% more in interest each year than U.S. Treasury bonds. BB± bonds paid between 0.78% and 4.23% more.

Carrying the highest country risk were the B or B− rated bonds of Venezuela at 4.73%, Ecuador at 7.15%, and finally, Argentina, with a country risk of 8.90%. What had some of these debtors done to deserve such bad grades? The Argentine government was still in the doghouse after the biggest default in history, although its country risk was falling (it had earlier been more than 60% at times!). The Venezuelan government of Hugo Chávez, despite healthy oil revenues, worried foreign investors with plans to nationalize industries and tax foreign companies' profits, and political stability

---

[6] The list is limited to privately issued bond and bank debts since 1980. Data from Eduardo Levy-Yeyati and Ugo G. Panizza, "The Elusive Costs of Sovereign Defaults," CIF Working Paper No. 11/2006. Dozens more countries, many in Africa, could be added to the list if we expanded the definition of default. For example, a number of very poor countries cannot make their payments on loans from international financial institutions like the World Bank. These debts may be mechanically rolled over, avoiding default by a technicality. In some cases, they are eventually "voluntarily" forgiven.

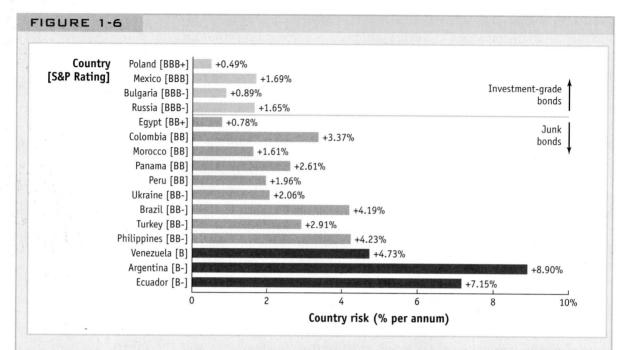

FIGURE 1-6

Country Risk Emerging markets typically pay higher interest rates on their debts. The greater the risk perceived by financial markets, the higher is the "country risk"—the size of the spread between a country's government bond interest rates and "safe" U.S. Treasury bond interest rates. The data shown are for June 2005.

Sources: EMBI+ spreads from cbonds.info, June 15, 2005; Standard & Poor's ratings, June 3, 2005.

appeared uncertain. In Ecuador, meanwhile, a default was starting to look possible, as the government raised objections to the restructuring terms agreed to following its previous default in 1999.

Key Topics Why do countries default? What happens when they do? What are the determinants of risk premiums? How do risk premiums affect macroeconomic outcomes such as output and exchange rates?

Summary

International flows of goods, services, income, and capital allow the global macroeconomy to operate, and we need to understand all these vital functions. In our course of study, we build up our understanding gradually, starting with basic accounting and measurement, then moving on to understand what causes imbalances in the flows and the accumulations of debts and credits and what the consequences of these imbalances might be. Along the way, our eyes will be opened to the gains from financial globalization, as well as some of the inherent risks of international finance.

Plan of Study The apparatus of national income accounts and international transactions is presented in Chapter 5. The **balance of payments** shows how the current account can be broken down into imbalances of goods and services, an important item known as the *trade balance,* plus imbalances on various kinds of income and transfers; it also shows how these transactions are financed by trade in assets. Chapter 6 considers the helpful functions that imbalances can play in a well-functioning economy in the long run, allowing us to see the potential long-run benefits of financial globalization. Chapter 7 then explores how imbalances play a role in short-run macroeconomic adjustment and in the workings of monetary and fiscal policies that are used to manage aggregate demand. In Chapter 8, we pay attention to the fact that assets traded internationally are often denominated in different currencies; we then see how wealth can be sensitive to exchange rate changes and what macroeconomic effects this might have. Chapter 9 examines the implications of risk premiums for exchange rates, allowing us to see some of the links between exchange rate crises and default crises. Chapter 11 explores in more detail topics such as global imbalances and default.

Buy now, pay later? The U.S. trade deficit is always in the news.

3 Government and Institutions: Of Policies and Performance

In theory, one could devise a course of study in international economics without reference to government, but the result might not shed much light on reality. As we know from other courses in economics, and as we have already started to see in this brief introduction, government actions influence economic outcomes in many ways. Governments affect exchange rates, they conduct monetary and fiscal policies, they can pay (or not pay) their debts, and so on.

To gain a deeper understanding of the global macroeconomy, economists look at government activity on two distinct levels. The more traditional approach requires that we study **policies.** Here we focus on the economic implications of various government actions, such as the specific macroeconomic policy choices that are made from time to time. This discussion takes us into familiar textbook topics such as changes in monetary and fiscal policy. However, economists are increasingly paying attention to the broader contexts in which policy choices are made. We might refer to these slightly larger policy spaces as sets of rules, or **regimes.** Beyond sets of rules that limit policy choices, recent research focuses on **institutions,** a term that refers to the very broad legal, political, and social structures that influence economic behavior.

We conclude our brief introduction to international macroeconomics by highlighting three important features of the broad macroeconomic environment that will play an important role in the remainder of this book: the rules that a government decides to apply to restrict or allow capital mobility; the decision that a government makes between a fixed and a floating exchange rate regime; and the institutional foundations of economic performance, such as the quality of governance that prevails in a country.

Integration and Capital Controls: The Regulation of International Finance

The United States is seen as one of the most financially open countries in the world, fully open to the global capital market. This is mostly true, but in recent years the U.S. government has blocked some foreign investment in ports, oil, and airlines. These are rather exceptional cases in the United States, but in many countries there are numerous, severe restrictions on cross-border financial transactions.

It is important to remember that globalization does not occur in a political vacuum. Globalization is often viewed as a technological phenomenon, a process driven by innovations in transport and communications such as container shipping and the Internet. But international economic integration has also occurred because some governments have allowed it to happen. In the past 50 years, international trade has grown as trade barriers have been slowly dismantled. More recently, international capital movement has been encouraged as barriers to financial transactions have been lifted.

Figure 1-7 documents some of the important features of the trend toward financial globalization since 1970. Panel (a) employs an index of financial openness, where 0% means fully closed with tight capital controls, and 100% means fully open with no controls. The index is compiled from measures of restriction on cross-border financial transactions. The average value of the index is shown for three groups of countries that will figure quite often in our analysis:

- **Advanced countries**—countries with high levels of income per person that are well integrated into the global economy
- **Emerging markets**—mainly middle-income countries that are growing and becoming more integrated into the global economy
- **Developing countries**—mainly low-income countries that are not yet well integrated into the global economy

Using these data to gauge policy changes over the past three decades, we can see that the trend toward financial openness started first, and went the furthest, in the advanced countries, with a rapid shift toward openness evident in the 1980s, when many countries abolished capital controls that had been in place since World War II. We can also see that in the 1990s, emerging markets also started to liberalize financially and, to a lesser degree, so too did some developing countries.

What were the consequences of these policy changes? Panel (b) looks at some economic outcomes and measures the extent of cross-border financial

FIGURE 1-7

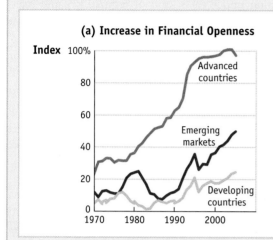

(a) Increase in Financial Openness

Index 100%

Advanced countries

Emerging markets

Developing countries

1970   1980   1990   2000

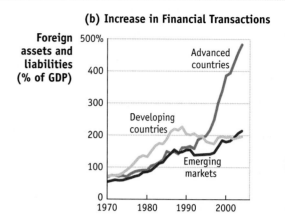

(b) Increase in Financial Transactions

Foreign assets and liabilities (% of GDP)   500%

Advanced countries

Developing countries

Emerging markets

1970   1980   1990   2000

Financial Globalization Since the 1970s, many restrictions on international financial transactions have been lifted, as shown by the time series chart in panel (a). The volume of transactions has also increased dramatically, as shown in panel (b). These trends have been strongest in the advanced countries, followed by the emerging markets and the developing countries.

Notes: The *advanced countries* are Australia, Austria, Belgium, Canada, Denmark, Finland, France, Germany, Greece, Iceland, Ireland, Italy, Japan, Luxembourg (excluded here), The Netherlands, New Zealand, Norway, Portugal, Spain, Sweden, Switzerland, The United Kingdom, and United States. The *emerging markets* are Argentina, Brazil, Chile, China, Colombia, The Czech

Republic, Egypt, Estonia, Hong Kong, Hungary, India, Indonesia, Israel, Korea, Latvia, Lithuania, Malaysia, Mexico, Pakistan, Peru, The Philippines, Poland, Russia, Saudi Arabia, Singapore, The Slovak Republic, Slovenia, South Africa, Thailand, Turkey, and Venezuela. All other countries are treated as *developing*.

Sources: *Gian Maria Milesi-Ferretti and Philip R. Lane, 2006, "The External Wealth of Nations Mark II: Revised and Extended Estimates of Foreign Assets and Liabilities, 1970–2004," IMF Working Papers 06/69. Menzie D. Chinn and Hiro Ito, 2006, "What Matters for Financial Development? Capital Controls, Institutions, and Interactions," Journal of Development Economics, 81(1), 163–192 (and updates). Country classifications are an extended version of those developed in M. Ayhan Kose, Eswar Prasad, Kenneth S. Rogoff and Shang-Jin Wei, 2006, "Financial Globalization: A Reappraisal," NBER Working Paper No. 12484.*

transactions by adding up total foreign assets and liabilities (expressed as a percentage of output) for the three country groups. As the world became more financially open, the extent of cross-border financial transactions increased by a factor of ten or more. As one might expect, this trend has gone the furthest in the more financially open advanced countries, but the emerging markets and developing countries follow a similar path.

Key Topics Why have so many countries made the choice to pursue policies of financial openness? What are the potential economic benefits of removing capital controls and adopting such liberalization policies? If there are benefits, why has this policy change been so slow to occur since the 1970s? Are there any potential costs that offset the benefits? If so, can capital controls really work?

Independence and Monetary Policy: The Choice of Exchange Rate Regimes

We have seen that there are two broad categories of exchange rate behavior, and we refer to these as fixed regimes and floating regimes. How common is each

Out of control: For years, Zimbabwe imposed capital controls. In theory, U.S. dollars could be traded for Zimbabwe dollars only through official channels at an official rate. On the street, the reality was different.

type? Figure 1-8 shows that there are many countries operating under each kind of regime. Because fixed and floating are both common regime choices, we have to understand both.

The choice of exchange rate regime is a major policy problem. If you have noticed even a small fraction of the attention given by journalists and policy makers in recent years to the exchange rate movements of the dollar, euro, yen, pound, yuan, and other currencies, you will be aware that these are major issues in debates on the global economy.

Exploring the evidence on exchange rate fluctuations, their impact, and their theoretical origins is a major goal of this book. On an intuitive level, whether we are confused travelers fumbling to change money at the bank or importers and exporters trying to conduct business in a predictable way, we have a sense that exchange rate fluctuations, especially if acute, could impose real economic costs. If everyone fixed their exchange rates, we could avoid those costs. Or, taking the argument to an extreme, we might wonder why different currencies even exist in the first place. All currency-related transaction costs could be avoided if we had a single world currency. But we are very far from that monetary utopia—at present more than 150 different currencies exist!

The existence of multiple currencies in the world dates back centuries, as numismatic history can confirm. This is understandable—for a state to possess its own currency has long been viewed as an almost essential aspect of sovereignty. Without control of its own national currency, a government's freedom to pursue its own monetary policy is sacrificed automatically. However, even with your own currency, it still remains to be seen how beneficial—and how feasible—such monetary independence might be.

FIGURE 1-8

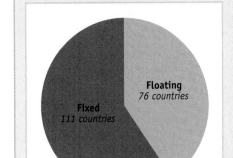

Exchange Rate Regimes of the World The pie chart shows a classification of exchange rate regimes around the world for the year 2006.

Notes: The fixed category includes countries with no separate legal tender (41 countries), currency boards (7), other fixed pegs (52), pegs within horizontal bands (6), and crawling pegs (5). The floating category includes managed floating with no predetermined path for the exchange rate (51) and independently floating (25). More details are shown in Chapter 2.

Source: IMF, De Facto Classification of Exchange Rate Regimes and Monetary Policy Framework, July 31, 2006, http://www.imf.org.

Despite this profusion of currencies, we also see newly emerging forms of order. Some groups of countries have sought to simplify their transactions through monetary union—the adoption of a **common currency** with shared policy responsibility. The most notable example is the Eurozone, a subset of the European Union currently comprising 13 countries in 2007 but with more members expected to join soon. Still other countries have chosen to use currencies over which they have no policy control, as with the recent cases of **dollarization** in countries such as El Salvador and Ecuador.

Key Topics Why do so many countries insist on the "barbarism" of having their own currency (as John Stuart Mill put it)? Why have a few, like the Eurozone, gone in the opposite direction by creating a common currency? Why have others dollarized? Why do some of the countries that have kept their own currencies then maintain a fixed exchange rate vis-à-vis another currency? And why do others permit their exchange rate to fluctuate over time, making a floating exchange rate their regime choice?

Institutions and Economic Performance: The Quality of Governance

Our final concern is not specific policy choices but the broader institutional context. Institutions consist of the legal, political, social, and other structures of a society that, through either formal mechanisms and rules or informal norms and culture, deliver a better or worse environment for economic prosperity and stability.

Figure 1-9 provides evidence of the importance of the quality of institutions or "governance" using national measures on six dimensions: voice and accountability, political stability, government effectiveness, regulatory quality, rule of law, and control of corruption. The figure shows that, across countries, an average or composite measure of all these dimensions is strongly correlated with economic outcomes (see **Headlines: The Wealth of Nations**).

First, we see that better institutions are correlated with more **income per person** in panel (a). A government that is unaccountable, unstable, ineffective, capricious, corrupt, and not based on laws is unlikely to encourage commerce, business, investment, or innovation. The effects of institutions on economic prosperity are very large. In the advanced countries at the top right of the figure, income per person is more than 50 times larger than in the poorest developing countries at the bottom left, probably the largest gap between rich and poor nations we have ever seen in history. Economists refer to this unequal outcome as **The Great Divergence.**

Lithuanians and Letts do it . . . and others are falling in love with the euro, too. Below are the proposed designs of euro coins for six aspiring members (left to right): Cyprus, Estonia, Latvia, Lithuania, Malta, and Slovakia.

FIGURE 1-9

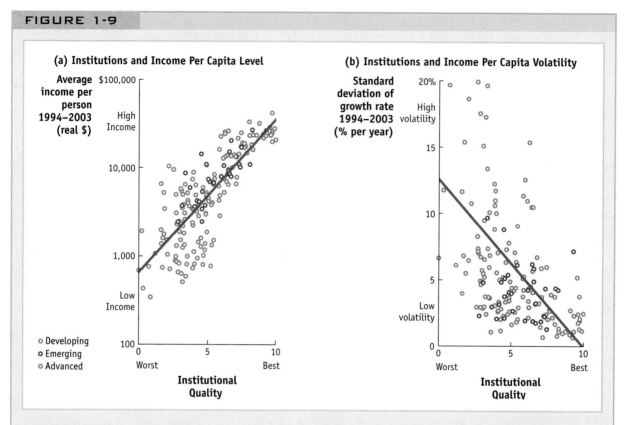

Institutions and Economic Performance The scatterplots show how an index measuring the quality of a country's institutions is positively correlated with the level of income per person as shown in panel (a) and is inversely correlated with the volatility of income per person as shown in panel (b).

Note: Several highly volatile countries (e.g., Afghanistan, Bosnia) are extreme outliers and are off the chart on the right.

Source: Real GDP per capita from Penn World Tables. Institutional quality from Daniel Kaufmann, Aart Kraay and Massimo Mastruzzi, 2006, "Governance Matters V: Governance Indicators for 1996–2005," World Bank Policy Research, September 2006.

We also see that better institutions are correlated with less **income volatility** (smaller fluctuations in income per capita). This result is shown in panel (b) and may also reflect the unpredictability of economic activity in poorly governed economies. There may be periodic shifts in political power, leading to big changes in economic policies. Or there may be internal conflict between groups that sporadically breaks out and leads to conflict over economic spoils. Or state capacity may be too weak to ensure that essential policies to stabilize the economy are carried out properly (e.g., bank regulation).

Recent research has documented these patterns and has sought to show that causality runs from institutions to outcomes and to explore the possible sources of institutional variation. Institutional change is typically very slow, taking decades or even centuries: vested interests may seek to block efficiency-enhancing reforms and so, as the institutional economist Thorstein Veblen famously pointed out, "Institutions are products of the past process, are adapted to past circumstances, and are therefore never in full accord with the requirements of the present." Consequently, much influential research seeks to find deep historical origins for the divergence of institutions (and hence incomes), including factors such as the following:

- Actions of colonizing powers (helpful in setting up good institutions in areas settled by Europeans but harmful in tropical areas where Europeans did not transplant their own institutions and "extractive" states developed);

- Types of legal codes that different countries developed (the British common law generally resulting in better outcomes than codes based on continental civil law);

- Patterns of resource endowments (tropical crops being more suitable for slave-based economies, limited power sharing, and extractive outcomes; temperate crops being more suited to small-scale farming, decentralized democratic power, and better governance).[7]

Key Topics Research shows that governance matters. It explains deep differences between countries in their macroeconomic outcomes. Poor governance generally means that a country is poorer and is subject to more macroeconomic shocks. It may also be subject to more political shocks and a general inability to conduct policy in a reliable and consistent way. These characteristics force us to think carefully about the formulation of optimal policies and policy regimes in rich and poor countries. One size may not fit all, and policies that work well in a stable, well-governed country may be less successful in an unstable, developing country with a record of low-quality government.

Summary

The functioning of the global macroeconomy is affected in many ways by the actions of governments. Throughout the book, we must pay attention to the possible actions that governments might take and try to understand their possible causes and consequences.

Plan of Study In Chapter 4, we encounter an important result: if a country is financially open, then a fixed exchange rate is incompatible with the exercise of monetary policy. Because both goals may be desirable, policy makers are often reluctant to face up to the difficult trade-offs implied by financial globalization. Despite these challenges, capital mobility is on the

---

[7] Daron Acemoglu, Simon Johnson and James A. Robinson, 2001, "The Colonial Origins of Comparative Development: An Empirical Investigation," *American Economic Review,* 91(5), December, 1369–1401. Stanley L. Engerman and Kenneth L. Sokoloff, 1997, "Factor Endowments, Institutions, and Differential Paths of Growth among New World Economies: A View from Economic Historians of the United States," in Stephen Haber, ed., *How Latin America Fell Behind,* Stanford, CA: Stanford University Press. Rafael La Porta, Florencio Lopez-de-Silanes, Andrei Shleifer and Robert Vishny, 1999, "The Quality of Government," *Journal of Law, Economics and Organization,* 15(1), April, 222–279.

HEADLINES

The Wealth of Nations

Social scientists have sought for centuries to understand the essential conditions that enable a nation to advance toward prosperity. In The Wealth of Nations, *Adam Smith said: "Little else is requisite to carry a state to the highest degree of opulence from the lowest barbarism, but peace, easy taxes, and a tolerable administration of justice; all the rest being brought about by the natural course of things." In many poor countries, basic institutional conditions are weak: politics are unstable, corruption is endemic, the quality of government services is low, and legal enforcement of property rights and contracts is nearly impossible. The following article discusses the poor quality of governance in the developing countries and the obstacle this poses to economic development.*

It takes 200 days to register a new business in Haiti and just two in Australia. This contrast perfectly encapsulates the gulf between one of the world's poorest countries and one of the richest. A sophisticated market economy is a uniquely powerful engine of prosperity. Yet, in far too many poor countries, the law's delays and the insolence of office prevent desperately needed improvements in economic performance.

That makes [the 2005] "World Development Report" among the most important the World Bank has ever produced.* It is about how to make market economies work. . . . The report is based on two big research projects: surveys of the investment climate . . . in 53 countries; and the "doing business" project, which identifies obstacles to business in 130 countries. . . . The argument starts with growth. As the report rightly notes: "With rising populations, economic growth is the only sustainable mechanism for increasing a society's standard of living." Happily, "investment climate improvements in China and India have driven the greatest reductions in poverty the world has ever seen." . . . Governmental failure is the most important obstacle business faces. Inadequate enforcement of contracts, inappropriate regulations, corruption, rampant crime and unreliable infrastructure can cost 25

per cent of sales. This is more than three times what businesses typically pay in taxes. Similarly, when asked to enumerate the obstacles they face, businesses list policy uncertainty, macroeconomic instability, taxes and corruption at the head of the list. What do these have in common? Incompetence and malfeasance by governments is again the answer. . . .

In many developing countries, the requirement is not less government but more and better directed government. What does this involve? Four requirements are listed: a reduction in the

"rent-seeking" that affects all countries but mars developing countries to an extreme extent; credibility in the making and execution of policy; the fostering of public trust and legitimacy; and the tailoring of policy responses to what works in local conditions.

One of the conclusions the report rightly draws from this list is that reform is not a one-off event but a process. What is involved is not just discrete and well-known policy changes (such as lower tariffs) but the fine-tuning of policy and the evolution of institutions. This is

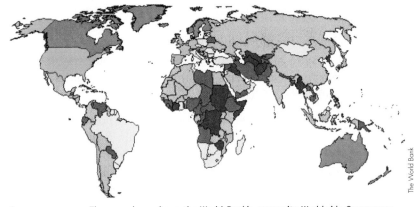

The World Bank

Green means grow: The map above shows the World Bank's composite Worldwide Governance Indicator in 2005. The index measures voice and accountability, political stability, government effectiveness, regulatory quality, rule of law, and control of corruption. Green indicates a country that is in the top 25% based on this measure, yellow next 25%, orange next 25%, and red bottom 25%. Dark green and dark red are the top and bottom 10%, respectively. The prosperity in Europe, North America, Australiasia, and Japan coincides with the best institutions of governance; the poverty in so much of Africa and parts of Asia with the poorest ones.

Continued on next page.

why, it suggests, the credibility of the government's journey, as in China, may be more important than the details of policy at each stage along the way.

Turning these broad objectives into specific policy is a tricky business. The Bank describes its core recommendation as "delivering the basics." These are: stability and security, which includes protection of property (see chart), facilitating contract enforcement, curbing crime and compensating for expropriation; better regulation and taxation, which means focusing intervention where it is needed, broadening the tax base and lowering tax rates, and reducing barriers to trade; better finance and infrastructure, which requires both more competition and better regulation; and transforming labour market regulation, to foster skills, while avoiding the counterproductive interventions that so often destroy employment in the formal sector. . . .

The world's wealthy countries can also help by lifting their many barriers to imports from developing countries and by targeting aid on improving the investment climate.

Governments then are both the disease and the cure. This is why development is so hard and so slow. The big advance is in the richness of our understanding of what makes an economy thrive. But that understanding also demonstrates the difficulties. The Bank's recognition of the nature of the disease is at least a first step towards the cure.

Source: Martin Wolf, "Sweep Away the Barriers to Growth," Financial Times, October 5, 2004.
*A Better Investment Climate for Everyone, World Development Report 2005. Oxford University Press and the World Bank.

rise, under both fixed and floating exchange rate regimes. Chapter 6 explores the economic rationales for financial liberalization: to smooth consumption, enhance efficiency, and diversify risk. On those grounds, financial openness is an unmitigated plus. So why are countries slow to liberalize? We explore exchange rate regime choice in detail in Chapter 8 and study the trade-offs involved. Then, in Chapter 9, we study crises. We see that if a country's policy makers cling to fixed exchange rates, there is a risk of suffering costly crises. The remarkable Euro project, discussed in Chapter 10, throws these issues into sharper perspective in the one region of the world where economic integration has arguably progressed the furthest in recent decades. The main lessons of our study are that policy makers need to acknowledge trade-offs, formulate sensible goals, and exercise careful judgment when deciding when and how to financially open their economies. Sadly, history shows that all too often they don't.

4 Conclusions

Today's global macroeconomy is an economic system characterized by increasingly integrated markets for goods, services, and capital. To effectively study macroeconomic outcomes in this context, we must understand the important economic linkages between different countries—their currencies, their trade, their capital flows, and so on. Only then can we understand some of the most important economic phenomena in the world today, such as the fluctuations in currencies, the causes of crises, the determinants of global imbalances, the problems of economic policy making, and the origins of the growing gap between rich and poor countries.

KEY POINTS

1. Countries have different currencies, and the price at which these currencies trade is known as the exchange rate. An important goal is to understand what determines this exchange rate and how the exchange rate is linked to the rest of the economy. Along the way, we confront various questions: Why do some countries have fixed exchange rates and others floating? Why do some go from one to the other, often via a crisis? Why do some countries have no currency of their own?

2. Countries are financially integrated, and this allows them to decouple their level of income from their level of expenditure, with the difference being known as the current account. An important goal is to understand what determines the current account and how the current account is linked to the rest of the economy.

Along the way, we confront various questions: How does the current account affect a country's wealth? How are the resulting credits and debts settled? Is the current account constrained in any way, and how does adjustment take place?

3. Countries are differentiated by the quality of their policy choices and in the quality of the deeper institutional context in which policies are made. An important goal is to understand how policy regimes and institutions affect policy choices and economic outcomes. Along the way, we confront various questions: How does quality of governance affect economic outcomes? Why might some policies, such as a fixed exchange rate, work better in some contexts than others? Do country characteristics affect the costs and benefits of financial globalization?

KEY TERMS

fixed exchange rate, p. 4
floating exchange rate, p. 4
exchange rate crisis, p. 6
default, p. 6
International Monetary Fund (IMF), p. 7
World Bank, p. 7
income, p. 10
expenditure, p. 10

deficit, p. 10
surplus, p. 10
wealth, p. 13
capital gains, p. 14
country risk, p. 15
balance of payments, p. 16
policies, p. 17
regimes, p. 17
institutions, p. 17

advanced countries, p. 18
emerging markets, p. 18
developing countries, p. 18
common currency, p. 21
dollarization, p. 21
income per person, p. 21
The Great Divergence, p. 21
income volatility, p. 22

PROBLEMS

1. The data in Table 1-1 end in 2006. Visit the U.S. Bureau of Economic Analysis at bea.gov to find information for the latest full calendar year (or for the last four quarters). What is the latest estimate of the size of the annual U.S. current account deficit in billions of dollars?

2. The data in Figure 1-1 end in 2007. Visit oanda.com and download data on the same exchange rates (yuan per dollar and dollar per euro) for the past 12 months. What are the rates today? What were they a year ago? By what percentage amount did the rates change? At the oanda.com website, click on "Currency Tools" and then "FXGraph" and use the tool to plot the last year of data for each exchange rate. Do you think the rates are floating or fixed?

3. The data in Figure 1-4 are for recent years. Find the IMF's World Economic Outlook Databases. (Hint: Google "World Economic Outlook Databases.") Use this interactive tool to obtain the latest data on current accounts in U.S. dollars for all countries (actual data or IMF estimates). Which countries had the ten largest deficits last year? Which countries had the ten largest surpluses last year?

4. Figure 1-6 presents data on country risk (emerging market interest-rate spreads) for 2005. Visit the *Financial Times* website (at ft.com; click on "Market data") to download data for country risk today. (Hint: Google "FT High yield emerging markets."). Which three emerging market countries have the highest spreads on their U.S. dollar debt? Which three have the lowest?

5. The map at the end of the chapter shows the World Bank's composite governance indicator. The World Bank has prepared other indicators to measure institutional differences among countries. Use the Internet to find the World Bank's "Ease of Doing Business Map." (Hint: Again, use Google.) Do you notice a correlation between the ease of doing business and the overall governance indicator? Can you find countries that rank high on the ease of doing business indicator but low on the governance indicator? Are these countries rich or poor? (Hint: Look up their GNI per person at the World Bank by googling "world bank gni per capita.")

6. The charts below show the growth of real GDP per capita in three pairs of geographically adjacent countries: North and South Korea, Argentina and Chile, Zimbabwe and Botswana (using data from the Penn World Table).

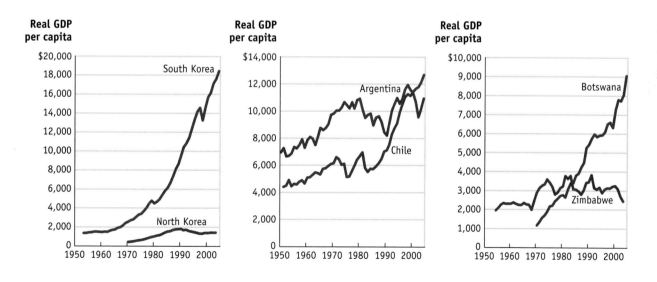

(a) Which country in each pair experienced faster growth in GDP per capita? Which one is now richest?

(b) The World Bank's World Governance Indicators for each country in 2000 were as below (higher is better).

Based on these data, do you think institutions can explain the divergent outcomes in these countries? Explain. Why do you think it helps to compare countries that are physically contiguous?

	Control of Corruption	Government Effectiveness	Political Stability and Absence of Violence	Rule of Law	Regulatory Quality	Voice and Accountability
South Korea	0.37	0.63	0.49	0.64	0.47	0.76
North Korea	−0.93	−1.10	−0.66	−1.08	−1.70	−2.02
Chile	1.56	1.34	0.85	1.31	1.38	0.56
Argentina	−0.34	0.28	0.48	0.17	0.45	0.44
Botswana	1.02	0.98	0.90	0.67	0.79	0.78
Zimbabwe	−0.87	−1.13	−1.21	−0.74	−1.61	−0.97

Introduction to Exchange Rates and the Foreign Exchange Market

The chapter on the Fall of the Rupee you may omit. It is somewhat too sensational.
—Miss Prism, in Oscar Wilde's The Importance of Being Earnest, 1895

The people who benefit from roiling the world currency market are speculators and as far as I am concerned they provide not much useful value.
—Paul O'Neill, U.S. Secretary of the Treasury, 2002

Every year or two, George, an American, takes a vacation in Paris. He tries to budget carefully, but his trip to France is always harder to plan financially than his trips within the United States. For example, in 2003 he stayed at a modest hotel that cost 100 euros (€100) per night in local currency. He did the same in 2005 and 2007 but each time with different impacts on his budget. George would buy foreign currency, or *foreign exchange,* to make purchases in France. He could trade his U.S. dollars for euros, the currency used in France, in the *market for foreign exchange* at the prevailing market *exchange rate.* When he went on his trip in 2003, 1 euro could be purchased for $1.10, so the €100 he spent on a night at the hotel cost him $110 in U.S. currency. In 2005 each euro cost $1.21, so each night cost $121, an increase of 10% over 2003. On his trip in early 2007, 1 euro cost $1.32, a further 10% increase, and each night made a large $132 dent in his vacation budget. George's hotel stay—and all his eating, drinking, and other activities in Paris—were getting more expensive in dollar terms. By this time, George was seriously thinking about cutting his trip short—or even taking his next vacation in Northern California, where he reckoned he might find equally good hotels, restaurants, fine food, and wine at prices that were more affordable.

Tourists like George are not the only people affected by exchange rates. Even today's armchair travelers may have dealings with foreign exchange, as they surf the Web and purchase items from foreign as well as domestic sellers. Much larger flows of international trade in goods and services move through traditional wholesale and retail channels. Such trade is affected by exchange rates because they influence the prices in different currencies of the imported goods and services we buy or the exported goods and services we sell. Foreign exchange also facilitates massive flows of international investment, including the direct investments made by multinationals in overseas firms as well as the stock and bond trades made by individual investors and fund managers seeking to diversify their portfolios.

Any given foreign exchange transaction may appear routine and far removed from deep macroeconomic and political consequences. In the aggregate, however, activity in the foreign exchange market can be responsible for "sensational" events (as Oscar Wilde suggested, albeit with irony) and has aroused strong passions over the course of history (Paul O'Neill being only one of the latest to criticize the activities of foreign exchange traders). In the foreign exchange market, the sums involved are enormous and the economic implications can be dramatic. In times of crisis, the fates of nations and their leaders seem to hang, in part, on the state of the currency market. Why is that so?

In this chapter, we begin our study of foreign exchange. We first survey exchange rate basics: the key definitions of exchange rates and related concepts. We then examine the evidence to see how exchange rates behave in the real world and establish some basic facts about exchange rate behavior that require explanation. We next look at the workings of the foreign exchange market, including the role of private participants as well as interventions by governments. Finally, we look in detail at how foreign exchange markets work, and we emphasize two key market mechanisms: *arbitrage* and *expectations*.

1 Exchange Rate Essentials

The **exchange rate** (E) is the price of some foreign currency expressed in terms of a home currency. Because an exchange rate is the relative price of two currencies, it may be quoted in either of two ways: how many units of home currency can be exchanged for one unit of foreign currency (e.g., $1.40 per euro, which can be written 1.40 $/€) or how many units of foreign currency can be exchanged for one unit of home currency (e.g., €0.71 per U.S. dollar, or 0.71 €/$). Knowing which form is being used is essential to avoid confusion, so a systematic rule is helpful, even if it is arbitrary.

Defining the Exchange Rate

It is common practice to quote the prices of items traded, whether goods or assets, as units of domestic currency per unit purchased. In the United States, coffee might be sold at 10 dollars per pound (\$/lb); in France, at 20 euros per kilogram (€/kg).[1]

The usual way to quote the price of foreign currency is no different: units of domestic currency per units of foreign currency. Still, confusion can arise because the price then depends on the perspective of the observer. Consider the dollar-euro exchange rate. For the U.S. citizen, who is used to prices expressed as \$/unit, the price of a foreign currency (say, the euro) is in terms of \$/€. For someone in the Eurozone, however, the convention is to quote prices as €/unit, so €/\$ would be the natural choice.

To avoid confusion, we must use careful notation and specify which country is the home country and which the foreign country. Throughout the remaining chapters of the book, when we refer to a particular country's exchange rate, we will be quoting it in terms of units of domestic currency per units of foreign currency.

From now on, $E_{1/2}$ will denote the exchange rate in units of country 1 currency per units of country 2 currency; it is country 1's exchange rate against currency 2. For example, $E_{\$/€}$ is the U.S. exchange rate (against the euro) in U.S. dollars per euro.

Different expressions of the same exchange rate can be seen all the time—even on the same page in the same publication! So it is important to keep things straight. Table 2-1 presents a typical display of exchange rate information as one might see it in the financial press.[2] Column (1) shows the reported price of U.S. dollars in various currencies (e.g., €/\$); columns (2) and (3) show, respectively, the most recent price of British pounds sterling (e.g., \$/£) and euros (e.g., \$/€) on June 1, 2007.[3] Thus, the first three entries show the Canadian dollar's exchange rate against the U.S. dollar, the pound, and the euro. For comparison, columns (4) to (6) show the same rates one year earlier.

Exchange rate humor.

Four entries in this table correspond to the dollar-euro exchange rate, and these have been highlighted. We see that on June 1, 2007, the euro was quoted at \$1.342 per euro. According to our definition, this is the price from the U.S. perspective and is sometimes called the "American terms." Conversely, the dollar is quoted at €0.745 per dollar, the "European terms."

---

[1] One could just as well conduct business with coffee quoted as 0.1 lb/\$ or 0.05 kg/€; this happens occasionally, but it is not the norm.

[2] These are typically *midrange* or *central* rates—an end-of-day average of buying and selling rates from the market. As we discuss later in the chapter, such rates do not allow for *spreads,* the commissions and fees that push buying prices above selling prices in any market in which intermediaries are present.

[3] The currency's price in terms of itself is equal to 1 and is omitted.

TABLE 2-1

Exchange Rate Quotations This table shows major exchange rates as they might appear in the financial media. Columns (1) to (3) show rates on June 1, 2007. For comparison, columns (4) to (6) show rates on June 1, 2006. For example, column (1) shows that on June 1, 2007, one U.S. dollar was worth 1.064 Canadian dollars, 5.551 Danish krone, 0.745 euros, and so on. The euro-dollar rates appear in bold type.

| Country (currency) | Currency Symbol | EXCHANGE RATES ON JUNE 1, 2007 | | | EXCHANGE RATES ON JUNE 1, 2006 *ONE YEAR PREVIOUSLY* | | |
| | | (1) | (2) | (3) | (4) | (5) | (6) |
		Per $	Per £	Per €	Per $	Per £	Per €
Canada (dollar)	C$	1.064	2.106	1.428	1.103	2.060	1.414
Denmark (krone)	DKr	5.551	10.99	7.449	5.819	10.87	7.458
Euro (euro)	€	**0.745**	1.475	—	**0.780**	1.457	—
Japan (yen)	¥	122.0	241.5	163.8	112.4	210.0	144.1
Norway (krone)	NKr	6.038	11.95	8.101	6.079	11.36	7.792
Sweden (krona)	SKr	6.945	13.74	9.318	7.220	13.49	9.254
Switzerland (franc)	SFr	1.231	2.436	1.652	1.218	2.276	1.562
United Kingdom (pound)	£	0.505	—	0.678	0.535	—	0.686
United States (dollar)	$	—	1.979	**1.342**	—	1.868	**1.282**

Source: ft.com.

We would write these exchange rates using mathematical symbols as follows, with care given to the explicit expression of the relevant units:

$E_{\$/€} = 1.342 =$ U.S. exchange rate (American terms)
$E_{€/\$} = 0.745 =$ Eurozone exchange rate (European terms)

Just as there is complete equivalence when we express the relative price of coffee and dollars at 10 $/lb or 0.1 lb/$, the price of the euro in terms of dollars is always equal to the reciprocal (or inverse) of the price of dollars in terms of euros. Hence

$$E_{\$/€} = \frac{1}{E_{€/\$}}$$

In our example,

$$1.342 = \frac{1}{0.745}$$

Similar calculations and notations would apply to any pair of currencies.

Appreciations and Depreciations

Like many financial tables, Table 2-1 includes information on how prices have changed over time. Over the previous 12 months, the Eurozone exchange rate *decreased* from $E_{€/\$} = 0.780$ a year ago to $E_{€/\$} = 0.745$ on June 1, 2007. The value of the euro relative to the dollar went up—fewer euros were needed to buy one dollar. This change is often described by saying that the euro got "stronger" against the dollar.

Symmetrically, the value of the dollar in euro terms also changed. We see this by computing the reciprocal American terms. Over the same year, the U.S exchange rate *increased* from $E_{\$/€} = 1/0.780 = 1.282$ a year ago to $E_{\$/€} = 1/0.745 = 1.342$ on June 1, 2007. One dollar bought fewer euros than it had a year previously—hence, we say that the dollar fell in value relative to the euro or got "weaker" against the euro.

To use more formal terms, if a currency buys more of another currency, we say it has experienced an **appreciation** or has *appreciated*. If a currency buys less of another currency, we say it has experienced a **depreciation** or has *depreciated*.

In our example, we can understand appreciation and depreciation from both the U.S. and European perspective; this lesson will generalize to all other currency pairs (see the **Net Work** exercise).

In U.S. terms, the following holds true:

■ When the U.S. exchange rate $E_{\$/€}$ *rises,* more dollars are needed to buy one euro. The price of one euro goes up in dollar terms, and the U.S. dollar experiences a depreciation.

■ When the U.S. exchange rate $E_{\$/€}$ *falls,* fewer dollars are needed to buy one euro. The price of one euro goes down in dollar terms, and the U.S. dollar experiences an appreciation.

Similarly, in European terms, the following holds true:

■ When the Eurozone exchange rate $E_{€/\$}$ *rises,* the price of one dollar goes up in euro terms and the euro experiences a depreciation.

■ When the Eurozone exchange rate $E_{€/\$}$ *falls,* the price of one dollar goes down in euro terms and the euro experiences an appreciation.

If the dollar is appreciating against the euro, the euro must simultaneously be depreciating against the dollar. Because they are the reciprocal of each other, changes in $E_{\$/€}$ and $E_{€/\$}$ must always move in opposite directions.

It can seem confusing or counterintuitive that a fall in the U.S. exchange rate means the dollar is appreciating. Yet it is reasonable because we express the price of foreign currency in dollars, just like the prices of other goods. When the price of coffee falls from $10 to $9 per pound, it seems sensible to say that coffee is depreciating or falling in value—but relative to what? The dollars—the currency in which the price is denominated. Conversely, dollars are *appreciating* against coffee! If we keep this analogy in mind, it makes sense that when the dollar price of a euro falls, the dollar has appreciated against the euro.

In addition to knowing whether a currency has appreciated or depreciated, we are often interested in knowing the size of an appreciation or depreciation. To do this, we can calculate the proportional change (or fractional change) in the foreign-currency value of the home currency. This proportional change is usually expressed in percentage terms.

N E T **W O R K**

Visit the ft.com website (or another financial website such as oanda.com or xe.com), and download the same exchange rates as shown in Table 2-1 for today's date. For all currencies (other than the dollar), compute the one-year percentage appreciation or depreciation against the dollar. For the dollar, compute the one-year percentage appreciation or depreciation against each currency. (Hint: Google "ft.com cross rates.")

In the previous example, we would denote these changes as follows:

- In 2006, at time t, the dollar value of the euro was $E_{\$/€,t} = \$1.282$.
- In 2007, at time $t + 1$, the dollar value of the euro was $E_{\$/€,t+1} = \$1.342$.
- The change in the dollar value of the euro was $\Delta E_{\$/€,t} = 1.342 - 1.282 = \$0.060$.
- The percentage change was $\Delta E_{\$/€,t}/E_{\$/€,t} = 0.060/1.282 = +4.7\%$.
- Thus, the euro *appreciated* against the dollar by 4.7%.

Similarly, over the same year:

- In 2006, at time t, the euro value of the dollar was $E_{€/\$,t} = €0.780$.
- In 2007, at time $t + 1$, the euro value of the dollar was $E_{€/\$,t+1} = €0.745$.
- The change in the value of the dollar was $\Delta E_{€/\$,t} = 0.78 - 0.95 = €-0.035$.
- The percentage change was $\Delta E_{€/\$,t}/E_{€/\$,t} = -0.035/0.780 = -4.5\%$.
- Thus, the dollar *depreciated* against the euro by 4.5%.

Note that the size of one country's appreciation (here 4.7%) will not exactly equal the size of the other country's depreciation (here 4.5%). However, for small changes, the opposing movements are *approximately* equal. For example, if the U.S. terms move slightly from $1.00 to $1.01 per euro, the European terms move from €1.00 to €0.99099; a 1% euro appreciation is approximately a 1% dollar depreciation.[4]

Multilateral Exchange Rates

Our discussion of exchange rates has focused on the simplest type of exchange rate between two countries or currencies, what economists refer to as a *bilateral* exchange rate. In reality, we live in a world of many countries and many currencies and it is of great practical importance to ask whether a particular currency has strengthened or weak-

---

[4] Suppose that the home exchange rate is a, so one unit of home currency buys $1/a$ units of foreign currency. Now the home exchange rate depreciates to $b > a$, and one unit of home currency buys $1/b$ units of foreign currency, with $1/b < 1/a$. The size of the depreciation D of the home currency is

$$D = \left(\frac{1}{a} - \frac{1}{b}\right)\Big/\left(\frac{1}{a}\right) = \left(1 - \frac{a}{b}\right) = \left(\frac{b - a}{b}\right).$$

Symmetrically, the foreign currency was initially worth a units of home currency but is now worth b. Thus, the size of the appreciation A of the foreign currency is

$$A = \frac{(b - a)}{a} = \frac{b}{a}D$$

The percentage appreciation A will be approximately equal to the percentage depreciation D when b/a is close to 1, or when b is approximately equal to a, that is, when the change in the exchange rate is small.

ened not just against one other currency, but against other currencies in general.

The answer is not always obvious. For example, the U.S. dollar may be depreciating against some currencies, while remaining fixed or appreciating against others. To aggregate these different trends in bilateral exchange rates into one measure, economists calculate *multilateral* exchange rate changes for baskets of currencies using *trade weights* to construct an average of all the bilateral changes for each currency in the basket. The resulting measure is referred to as the change in the **effective exchange rate.**

For example, suppose 40% of home trade is with country 1 and 60% is with country 2; home's currency appreciates 10% against 1 but depreciates 30% against 2. To calculate the change in home's effective exchange rate, we multiply each exchange rate change by the corresponding trade share and then add up: $(-10\% \times 40\%) + (30\% \times 60\%) = (-0.1 \times 0.4) + (0.3 \times 0.6) = -0.04 + 0.18 = 0.14 = +14\%$. In this example, home's effective exchange rate has depreciated by 14%.

In general, suppose there are N currencies in the basket, and home's trade with the N partners is $\text{Trade} = \text{Trade}_1 + \text{Trade}_2 + \ldots + \text{Trade}_N$. Applying trade weights to each bilateral exchange rate change, the change in home's effective exchange rate ($E_{\text{effective}}$) is

$$\frac{\Delta E_{\text{effective}}}{E_{\text{effective}}} = \underbrace{\frac{\Delta E_1}{E_1} \frac{\text{Trade}_1}{\text{Trade}} + \frac{\Delta E_2}{E_2} \frac{\text{Trade}_2}{\text{Trade}} + \ldots + \frac{\Delta E_N}{E_N} \frac{\text{Trade}_N}{\text{Trade}}}_{\text{Trade–weighted average of bilateral nominal exchange rate exchanges}}$$

Many discussions in the financial press focus on the effective exchange rate (see **Headlines: By How Much Has the Dollar Fallen?**).

Example: Using Exchange Rates to Compare Prices in a Common Currency

To make comparisons of prices across nations, we must convert prices to a common currency. The following examples show how we use exchange rates to accomplish this task.

James Bond is back from another mission and, what with all the explosions, his wardrobe is looking ragged. He needs a new tuxedo. Bond will be in numerous cities On Her Majesty's Secret Service in the next few days, so he can shop around the globe. Although style is important, price is a key factor in Bond's choice, given the paltry MI6 clothing allowance. Should he visit the new tailor in Manhattan? Go back to his favorite cutter in Hong Kong? Or simply nip around the corner to Savile Row in London?

The London tailor sells a tux for £2,000; the Hong Kong shop asks HK$30,000; in New York, the going rate is $4,000. In the near future, when the decision must be made, these prices are fixed in their respective home currencies. Which tux will 007 choose?

HEADLINES

....

By How Much Has the Dollar Fallen?

If you had read the financial press in 2002 to 2004, you would have known that the U.S. dollar had suffered a dramatic depreciation. It lost value against many well-known major currencies, such as the euro, the pound sterling, the Canadian dollar, and the Swiss franc. But on average, the weakening of the dollar was not as pronounced when measured against all U.S. trading partners.

The simple reason for this was the fact that Japan and China, along with several other developing countries in Asia, sought to control their exchange rates in such a way as to limit their appreciation against the dollar. Moreover, Mexico—a major U.S. trading partner—actually saw its peso fall against the dollar, when almost every other currency was rising. Thus, in multilateral terms, the fall in the value of the dollar (measured against a base of 100 in January 2002) was not as dramatic as many headlines suggested, as was pointed out by the Economist *newspaper.*

In January 2002 one euro bought 86 cents: this week it was worth almost $1.32. The dollar has thus lost 35% against the euro, but by how much has it fallen against a basket of currencies, weighted by their importance in America's trade? Some say that since early 2002 the dollar's trade-weighted value has fallen by 27%; others insist on only 14%. Confusion arises because there are competing indices, including different currencies with different weights.

The chart (Figure 2-1) shows the two indices published by America's Federal Reserve. The lower line shows the dollar's average fall against seven major currencies, such as the euro, the Canadian dollar and the pound. The upper line, the Fed's broad index, tracks the dollar against 26 currencies, including those of emerging economies, such as Mexico and China.

This makes a huge difference: the euro (against which the dollar has fallen by most) has a weight of 34% in the narrow index but only 19% in the broad index. But the dollar has risen against the Mexican peso in the past couple of years and has been fixed against the Chinese yuan. Together these have a weight of 21% in the broad index, so including them yields a smaller drop in the dollar.

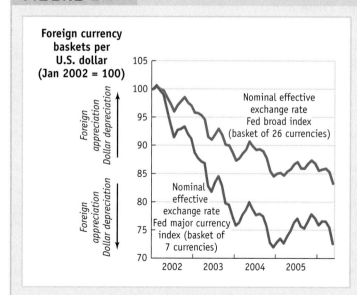

FIGURE 2-1

Foreign currency baskets per U.S. dollar (Jan 2002 = 100)

Nominal effective exchange rate Fed broad index (basket of 26 currencies)

Nominal effective exchange rate Fed major currency index (basket of 7 currencies)

Effective Exchange Rates: Change in the Value of the U.S. Dollar, 2002–2006 The chart shows the value of the dollar measured by the U.S. Federal Reserve using two different baskets of foreign currencies, starting with the index set to 100 foreign baskets in January 2002. Against a basket of 7 major currencies, the dollar had depreciated by more than 25% by late 2004. Against a broad basket of 26 currencies, the dollar had lost only 15% of its value. This is because the dollar was floating against the major currencies, but the broad basket included important U.S. trading partners (such as China and other Asian economies) that maintained fixed or tightly managed exchange rates against the dollar.

Note: Seven of the 26 currencies in the broad index—the euro, Canadian dollar, Japanese yen, British pound, Swiss franc, Australian dollar, and Swedish krona—trade widely in currency markets outside their home areas, and (along with the U.S. dollar) they are referred to by the Federal Reserve Board as "major" currencies.

Source: U.S. Federal Reserve.

Source: Excerpted from "By How Much Has the Dollar Fallen?" Economist, November 25, 2004. Corrected.

....

To choose among goods priced in different currencies, Bond must first convert all the prices into a common currency; for this he uses the exchange rate (and a calculator disguised as a toothbrush). Table 2-2 shows the prices, in local currency and converted into pounds, under different hypothetical exchange rates.

Scenario 1 In the first column, the Hong Kong suit costs HK$30,000 and the exchange rate is HK$15 per pound. Dividing 30,000 by 15, we find that this suit costs £2,000 in British currency. The U.S. suit has a price of $4,000, and at an exchange rate of $2 per pound we obtain a British currency price of £2,000. Thus, in this special case, the exchange rates are such that all locations offer the same price when measured in a common currency (pounds in this case). Bond will have a difficult choice.

Scenario 2 Moving to the next column, the Hong Kong dollar has depreciated against the pound compared with scenario 1: it now takes more HK$ (16 instead of 15) to buy £1. In contrast, the U.S. dollar has appreciated against the pound: it takes fewer dollars (1.9 instead of 2.0) to buy £1. At the new exchange rates, the cost of the New York tux has gone up to £2,105 (4,000/1.9), and the Hong Kong tux has fallen to £1,875 (30,000/16). Hong Kong has the lowest price.

Scenario 3 Here, compared with scenario 1, the Hong Kong dollar has appreciated: it now takes fewer $HK to buy £1 (14 instead of 15), and the price of the Hong Kong tux has risen to £2,143 (30,000/14). At the same time, however, the U.S. dollar has depreciated: it now takes more dollars (2.1 instead of 2) to buy £1. With the dollar's depreciation, New York now has the best price of £1,905 (4,000/2.1).

Scenario 4 In this case, compared with scenario 1, the pound has depreciated against the other two currencies, and they have each appreciated against the

TABLE 2-2

Using the Exchange Rate to Compare Prices in a Common Currency Now pay attention 007! This table shows how the hypothetical cost of James Bond's next tuxedo in different locations depends on the exchange rates that prevail.

Scenario		1	2	3	4
Cost of the tuxedo in local currency	London	£2,000	£2,000	£2,000	£2,000
	Hong Kong	HK$30,000	HK$30,000	HK$30,000	HK$30,000
	New York	$4,000	$4,000	$4,000	$4,000
Exchange rates	HK$/£	15	16	14	14
	$/£	2.0	1.9	2.1	1.9
Cost of the tuxedo in pounds	London	£2,000	£2,000	£2,000	£2,000
	Hong Kong	£2,000	£1,875	£2,143	£2,143
	New York	£2,000	£2,105	£1,905	£2,105

$4,000 and counting: Cross-border shopping need not be a shot in the dark.

pound. It takes fewer Hong Kong dollars (14 instead of 15) and also fewer U.S. dollars (1.9 instead of 2.0) to buy £1. Based on the calculations in scenarios 2 and 3, you should be able to figure out the prices in pounds for this case. You will find that London has the bargain price of £2,000, and the other cities have a higher price.

This example illustrates a key point. We assumed that while exchange rates may change, domestic-currency goods prices are fixed in the short run. An economist would say the prices are *sticky* in the short run. (As we see later, this may not be an unreasonable assumption.) With these assumptions, fluctuations in the exchange rate cause fluctuations in the common-currency prices of goods from different countries.

Generalizing The same logic applies to any exchange rate. All else equal, when the prices of goods are constant in domestic currencies, the following conclusions will apply:

■ *Changes in the exchange rate cause changes in prices of foreign goods expressed in the home currency* (e.g., fluctuations in the $/£ exchange rate cause fluctuations in the £ price of the New York suit).

■ *Changes in the exchange rate cause changes in the relative prices of goods produced in different countries* (e.g., fluctuations in the $/£ and HK$/£ exchange rates cause fluctuations in the price of the New York suit compared with the Hong Kong suit).

■ *When the home country's exchange rate depreciates against the foreign country, home exports become less expensive as imports to foreigners, and foreign exports become more expensive as imports to home residents* (e.g., when the £ depreciates against the HK$, the London suit is cheaper in £ terms).

■ *When the home country's exchange rate appreciates against the foreign country, home export goods become more expensive as imports to foreigners, and foreign export goods become less expensive as imports to home residents* (e.g., when the £ appreciates against the $, the New York suit is cheaper in £ terms).

2 Exchange Rates in Practice

Having seen Table 2-1, it might be tempting to use the same figures as a guide to today's exchange rates between countries, but this would be a big mistake. Exchange rates fluctuate. They depreciate and appreciate. A lot. On a single day, in a matter of hours or even minutes, they can change substantially. Over a year, they can move up and down, but they may still drift considerably in one direction or another. In this section, we examine the behavior of exchange rates using data from the foreign exchange market from the recent past.

Exchange Rate Regimes: Fixed versus Floating

Any complete theory of exchange rate determination must account for observed behavior, so we should familiarize ourselves with the various patterns we seek to explain. Economists group different patterns of exchange rate behavior into categories known as **exchange rate regimes.** These regimes reflect policy choices made by governments, and their causes and consequences are a major focus of our study.

Two major categories stand out:

- **Fixed** (or **pegged**) exchange rate regimes are those in which a country's exchange rate fluctuates in a narrow range (or not at all) against some *base currency* over a sustained period, usually a year or longer. A country's exchange rate can remain rigidly fixed for long periods only if the government intervenes in the foreign exchange market in one or both countries.

- **Floating** (or **flexible**) exchange rate regimes are all the other cases in which a country's exchange rate fluctuates in a wider range, and the government makes no attempt to fix it against any other base currency. Appreciations and depreciations may occur from year to year, each month, by the day, or every minute.

For example, in Chapter 1, Figure 1-1, we saw data for two of the most talked about exchange rates in the world today: the U.S. dollar-euro and the Chinese yuan-U.S. dollar rates. The dollar-euro rate fluctuated considerably and was said to be floating; the yuan-dollar rate was steady, or changed very slowly, and was said to be fixed.

However, the "fixed versus floating" classification is not without its problems. First, in practice, to judge whether a regime is fixed or floating, we have to decide where we draw the line between "narrow" and "wide" fluctuations. One rule of thumb is to use annual variations in excess of ±2% or ±1% as the sign of a floating regime. Second, because of its simplicity, "fixed versus floating" is only a very coarse description of exchange rate regimes. In reality, the distinctions may not be so cut and dried. Fixed and floating provide benchmarks throughout this book and deliver great insights, but we sometimes need more precise ways of describing *intermediate regimes,* as the following application illustrates.

APPLICATION

Recent Exchange Rate Experiences

If we spend a moment looking at recent exchange rate experiences in a variety of countries, we will not only find some helpful illustrations of the differences between floating and fixed rate regimes but also see some of the different varieties of fixed and floating behavior. We will also encounter the phenomenon of regime change, in which one type of regime gives way to another, either smoothly or catastrophically.

Evidence from Developed Countries Figure 2-2 shows the daily exchange rates from 1996 to 2007 for various currency pairs. The top row shows the U.S. dollar exchange rate against two major currencies (the Japanese yen, the British pound) and against the currency of a neighboring country (the Canadian dollar, also called the *loonie* because it has a loon on it). The bottom row shows the exchange rate of the euro against the yen and the pound and against the currency of a neighboring country, the Danish krone. In all six charts, the vertical scale varies by a factor of two from maximum to minimum,

FIGURE 2-2

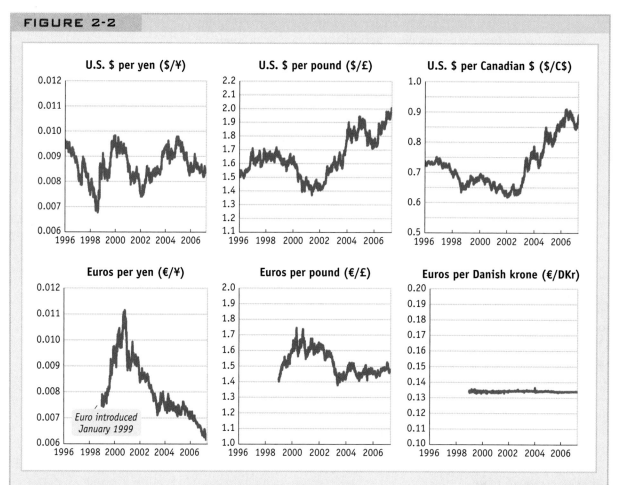

Exchange Rate Behavior: Selected Developed Countries, 1996–2007 This figure shows exchange rates of three currencies against the U.S. dollar and three against the euro. The euro rates begin in 1999 when the currency was introduced. The yen, pound, and Canadian dollar all float against the U.S. dollar. The pound and yen float against the euro. The Danish krone is fixed against the euro. The vertical scale ranges by a factor of two on all charts.

Source: oanda.com.

so all of these charts are comparable in terms of their representation of these exchange rates' volatility.

We can clearly see that the U.S. dollar is in a floating relationship with all three foreign currencies shown in the top row—the yen, pound, and loonie. How volatile are the exchange rates? The range of variation in each case is about the same, with the maximum being about one and a half times the minimum: the yen ranges from about $0.0065 to $0.010, the pound from $1.3 to almost $1.95, the loonie from $0.6 to about $0.85. The movements between these peaks and troughs may take many months or years to occur, but the exchange rate also shows a great deal of short-run volatility, with lots of up-and-down movement from day to day. A floating regime of this sort is called a **free float.**

A similar picture emerges for the euro in the bottom row of Figure 2-2, which looks at the euro's variation against the yen and the pound. Again, these currencies are clearly floating against each other, and the range of variation is similar, although the euro-pound rate varies a bit less than the euro-yen rate. In the sixth and final chart, the Danish krone provides a contrast—an example of a fixed exchange rate in a developed country. Denmark is part of the European Union, but like Britain, it has kept its own national currency, at least for now, and does not use the euro as its currency. Unlike Britain, Denmark has fixed its exchange rate against the euro, keeping it very close to 7.44 krone per euro (0.134 euro per krone). There is some variation around this rate, but it is small—no more than plus or minus 2%. This type of fixed regime is known as a **band.**

Evidence from Developing Countries Figure 2-3 shows the daily exchange rates against the U.S. dollar from 1996 to 2007 for some developing countries. Exchange rates in developing countries can be much more volatile than those in developed countries. The charts in the top row illustrate exchange rate behavior in three Asian countries: India, Thailand, and South Korea. These exchange rates exhibit a much larger range of variation than those in Figure 2-2: the maximum on the vertical axis is three times the minimum.

India had what looked like a fixed rate of close to 35 rupees per dollar until late 1997; there was then a depreciation followed by a period of more pronounced movement more like a float. However, the Indian government still exercised some control to prevent abrupt currency movements even after 1997. This middle ground, somewhere between a fixed rate and a free float, is called a **managed float** (also known as a *dirty float,* or a policy of *limited flexibility*).

Thailand and South Korea show more extreme versions of the same pattern, except that in these cases the depreciation in 1997 was large and sudden, with the baht and the won exchange rates more than doubling in a matter of weeks. Such dramatic depreciations are called **exchange rate crises.** They are more common in developing countries than in developed countries, and 1997 was a year in which many crises occurred, a phenomenon we shall study later in the book.

FIGURE 2-3

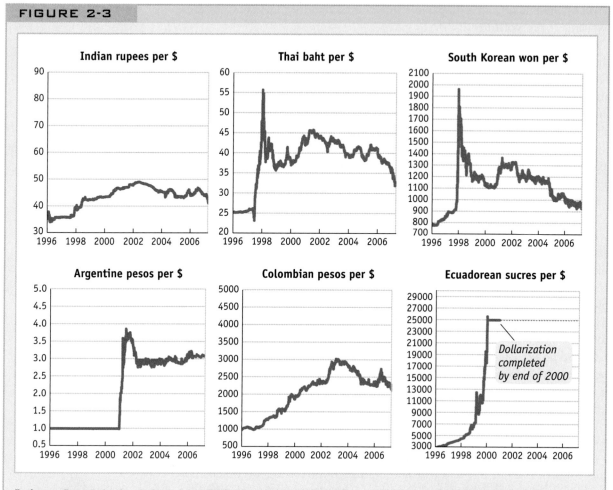

Exchange Rate Behavior: Selected Developing Countries, 1996–2007 Exchange rates in developing countries show a wide variety of experiences and greater volatility. Pegging is common but is punctuated by periodic crises (you can see the effects of these crises in graphs for Thailand, South Korea, and Argentina). Rates that are unpegged may show some flexibility (India). Some rates crawl gradually (Colombia). Dollarization can occur (Ecuador). The vertical scale ranges by a factor of three on the upper charts and by a factor of ten on the lower charts.

Source: oanda.com.

In the bottom row of Figure 2-3, we move to Latin America and find even more varieties of exchange rate experience. The vertical scale now expands even further—the maximum on the scale is ten times the minimum, a change made necessary by the even more volatile exchange rates in this region.

Argentina initially had a fixed rate (of one peso per dollar), followed in 2001 by an exchange rate crisis. After a period of limited flexibility, Argentina returned to an almost fixed rate with a band that appears to be centered at about three pesos per dollar from 2003 to 2007.

In the next figure, Colombia presents an example of a different kind of fixed exchange rate, one that follows not a predetermined target level but a predetermined target trend. Here the authorities kept the Colombian peso steadily depreciating at an almost constant rate from 1996 to 2002. This type of fixed arrangement is called a **crawl** (if the exchange rate follows a simple trend, it is a *crawling peg;* if some variation about the trend is allowed, it is termed a *crawling band*).

In the final figure, Ecuador displays a different crisis pattern. Here a period of floating was followed by a fixed rate rather than the other way around (compare with Thailand or Argentina). Initially, depreciation was very fast. Because episodes of severe depreciation like this represent a distinct form of exchange rate behavior, some economists have suggested, not jokingly, that these regimes be identified separately as *freely falling* exchange rate regimes.[5] The Ecuadorean sucre stabilized at a fixed rate of 25,000 sucres per dollar, but Ecuador took the remarkable step of abolishing its own national currency and unilaterally adopting the currency of another country, the U.S. dollar, as its legal tender. The sucre ceased to be. This kind of policy is often referred to as **dollarization,** even in cases in which the adopted currency is not the U.S. dollar (see **Side Bar: Currency Unions and Dollarization**).

Exchange Rate Regimes of the World   To move beyond specific examples, Figure 2-4 shows the IMF's classification of exchange rate regimes around the world, which allows us to see the prevalence of different regime types across the whole spectrum from fixed to floating. The IMF now uses an unofficial classification based on observed exchange rate behavior. Most economists prefer this type of classification to the often misleading official classifications that were based on countries' official policy announcements. For example, as we saw in Figure 2-3, Thailand pegged to the dollar before the 1997 crisis, even though official statements denied this and the Thai authorities claimed the baht was floating.[6]

The classification in Figure 2-4 covers 187 economies for the year 2006, and regimes are ordered from the most rigidly fixed to the most freely floating. The first 41 countries are those that have no currency of their own. Next are 7 countries using an ultrahard peg called a **currency board,** a type of fixed regime that has special legal and procedural rules designed to make the peg "harder"—that is, more durable. Then come 52 conventional pegs, with variations of less than ±1%, some fixed to a single currency and a few pegging against a basket of currencies. These are followed by the less rigidly fixed arrangements such as the 6 bands and the 5 crawling pegs. We then encounter two kinds of flexible regimes: the 51 regimes of managed floating rates, in which the authorities seem to restrict

---

[5] Carmen M. Reinhart and Kenneth S. Rogoff, 2004, "The Modern History of Exchange Rate Arrangements: A Reinterpretation," *Quarterly Journal of Economics,* 119(1), February, 1–48.

[6] On unofficial or de facto classifications, see Carmen M. Reinhart and Kenneth S. Rogoff, 2004, "The Modern History of Exchange Rate Arrangements: A Reinterpretation," *Quarterly Journal of Economics,* 119(1), February, 1–48; Jay C. Shambaugh, 2004, "The Effect of Fixed Exchange Rates on Monetary Policy," *Quarterly Journal of Economics,* 119(1), February, 301–352; and Eduardo Levy Yeyati and Federico Sturzenegger, 2005, "Classifying Exchange Rate Regimes: Deeds vs. Words," *European Economic Review,* 49(6), August, 1603–1635.

FIGURE 2-4

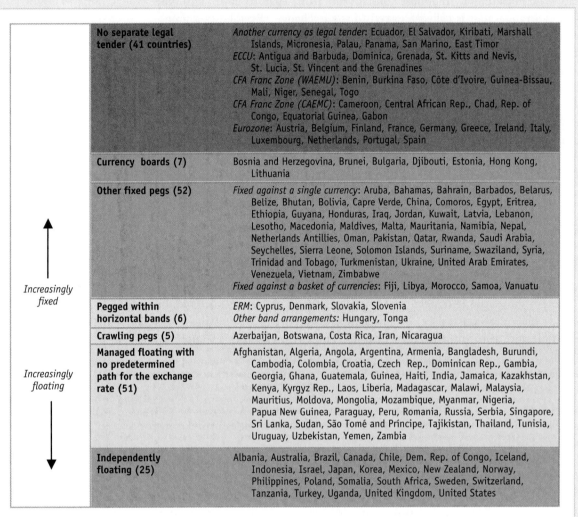

A Spectrum of Exchange Rate Regimes The chart shows the spectrum of exchange rate regimes around the world as of July 31, 2006.

Source: IMF, De Facto Classification of Exchange Rate Regimes and Monetary Policy Framework, July 31, 2006.

exchange rate movements to a noticeable degree, and lastly the 25 independently floating regimes.

Looking Ahead This brief look at the evidence supplies important motivation for the analysis in the remainder of this book. First, the world is divided into fixed and floating rate regimes, so we need to understand how *both* types of regime work. Studying fixed and floating regimes side by side will occupy much of our attention until Chapter 7. Second, when we look at who is fixed and who is floating, we start to notice patterns. Most of the floaters are advanced countries (with the exception of the euro area), and most of the

SIDE BAR

Currency Unions and Dollarization

Almost every economy issues its own currency and jealously guards this sovereign right. There are only two exceptions: groups of economies that agree to form a currency or monetary union and adopt a common currency and individual economies that dollarize by adopting the currency of another country as their own.

Under a *currency union* (or monetary union), there is some form of transnational structure, including, at the very least, a single central bank or monetary authority that is accountable to the member nations. The most prominent example of a currency union is the Eurozone. Other currency unions include the CFA and CFP Franc zones (among some former French colonies in Africa and the Pacific) and the Eastern Caribbean Currency Union of nine member states.

Under *dollarization,* one country unilaterally adopts the currency of another, often without any formal agreement and certainly with no sharing of power with respect to monetary policy. The reasons for this choice can vary. The adopting country may be very small, so the costs of running its own central bank and issuing its own currency may be prohibitive. Such is the case, for example, for the 42 Pitcairn Islanders (who use New Zealand or U.S. dollars as currency). Other countries may have a poor record of managing their own monetary affairs and may believe that they can "import" a better policy from, say, the U.S. Federal Reserve. The currency changeover could be a de jure policy choice; or it may happen de facto if people are so fed up that they stop using the national currency and switch en masse to an alternative. Many of these economies use the U.S. dollar, but other popular choices include the euro (for small states in Europe) and the Australian and New Zealand dollars (for small states in Oceania).

---

fixers are developing countries (with the exception of the euro area). The question of why some countries fix while others float is covered in more detail in Chapters 8 to 10. (See the **Net Work** exercise.) ■

3 The Market for Foreign Exchange

Day by day, minute by minute, and second by second, exchange rates the world over are set in the **foreign exchange market** (or *forex market* or *FX market*), which, like any market, is a collection of private individuals, corporations, and some public institutions that buy and sell. When two currencies are traded for each other in a market, the exchange rate is the price at which the trade was done, a price that is determined by market forces.

The forex market is not an organized exchange: trade is conducted "over the counter" between parties at numerous interlinked locations around the world. The forex market is massive and has grown dramatically in recent years. According to the Bank for International Settlements, in April 2007 the global forex market traded $3,210 billion per day in currency, 70% more than in 2004 and 290% more than in 1992. The three major foreign exchange centers—the United Kingdom ($1,359 billion per day, almost all in London), the United States ($664 billion, mostly in New York), and Japan ($238 billion, principally in Tokyo)—played home to more than half of the trade.[7] Other

---

[7] Data from Bank for International Settlements, Triennial Central Bank Survey of Foreign Exchange and Derivatives Market Activity in April 2007 (Basel: Bank for International Settlements, September 2007).

important centers for forex trade include Hong Kong, Paris, Singapore, Sydney, and Zurich. Thanks to time-zone differences, when all trading centers are included, there is not a moment of the day when foreign exchange is not being traded somewhere in the world. This section briefly examines the basic workings of this market.

The Spot Contract

The simplest forex transaction we can imagine is a contract for the immediate exchange of one currency for another between two parties. This type of transaction is known as a **spot contract** because it happens "on the spot." Accordingly, the exchange rate for this transaction is often called the **spot exchange rate.** In this book, the use of the term "exchange rate" always refers to the spot rate. Thanks to recent technological advances, actual settlement for most spot trades is usually done continuously in real time and the risk of one party failing to deliver on its part of the transaction (the *default risk* or *settlement risk*) is essentially zero.[8]

Most of our personal transactions in the forex market are small spot transactions via retail channels, but this activity represents just a tiny fraction of the total transactions in foreign exchange that take place each day. The vast majority of trading volume involves commercial banks in major financial centers around the world. But even there the spot contract is the most common type of trade and appears in almost 90% of all forex transactions, either on its own as a single contract or in trades where it is combined with other forex contracts.

Transaction Costs

When individuals buy a foreign currency through a retail channel (such as a bank), they pay a higher price than the midrange quote typically seen in the press; and when they sell, they are paid a lower price. The difference or **spread** between the "buy at" and "sell for" prices may be large, perhaps 2% to 5%. These fees and commissions go to the many middlemen that stand between the person on the street and the forex market. But when a big firm or a bank needs to exchange millions of dollars, the spreads and commissions are very small. Spreads are usually less than one-tenth of 1%, and for actively traded major currencies, they are approximately 0.01% to 0.03%.

Spreads are an important example of a **market friction** or **transaction cost.** These frictions create a wedge between the price paid by the buyer and the price received by the seller. Although spreads are potentially important for any microeconomic analysis of the forex market, macroeconomic

---

[8] Until recently, spot trades in the forex market took two days for clearing or settlement. If a bank failed in that two-day window, spot trades could suffer occasional settlement failure. However, since 1997 a *continuously linked settlement* (CLS) system has been used by the major trading banks and covers a substantial majority of cross-currency transactions all over the world. The system allows simultaneous settlement across the globe, eliminating the settlement risk caused by delays arising from time-zone differences. Fifteen currencies are currently eligible for CLS settlement. They are U.S. dollar, euro, U.K. pound, Japanese yen, Swiss franc, Canadian dollar, Australian dollar, Swedish krona, Danish krone, Norwegian krone, Singapore dollar, Hong Kong dollar, New Zealand dollar, Korean won, and South African rand (http://www.cls-services.com/about_cls/).

analysis usually proceeds on the assumption that, in today's world of low-cost trading, the transaction-cost spreads in markets are so low that they can be ignored in most macroeconomic analyses.

Derivatives

The spot contract is undoubtedly the most important contract in the forex market, but there are many other related forex contracts. These contracts include *forwards, swaps, futures,* and *options.* Collectively, all these related forex contracts are termed **derivatives** because the contracts and their pricing are derived from the spot rate.

The forex derivatives market is small relative to the entire global forex market. According to April 2007 data from the Bank for International Settlements, the trade in spot contracts amounted to $1,005 billion per day, while the trade in forward contracts (including swaps) was $2,076 billion per day. All other forex derivative trades amounted to just $291 billion per day, or less than 10% of all forex trades.

For the rest of this chapter, we focus on the two most important contracts—the spot and the forward. Figure 2-5 shows recent trends in the spot and forward rates in the dollar-euro market. The forward rate tends to track the spot rate fairly closely, and we will explore this relationship further in a moment.

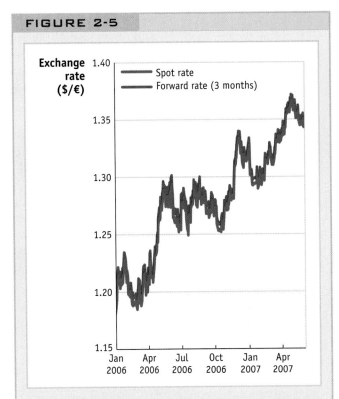

FIGURE 2-5

Spot and Forward Rates The chart shows the U.S. spot and three-month forward exchange rates for the euro in dollars per euro between January 2006 and June 2007. The spot and forward rates closely track each other.

Source: Federal Reserve Bank of New York.

The full study of derivative markets requires an in-depth analysis of risk that is beyond the scope of a course in international macroeconomics. Such topics are reserved for advanced courses in finance that explore a rich variety of derivative contracts in great detail. The following application supplies a basic guide to derivatives.

APPLICATION

Foreign Exchange Derivatives

There are many derivative contracts in the foreign exchange market, of which the following are the most common:

Forwards A **forward** contract differs from a spot contract in that the two parties make the contract today, but the *settlement date* for the delivery of the currencies is in the future, or forward. The time to delivery, or *maturity,* varies—30 days, 90 days, six months, a year, or even longer—depending on the contract. However, because the price is fixed as of today, the contract carries no risk.

Swaps A **swap** contract combines a spot sale of foreign currency with a forward repurchase of the same currency. This is a common contract for counterparties dealing in the same currency pair over and over again. Combining two transactions reduces transactions costs because the broker's fees and commissions are lower than on a spot and forward purchased separately.

Futures A **futures** contract is a promise that the two parties holding the contract will deliver currencies to each other at some future date at a prespecified exchange rate, just like a forward contract. Unlike the forward contract, futures contracts are standardized, mature at certain arranged dates, and can be traded on an organized futures exchange. Hence, the futures contract does not require that the parties involved at the delivery date be the same two parties that originally made the deal.

Options An **option** provides one party, the buyer, with the right to buy (*call*) or sell (*put*) a currency in exchange for another at a prespecified exchange rate at a future date. The other party, the seller, must perform the trade if asked to do so by the buyer, but a buyer is under no obligation to trade and, in particular, will not exercise the option if the spot price on the expiration date turns out to be more favorable.

All of these products exist to allow investors to trade foreign currency for delivery at different times or with different contingencies. Thus, derivatives allow investors to engage in *hedging* (risk avoidance) and *speculation* (risk taking).

- Example 1: Hedging. As chief financial officer of a U.S. firm, you expect to receive payment of €1 million in 90 days for exports to France. The current spot rate is $1.40 per euro. Losses will be incurred on the deal if the dollar strengthens to less than $1.30 per euro. You advise that the firm buy €1 million in call options on dollars at a rate of $1.35 per euro, ensuring that the firm's euro receipts will sell for at least this rate. This locks in a decent profit even if the spot rate falls below $1.35. This is hedging.

- Example 2: Speculation. The market currently prices one-year euro futures at $1.40, but you think the dollar will weaken to $1.54 in the next 12 months. If you wish to make a bet, you would buy these futures, and if you are proved right, you will realize a 10% profit. Any level above $1.40 will generate a profit. If the dollar is at or below $1.40 a year from now, however, your investment in futures will be a total loss. This is speculation.

Private Actors

The key actors in the forex market are the traders. Most forex traders work for **commercial banks.** These banks trade for themselves and also serve clients who want to import or export goods, services, or assets. International trade and investment require payments to be made across borders, which often involve a change of currency. Commercial banks are the principal financial intermediaries that provide this service.

For example, suppose the U.S.-based Apple Computer Inc. has sold €1 million worth of computers to a German distributor and wishes to receive payment for them in U.S. dollars. The German distributor informs its commercial bank, Deutsche Bank, and receives an exchange rate quote of $1.4 per euro, based on the spot exchange rate. If the distributor authorizes the transaction, Deutsche Bank debits €1 million from the distributor's bank account, sells this €1 million bank deposit in the forex market in exchange for a $1.4 million deposit, credits that $1.4 million to Apple's bank in California, which, in turn, deposits $1.4 million into Apple's bank account. No money has physically moved in this process, and all the transactions can be accomplished in less than a minute with a few keystrokes. The transaction alters the deposit balances of the two parties as expected, but the banks pay each other through transfers of deposits.

This example illustrates **interbank trading,** whereby two banks exchange deposits with one another. This business is highly concentrated: about three-quarters of all forex market transactions globally are handled by just ten banks, led by names such as Deutsche Bank, UBS, Citigroup, HSBC, and Barclays. They trade currencies not just for their clients but also on their own account in search of profit. The vast majority of forex transactions are profit-driven interbank trades of this kind, and it is the exchange rates for interbank trades that are quoted in the press. Consequently, we focus on interbank trading of deposits as the key influence in the forex market and in the determination of the spot exchange rate.

Other actors are increasingly participating directly in the forex market. Some **corporations** may enter the market if they are engaged in extensive transactions either to buy inputs or sell products in foreign markets. By trading directly in the market themselves, these corporations effectively bypass the fees and commissions charged by the commercial banks. If the volume of transactions is large enough, these savings could easily offset the costs of running an in-house currency trading operation. Similarly **nonbank financial institutions** such as mutual fund companies may invest so much overseas that they can justify having their own foreign exchange trading operation.

Government Actions

We have so far described the forex market in terms of the private actors. Our discussion of the forex market is incomplete, however, without mention of actions taken by government authorities. Such activities are by no means present in every market at all times, but they are sufficiently frequent that we need to fully understand them. In essence, there are two primary types of actions taken by authorities in the forex market.

At one extreme, it is possible for a government to try to completely control the market by preventing its free operation, by restricting trading or movement of forex, or by allowing the trading of forex only through government channels. Policies of this kind are a form of **capital control,** a restriction on cross-border financial transactions. A recent example was the decision of the Malaysian government to temporarily impose controls in the wake of the 1997 Asian exchange rate crisis, an event that prompted Prime Minister Mahathir Mohamad to declare that "currency trading is unnecessary, unproductive and totally immoral. It should be stopped, it should be made illegal."[9]

Capital controls are never 100% successful, however. Illegal trades will inevitably occur and are almost impossible to stop. The government may set up an **official market** for foreign exchange and issue a law requiring people to buy and sell in that market at officially set rates. But illicit dealings can persist "on the street" where individuals may trade at exchange rates unconstrained by the government in **black markets** or *parallel markets*. For example, in Italy in the 1930s, the Mussolini regime set harsh punishments for trading in foreign currency that gradually rose to include the death penalty, but trading still continued on the black market.

A less drastic action taken by the authorities is to let the private market for foreign exchange function but to fix or control forex prices in the market through **intervention,** a job typically given to a nation's central bank.

Looking Ahead How do central banks intervene in the forex market? Indeed, how can a government control a price in any market? This is an age-old problem. Consider the issue of food supply in medieval and premodern Europe, one of the earliest examples of government intervention in markets. Rulers faced the problem that populations, especially in cities, depended on low and stable prices of wheat to survive. Droughts or harvest failures could decimate the crop locally, or even regionally, leading to famine—and political unrest. Governments reacted by establishing state-run granaries, where wheat would be stored up in years of plenty and then released to the market in years of scarcity. The price could even be fixed if the government stood ready to buy or sell grain at a preset price—*and always had enough grain in reserve to do so*. Some authorities successfully followed this strategy for many years. Others failed when they ran out of grain reserves. Once a reserve is gone, market forces take over. If there is a heavy demand that is no longer being met by the state, a rapid price increase will inevitably follow.

Foreign exchange market intervention works similarly. If a government wishes to maintain a fixed exchange rate, the central bank must stand ready to buy or sell its own currency, in exchange for foreign currency, at a fixed price. As we shall see, this means keeping some foreign currency reserves as a buffer. But having this buffer raises many problems. For one thing, it is costly—resources are tied up in foreign currency when they could be invested in more profitable activities. Second, forex reserves are not an unlimited buffer, and if they run out, the game is up. A major task for us later in the book is to understand why countries peg, how a peg is maintained, and under what circumstances pegs fail, leading to an exchange rate crisis.

---

[9] From a speech at the World Bank meeting in Hong Kong, September 20, 1997, in which Mr. Mohamad also referred to the legendary currency trader George Soros as a "moron." See Edward A. Gargan, "Premier of Malaysia Spars with Currency Dealer; Mahathir Says Soros and His Ilk Are 'Impoverishing Others' for Profit," *New York Times,* September 22, 1997, A1.

Summary To conclude, the extent of government intervention can vary. However, even with complete and watertight capital controls, including the suppression of the black market, private actors are always present in the market. Our first task is to understand their economic motives and actions.

4 Arbitrage and Spot Exchange Rates

The most basic of activities pursued by private actors in any market is **arbitrage,** a trading strategy that exploits any profit opportunities arising from price differences. Understanding arbitrage is one of the keys to thinking like an economist in any situation and is an essential tool in the study of exchange rates.

In the simplest terms, arbitrage means to buy low and sell high. If such profit opportunities exist, then the market is considered to be out of equilibrium. If no such profit opportunities exist, there will be no arbitrage and the market is in **equilibrium** and satisfies a **no–arbitrage condition.**

Arbitrage with Two Currencies Suppose you trade dollars and pounds for a bank with branches in New York and London. You can electronically transfer the funds cost free between the two branch locations. Forex trading commissions are the same in each city and so small as to be negligible. Suppose the exchange rate in New York is $E_{£/\$}^{\text{N.Y.}} = £0.50$ per dollar, in London $E_{£/\$}^{\text{London}} = £0.55$ per dollar. Can you make a profit for the bank?

Yes. You can buy \$1 for £0.50 in New York and sell it for £0.55 in London for an instant, riskless profit. Indeed, everyone would buy in New York and sell in London.

In general, one of the three possibilities can occur. The spot rate can be higher in London: $E_{£/\$}^{\text{N.Y.}} < E_{£/\$}^{\text{London}}$; the spot rate can be higher in New York: $E_{£/\$}^{\text{N.Y.}} > E_{£/\$}^{\text{London}}$; or the spot rate can be equal in both locations: $E_{£/\$}^{\text{N.Y.}} = E_{£/\$}^{\text{London}}$. Arbitrage will occur in the first two cases. Only in the last case, in which spot rates are equal, does no arbitrage occur. Hence, the no-arbitrage condition for spot rates is

$$E_{£/\$}^{\text{N.Y.}} = E_{£/\$}^{\text{London}}$$

The no-arbitrage condition is shown diagrammatically in Figure 2-6. Following both sets of arrows, we see that on each path we start with a dollar and end up with pounds, but we are indifferent between these paths only when the end result is identical. This is when no arbitrage is possible.

If the market were out of equilibrium, arbitrage would drive up the price in the low-price market and drive down the price in the high-price market. In our example, everyone buying dollars in New York and selling them in London would

Forex traders at their desks in London and money changers on the street in Kabul.

FIGURE 2-6

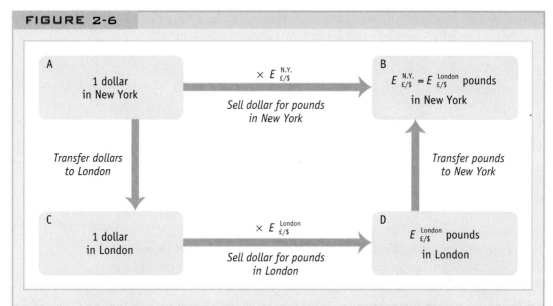

Arbitrage and Spot Rates Arbitrage ensures that the trade of currencies in New York along the path AB occurs at the same exchange rate as via London along path ACDB. At B the pounds received must be the same. Regardless of the route taken to get to B, $E_{£/\$}^{N.Y.} = E_{£/\$}^{London}$.

bid up the spot rate in New York from £0.50 and would bid down the spot rate in London from £0.55. This process would continue until the prices converged, arbitrage ceased, and equilibrium was attained. In forex markets, these adjustments happen nearly instantaneously, whether in the high-tech electronic markets of world financial centers or in the markets on street corners in the developing world.

Arbitrage with Three Currencies The same logic that we just applied to transactions between two currencies can also be applied to transactions involving three currencies. Again, as the trader in New York, you are considering trading dollars and pounds, but you also consider indirect or "triangular" trade via a third currency, say, the euro. Triangular arbitrage works as follows: you sell dollars in exchange for euros, then immediately sell the same euros in exchange for pounds. This may be a roundabout way to acquire pounds, yet it is perfectly feasible. But is it sensible? Perhaps.

For example, suppose euros can be obtained at $E_{€/\$} = €0.8$ per dollar, and pounds can be obtained at $E_{£/€} = £0.7$ per euro. Starting with $1, you can obtain 0.8 euros, and with those 0.8 euros, you can obtain 0.7×0.8 pounds. Thus, setting aside the negligibly small commissions, the resulting pound–dollar exchange rate on the combined trade is $E_{£/€} \times E_{€/\$} = 0.7 \times 0.8 = 0.56$ pounds per dollar. If, say, the exchange rate on the direct trade from dollars to pounds is a less favorable $E_{£/\$} = 0.5$, we can trade $1 for £0.56 via the euro, and then trade the £0.56 for $1.12 by way of a direct trade (because $1.12 = 0.56/0.5$), a riskless profit of 12¢.

In general, three cases are again possible. The direct trade from dollars to pounds has a better rate: $E_{£/\$} > E_{£/€}E_{€/\$}$; the indirect trade has a better rate:

$E_{£/\$} < E_{£/€}E_{€/\$}$; or the two trades have the same rate and yield the same result: $E_{£/\$} = E_{£/€}E_{€/\$}$. Only in the last case are there no profit opportunities. This no-arbitrage condition can be written in two ways:

$$\underbrace{E_{£/\$}}_{\substack{\text{Direct} \\ \text{exchange rate}}} = E_{£/€}E_{€/\$} = \underbrace{\frac{E_{£/€}}{E_{\$/€}}}_{\text{Cross rate}}$$

The right-hand expression, a ratio of two exchange rates, is referred to as a **cross rate.** Examine the units carefully and notice how the € cancels out. The no-arbitrage condition applies to all currency combinations. It is shown diagrammatically in Figure 2-7, and you can see why it is called *triangular arbitrage*.

The cross rate formula is very convenient. It means that we do not need to keep track of the exchange rate of every currency at all times. For example, if we know the exchange rates against, say, the dollar, for every currency, then for *any* pair of currencies A and B we can use the dollar rates of each currency and the cross rate formula to work out the rate at which the two currencies will trade: $E_{A/B} = E_{A/\$}/E_{B/\$}$. In practice, this is how most exchange rates are calculated.

Cross Rates and Vehicle Currencies

The study of cross rates is not just an academic exercise because the vast majority of currency pairs are exchanged for one another through a third currency. There are 162 distinct currencies in the world at the time of this writing. If you write down every possible currency pair, then count them up (this may take some time), and infer that each pair could be directly traded in some forex

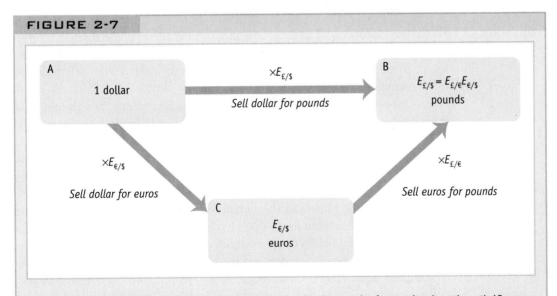

FIGURE 2-7

Arbitrage and Cross Rates Triangular arbitrage ensures that the direct trade of currencies along the path AB occurs at the same exchange rate as via a third currency along path ACB. The euros received at B must be the same on both paths, and $E_{£/\$} = E_{£/€}E_{€/\$}$.

market, you would be expecting to see 13,041 forex markets in operation. You would be disappointed, however, and find only a fraction of this number. Why?

Most currencies trade directly with only one or two of the major currencies, such as the dollar, euro, yen, or pound, and perhaps a few other currencies from neighboring countries. This is not too surprising. After all, to take some extreme examples, how often does somebody want to trade a Kenyan shilling for a Paraguayan guaraní? Or Mauritanian ouguiya for a Tongan pa'anga? These are small, far-apart countries between which there is very little international trade or investment. It is hard to find counterparties for forex trade in these currencies—so hard that the costs of trading become prohibitive. And there is no need to bear these costs because, to continue our example, Kenya, Paraguay, Mauritania, and Tonga do conduct a lot of business in major currencies such as the U.S. dollar, so individuals always have the option to engage in a triangular trade at the cross rate to convert shillings to dollars to guaraníes (or ouguiyas to dollars to pa'angas), all for a reasonable commission.

The vast majority of the world's currencies are traded in this indirect fashion. When a third currency, such as the U.S. dollar, is used in these transactions, it is referred to a **vehicle currency** because it is not the home currency of either of the parties involved in the trade and is just used for intermediation. Market data illustrate the importance of vehicle currencies. According to April 2007 data from the Bank for International Settlements, the most common vehicle currency is the U.S. dollar, which appears on one side of more than 86% of all global trades. The euro is second, playing a role in 37% of all trades (many of them with the U.S. dollar). The Japanese yen appears in 17% of all trades and the British pound in 15% of all trades (many of those trades with the U.S. dollar and the euro).

5 Arbitrage and Interest Rates

So far, our discussion of arbitrage has shown how actors in the forex market—for example, the banks—exploit profit opportunities if currencies trade at different prices. But this is not the only type of arbitrage activity affecting the forex market.

An important question for investors is in which currency they should hold their liquid cash balances. Their cash can be placed in bank deposit accounts denominated in various currencies where it will earn a modest interest rate. For example, a trader working for a major bank in New York could leave the bank's cash in a euro deposit for one year earning a 2% euro interest rate, or she could put the money in a U.S. dollar deposit for one year earning a 4% dollar interest rate. How can she decide which asset, the euro or the dollar deposit, is the best investment?

This is the final problem that we address in this chapter, and this analysis provides the tools we need to understand the forex market in the rest of this book. The analysis again centers on arbitrage. Would selling euro deposits and buying dollar deposits make a profit for the banker? Decisions like these drive the demand for dollars versus euros and the exchange rate between the two currencies.

The Problem of Risk A key issue for the trader is the problem of exchange rate risk. The trader is in New York, and her bank cares about returns in U.S.

dollars. The dollar deposit pays a return in dollars. But the euro deposit pays a return in euros, and one year from now we cannot know for sure what the dollar-euro exchange rate will be. Thus, how we analyze the arbitrage problem in the sections that follow depends on how risk is handled by the investor. We consider two ways to deal with the risk:

- On the one hand, we know a simple way to avoid exchange risk. One can hedge it or "cover" it by using a forward contract. When investors compare returns in this case, all exchange risk is covered, and the problem is one of *riskless arbitrage*. This approach leads to a no-arbitrage condition known as *covered interest parity (CIP)*.

- On the other hand, one can proceed with exchange risk unhedged or "uncovered" by employing only spot contracts. When investors compare returns in this case, the problem is one of *risky arbitrage*. This approach leads to a no-arbitrage condition known as *uncovered interest parity (UIP)*.

These two parity conditions are closely related to each other and will help us understand the determinants of exchange rates for the two main contracts in the forex market, the spot and the forward.

Riskless Arbitrage: Covered Interest Parity

Suppose that contracts to exchange euros for dollars in one year carry an exchange rate of $F_{\$/€}$ dollars per euro. This is known as the **forward exchange rate,** and it allows investors to be absolutely sure of the price at which they can trade forex in the future.

Assume you are trading for the bank in New York, and you have to decide whether to invest \$1 for one year in either a dollar or euro bank deposit that pays interest. The interest rate offered in New York on dollar deposits is $i_\$$, and in Europe the interest rate offered on euro deposits is $i_€$. Which investment offers the higher return?

If you invest in a dollar deposit, your \$1 placed in a U.S. bank account will be worth $(1 + i_\$)$ dollars in one year's time. This would be the dollar value of principal and interest for the U.S. dollar bank deposit: we refer to this as the *dollar return*. Note that we explicitly specify in what currency the return is measured, for purposes of comparability.

If you invest in a euro deposit, you first need to convert the dollar to euros. Using the spot exchange rate, \$1 buys $1/E_{\$/€}$ euros today. These $1/E_{\$/€}$ euros would be placed in a euro account earning $i_€$, so in a year's time they would be worth $(1 + i_€)/E_{\$/€}$ euros. You would then convert them back into dollars, but the future spot rate cannot be known for sure. To avoid that risk, you engage in a forward contract today to make the future transaction at a forward rate $F_{\$/€}$. The $(1 + i_€)/E_{\$/€}$ euros you will have in one year's time can then be exchanged for $(1 + i_€)F_{\$/€}/E_{\$/€}$ dollars, and this would be the dollar value of principal and interest, or dollar return, on the euro bank deposit.[10]

---

[10] Note that this arbitrage strategy requires a spot and a forward contract. The two could be combined in a swap contract, and this helps explain the prevalence of swaps in the forex market.

Three cases are possible as you compare the dollar returns from the two deposits. The U.S. deposit has a higher dollar return, the euro deposit has a higher dollar return, or both deposits have the same dollar return. In the first case, you would advise your bank to sell its euro deposits and buy dollar deposits; your reaction in the second case would be to advise the opposite trades. Only in the third case is there no expected profit from arbitrage, so the relevant no-arbitrage condition can be written as follows:

$$(2\text{-}1) \qquad \text{Covered interest parity (CIP):} \underbrace{(1 + i_\$)}_{\substack{\text{Dollar return on} \\ \text{dollar deposits}}} = \underbrace{(1 + i_\epsilon)\frac{F_{\$/\epsilon}}{E_{\$/\epsilon}}}_{\substack{\text{Dollar return on} \\ \text{euro deposits}}}$$

This expression is called **covered interest parity (CIP)** because all exchange rate risk on the euro side has been "covered" by use of the forward contract. We say that such a trade employs *forward cover*. The condition is illustrated in Figure 2-8.

Summary Covered interest parity is a no-arbitrage condition that describes an equilibrium in which investors are indifferent between interest-bearing bank deposits in two currencies and exchange risk has been eliminated by the use of a forward contract.

FIGURE 2-8

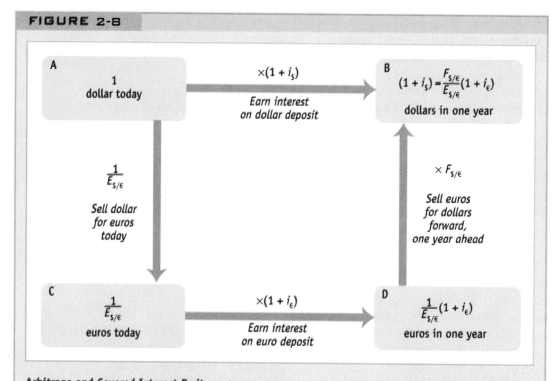

Arbitrage and Covered Interest Parity Under CIP, returns to holding dollar deposits accruing interest going along the path AB must equal the returns from investing in euros going along the path ACDB with risk removed by use of a forward contract. Hence, at B, the riskless payoff must be the same on both paths, and $(1 + i_\$) = \frac{F_{\$/\epsilon}}{E_{\$/\epsilon}}(1 + i_\epsilon)$.

Covered interest parity also provides a theory of what determines the forward exchange rate. We can rearrange the above equation and solve for the forward rate:

$$F_{\$/\epsilon} = E_{\$/\epsilon}\frac{1 + i_{\$}}{1 + i_{\epsilon}}$$

Thus, if covered interest parity holds, we can calculate the forward rate if we know all three right-hand side variables: the spot rate $E_{\$/\epsilon}$, the dollar interest rate $i_{\$}$, and the euro interest rate i_{ϵ}. For example, suppose the euro interest rate is 3%, the dollar interest rate is 5%, and the spot rate is \$1.30 per euro. Then the preceding equation says the forward rate would be 1.30 × (1.05)/(1.03) = \$1.3252 per euro.

In practice, this is exactly how the market works and how the price of the forward contract is set. Watching their screens, traders all around the world can see the interest rates on bank deposits in each currency, and the spot exchange rate. We can now also see why the forward contract is called a "derivative" contract: to establish the price of the forward contract (the forward rate F), we first need to know the price of the spot contract (the spot rate E). That is, the pricing of the forward contract is derived from the pricing of the underlying spot contract, using additional information on interest rates.

This result raises a new question: How are the interest rates and the spot rate determined? We return to that question in a moment, after looking at some evidence to verify that covered interest parity does indeed hold.

APPLICATION

Evidence on Covered Interest Parity

Does covered interest parity hold? We expect returns to be equalized only if arbitrage is possible. This is not always the case. If governments impose capital controls, there is no way for traders to exploit profit opportunities and no reason for the returns on different currencies to equalize. For example, Figure 2-9 shows that in recent years covered interest parity holds very closely in practice between the United Kingdom and Germany, ever since the two countries abolished their capital controls in the period from 1979 to 1981. (The German deposits shown here were denominated in marks prior to 1999. The same result holds after 1999, when the euro replaced the mark as the German currency.)

The line on the chart shows the profit that could have been made (measured in percent per annum in British currency, before transaction costs) if the investor had been able to move funds from the United Kingdom to Germany with forward cover (or, when the line is in negative territory, the profit from moving funds from Germany to the United Kingdom). From Equation (2-1), we know that the hypothetical profit from this riskless arbitrage would be

$$\text{Profit} = \underbrace{(1 + i_{GER})\frac{F_{UK/GER}}{E_{UK/GER}}}_{\substack{\text{Pound return on} \\ \text{German deposits}}} - \underbrace{(1 + i_{UK})}_{\substack{\text{Pound return on} \\ \text{U.K. deposits}}}$$

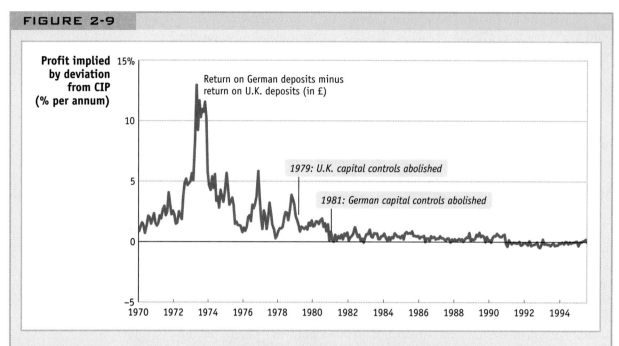

Profit implied by deviation from CIP (% per annum)

Return on German deposits minus return on U.K. deposits (in £)

1979: U.K. capital controls abolished

1981: German capital controls abolished

Financial Liberalization and Covered Interest Parity: Arbitrage between United Kingdom and Germany The chart shows the difference in monthly pound returns on deposits in British pounds and German marks using forward cover from 1970 to 1995. The implied profit from arbitrage is given by $(1 + i_{GER})F_{UK/GER}/E_{UK/GER} - (1 + i_{UK})$. In the 1970s, the difference was positive and often large: traders would have profited from arbitrage by moving money from pound deposits to mark deposits, but capital controls prevented them from freely doing so. After financial liberalization, these profits essentially vanished, and no arbitrage opportunities remained. The CIP condition held, aside from small deviations resulting from transactions costs and measurement errors.

Source: Maurice Obstfeld and Alan M. Taylor, 2004, Global Capital Markets: Integration, Crisis, and Growth, Japan-U.S. Center Sanwa Monographs on International Financial Markets, Cambridge: Cambridge University Press.

This profit would be zero if and only if covered interest parity held. In the 1960s and 1970s, the hypothetical profits implied by this expression were large—or would have been had arbitrage been allowed. Instead, capital controls in both countries prevented arbitrage. Covered interest parity therefore failed to hold. But arbitrage became possible following financial liberalization. From that time until the present, profits have been essentially zero. Computed profits are not exactly zero because of regulations, fees, other transaction costs, and measurement error. Once we allow for these factors, there are no profit opportunities left. Covered interest parity does hold when capital markets are open, and this can be confirmed for all freely traded currencies today. ■

Risky Arbitrage: Uncovered Interest Parity

To understand how the spot exchange rate is determined, we now turn to the other form of interest arbitrage mentioned earlier, risky arbitrage. To keep things simple, let us suppose, for now, that investors focus *exclusively* on the expected dollar return of the two bank deposits. (See **Side Bar: Assets and Their Attributes**.)

SIDE BAR

Assets and Their Attributes

The bank deposits traded in the forex market pay interest and are part of the wider portfolio of assets held by banks and other private actors. As we have argued, the forex market is heavily influenced by the demand for these deposits as assets.

An investor's entire portfolio of assets may include stocks, bonds, real estate, art, bank deposits in various currencies, and so on. What influences the demand for such assets? Viewed from a financial viewpoint (that is, setting aside the beauty of a painting or château), all assets have three key attributes that influence demand: return, risk, and liquidity.

An asset's **rate of return** is the total net increase in wealth (measured in a given currency) resulting from holding the asset for a specified period of time, typically one year. For example, you start the year by buying one share of DotBomb Inc., a hot Internet stock, for $100. At year's end, the share is worth $150 and has paid you a dividend of $5. Your total return is $55: a $50 capital gain from the change in the stock price and a $5 dividend. Your total annual rate of return is 55/100, or 55%. The next year, the stock falls from $150 to $75 and pays no dividend. You lost half of your money in the second year: your rate of return for that year was −75/150, or −50%. All else equal, investors prefer investments with high returns.

The *risk* of an asset refers to the volatility of its rate of return. The **liquidity** of an asset refers to the ease and speed with which it can be liquidated, or sold. A stock may seem to have high risk because its rate of return bounces up and down quite a lot, but its risk must be considered in relation to the riskiness of other investments. Its degree of risk could be contrasted with the rate of interest your bank offers on a money market deposit, a return that is usually very stable over time. You will lose your bank deposit only if your bank fails, which is usually very unlikely. Your bank deposit is also very liquid. You can go to a cash machine or write a check to access that form of wealth. A work of art, for example, is much less liquid. To get a sale, you will need the services of an auctioneer. Art is also risky. Different works can go in and out of fashion. All else equal, investors prefer assets with low risk and high liquidity.

Two observations follow. First, because all else is never equal, investors are willing to trade off among these attributes. You may be willing to hold a relatively risky and illiquid asset if you expect it will pay a relatively high return. Second, what you expect matters. Most investments, like stocks or art, do not have a fixed, predictable, guaranteed rate of return. Instead, all investors have to forecast. We refer to the forecast of the rate of return as the **expected rate of return.**

Imagine you are once again trading for a bank in New York, and you must decide whether to invest $1 for one year in a dollar or euro bank deposit that pays interest. However, this time you use spot contracts only and make no use of the forward contract to hedge against the riskiness of the future exchange rate.

The $1 invested in a dollar deposit will be worth $(1 + i_\$)$ in one year's time, and this would be the dollar return, as before.

If you invest in a euro deposit, a dollar buys $1/E_{\$/\euro}$ euros. With interest, these would be worth $(1 + i_\euro)/E_{\$/\euro}$ euros in a year's time. You will convert them back into dollars using a spot contract at the exchange rate that will prevail in one year's time. In this case, traders like you face exchange rate risk and must make a *forecast* of the future spot rate. We refer to the forecast as $E^e_{\$/\euro}$, which we call the **expected exchange rate.** Based on the forecast, you expect that the $(1 + i_\euro)/E_{\$/\euro}$ euros you will have in one year's time will be worth $(1 + i_\euro)E^e_{\$/\euro}/E_{\$/\euro}$ when converted into dollars, and this is the *expected dollar return*, the expected dollar value of principal and interest for euro deposits.

Again, three cases are possible: the U.S. deposit has a higher expected dollar return, the euro deposit has a higher expected dollar return, or both deposits have the same expected dollar return.

We have assumed that investors like you are indifferent to risk and care only about expected returns. Thus, in the first two cases, you have expected profit opportunities and risky arbitrage would be possible: you would sell the deposit with the low expected return and buy the deposit with the higher expected return. Only in the third case is there no expected profit from arbitrage, so the no-arbitrage condition here can be written as follows:

Uncovered interest parity (UIP):

$$(2\text{-}2) \qquad \underbrace{(1 + i_\$)}_{\substack{\text{Dollar return on} \\ \text{dollar deposits}}} = \underbrace{(1 + i_\euro)\frac{E^e_{\$/\euro}}{E_{\$/\euro}}}_{\substack{\text{Expected dollar return} \\ \text{on euro deposits}}}$$

This expression is called **uncovered interest parity (UIP)** because exchange rate risk has been left "uncovered" by the decision to eschew forward cover and instead simply wait to use a spot contract in a year's time. The condition is illustrated in Figure 2-10.

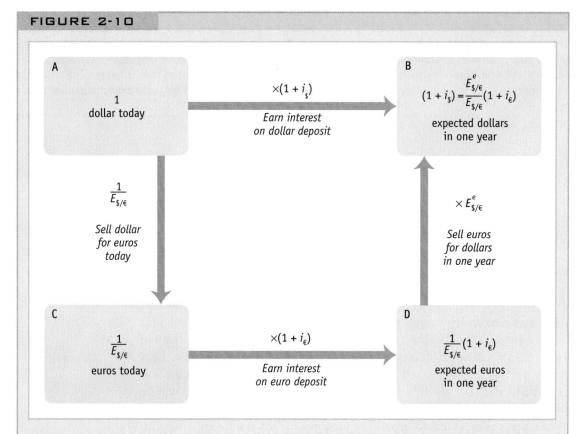

FIGURE 2-10

Arbitrage and Uncovered Interest Parity Under UIP, returns to holding dollar deposits accruing interest going along the path AB must equal the *expected* returns from investing in euros going along the risky path ACDB. Hence, at B, the expected payoff must be the same on both paths, and $(1 + i_\$) = \dfrac{E^e_{\$/\euro}}{E_{\$/\euro}}(1 + i_\euro)$.

Summary Uncovered interest parity is a no-arbitrage condition that describes an equilibrium in which investors are indifferent between interest-bearing bank deposits in two currencies *without* the use of forward contracts to cover exchange rate risk.

Uncovered interest parity provides us with a theory of what determines the spot exchange rate. We can rearrange the previous equation and solve for the spot rate:

$$E_{\$/€} = E_{\$/€}^e \frac{1 + i_€}{1 + i_\$}$$

Thus, if uncovered interest parity holds, we can calculate today's spot rate if we know all three right-hand side variables: the expected spot rate in the future, $E_{\$/€}^e$; the dollar interest rate, $i_\$$; and the euro interest rate, $i_€$. For example, suppose the euro interest rate is 2%, the dollar interest rate is 4%, and the expected future spot rate is \$1.40 per euro. Then the preceding equation says today's spot rate would be $1.40 \times (1.02)/(1.04) = \$1.3731$ per euro.

This result still raises more questions: How can the expected future exchange rate be forecast? And, as in the case of covered interest parity, we still do not know how interest rates are determined.

We address these still-unanswered questions in the next two chapters. Chapter 3 looks at the determinants of the expected future exchange rate $E_{\$/€}^e$ by developing a model of exchange rates in the long run. Chapter 4 looks at the determinants of the interest rates $i_\$$ and $i_€$ and, with all the parts in place, leads to a unified theory of exchange rates.

APPLICATION

Evidence on Uncovered Interest Parity

Does uncovered interest parity hold? The two interest parity equations seen previously are very similar. Equation (2-1), the CIP equation, uses the forward rate; Equation (2-2), the UIP equation, uses the expected future spot rate. To recap:

$$\text{CIP:} \ (1 + i_\$) = (1 + i_€)\frac{F_{\$/€}}{E_{\$/€}}$$

$$\text{UIP:} \ (1 + i_\$) = (1 + i_€)\frac{E_{\$/€}^e}{E_{\$/€}}$$

Dividing the second equation by the first, we obtain $1 = E_{\$/€}^e / F_{\$/€}$, or

$$F_{\$/€} = E_{\$/€}^e$$

Thus, if *both* covered interest parity *and* uncovered interest parity hold, an important relationship emerges: *The forward rate must equal the expected future spot rate.* The result is intuitive. In equilibrium, if investors do not care about risk (as we have assumed), then they have no reason to prefer to avoid risk by using the forward rate rather than waiting for the expected future spot rate to materialize.

Since the evidence in favor of covered interest parity is strong, we may assume that it holds. The previous equation then provides a test for whether uncovered interest parity holds. But if the forward rate equals the expected spot rate, then we also know that

$$\underbrace{\frac{F_{\$/\epsilon}}{E_{\$/\epsilon}} - 1}_{\text{Forward premium}} = \underbrace{\frac{E^e_{\$/\epsilon}}{E_{\$/\epsilon}} - 1}_{\substack{\text{Expected rate} \\ \text{of depreciation}}}$$

and we see that some convenient terms appear here when we divide by the spot rate and subtract 1. The last equation says that the expected rate of depreciation equals the **forward premium** (the proportional difference between the forward and spot rates). For example, if the spot rate is $1.00 per euro, and the forward rate is $1.05, the forward premium is 5%. But if $F_{\$/\epsilon} = E^e_{\$/\epsilon}$, the expected future spot rate is also $1.05, and there is a 5% expected rate of depreciation.

The left-hand side of the preceding equation, the forward premium, is easily observed. The difficulty is on the right-hand side: expectations are typically unobserved. Still, the test can be attempted using surveys in which traders are asked to report their expectations. Using data from one such test, Figure 2-11 shows a strong correlation between expected rates of depreciation and the forward premium, with a slope close to 1. Still, the points do not lie exactly on the 45-degree line, so sometimes expected depreciation is not equal to the interest differential. Does this mean that arbitrage is not working? Not necessarily. The deviations may be caused by sampling errors and the fact that individual traders may have different expectations. In addition, there may be limits to risky arbitrage in reality because of various factors such as transactions costs (market frictions) and aversion to risk, which we have so far neglected, but which we discuss in more detail in later chapters (see Chapter 11). ■

Uncovered Interest Parity: A Useful Approximation

Because it provides a theory of the spot exchange rate, the uncovered interest parity equation, Equation (2-2) is one of the most important conditions in international macroeconomics. Yet for most purposes, a simpler and more convenient approximation can be employed.

The intuition behind the approximation is as follows. Holding dollar deposits rewards the investor with dollar interest. Holding euro deposits rewards investors in two ways: they receive euro interest, but they also receive a gain (or loss) on euros equal to the rate of euro appreciation (i.e., approximately the rate of dollar depreciation). Thus, if UIP is to hold, and an investor is to be indifferent between dollar deposits and euro deposits, then any interest shortfall (excess) on the euro side must be offset by an expected gain (loss) in the form of euro appreciation (or dollar depreciation).

We can write the approximation formally as follows:

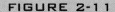

FIGURE 2-11

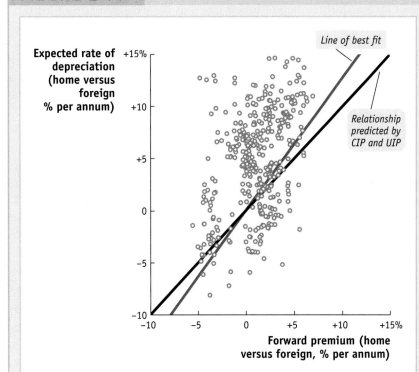

Expected rate of depreciation (home versus foreign % per annum)

Line of best fit

Relationship predicted by CIP and UIP

Forward premium (home versus foreign, % per annum)

Evidence on Interest Parity When UIP and CIP hold, the 12-month forward premium ($F_{\$/\euro}/E_{\$/\euro} - 1$) should equal the 12-month expected rate of depreciation ($E_{\$/\euro}^e/E_{\$/\euro} - 1$). A scatterplot showing these two variables should be close to the 45-degree line. It is hard to obtain data on market expectations, but this has been attempted using evidence from surveys of individual forex traders' expectations over the period 1988 to 1993. UIP finds some support in these data, as the slope is not too far from 1.

Notes: Line of best fit is through the origin. Data shown are monthly for the German mark, Swiss franc, Japanese yen, British pound, and Canadian dollar against the U.S. dollar from February 1988 to October 1993.

Source: From Menzie Chinn and Jeffrey A. Frankel, 2002, "Survey Data on Exchange Rate Expectations: More Currencies, More Horizons, More Tests," in W. Allen and D. Dickinson, eds., Monetary Policy, Capital Flows and Financial Market Developments in the Era of Financial Globalisation: Essays in Honour of Max Fry, London: Routledge, 145–167.

(2-3)   UIP approximation: $\underbrace{i_{\$}}_{\substack{\text{Interest rate on} \\ \text{dollar deposits} \\ = \\ \text{Dollar rate of} \\ \text{return on dollar} \\ \text{deposits}}} = \underbrace{\underbrace{i_{\euro}}_{\substack{\text{Interest rate on} \\ \text{euro deposits}}} + \underbrace{\dfrac{\Delta E_{\$/\euro}^e}{E_{\$/\euro}}}_{\substack{\text{Expected rate of} \\ \text{depreciation of the} \\ \text{dollar}}}}_{\substack{\text{Expected dollar rate of return on} \\ \text{euro deposits}}}.$

There are three terms in this equation. The left-hand side is the interest rate on dollar deposits. The first term on the right is the interest rate on euro deposits. The second term on the right can be expanded as $\Delta E_{\$/\euro}^e/E_{\$/\euro} = (E_{\$/\euro}^e - E_{\$/\euro})/E_{\$/\euro}$ and is the expected fractional change in the euro's value, or the expected rate of appreciation of the euro. As we have seen, this expression equals the appreciation of the euro exactly, but for small changes it is approximately equal to the **expected rate of depreciation** of the dollar.[11]

---

[11] To derive Equation (2-3), we can write $E_{\$/\euro}^e/E_{\$/\euro} = (1 + \Delta E_{\$/\euro}^e/E_{\$/\euro})$, and so the equation becomes

$$1 + i_{\$} = (1 + i_{\euro})\left(1 + \frac{\Delta E_{\$/\euro}^e}{E_{\$/\euro}}\right) = 1 + i_{\euro} + \frac{\Delta E_{\$/\euro}^e}{E_{\$/\euro}} + \left[i_{\euro}\frac{\Delta E_{\$/\euro}^e}{E_{\$/\euro}}\right]$$

When the euro interest rate and the expected rate of depreciation are small, the last term in brackets is very small and may be neglected in an approximation. We can then cancel out the 1 that appears on each side of the above equation to obtain Equation (2-3).

The UIP approximation equation, Equation (2-3), says that the home interest rate equals the foreign interest rate plus the expected rate of depreciation of the home currency.

A numerical example illustrates the UIP approximation formula. Suppose the dollar interest rate is 4% per year and the euro interest rate 3% per year. If UIP is to hold, then the expected rate of dollar depreciation over a year must be 1%. In that case, a dollar investment put into euros for a year will grow by 3% due to euro interest and (in dollar terms) will grow by an extra 1% due to euro appreciation, so the total dollar return on the euro deposit is approximately equal to the 4% that is offered by dollar deposits.[12]

To sum up, the uncovered interest parity condition, whether in exact form (Equation 2-2) or approximate form (Equation 2-3), states that there must be parity between expected returns, *expressed in a common currency,* in the two markets.

Summary

All economic models produce an output (some unknown or *endogenous* variable to be explained) and require a set of inputs (some known or *exogenous* variables that are treated as given). The two interest parity conditions provide us with models that explain how the prices of the two most important forex contracts are determined. Uncovered interest parity applies to the spot market and determines the spot rate, based on interest rates and exchange rate expectations. Covered interest parity applies to the forward market and determines the forward rate based on interest rates and the spot rate. Figure 2-12 sums up what we have learned.

6 Conclusions

The foreign exchange market has a long and often tumultuous record and, in today's globalized world, exchange rates matter more than ever. They affect the prices of international transactions, they can be a focus of government policy, and they often play a major role in economic and political crises.

This chapter has set the stage for our study of exchange rates. We first learned what exchange rates are, how they are used, and the ways in which they have behaved in reality under different exchange rate regimes. History offers the only laboratory for study and illustrates a vast range of experiences past and present. At some point, almost all possible exchange rate regimes have been tried, and this experimentation continues.

These observations underscore the importance of trying to understand different regimes and their causes and consequences. We have prepared ourselves by examining the workings of the foreign exchange market in some detail. Government intervention (or its absence) in this market determines the

---

[12] Note that the $1 investment in euros will be worth $(1.03) \times (1.01) = \$1.0403$ after one year, which is very close to $1.04, the value of the dollar deposit after one year. The difference is just the approximation error. See the previous footnote.

FIGURE 2-12

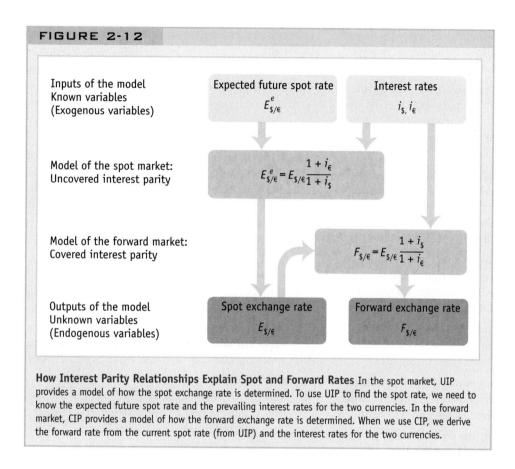

How Interest Parity Relationships Explain Spot and Forward Rates In the spot market, UIP provides a model of how the spot exchange rate is determined. To use UIP to find the spot rate, we need to know the expected future spot rate and the prevailing interest rates for the two currencies. In the forward market, CIP provides a model of how the forward exchange rate is determined. When we use CIP, we derive the forward rate from the current spot rate (from UIP) and the interest rates for the two currencies.

nature of the exchange rate regime in operation, from fixed to floating. The workings of actors in this market then ultimately determine economic outcomes in equilibrium, including the exchange rate.

How is forex market equilibrium determined? We argued that two key forces operate in the foreign exchange market: arbitrage and expectations. Through expectations, news about the future can affect expected returns. Through arbitrage, differences in expected returns are equalized, as summed up by the two important interest parity conditions. In the next two chapters, we build on these ideas further to develop a complete theory of exchange rates.

KEY POINTS

1. The exchange rate in a country is the price of a unit of foreign currency expressed in terms of the domestic currency. This price is determined in the spot market for foreign exchange.

2. When the home exchange rate rises, less foreign currency is bought/sold per unit of home currency; the home currency has depreciated. If home currency buys (x%) less foreign currency, the home currency is said to have depreciated (by x%).

3. When the home exchange rate falls, more foreign currency is bought/sold per unit of home currency; the home currency has appreciated. If home currency buys (x%) more foreign currency, the home currency is said to have appreciated (by x%).

4. The exchange rate is used to convert the prices of goods and assets into a common currency to allow meaningful price comparisons.

5. Exchange rates may be stable over time or they may fluctuate. History supplies examples of the former (fixed exchange rate regimes) and the latter (floating exchange rate regimes) as well as a number of intermediate regime types.

6. An exchange rate crisis occurs when the exchange rate experiences a sudden and large depreciation. These events are often associated with broader economic and political turmoil, especially in developing countries, and deserve special attention.

7. Some countries may forgo a national currency to form a currency union with other nations (e.g., the Eurozone), or they may unilaterally adopt the currency of another country ("dollarization").

8. Looking across all countries today, numerous fixed and floating rate regimes are observed, so we must understand both types of regime.

9. The forex market is dominated by spot transactions, but many other derivative contracts exist, such as forwards, swaps, futures, and options.

10. The main actors in the market are private investors and (frequently) the government

authorities, represented usually by the central bank.

11. Arbitrage on currencies means that spot exchange rates are approximately equal in different forex markets. Cross rates (for indirect trades) and spot rates (for direct trades) are also approximately equal.

12. Riskless interest arbitrage leads to the covered interest parity (CIP) condition. CIP says that the dollar return on dollar deposits must equal the dollar return on euro deposits, where forward contracts are used to cover exchange rate risk.

13. Covered interest parity explains how the forward rate is determined by the home and foreign interest rates and the spot exchange rate.

14. Risky interest arbitrage leads to the uncovered interest parity (UIP) condition. UIP says that the dollar return on dollar deposits must equal the expected dollar returns on euro deposits, where spot contracts are used and exchange rate risk is not covered.

15. Uncovered interest parity explains how the spot rate is determined by the two interest rates and the expected future spot exchange rate.

KEY TERMS

exchange rate, p. 30
appreciation, p. 33
depreciation, p. 33
effective exchange rate, p. 35
exchange rate regimes, p. 39
fixed (or pegged) exchange rate regime, p. 39
floating (or flexible) exchange rate regime, p. 39
free float exchange rate regime, p. 41
band, p. 41
managed float, p. 41
exchange rate crises, p. 41
crawl, p. 43
dollarization, p. 43
currency board, p. 43

currency (or monetary) union, p. 45
foreign exchange (forex) market, p. 45
spot contract, p. 46
spot exchange rate, p. 46
spread, p. 46
market friction, p. 46
transaction cost, p. 46
derivatives, p. 47
forward, p. 47
swap, p. 48
futures, p. 48
option, p. 48
commercial banks, p. 48
interbank trading, p. 49
corporations, p. 49

nonbank financial institutions, p. 49
capital control, p. 49
official market, p. 50
black market, p. 50
intervention, p. 50
arbitrage, p. 51
equilibrium, p. 51
no-arbitrage condition, p. 51
cross rate, p. 53
vehicle currency, p. 54
forward exchange rate, p. 55
covered interest parity, p. 56
rate of return, p. 59
risk, p. 59
liquidity, p. 59

expected rate of return, p. 59

expected exchange rate, p. 59

uncovered interest parity, p. 60

forward premium, p. 62

expected rate of depreciation, p. 63

PROBLEMS

1. Refer to the exchange rates from November 6, 2006, given in the following table.

Country	Today November 6, 2006 Per $	Per £	One Year Ago November 6, 2005 Per €	Per $
Australia	1.289	2.461	1.650	1.366
Canada	1.128	2.153	1.444	1.190
Denmark	5.823	11.121	7.457	6.328
Euro	0.781	1.491	1.000	0.848
Hong Kong	7.785	14.867	9.969	7.752
India	44.620	85.215	57.140	45.780
Japan	117.440	224.287	150.394	117.570
Mexico	10.811	20.647	13.845	3.778
Sweden	7.138	13.632	9.141	10.706
United Kingdom	0.524	1.000	0.671	0.573
United States	1.000	1.910	1.281	1.000

Source: U.S. Federal Reserve Board of Governors, H.10 release: Foreign Exchange Rates.

Based on the table provided, answer the following questions.

a. Compute the U.S. dollar-yen exchange rate, $E_{\$/¥}$, and the U.S. dollar-Canadian dollar exchange rate, $E_{\$/C\$}$, on November 6, 2005, and November 6, 2006.

b. What happened to the value of the U.S. dollar relative to the Japanese yen and Canadian dollar between November 6, 2005, and November 6, 2006? Compute the percentage change in the value of the U.S. dollar relative to each currency using the U.S. dollar-foreign currency exchange rates you computed in (a).

c. Using the information in the table for November 2006, compute the Danish krone-Canadian dollar exchange rate, $E_{krone/C\$}$.

d. Visit the website of the Board of Governors of the Federal Reserve System at http://www.federalreserve.gov/. Click on "Economic Research and Data" and then "Statistical Releases and Historical Data."

Download the H.10 release Foreign Exchange Rates (daily). What has happened to the value of the U.S. dollar relative to the Canadian dollar, Japanese yen, and Danish krone since November 2006?

e. Using the information from (d), what has happened to the value of the U.S. dollar relative to the British pound and the euro? Note: the H.10 release quotes these exchange rates as U.S. dollars per unit of foreign currency in line with long-standing market conventions.

2. Consider the United States and the countries it trades with the most (measured in trade volume): Canada, Mexico, China, and Japan. For simplicity, assume these are the only four countries with which the United States trades. Trade shares and exchange rates for these four countries are as follows:

Country (currency)	Share of Trade	$ per FX in 2002	$ per FX in 2003
Canada (dollar)	36%	0.641	0.763
Mexico (peso)	28%	0.098	0.089
China (yuan)	20%	0.121	0.121
Japan (yen)	16%	0.008	0.009

a. Compute the percentage change from 2002 to 2003 in the four U.S. bilateral exchange rates (defined as U.S. dollars per units of foreign exchange, or FX) in the table provided.

b. Use the trade shares as weights to compute the percentage change in the nominal effective exchange rate for the United States between 2002 and 2003 (in U.S. dollars per foreign currency basket).

c. Based on your answer to (b), what happened to the value of the U.S. dollar against this basket between 2002 and 2003? How does this compare with the change in the value of the U.S. dollar relative to the Mexican peso? Explain your answer.

3. Go to the website for Federal Reserve Economic Data (FRED): http://research.stlouisfed.org/fred2/. Locate the monthly exchange rate data for the following:

   a. Canada (dollar), 1980–2006
   b. China (yuan), 1999–2005
   c. Mexico (peso), 1993–1995 and 1995–2006
   d. Thailand (baht), 1986–1997 and 1997–2006
   e. Venezuela (bolivar), 2003–2006

   Look at the graphs and make a judgment as to whether each currency was fixed (peg or band), crawling (peg or band), or floating relative to the U.S. dollar during each time frame given.

4. Describe the different ways in which the government may intervene in the foreign exchange market. Why does the government have the ability to intervene in this way while private actors do not?

5. Suppose quotes for the dollar-euro exchange rate, $E_{\$/\epsilon}$, are as follows: in New York $1.50 per euro, and in Tokyo $1.55 per euro. Describe how investors use arbitrage to take advantage of the difference in exchange rates. Explain how this process will affect the dollar price of the euro in New York and Tokyo.

6. Consider a Dutch investor with 1,000 euros to place in a bank deposit in either the Netherlands or Great Britain. The (one-year) interest rate on bank deposits is 2% in Britain and 4.04% in the Netherlands. The (one-year) forward euro-pound exchange rate is 1.575 euros per pound and the spot rate is 1.5 euros per pound. Answer the following questions, using the *exact* equations for UIP and CIP as necessary.

   a. What is the euro-denominated return on Dutch deposits for this investor?
   b. What is the (riskless) euro-denominated return on British deposits for this investor using forward cover?
   c. Is there an arbitrage opportunity here? Explain why or why not. Is this an equilibrium in the forward exchange rate market?
   d. If the spot rate is 1.5 euros per pound, and interest rates are as stated previously, what is the equilibrium forward rate, according to covered interest parity (CIP)?

   e. Suppose the forward rate takes the value given by your answer to (d). Compute the forward premium on the British pound for the Dutch investor (where exchange rates are in euros per pound). Is it positive or negative? Why do investors require this premium/discount in equilibrium?
   f. If uncovered interest parity (UIP) holds, what is the expected depreciation of the euro (against the pound) over one year?
   g. Based on your answer to (f), what is the expected euro-pound exchange rate one year ahead?

7. You are a financial adviser to a U.S. corporation that expects to receive a payment of 40 million Japanese yen in 180 days for goods exported to Japan. The current spot rate is 100 yen per U.S. dollar ($E_{\$/\yen} = 0.0100$). You are concerned that the U.S. dollar is going to appreciate against the yen over the next six months.

   a. Assuming the exchange rate remains unchanged, how much does your firm expect to receive in U.S. dollars?
   b. How much would your firm receive (in U.S. dollars) if the dollar appreciated to 110 yen per U.S. dollar ($E_{\$/\yen} = 0.00909$)?
   c. Describe how you could use an options contract to hedge against the risk of losses associated with the potential appreciation in the U.S. dollar.

8. Consider how transactions costs affect foreign currency exchange. Rank each of the following foreign exchanges according to their probable spread (between the "buy at" and "sell for" bilateral exchange rates) and justify your ranking.

   a. An American returning from a trip to Turkey wants to exchange his Turkish lira for U.S. dollars at the airport.
   b. Citigroup and HSBC, both large commercial banks located in the United States and United Kingdom, respectively, need to clear several large checks drawn on accounts held by each bank.
   c. Honda Motor Company needs to exchange yen for U.S. dollars to pay American workers at its Ohio manufacturing plant.
   d. A Canadian tourist in Germany pays for her hotel room using a credit card.

Exchange Rates I: The Monetary Approach in the Long Run

Our willingness to pay a certain price for foreign money must ultimately and essentially be due to the fact that this money possesses a purchasing power as against commodities and services in that foreign country.

Gustav Cassel, of the Swedish school of economics, 1922

The fundamental things apply / As time goes by.

Herman Hupfeld, songwriter, 1931
(from the film *Casablanca*, 1942)

The cost of living is usually rising, but it rises in some places more than others. From 1970 to 1990, for example, a standardized Canadian basket of consumer goods rose in price considerably. In 1970 a Canadian would have spent C\$100 (100 Canadian dollars) to purchase this basket; by 1990 the same basket cost C\$392. Thus, Canadian prices rose by 292%. Over the same period, in the United States, a basket of goods that initially cost \$100 in 1970 had risen in cost to \$336 by 1990. Thus, U.S. prices rose by 236%. Both countries witnessed serious inflation, but Canadian prices rose more.

So did Canadian goods end up more expensive in 1990? Did higher inflation in Canada cause Canadians to start spending more on U.S. goods? Did it cause Americans to spend less on Canadian goods?

The answer to all three questions is no. In 1970 C\$1 was worth almost exactly \$1 (1 U.S. dollar). So in 1970 both baskets cost the same *when their cost was expressed in a common currency,* about C\$100 = \$100. By 1990, however, the Canadian dollar (also called the loonie) had depreciated relative to its 1970 value and C\$1.16 was needed to buy \$1.00. Thus the \$336 U.S. basket in 1990 actually cost \$336 × 1.16 = C\$390 when expressed in Canadian currency—almost the same price as the C\$392 Canadian basket! (Conversely, expressed in U.S. currency, the Canadian basket cost about 392/1.16 = \$338, almost the same as the \$336 U.S. basket.)

In this example, although Canadian prices rose about 16% more than U.S. prices, U.S. residents also found that each of their U.S. dollars could buy about 16% more loonies. From the U.S. point of view, the cost of the baskets in each country *expressed in U.S. dollars* rose by about the same amount. The same was true from the Canadian perspective with all prices expressed in loonies. Economists (such as Gustav Cassel, quoted previously) would say that the relative *purchasing power* of each currency (in terms of U.S. versus Canadian goods) had remained the same.

The loonie.

Is it a coincidence that the changes in prices and exchange rates just happened to turn out that way? A fundamental economic hypothesis asserts that this outcome is *not* a coincidence at all—and that *in the long run,* this relationship between prices and exchange rates will always prevail. This observation provides another building block in the theory of how exchange rates are determined. How?

In Chapter 2, uncovered interest parity provided us with a theory of how the spot exchange rate is determined, given knowledge of three variables: the expected future exchange rate, the home interest rate, and the foreign interest rate. The next two chapters explain how all three variables are determined and provide a complete theory of exchange rates. Chapter 4 discusses the determinants of interest rates in each country. In this chapter, we focus on the determinants of the expected future exchange rate.

If investors are to make forecasts of future exchange rates, they need a plausible long-run theory of the exchange rate. The theory we develop in this chapter has two parts. In the first part, we develop a theory of purchasing power, which links the exchange rate to price levels in each country in the long run. This theory provides a partial answer but raises another question: Where do price levels come from? In the second part of the chapter, we explore how price levels are related to monetary conditions in each country. Combining the monetary theory of price levels with the purchasing power theory, we emerge with a *long-run* theory known as the **monetary approach to exchange rates.** The goal of this chapter is to set out this approach so that we can understand the long-run relationship between money, prices, and exchange rates.

1 Exchange Rates and Prices in the Long Run: Purchasing Power Parity and Goods Market Equilibrium

Just as arbitrage occurs in the international market for financial assets, it also occurs in the international markets for goods. The result of goods market arbitrage is that the prices of goods in different countries expressed in a common currency must be equalized. Applied to a single good, this idea is referred to as the *law of one price;* applied to an entire basket of goods, it is called the theory of *purchasing power parity*.

Why should these "laws" hold? If the price of a good were not the same in two locations, buyers would rush to buy at the cheap location (forcing prices up there) and would shy away from the expensive location (forcing prices down there). Some factors, such as the costs of transporting the goods from one location to another, may hinder the process of arbitrage, and later on we will study models that take transaction costs into account. For now, however, our goal is to develop a simple yet useful theory based on an idealized world of *frictionless trade,* that is, a world in which transaction costs can be neglected. We start at the microeconomic level with single goods and the law of one price. We then work up to the macroeconomic level to consider baskets of goods and purchasing power parity.

The Law of One Price

The **law of one price (LOOP)** states that in the absence of trade frictions (such as transport costs and tariffs) and under conditions of free competition (where no individual sellers or buyers have power to manipulate prices), identical goods sold in different locations must sell for the same price when the prices are expressed in a common currency.

To see how the law of one price operates, consider the trade in diamonds that takes place between the United States and the Netherlands. Suppose that a diamond of a given quality is priced at €2,000 in the Amsterdam market, and the exchange rate is $1.40 per euro. If the law of one price holds, the same-quality diamond should sell in New York for (€2,000 per diamond) × (1.40 $/€) = $2,800 per diamond.

Why will the prices be the same? Under competitive conditions and frictionless trade, arbitrage will ensure this outcome. If diamonds were more expensive in New York, arbitragers would buy at a low price in Holland and sell at a high price in Manhattan. If Dutch prices were higher, arbitragers would profit from the reverse trade. *By definition,* in a market equilibrium there are no arbitrage opportunities. If diamonds can be freely moved between New York and Amsterdam, both markets must offer the same price. Economists refer to this situation in the two locations as an *integrated market*.

We can mathematically state the law of one price as follows, for the case of any good g sold in two locations, say, Europe (EUR, meaning the Eurozone) and the United States (US). The *relative price* of good g (denoted $q^g_{EUR/US}$) is the ratio of the good's price in Europe relative to the good's price in the United States where both prices are expressed in a common currency. Using subscripts, as before, to indicate locations and currencies, the law of one price states that

$$q^g_{EUR/US} \;=\; (E_{\$/€}\, P^g_{EUR})\,/\; P^g_{US},$$

<table>
<tr><td>Relative price of good g
in Europe versus U.S.</td><td>European price
of good g in $</td><td>U.S. price
of good g in $</td></tr>
</table>

where P^g_{US} is the good's price in the United States, P^g_{EUR} is the good's price in Europe, and $E_{\$/\epsilon}$ is the dollar-euro exchange rate used to convert euro prices into dollar prices.

The law of one price may or may not hold. Recall from Chapter 2 that there are three possibilities in an arbitrage situation of this kind: the ratio exceeds 1 and the good is cheaper in the United States; the ratio is less than 1 and the good is cheaper in Europe; or, $E_{\$/\epsilon} P^g_{EUR} = P^g_{US}$, and the ratio is 1, $q^g_{EUR/US} = 1$, so that the good is the same price in both locations.

Again, as in Chapter 2, only one of these cases is a market equilibrium: in the first case, arbitrage will occur since the good is cheaper in the United States; in the second case, arbitrage will occur because the good is cheaper in Europe; only in the final case is there no arbitrage, the condition that defines market equilibrium. In equilibrium, European and U.S. prices, expressed in the same currency, are equal; the relative price of the good in the two locations is equal to 1, and the law of one price holds.

How can the law of one price further our understanding of exchange rates? We can rearrange the equation for price equality, $E_{\$/\epsilon} P^g_{EUR} = P^g_{US}$, to show that if the law of one price holds, then the exchange rate must equal the ratio of the goods' prices expressed in the two currencies:

$$\underbrace{E_{\$/\epsilon}}_{\substack{\text{Exchange} \\ \text{rate}}} = \underbrace{P^g_{US}/P^g_{EUR}}_{\substack{\text{Ratio of} \\ \text{goods' prices}}}.$$

One final word of caution: given our concerns in Chapter 2 about the right way to define the exchange rate, we must take care when using expressions that are ratios to ensure that the units on each side of the equation correspond. In the last equation, we know we have it right because the left-hand side is expressed in dollars per euro and the right-hand side is also a ratio of dollars to euros ($ per unit of goods divided by € per unit of goods).

Purchasing Power Parity

The principle of **purchasing power parity (PPP)** is essentially the macro-economic counterpart to the microeconomic law of one price (LOOP). The law of one price relates exchange rates to the relative prices of individual goods, while purchasing power parity relates exchange rates to relative price levels for a basket of goods. In studying international macroeconomics, purchasing power parity is the more relevant concept.

Suppose we compute a *price level* (denoted P) in each location as a weighted average of the prices of all goods g in a basket, using the same goods and weights in both locations. Let P_{US} be the basket's price in the United States and P_{EUR} the basket's price in Europe. If the law of one price holds for each good in the basket, it will also hold for the price of the basket as a whole.[1]

---

[1] For example, if the law of one price holds and $P^g_{US} = (E_{\$/\epsilon}) \times (P^g_{EUR})$ for all goods g, this implies that for N goods, the *arithmetic* weighted average satisfies $\Sigma^N_{g=1}\omega^g P^g_{US} = (E_{\$/\epsilon}) \times \Sigma^N_{g=1}\omega^g P^g_{EUR}$ for any set of weights ω^g that sum to 1, so PPP holds. The same is also true for *geometric* averages. Technically speaking, this follows for *any* price index definition that satisfies the usually required property that the index be homogeneous of degree 1 in the individual goods' prices.

To express PPP algebraically, we can compute the relative price of the two baskets of goods in each location, denoted $q_{EUR/US}$:

$$\underbrace{q_{EUR/US}}_{\substack{\text{Relative price of} \\ \text{basket in Europe} \\ \text{versus U.S.}}} = \underbrace{(E_{\$/€} \, P_{EUR})}_{\substack{\text{European price} \\ \text{of basket} \\ \text{expressed in \$}}} / \underbrace{P_{US}^{g}.}_{\substack{\text{U.S. price} \\ \text{of basket} \\ \text{expressed in \$}}}$$

Just as there were three cases for the law of one price, there are three cases for PPP: the basket is cheaper in the United States; or the basket is cheaper in Europe; or $E_{\$/€} \, P_{EUR} = P_{US}$, or $q_{EUR/US} = 1$, and the basket is the same price in both locations. In the first two cases, the basket is cheaper in one location and profitable arbitrage on the baskets is possible. Only in the third case is there no arbitrage. PPP holds *when price levels in two countries are equal when expressed in a common currency.* This statement about equality of price levels is also called **absolute PPP.**

For example, suppose the European basket costs €400, and the exchange rate is $1.25 per euro. For PPP to hold, the U.S. basket would have to cost $1.25 \times 400 = \$500$.

The Real Exchange Rate

The relative price of the two countries' baskets (denoted q) is the macro-economic counterpart to the microeconomic relative price of individual goods (q^g). The relative price of the baskets is one of the most important variables in international macroeconomics, and it has a special name: it is known as the **real exchange rate.** The real exchange rate, defined as $q_{EUR/US} = E_{\$/€} \, P_{EUR}/P_{US}$, tells us how many U.S. baskets are needed to purchase one European basket.

As with the nominal exchange rate, we need to be careful about what is in the numerator of the real exchange rate and what is in the denominator. According to our definition (based on the case we just examined), we will refer to $q_{EUR/US} = E_{\$/€} \, P_{EUR}/P_{US}$ as the home country, or U.S. real exchange rate: it is the price of the European basket in terms of the U.S. basket (or, in a Home-Foreign example, the price of a Foreign basket in terms of a Home basket).

To avoid confusion, it is essential to understand the difference between nominal exchange rates (which we have studied so far) and real exchange rates. The exchange rate for currencies is a *nominal* concept; it says how many dollars trade for one euro. The real exchange rate is a *real* concept; it says how many U.S. baskets trade for one European basket.

The real exchange rate has some terminology similar to that used with the nominal exchange rate:

- If the real exchange rate rises (more Home goods are needed in exchange for Foreign goods), we say Home has experienced a **real depreciation.**

- If the real exchange rate falls (fewer Home goods are needed in exchange for Foreign goods), we say Home has experienced a **real appreciation.**

Absolute PPP and the Real Exchange Rate

We can restate absolute PPP in terms of real exchange rates: *purchasing power parity states that the real exchange rate is equal to 1.* Under absolute PPP, all baskets have the same price when expressed in a common currency, so their relative price is 1.

It is common practice to use the absolute PPP-implied level of 1 as a benchmark or reference level for the real exchange rate. This leads naturally to some new terminology:

- If the real exchange rate $q_{EUR/US}$ is below 1 by $x\%$, then Foreign goods are relatively cheap, $x\%$ cheaper than Home goods, the Home currency (the dollar) is said to be *strong,* the euro is *weak,* and we say the euro is **undervalued** by $x\%$.

- If the real exchange rate $q_{EUR/US}$ is above 1 by $x\%$, then Foreign goods are relatively expensive, $x\%$ more expensive than Home goods, the Home currency (the dollar) is said to be *weak,* the euro is *strong,* and we say the euro is **overvalued** by $x\%$.

For example, if the European basket costs $E_{\$/€} P_{EUR} = \$550$ in dollar terms, and the U.S. basket costs only $P_{US} = \$500$, then $q_{EUR/US} = E_{\$/€} P_{EUR}/P_{US} = \$550/\$500 = 1.10$, and the euro is 10% overvalued against the dollar.

Absolute PPP, Prices, and the Nominal Exchange Rate

Finally, just as we did with the law of one price, we can rearrange the equation for the equality of price levels, $E_{\$/€} P_{EUR} = P_{US}$, to solve for the exchange rate that would be implied by absolute PPP:

(3-1)   Absolute PPP: $\underbrace{E_{\$/€}}_{\text{Exchange rate}} = \underbrace{P_{US}/P_{EUR}}_{\text{Ratio of price levels}}.$

This is one of the most important equations in the book because it shows how PPP (or absolute PPP) makes a clear prediction about exchange rates:

Purchasing power parity implies that the exchange rate at which two currencies trade is equal to the relative price levels of the two countries.

For example, if a basket of goods costs $520 in the United States and the same basket costs €400 in Europe, the theory of PPP would predict an exchange rate of $520/€400 = $1.30 per euro.

Thus, if we know the price levels in different locations, we can use PPP to determine the exchange rate. PPP applies at any point in time, and applied to the future it means that if we can forecast future price levels, then we can forecast the expected future exchange rate, which is the main goal of this chapter. Here, then, is a key building block in our theory, as shown in Figure 3-1.

Relative PPP, Inflation, and Exchange Rate Depreciation

PPP in its absolute PPP form involves price levels, but in macroeconomics we are often more interested in the rate at which price levels change than we are in the price levels themselves. The rate of change of the price level is known as the *rate of inflation,* or simply **inflation.** For example, if the price level today is 100 and next year it is 123, then the rate of inflation is 23% (per year).

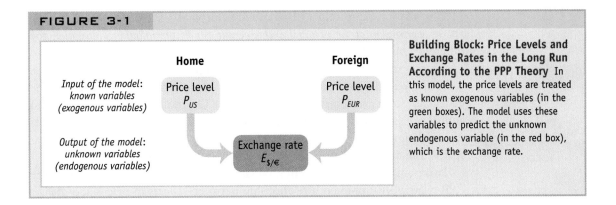

FIGURE 3-1

Building Block: Price Levels and Exchange Rates in the Long Run According to the PPP Theory In this model, the price levels are treated as known exogenous variables (in the green boxes). The model uses these variables to predict the unknown endogenous variable (in the red box), which is the exchange rate.

Because inflation is such an important variable in macroeconomics, we examine the implications of PPP for the study of inflation.

To consider changes over time, we introduce a subscript t to denote the time period, and calculate the rate of change of both sides of Equation (3-1). On the left-hand side, the rate of change of the exchange rate in Home is the rate of exchange rate depreciation in Home given by[2]

$$\underbrace{\frac{\Delta E_{\$/€,t}}{E_{\$/€,t}}}_{\text{Rate of depreciation of the nominal exchange rate}} = \frac{E_{\$/€,t+1} - E_{\$/€,t}}{E_{\$/€,t}}.$$

On the right of Equation (3-1), the rate of change of the ratio of two price levels equals the rate of change of the numerator minus the rate of change of the denominator:[3]

$$\frac{\Delta(P_{US}/P_{EUR})}{(P_{US}/P_{EUR})} = \frac{\Delta P_{US,t}}{P_{US,t}} - \frac{\Delta P_{EUR,t}}{P_{EUR,t}}$$

$$= \underbrace{\left(\frac{P_{US,t+1} - P_{US,t}}{P_{US,t}}\right)}_{\substack{\text{Rate of inflation in} \\ \text{U.S. } \pi_{US,t}}} - \underbrace{\left(\frac{P_{EUR,t+1} - P_{EUR,t}}{P_{EUR,t}}\right)}_{\substack{\text{Rate of inflation in} \\ \text{Europe } \pi_{EUR,t}}} = \pi_{US,t} - \pi_{EUR,t},$$

where the terms in brackets are the inflation rates in each location, denoted π_{US} and π_{EUR}, respectively.

If Equation (3-1) holds for levels of exchange rates and prices, then it must also hold for rates of change in these variables. By combining the last two expressions, we obtain

(3-2)   Relative PPP: $$\underbrace{\frac{\Delta E_{\$/€,t}}{E_{\$/€,t}}}_{\substack{\text{Rate of depreciation of} \\ \text{the nominal exchange rate}}} = \underbrace{\pi_{US,t} - \pi_{EUR,t}.}_{\text{Inflation differential}}$$

---

[2] The rate of depreciation at Home and the rate of appreciation in Foreign are equal, as an approximation, as we saw in Chapter 2.
[3] The first equality is exact for small changes and otherwise holds true as an approximation.

This way of expressing PPP is called **relative PPP,** and it *implies that the rate of depreciation of the nominal exchange rate equals the inflation differential,* the difference between the inflation rates of two countries.

We saw relative PPP in action in the example at the start of this chapter. Over 20 years, Canadian prices rose 16% more than U.S. prices, and the Canadian dollar depreciated 16% against the U.S. dollar. Converting these to annual rates, Canadian prices rose by 0.75% per year more than U.S. prices (the inflation differential), and the loonie depreciated by 0.75% per year against the dollar. Relative PPP held in this case.[4]

Two points should be kept in mind about relative PPP. First, unlike absolute PPP, relative PPP predicts a relationship between *changes* in prices and *changes* in exchange rates, rather than a relationship between their levels. Second, remember that relative PPP is derived from absolute PPP. Hence, the latter implies the former. *If absolute PPP holds, then relative PPP must hold also.* But the converse need not be true. For example, imagine that all goods consistently cost 20% more in country A than in country B, so absolute PPP fails; but it still can be the case that the inflation differential between A and B (say 5%) is equal to the rate of depreciation (say 5%), so relative PPP may still hold.

Summary

The purchasing power parity theory, whether in the absolute PPP or relative PPP form, suggests that price levels in different countries and exchange rates are tightly linked, either in their absolute levels or in the rate at which they change. To assess how useful this theory is, let's look at some empirical evidence to see how well the theory matches reality. We then reexamine the workings of PPP and reassess its underlying assumptions.

APPLICATION

Evidence for PPP in the Long Run and Short Run

Is there evidence for PPP? The data offer some support for relative PPP most clearly over the long run, when even moderate inflation mounts up and leads to large cumulative changes in price levels and, hence, substantial cumulative inflation differentials.

The scatter plot in Figure 3-2 shows average rates of depreciation and inflation differentials for a sample of countries compared with the United States over three decades from 1975 to 2005. If relative PPP were true, then the depreciation of each country's currency would exactly equal the inflation differential, and the data would line up on the 45-degree line. We see that this is not literally true in the data, but the correlation is close. Relative PPP is an approximate, useful guide to the relationship between prices and exchange rates in the long run, over horizons of many years or decades.

But the purchasing power theory turns out to be a pretty useless theory in the short run, over horizons of just a few years. This is easily seen by examining the

---

[4] Note that the rates of change are approximate, with $1.0075^{20} = 1.16$.

FIGURE 3-2

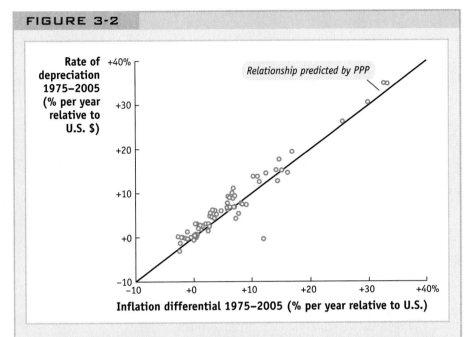

Inflation Differentials and the Exchange Rate, 1975–2005 This scatter plot shows the relationship between the rate of exchange-rate depreciation against the U.S. dollar (the vertical axis) and the inflation differential against the United States (horizontal axis) over the long run, based on data for a sample of 82 countries. The correlation between the two variables is strong and bears a close resemblance to the theoretical prediction of PPP that all data points would appear on the 45-degree line.

Source: International Monetary Fund (IMF), International Financial Statistics.

time series of relative price ratio and exchange rates for any pair of countries, and looking at the behavior of these variables from year to year and not just over the entire period. If absolute PPP held at all times, then the exchange rate would always be equal to the relative price ratio. Figure 3-3 shows 30 years of data for the United States and United Kingdom from 1975 to 2004. While this figure reinforces the relevance of PPP in the long run, it shows substantial and persistent deviations from PPP in the short run. The two series drift together over 30 years, but in any given year the differences between the two can be 10%, 20%, or more. Differences in levels show that absolute PPP fails; not surprisingly, relative PPP fails too. For example, from 1980 to 1985, the pound depreciated by 45% (from $2.32 to $1.28), but the cumulative inflation differential over these five years was only 9%. ■

How Slow Is Convergence to PPP?

The evidence suggests that PPP works better in the long run but not in the short run. If PPP were taken as a strict proposition for the short run, it would require price adjustment via arbitrage to happen fully and instantaneously, rapidly closing the gap between common-currency prices in different countries for all goods in the basket. This doesn't happen.

FIGURE 3-3

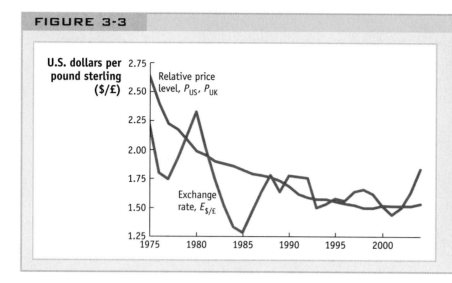

Exchange Rates and Relative Price Levels Data for the United States and United Kingdom for 1975 to 2004 show that the exchange rate and relative price levels do not always move together in the short run. Relative price levels tend to change slowly and have a small range of movement; exchange rates move more abruptly and experience large fluctuations. Therefore, relative PPP does *not* hold in the short run. However, it is a better guide to the long run, and we can see that the two series do tend to drift together over the decades.

Source: Penn World Tables, version 6.2.

SIDE BAR

Forecasting When the Real Exchange Rate Is Undervalued or Overvalued

Relative PPP makes forecasting exchange rate changes simple: just compute the inflation differential. But what about situations in which PPP doesn't hold, as is often the case? Even if the real exchange rate is not equal to 1, knowledge of the real exchange rate and the convergence speed may still allow us to construct a forecast of real and nominal exchange rates.

To see how, let's take an example. Start with the definition of the real exchange rate, $q_{EUR/US} = E_{\$/€}P_{EUR}/P_{US}$. Rearranging, we find $E_{\$/€} = q_{EUR/US} \times (P_{US}/P_{EUR})$. By taking the rate of change of that expression, we find that the rate of change of the nominal exchange rate equals the rate of change of the real exchange rate plus home inflation minus foreign inflation:

$$\underbrace{\frac{\Delta E_{\$/€,t}}{E_{\$/€,t}}}_{\substack{\text{Rate of depreciation} \\ \text{of the nominal} \\ \text{exchange rate}}} = \underbrace{\frac{\Delta q_{EUR/US,t}}{q_{EUR/US,t}}}_{\substack{\text{Rate of depreciation} \\ \text{of the real} \\ \text{exchange rate}}} + \underbrace{\pi_{US,t} - \pi_{EUR,t}.}_{\text{Inflation differential}}$$

When q is constant, the first term on the right is zero and we are back to the simple world of relative PPP and Equation (3-2). For forecasting purposes, the predicted nominal depreciation is then just the second term on the right, the inflation differential. For example, if the forecast is for U.S. inflation to be 3% next year and European inflation to be 1%, then the inflation differential is +2% and we would forecast a U.S. dollar depreciation, or rise in $E_{\$/€}$, of +2% next year.

What if q isn't constant and PPP fails? If there is currently a deviation from absolute PPP, but we still think that there will

be convergence to absolute PPP in the long run, the first term on the right of the formula is nonzero. However, we can still estimate it given the right information.

To continue the example, suppose you are told that a U.S. basket of goods currently costs $100, but the European basket of the same goods costs $130. You would compute a U.S. real exchange rate, $q_{EUR/US}$, of 1.30 today. But what will it be next year? If you expect absolute PPP to hold in the long run, the U.S. real exchange rate will move toward 1. How fast? Now we need to know the convergence speed. Using the 15% rule of thumb, we would estimate that 15% of the 0.3 gap between 1 and 1.3 (i.e., 0.045) would dissipate over one year. Hence, the U.S. real exchange would be forecast to fall from 1.3 to 1.255, implying a change of −3.46% in the next year. In this case, adding the two terms on the right of the expression given previously, we would forecast that the approximate change in E next year would be the change in $q_{EUR/US}$ of −3.46% plus the inflation differential of +2%, for a total of −1.46%, a dollar appreciation of 1.46% against the euro.

The intuition for the result is as follows: the U.S. dollar is undervalued against the euro. If convergence to PPP is to happen, then some of that undervaluation will dissipate over the course of the year through a real appreciation of the dollar (predicted to be 3.46%). That real appreciation can be broken down into two components: U.S. goods may experience higher inflation than European goods (predicted to be +2%), and the rest has to be accomplished via nominal dollar appreciation (thus predicted to be 1.46%).

In reality, research shows that price differences, the deviations from PPP, can be large and persistent in the short run. Estimates suggest that these deviations may die out at a rate of about 15% per year. This kind of measure is often referred to as a *speed of convergence:* in this case, it implies that after one year, 85% (0.85) of an initial price difference persists; compounding, after two years 72% of the gap persists ($0.72 = 0.85^2$); and after four years, 52% ($0.52 = 0.85^4$). Thus approximately half of any PPP deviation still remains after four years: economists would refer to this as a four-year *half-life*.

Such estimates provide a rule of thumb that is useful as a guide to forecasting real exchange rates. For example, suppose the home basket costs $100 and the foreign basket $90, in home currency. Home's real exchange rate is 0.9, and the home currency is overvalued, with foreign goods less expensive than home goods. The deviation of the real exchange rate from the PPP-implied level of 1 is equal to −0.1. Our rule of thumb tells us that next year 15% of this deviation will have disappeared, so it would be only −0.085, meaning that home's real exchange rate would be forecast to be 0.915 next year and thus end up a little bit closer to 1, after a small depreciation. (See **Side Bar: Forecasting when the Real Exchange Rate Is Undervalued or Overvalued.**)

What Explains Deviations from PPP?

It is a slow process when it takes four years for even half of any given price difference to dissipate, but economists have found a variety of reasons why the tendency for PPP to hold is relatively weak in the short run:

■ *Transaction costs.* Trade is not frictionless because costs of international transportation are significant for most goods and because some goods also bear additional costs, such as tariffs and duties, when they cross borders. By some recent estimates, transportation costs may add about 20% on average to the price of goods moving internationally, while tariffs (and other policy barriers) may add another 10%.[5] Other costs arise due to the time it takes to ship goods and the costs and time delays associated with developing distribution networks and satisfying legal and regulatory requirements in foreign markets.

■ *Nontraded goods.* Some goods are inherently nontradable; one can think of them as having infinitely high transaction costs. Most goods and services fall somewhere between tradable and nontradable. Consider a restaurant meal; it includes traded goods such as some raw foods and nontraded goods such as the work of the chef. As a result, PPP may not hold. (See **Headlines: The Big Mac Index.**)

---

[5] There is also evidence of other significant border-related barriers to trade. See James Anderson and Eric van Wincoop, 2004, "Trade Costs," *Journal of Economic Literature,* 42, September, 691–751.

■ *Imperfect competition and legal obstacles.* Many goods are not simple undifferentiated commodities, as LOOP and PPP assume, but are differentiated products with brand names, copyrights, and legal protection. For example, consumers have the choice of cheaper generic acetaminophen or a pricier brand-name product such as Tylenol, but these are not seen as perfect substitutes. Such differentiated goods create conditions of *imperfect competition* because firms have some power to set the price of their good. With this kind of *market power,* firms can charge different prices not just across brands but also across countries (pharmaceutical companies, for example, charge different prices for drugs in different countries). This practice is possible because arbitrage can be shut down by legal threats or regulations. If you try to import large quantities of a firm's pharmaceutical and resell them, then, as an unauthorized distributor, you will probably hear very quickly from the firm's lawyers and/or from the government regulators. The same would apply to many other goods such as automobiles and consumer electronics.

HEADLINES

The Big Mac Index

For more than 20 years, the Economist newspaper has been engaged in a whimsical attempt to judge PPP theory based on a well-known, globally uniform consumer good: the McDonald's Big Mac. The over- or undervaluation of a currency against the U.S. dollar is gauged by comparing the relative prices of a burger in a common currency, and expressing the difference as a percentage deviation:

$$\text{Big Mac Index} = q^{\text{Big Mac}} - 1 = \left(\frac{E_{\text{\$/local currency}} P_{\text{local}}^{\text{Big Mac}}}{P_{\text{US}}^{\text{Big Mac}}} \right) - 1.$$

Table 3-1 shows the 2007 survey results, and you can read in the following excerpt the Economist's attempt to digest these findings.

Home of the undervalued burger?

The Economist's Big Mac index is based on the theory of purchasing-power parity (PPP), according to which exchange rates should adjust to equalise the price of a basket of goods and services around the world. Our basket is a burger: a McDonald's Big Mac.

The table below shows by how much, in Big Mac PPP terms, selected currencies were over- or undervalued at the end of January. Broadly, the pattern is such as it was last spring, the previous time this table was compiled. The most

overvalued currency is the Icelandic krona: the exchange rate that would equalise the price of an Icelandic Big Mac with an American one is 158 kronur to the dollar; the actual rate is 68.4, making the krona 131% too dear. The most undervalued currency is the Chinese yuan, at 56% below its PPP rate; several other Asian currencies also appear to be 40–50% undervalued.

The index is supposed to give a guide to the direction in which currencies should, in theory, head in the long run.

It is only a rough guide, because its price reflects non-tradable elements— such as rent and labour. For that reason, it is probably least rough when comparing countries at roughly the same stage of development. Perhaps the most telling numbers in this table are therefore those for the Japanese yen, which is 28% undervalued against the dollar, and the euro, which is 19% overvalued. Hence European finance ministers' beef with the low level of the yen.

Source: "The Big Mac Index," Economist, February 1, 2007.

Continued on next page.

TABLE 3-1

The Big Mac Index The table shows the price of a Big Mac in January 2007 in local currency (column 1) and converted to U.S. dollars (column 2) using the actual exchange rate (column 4). The dollar price can then be compared with the average price of a Big Mac in the United States ($3.22 in column 1, row 1). The difference (column 5) is a measure of the overvaluation (+) or undervaluation (−) of the local currency against the U.S. dollar. The exchange rate against the dollar implied by PPP (column 3) is the hypothetical price of dollars in local currency that would have equalized burger prices, which may be compared with the actual observed exchange rate (column 4).

	Big Mac Prices		Exchange rate (local currency per U.S. dollar)		Over (+)/ under (−) valuation
	In local currency (1)	In U.S. dollars (2)	Implied by PPP (3)	Actual, Jan 31st (4)	against dollar, % (5)
United States	$3.22	3.22	—	—	—
Argentina	Peso 8.25	2.65	2.56	3.11	−18
Australia	A$3.45	2.67	1.07	1.29	−17
Brazil	Real 6.40	3.01	1.99	2.13	−6
Britain	£1.99	3.90	0.62	0.51	+21
Canada	C$3.63	3.08	1.13	1.18	−4
Chile	Peso 1670	3.07	519	544	−5
China	Yuan 11.0	1.41	3.42	7.77	−56
Columbia	Peso 6900	3.06	2,143	2,254	−5
Costa Rica	Colones 1130	2.18	351	519	−32
Czech Republic	Koruna 52.1	2.41	16.2	21.6	−25
Denmark	DKr27.75	4.84	8.62	5.74	+50
Egypt	Pound 9.09	1.60	2.82	5.70	−50
Estonia	Kroon 30	2.49	9.32	12.0	−23
Euro area	2.94	3.82	0.91	0.77	+19
Hong Kong	HK$12.00	1.54	3.73	7.81	−52
Hungary	Forint 590	3.00	183	197	−7
Iceland	Kronur 509	7.44	158	68.4	+131
Indonesia	Rupiah 15,900	1.75	4,938	9,100	−46
Japan	¥280	2.31	87.0	121	−28
Latvia	Lats 1.35	2.52	0.42	0.54	−22
Lithuania	Litas 6.50	2.45	2.02	2.66	−24
Malaysia	M$5.50	1.57	1.71	3.50	−51
Mexico	Peso 29.0	2.66	9.01	10.9	−17
New Zealand	NZ$4.60	3.16	1.43	1.45	−2
Norway	Kroner 41.5	6.63	12.9	6.26	+106
Pakistan	Rupee 140	2.31	43.5	60.7	−28
Paraguay	Guarani 10,000	1.90	3,106	5,250	−41
Peru	New Sol 9.50	2.97	2.95	3.20	−8
Philippines	Peso 85.0	1.74	26.4	48.9	−46
Poland	Zloty 6.90	2.29	2.14	3.01	−29
Russia	Rouble 49.00	1.85	15.2	26.5	−43
Saudi Arabia	Riyal 9.00	2.40	2.80	3.75	−25
Singapore	S$3.60	2.34	1.12	1.54	−27
Slovakia	Crown 57.98	2.13	18.0	27.2	−34
South Africa	Rand 15.5	2.14	4.81	7.25	−34
South Korea	Won 2,900	3.08	901	942	−4
Sri Lanka	Rupee 190	1.75	59.0	109	−46
Sweden	SKr 32.0	4.59	9.94	6.97	+43
Switzerland	SFr 6.30	5.05	1.96	1.25	+57
Taiwan	NT$75.00	2.28	23.3	32.9	−29
Thailand	Baht 62.0	1.78	19.3	34.7	−45
Turkey	Lire 4.55	3.22	1.41	1.41	+0
UAE	Dirhams 10.0	2.72	3.11	3.67	−15
Ukraine	Hryvnia 9.00	1.71	2.80	5.27	−47
Uruguay	Peso 55.0	2.17	17.1	25.3	−33
Venezuela	Bolivar 6,800	1.58	2,112	4,307	−51

Source: "The Big Mac index," The Economist, February 1, 2007.

NET WORK

The Big Mac Index isn't alone. In 2004 the *Economist* made a Starbuck's Tall Latte Index, which you can try to find online. (Hint: Google "cnn tall latte index.") In 2007 two new indices appeared: the iPod Index (based on the local prices of Apple's iPod music player) and iTunes Index (based on the local prices of a single song downloaded from Apple's iTunes store). Find those indices online and the discussions surrounding them. (Hint: Google "ipod itunes index big mac.") Do you think that either the iPod Index or iTunes Index is a better guide to currency overvaluation/undervaluation than the Big Mac Index?

■ *Price stickiness.* One of the most common assumptions of macroeconomics is that prices are "sticky" in the short run—that is, they do not or cannot adjust quickly and flexibly to changes in market conditions. PPP assumes that arbitrage can force prices to adjust, but adjustment will be slowed down by price stickiness. Empirical evidence shows that many goods' prices do not adjust quickly in the short run. For example, in Figure 3-3, we saw that the nominal exchange rate moves up and down in a very dramatic fashion but that price levels are much more sluggish in their movements and do not fully match exchange rate changes.

Despite these problems, the evidence suggests that as a long-run theory of exchange rates, PPP is still a useful approach.[6] And PPP may become even more relevant in the future as arbitrage becomes more efficient and more goods and services are traded. Years ago we might have taken it for granted that certain goods and services (such as pharmaceuticals, customer support, health care services) were strictly nontraded and thus not subject to arbitrage, at the international level. Today, many consumers shop for pharmaceuticals overseas to save money. If you dial a U.S. software support call center, you may find yourself being assisted by an operator in India. In some countries, citizens motivated by cost considerations may travel overseas for dental treatment, eye care, hip replacements, and other health services (so-called "medical tourism" or "health tourism"). These globalization trends may well continue.

2 Money, Prices, and Exchange Rates in the Long Run: Money Market Equilibrium in a Simple Model

It is time to take stock of the theory developed so far in this chapter. Up to now, we have concentrated on PPP, which says that in the long run the exchange rate is determined by the ratio of the price levels in two countries. But what determines those price levels?

Monetary theory supplies an answer: according to this theory, in the long run, price levels are determined in each country by the relative demand and supply of money. You may recall this theory from previous macroeconomics courses in the context of a closed economy. This section recaps the essential elements of monetary theory and shows how they fit into our theory of exchange rates in the long run.

What Is Money?

We recall the distinguishing features of this peculiar asset that is so central to our everyday economic life. Economists think of **money** as performing three key functions in an economy:

---

[6] Alan M. Taylor and Mark P. Taylor, 2004, "The Purchasing Power Parity Debate," *Journal of Economic Perspectives,* 8, Fall, 135–158.

1. Money is a *store of value* because, as with any asset, money held from today until tomorrow can still be used to buy goods and services in the future. Money's rate of return is low compared with many other assets. Because we earn no interest on it, there is an opportunity cost to holding money. If this cost is low, we will hold money more willingly than we hold other assets (stocks, bonds, and so on).

2. Money also gives us a *unit of account* in which all prices in the economy are quoted. When we enter a store in France, we expect to see the prices of goods to read something like "100 euros"—not "10,000 Japanese yen" or "500 bananas," even though, in principle, the yen or the banana could also function as a unit of account in France (bananas would, however, be a poor store of value).

3. Money is a *medium of exchange* that allows us to buy and sell goods and services without the need to engage in inefficient barter (direct swaps of goods). The ease with which we can convert money into goods and services is a measure of how *liquid* money is compared with the many illiquid assets in our portfolios (such as real estate). Money is the most liquid asset of all.

The Measurement of Money

What counts as money? Clearly the currency we hold is money. But do checking accounts count as money? What about savings accounts, mutual funds, and other securities? Figure 3-4 depicts the most widely used measures of the money supply and illustrates their relative magnitudes with recent data from the United States. The narrowest definition of money includes only currency, and it is called M0 (or "base money"). The next measure of money, M1, includes highly liquid instruments such as demand deposits in checking accounts and traveler's checks. The broad measure of money, M2, includes slightly less liquid assets such as savings and small time deposits.[7]

For our purposes, money is defined as the *stock of liquid assets that are routinely used to finance transactions,* in the sense implied by the "medium of exchange" function of money. When we speak of money (denoted M), we will generally mean M1, currency plus demand deposits. Many important assets are excluded from M1, including longer-term assets held by individuals and the voluminous interbank deposits used in the foreign exchange market discussed in Chapter 2. These assets do not count as money in the sense used here because they are relatively illiquid and not used routinely for transactions.

---

[7] There is little consensus on the right broad measure of money. Until 2006 the U.S. Federal Reserve collected data on M3, which included large time deposits, repurchase agreements, and money market funds. This was discontinued because the data were costly to collect and of limited use to policy makers. In the United Kingdom, a slightly different broad measure, M4, is still used. Some economists now prefer a money aggregate called MZM, or "money of zero maturity," as the right broad measure, but its use is not widespread.

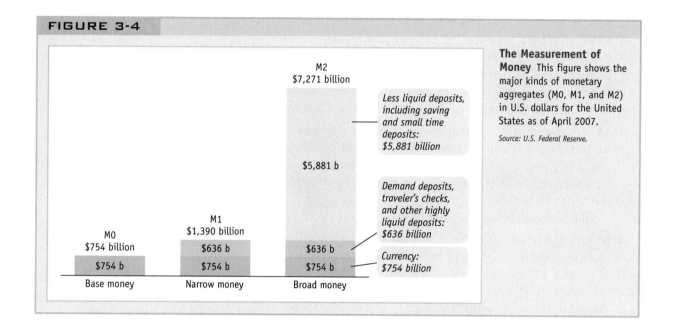

FIGURE 3-4

M2
$7,271 billion

Less liquid deposits,
including saving
and small time
deposits:
$5,881 billion

$5,881 b

M1
$1,390 billion

Demand deposits,
traveler's checks,
and other highly
liquid deposits:
$636 billion

M0
$754 billion

$636 b $636 b

Currency:
$754 billion

$754 b $754 b $754 b

Base money   Narrow money   Broad money

**The Measurement of
Money** This figure shows the
major kinds of monetary
aggregates (M0, M1, and M2)
in U.S. dollars for the United
States as of April 2007.

Source: U.S. Federal Reserve.

The Supply of Money

How is the supply of money determined? In practice, a country's **central
bank** controls the **money supply.** Strictly speaking, by issuing notes and
coins, the central bank controls directly only the level of M0, or base money,
the amount of currency in the economy. However, it can *indirectly* control the
level of M1 by using monetary policy to influence the behavior of the private
banks that are responsible for checking deposits. The intricate mechanisms by
which monetary policy affects M1 are beyond the scope of this book. We
make the simplifying assumption that the central bank's policy tools are sufficient to allow it to control indirectly, but accurately, the level of M1.[8]

The Demand for Money: A Simple Model

A simple theory of household money demand is motivated by the assumption that the need to conduct transactions is in proportion to an individual's
income. For example, if an individual's income doubles from $20,000 to
$40,000, we expect his or her demand for money (expressed in dollars) to
double also.

Moving from the individual or household level up to the aggregate or
macroeconomic level, we can infer that the aggregate **money demand**
will behave similarly. *All else equal, a rise in national dollar income (nominal
income) will cause a proportional increase in transactions and, hence, in aggregate
money demand.*

---

[8] A full treatment of this topic can be found in a textbook on money and banking. See Laurence M. Ball,
The Financial System, Money and the Global Economy, New York: Worth, forthcoming.

This insight suggests a simple model in which the demand for money is proportional to dollar income. This model is known as the **quantity theory of money:**

$$\underbrace{M^d}_{\substack{\text{Demand for} \\ \text{money (\$)}}} = \underbrace{\overline{L}}_{\text{A constant}} \times \underbrace{PY}_{\substack{\text{Nominal} \\ \text{income (\$)}}}.$$

Here, PY measures the total nominal dollar value of income in the economy, equal to the price level P times real income Y. The term $\overline{L}$ is a constant that measures how much demand for liquidity is generated for each dollar of nominal income. To emphasize this point, we assume for now that every \$1 of nominal income requires \$ $\overline{L}$ of money for transactions purposes and that this relationship is constant. (Later, we can relax this assumption.)

If the price level rises by 10% and real income is fixed, we are paying a 10% higher price for all goods, so the dollar cost of transactions rises by 10%. Similarly, if real income rises by 10% but prices stay fixed, the dollar amount of transactions will rise by 10%. Hence, the *demand for nominal money balances,* M^d, is proportional to the *nominal* income, PY.

Another way to look at the quantity theory is to convert all quantities into real quantities by dividing the previous equation by P, the price level (the price of a basket of goods). Quantities are then converted from nominal dollars to real units (specifically, into units of baskets of goods). This allows us to derive the *demand for real money balances:*

$$\underbrace{\frac{M^d}{P}}_{\substack{\text{Demand for} \\ \text{real money}}} = \underbrace{\overline{L}}_{\text{A constant}} \times \underbrace{Y}_{\text{Real income}}.$$

Real money balances are simply a measure of the purchasing power of the stock of money in terms of goods and services. The expression just given says simply that the demand for real money balances is proportional to real income. The more real income we have, the more real transactions we have to perform and the more real money we need. Moreover, the relationship is assumed to be one of strict proportionality: a 10% increase in real income would imply a 10% increase in real money demand.

Equilibrium in the Money Market

The condition for equilibrium in the money market is simple to state: the demand for money M^d must equal the supply of money M, which we assume to be under the control of the central bank. Imposing this condition on the last two equations, we find that nominal money supply equals nominal money demand:

$$M = \overline{L}PY,$$

and that real money supply equals real money demand:

$$\frac{M}{P} = \overline{L}Y.$$

A Simple Monetary Model of Prices

We are now in a position to put together a simple model of the exchange rate, using two building blocks. The first building block is a model that links prices to monetary conditions—the quantity theory. The second building block is a model that links exchange rates to prices—PPP.

We consider two countries, as before, and for simplicity we will consider the United States as the home country and Europe as the foreign country. (The model generalizes to any pair of countries.)

Let's consider the last equation given and apply it to the United States, adding U.S. subscripts for clarity. We can rearrange this formula to obtain an expression for the U.S. price level:

$$P_{US} = \frac{M_{US}}{\overline{L}_{US}Y_{US}}.$$

Note that the price level is determined by how much nominal money is issued relative to the demand for real money balances: the numerator on the right-hand side is the total supply of *nominal* money; the denominator is the total demand for *real* money balances.

We can do the same rearrangement for Europe to obtain the analogous expression for the European price level:

$$P_{EUR} = \frac{M_{EUR}}{\overline{L}_{EUR}Y_{EUR}}.$$

The last two equations are examples of the **fundamental equation of the monetary model of the price level.** Two such equations, one for each country, give us another important building block for our theory of prices and exchange rates as shown in Figure 3-5.

In the long run, we assume prices are flexible and will adjust to put the money market in equilibrium. For example, if the amount of money in circulation (the nominal money supply) rises, say, by a factor of 100, and real

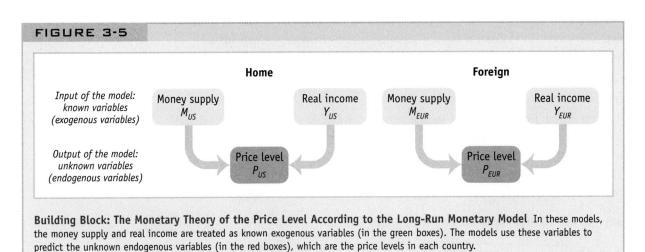

FIGURE 3-5

Building Block: The Monetary Theory of the Price Level According to the Long-Run Monetary Model In these models, the money supply and real income are treated as known exogenous variables (in the green boxes). The models use these variables to predict the unknown endogenous variables (in the red boxes), which are the price levels in each country.

income stays the same, then there will be "more money chasing the same quantity of goods." This leads to inflation, and in the long run, the price level will rise by a factor of 100. In other words, we will be in the same economy as before except that all prices will have two zeroes tacked on to them.

A Simple Monetary Model of the Exchange Rate

A long-run model of the exchange rate is close at hand. If we take the last two equations, which use the monetary model to find the price level in each country, and plug them into Equation (3-1), we can use absolute PPP to solve for the exchange rate:

$$
(3\text{-}3) \quad \underbrace{E_{\$/€}}_{\substack{\text{Exchange}\\\text{rate}}} = \underbrace{\frac{P_{US}}{P_{EUR}}}_{\substack{\text{Ratio of}\\\text{price}\\\text{levels}}} = \frac{\left(\dfrac{M_{US}}{\overline{L}_{US}Y_{US}}\right)}{\left(\dfrac{M_{EUR}}{\overline{L}_{EUR}Y_{EUR}}\right)} = \underbrace{\frac{(M_{US}/M_{EUR})}{(\overline{L}_{US}Y_{US}/\overline{L}_{EUR}Y_{EUR})}}_{\substack{\text{Relative nominal money}\\\text{supplies divided by relative}\\\text{real money demands}}}.
$$

This is the **fundamental equation of the monetary approach to exchange rates.** By substituting the price levels from the monetary model into PPP, we have put together the two building blocks from Figures 3-1 and 3-5. The implications of this equation are intuitive.

■ Suppose the U.S. money supply increases, all else equal. The right-hand side increases (the U.S. nominal money supply increases relative to Europe), causing the exchange rate to increase (the U.S. dollar depreciates against the euro). For example, if the U.S. money supply doubles, then all else equal, the U.S. price level doubles. That is, a bigger U.S. supply of money leads to a weaker dollar. That makes sense—there are more dollars around, so you expect each dollar to be worth less.

■ Now suppose the U.S. real income level increases, all else equal. Then the right-hand side decreases (the U.S. real money demand increases relative to Europe), causing the exchange rate to decrease (the U.S. dollar appreciates against the euro). For example, if the U.S. real income doubles, then all else equal, the U.S. price level falls by a factor of one-half. That is, a stronger U.S. economy leads to a stronger dollar. That makes sense—there is more demand for the same quantity of dollars, so you expect each dollar to be worth more.

Money Growth, Inflation, and Depreciation

The model just presented uses absolute PPP to link the level of the exchange rate to the level of prices and uses the quantity theory to link prices to monetary conditions in each country. But as we have said before, macroeconomists are often more interested in rates of change of variables (e.g., inflation) rather than levels.

Can our theory be extended for this purpose? Yes, but this task takes a little work. We convert Equation (3-3) into growth rates by taking the rate of change of each term.

The first term of Equation (3-3) is the exchange rate $E_{\$/€}$. Its rate of change is the rate of depreciation, $\Delta E_{\$/€}/E_{\$/€}$. When this term is positive, say 1%, the dollar is depreciating at 1% per year; if negative, say −2%, the dollar is appreciating at 2% per year.

The second term of Equation (3-3) is the ratio of the price levels P_{US}/P_{EUR}, and as we saw when we derived relative PPP at Equation (3-2), its rate of change is the rate of change of the numerator (U.S. inflation) minus the rate of change of the denominator (European inflation), which equals the inflation differential $\pi_{US,t} - \pi_{EUR,t}$.

What is the rate of change of the third term in Equation (3-3)? The numerator represents the U.S. price level, $P_{US} = M_{US}/\overline{L}_{US}Y_{US}$. Again, the growth rate of a fraction equals the growth rate of the numerator minus the growth rate of the denominator. In this case, the numerator is the money supply M_{US}, and its growth rate is μ_{US},

$$\mu_{US,t} = \underbrace{\frac{M_{US,t+1} - M_{US,t}}{M_{US,t}}}_{\text{Rate of money supply growth in U.S.}}.$$

The denominator is $\overline{L}_{US}Y_{US}$, which is a constant $\overline{L}_{US}$ times real income Y_{US}. Thus, $\overline{L}_{US}Y_{US}$ grows at a rate equal to the growth rate of real income, g_{US}:

$$g_{US,t} = \underbrace{\frac{Y_{US,t+1} - Y_{US,t}}{Y_{US,t}}}_{\text{Rate of real income growth in U.S.}}.$$

Putting all the pieces together, the growth rate of $P_{US} = M_{US}/\overline{L}_{US}Y_{US}$ equals the money supply growth rate μ_{US} minus the real income growth rate g_{US}. We have already seen that the growth rate of P_{US} on the left-hand side is the inflation rate π_{US}. Thus, we know that

(3-4) $\pi_{US,t} = \mu_{US,t} - g_{US,t}$.

The denominator of the third term of Equation (3-3) represents the European price level, $P_{EUR} = M_{EUR}/\overline{L}_{EUR}Y_{EUR}$, and its rate of change is calculated similarly:

(3-5) $\pi_{EUR,t} = \mu_{EUR,t} - g_{EUR,t}$.

The intuition for these expressions echoes what we said previously. When money growth is higher than income growth, we have "more money chasing fewer goods" and this leads to inflation.

Combining Equation (3-4) and Equation (3-5), we can now solve for the inflation differential in terms of monetary fundamentals and finish our task of computing the rate of depreciation of the exchange rate:

(3-6)
$$\underbrace{\frac{\Delta E_{\$/\text{€},t}}{E_{\$/\text{€},t}}}_{\substack{\text{Rate of depreciation of} \\ \text{the nominal exchange rate}}} = \underbrace{\pi_{US,t} - \pi_{EUR,t}}_{\text{Inflation differential}} = (\mu_{US,t} - g_{US,t}) - (\mu_{EUR,t} - g_{EUR,t})$$

$$= \underbrace{(\mu_{US,t} - \mu_{EUR,t})}_{\substack{\text{Differential in} \\ \text{nominal money supply} \\ \text{growth rates}}} - \underbrace{(g_{US,t} - g_{EUR,t})}_{\substack{\text{Differential in real} \\ \text{output growth rates}}}.$$

The last term here is the rate of change of the fourth term in Equation (3-3).

Equation (3-6) is the fundamental equation of the monetary approach to exchange rates expressed in rates of change, and much of the same intuition we applied in explaining Equation (3-3) carries over here.

■ If the United States runs a looser monetary policy in the long run measured by a faster money growth rate, the dollar will depreciate more rapidly, all else equal. For example, suppose Europe has a 5% annual rate of change of money and a 2% rate of change of real income; then its inflation would be the difference, 5% minus 2% equals 3%. Now suppose the United States has a 6% rate of change of money and a 2% rate of change of real income, then its inflation would be the difference, 6% minus 2% equals 4%. And the rate of depreciation of the dollar would be U.S. inflation minus European inflation, 4% minus 3%, or 1% per year.

■ If the U.S. economy grows faster in the long run, the dollar will appreciate more rapidly, all else equal. In the last numerical example, suppose the U.S. growth rate of real income in the long run increases from 2% to 5%, all else equal. Now U.S. inflation equals the money growth rate of 6% minus the new real income growth rate of 5%, so inflation is just 1% per year. Now the rate of dollar depreciation is U.S. inflation minus European inflation, that is, 1% minus 3%, or −2% per year (meaning the U.S. dollar would now appreciate at 2% per year).

With a change of notation to make the United States the foreign country, the same lessons could be derived for Europe and the euro.

3 The Monetary Approach: Implications and Evidence

The monetary approach to exchange rates is a workhorse model with many practical applications in the study of long-run exchange rate movements. In this section, we illustrate its main application to forecasting and examine some empirical evidence.

Exchange Rate Forecasts Using the Simple Model

The most important practical application for us, presently, is to understand how the monetary approach can be used to forecast the future exchange rate. Remember from Chapter 2 that forex market arbitragers need to form such a forecast to be able to make arbitrage calculations using uncovered interest parity. If we use the monetary model to forecast exchange rates, then Equation (3-3) says that a forecast of future exchange rates (the left-hand side) can be constructed as long as we know how to make a forecast of future money supplies and real income.

In practice, this is why expectations about money and real income in the future are so widely reported in the financial media, and especially in the forex market. The discussion returns with obsessive regularity to two questions. The first question, "What are central banks going to do?" leads to all manner of attempts to decode the statements and remarks of central bank officials. The second question, "How is the economy expected to grow in real terms?" leads to a keen interest in any indicators such as productivity data or investment activity that might hint at changes in the rate of growth. There is great uncertainty in trying to answer these questions, and forecasts of economic variables years in the future are likely to be subject to large errors. Nonetheless, this is one of the key tasks of financial markets.

Note that if one uses the monetary model for forecasting, one is answering a hypothetical question that the forecaster might ask: What path would exchange rates follow from now on *if prices were flexible and PPP held*? Admittedly, as we know, and as any forecaster knows, in the short run, there might be deviations from this prediction about exchange rate changes, but in the longer run, the prediction will supply a more reasonable guide.

Forecasting Exchange Rates: An Example To see how forecasting might work, let's look at a simple scenario. Assume that U.S. and European real income growth rates are identical and equal to zero (0%) so that real income levels are constant. Assume also that the European money supply is constant. If the money supply and real income in Europe are constant, then the European price level is constant, and European inflation is zero, as we can see from Equation (3-5). These assumptions allow us to perform a controlled thought-experiment, and focus on changes on the U.S. side of the model, all else equal. Let's look at two cases.

Case 1: A one-time increase in the money supply. In the first, and simpler, case, suppose at some time T that the U.S. money supply has risen by a fixed proportion, say 10%, all else equal. Assuming that prices are flexible, what does our model predict will happen to the level of the exchange rate after time T? To spell out the argument in detail, we look at the implications of our model for some key variables.

a. There is a 10% increase in the money supply M.

b. Real money balances M/P remain constant, because real income is constant.

c. These last two statements imply that price level P and money supply M must move in the same proportion, so there is a 10% increase in the price level P.

d. PPP implies that the exchange rate E and price level P must move in the same proportion, so there is a 10% increase in the exchange rate E; that is, the dollar depreciates by 10%.

A quicker solution uses the fundamental equation of the monetary approach at Equation (3-3): the price level and exchange rate are proportional to the money supply, all else equal.

Case 2: An increase in the rate of money growth. The model also applies to more complex scenarios. Consider a second case in which U.S. money supply is not constant but grows at a steady fixed rate μ. Then suppose we learn at time T that the United States will raise the rate of money supply growth from some previously fixed rate μ to a slightly higher rate. How would people expect the exchange rate to behave assuming price flexibility? Let's work through this case step by step:

a. Money supply is growing at a constant rate.

b. Real money balances M/P remain constant, as before.

c. These last two statements imply that price level P and money supply M must move in the same proportion, so M is always a constant multiple of P.

d. PPP implies that the exchange rate E and price level P must move in the same proportion, so E is always a constant multiple of P (and hence of M).

Corresponding to these four steps, the four panels of Figure 3-6 illustrate the path of the key variables in this example. This figure shows that if we can

FIGURE 3-6

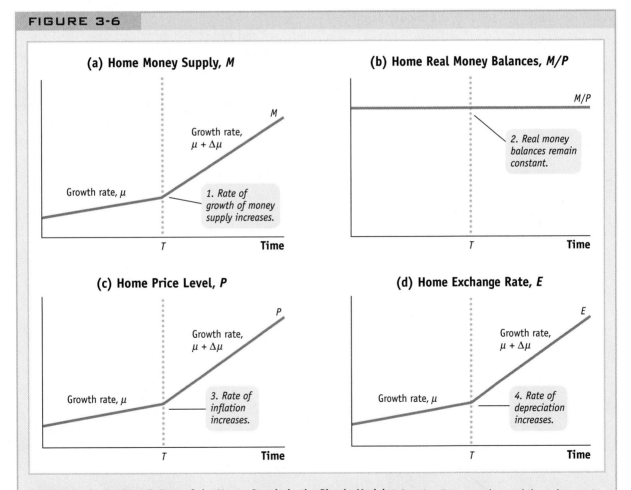

An Increase in the Growth Rate of the Money Supply in the Simple Model Before time T, money, prices, and the exchange rate all grow at rate μ. Foreign prices are constant. In panel (a), we suppose at time T there is an increase $\Delta\mu$ in the rate of growth of home money supply M. In panel (b), the quantity theory assumes that the level of real money balances remains unchanged. After time T, if real money balances (M/P) are constant, then money M and prices P still grow at the same rate, which is now $\mu + \Delta\mu$, so the rate of inflation rises by $\Delta\mu$, as shown in panel (c). PPP and an assumed stable foreign price level imply that the exchange rate will follow a path similar to that of the domestic price level, so E also grows at the new rate $\mu + \Delta\mu$, and the rate of depreciation rises by $\Delta\mu$, as shown in panel (d).

forecast the money supply at any future period as in (a), and if we know real money balances remain constant as in (b), then we can forecast prices as in (c) and exchange rates as in (d). These forecasts are good in any future period, under the assumptions of the monetary approach. Again, the fundamental equation (3-3) supplies the answer more quickly; under the assumptions we have made, money, prices, and exchange rates all move in proportion to one another.

APPLICATION

Evidence for the Monetary Approach

The monetary approach to prices and exchange rates suggests that, all else equal, increases in the rate of money supply growth should be the same size as increases in the rate of inflation and the rate of exchange rate depreciation. Looking for evidence of this relationship in real-world data is one way to put this theory to the test.

The scatter plots in Figure 3-7 and Figure 3-8 show data from the 1975 to 2005 period for a large sample of countries. The results offer fairly strong support for the monetary theory. Equation (3-6) predicts that an $x\%$ difference in money growth rates (relative to the United States) should be associated with an $x\%$ difference in inflation rates (relative to the United States) and an $x\%$ depreciation of the home exchange rate (against the U.S. dollar). If this association were literally true in the data, then the scatter plots would show each country on the 45-degree line. This is not exactly true, but the actual relationship is very close and offers some support for the monetary approach.

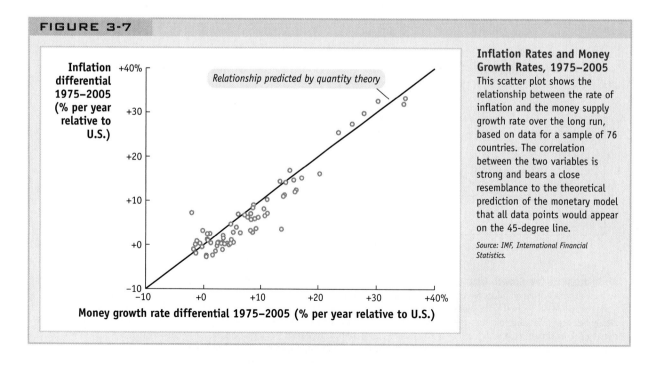

FIGURE 3-7

Inflation Rates and Money Growth Rates, 1975–2005 This scatter plot shows the relationship between the rate of inflation and the money supply growth rate over the long run, based on data for a sample of 76 countries. The correlation between the two variables is strong and bears a close resemblance to the theoretical prediction of the monetary model that all data points would appear on the 45-degree line.

Source: IMF, International Financial Statistics.

FIGURE 3-8

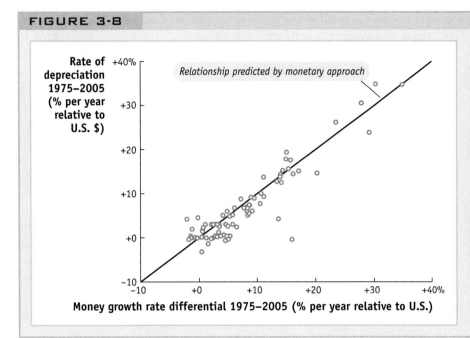

Money Growth Rates and the Exchange Rate, 1975–2005 This scatter plot shows the relationship between the rate of exchange-rate depreciation against the U.S. dollar and the money growth rate differential versus the United States over the long run, based on data for a sample of 82 countries. The data show a strong correlation between the two variables and a close resemblance to the theoretical prediction of the monetary approach to exchange rates, which would predict that all data points would appear on the 45-degree line.

Source: IMF, International Financial Statistics.

One reason the data do not sit on the 45-degree line is that all else is *not* equal in this sample of countries. In Equation (3-6), countries differ not only in their relative money supply growth rates but also in their real income growth rates. Another explanation is that we have been assuming that the money demand parameter L is constant, and this may not be true in reality. This is an issue we must now confront.[9] ■

Hyperinflations of the Twentieth Century

The monetary approach assumes long-run PPP, which has some support. But we have been careful to note, again, that PPP works poorly in the short run. However, there is one notable exception to this general principle: hyperinflations.

Economists traditionally define a **hyperinflation** as occurring when the inflation rises to a sustained rate of more than 50% per month (which means that prices are doubling every 51 days). In common usage, some lower inflation episodes are also called hyperinflations; for example, an annual inflation rate of 1,000% is a common rule of thumb (when inflation is "only" 22% per month).

There have been many hyperinflations worldwide since the early twentieth century, usually when governments face a budget crisis, are unable to borrow to finance a deficit, and instead choose to print money to cover their

---

[9] Economists can use sophisticated statistical techniques to address these issues and still find results favorable to the monetary approach in the long run. See David E. Rapach and Mark E. Wohar, 2002, "Testing the Monetary Model of Exchange Rate Determination: New Evidence from a Century of Data," *Journal of International Economics*, 58(2), 359–385.

financing needs. The situation is not sustainable and usually leads to economic, social, and political crisis, which is eventually resolved with a return to price stability. Nonetheless, each crisis provides a unique laboratory for testing the predictions of the PPP theory.

The scatter plot in Figure 3-9 looks at the data using changes in levels (from start to finish, expressed as multiples). The change in the exchange rate (with the United States) is on the vertical axis and the change in the price level (compared with the United States) is on the horizontal axis. Because of the huge changes involved, both axes use log scales in powers of 10. For example, 10^{12} on the vertical axis means the exchange rate rose (the currency depreciated) by a factor of a trillion against the U.S. dollar during the hyperinflation.

PPP would imply that changes in prices and exchange rates should be equal. If so, all observations would be on the 45-degree line, and mostly they do follow this pattern, providing support for PPP. What the hyperinflations have in common is that a very large depreciation was about equal to a very large inflation differential. In an economy with fairly stable prices and exchange rates, large changes in exchange rates and prices only develop over

FIGURE 3-9

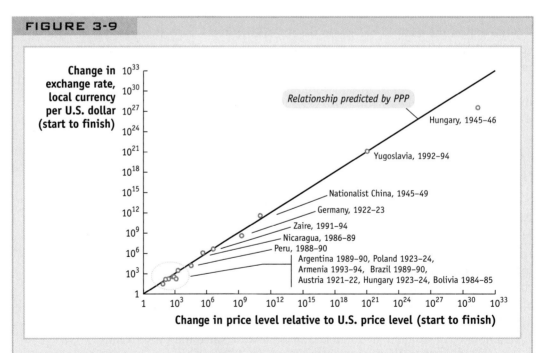

Purchasing Power Parity during Hyperinflations The scatter plot shows the relationship between the cumulative start-to-finish exchange-rate depreciation against the U.S. dollar and the cumulative start-to-finish rise in the local price level for hyperinflations in the twentieth century. Note the use of logarithmic scales. The data show a strong correlation between the two variables and a *very* close resemblance to the theoretical prediction of PPP that all data points would appear on the 45-degree line.

Sources: IMF, International Financial Statistics; Global Financial Data; Phillip Cagan, "The Monetary Dynamics of Hyperinflation," in Milton Friedman, ed., 1956, Studies in the Quantity Theory of Money, Chicago: University of Chicago Press, pp. 25–117; Pavle Petrovic and Zorica Mladenovic, 2000, "Money Demand and Exchange Rate Determination under Hyperinflation: Conceptual Issues and Evidence from Yugoslavia," Journal of Money, Credit and Banking, 32, 785–806.

the very long run of years and decades; but in a hyperinflation, large inflations and large depreciations are compressed into the short run of years or months.

Some price changes were outrageously large. Austria's hyperinflation of 1921 to 1922 was the first on record, and prices rose by a factor of about 100 (10^2). In Germany from 1922 to 1923, prices rose by a factor of about 20 billion (2×10^{10}); in the worst month, prices were doubling on average every two days. In Hungary from 1945 to 1946, pengö prices rose by a factor of about 10^{31}, the current record, and in July 1946, prices were doubling on average every 15 hours. Serbia's inflation from 1992 to 1994 came close to breaking the record for cumulative price changes. In comparison, Argentina's 700-fold inflation and Brazil's 200-fold inflation in 1989 to 1990 look deceptively modest. (For more discussion of hyperinflation and its consequences see **Side Bar: Currency Reform** and **Headlines: The First Hyperinflation of the Twenty-First Century.**)

There is one other important lesson to be learned from hyperinflations. In our simple monetary model, the money demand parameter L was assumed to be *constant* and equal to $\overline{L}$. This implied that real money balances were proportional to real income, with $M/P = \overline{L}\,Y$ as shown in Equation (3-5). Is this assumption of stable real money balances justified?

SIDE BAR

Currency Reform

Hyperinflations help us understand how some currencies become extinct if they cease to function well and lose value rapidly. Dollarization in Ecuador is a recent example. Other currencies survive such travails, only to be reborn. But the low denomination bills—the ones, fives, tens—usually become essentially worthless and normal transactions can require you to be a millionaire. The eradication of a few pesky zeroes might then be a good idea. A new unit of currency defined as 10^N (10 raised to the power N) old units may then be created by the authorities.

Sometimes N can get quite large. In the 1980s, Argentina suffered hyperinflation. On June 1, 1983, the *peso argentino* replaced the (old) peso at a rate of 10,000 to 1. Then on June 14, 1985, the *austral* replaced the peso argentino at 1,000 to 1. Finally, on January 1, 1992, the *convertible peso* replaced the austral at a rate of 10,000 to 1 (i.e., 10,000,000,000 old pesos). After all this, if you had owned 1 new peso in 1983 (and had changed it into the later monies), it would have lost 99.99997% of its U.S. dollar value by 2003.

In 1946 the Hungarian *pengö* became so worthless that the authorities no longer printed the denomination on each note in numbers, but only in words—perhaps to avert distrust (unsuccessful), to hide embarrassment (also unsuccessful), or simply because there wasn't room to print all those zeroes. By July 15, 1946, there were 76,041,000,000,000,000,000,000,000 pengö in circulation. A stable new currency, the *forint,* was finally introduced on July 26, 1946, with each forint worth 400,000 quadrillion pengö ($4 \times 10^{20} = 400,000,000,000,000,000,000$ pengö).

Above left to right are an Argentine 500,000 austral bill of 1990; a 500,000,000,000 Yugoslav dinara of 1993, a record for the most zeroes on a banknote; a 1923 one billion German mark note (1 German billion = 1 U.S. trillion); and a Hungarian 100 Million B-pengö of 1946, with the "B" denoting the Hungarian billion, or a million million: this 100,000,000,000,000,000,000 pengö note is the highest denomination of currency ever issued by any country.

The evidence shown in Figure 3-10 suggests this assumption is not justified, based on a subset of the hyperinflations. For each point, on the horizontal axis of this figure we see the peak monthly inflation rate (the moment when prices were rising most rapidly); on the vertical axis, we see the level of real money balances in that month relative to their initial level (in the month just before the hyperinflation began). If real money balances were stable, there ought to be no variation in the vertical dimension aside from fluctuations in real income. But there is, and with a clear pattern: the higher the level of inflation, the lower the level of real money balances. These declines are far too severe to be explained by just the fall in real incomes experienced during hyperinflations, though such income declines did occur.

This finding may not strike you as very surprising. If prices are doubling every few days (or every few hours), the money in people's pockets is rapidly turning into worthless pieces of paper. They will try to minimize their money holdings—and will do so even more as inflation rises higher and higher, just as the figure shows. It becomes just too costly to hold very much money, despite one's need to use it for transactions.

If you thought along these lines, you have an accurate sense of how people behave during hyperinflations. You also anticipated the extensions to the simple model that we make in the next section to make it more realistic. Even during "normal" inflations—situations that are less pathological than a hyperinflation—it is implausible to assume that real money balances are perfectly stable. Instead, we will assume that people make the trade-off highlighted previously: comparing the benefits of holding money for transactions purposes with the costs of holding money as compared with other assets. ■

FIGURE 3-10

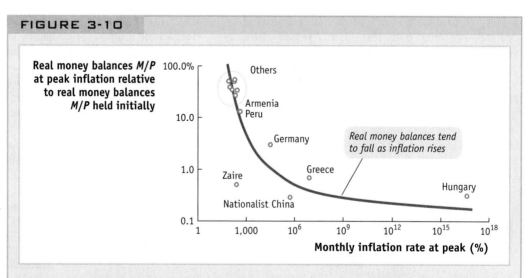

The Collapse of Real Money Balances during Hyperinflations This figure shows that real money balances tend to collapse in hyperinflations as people economize by reducing their holdings of rapidly depreciating notes. The horizontal axis shows the peak monthly inflation rate (%), and the vertical axis shows the ratio of real money balances in that peak month relative to real money balances at the start of the hyperinflationary period. The data are shown using log scales for clarity.

Sources: Global Financial Data; Phillip Cagan, "The Monetary Dynamics of Hyperinflation," in Milton Friedman, ed., 1956, Studies in the Quantity Theory of Money, Chicago: University of Chicago Press, pp. 25–117.

HEADLINES

The First Hyperinflation of the Twenty-First Century

By 2007 the long-suffering people of Zimbabwe faced an accelerating descent into economic chaos. The country was almost at a standstill, except for the printing presses churning out the banknotes. A creeping inflation—58% in 1999, 132% in 2001, 385% in 2003, and 586% in 2005—was about to become hyperinflation.

Zimbabwe's annual inflation rate surged to an unprecedented 3,714 percent at the end of April, the official state newspaper reported Thursday, as the government set up a new commission to try to bring price hikes down to single digit levels.

Prices more than doubled last month as shown by a 100.7 percent increase—the highest on record—in the consumer price index calculated by the state Central Statistical Office, the *Herald* newspaper said. In the past year they increased 36-fold.

The *Herald* said that President Robert Mugabe on Monday signed into law new regulations to enforce wage and price controls through "comprehensive price surveys and inspections," with a penalty of up to five years in jail for violators. The ultimate aim would be to bring inflation into single digits.

In recent years, the government has tried to freeze prices for corn meal, bread, cooking oil, meat, school fees and transport costs with little success. Socialist-style controls have driven a thriving black market in scarce commodities.

For instance sugar, unavailable in regular stores for weeks, fetches at least 10 times the government's designated price

at a dirty, seething market in Harare's impoverished western township of Mbare.

Minibus drivers, the country's main commuter transport, routinely ignore government directives on fares, citing soaring black market prices for gasoline. Commuters questioned at police roadblocks often lie about the fare they paid or risk being thrown off the bus and left stranded.

The independent Confederation of Zimbabwe Industries estimates most factories across the country are running at around 30 percent capacity or less, and countless businesses have shut down, fueling record unemployment of about 80 percent.

Many consumer items have disappeared altogether, forcing supermarkets to fill out their shelves with empty packaging behind the few goods on display.

The worst economic crisis since independence in 1980 is blamed on corruption, mismanagement and the often-violent seizures of thousands of white-owned commercial farms since 2000 that disrupted the agriculture-based economy.

Hikes in prices of power, other fuels, passenger transport, vegetables and meat contributed to April's surge in the consumer price index, which was double

the increase in March of 50.3 percent, the Central Statistical Office said, according to the *Herald*.

The international benchmark for hyperinflation is a 50 percent month-on-month increase.

The government warned Wednesday that the price of bread is likely to rise because only a fraction of the normal wheat crop has been planted. . . .

On Monday, the state postal service upped its charges by 600 percent, the second increase in three months. A stamp for a local letter weighing 20 grams (0.7 of an ounce) went up to Zimbabwean $40,000, or US$2.60 (€1.90). . . .

The Reserve Bank last year introduced sweeping currency reforms knocking off the final three digits—thus Zimbabwean $250,000 became Zimbabwean $250—in a vain attempt to tame inflation.

Even so, consumers are still forced to carry around huge bricks of notes to pay for scarce supplies and basic services.

For example, a pest control service on Wednesday charged Zimbabwean $1 million as a callout charge to a homeowner whose house was plagued by the rats which are thriving as the country's sanitation and garbage collection collapses.

Ink on their hands: Under President Robert Mugabe and Central Bank Governor Gideon Gono, Zimbabwe is the latest country to join a rather exclusive club. On the right, a Z$100,000 note.

Source: Excerpted from the Associated Press, "Inflation in Zimbabwe Surges to Record 3,714 Percent, the Highest in the World," International Herald Tribune, May 17, 2007.

4 Money, Interest, and Prices in the Long Run: A General Model

So far we have a theory that links exchange rates to the price levels in each country: PPP. We also have a simple monetary model that links price levels in each country to underlying conditions of money supply and demand: the *quantity theory*. The quantity theory provides basic intuition for the links between money, prices, and exchange rates.

The trouble is that the quantity theory makes what seems to be an implausible assumption about the stability of the demand for money. In this section, we explore a general model of money demand that addresses this shortcoming by allowing money demand to vary with the nominal interest rate. This theory, in turn, brings another variable into play: How is the nominal interest rate determined in the long run? Answering this question will lead us to consider the links between inflation and the nominal interest rate in an open economy. With these new models in hand, we then return to the question of how best to forecast exchange rates in the long run.

The Demand for Money: The General Model

The general model of money demand is motivated by two insights, the first of which carries over from the simple model we studied earlier in this chapter, the quantity theory.

- *Benefits of holding money.* As before, the benefit of money is that individuals can conduct transactions with it. As in the simple quantity theory, we continue to assume that transactions demand is in proportion to income, all else equal.

- *Costs of holding money.* The nominal interest rate on money is zero, $i_{money} = 0$. By holding money and not earning interest, people incur the opportunity cost of holding money. For example, an individual could hold an interest-earning asset paying $i_\$$. The difference in nominal returns between this asset and money would be $i_\$ - i_{money} = i_\$ > 0$. This is one way of expressing the opportunity cost.

Moving from the individual or household level up to the macroeconomic level, we can infer that aggregate money demand in the economy as a whole will behave similarly:

All else equal, a rise in national dollar income (nominal income) will cause a proportional increase in transactions and, hence, in aggregate money demand.

All else equal, a rise in the nominal interest rate will cause the aggregate demand for money to fall.

Based on these insights, we arrive at the general model of the demand for money, in which demand is proportional to nominal income and a decreasing function of the nominal interest rate:

$$M^d = \underbrace{L(i)}_{\substack{\text{A decreasing} \\ \text{function}}} \times \underbrace{P \times Y.}_{\substack{\text{Nominal} \\ \text{income (\$)}}}$$

$$\underbrace{M^d}_{\substack{\text{Demand for} \\ \text{money (\$)}}}$$

Formerly, in the quantity theory, the parameter L (the liquidity ratio, the amount of money needed for transactions per dollar of nominal GDP) was a constant. But now we assume it is a decreasing function of the nominal interest rate i. Dividing by P, we can derive the demand for real money balances:

$$\underbrace{\frac{M^d}{P}}_{\substack{\text{Demand for} \\ \text{real money}}} = \underbrace{L(i)}_{\substack{\text{A decreasing} \\ \text{function}}} \times \underbrace{Y}_{\substack{\text{Real} \\ \text{income}}}.$$

Figure 3-11(a) shows a typical **real money demand function** of this form, with the quantity of real money balances demanded on the horizontal axis and the nominal interest rate on the vertical axis. The downward slope of the demand curve reflects the inverse relationship between the demand for real money balances and the nominal interest rate *at a given level of real income* (Y).

Figure 3-11(b) shows what happens when real income increases from Y_1 to Y_2. When real income increases (by $x\%$), the demand for real money balances increases (by $x\%$) at each level of the nominal interest rate.

Long-Run Equilibrium in the Money Market

The money market is in equilibrium when the real money supply (determined by the central bank) equals the demand for real money balances:

(3-7)
$$\underbrace{\frac{M}{P}}_{\text{Real money supply}} = \underbrace{L(i)\,Y.}_{\text{Real money demand}}$$

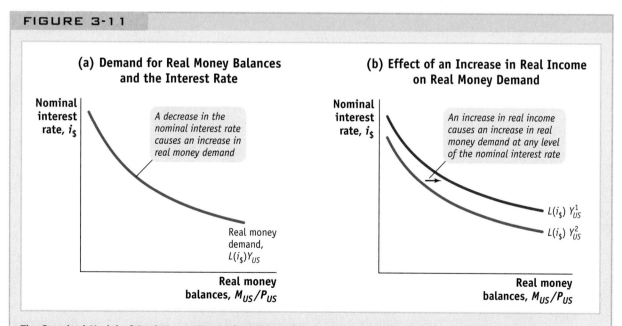

FIGURE 3-11

(a) Demand for Real Money Balances and the Interest Rate

Nominal interest rate, $i_\$$

A decrease in the nominal interest rate causes an increase in real money demand

Real money demand, $L(i_\$)Y_{US}$

Real money balances, M_{US}/P_{US}

(b) Effect of an Increase in Real Income on Real Money Demand

Nominal interest rate, $i_\$$

An increase in real income causes an increase in real money demand at any level of the nominal interest rate

$L(i_\$)\,Y_{US}^1$

$L(i_\$)\,Y_{US}^2$

Real money balances, M_{US}/P_{US}

The Standard Model of Real Money Demand Panel (a) shows the real money demand function for the United States. The downward slope implies that the quantity of real money demand rises as the nominal interest rate $i_\$$ falls. Panel (b) shows that an increase in real income from Y_{US}^1 to Y_{US}^2 causes real money demand to rise at all levels of the nominal interest rate $i_\$$.

We will continue to assume that prices are flexible in the long run and that they adjust to ensure that equilibrium is maintained.

This all looks familiar. There is just one small problem remaining. Under the quantity theory, the nominal interest rate was ignored. Now it is a key variable in the determination of money demand. So now we need a theory to tell us what the level of the nominal interest rate i will be in the long run. Once we have solved this problem, we will be able to apply this new model of the money market to the analysis of exchange rate determination in the long run.

Inflation and Interest Rates in the Long Run

The tools we need to determine the nominal interest rate in an open economy are already at hand. So far in this chapter, we have developed the idea of purchasing power parity (PPP), which links prices and exchange rates. In the last chapter, we developed another parity idea, uncovered interest parity (UIP), which links exchange rates and interest rates. With only these two relationships in hand, PPP and UIP, we can derive a powerful and striking result concerning interest rates with profound implications for our study of open economy macroeconomics.

Relative PPP, as stated in Equation (3-2), states that the rate of depreciation equals the inflation differential. When market actors use this equation to make a forecast of future exchange rates, we refer to the forecast as the expected exchange rate, meaning that a statistical expectation has been used as a predictor. Thus, we use a superscript e to denote such expectations in Equation (3–2) and obtain

$$\underbrace{\frac{\Delta E^e}{E_{\$/€,t}}}_{\text{Expected rate of dollar depreciation}} = \underbrace{\pi^e_{US,t} - \pi^e_{EUR,t}.}_{\text{Expected inflation differential}}$$

Next we recall that uncovered interest parity (UIP) in its simplified approximate form (Equation 2–3) can be slightly rearranged to show that the expected rate of depreciation equals the interest differential:

$$\underbrace{\frac{\Delta E^e_{\$/€}}{E_{\$/€}}}_{\text{Expected rate of dollar depreciation}} = \underbrace{i_{\$}}_{\substack{\text{Net dollar} \\ \text{interest rate}}} - \underbrace{i_{€}.}_{\substack{\text{Net euro} \\ \text{interest rate}}}$$

This way of writing the UIP equation says that traders will be indifferent to a higher U.S. interest rate relative to the euro interest rates (making U.S. deposits look more attractive) only if it is offset by an expected dollar depreciation (making U.S. deposits look less attractive). For example, if the U.S. interest rate is 4% and the euro interest rate is 2%, the interest differential is 2% and the forex market can be in equilibrium only if traders expect a 2% depreciation of the U.S. dollar against the euro, which would exactly offset the higher U.S. interest rate.

The Fisher Effect

Because the left sides of the previous two equations are equal, the right sides must also be equal. Thus, the nominal interest differential equals the expected inflation differential:

(3-8)
$$\underbrace{i_\$ - i_\text{€}}_{\text{Nominal interest rate differential}} = \underbrace{\pi_{US}^e - \pi_{EUR}^e.}_{\text{Nominal inflation rate differential (expected)}}$$

What does this important result say? To take an example, suppose expected inflation is 2% in the United States and 4% in Europe. The inflation differential on the right is then −2%. If interest rates in Europe are 3%, then to make the interest differential the same as the inflation differential, −2%, the interest rate in the United States must equal 1% (1% − 3% = −2%).

Now suppose expected inflation in the United States changes, rising by 1 percentage point to 3%. If the equation is to still hold, and nothing changes in Europe, then the U.S. interest rate must also rise by 1 percentage point to 2%. In general, this equation predicts that changes in the expected rate of inflation will be fully incorporated (one for one) into changes in nominal interest rates.

All else equal, a rise in the expected inflation rate in a country will lead to an equal rise in its nominal interest rate.

This result is known as the **Fisher effect,** named for the American economist Irving Fisher (1867–1947). Because this result depends on an assumption of PPP, it is therefore likely to hold only in the long run.

The Fisher effect makes clear the link between nominal inflation and interest rates under flexible prices, a finding that is widely applicable. For a start, it makes sense of the evidence we just saw on money holdings during hyperinflations (see Figure 3-10). As inflation rises, the Fisher effect tells us that the nominal interest rate i must rise by the same amount; the general model of money demand then tells us that $L(i)$ must fall because it is a decreasing function of i; thus, for a given level of real income, real money balances must fall.

In other words, the Fisher effect predicts that the change in the opportunity cost of money is equal not just to the change in the nominal interest rate but also to the change in the inflation rate. In times of very high inflation, people should, therefore, want to reduce their money holdings—and they do.

Real Interest Parity

As just described, the Fisher effect tells us something about nominal interest rates, but we can quickly derive the implications for real interest rates, too. Rearranging the last equation we find

$$i_\$ - \pi_{US}^e = i_\text{€} - \pi_{EUR}^e.$$

The expressions on either side of this equation might look familiar from previous courses in macroeconomics. When the inflation rate (π) is subtracted from a *nominal* interest rate (i), the result is a **real interest rate** (r), the inflation-adjusted return on an interest-bearing asset. Given this definition, we can simplify the last equation further. On the left is the expected real interest rate in the United States, ($r^e_{US} = i_\$ - \pi^e_{US}$). On the right is the expected real interest rate in Europe, ($r^e_{EUR} = i_€ - \pi^e_{EUR}$).

Thus, using only two assumptions, PPP and UIP, we can show that

(3-9)
$$r^e_{US} = r^e_{EUR}.$$

This remarkable result states the following: *If PPP and UIP hold, then expected real interest rates are equalized across countries.*

This powerful condition is called **real interest parity** because it depends on an assumption of PPP; it is therefore likely to hold only in the long run.[10]

We have arrived at a strong conclusion about the potential for globalization to cause convergence in economic outcomes, since real interest parity implies the following: *Arbitrage in goods and financial markets alone is sufficient, in the long run, to cause the equalization of real interest rates across countries.*

We have considered two countries, but this argument applies to all countries integrated into the global capital market. In the long run, they will all share a common expected real interest rate, the long-run expected **world real interest rate** denoted r^*, so

$$r^e_{US} = r^e_{EUR} = r^*.$$

From now on, unless indicated otherwise, we treat r^* as a given, exogenous variable, something outside the control of a policy maker in any particular country.[11]

Under these conditions, the Fisher effect is even clearer, since, by definition,

$$i_\$ = r^e_{US} + \pi^e_{US} = r^* + \pi^e_{US}, \qquad i_€ = r^e_{EUR} + \pi^e_{EUR} = r^* + \pi^e_{EUR}.$$

In each country, the long-run expected nominal interest rate is the long-run world real interest rate plus that country's expected long-run inflation rate. For example, if the world real interest rate is $r^* = 2\%$, and the country's long-run inflation rate goes up by 2 percentage points from 3% to 5%, then its long-run nominal interest rate also goes up by 2 percentage points from the old level of 2 + 3 = 5% to a new level of 2 + 5 = 7%.

APPLICATION

Evidence on the Fisher Effect

Are the Fisher effect and real interest parity supported by empirical evidence? One might expect a problem here. We derived them from purchasing power parity. The evidence we have seen on PPP offers support only in the long run. Thus, we do not expect the Fisher effect and real interest parity to hold exactly and in the short run either but only as a long-run approximation.

---

[10] You may have encountered other theories in which real interest rates are equalized across countries by other means. Countries may share common technologies (due to technology diffusion) or might have similar saving behavior (due to similar preferences). Such assumptions could lead to identical real interest rates even in two *closed* economies. But here we have derived the RIP condition *only* from UIP and PPP, meaning that, in *open* economies, these are *sufficient* conditions for real interest rates to be equalized. No other assumptions are needed!

[11] In advanced economic theories, the determinants of the world real interest rate are explored, with reference to consumption preferences of households and the extent to which they discount the future.

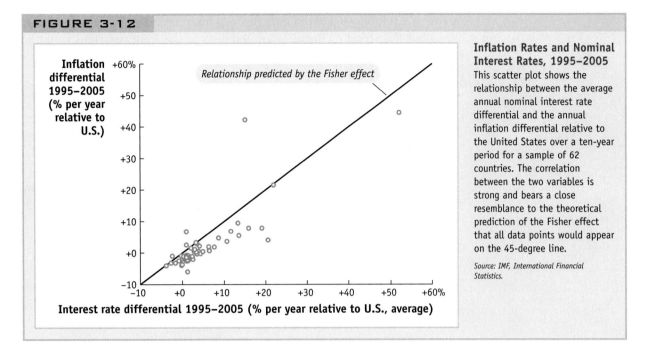

FIGURE 3-12

Inflation Rates and Nominal Interest Rates, 1995–2005 This scatter plot shows the relationship between the average annual nominal interest rate differential and the annual inflation differential relative to the United States over a ten-year period for a sample of 62 countries. The correlation between the two variables is strong and bears a close resemblance to the theoretical prediction of the Fisher effect that all data points would appear on the 45-degree line.

Source: IMF, International Financial Statistics.

Figure 3-12 shows that the Fisher effect is close to reality in the long run: on average, countries with higher inflation rates tend to have higher nominal interest rates, and the data line up fairly well with the predictions of the theory. Figure 3-13 shows that, for three developed countries, real interest

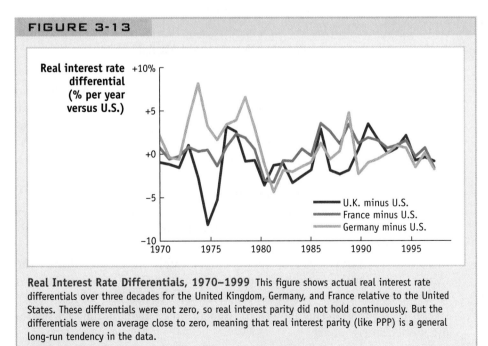

FIGURE 3-13

Real Interest Rate Differentials, 1970–1999 This figure shows actual real interest rate differentials over three decades for the United Kingdom, Germany, and France relative to the United States. These differentials were not zero, so real interest parity did not hold continuously. But the differentials were on average close to zero, meaning that real interest parity (like PPP) is a general long-run tendency in the data.

Source: Maurice Obstfeld and Alan M. Taylor, 2004, Global Capital Markets: Integration, Crisis, and Growth, Japan-U.S. Center Sanwa Monographs on International Financial Markets, Cambridge: Cambridge University Press.

parity holds fairly well in the long run: real interest differentials are not always zero, but they tend to fluctuate around zero in the long run. This could be seen as evidence in favor of long-run real interest parity. ■

The Fundamental Equation under the General Model

Now that we have an understanding of how the nominal interest rate is determined in the long run, we can apply the general model. This model differs from the simple model (the quantity theory) *only* by allowing L to vary as a function of the nominal interest rate i.

We can update our fundamental equations to allow for this change in how we treat L. For example, the fundamental equation of the monetary approach to exchange rates, Equation (3-3), can now be rewritten:

$$(3\text{-}10) \quad \underbrace{E_{\$/€}}_{\substack{\text{Exchange}\\\text{rate}}} = \underbrace{\frac{P_{US}}{P_{EUR}}}_{\substack{\text{Ratio of}\\\text{price}\\\text{levels}}} = \frac{\left(\dfrac{M_{US}}{L_{US}(i_\$)Y_{US}}\right)}{\left(\dfrac{M_{EUR}}{L_{EUR}(i_€)Y_{EUR}}\right)} = \underbrace{\frac{(M_{US}/M_{EUR})}{(L_{US}(i_\$)Y_{US}/L_{EUR}(i_€)Y_{EUR})}}_{\substack{\text{Relative nominal money supplies divided}\\\text{by relative real money demands}}}.$$

What have we gained from this refinement? We know that the simple model will remain valid in cases in which nominal interest rates remain unchanged in the long run. It is only when nominal interest rates change that the general model has different implications, and we now have the right tools for that situation. To explore those differences, we revisit one of the exchange rate forecasting problems we studied earlier.

Exchange Rate Forecasts Using the General Model

Earlier in the chapter, we looked at two forecasting problems *under the assumption of flexible prices*. The first was a one-time change in an otherwise constant U.S. money supply. Under the assumptions we made (stable real income in both countries and stable European money supply), this change caused a one-time increase in the U.S. price level but did not lead to a change in U.S. inflation (which was zero before and after the event). The Fisher effect tells us that if inflation rates are unchanged, then, in the long run, nominal interest rates remain unchanged. Thus, the predictions of the simple model remain valid. The more complex forecasting problem involved a change in U.S. money growth rates and it did lead to a change in inflation. It is here that the general model makes different predictions.

Recall, we assumed that U.S. and European real income growth rates are identical and equal to zero (0%), so real income levels are constant. We also assumed that European money supply is constant, so that the European price level is constant, too. This allowed us to focus on changes on the U.S. side of the model, all else equal.

We now reexamine the forecasting problem for the case in which there is an increase in the U.S. rate of money growth. We learn at time T that the

United States will raise the rate of money supply growth from some fixed rate μ to a slightly higher rate, $\mu + \Delta\mu$.

For example, imagine an increase from 2% to 3% growth, so $\Delta\mu = 1\%$. How will the exchange rate behave in the long run? To solve the model, we make a provisional assumption that U.S. inflation rates and interest rates are constant before and after time T and focus on the differences between the two periods caused by the change in money supply growth. The story is told in Figure 3-14:

a. The money supply is growing at a constant rate. If the interest rate is constant in each period, then real money balances M/P remain constant, by assumption, since $L(i)Y$ is then a constant. If real money

FIGURE 3-14

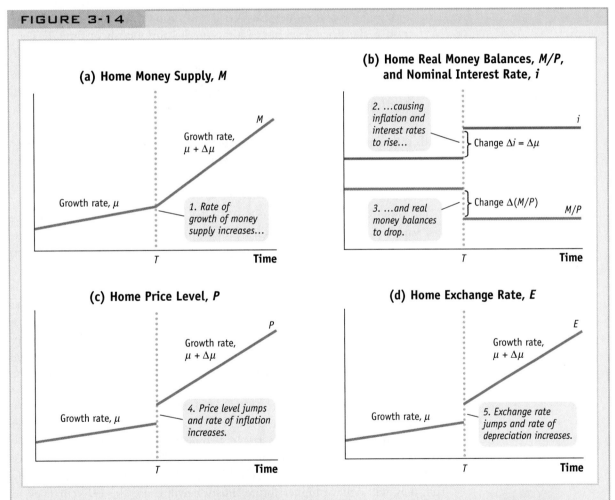

An Increase in the Growth Rate of the Money Supply in the Standard Model Before time T, money, prices, and the exchange rate all grow at rate μ. Foreign prices are constant. In panel (a), we suppose at time T there is an increase $\Delta\mu$ in the rate of growth of home money supply M. This causes an increase $\Delta\mu$ in the rate of inflation; the Fisher effect means that there will be a $\Delta\mu$ increase in the nominal interest rate; as a result, as shown in panel (b), real money demand falls with a discrete jump at T. If real money balances are to fall when the nominal money supply expands continuously, then the domestic price level must make a discrete jump up at time T, as shown in panel (c). Subsequently, prices grow at the new higher rate of inflation; and given the stable foreign price level, PPP implies that the exchange rate follows a similar path to the domestic price level, as shown in panel (d).

balances are constant, then M and P grow at the same rate. Before T that rate is $\mu = 2\%$; after T that rate is $\mu + \Delta\mu = 3\%$. That is, U.S. inflation rises by an amount $\Delta\mu = 1\%$ at time T.

b. As a result of the Fisher effect, U.S. interest rates rise by $\Delta\mu = 1\%$ at time T. Consequently, real money balances M/P must fall at time T because $L(i)Y$ will decrease as i increases.

c. In (a) we have described the path of M. In (b) we found that M/P is constant up to T, then drops suddenly, and then is constant after time T. What path must the price level P follow? Up to time T, it is a constant multiple of M; the same applies after time T, but the constant has increased. Why? The nominal money supply grows smoothly, without a jump. So if real money balances are to drop down discontinuously at time T, the price level has to jump up discontinuously at time T. The intuition for this is that the rise in inflation and interest rates at time T prompts people to instantaneously demand less real money, but because the supply of nominal money is unchanged, the price level has to rise. Apart from this jump, P grows at a constant rate; before T that rate is $\mu = 2\%$; after T that rate is $\mu + \Delta\mu = 3\%$.

d. PPP implies that E and P must move in the same proportion, so E is always a constant multiple of P. Thus, E jumps like P at time T. Apart from this jump, E grows at a constant rate; before T that rate is $\mu = 2\%$; after T that rate is $\mu + \Delta\mu = 3\%$.

Corresponding to these four steps, Figure 3-14 illustrates the path of the key variables in this example. (Our provisional assumption of constant inflation rates and interest rates in each period is satisfied, so the proposed solution is internally consistent.)

Comparing Figure 3-14 with Figure 3-6, we can observe the subtle qualitative differences between the predictions of the simple quantity theory and those of the more general model. Shifts in the interest rate introduce jumps in real money demand. Because money supplies evolve smoothly, these jumps end up being reflected in the price levels and hence—via PPP—in exchange rates. The Fisher effect tells us that these interest rate effects are ultimately the result of changes in expected inflation.

Looking Ahead We can learn a little more by thinking through the market mechanism that produces this result. People learn at time T that money growth will be more rapid in the United States. This creates expectations of higher inflation in the United States. If people believe PPP holds in the long run, they will believe higher future inflation will cause the U.S. currency to depreciate in the future. This prospect makes holding dollars less attractive, by UIP. People try to sell dollars, and invest in euros. This creates immediate downward pressure on the dollar—even though at time T itself the supply of dollars does not change at all! This lesson underlines yet again the importance of expectations in determining the exchange rate. *Even if actual economic conditions today are completely unchanged, news about the future affects today's exchange* *rate.* This crucial insight can help us explain many phenomena relating to the volatility and instability in spot exchange rates, an idea we develop further in the chapters that follow.

5 Monetary Regimes and Exchange Rate Regimes

The monetary approach shows that, in the long run, all nominal variables—the money supply, interest rate, price level, and exchange rate—are interlinked. The approach also highlights important challenges for long-run economic policy design, to which we now turn. This is not mere digression. How these problems are solved will, in turn, have implications for exchange rate behavior and hence for the problem of forecasting the future exchange rate that we have examined.

We have repeatedly stressed the importance of inflation as an economic variable. Why is it so important? High or volatile inflation rates are considered undesirable. They may destabilize an economy or retard its growth.[12] Economies with low and stable inflation generally grow faster than those with high or volatile inflation. Inflationary crises, in which inflation jumps to a high or hyperinflationary level, are very damaging.[13]

Policy makers therefore aim to keep the price level or inflation within certain bounds. Economists would describe this kind of objective as an **inflation target,** which we can think of as an overarching aspect of the monetary policy framework. To achieve such an objective requires that policy makers be subject to some kind of constraint in the long run. Such constraints are called **nominal anchors** because they attempt to tie down a nominal variable that is potentially under the policy makers' control.

Policy makers cannot directly control prices, so the attainment of price stability in the *short run* is not feasible. The question is what can policy makers do to try to ensure that price stability is achieved in the long run and what tolerance for flexibility in policies will be allowed in the short run. Long-run nominal anchoring and short-run flexibility are the characteristics of the policy framework that economists call the **monetary regime.** In this section, we examine different types of monetary regimes in the open economy and their relationship to the exchange rate.

---

[12] Macroeconomists can list numerous potential costs of inflation. Expected inflation generates a cost of holding money, a tax on transactions that adds friction to the economy; firms and workers use nominal contracts for prices and would have to change prices and recontract more often; inflation also distorts the economy when a tax system has significant nominal provisions (e.g., fixed deductions and exemptions). Unexpected inflation creates arbitrary redistributions from creditors to debtors, and this introduces risk into borrowing and lending, making interest rates and investment more costly. In short, if inflation is other than low and stable, economic life becomes at best inconvenient and at worst (as in a hyperinflation) dysfunctional. See N. Gregory Mankiw, 2007, *Macroeconomics,* 6th ed., ch. 4, New York: Worth.

[13] This evidence is merely suggestive: high inflation and slow growth may each be caused by other factors, such as weak institutions. Some studies have used sophisticated econometrics to address this problem. See Stanley Fischer, 1993, "The Role of Macroeconomic Factors in Growth," *Journal of Monetary Economics,* 32, 485–511; Robert J. Barro, 1997, *Determinants of Economic Growth,* Cambridge, MA: MIT Press; Michael Bruno and William Easterly, 1998, "Inflation Crises and Long-Run Growth," *Journal of Monetary Economics,* 41, 3–26.

The Long Run: The Nominal Anchor

Which variables could policy makers use as anchors to achieve an inflation objective in the long run? To answer the question, we can go back and rearrange the equations for relative PPP at Equation (3-2), the quantity theory in rates of change at Equation (3-6), and the Fisher effect at Equation (3-8), to obtain alternative expressions for the rate of inflation in the home country. To emphasize that these findings apply quite generally to all countries, we relabel the countries home (H) and foreign (F) instead of United States and Europe.

The three main nominal anchor choices are as follows:

■ **Exchange rate target:** Relative PPP at Equation (3-2) says that the rate of depreciation equals the inflation differential, or $\Delta E_{H/F}/E_{H/F} = \pi_H - \pi_F$. Rearranging this expression suggests one way to anchor inflation is as follows:

$$\underbrace{\pi_H}_{\text{Inflation}} = \underbrace{\frac{\Delta E_{H/F}}{E_{H/F}}}_{\substack{\text{Rate of} \\ \text{depreciation}}} + \underbrace{\pi_F.}_{\substack{\text{Foreign} \\ \text{inflation}}}$$

Anchor variable

Relative PPP says that home inflation equals the rate of depreciation plus foreign inflation. A simple rule would be to set the rate of depreciation equal to a constant. Under a fixed exchange rate, that constant is set at zero (a peg). Under a crawl, it is nonzero. Alternatively, there may be room for movement about a target (a band). Or there may be a vague goal to allow the exchange rate "limited flexibility." Such policies can deliver stable home inflation if PPP works well and if policy makers keep their commitment. The drawback is that PPP implies that over the long run the home country "imports" inflation from the foreign country over and above the chosen rate of depreciation. For example, under a peg, if foreign inflation rises by 1% per year, then so, too, does home inflation. Thus, countries almost invariably peg to a country with a reputation for price stability (e.g., the United States). This is a common policy choice: fixed exchange rates of some form are in use in more than half of the world's countries.

■ **Money supply target:** The quantity theory suggests another way to anchor because the fundamental equation for the price level in the monetary approach says that inflation equals the excess of the rate of money supply growth over and above the rate of real income growth:

$$\underbrace{\pi_H}_{\text{Inflation}} = \underbrace{\mu_H}_{\text{Money supply growth}} - \underbrace{g_H.}_{\text{Real output growth}}$$

Anchor variable

A simple rule of this sort is: set the growth rate of the money supply equal to a constant, say 2% per annum. The printing presses are put on automatic pilot, and no human interference should be allowed. Essentially, the central bank is run by robots. This would be a truly hard rule, if applied. The drawback is that real income growth, the final term in the previous equation, can be unstable. In periods of high growth, inflation will be below target. In periods of low growth, inflation will be above target. For this reason, money supply targets are waning in popularity or are used in conjunction with other targets. For example, the European Central Bank claims to use monetary growth rates as a partial guide to policy, but nobody is quite sure how serious it is.

■ **Inflation target plus interest rate policy:** The Fisher effect suggests yet another anchoring method:

$$\underbrace{\pi_H^e}_{\substack{\text{Inflation} \\ \text{(expected)}}} = \underbrace{i_H}_{\text{Nominal interest rate}} - \underbrace{r^*}_{\text{World real interest rate}}.$$

Anchor variable

The Fisher effect says that home inflation is the home nominal interest rate minus the foreign real interest rate. If the latter can be assumed to be constant, then as long as the average nominal interest rate is kept stable, inflation can also be kept stable. This type of nominal anchoring framework is an increasingly common policy choice. Assuming a stable world real interest rate turns out not to be a bad assumption. (And in principle, the target level of the nominal interest rate could be adjusted if necessary.) More or less hard versions of the rule can be imagined. A central bank could peg the nominal interest rate at a fixed level at all times, but such rigidity is rarely seen and central banks usually adjust interest rates in the short run to meet other goals. For example, if the world real interest rate is $r^* = 2.5\%$, and the country's long-run inflation target is 2%, then its long-run nominal interest rate ought to be on average equal to 4.5% (because 2.5 = 4.5 minus 2). This would be termed the *neutral* level of the nominal interest rate. But in the short run, the central bank might use some discretion to set interest rates above or below this neutral level.

The Choice of a Nominal Anchor and Its Implications Under the assumptions we have made, any of the three nominal anchor choices are valid. If a particular long-run inflation objective is to be met, then, all else equal, the first equation says it will be consistent with one particular rate of depreciation; the second equation says it will be consistent with one particular rate of money supply growth; the third equation says it will be consistent with one particular rate of interest. But if policy makers announced targets for all three variables, they would be able to match all three consistently only by chance. Two observations follow.

First, using more than one target may be problematic. Under a fixed exchange rate regime, policy makers cannot employ any target other than the exchange rate. However, they may be able to use a mix of different targets

N E T W O R K

Visit the websites of some central banks around the world, for example, the U.S. Federal Reserve (http://www.federalreserve.gov/) and the European Central Bank (http://www.ecb.int/). Read their main statements of policy. Try to find out what their policy goals are *in the long run*. Who sets them? Is there more than one goal? What about a nominal anchor—is controlling inflation a long-run goal? If so, what policy is used to try to ensure that the long-run inflation goal will be met? In the short run, is the main tool they use for implementing their policy the quantity of money, the exchange rate, or the interest rate?

SIDE BAR

Nominal Anchors in Theory and Practice

An appreciation of the importance of nominal anchors has transformed monetary policy making and inflation performance throughout the global economy in recent decades.

In the 1970s, most of the world was struggling with high inflation. An economic slowdown prompted central banks everywhere to loosen monetary policy. In advanced countries, a move to floating exchange rates allowed great freedom for them to loosen their monetary policy. Developing countries had already proven vulnerable to high inflation and now many of these countries were exposed to even worse inflation. Those who were pegged to major currencies imported high inflation via PPP. Those who weren't pegged struggled to find a credible nominal anchor as they faced economic downturns of their own. High oil prices everywhere contributed to inflationary pressure.

In the 1980s, inflationary pressure continued in many developed countries, and in many developing countries high levels of inflation, and even hyperinflations, were not uncommon. Governments were forced to respond to public demands for a more stable inflation environment. In the 1990s, policies designed to create effective nominal anchors were put in place in many countries.

One study found that the use of explicit targets, whether for the exchange rate, money, or inflation, grew markedly in the 1990s, replacing regimes in which there had previously been no explicit nominal anchor:

- The number of countries in the study with exchange rate targets increased from 30 to 47. The number with money targets increased from 18 to 39. The number with inflation targets increased most dramatically, almost sevenfold, from 8 to 54.

- Many countries had more than one target in use: in 1998 55% of the sample announced an explicit target (or monitoring range) for more than one of the exchange rate, money, and inflation.*

Most, but not all, of those policies have turned out to be credible, too, thanks to political developments in many countries that have fostered **central-bank independence.** Independent central banks stand apart from the interference of politicians: they have operational freedom to try to achieve the inflation target, and they may even play a role in setting that target.

Overall, these efforts are judged to have achieved at least some success, although in many countries inflation had already been brought down substantially in the early to mid-1980s before inflation targets and institutional changes were implemented.

Table 3-2 shows a steady decline in average levels of inflation since the early 1980s. The lowest levels of inflation are seen in the advanced economies, although developing countries have also started to make some limited progress. In the industrial countries, central-bank independence is now commonplace (it was not in the 1970s), but in developing countries it is still relatively rare.

TABLE 3-2

Global Disinflation Cross-country data from 1980 to 2004 show the gradual reduction in the annual rate of inflation around the world. This disinflation process began in the rich, advanced economies in the early 1980s. The poorer emerging markets and developing countries suffered from even higher rates of inflation, although these finally began to fall in the 1990s.

	Annual Inflation Rate (%)				
	1980–1984	1985–1989	1990–1994	1995–1999	2000–2004
World	14.1	15.5	30.4	8.4	3.9
Advanced economies	8.7	3.9	3.8	2.0	1.8
Emerging markets and developing countries	31.4	48.0	53.2	13.1	5.6

Source: Kenneth Rogoff, 2003, "Globalization and Global Disinflation," Economic Review, Federal Reserve Bank of Kansas City, IV, 45–78.

* Gabriel Sterne, 1999, "The Use of Explicit Targets for Monetary Policy: Practical Experiences of 91 Economies in the 1990s," Bank of England Quarterly Bulletin, 39(3), August, 272–281.

TABLE 3-3

Exchange Rate Regimes and Nominal Anchors This table illustrates the possible exchange rate regimes that are consistent with various types of nominal anchors. Countries that are dollarized or in a currency union have a "superfixed" exchange rate target. Pegs, bands, and crawls also target the exchange rate. Managed floats have no preset path for the exchange rate, which allows other targets to be employed. Countries that float freely or independently are judged to pay no serious attention to exchange rate targets; if they have anchors, they will involve monetary targets or inflation targets with an interest rate policy. The countries with "freely falling" exchange rates have no serious target and have high rates of inflation and depreciation. It should be noted that many countries engage in implicit targeting (e.g., inflation targeting) without announcing an explicit target and that some countries may use a mix of more than one target.

	Compatible Exchange Rate Regimes				
Type of Nominal Anchor	**Countries Without a Currency of Their Own**	**Pegs/ Bands/Crawls**	**Managed Floating**	**Freely Floating**	**Freely Falling (rapid depreciation)**
Exchange rate target	✔	✔	✔		
Money supply target			✔	✔	
Inflation target (plus interest rate policy)			✔	✔	
None				✔	✔

by adopting an intermediate regime, such as a managed exchange rate with limited flexibility. Table 3-3 shows how the choice of a target as a nominal anchor affects the choice of exchange rate regime. Obviously, these are not independent choices. But a variety of choices do exist. Thus: *Nominal anchoring is possible with a variety of exchange rate regimes.*

Second, whatever target choice is made, a country that commits to a target as a way of nominal anchoring is committing itself to set future money supplies and/or interest rates in such a way as to meet the target. Only one such policy choice will be compatible with the target. Thus: *A country with a nominal anchor sacrifices monetary policy autonomy in the long run.* (See **Side Bar: Nominal Anchors in Theory and Practice.**)

6 Conclusions

This chapter emphasized the determinants of exchange rates in the long run using the monetary approach. We employed purchasing power parity and a simple monetary model (the quantity theory) to study an equilibrium in which goods are arbitraged and prices are flexible. Under these assumptions, in the home country, changes in the money supply pass through into proportional changes in the price level and the exchange rate.

We also found that uncovered interest parity and purchasing power parity implied that real interest rates are equalized across countries. This helped us develop a monetary model that was more complex—and more realistic—because it allowed money demand to fluctuate in response to changes in the interest rate. In that setting, increases in money growth lead to higher inflation and a higher nominal interest rate and, hence, via decreases in money demand, to even higher price levels. Still, the same basic intuition holds, and one-time changes in the money supply still lead to proportionate changes in prices and exchange rates.

The monetary approach to exchange rates provides a basis for certain kinds of forecasting and policy analysis using the flexible-price model in the long run. But such forecasts matter even in the short run because today's spot exchange rate depends, like all asset prices, on the exchange rate expected to prevail in the future. To make these connections clear, in the next chapter we bring ideas from Chapters 2 and 3 together to form a complete model of the exchange rate.

KEY POINTS

1. Purchasing power parity (PPP) implies that the exchange rate should equal the relative price level in the two countries, and the real exchange rate should equal 1.

2. Evidence for PPP is weak in the short run and more favorable in the long run. In the short run, deviations are common and changes in the real exchange rate do occur. The failure of PPP in the short run is primarily the result of price stickiness, and market frictions and imperfections that limit arbitrage.

3. A simple monetary model (the quantity theory) explains price levels in terms of money supply levels and real income levels. Because PPP can explain exchange rates in terms of price levels, the two together can be used to develop a monetary approach to the exchange rate.

4. If we can forecast money supply and income, we can use the monetary approach to forecast the level of the exchange rate at any time in the future. However, the monetary approach is valid only under the assumption that prices are flexible. This assumption is more likely to hold in the long run, so the short-run forecast is not reliable. Evidence for PPP and the monetary approach is more favorable in the long run.

5. PPP theory, combined with uncovered interest parity, leads to the strong implications of the Fisher effect (interest differentials between countries should equal inflation differentials). The Fisher effect says that changes in local inflation rates pass through one for one into changes in local nominal interest rates. The result implies real interest parity (expected real interest rates should be equalized across countries). Because these results rest on PPP, they should be viewed only as long-run results, and the evidence is somewhat favorable.

6. We can augment the simple monetary model (quantity theory) to allow for the demand for real money balances to decrease as the nominal interest rate rises. This leads to the general monetary model. Its predictions are similar to those of the simple model, except that a one-time rise in money growth rates leads to a one-time rise in inflation, which leads to a one-time drop in real money demand, which in turn causes a one-time jump in the price level and the exchange rate.

7. The monetary approach to exchange rate determination in the long run has implications for economic policy. Policy makers and the public generally prefer a low-inflation environment. Various policies based on exchange rates, money growth, or interest rates have been proposed as nominal anchors. Recent decades have seen a worldwide decline in inflation thanks to the explicit recognition of the need for nominal anchors.

KEY TERMS

monetary approach to exchange rates, p. 70

law of one price (LOOP), p. 71

purchasing power parity (PPP), p. 71

absolute PPP, p. 73

real exchange rate, p. 73

real depreciation, p. 73

real appreciation, p. 73

undervalued, p. 74

overvalued, p. 74

inflation, p. 74

relative PPP, p. 76

PROBLEMS

1. Suppose that two countries, Vietnam and Côte d'Ivoire, produce coffee. The currency unit used in Vietnam is the dong (VND). Côte d'Ivoire is a member of Communaute Financiere Africaine (CFA), a currency union of West African countries that use the CFA franc (XOF). In Vietnam, coffee sells for 5,000 dong (VND) per pound of coffee. The exchange rate is 30 VND per 1 CFA franc, $E_{VND/XOF} = 30$.

   a. If the law of one price holds, what is the price of coffee in Côte d'Ivoire, measured in CFA francs?

   b. Assume the price of coffee in Côte d'Ivoire is actually 160 CFA francs per pound of coffee. Compute the relative price of coffee in Côte d'Ivoire versus Vietnam. Where will coffee traders buy coffee? Where will they sell coffee in this case? How will these transactions affect the price of coffee in Vietnam? In Côte d'Ivoire?

2. Consider each of the following goods and services. For each, identify whether the law of one price will hold, and state whether the relative price $q^g_{Foreign/US}$ is greater than, less than, or equal to 1. Explain your answer in terms of the assumptions we make when using the law of one price.

   a. Rice traded freely in the United States and Canada

   b. Sugar traded in the United States and Mexico; the U.S. government imposes a quota on sugar imports into the United States

   c. The McDonald's Big Mac sold in the United States and Japan

   d. Haircuts in the United States and the United Kingdom

3. Use the table that follows to answer this question. Suppose the cost of the market basket in the United States is $P_{US} = \$190$. Check to see whether purchasing power parity (PPP) holds for each of the countries listed, and determine whether we should expect a real appreciation or real depreciation for each country (relative to the United States) in the long run. For the answer, create a table similar to the one shown and fill in the blank cells. (Hint: Use a spreadsheet application such as Excel.)

Country (currency measured in FX units)	Per $, $E_{FX/\$}$	Price of Market Basket (in FX)	Price of U.S. Basket in FX (P_{us} times $E_{FX/\$}$)	Real Exchange Rate, q	Does PPP Hold? (yes/no)	Is FX Currency Overvalued or Undervalued?	Is FX Currency Expected to Have Real Appreciation or Depreciation?
Brazil (real)	2.1893	520					
Cyprus (Cy£)	0.45	75					
India (rupee)	46.6672	12,000					
Mexico (peso)	11.0131	1,800					
South Africa (rand)	6.9294	800					
Zimbabwe (ZW$)	101,347	4,000,000					

4. Table 3-1 in the text shows the percentage undervaluation or overvaluation in the Big Mac, based on exchange rates in February 2007. Suppose purchasing power parity holds in the long run, so that these deviations would be expected to disappear. Suppose the local currency prices of the Big Mac remained unchanged. Exchange rates in June 2007 were as follows:

Country	Per U.S. $
Australia (A$)	1.20
Brazil (real)	2.02
Canada (C$)	1.12
Denmark (krone)	5.49
Eurozone (euro)	0.736
Japan (yen)	118.47
Mexico (peso)	10.97
Sweden (krona)	6.77

Based on the these data and Table 3-1, for which countries were the PPP-based exchange rate predictions derived from the Big Mac Index correct? For which were they incorrect? How might you explain the failure of the Big Mac Index to correctly predict the change in the nominal exchange rate between February and June 2007?

5. You are given the following information. The current dollar-pound exchange rate is $2 per pound. A U.S. basket that costs $100 would cost $120 in the United Kingdom. For the next year, the Fed is predicted to keep U.S. inflation at 2% and the Bank of England is predicted to keep U.K. inflation at 3%. The speed of convergence to absolute PPP is 15% per year.

a. What is the expected U.S. minus U.K. inflation differential for the coming year?

b. What is the current U.S. real exchange rate $q_{UK/US}$ with the United Kingdom?

c. How much is the dollar overvalued/undervalued?

d. What do you predict the U.S. real exchange rate with the United Kingdom will be in one year's time?

e. What is the expected rate of real depreciation for the United States (versus the United Kingdom)?

f. What is the expected rate of nominal depreciation for the United States (versus the United Kingdom)?

g. What do you predict will be the dollar price of one pound a year from now?

6. Describe how each of the following factors might explain why PPP is a better guide for exchange rate movements in the long run, versus the short run: (i) transactions costs, (ii) nontraded goods, (iii) imperfect competition, (iv) price stickiness. As markets become increasingly integrated, do you suspect PPP will become a more useful guide in the future? Why or why not?

7. Consider two countries: Japan and Korea. In 1996 Japan experienced relatively slow output growth (1%), while Korea had relatively robust output growth (6%). Suppose the Bank of Japan allowed the money supply to grow by 2% each year, while the Bank of Korea chose to maintain relatively high money growth of 12% per year.

For the following questions, use the simple monetary model (where L is constant). You will find it easiest to treat Korea as the home country and Japan as the foreign country.

a. What is the inflation rate in Korea? In Japan?

b. What is the expected rate of depreciation in the Korean won relative to the Japanese yen?

c. Suppose the Bank of Korea increases the money growth rate from 12% to 15%. If nothing in Japan changes, what is the new inflation rate in Korea?

d. Using time series diagrams, illustrate how this increase in the money growth rate affects the money supply M_K, Korea's interest rate, prices P_K, real money supply, and $E_{won/¥}$ over time. (Plot each variable on the vertical axis and time on the horizontal axis.)

e. Suppose the Bank of Korea wants to maintain an exchange rate peg with the Japanese yen. What money growth rate would the Bank of Korea have to choose to keep the value of the won fixed relative to the yen?

f. Suppose the Bank of Korea sought to implement policy that would cause the Korean won to appreciate relative to the Japanese yen. What ranges of the money growth rate (assuming positive values) would allow the Bank of Korea to achieve this objective?

8. This question uses the general monetary model, where L is no longer assumed constant, and money demand is inversely related to the nominal interest rate. Consider the same scenario described in the beginning of the previous question. In addition, the bank deposits in Japan pay 3% interest, $i_¥ = 3\%$.

   a. Compute the interest rate paid on Korean deposits.

   b. Using the definition of the real interest rate (nominal interest rate adjusted for inflation), show that the real interest rate in Korea is equal to the real interest rate in Japan. (Note that the inflation rates you computed in the previous question will be the same in this question.)

   c. Suppose the Bank of Korea increases the money growth rate from 12% to 15% and the inflation rate rises proportionately (one for one) with this increase. If the nominal interest rate in Japan remains unchanged, what happens to the interest rate paid on Korean deposits?

   d. Using time series diagrams, illustrate how this increase in the money growth rate affects the money supply, M_K; Korea's interest rate; prices, P_K; real money supply; and $E_{won/¥}$ over time. (Plot each variable on the vertical axis and time on the horizontal axis.)

9. Both advanced economies and developing countries have experienced a decrease in inflation since the 1980s (see Table 3-2 in the text). This question considers how the choice of policy regime has influenced this global disinflation. Use the monetary model to answer this question.

   a. The Swiss Central Bank currently targets its money growth rate to achieve policy objectives. Suppose Switzerland has output growth of 3% and money growth of 8% each year. What is Switzerland's inflation rate in this case? Describe how the Swiss Central Bank could achieve an inflation rate of 2% in the long run through the use of a nominal anchor.

   b. Like the Federal Reserve, the Reserve Bank of New Zealand uses an interest rate target. Suppose the Reserve Bank of New Zealand maintains a 6% interest rate target and the world *real* interest rate is 1.5%. What is the New Zealand inflation rate in the long run? In 1997 New Zealand adopted a policy agreement that required the bank to maintain an inflation rate no higher than 2.5%. What interest rate targets would achieve this objective?

   c. The National Bank of Slovakia maintains an exchange rate band relative to the euro. This is a prerequisite for joining the Eurozone. The Slovak Republic must keep its exchange rate within ±15% of the central parity of 35.4424 koruna per euro. Compute the exchange rate values corresponding to the upper and lower edges of this band. Suppose PPP holds. If Eurozone inflation is currently 2% per year and inflation in Slovakia is 5%, compute the rate of depreciation of the koruna. Will Slovakia be able to maintain the band requirement? For how long? Does your answer depend on where in the band the exchange rate currently sits? A primary objective of the European Central Bank is price stability (low inflation) in the current and future Eurozone. Is an exchange rate band a necessary or sufficient condition for the attainment of this objective?

10. Several countries that have experienced hyperinflation adopt dollarization as a way to control domestic inflation. For example, Ecuador has used the U.S. dollar as its domestic currency since 2000. What does dollarization imply about the exchange rate between Ecuador and the United States? Why might countries experiencing hyperinflation adopt dollarization? Why might they do this rather than just fixing their exchange rate?

11. You are the central banker for a country that is considering the adoption of a new nominal anchor. When you take the position as chairperson, the inflation rate is 4% and your position as the central bank chairperson requires that you achieve a 2.5% inflation target within the next year. The economy's growth in real output is currently 3%. The world real interest rate is currently 1.5%. The currency used in your country is the lira. *Assume prices are flexible.*

a. Why is having a nominal anchor important for you to achieve the inflation target? What is the drawback of using a nominal anchor?

b. What is the growth rate of the money supply in this economy? If you choose to adopt a money supply target, which money supply growth rate will allow you to meet your inflation target?

c. Suppose the inflation rate in the United States is currently 2% and you adopt an exchange rate target relative to the U.S. dol-lar. Compute the percent appreciation/depreciation in the lira needed for you to achieve your inflation target. Will the lira appreciate or depreciate relative to the U.S. dollar?

d. Your final option is to achieve your inflation target using interest rate policy. Using the Fisher equation, compute the current nominal interest rate in your country. What nominal interest rate will allow you to achieve the inflation target?

4

Exchange Rates II: The Asset Approach in the Short Run

The long run is a misleading guide to current affairs. In the long run we are all dead. Economists set themselves too easy, too useless a task if in tempestuous seasons they can only tell us that when the storm is past the ocean is flat again.

John Maynard Keynes, *A Tract on Monetary Reform,* 1923

As we saw in the last chapter, the monetary approach to exchange rates may work in the long run, but it is a poor guide to what happens in the short run. To recap this distinction, let's return to the Canada-U.S. comparison with which we opened the last chapter, only this time we'll look at what has been happening in the short run.

From March 2005 to March 2006, the Canadian price level (measured by the consumer price index) rose from 126.5 to 129.3, an increase of 2.2%. The U.S. price level rose from 193.3 to 199.8, an increase of 3.4%. U.S. prices therefore increased 1.2% more than Canadian prices. But over the same period, the loonie (Canadian dollar) rose in value from $0.8267 to $0.8568, an appreciation of 3.6%.[1]

Since Canadian baskets cost 2.2% more in loonie terms, and each loonie cost 3.6% more in U.S. dollar terms, the change in the U.S. dollar price of the Canadian basket was approximately the sum of these two changes, or about 5.8%. But over the same period, the U.S. dollar price of U.S. baskets rose only 3.4%. Taking the difference, Canadian baskets ended up 2.4% more expensive than U.S. baskets, meaning that the U.S. *real* exchange rate with Canada rose by 2.4%, a real depreciation. This pattern was not unusual. In the previous year from March

---

[1] Data for this example are taken from the Bank of Canada and U.S. Bureau of Labor Statistics.

2004 to March 2005, the real depreciation had been even larger, at 7.5%, so over two years Canadian goods rose in price by about 10% compared with U.S. goods.

Evidence of this kind suggests that substantial deviations from purchasing power parity (PPP) occur in the short run: the same basket of goods generally does not cost the same everywhere. These short-run failures of the monetary approach prompted economists to formulate an alternative theory to explain exchange rates in the short run: the **asset approach to exchange rates,** the subject of this chapter.

The asset approach is based on the idea that currencies are assets. The price of the asset in this case is the spot exchange rate, the price of one unit of foreign exchange. Here we can draw on insights first seen in Chapter 2, where we saw how arbitrage plays a major role in the forex market by forcing the expected returns of two assets in different currencies to be equal. This insight led us to derive the uncovered interest parity (UIP) condition. Because it characterizes a forex market equilibrium, UIP will be further explored and extensively applied in this chapter.

The asset approach differs from the monetary approach in its time frame and assumptions. In the monetary approach, we envisage a long run that takes several years; in the asset approach, we are typically thinking of a short run of a matter of weeks or months, or perhaps a year or so at most. In the monetary approach, we treat goods prices as perfectly flexible, an assumption that might be plausible in the long run; in the asset approach, we assume that goods prices are sticky, an assumption that might be appropriate in the short run. Each theory is valid but only in the right context. Thus, rather than supplanting the monetary approach, the asset approach complements it, and it provides us with the final building blocks necessary to construct a complete theory of exchange rates.

All of our theoretical building blocks assume that exchange rates are determined by market forces in the goods, money, and foreign exchange markets, so we know they apply when the exchange rate floats, and the authorities leave it to find its own market-determined level. Can our theory tell us anything about fixed exchange rates? Yes. At the end of the chapter, we see how the same theoretical framework can be applied to a fixed exchange rate regime.

1 Exchange Rates and Interest Rates in the Short Run: UIP and FX Market Equilibrium

We now recap the crucial equilibrium condition for the forex (or FX) market. In Chapter 2, we considered a U.S. investor with two alternative investment strategies: a one-year domestic investment in a U.S. dollar account with an interest rate $i_\$$, or a one-year overseas investment in a euro account with an interest rate $i_\unicode{x20AC}$. Let us recap the essentials.

Risky Arbitrage

As before, we assume the Home country is the United States (US); the Foreign country is Europe (EUR, meaning the Eurozone). Appealing to the idea of risky arbitrage, we argued that the foreign exchange market would be in equilibrium only if there were no expected differences in the rates of return offered by the two types of investment. As we saw in the approximate uncovered interest parity condition—Equation (2–3), and repeated in this section as Equation (4-1)—this outcome requires that the dollar rate of return on the Home investment (the dollar deposit) equal the expected dollar rate of return on the Foreign investment (the euro deposit):

(4-1)
$$ \underbrace{i_\$}_{\substack{\text{Interest rate} \\ \text{on dollar deposits} \\ = \\ \text{Dollar rate of return} \\ \text{on dollar deposits}}} = \underbrace{\underbrace{i_\euro}_{\substack{\text{Interest rate} \\ \text{on euro deposits}}} + \underbrace{\frac{(E^e_{\$/\euro} - E_{\$/\euro})}{E_{\$/\euro}}}_{\substack{\text{Expected rate of} \\ \text{depreciation of the dollar}}}}_{\substack{\text{Expected dollar rate of return} \\ \text{on euro deposits}}}. $$

where each interest rate is an annual rate, $E_{\$/\euro}$ is today's exchange rate (the spot rate), and $E^e_{\$/\euro}$ is the expected future exchange rate that will prevail one year ahead.

The uncovered interest parity (UIP) equation is the **fundamental equation of the asset approach to exchange rates,** and from now on, we will use it in the form of Equation (4-1). As we have seen, by rearranging this equation, we can solve it for the spot exchange rate, provided we know all of the other variables. Thus, the asset approach employs the UIP equation as a way to determine today's spot exchange rate, as illustrated in Figure 4-1. Hence, the theory is useful only if we can assume knowledge of interest rates and the future expected exchange rate. Where does that knowledge come from?

Exchange Rate Expectations First, we need a forecast of the future level of the exchange rate $E^e_{\$/\euro}$. The asset approach itself does not provide the answer, so we must look elsewhere. But there is an obvious forecasting method available to us right now: we can form expectations of the future exchange rate using the long-run monetary approach to the exchange rate presented in Chapter 3. We can now see how the asset approach and monetary approach fit together.

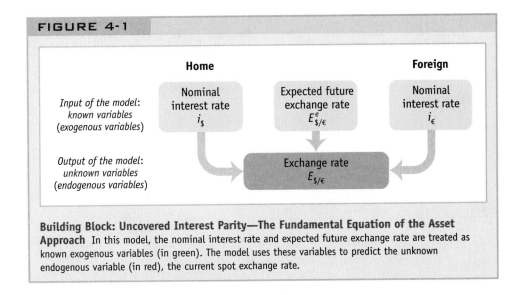

FIGURE 4-1

Building Block: Uncovered Interest Parity—The Fundamental Equation of the Asset Approach In this model, the nominal interest rate and expected future exchange rate are treated as known exogenous variables (in green). The model uses these variables to predict the unknown endogenous variable (in red), the current spot exchange rate.

Short-Term Interest Rates The other assumption in the asset approach is that we know today's interest rates on deposit accounts in each country, the dollar interest rate $i_\$$, and the euro account interest rate $i_€$. These short-term interest rates are observable by market participants. But how are these interest rates determined, and, in particular, what is their relation to economic policy? In the next section, we explore that question to develop a fuller understanding of how exchange rates are determined.

Equilibrium in the FX Market: An Example

To explore the concepts we've just studied, let's work through a numerical example to show how equilibrium in the foreign exchange market is determined.

Suppose we have made a forecast (using Chapter 3's monetary model) that the expected future exchange rate $E^e_{\$/€}$ (in one year's time) is 1.224 dollars per euro. Suppose the current European interest rate $i_€$ is 3%, and the current U.S. interest rate $i_\$$ is 5%.

For various values of the spot exchange rate $E_{\$/€}$, Table 4-1 calculates the domestic rate of return and expected foreign rate of return in U.S. dollars for a U.S. investor. (Remember that 5% = 0.05, 3% = 0.03, and so on.) In the table, the foreign returns have two components, one due to the

TABLE 4-1

Interest Rates, Exchange Rates, Expected Returns, and FX Market Equilibrium: A Numerical Example The foreign exchange (FX) market is in equilibrium when the domestic and foreign returns are equal. In this example, the dollar interest rate is 5%, the euro interest rate is 3%, and the expected future exchange rate (one year ahead) is $E^e_{\$/€} = 1.224$ $/€. The equilibrium is highlighted in bold type, where both returns are 5% in annual dollar terms. Figure 4-2 plots the domestic and foreign returns (columns 1 and 6) against the spot exchange rate (column 3). Figures are rounded in this table.

(1)	(2)	(3)	(4)	(5)	(6) = (2) + (5)
Interest Rate on Dollar Deposits (annual)	Interest Rate on Euro Deposits (annual)	Spot Exchange Rate (today)	Expected Future Exchange Rate (in 1 year)	Expected Euro Appreciation against Dollar (in 1 year)	Expected Dollar Return on Euro Deposits (annual)
Domestic Return ($)					Foreign Expected Return ($)
$i_\$$	$i_€$	$E_{\$/€}$	$E^e_{\$/€}$	$\dfrac{E^e_{\$/€} - E_{\$/€}}{E_{\$/€}}$	$i_€ + \dfrac{E^e_{\$/€} - E_{\$/€}}{E_{\$/€}}$
0.05	0.03	1.16	1.224	0.0552	0.0852
0.05	0.03	1.18	1.224	0.0373	0.0673
0.05	**0.03**	**1.20**	**1.224**	**0.02**	**0.05**
0.05	0.03	1.22	1.224	0.0033	0.0333
0.05	0.03	1.24	1.224	−0.0129	0.0171

Market equilibrium

European interest rate $i_€$ and the other due to the expected rate of depreciation of the dollar, as in Equation (4-1).

Figure 4-2 presents an **FX market diagram,** a graphical representation of the forex market. We plot the expected domestic and foreign returns (on the vertical axis) against today's spot exchange rate (on the horizontal axis). The domestic dollar return (DR) is fixed at 5% = 0.05 and is independent of the spot exchange rate. It is just the Home nominal interest rate.

The foreign expected dollar return (FR) depends on the spot exchange rate according to Equation (4-1) and as shown in Table 4-1. For example, we see from the table that a spot exchange rate of 1.224 implies a foreign return of 3% = 0.03. Hence, the point (1.224, 0.03) is on the FR line, as shown. This is the special case in which there is no expected depreciation (spot and expected future exchange rates are equal to 1.224), so the foreign return equals the Foreign interest rate, 3%.

More generally, we see that the foreign return falls as the spot exchange rate $E_{\$/€}$ increases, all else equal. This is clear mathematically from the right side of Equation (4-1). The intuition is as follows. If the dollar depreciates today, $E_{\$/€}$ rises, and $1 moved into a European account is worth fewer euros today; this in turn leaves fewer euro proceeds in a year's time after euro interest has accrued; and if expectations are fixed so that the future euro–dollar exchange rate $E^e_{\$/€}$ is known and unchanged, then those fewer future euros will be worth fewer future dollars. Thus, the foreign return (in dollars) goes down as $E_{\$/€}$ rises, *all else equal*. The FR curve is downward sloping.

What is the equilibrium level of the spot exchange rate? According to Table 4-1, the equilibrium exchange rate is 1.20 $/€. Only then are domestic returns and foreign returns equalized. To illustrate the solution graphically, domestic and foreign returns are plotted in Figure 4-2. The FX market is in equilibrium, and foreign and domestic returns are equal, at the point at which the FR and DR curves intersect. This is labeled as point 1.

FIGURE 4-2

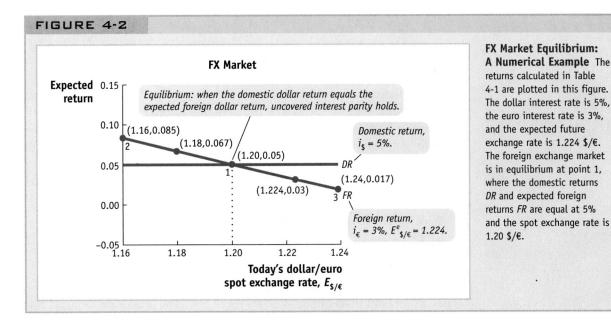

FX Market Equilibrium: A Numerical Example The returns calculated in Table 4-1 are plotted in this figure. The dollar interest rate is 5%, the euro interest rate is 3%, and the expected future exchange rate is 1.224 $/€. The foreign exchange market is in equilibrium at point 1, where the domestic returns DR and expected foreign returns FR are equal at 5% and the spot exchange rate is 1.20 $/€.

Adjustment to FX Market Equilibrium

Our FX market equilibrium condition and its graphical representation should now be clear. But how is this equilibrium reached? It turns out that arbitrage automatically pushes the level of the exchange rate toward its equilibrium value.

To see this, suppose that the market is initially out of equilibrium, with the spot $E_{\$/€}$ exchange rate at a level too low, so that the foreign return—the right-hand side of Equation (4-1)—exceeds the domestic return (the left-hand side).

At point 2 in Figure 4-2, foreign returns are well above domestic returns. With the spot exchange rate of 1.16 $/€ and (from Table 4-1) an expected future exchange rate as high as 1.224 $/€, the euro is expected to *appreciate* by $5.5\% = 0.055$ $[= (1.224/1.16) - 1]$. In addition, euros earn at an interest rate of 3%, for a whopping foreign expected return of $5.5\% + 3\% = 8.5\% = 0.085$, which far exceeds the domestic return of 5%. At point 2, in other words, the euro offers too high a return; equivalently, it is too cheap. Traders want to sell dollars and buy euros. These market pressures bid up the price of a euro: the dollar starts to depreciate against the euro, causing $E_{\$/€}$ to rise, which moves foreign and domestic returns into equality and forces the exchange rate back toward equilibrium at point 1.

The same idea applies to a situation in which the spot exchange rate $E_{\$/€}$ is initially too high. At point 3 in Figure 4-2, foreign and domestic returns are not equal: the exchange rate is 1.24 $/€. Given where the exchange rate is expected to be in a year's time (1.224 $/€), paying a high price of 1.24 $/€ today means the euro is expected to *depreciate* by about $1.3\% = 0.013$ $[= (1.224/1.24) - 1]$. If euro deposits pay 3%, and euros are expected to depreciate 1.3%, this makes for a net foreign return of just 1.7%, well below the domestic return of $5\% = 0.05$. In other words, at point 3, the euro offers too low a return; equivalently, it is too expensive today. Traders will want to sell euros.

Only at point 1 is the euro trading at a price at which the foreign return equals the domestic return. At point 1, the euro is neither too cheap nor too expensive—its price is just right for uncovered interest parity to hold, for arbitrage to cease, and for the FX market to be in equilibrium.

Changes in Domestic and Foreign Returns and FX Market Equilibrium

When economic conditions change, the two curves depicting domestic and foreign returns shift. In the case of the domestic return curve, the movements are fairly transparent. This curve is a horizontal line that intersects the vertical axis at a level equal to the domestic interest rate. Shifts in the foreign returns curve are a bit more complicated.

To gain greater familiarity with the model, let's see how the FX market example shown in Figure 4-2 responds to three separate shocks:

- A higher domestic interest rate, $i_\$ = 7\%$
- A lower foreign interest rate, $i_€ = 1\%$
- A lower expected future exchange rate, $E^e_{\$/€} = 1.20$ $/€

These three cases are shown in Figure 4-3, panels (a), (b), and (c). In all three cases, the shocks make dollar deposits more attractive than euro deposits, but

FIGURE 4-3

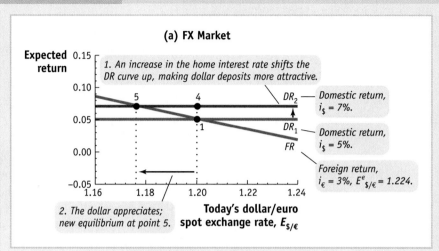

(a) FX Market

1. An increase in the home interest rate shifts the DR curve up, making dollar deposits more attractive.

Domestic return, $i_\$ = 7\%$.
Domestic return, $i_\$ = 5\%$.
Foreign return, $i_\epsilon = 3\%$, $E^e_{\$/\epsilon} = 1.224$.

2. The dollar appreciates; new equilibrium at point 5.

Today's dollar/euro spot exchange rate, $E_{\$/\epsilon}$

(a) A Change in the Home Interest Rate A rise in the dollar interest rate from 5% to 7% increases domestic returns, shifting the DR curve up from DR_1 to DR_2. At the initial equilibrium exchange rate of 1.20 $/€ on DR_2, domestic returns are above foreign returns at point 4. Dollar deposits are more attractive and the dollar appreciates from 1.20 $/€ to 1.177 $/€. The new equilibrium is at point 5.

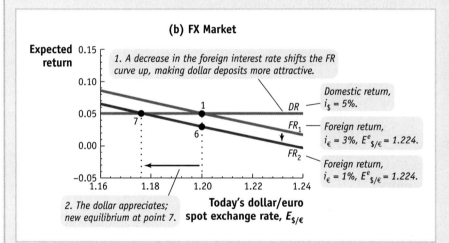

(b) FX Market

1. A decrease in the foreign interest rate shifts the FR curve up, making dollar deposits more attractive.

Domestic return, $i_\$ = 5\%$.
Foreign return, $i_\epsilon = 3\%$, $E^e_{\$/\epsilon} = 1.224$.
Foreign return, $i_\epsilon = 1\%$, $E^e_{\$/\epsilon} = 1.224$.

2. The dollar appreciates; new equilibrium at point 7.

Today's dollar/euro spot exchange rate, $E_{\$/\epsilon}$

(b) A Change in the Foreign Interest Rate A fall in the euro interest rate from 3% to 1% lowers foreign expected dollar returns, shifting the FR curve down from FR_1 to FR_2. At the initial equilibrium exchange rate of 1.20 $/€ on FR_2, foreign returns are below domestic returns at point 6. Dollar deposits are more attractive and the dollar appreciates from 1.20 $/€ to 1.177 $/€. The new equilibrium is at point 7.

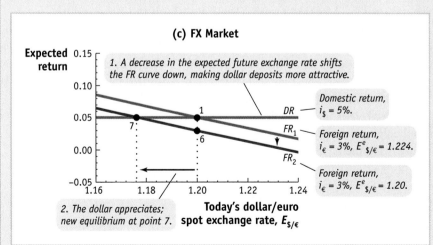

(c) FX Market

1. A decrease in the expected future exchange rate shifts the FR curve down, making dollar deposits more attractive.

Domestic return, $i_\$ = 5\%$.
Foreign return, $i_\epsilon = 3\%$, $E^e_{\$/\epsilon} = 1.224$.
Foreign return, $i_\epsilon = 3\%$, $E^e_{\$/\epsilon} = 1.20$.

2. The dollar appreciates; new equilibrium at point 7.

Today's dollar/euro spot exchange rate, $E_{\$/\epsilon}$

(c) A Change in the Expected Future Exchange Rate A fall in the expected future exchange rate from 1.224 to 1.20 lowers foreign expected dollar returns, shifting the FR curve down from FR_1 to FR_2. At the initial equilibrium exchange rate of 1.20 $/€ on FR_2, foreign returns are below domestic returns at point 6. Dollar deposits are more attractive and the dollar appreciates from 1.20 $/€ to 1.177 $/€. The new equilibrium is at point 7.

for different reasons. Regardless of the reason, however, the shocks we examine all lead to dollar appreciations.

A Change in the Domestic Interest Rate In Figure 4-3, panel (a), when $i_\$$ rises to 7%, the domestic return is increased by 2% so the domestic return curve DR shifts up by 2% = 0.02 from DR_1 to DR_2. The foreign return is unaffected. Now, at the old equilibrium spot exchange rate of 1.20 $/€, the domestic return (point 4) is higher than the foreign return. Traders sell euros and buy dollars; the dollar appreciates to 1.177 $/€ at the new equilibrium, point 5. The foreign return and domestic return are equal once again and UIP holds once more.

A Change in the Foreign Interest Rate In Figure 4-3, panel (b), when $i_€$ falls to 1%, euro deposits now pay a lower interest rate (1% versus 3%). The foreign return curve FR shifts down by 2% = 0.02 from FR_1 to FR_2. The domestic return is unaffected. Now, at the old equilibrium rate of 1.20 $/€, the foreign return (point 6) is lower than the domestic return. Traders sell euros and buy dollars; the dollar appreciates to 1.177 $/€ at the new equilibrium, point 7, and UIP holds once more.

A Change in the Expected Future Exchange Rate In Figure 4-3, panel (c), a decrease in the expected future exchange rate $E^e_{\$/€}$ lowers the foreign return because a euro is expected to be worth fewer dollars in the future. The foreign return curve FR shifts down from FR_1 to FR_2. The domestic return is unaffected. At the old equilibrium rate of 1.20 $/€, the foreign return (point 6) is lower than the domestic return. Again, traders sell euros and buy dollars, causing the dollar to appreciate and the spot exchange rate to fall to 1.177 $/€. The new equilibrium is point 7.

Summary

The FX market diagram, with its representation of domestic returns and foreign returns, is central to our analysis in this chapter and later in the book. Ensure that you have an intuitive grasp of the ways in which domestic returns depend on $i_\$$ and foreign returns depend on both the Foreign interest rate $i_€$ *and* the expected future exchange rate $E^e_{\$/€}$. Try to remember how any change that raises (lowers) the foreign return relative to the domestic return makes euro deposits more (less) attractive to investors, so that traders will buy (sell) euro deposits, pushing the FX market toward a new equilibrium at which the dollar will have depreciated (appreciated) against the euro.

To check your understanding, you might wish to rework the three examples and the figures for the cases of a *decrease* in $i_\$$, an *increase* in $i_€$, and an *increase* in $E^e_{\$/€}$; constructing the equivalent of Table 4-1 for each case may also prove helpful.

2 Interest Rates in the Short Run: Money Market Equilibrium

The previous section has laid out the essentials of the asset approach to exchange rates. Figure 4-1 sums up the uncovered interest parity relationship at the heart of the asset approach. The spot exchange rate is the output (endogenous variable) of this model, and the expected exchange rate and the two interest rates are the inputs (exogenous variables). But where do the expected exchange rate and the two interest rates come from? In the last chapter, we developed a theory of the long-run exchange rate, the monetary approach, which can be used to forecast the future exchange rate. That leaves us with just one unanswered question: How are current interest rates determined?

Money Market Equilibrium in the Short Run: How Nominal Interest Rates Are Determined

We are already familiar with the mechanics of money supply and money demand from Chapter 3 and build on that foundation here. We consider two money markets in two locations and their respective equilibria in which money demand equals money supply. As before, for this example, the two markets are the United States and Europe. In both countries, the money supply is controlled by the central bank and is taken as given; money demand is governed by the general model seen in Chapter 3, in which the demand for real money balances $M/P = L(i)Y$ is a function of the interest rate i and real income Y.

The Assumptions It is important to understand the key difference between the way we approach money market equilibrium in the short run (in this chapter) and the way we approached it in the long run (in the last chapter).

In Chapter 3, we made the following *long-run* assumptions:

■ In the long run, the price level P is fully flexible and adjusts to bring the money market to equilibrium.

■ In the long run, the nominal interest rate i equals the world real interest rate plus domestic inflation.

In this chapter, we make quite different *short-run* assumptions:

■ In the short run, the price level is sticky; it is a known predetermined variable, fixed at $P = \bar{P}$ (the bar indicates a fixed value).

■ In the short run, the nominal interest rate i is fully flexible and adjusts to bring the money market to equilibrium.

Why do we make different assumptions in the short run?

First, why assume prices are now sticky? The assumption of sticky prices, also called **nominal rigidity,** is common to the study of macroeconomics in the short run. Economists have many explanations for price stickiness. Nominal wages may be sticky because of long-term labor contracts. Nominal product prices may be sticky because of *menu costs,* that is, firms find it costly to frequently change their output prices. Thus, while we think it is reasonable to assume all prices are flexible in the long run, this cannot be taken for granted in the short run.

Second, why assume that interest rates are now flexible? In Chapter 3, we showed that nominal interest rates are pinned down by the Fisher effect (or real interest parity) in the long run. However, this result does not apply in the short run because it is derived from purchasing power parity—which, as we know, fails to hold in the short run. Indeed, we saw evidence that real interest rates fluctuate in ways that deviate from real interest parity in the short run.

The Model With these explanations of our short-run assumptions in hand, we can now use the same general monetary model of Chapter 3 and write down expressions for money market equilibrium in the two countries as follows:

(4-2)
$$\underbrace{\frac{M_{US}}{\overline{P}_{US}}}_{\substack{\text{U.S. supply of}\\\text{real money balances}}} = \underbrace{L(i_{\$}) \times Y_{US},}_{\substack{\text{U.S. demand for}\\\text{real money balances}}}$$

(4-3)
$$\underbrace{\frac{M_{EUR}}{\overline{P}_{EUR}}}_{\substack{\text{European supply of}\\\text{real money balances}}} = \underbrace{L(i_{\text{€}}) \times Y_{EUR}.}_{\substack{\text{European demand for}\\\text{real money balances}}}$$

To recapitulate, let's be clear on how these money market equilibria are achieved. In the long run, we relied on prices to adjust to clear the money market and bring money demand and money supply into line. In the short run, when prices are sticky, no such adjustment is possible. However, nominal interest rates *are* free to adjust. In the short run, it is the nominal interest rate in each country that adjusts to bring money supply and money demand into equilibrium.

Money Market Equilibrium in the Short Run: Graphical Solution

Figure 4-4 represents the U.S. money market (a similar diagram applies to the European market). On the horizontal axis is the quantity of U.S. real money balances M_{US}/P_{US} and on the vertical axis is the U.S. nominal interest rate $i_{\$}$.

FIGURE 4-4

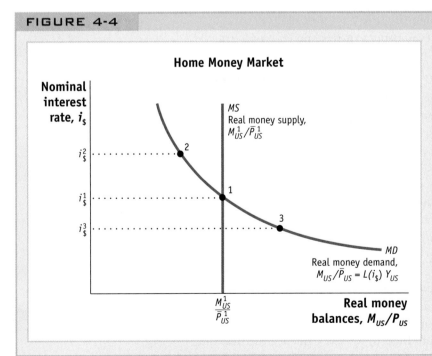

Home Money Market

Nominal interest rate, $i_{\$}$

$i_{\$}^2$

$i_{\$}^1$

$i_{\$}^3$

MS
Real money supply,
$M_{US}^1/\overline{P}_{US}^1$

2

1

3

MD
Real money demand,
$M_{US}/\overline{P}_{US} = L(i_{\$}) Y_{US}$

$\dfrac{M_{US}^1}{\overline{P}_{US}^1}$

Real money balances, M_{US}/P_{US}

Equilibrium in the Home Money Market The supply and demand for real money balances determine the nominal interest rate. The money supply curve (*MS*) is vertical at $M_{US}^1/\overline{P}_{US}^1$ because the quantity of money supplied does not depend on the interest rate. The money demand curve (*MD*) is downward sloping because an increase in the interest rate raises the cost of holding money, thus lowering the quantity demanded. The money market is in equilibrium when the nominal interest rate $i_{\$}^1$ is such that real money demand equals real money supply (point 1). At points 2 and 3, demand does not equal supply and the interest rate will adjust until the money market returns to equilibrium.

The vertical line represents the supply of real money balances; this supply is fixed by the central bank at the level $M^1_{US}/\overline{P}^1_{US}$ and is independent of the level of the interest rate. The downward-sloping line represents the demand for real money balances, $L(i_\$) \times Y_{US}$. Demand decreases as the U.S. nominal interest rate increases because the opportunity cost of holding money rises and people don't want to hold high money balances. The money market is in equilibrium at point 1: the demand and supply of real money balances are equal at $M^1_{US}/\overline{P}^1_{US}$ and at a nominal interest rate $i^1_\$$.

Adjustment to Money Market Equilibrium in the Short Run

If interest rates are flexible in the short run, as we assume they are, there is nothing to prevent them from adjusting to clear the money market. But how do market forces ensure that a nominal interest rate $i^1_\$$ is attained? The adjustment process works as follows.

Suppose instead that the interest rate was $i^2_\$$, so that we were at point 2 on the real money demand curve. At this interest rate, real money demand is less than real money supply. In the aggregate, the central bank has put more money in the hands of the public than the public wishes to hold. The public will desire to reduce its cash holdings by exchanging money for assets such as bonds, saving accounts, and so on. That is, they will save more and seek to lend their money to borrowers. But borrowers will not want to borrow more unless the cost of borrowing falls. So the interest rate will be driven down as eager lenders compete to attract scarce borrowers. As this happens, back in the money market, in Figure 4-4, we move from point 2 back toward equilibrium at point 1.

A similar story can be told if the money market is initially at point 3, where there is an excess demand for money. In this case, the public wishes to reduce their savings in the form of interest-bearing assets and turn them into cash. Now fewer loans are extended. The loan market will suffer an excess demand. But borrowers will not want to borrow less unless the cost of borrowing rises. So the interest rate will be driven up as eager borrowers compete to attract scarce lenders. These adjustments come to a halt only when there is no excess supply of real money balances—namely, when point 1 is reached.

Another Building Block: Short-Run Money Market Equilibrium

This model of the money market may be familiar from previous courses in macroeconomics. The lessons that are important for our theory of exchange rates are summed up in Figure 4-5. We treat the price level in each country as fixed and known in the short run. We assume that the money supply and real income in each country are known. The money market equilibrium equations—Equations (4-2) and (4-3)—can be solved for the interest rates in each country. Once they are known, these interest rates can be plugged into the fundamental equation of the asset approach to exchange

FIGURE 4-5

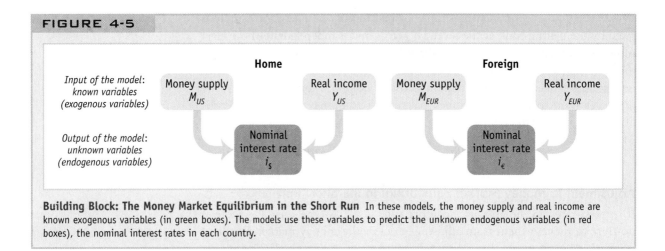

Building Block: The Money Market Equilibrium in the Short Run In these models, the money supply and real income are known exogenous variables (in green boxes). The models use these variables to predict the unknown endogenous variables (in red boxes), the nominal interest rates in each country.

rate determination—Equation (4-1)—along with the future expected exchange rate derived from a forecast based on the monetary model of Chapter 3.

Changes in Money Supply and the Nominal Interest Rate

Money market equilibrium depends on money supply and money demand. If either changes, the equilibrium will change, and we need to understand how these changes occur.

Figure 4-6, panel (a), shows how the money market responds to a monetary policy change consisting of an increase in the Home (U.S.) nominal money supply from M_{US}^1 to M_{US}^2. Because, by assumption, the U.S. price level is fixed in the short run at $\overline{P}_{US}^1$, the increase in nominal money supply causes an increase in real money supply from $M_{US}^1/\overline{P}_{US}^1$ to $M_{US}^2/\overline{P}_{US}^1$. The money supply curve shifts to the right from MS_1 to MS_2. Clearly, point 1 is no longer an equilibrium; at the interest rate $i_\$^1$, there is now an excess supply of real money balances. As people move their dollars into interest-bearing assets to be loaned out, the interest rate must fall. The interest rate falls from $i_\$^1$ to $i_\$^2$, at which point the money market is again in equilibrium at point 2. By the same logic, a reduction in the nominal money supply will raise the interest rate.

To sum up, *in the short run, all else equal, an increase in a country's money supply will lower the country's nominal interest rate; a decrease in a country's money supply will raise the country's nominal interest rate.*

Fortunately, our graphical analysis shows that, for a *given* money demand curve, setting a money supply level uniquely determines the interest rate and vice versa. Hence, for many purposes, *it is equivalent to consider either the money supply or the interest rate as the policy instrument,* and we proceed accordingly in our theoretical analysis. In practice, most central banks tend to use the interest rate as their policy instrument because the money demand curve may not be stable, and these fluctuations would lead to unstable interest rates if the money supply were set at a given level as the policy instrument.

NET WORK

Visit some of the major central bank websites, such as the U.S. Federal Reserve, the Bank of England, the Bank of Canada, or the European Central Bank. Look at their recent policy actions. Do they take the form of changes in money supply or changes in interest rates? Can you find any reference to the money supply in these central banks' policy statements?

FIGURE 4-6

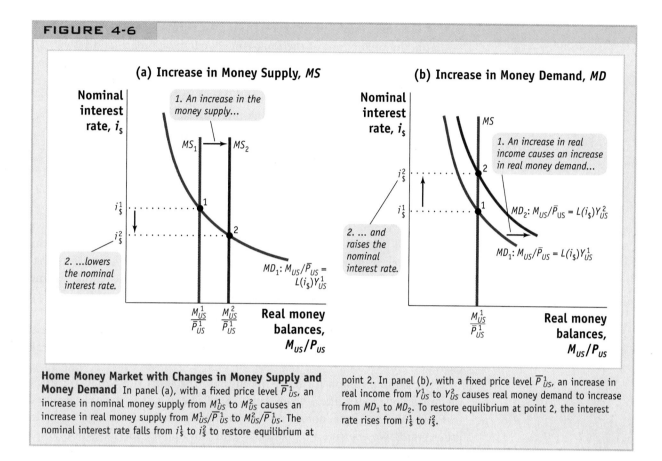

(a) Increase in Money Supply, MS

Nominal interest rate, $i_\$$

1. *An increase in the money supply...*

$MS_1 \longrightarrow MS_2$

1

$i_\$^1$ ....

$i_\$^2$ 2

2. *...lowers the nominal interest rate.*

$MD_1: M_{US}/\bar{P}_{US} = L(i_\$)Y_{US}^1$

$\dfrac{M_{US}^1}{\bar{P}_{US}^1}$ $\dfrac{M_{US}^2}{\bar{P}_{US}^1}$ **Real money balances, M_{US}/P_{US}**

(b) Increase in Money Demand, MD

Nominal interest rate, $i_\$$

MS

1. *An increase in real income causes an increase in real money demand...*

$i_\$^2$ 2

$i_\$^1$ 1

2. *... and raises the nominal interest rate.*

$MD_2: M_{US}/\bar{P}_{US} = L(i_\$)Y_{US}^2$

$MD_1: M_{US}/\bar{P}_{US} = L(i_\$)Y_{US}^1$

$\dfrac{M_{US}^1}{\bar{P}_{US}^1}$ **Real money balances, M_{US}/P_{US}**

Home Money Market with Changes in Money Supply and Money Demand In panel (a), with a fixed price level $\bar{P}_{US}^1$, an increase in nominal money supply from M_{US}^1 to M_{US}^2 causes an increase in real money supply from $M_{US}^1/\bar{P}_{US}^1$ to $M_{US}^2/\bar{P}_{US}^1$. The nominal interest rate falls from $i_\$^1$ to $i_\$^2$ to restore equilibrium at point 2. In panel (b), with a fixed price level $\bar{P}_{US}^1$, an increase in real income from Y_{US}^1 to Y_{US}^2 causes real money demand to increase from MD_1 to MD_2. To restore equilibrium at point 2, the interest rate rises from $i_\$^1$ to $i_\$^2$.

Changes in Real Income and the Nominal Interest Rate

Figure 4-6, panel (b), shows how the money market responds to an increase in Home (U.S.) real income from Y_{US}^1 to Y_{US}^2. The increase in real income causes real money demand to increase as reflected in the shift from MD_1 to MD_2. At the initial interest rate $i_\$^1$, there is now an excess demand for real money balances. To restore equilibrium at point 2, the interest rate rises from $i_\$^1$ to $i_\$^2$ to encourage people to hold lower dollar balances. Similarly, a reduction in real income will lower the interest rate.

To sum up, *in the short run, all else equal, an increase in a country's real income will raise the country's nominal interest rate; a decrease in a country's real income will lower the country's nominal interest rate.*

The Monetary Model: The Short Run versus the Long Run

The short-run implications of the model we have just discussed stand in marked contrast to the long-run implications of the monetary approach we presented in the previous chapter. Let's look at these differences, and understand how they arise.

Consider the following example: the Home central bank that previously kept the money supply constant suddenly switches to an expansionary policy. In the following year, it allows the money supply to grow at a rate of 5%.

■ If such expansions were expected to be a permanent policy in the long run, the predictions of the long-run monetary approach and Fisher effect are clear. All else equal, a 5 percentage point increase in the rate of Home money growth causes a 5 percentage point increase in the rate of Home inflation and a 5 percentage point increase in the Home nominal interest rate. The Home interest rate will *rise* in the long run.

■ If this expansion were expected to be temporary, then the short-run model we have just studied in this chapter tells a very different story. All else equal, if the Home money supply expands, the immediate effect is an excess supply of real money balances. The Home interest rate will then *fall* in the short run.

These different outcomes illustrate the importance of the assumptions we make about price flexibility. They also underscore the importance of the nominal anchor in monetary policy formulation and the constraints that central banks have to confront. The different outcomes also explain some apparently puzzling linkages among money, interest rates, and exchange rates. In both of the previous cases, an expanded money supply leads to a weaker currency. However, in the short run, low interest rates and a weak currency go together, whereas in the long run, high interest rates and a weak currency go together.

What is the intuition for these findings? In the short run, when we study the impact of a lower interest rate and we say "all else equal," we have assumed that expectations have not changed concerning future exchange rates. In other words, we envisage (implicitly) a temporary policy that does not tamper with the nominal anchor. In the long run, if the policy turns out to be permanent, this assumption is inappropriate; prices are flexible and money growth, inflation, and expected depreciation now all move in concert—in other words, the "all else" is no longer equal.

A good grasp of these key differences between the short- and long-run approaches is essential to understanding the determinants of exchange rates. To cement our understanding, in the rest of the chapter we will explore the different implications of temporary and permanent policy changes. To facilitate our applied work, we lay out the short-run model in a succinct, graphical form.

3 The Asset Approach: Applications and Evidence

To simplify the graphical presentation of the asset approach, we focus on conditions in the Home economy; a similar approach can be used for the Foreign economy. For illustration we again assume that Home is the United States and Foreign is Europe.

The Asset Approach to Exchange Rates: Graphical Solution

Figure 4-7 shows two markets: panel (a) shows the Home money market (for the United States), and panel (b) shows the FX market diagram (for the dollar-euro market). This figure summarizes the asset approach in the short run.

FIGURE 4-7

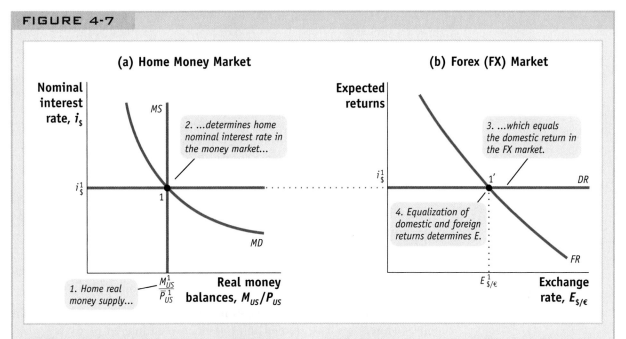

(a) Home Money Market

Nominal interest rate, $i_\$$

MS

2. ...determines home nominal interest rate in the money market...

$i_\$^1$

1

MD

1. Home real money supply...

$\frac{M_{US}^1}{\overline{P}_{US}^1}$

Real money balances, M_{US}/P_{US}

(b) Forex (FX) Market

Expected returns

3. ...which equals the domestic return in the FX market.

$i_\$^1$

1'

DR

4. Equalization of domestic and foreign returns determines E.

FR

$E_{\$/€}^1$

Exchange rate, $E_{\$/€}$

Equilibrium in the Money Market and the FX Market The figure summarizes the equilibria in the two asset markets in one diagram. In panel (a), in the home (U.S.) money market, the home nominal interest rate $i_\$^1$ is determined by the levels of real money supply *MS* and demand *MD* with equilibrium at point 1. In panel (b), in the dollar-euro FX market, the spot exchange rate $E_{\$/€}^1$ is determined by foreign and domestic expected returns, with equilibrium at point 1'. Arbitrage forces the domestic and foreign returns in the FX market to be equal, a result that depends on capital mobility.

The U.S. Money Market Panel (a) depicts equilibrium in the U.S. money market. The horizontal axis shows the quantity of U.S. real money balances demanded or supplied, M_{US}/P_{US}. The vertical axis shows the U.S. nominal interest rate, $i_\$$. Two relationships are shown:

1. The vertical line *MS* represents the U.S. real money supply. The line is vertical because (i) the nominal U.S. money supply M_{US} is treated as exogenous (known), since it is set by the Home central bank, and (ii) the U.S. price level $\overline{P}_{US}$ is treated as exogenous (known) in the short run due to price stickiness.

2. The curve *MD* on the diagram represents the U.S. demand for real money balances, $L(i_\$)Y_{US}$. It slopes down because, when the Home nominal interest rate $i_\$$ rises, the opportunity cost of holding money increases, and demand falls. For now, we also assume that the U.S. real income level Y_{US} is exogenous (given) and fixed in the short run. (We relax this assumption in Chapter 7.)

In equilibrium, money demand equals money supply, the quantity of real money demanded and supplied is $M_{US}^1/\overline{P}_{US}^1$, and the nominal interest rate is $i_\$^1$ (point 1).

The Market for Foreign Exchange Panel (b) depicts equilibrium in the FX market. The horizontal axis shows the spot exchange rate, $E_{\$/€}$. The vertical axis shows U.S. dollar returns on Home and Foreign deposits. Two relationships are shown:

1. The downward-sloping foreign return curve *FR* shows the relationship between the exchange rate and the expected dollar rate of return on foreign deposits $[i_{€} + (E^e_{\$/€} - E_{\$/€})/E_{\$/€}]$. The European interest rate $i_{€}$ is treated as exogenous (given); it is determined in the European money market, which is not shown in this figure. The expected future exchange rate $E^e_{\$/€}$ is treated as exogenous (given); it is determined by a forecast from the long-run model of Chapter 3.

2. The horizontal domestic return line *DR* shows the dollar rate of return on U.S. deposits, which is the U.S. nominal interest rate $i_{\$}$. It is horizontal at $i^1_{\$}$ because this is the U.S. interest rate determined in the Home money market in panel (a), and it is the same regardless of the spot exchange rate.

In equilibrium, foreign and domestic returns are equal (uncovered interest parity holds) and the FX market is in equilibrium at point $1'$.

Capital Mobility Is Crucial We assume that the FX market is subject to the arbitrage forces we have studied and that uncovered interest parity will hold. But this is true only if there are no capital controls: as long as capital can move freely between Home and Foreign capital markets, domestic and foreign returns will be equalized. Our assumption that *DR* equals *FR* depends on capital mobility. If capital controls are imposed, there is no arbitrage and no reason why *DR* has to equal *FR*.

Putting the Model to Work With this graphical apparatus in place, it is relatively straightforward to solve for the exchange rate given knowledge of all the known (exogenous) variables we have specified previously.

To solve for the exchange rate, we start in the Home money market in panel (a) on the horizontal axis, at the level of real money supply $M^1_{US}/\overline{P}^1_{US}$; we trace upward along *MS* to *MD* at point 1, to find the current Home interest rate $i^1_{\$}$. We then trace right and move across from the Home money market to the FX market in panel (b), since the Home interest rate is the same as domestic return *DR* in the FX market. We eventually meet the *FR* curve at point $1'$. We then trace down and read off the equilibrium exchange rate $E^1_{\$/€}$.

Our graphical treatment shows that solving the model is as simple as tracing a path around the diagrams. While we gain in simplicity, we also lose some generality because one market, the foreign money market, has been left out of the analysis. However, the same analysis also applies to the foreign country. As a quick check that you understand the logic of the asset approach to exchange rates, you might try to construct the equivalent of Figure 4-7 under the assumption that Europe is the Home economy and the United States is the Foreign economy. (Hint: In the FX market, you will need to treat the Home [European] expected future exchange rate $E^e_{€/\$}$ and the Foreign [U.S.] interest rate $i_{\$}$ as given. Take care with the currency units of every variable.)

Short-Run Policy Analysis

The graphical exposition in Figure 4-7 shows how the asset approach works to determine the exchange rate. This approach can be used to analyze the impacts of economic policy or other shocks to the economy.

The most straightforward shocks we can analyze are temporary shocks because they affect only the current state of the money and foreign exchange markets and do not affect expectations about the future. In this section, we use the model to see what happens when there is a temporary, short-run increase in the money supply by the central bank.

A Temporary Shock to the Home Money Supply We take the model of Figure 4-7 and assume that, apart from the Home money supply, all exogenous variables remain unchanged and fixed at the same level. Thus, Foreign money supply, Home and Foreign real income and price levels, and the expected future exchange rate are all fixed.

The initial state of all markets is shown in Figure 4-8. The Home money market is in equilibrium at point 1 where Home money supply MS and money demand MR are equal at the Home nominal interest rate $i_\$^1$. The foreign exchange market is in equilibrium at point $1'$, where domestic return DR equals foreign return FR, where $i_\$^1 = i_\in^1 + (E_{\$/\in}^e - E_{\$/\in}^1)/E_{\$/\in}^1$, and the spot exchange rate is $E_{\$/\in}^1$.

FIGURE 4-8

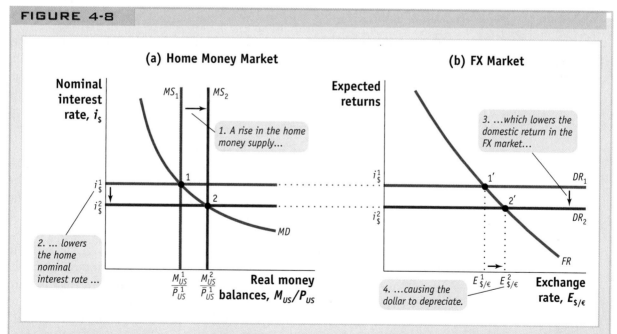

Temporary Expansion of the Home Money Supply In panel (a), in the Home money market, an increase in Home money supply from M_{US}^1 to M_{US}^2 causes an increase in real money supply from $M_{US}^1/\overline{P}_{US}^1$ to $M_{US}^2/\overline{P}_{US}^1$. To keep real money demand equal to real money supply, the interest rate falls from $i_\$^1$ to $i_\$^2$, and the new money market equilibrium is at point 2. In panel (b), in the FX market, to maintain the equality of domestic and foreign expected returns, the exchange rate rises (the dollar depreciates) from $E_{\$/\in}^1$ to $E_{\$/\in}^2$, and the new FX market equilibrium is at point $2'$.

Suppose the U.S. money supply is increased temporarily from M_{US}^1 to M_{US}^2. Under the assumption of sticky prices, $\overline{P}_{US}^1$ does not change, so the U.S. real money supply will increase to M_{US}^2/P_{US}^1, and the real money supply curve shifts from MS_1 to MS_2 in panel (a). U.S. real money demand is unchanged, so the money market equilibrium shifts from point 1 to point 2 and the nominal interest rate falls from $i_\$^1$ to $i_\$^2$. The expansion of the U.S. money supply causes the U.S. nominal interest rate to fall.

A *temporary* monetary policy shock leaves the long-run expected exchange rate $E_{\$/€}^e$ unchanged. Assuming all else equal, European monetary policy is also unchanged, and the euro interest rate remains fixed at $i_€$. If $E_{\$/€}^e$ and $i_€$ are unchanged, then the foreign return FR curve in panel (b) is unchanged and the new FX market equilibrium is at point $2'$. The lower domestic return $i_\$^2$ is matched by a lower foreign return. The foreign return is lower because the U.S. dollar has depreciated from $E_{\$/€}^1$ to $E_{\$/€}^2$.

The result is intuitive, and we have seen each of the steps previously. We now just put them all together: A Home monetary expansion lowers the Home nominal interest rate, which is also the domestic return in the FX market. This makes Foreign deposits more attractive and makes traders wish to sell Home deposits and buy Foreign deposits. This in turn makes the Home exchange rate increase (depreciate). However, this depreciation makes Foreign deposits less attractive (all else equal). Eventually the equality of foreign and domestic returns is restored, uncovered interest parity holds again, and the foreign exchange market reaches a new short-run equilibrium.

A Temporary Shock to the Foreign Money Supply We now repeat the previous analysis for a shock to the *Foreign* money supply. All other exogenous variables remain unchanged and fixed at their initial levels. Thus, Foreign money supply, Home and Foreign real income and price levels, and the expected future exchange rate are all fixed. The initial state of all markets is shown in Figure 4-9: the Home money market is in equilibrium at point 1 and the FX market is in equilibrium at point 2.

Let's see what happens when the Foreign money supply increases temporarily. Because changes in the Foreign money supply have no effect on the Home money market in panel (a), equilibrium remains at point 1 and the Home nominal interest rate stays at $i_\$^1$.

The shock is temporary, so long-run expectations are unchanged, and the expected exchange rate $E_{\$/€}^e$ stays fixed in panel (b). However, because the Foreign money supply has expanded temporarily, the euro interest rate falls from $i_€^1$ to $i_€^2$. Foreign returns are diminished, all else equal, by a fall in euro interest rates, so the foreign return curve FR shifts downward from FR_1 to FR_2. On the horizontal axis in panel (b), we can see that at the new FX market equilibrium (point $2'$) the Home exchange rate has decreased (the U.S. dollar has appreciated) from $E_{\$/€}^1$ to $E_{\$/€}^2$.

This result is also intuitive. A Foreign monetary expansion lowers the Foreign nominal interest rate, which lowers the foreign return in the FX market. This makes Foreign deposits less attractive and makes traders wish to buy

FIGURE 4-9

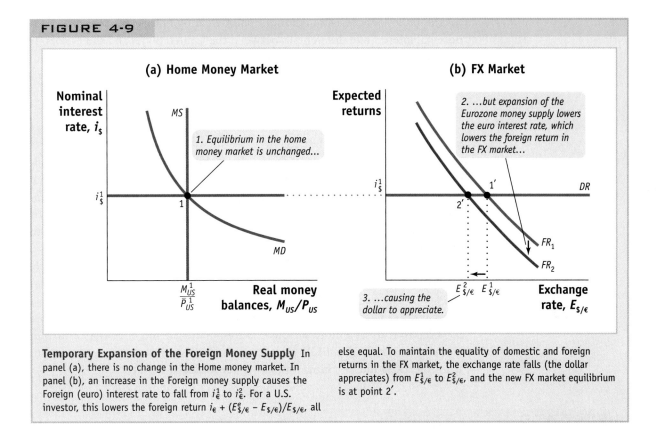

(a) Home Money Market

Nominal interest rate, $i_\$$

MS

1. *Equilibrium in the home money market is unchanged...*

$i_\$^1$

1

MD

$\dfrac{M_{US}^1}{\overline{P}_{US}^1}$

Real money balances, M_{US}/P_{US}

(b) FX Market

Expected returns

2. *...but expansion of the Eurozone money supply lowers the euro interest rate, which lowers the foreign return in the FX market...*

$i_\$^1$

1′

DR

2′

FR_1

FR_2

3. *...causing the dollar to appreciate.*

$E_{\$/€}^2$ $E_{\$/€}^1$

Exchange rate, $E_{\$/€}$

Temporary Expansion of the Foreign Money Supply In panel (a), there is no change in the Home money market. In panel (b), an increase in the Foreign money supply causes the Foreign (euro) interest rate to fall from $i_€^1$ to $i_€^2$. For a U.S. investor, this lowers the foreign return $i_€ + (E_{\$/€}^e - E_{\$/€})/E_{\$/€}$, all else equal. To maintain the equality of domestic and foreign returns in the FX market, the exchange rate falls (the dollar appreciates) from $E_{\$/€}^1$ to $E_{\$/€}^2$, and the new FX market equilibrium is at point 2′.

Home deposits and sell Foreign deposits. This in turn makes the Home exchange rate decrease (appreciate). However, this appreciation makes Foreign deposits more attractive (all else equal). Eventually the equality of foreign and domestic returns is restored, uncovered interest parity holds again, and the foreign exchange market reaches a new short-run equilibrium.

To ensure you have grasped the model fully, you might try two exercises. First, derive the predictions of the model for temporary *contractions* in the Home or Foreign money supplies. Second, go back to the version of Figure 4-6 that you constructed from the European perspective and generate predictions using that version of the model, first for a temporary expansion of the money supply in Europe and then for a temporary expansion in the United States. Do you get the same answers?

APPLICATION

The Rise and Fall of the Dollar, 1999–2004

In the 1990s, many developed countries adopted monetary policies that established clear, long-run nominal anchors. The European Central Bank (ECB), for example, adopted an explicit inflation target. The Federal Reserve in the United States operated with a more implicit target, but nonetheless could claim to have a credible anchor, too.

The Fisher effect tells us that nominal anchoring of this kind ought to keep nominal interest rate differentials between the United States and the Eurozone roughly constant in the long run. But in the short run, this constraint does not apply, so central banks have some freedom to temporarily change their monetary policies. In the years 2000 to 2004, such flexibility was put to use and interest rates in the United States and Europe followed very different tracks.

In later chapters, we study in more detail why central banks alter monetary policy in the short run, but for now we focus on how such changes affect exchange rates. As Figure 4-10 shows, the Fed raised interest rates in the period from 1999 to 2001 faster than the ECB (the Fed was more worried about the U.S. economy "overheating" with higher inflation). In this period of global economic boom, the ECB's policy also tightened over time, as measured by changes in the Euro interest rate—the refinancing rate set by the ECB. But the changes were more restrained and slower in coming.

As Figure 4-10 also shows, the Fed then lowered interest rates aggressively in the period from 2001 to 2004, with rates falling as low as 1% in 2003 to 2004 (the U.S. economy had slowed after the boom and the Fed hoped that lower interest rates would avert a recession; the terrorist attacks of September 2001 led to fears of a more serious economic setback and encouraged further monetary easing). The ECB also acted similarly to lower interest rates, but again the ECB did not move rates as far or as fast as the Fed.

FIGURE 4-10

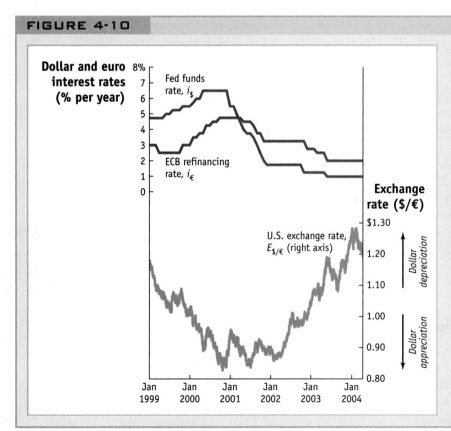

U.S.-Eurozone Interest Rates and Exchange Rates, 1999–2004 From the euro's birth in 1999 until 2001, the dollar steadily appreciated against the euro, as interest rates in the United States were raised well above those in Europe. In early 2001, however, the Federal Reserve began a long series of interest rate reductions. By 2002 the Fed Funds rate was well below the ECB's refinancing rate. Theory predicts a dollar appreciation (1999–2001) when U.S. interest rates were relatively high, followed by a dollar depreciation (2001–2004) when U.S. interest rates were relatively low. Looking at the figure, you will see that this is what occurred.

Sources: Websites of central banks; OANDA. Exchange rate is monthly average.

As a result, the ECB's interest rate, previously lower than the Fed's rate, was soon higher than the U.S. rate in 2001 and remained higher through 2004. Investors most likely viewed these policy changes as a temporary shift in monetary policy in both countries. Hence, they might be considered as an example of temporary monetary policy shocks. Do our model's predictions accord well with reality?

Up until 2001, the policy of higher rates in the United States could be seen as a temporary Home monetary contraction (relative to Foreign), and our model would predict a dollar appreciation in the short run. After 2001 the aggressive reductions in U.S. interest rates could be seen as a temporary Home monetary expansion (relative to Foreign), and our model predicts a dollar depreciation in the short run. Looking at the path of the dollar-euro exchange rate in the figure, we can see that the model accords well with reality. ■

4 A Complete Theory: Unifying the Monetary and Asset Approaches

In this section, we extend our analysis from the short run to the long run, allowing us to examine permanent as well as temporary shocks. To do this, we put together a complete theory of exchange rates that couples the long-run and short-run approaches, as shown schematically in Figure 4-11:

■ We need the asset approach (this chapter)—short-run money market equilibrium and uncovered interest parity:

(4-4)
$$\left. \begin{array}{l} \overline{P}_{US} = M_{US}/[L_{US}\,(i_\$)\,Y_{US}] \\ \overline{P}_{EUR} = M_{EUR}/[L_{EUR}\,(i_\euro)\,Y_{EUR}] \\ i_\$ = i_\euro + \dfrac{E^e_{\$/\euro} - E_{\$/\euro}}{E_{\$/\euro}} \end{array} \right\} \quad \text{The asset approach.}$$

There are three equations and three unknowns (two short-run nominal interest rates and the spot exchange rate). The future expected exchange rate must be known, as must the current levels of money and real income. (The price level is also treated as given.)

■ But to forecast the future expected exchange rate, we also need the long-run monetary approach (Chapter 3)—a long-run monetary model and purchasing power parity:

(4-5)
$$\left. \begin{array}{l} P^e_{US} = M^e_{US}/[L_{US}(i^e_\$)\,Y^e_{US}] \\ P^e_{EUR} = M^e_{EUR}/[L_{EUR}\,(i^e_\euro)\,Y^e_{EUR}] \\ E^e_{\$/\euro} = P^e_{US}/P^e_{EUR} \end{array} \right\} \quad \text{The monetary approach.}$$

There are three equations and three unknowns (two price levels and the exchange rate). Note that all variables here have a superscript e to denote future expected values or forecasts. We assume that forecasts of future money, real income, and nominal interest rates are known. This

FIGURE 4-11

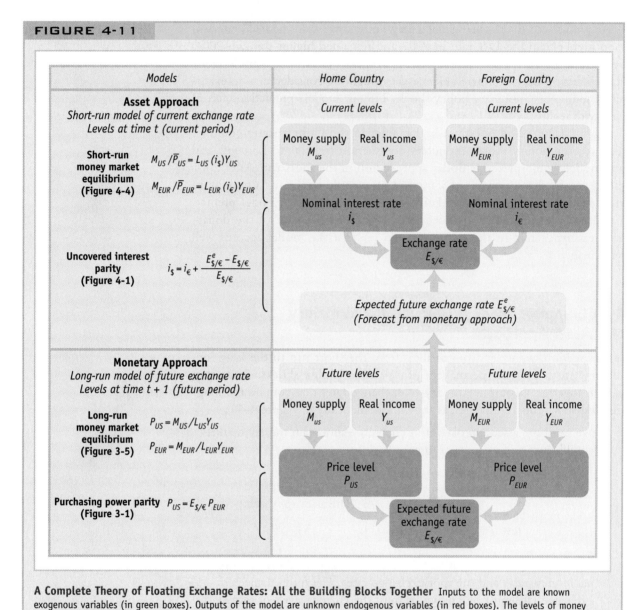

A Complete Theory of Floating Exchange Rates: All the Building Blocks Together Inputs to the model are known exogenous variables (in green boxes). Outputs of the model are unknown endogenous variables (in red boxes). The levels of money supply and real income determine exchange rates.

model can then be applied to obtain price forecasts and, hence, a forecast of the future expected exchange rate.[2]

Figure 4-11 sums up all the theory we have learned so far in the past two chapters. It shows how all the pieces fit together. In total we have six equations and six unknowns.

---

[2] Recall that Chapter 3 also showed us how real interest parity can be used to solve for the long-run nominal interest rate i in each country, the so-called *neutral level* of the nominal interest rate. For example, restricting our attention to the case of a stable long-run inflation rate (e.g., under nominal anchoring in which an announced inflation target is expected to be hit in each country), we have

$$\left. \begin{array}{l} i_\$ = \pi_{US,\,\text{target}} + r^* \\ i_\euro = \pi_{EUR,\,\text{target}} + r^* \end{array} \right\} \quad \text{Real interest parity.}$$

It is only now, with all the building blocks in place, that we can fully appreciate how the two key mechanisms of *expectations* and *arbitrage* operate in a variety of ways to determine exchange rates in both the short run and the long run. Ensure you are comfortable with all of the building blocks—how they work individually and how they connect.

After no little effort, we have arrived at a complete theory to explain exchange rates in both the short run and the long run. The model incorporates all of the key economic fundamentals that affect exchange rates and, in practice, and although forex markets exhibit a great deal of turbulence and uncertainty, there is evidence that these fundamentals play a major role in shaping traders' decisions (see **Side Bar: Confessions of a Forex Trader**).

NET WORK

Search the Internet for websites and services offering exchange rate forecasts. (Hint: Google "exchange rate forecast.") How far ahead is the forecast made? What do the forecasters say about the methods that they use, if anything? Is the forecast based on fundamentals or technical methods? How much credence would you give to the forecast?

SIDE BAR

Confessions of a Forex Trader

Trying to forecast exchange rates is a major enterprise in financial markets and serves as the basis of any trading strategy. A tour of the industry would find many firms offering forecasting services at short, medium, and long horizons. Forecasts are generally based on three methodologies (or some mix of all three):

1. *Economic fundamentals.* Forecasts are based on ideas developed in the past two chapters. Exchange rates are determined by factors such as money, output, interest rates, and so on; hence, forecasters try to develop long- and short-range predictions of these deep, "fundamental" variables. Example: "The exchange rate will depreciate because a looser monetary policy is expected."

2. *Politics.* Forecasts recognize that some factors that are not purely economic can affect exchange rates. One is the outbreak of war (see the application at the end of this chapter). Political crises might matter, too, if they affect perceptions of risk. Changes in risk interfere with simple interest parity and can move exchange rates (see Chapter 9). Making such forecasts is more qualitative and subjective but is still concerned with fundamental determinants in our theory. Example: "The exchange rate will depreciate because a conflict with a neighboring state raises the probability of war and inflation."

3. *Technical methods.* Forecasts rely on extrapolations from past behavior. Trends may be assumed to continue ("momentum"), or recent maximum and minimum values may be assumed to be binding. These trading strategies assume that financial markets exhibit some persistence and, if followed, may make such an assumption self-fulfilling for a time. Nonetheless, large crashes that return asset prices back to fundamental levels can burst such

bubbles. Example: "The exchange rate has hit this level three times this year but never gone further; it will not go further this time."

A recent survey of U.K. forex traders provided some interesting insights into this world.[*] One-third described their trading as "technical based," and one-third said their trades were "fundamentals based"; others were jobbing or trading for clients.

The survey revealed that insights from economic theory mattered little from one hour to the next. In the very short run, within the day, traders confessed that many factors unrelated to economic fundamentals affected exchange rates in the market: 29% cited "bandwagon effects," and 33% mentioned "overreaction to news." Concerning within-day changes in exchange rates, when asked "do you believe exchange rate movements accurately reflect changes in the fundamental value," fully 97% of the traders responded no and only 3% yes. However, in the medium run, described as within six months, 58% responded yes. And in the long run, described as more than six months, 87% thought that changes reflected fundamentals.

Which economic fundamentals mattered? News about money supplies, interest rates, and GDP levels was quickly incorporated into trading, usually in less than a minute or even in a matter of seconds. All of these are key variables in our complete model. As we would expect, PPP was deemed irrelevant within the day, but 16% thought it mattered in the medium run, and 44% in the long run. The lack of unanimity about PPP may reflect legitimate concerns about its shortcomings (see Chapters 3 and 11).

[*] *Yin-Wong Cheung, Menzie D. Chinn, and Ian W. Marsh, 2004, "How Do UK-Based Foreign Exchange Dealers Think Their Market Operates?" International Journal of Finance & Economics, 9(4), 289–306.*

Long-Run Policy Analysis

When and how can we apply the complete model? The downside of working with the complete model is that we have to keep track of multiple mechanisms and variables; the upside is that the theory is fully developed and can be applied to short-run and long-run policy shocks.

As the last section indicated, temporary shocks represent one kind of monetary policy change, one that does not affect the long-run nominal anchor. This allowed us to conduct all of the analysis under the assumption that the long-run expected level of the exchange rate remained unchanged.

When the monetary authorities decide to make a *permanent* change, however, this assumption of unchanged expectations will be violated. Under such a change, the authorities would cause an enduring change in all nominal variables; that is, they would be electing to change their nominal anchor policy in some way. Thus, when a monetary policy shock is permanent, the long-run expectation of the level of the exchange rate must adjust. This change will, in turn, cause the exchange rate predictions of the short-run model to differ from those made when the policy shock was only temporary.

These insights guide our analysis of permanent policy shocks. They also tell us that we cannot approach such analysis chronologically. Before we can figure out what happens in the short run, we have to know expectations, that is, what is going to happen in the long run. Thus, we have to use a technique that is common in forward-looking economic problems, and *solve backward* from the future to the present. (This ordering mirrors the presentation of the material in this textbook—we must understand the long run before we can understand the short run.)

A Permanent Shock to the Home Money Supply

We start our analysis of the Home (United States) and Foreign (Europe) economies with each economy currently at a long-run equilibrium in which all variables are steady. In this equilibrium, we assume that each country has a fixed real income, a fixed money supply, and a zero rate of inflation. Hence, there is a zero rate of depreciation because the equilibrium is characterized by purchasing power parity, and interest rates in each country are the same because the equilibrium is characterized by uncovered interest parity.

Our analysis is shown Figure 4-12. Panels (a) and (b) show the short-run impacts of a permanent increase in the money supply in the Home (U.S.) money and FX markets; panels (c) and (d) show the long-run impacts and the adjustment from the short run to the long run. We examine each of these three aspects in turn.

As shown in panels (a), (b), (c), and (d), we suppose the Home economy starts with initial equilibria in the home money and FX markets shown by points 1 and 1′, respectively. In the money market, in panels (a) and (c), at point 1, the home money market is initially in equilibrium: MS_1 corresponds to an initial real money supply of M^1_{US}/P^1_{US}; given real money demand MD, the nominal interest rate is $i^1_\$$. In the FX market, in panels (b) and (d), at point 1′, the domestic return DR_1 is the nominal interest rate $i^1_\$$. Given the foreign

FIGURE 4-12

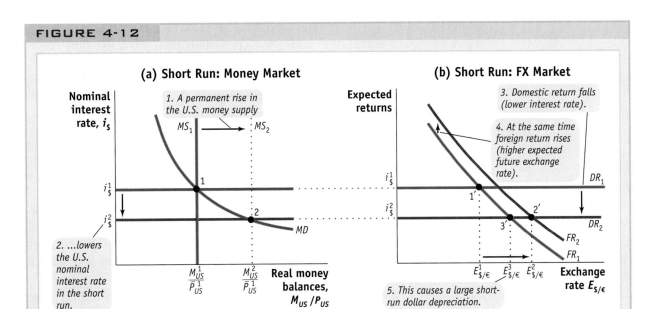

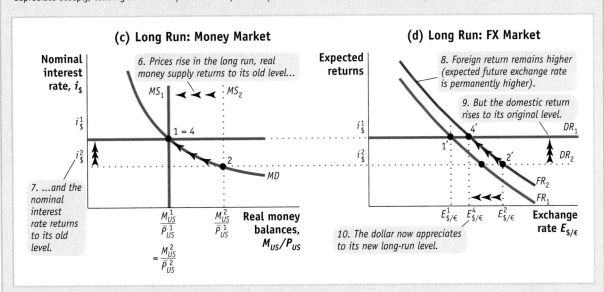

Permanent Expansion of the Home Money Supply
Short-Run Impact: In panel (a), the home price level is fixed, but the supply of dollar balances increases and real money supply shifts out. To restore equilibrium at point 2, the interest rate falls from $i_\$^1$ to $i_\$^2$. In panel (b), in the FX market, the home interest rate falls, so the domestic return decreases and DR shifts down. In addition, the permanent change in the home money supply implies a permanent, long-run depreciation of the dollar. Hence, there is also a permanent rise in $E_{\$/€}^e$, which causes a permanent increase in the foreign return $i_€ + (E_{\$/€}^e - E_{\$/€})E_{\$/€}$, all else equal; FR shifts up from FR_1 to FR_2. The simultaneous fall in DR and rise in FR cause the home currency to depreciate steeply, leading to a new equilibrium at point 2' (and not at 3', which would be the equilibrium if the policy were temporary).

Long-Run Adjustment: In panel (c), in the long run, prices are flexible, so the home price level and the exchange rate both rise in proportion with the money supply. Prices rise to P_{US}^2, and real money supply returns to its original level M_{US}^1/P_{US}^1. The money market gradually shifts back to equilibrium at point 4 (the same as point 1). In panel (d), in the FX market, the domestic return DR, which equals the home interest rate, gradually shifts back to its original level. The foreign return curve FR does not move at all; there are no further changes in the Foreign interest rate or in the future expected exchange rate. The FX market equilibrium shifts gradually to point 4'. The exchange rate falls (and the dollar appreciates) from $E_{\$/€}^2$ to $E_{\$/€}^4$. Arrows in both graphs show the path of gradual adjustment.

return curve FR_1, the equilibrium exchange rate is $E^1_{\$/\epsilon}$. If both economies are at a long-run equilibrium with zero depreciation, then this is also the expected future exchange rate $E^{e1}_{\$/\epsilon} = E^1_{\$/\epsilon}$.

We now start to figure out what happens after the policy shock hits today, working backward from the future to the present.

The Long Run Refer to panels (c) and (d) of Figure 4-12. We understand from Chapter 3 that, in the long run, an increase in the money supply will eventually lead to a proportionate increase in the price level and the exchange rate. If the money supply increases from M^1_{US} to M^2_{US} today, then the price level will *eventually* increase by the same proportion from P^1_{US} to P^2_{US}, and, to maintain PPP, the exchange rate will *eventually* rise by the same proportion (and the dollar will depreciate) from $E^1_{\$/\epsilon}$ to its long-run level $E^4_{\$/\epsilon}$, in panel (d), where $E^4_{\$/\epsilon}/E^1_{\$/\epsilon} = P^2_{US}/P^1_{US} = M^2_{US}/M^1_{US} > 1$. (We use "4" to denote long-run exchange rate values because there will be some short-run responses to consider in just a moment.)

Thus, in the long run, in panel (c), if money and prices both rise in the same proportion, then the real money supply will be unchanged at its original level $M^1_{US}/P^1_{US} = M^2_{US}/P^2_{US}$, the real money supply curve will still be in its original position MS_1, and the nominal interest rate will again be $i^1_\$$. In the long run, the money market returns to where it started: long-run equilibrium is at point 4 (same as point 1).

In the FX market, however, a permanent money supply shock causes some permanent changes in the long run. One thing that does not change is the domestic return, DR_1, since in the long run it returns to $i^1_\$$. But the exchange rate will rise from the initial long-run exchange rate, $E^1_{\$/\epsilon}$, to a new long-run level, $E^4_{\$/\epsilon}$. Because $E^4_{\$/\epsilon}$ is also a long-run stable level, it is also the new expected level of the exchange rate $E^{4e}_{\$/\epsilon}$ that will prevail in the future. That is, the future will look like the present, under our assumptions, except that the exchange rate will be sitting at $E^4_{\$/\epsilon}$ instead of $E^1_{\$/\epsilon}$. What does this change do to the foreign return curve, FR? As we know, when the expected exchange rate increases, foreign returns are higher, so the FR curve shifts up, from FR_1 to FR_2. Because in the long run $E^4_{\$/\epsilon}$ is the new stable equilibrium exchange rate, and $i^1_\$$ is the interest rate, the new FX market equilibrium is at point 4' where FR_2 intersects DR_1.

The Short Run Only now that we have changes in expectations worked out can we work back through panels (a) and (b) of Figure 4-12 to see what will happen in the short run.

Look first at the FX market in panel (b). Because expectations about the future exchange rate have changed with today's policy announcement, the FX market is affected immediately. Everyone knows that the exchange rate will be $E^4_{\$/\epsilon}$ in the future. The foreign return curve shifts when the expected exchange rate changes; it rises from FR_1 to FR_2. This is the same shift we just saw in the long-run panel (d). The dollar is expected to depreciate to $E^4_{\$/\epsilon}$ (relative to $E^1_{\$/\epsilon}$) in the future, so euro deposits are more attractive today.

Now consider the impact of the change in monetary policy in the short run. Look at the money market in panel (a). In the short run, if the money supply increases from M_{US}^1 to M_{US}^2 but prices are sticky at P_{US}^1, then real money balances rise from M_{US}^1/P_{US}^1 to M_{US}^2/P_{US}^1. The real money supply shifts from MS_1 to MS_2 and the home interest rate falls from $i_\$^1$ to $i_\$^2$, leading to a new short-run money market equilibrium at point 2.

Now look back to the FX market in panel (b). If this were a *temporary* monetary policy shock, expectations would be unchanged, and the FR_1 curve would still describe foreign returns, but domestic returns would fall from DR_1 to DR_2 as the interest rate fell and the home currency would depreciate to the level $E_{\$/€}^3$. The FX market equilibrium, after a temporary money supply shock, would be at point 3′, as we have seen before.

But this is not the case now. This time we are looking at a permanent shock to money supply. It has *two* effects on today's FX market. One impact of the money supply shock is to lower the home interest rate, decreasing domestic returns in today's FX market from DR_1 to DR_2. The other impact of the money supply shock is to increase the future expected exchange rate, increasing foreign returns in today's FX market from FR_1 to FR_2. Hence, the FX market equilibrium in the short run is where DR_2 and FR_2 intersect, now at point 2′, and the exchange rate depreciates all the way to $E_{\$/€}^2$.

Note that the short-run equilibrium level of the exchange rate ($E_{\$/€}^2$) is higher than the level that would be observed under a temporary shock ($E_{\$/€}^3$) and also higher than the level that will be observed in the long run ($E_{\$/€}^4$). To sum up, *in the short run, the permanent shock causes the exchange rate to depreciate more than it would under a temporary shock and more than it will end up depreciating in the long run.*

Adjustment from Short Run to Long Run The arrows in panels (c) and (d) of Figure 4-12 trace what happens as we move from the short run to the long run. Prices that were initially sticky in the short run become unstuck. The price level rises from P_{US}^1 to P_{US}^2, and this pushes the real money supply back to its initial level, from MS_2 back to MS_1. Money demand, MD, is unchanged. Hence, in the home money market of panel (c), the economy moves from the short-run equilibrium at point 2 to the long-run equilibrium, which is again at point 1, following the path shown by the arrows. Hence, the interest rate gradually rises from $i_\$^2$ back to $i_\$^1$. This raises the domestic returns over in the FX market of panel (d) from DR_2 back to DR_1. So the FX market moves from the short-run equilibrium at point 2′ to the long-run equilibrium, which is again at point 4′.

An Example Let's make this very tricky experiment a bit more concrete with a numerical example. Suppose you are told that, all else equal, (i) the home money supply permanently increases by 5% today; (ii) prices are sticky in the short run, so this also causes an increase in real money supply that lowers domestic interest rates by 4 percentage points from 6% to 2%; (iii) prices will fully adjust in one year's time to today's monetary expansion and PPP will hold again. Based on this information, can you predict what will happen to prices and the exchange rate today and in a year's time?

Yes. Work backward from the long run to the short run, as before. In the long run, a 5% increase in M means a 5% increase in P that will be achieved in one

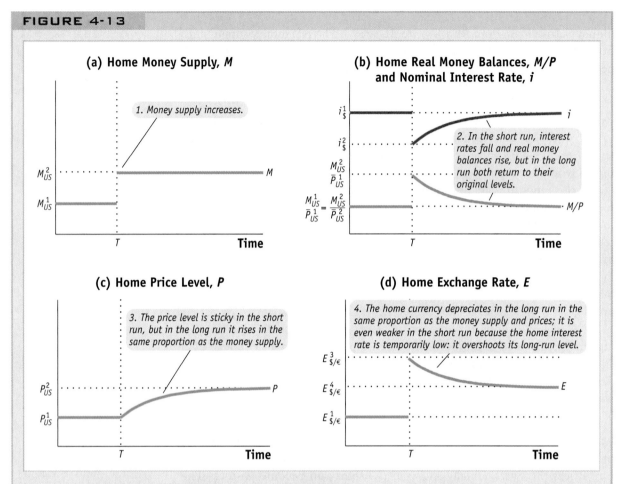

FIGURE 4-13

(a) Home Money Supply, *M*

1. Money supply increases.

(b) Home Real Money Balances, *M/P* and Nominal Interest Rate, *i*

2. In the short run, interest rates fall and real money balances rise, but in the long run both return to their original levels.

(c) Home Price Level, *P*

3. The price level is sticky in the short run, but in the long run it rises in the same proportion as the money supply.

(d) Home Exchange Rate, *E*

4. The home currency depreciates in the long run in the same proportion as the money supply and prices; it is even weaker in the short run because the home interest rate is temporarily low: it overshoots its long-run level.

Responses to a Permanent Expansion of the Home Money Supply In panel (a), there is a one-time permanent increase in home (U.S.) nominal money supply at time *T*. In panel (b), prices are sticky in the short run, so there is a short-run increase in the real money supply and a fall in the home interest rate. In panel (c), in the long run, prices rise in the same proportion as the money supply. In panel (d), in the short run, the exchange rate overshoots its long-run value (the dollar depreciates by a large amount), but in the long run, the exchange rate will have risen only in proportion to changes in money and prices.

year. By PPP, this 5% increase in P implies a 5% rise in E (a 5% depreciation in the dollar's value) over the same period. In other words, over the next year E will rise at 5% per year, which will be the rate of depreciation. Finally, in the short run, UIP tells us what happens to the exchange rate today: to compensate investors for the 4 percentage point decrease in the domestic interest rate, arbitrage in the FX market requires that the value of the home currency be expected to appreciate at 4% per year; that is, E must fall 4% in the year ahead. However, if E has to fall 4% in the next year and still end up 5% above its level at the start of today, then it must jump up 9% today: it overshoots its long-run level.

Overshooting

Compared with the temporary expansion of money supply we studied before, the permanent shock has a much greater impact on the exchange rate in the short run.

Under the temporary shock, domestic returns go down; traders want to sell the dollar for one reason only—temporarily lower dollar interest rates make dollar deposits less attractive. Under the permanent shock, domestic returns go down and foreign returns go up; traders want to sell the dollar for two reasons—temporarily lower dollar interest rates and an expected dollar depreciation make dollar deposits *much* less attractive. In the short run, the interest rate and exchange rate effects combine to create an instantaneous "double whammy" for the dollar, which gives rise to a phenomenon that economists refer to as exchange rate **overshooting.**

To better visualize the overshooting phenomenon, we show in Figure 4-13 the time path over which the key economic variables change after the permanent shock we just studied using Figure 4-12. We see the following:

a. The nominal money supply is subject to a one-time increase at time *T*.

b. Real money balances rise instantaneously but revert to their initial level in the long run; the nominal interest rate falls instantaneously but reverts to its initial level in the long run.

c. The price level is sticky in the short run but rises to a new higher level in the long run, increasing in the same proportion as the nominal money supply.

d. The exchange rate rises (depreciates) to a new higher level in the long run, rising in the same proportion as the nominal money supply. In the short run, however, the exchange rate rises even more, overshooting its long-run level, then gradually decreasing to its long-run level (which is still higher than the initial level).

The overshooting result adds yet another argument for the importance of a sound long-run nominal anchor: without it, exchange rates are likely to be more volatile, creating instability in the forex market and possibly in the wider economy. The wild fluctuations of exchange rates in the 1970s, at a time when exchange rate anchors were ripped loose, exposed these linkages with great clarity (see **Side Bar: Overshooting in Practice**). And new research provides evidence that the shift to a new form of anchoring, inflation targeting, might be helping to bring down exchange rate volatility in recent years.[3]

APPLICATION

Bernanke's Bold Move

We now have the tools to analyze the impacts of both temporary and permanent changes in monetary policy. But in each case we have stressed that these predictions apply *only* to unexpected changes in monetary policy. It is important to remember why this is the case.

Suppose you are a U.S. investor, and when you wake up the U.S. interest rate is 3%. Is that the relevant domestic return for your calculations? It

[3] Andrew K. Rose, 2007, "A Stable International Monetary System Emerges: Inflation Targeting Is Bretton Woods, Reversed," *Journal of International Money and Finance*, 26(5), 663–681.

SIDE BAR

Overshooting in Practice

Overshooting can happen in theory, but does it happen in the real world? Permanent shocks to monetary policy may play a large or a small role in the real world, depending on the extent to which a country is truly committed to a nominal anchor and on what form that anchor takes. Countries with a nominal anchor are in principle committing to a given level for all future nominal variables, including prices and exchange rates, all else equal. Such a commitment, if kept, would rule out permanent policy changes that would change the long-run equilibrium levels of prices and exchange rates.

Hence, the model of overshooting tells us that if there is a tendency for monetary policy shocks to be more permanent than temporary, then there will be a tendency for the exchange rate to be more volatile (since overshooting means that each permanent policy shock would cause a far bigger fluctuation in the exchange rate than a corresponding temporary policy shock). Thus, we might expect to see a serious increase in exchange rate volatility whenever a nominal anchoring system breaks down. Indeed, such conditions were seen in the 1970s, which is precisely when the overshooting phenomenon was discovered. How did this happen?

From the 1870s until the 1970s, except during major crises and wars, the world's major currencies were fixed against one another. Floating rates were considered anathema by policy makers and economists. Later in this book, we study the gold standard regime that began circa 1870 and fizzled out in the 1930s and the subsequent "dollar standard" of the 1950s and 1960s that was devised at a conference at Bretton Woods, New Hampshire, in 1944. As we shall see, the Bretton Woods system did not survive long for various reasons.

When floating rates reappeared in the 1970s, fears of instability returned. Concern mounted as floating exchange rates proved much more volatile than could be explained according to the prevailing flexible-price monetary approach: the models said that money supplies and real income were simply too stable to be able to generate such large fluctuations (as seen in Figure 4-14). Some feared that this was a case of *animal spirits,* John Maynard Keynes' term for irrational forces, especially in asset markets like that for foreign exchange. The challenge to economists was to derive a new model that could account for the wild swings in exchange rates.

Enter economist Rudiger Dornbusch of MIT. Building on Keynesian foundations, he published a paper in 1976 in which he showed that sticky prices and flexible exchange rates implied exchange rate overshooting.[*] Dornbusch's seminal work was a fortuitous case of a theory arriving at just the right time. In the 1970s, countries abandoned exchange rate anchors and groped for new ways to conduct monetary policy in a new economic environment. Policies varied and inflation rates grew, diverged, and persisted. Overshooting helps make sense of all this: if traders saw policies as having no well-defined anchor, monetary policy shocks might no longer be guaranteed to be temporary, so long-run expectations could swing wildly with every piece of policy news.

Rudiger Dornbusch, 1976, "Expectations and Exchange Rate Dynamics," Journal of Political Economy, 84, December, 1161–1176.

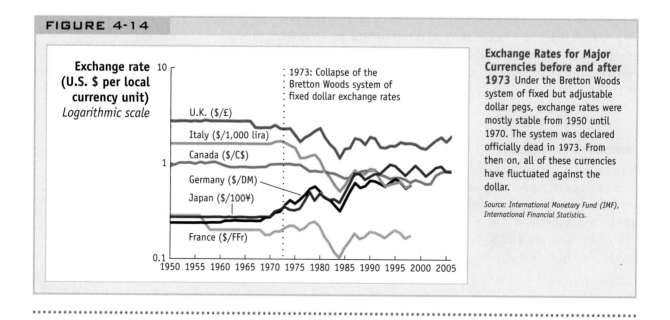

FIGURE 4-14

Exchange rate (U.S. $ per local currency unit)
Logarithmic scale

1973: Collapse of the Bretton Woods system of fixed dollar exchange rates

U.K. ($/£)
Italy ($/1,000 lira)
Canada ($/C$)
Germany ($/DM)
Japan ($/100¥)
France ($/FFr)

Exchange Rates for Major Currencies before and after 1973 Under the Bretton Woods system of fixed but adjustable dollar pegs, exchange rates were mostly stable from 1950 until 1970. The system was declared officially dead in 1973. From then on, all of these currencies have fluctuated against the dollar.

Source: International Monetary Fund (IMF), International Financial Statistics.

depends on your time horizon. Suppose you expect that by tomorrow, this interest rate will have changed to 2% and will remain at that level for the next 12 months. If you are investing in overnight money market deposits, then that one day of interest you earn at 3% is of little import. What matters is the average interest rate you receive over the length of the investment. And in this case it will be very close to 2%. But if you expect the 2% rate already, the announcement of the policy change tomorrow will not affect your calculations: you and all the other investors have already factored that decline in the interest rate into your decisions. An expected announcement is not *news* (in the way economists define news, as something unexpected).

This illustration is by no means a contrived example—it shows how to apply the simplified economic model in practice. In the real world, policymakers such as the Fed or ECB do not set 12-month interest rates; they target the overnight rate. Given the benchmark overnight rate, and expectations of future central bank actions, the market then formulates an expectation of interest rates at all maturities: weekly, 1 month, 3 month, 12 month, and so on.

To give a concrete example, consider Federal Reserve policymaking in 2006–2007. By June 2006 the Fed had raised interest rates by 0.25% at each of 17 straight meetings, taking the Fed funds rate up a staircase from 1% in June 2004 to 5.25% in June 2006. Then the Fed stood still for over a year and left the rate unchanged. There was speculation about changes at various times, but no compelling economic data arrived to suggest action, so nobody expected a change in policy. Our logic says that the forex market would not react to an expected action (or nonaction) by the Fed, and indeed this was the case. Over this two-year period, markets were not dramatically affected by Fed announcements.

But every so often a Fed meeting comes along where the action that the Fed will take is not clearly predictable. This happened for the first time under the Chairmanship of Ben Bernanke on September 18, 2007. Although inflation had been worryingly high, other data (notably housing price declines) appeared to suggest a weakening economy. At the same time, a sudden wave of credit-market turmoil due to mortgage defaults was putting a squeeze on lending. Wall Street was crying for help in the form of cheaper credit. A bank run in the United Kingdom the week before had frayed nerves further and market expectations shifted to the belief that a rate cut was a certainty. But there agreement ended: polls and surveys in the days before the Fed meeting showed that forecasts were evenly divided between a 0.25% cut in the Fed Funds rate, and a bold 0.5% cut. (The Fed only moves in $\frac{1}{4}$ point increments.)[4]

A surprise was therefore in store, one way or another: and in the end the Bernanke Fed went for the bold half point cut, by a unanimous vote of the Federal Open Market Committee. When the announcement hit at 2 p.m.,

[4] See, for example, press reports just before the Fed meeting. See also the entries on the economics blog econbrowser.com on the 18th for a discussion of expectations and market reactions.

Market reaction at 2 p.m. Eastern time, September 18, 2007: traders in the Chicago pit and the euro-dollar spot rate at 5-minute intervals over 48 hours from an xe.com trading screen (can you spot the policy announcement?).

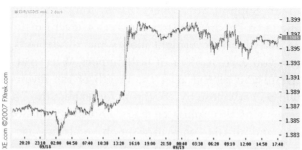

economists were standing by to see if their theories would hold up. The computers on forex trading desks whirred into action, the traders in futures pits went into a frenzy, and within minutes the dollar had lost nearly 1% of its value against the euro and other currencies. Indeed, this was a bigger fall than just the interest rate alone would have suggested: the domestic return only moved by 0.125% more than was expected, if we take the market expectation to be 0.375%, halfway between 0.25% and 0.5%. Why the big reaction?

Two explanations follow from what we have learned. First, the Fed signaled that it might be willing to lower rates more aggressively than most people had expected. The market then factored in a new belief that there could be even lower rates announced at future Fed meetings. Short-term market interest rates at all maturities up to a year therefore fell on this news—and they fell much more than the unexpected 0.125% drop in the policy rate:[5]

	Fed funds		Overnight	1 week	1 month	3 month	6 month	12 month
Before (Sep. 18)	5.25%		5.33%	5.26%	5.50%	5.59%	5.42%	5.11%
After (Sep. 19)	4.75%		4.94%	4.97%	5.15%	5.24%	5.11%	4.88%
Change	−0.50% actual		−0.39%	−0.29%	−0.35%	−0.35%	−0.31%	−0.23%
	−0.125% unexpected							

In addition, if future monetary easing was expected, the market also feared that the Fed might have made a permanent change to easier monetary policy, or a higher tolerance for inflation (than its counterparts at the ECB). Our theory tells us that a permanent change of that sort would lead to overshooting in the exchange rate, which could explain the very large jump in the exchange rate—and the animated behavior of the traders. ■

5 Fixed Exchange Rates and the Trilemma

We have developed a complete theory of exchange rates, based on the assumption that market forces in the money market and the foreign exchange market determine exchange rates. Our models have the most obvious application to

---

[5] The data are London Interbank Offered Rate (LIBOR) rates for the U.S. dollar from bba.org.uk. LIBOR fixing is at 12 noon, London time, so the last quote prior to the Fed announcement was on the 18th.

the case of floating exchange rate regimes. Under a float, there is no doubt that the market is being left to its own devices. But as we have seen, not every country floats. Can our theory also be applied to the equally important case of fixed exchange rate regimes and to other intermediate regimes? The answer is yes, and we conclude this chapter by adapting our existing theory for the case of fixed regimes.

What Is a Fixed Exchange Rate Regime?

To understand the crucial difference between fixing and floating, we contrast the polar cases of tight fixing (hard pegs including narrow bands) and free floating.

We also set aside regimes that include controls on arbitrage (*capital controls*) because such extremes of government intervention render our theory superfluous. Instead, we focus on the case of a fixed-rate regime without controls so that capital is mobile and is free to operate in the foreign exchange market. Under these conditions, the government allows the exchange rate to be subject to these market forces. In a fixed regime, the government itself becomes an actor in the foreign exchange market and uses intervention in the market to influence the market rate. Exchange rate intervention takes the form of the central bank buying and selling foreign currency at a fixed price, thus holding the market rate at a fixed level denoted $\overline{E}$.

Let us now explore the implications of that policy in the short run and the long run using the familiar building blocks of our theory. To give a concrete flavor to these derivations, we replace the United States and the Eurozone (whose currencies float against each other) with an example of an actual fixed exchange rate regime. The Foreign country remains the Eurozone, and the Home country is now Denmark.

We now examine the implications of Denmark's decision to peg its currency, the krone, to the euro at a fixed rate $\overline{E}_{DKr/€}$ rather than float.[6]

We have seen that, in the long run, fixing the exchange rate is one kind of nominal anchor. Even if it allowed the krone to float but had *some* nominal anchor, Denmark's monetary policy would still be constrained in the long run by the need to achieve its chosen nominal target. We know that any country with a nominal anchor faces long-run monetary policy constraints of some kind. *What we now show is that a country with a fixed exchange rate faces monetary policy constraints not just in the long run but also in the short run.*

Pegging Sacrifices Monetary Policy Autonomy in the Short Run: Example

By assumption, equilibrium in the krone-euro foreign exchange market requires that the Danish interest rate be equal to the Eurozone interest rate

---

[6] The actual arrangement is a "narrow band" centered on 7.46038 DKr/€ and officially of width ±2.25%, according to the ERM arrangement between Denmark and the Eurozone that has been in effect since 1999. In practice, the krone usually stays within ±1% of the central rate.

plus the expected rate of depreciation of the krone. But under a peg, the expected rate of depreciation is zero.

Here, uncovered interest parity reduces to the simple condition that the Danish central bank must set its interest rate equal to $i_{\unicode{x20AC}}$, the rate set by the European Central Bank (ECB):

$$i_{DKr} = i_{\unicode{x20AC}} + \underbrace{\frac{E^e_{DKr/\unicode{x20AC}} - E_{DKr/\unicode{x20AC}}}{E_{DKr/\unicode{x20AC}}}}_{\substack{\text{Equals zero} \\ \text{for a credible} \\ \text{fixed exchange rate}}} = i_{\unicode{x20AC}}.$$

Denmark cannot use its monetary policy to change its interest rate policy under a peg.

The same is true of money supply policy. Short-run equilibrium in Denmark's money market requires that money supply equal money demand; but once Denmark's interest rate is set equal to the Eurozone interest rate, $i_{\unicode{x20AC}}$, there is only one feasible level for money supply, as we see by imposing $i_{\unicode{x20AC}}$ as the Danish interest rate in money market equilibrium:

$$M_{DEN} = \overline{P}_{DEN} L_{DEN}(i_{DKr}) Y_{DEN} = \overline{P}_{DEN} L_{DEN}(i_{\unicode{x20AC}}) Y_{DEN}.$$

The implications are stark. The final expression contains the euro interest rate (exogenous, as far as the Danes are concerned), the fixed price level (exogenous by assumption), and output (also exogenous by assumption). No variable in this expression is under the control of the Danish authorities in the short run, and this is the only level of the Danish money supply consistent with equilibrium in the money and forex markets at the pegged rate $\overline{E}_{DKr/\unicode{x20AC}}$. If the Danish central bank is to maintain the peg, then in the short run it must choose the level of money supply implied by the last equation.

What's going on? Arbitrage is the key force. For example, if the Danish central bank tried to print more krone and lower interest rates, it would be foiled by arbitrage. Danes would want to sell krone deposits and buy higher-yield euro deposits, applying downward pressure on the krone; to maintain the peg, the Danish central bank would then have to act as a buyer. Whatever krone it had tried to pump into circulation, it would promptly have to buy back in the foreign exchange market.

Thus, *our short-run theory still applies, just with a different chain of causality:*

■ Under a float, the home monetary authorities pick the money supply M. In the short run, the choice of M determines the interest rate i in the money market; in turn, via UIP, the level of i determines the exchange rate E. The money supply is an input in the model (an exogenous variable), and the exchange rate is an output of the model (an endogenous variable).

■ Under a fix, this logic is reversed. Home monetary authorities pick the exchange rate E. In the short run, the choice of E determines the interest rate i via UIP; in turn, the level of i determines the necessary level of the money supply M. The exchange rate is an input in the model (an exogenous variable), and the money supply is an output of the model (an endogenous variable).

This reversal of short-run causality is shown in a new schematic in the top part of Figure 4-15.

Pegging Sacrifices Monetary Policy Autonomy in the Long Run: Example

As we have noted, choosing a nominal anchor implies a loss of long-run monetary policy autonomy. Let's quickly see how that works when the anchor is a fixed exchange rate.

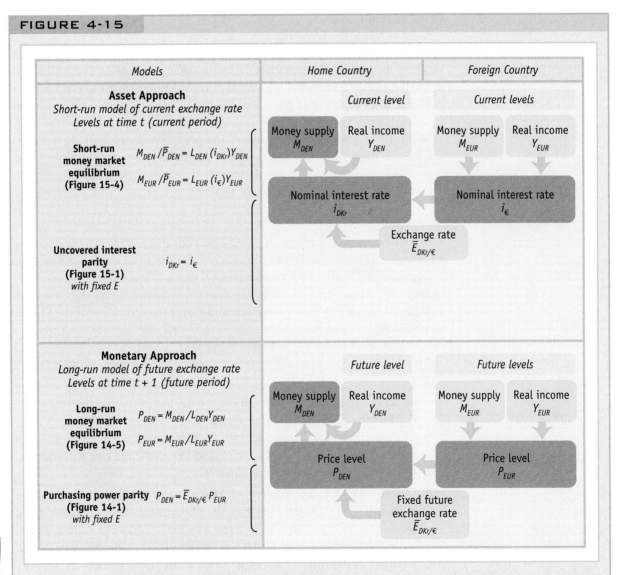

FIGURE 4-15

A Complete Theory of Fixed Exchange Rates: Same Building Blocks, Different Known and Unknown Variables Unlike in Figure 4-10, the Home country is now assumed to fix its exchange rate with the Foreign country. Inputs to the model are known exogenous variables (in green boxes). Outputs of the model are unknown endogenous variables (in red boxes). The levels of real income and the fixed exchange rate determine the Home money supply levels, given outcomes in the Foreign country.

Following our discussion of the standard monetary model, we must first ask what the nominal interest rate is going to be in Denmark in the long run. But we have already answered that question; it is going to be tied down the same way as in the short run, at the level set by the ECB, namely i_ε. We might question, in turn, where *that* level i_ε comes from (the answer is that it will be related to the "neutral" level of the nominal interest rate consistent with the ECB's own nominal anchor, its inflation target for the Eurozone). But that is beside the point: all that matters is that i_ε is as much out of Denmark's control in the long run as it is in the short run.

Next we turn to the price level in Denmark, which is determined in the long run by PPP. But if the exchange rate is pegged, we can write long-run PPP for Denmark as

$$P_{DEN} = \overline{E}_{DKr/\varepsilon} \, P_{EUR}.$$

Here we encounter another variable that is totally outside of Danish control in the long run. Under PPP, pegging to the euro means that the Danish price level is a fixed multiple of the Eurozone price level (which is exogenous, as far as the Danes are concerned).

With the long-run nominal interest and price level outside of Danish control, we can show, as before, that monetary policy autonomy is out of the question. We just substitute $i_{DKr} = i_\varepsilon$ and $P_{DEN} = \overline{E}_{DKr/\varepsilon} P_{EUR}$ into Denmark's long-run money market equilibrium to obtain

$$M_{DEN} = P_{DEN} L_{DEN}(i_{DKr}) Y_{DEN} = \overline{E}_{DKr/\varepsilon} \, P_{EUR} L_{DEN}(i_\varepsilon) Y_{DEN}.$$

The final expression contains the long-run euro interest rate and price levels (exogenous, as far as the Danes are concerned), the fixed exchange rate level (exogenous by assumption), and long-run Danish output (also exogenous by assumption). Again, no variable in the final expression is under the control of the Danish authorities in the long run, and this is the only level of the Danish money supply consistent with equilibrium in the money and foreign exchange market at the pegged rate of $\overline{E}_{DKr/\varepsilon}$.

Thus, *our long-run theory still applies, just with a different chain of causality*:

■ Under a float, the home monetary authorities pick the money supply M. In the long run, the growth of M determines the interest rate i via the Fisher effect and also the price level P; in turn, via PPP, the level of P determines the exchange rate E. The money supply is an input in the model (an exogenous variable), and the exchange rate is an output of the model (an endogenous variable).

■ Under a fix, this logic is reversed. Home monetary authorities pick the exchange rate E. In the long run, the choice of E determines the price level P via PPP, and also the interest rate i via UIP; these in turn determine the necessary level of the money supply M. The exchange rate is an input in the model (an exogenous variable), and the money supply is an output of the model (an endogenous variable).

This reversal of long-run causality is also shown in the new schematic in the bottom part of Figure 4-15.

The Trilemma

Our findings lead to the conclusion that policy makers face some tough choices. Not all desirable policy goals can be simultaneously met. These constraints are summed up in one of the most important principles in open-economy macroeconomics.

Consider the following three equations and parallel statements about desirable *policy goals*. For illustration we return to the Denmark-Eurozone example:

1. $\dfrac{E^e_{DKr/€} - E_{DKr/€}}{E_{DKr/€}} = 0$ *A fixed exchange rate*
   - Which may be desired as a means to promote stability in trade and investment
   - Represented here by zero expected depreciation

2. $i_{DKr} = i_€ + \dfrac{E^e_{DKr/€} - E_{DKr/€}}{E_{DKr/€}}$ *International capital mobility*
   - Which may be desired as a means to promote integration, efficiency, and risk sharing
   - Represented here by uncovered interest parity, which results from arbitrage

3. $i_{DKr} \neq i_€$ *Monetary policy autonomy*
   - Which may be desired as a means to manage the Home economy's business cycle
   - Represented here by the ability to set the Home interest rate independently of the Foreign interest rate

For a variety of reasons, as noted, governments may want to pursue all three of these policy goals. But they can't: formulae 1, 2, and 3 show that it is a *mathematical impossibility*! We simply note the following:

- 1 and 2 imply not 3 (1 and 2 imply interest equality, contradicting 3)
- 2 and 3 imply not 1 (2 and 3 imply an expected change in *E,* contradicting 1)
- 3 and 1 imply not 2 (3 and 1 imply a difference between domestic and foreign returns, contradicting 2)

This result, known as the **trilemma,** is one of the most important ideas in international macroeconomics.[7] It tells us that the three policy goals just outlined are simply mutually incompatible: you cannot have all three at once. You must choose to drop one of the three (or, equivalently, you must adopt one of three pairs: 1 and 2, 2 and 3, or 3 and 1).

---

[7] A definition: "Trilemma *noun* 1. a quandary posed by three alternative courses of action" (*Collins English Dictionary* online).

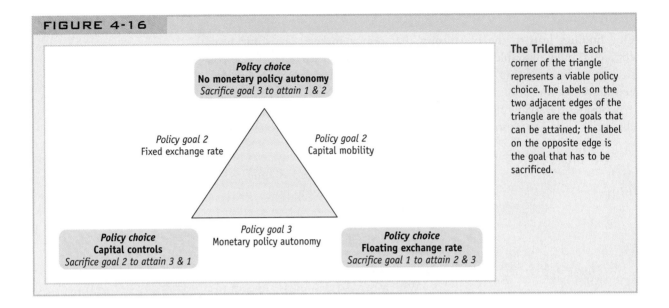

FIGURE 4-16

Policy choice
No monetary policy autonomy
Sacrifice goal 3 to attain 1 & 2

Policy goal 2
Fixed exchange rate

Policy goal 2
Capital mobility

Policy goal 3
Monetary policy autonomy

Policy choice
Capital controls
Sacrifice goal 2 to attain 3 & 1

Policy choice
Floating exchange rate
Sacrifice goal 1 to attain 2 & 3

The Trilemma Each corner of the triangle represents a viable policy choice. The labels on the two adjacent edges of the triangle are the goals that can be attained; the label on the opposite edge is the goal that has to be sacrificed.

The trilemma is simple and powerful, and we will explore its practical importance later in the book. For now, it suffices to say that history is replete with economic disasters stemming from some basic policy-making failure that ignores this fundamental precept.

The trilemma can be illustrated graphically as in Figure 4-16. Each corner of the triangle represents a viable policy choice. For each corner, the label at the vertex indicates the goal that has been sacrificed, while the labels on each adjacent edge of the triangle explain the goals that can be attained (see **Side Bar: Intermediate Regimes**).

APPLICATION

The Trilemma in Europe

We motivated the trilemma with the case of Denmark. Denmark has chosen policy goals 1 and 2. As a member of the European Union (EU), Denmark adheres to the single-market legislation that requires free movement of capital within the bloc. It also unilaterally pegs its krone to the euro under the EU's Exchange Rate Mechanism (ERM), an agreement that serves as a stepping-stone to Eurozone membership. Consequently, the Danish central bank must set an interest rate at the same level as that set by the ECB; it has lost option 3.

The Danes could make one of two choices if they wished to gain monetary independence from the ECB: they could abandon their commitment to the EU treaties on capital mobility (drop 2 to get 3), which is extremely unlikely, or they could abandon their ERM commitment and let the krone float against the euro (drop 1 to get 3), which is also fairly unlikely. Floating is, however, the choice of the United Kingdom, an EU country that has withdrawn from the ERM and that allows the pound to float against the euro.

SIDE BAR

Intermediate Regimes

The lessons of the trilemma most clearly apply when the policies are dichotomous, either on or off: a hard peg or a float, perfect capital mobility or immobility, complete autonomy or none at all. But sometimes a country may not be fully in one of the three corners: the rigidity of the peg, the degree of capital mobility, and the independence of monetary policy could be partial rather than full.

For example, in a band arrangement, the exchange rate is maintained within a range of $\pm X\%$ of some central rate. The significance of the band is that it allows some nonzero rate of expected depreciation—that is, a little bit of floating. As a result, a limited interest differential can open up between the two countries. For example, suppose the band is of width 2% (i.e., ±1% around a central rate). To compute home interest rates, UIP tells us that we must add the foreign interest rate (let's suppose it is 5%) to the expected rate of depreciation (which is ±2% in the extreme if the exchange rate moves from one band edge to the other). Thus, Home may "fix" this way and still have the freedom to set 12-month interest rates in the range between 3% and 7%. But the home country cannot evade the trilemma forever: on average, over time, the rate of depre-

ciation will have to be zero to keep the exchange rate within the narrow band, meaning that the Home interest rate must track the Foreign interest rate apart from small deviations.

Similar qualifications to the trilemma could result from partial capital mobility, where barriers to arbitrage could also lead to interest differentials. And with such differentials emerging, the desire for partial monetary autonomy can be accommodated.

In practice, once these distinctions are understood, it is usually possible to make some kind of judgment about which corner best describes the country's policy choice. For example, in 2007 both Slovakia and Denmark were supposedly pegged to the euro as members of the EU's Exchange Rate Mechanism (ERM). But the similarities ended there. The Danish krone has been operating in ERM bands of official width ±2.25%, but closer to ±1% in practice, a pretty hard peg and a rate that has never changed. The Slovak koruna operates with ±15% bands and shifted that band by appreciating its central rate by 8.5% in March 2007. With its narrow bands around the peg, Denmark's regime is clearly fixed. With its very wide (and adjustable) bands, Slovakia's regime has been more like managed floating.

Figure 4-17 shows evidence for the trilemma. Since 1999 the United Kingdom has had the ability to set interest rates independently of the ECB. But Denmark has not: since 1999 the Danish interest rate has tracked the ECB's rate almost exactly. Before 1999 Denmark, and some countries such as Austria and the Netherlands, pegged to the German mark with the same result: their interest rates had to track the German interest rate, but the U.K. interest rate did not. One difference is that Austria and the Netherlands have formally abolished their national currencies, the schilling and the guilder, and have adopted the euro—an extreme and explicit renunciation of monetary independence. Meanwhile the Danish krone lives on, showing that a national currency can suggest monetary sovereignty in theory but may deliver nothing of the sort in practice. ■

6 Conclusions

In this chapter, we drew together everything we have learned so far about exchange rates. We built on the insights of Chapter 2, in which we first learned about arbitrage and equilibrium in the foreign exchange (FX) market in the short run, taking expectations as given and applying uncovered interest

FIGURE 4-17

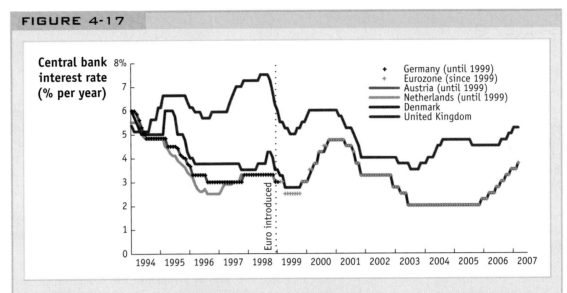

The Trilemma in Europe The figure shows selected central banks' base interest rates for the period 1994 to 2007 with reference to the German mark and euro base rates. In this period, the British made a policy choice to float against the German mark and (after 1999) against the euro. This permitted monetary independence because interest rates set by the Bank of England could diverge from those set in Frankfurt. No such independence in policy making was afforded by the Danish decision to peg the krone first to the mark and then to the euro. Since 1999 the Danish interest rate has moved almost exactly in line with the ECB rate. Similar forces operated pre-1999 for other countries pegging to the mark such as the Netherlands and Austria. Until they joined the Eurozone in 1999, their interest rates, like that of Denmark, closely tracked the German rate.

Sources: Websites of the central banks.

parity. We also relied on Chapter 3, in which we developed the purchasing power parity theory as a guide to exchange rate determination in the long run. Putting all these building blocks together provides a complete and internally consistent theory of exchange rate determination.

Exchange rates are an interesting topic in and of themselves, but at the end of the day, we also care about what they mean for the wider economy, how they relate to macroeconomic performance, and the part they play in the international monetary system. That is our next goal, and in Chapters 5 to 10, we will apply our exchange rate theories in a wider framework to help us understand how exchange rates function in the national and international economy. We also must acknowledge that our theory is a very simple and imperfect description of reality. There are still many puzzles and controversies in exchange rate economics, and these have prompted further research and more refined theories, topics we take up in Chapter 11.

Even so, the basic theory covered in the past three chapters is the first tool that applied economists and policy makers pick up when studying a problem involving exchange rates. As a first approximation, this theory has served well as a benchmark model of exchange rates in both rich and poor countries, whether in periods of economic stability or turbulence. Remarkably, it has even been applied in wartime, and we end this chapter with some unusual illustrations of the theory from conflicts past and present.

APPLICATION

News and the Foreign Exchange Market in Wartime

Our theory of exchange rates places expectations at center stage, but demonstrating the effect of changing expectations empirically is a challenge. However, wars dramatically expose the power of expectations to change exchange rates. War raises the risk that a currency may depreciate rapidly in the future. For one thing, the government may need to print money to finance its war effort, but how much inflation this practice will generate may be unclear. In addition, there is a risk of defeat and a decision by the victor to impose new economic arrangements such as a new currency; the existing currency may then be converted into the new currency at a rate dictated by the victors or, in a worst-case scenario, it may be declared totally worthless, that is, not legal tender. Demand for the currency will then collapse to zero and, hence, so will its value. Economic agents in the foreign exchange market are continually updating their forecasts about the war's possible outcomes, and, as a result, the path of an exchange rate during wartime usually reveals a clear influence of the effects of news.

The U.S. Civil War, 1861–1865 For four years, beginning April 12, 1861, a war raged between the Union (North) and Confederate (South) forces. An important economic dimension of this conflict was the decision by the Confederate states to issue their own currency, the Confederate dollar, to help gain economic autonomy from the North and finance their war effort. The exchange rate of the Confederate dollar against the U.S. dollar is shown in Figure 4-18.

How should we interpret these data? The two currencies differed in one important respect. If the South had won, and the Confederate states had gained independence, they would have kept their Confederate dollar, and the northern United States would have kept its U.S. dollar, too. Instead, the South was defeated, and, as expected in these circumstances, the U.S. dollar was imposed as the sole currency of the unified country; the Confederate dollar, like all liabilities of the Confederate nation, was repudiated by the victors and, hence, became worthless.

War news regularly influenced the exchange rate.[8] As the South headed for defeat, the value of the Confederate dollar shrank. The overall trend was

---

[8] This correlation was noted by Wesley Mitchell, 1903, *A History of the Greenbacks,* Chicago: University of Chicago Press. For recent econometric studies that examine this phenomenon, see George T. McCandless Jr., 1996, "Money, Expectations, and U.S. Civil War," *American Economic Review,* 86(3), 661–671; and Kristen L. Willard, Timothy W. Guinnane and Harvey S. Rosen, 1996, "Turning Points in the Civil War: Views from the Greenback Market," *American Economic Review,* 86(4), 1001–1018.

FIGURE 4-18

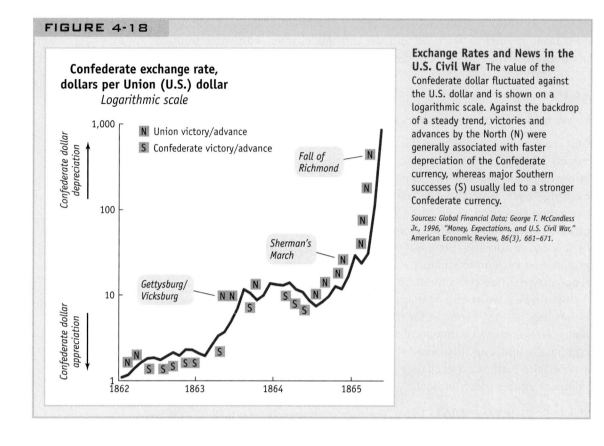

Confederate exchange rate, dollars per Union (U.S.) dollar
Logarithmic scale

Confederate dollar depreciation

N Union victory/advance
S Confederate victory/advance

Fall of Richmond

Sherman's March

Gettysburg/ Vicksburg

Confederate dollar appreciation

Exchange Rates and News in the U.S. Civil War The value of the Confederate dollar fluctuated against the U.S. dollar and is shown on a logarithmic scale. Against the backdrop of a steady trend, victories and advances by the North (N) were generally associated with faster depreciation of the Confederate currency, whereas major Southern successes (S) usually led to a stronger Confederate currency.

Sources: Global Financial Data; George T. McCandless Jr., 1996, "Money, Expectations, and U.S. Civil War," American Economic Review, 86(3), 661–671.

driven partly by inflationary war finance and partly by the probability of defeat. Major Northern victories marked "N" tended to coincide with depreciations of the Confederate dollar. Major Southern victories marked "S" were associated with appreciations or, at least, a slower depreciation. The key Union victory at Gettysburg, July 1–3, 1863, and the near simultaneous fall of Vicksburg on July 4 were followed by a dramatic depreciation of the Confederate dollar. By contrast, Southern victories (in the winter of 1862 to 1863 and the spring of 1864) were periods when the Southern currency held steady or even appreciated. But by the fall of 1864, and particularly after Sherman's March, the writing was on the wall, and the Confederate dollar began its final decline.

Currency traders in New York did good business either way. They were known to whistle "John Brown's Body" after a Union victory and "Dixie" after Confederate success, making profits all the while as they traded dollars for gold and vice versa. Abraham Lincoln was not impressed, declaring, "What do you think of those fellows in Wall Street, who are gambling in gold at such a time as this? . . . For my part, I wish every one of them had his devilish head shot off."

The Iraq War, 2003 The Civil War is not the only example of such phenomena. In 2003 Iraq was invaded by a U.S.-led coalition of forces intent on overthrowing the regime of Saddam Hussein, and the effects of war on currencies were again visible.[9]

Our analysis of this case is made a little more complicated by the fact that at the time of the invasion there were *two* currencies in Iraq. Indeed, some might say there were two Iraqs. Following a 1991 war, Iraq had been divided: in the North, a de facto Kurdish government was protected by a no-fly-zone enforced by the Royal Air Force and U.S. Air Force; in the South, Saddam's regime continued. The two regions developed into two distinct economies, and each had its own currency. In the North, Iraqi dinar notes called "Swiss" dinars circulated.[10] In the South, a new currency, the "Saddam" or "print" dinar, was introduced.[11]

Figure 4-19 shows the close correlation between wartime news and exchange rate movements for this modern episode. We can compare exchange rate movements with well-known events, but panel (a) allows another interesting comparison. In 2002 a company called TradeSports Exchange allowed bets on Saddam's destiny by setting up a market in contracts that paid $1 if he was deposed by a certain date, and the prices of these contracts are shown using the left scale. After he was deposed, contracts that paid out upon his capture were traded, and these are also shown. If such a contract had a price of, say, 80¢, then this implied that "the market" believed the probability of overthrow or apprehension was 80%.

In panel (b), we see the exchange rates of the Swiss dinar against the U.S. dollar and the Saddam dinar in 2002 to 2003. The Kurds' Swiss dinar-U.S. dollar rate had held at 18 per U.S. dollar for several years but steadily appreciated in 2002 to 2003 as the prospect of a war to depose Saddam became more likely. By May 2003, when the invasion phase of the war ended and Saddam had been deposed, it had appreciated as far as 6 to the dollar. The war clearly drove this trend: the more likely the removal of Saddam, the more durable would be Kurdish autonomy, and the more likely it would be that a postwar currency would be created that would respect the value of the Kurds' Swiss dinars. Notice how the rise in the value of the Swiss dinar tracked the odds of regime change until mid-2003.

After Baghdad fell, the coalition sought to capture Saddam, who had gone into hiding. As the hunt wore on, and a militant/terrorist insurgency began, fears mounted that he would never be found and his regime might survive underground and reappear. The odds on capture fell, and, moving in parallel, so did the value of the Swiss dinar. The Kurds now faced a rising probability that the whole

---

[9] This case study draws on Mervyn King, 2004, "The Institutions of Monetary Policy," *American Economic Review,* 94(2), May, 1–13.

[10] The notes were printed in Britain using plates of Swiss manufacture. The Kurds issued no new notes of their own; indeed, they had no means to do so and simply used this legacy currency after 1991. No new Swiss dinars were issued after 1989 in the South either.

[11] Once economic sanctions were imposed after the 1991 war, Baghdad had no access to the high-security technology and papers used to make modern banknotes. Instead, the Swiss dinar was retired, and the Saddam regime issued new legal tender notes in a form that it *could* print, using low-technology offset litho techniques that your local printer might use. These were the so-called "Saddam" or "print" dinars. Circulation of these notes exploded: a large volume of notes was printed by the Iraqi Central Bank and counterfeits added to this number. For these reasons, the northern currency, the Swiss dinar, was much more stable in the 1990s than the Saddam dinar.

FIGURE 4-19

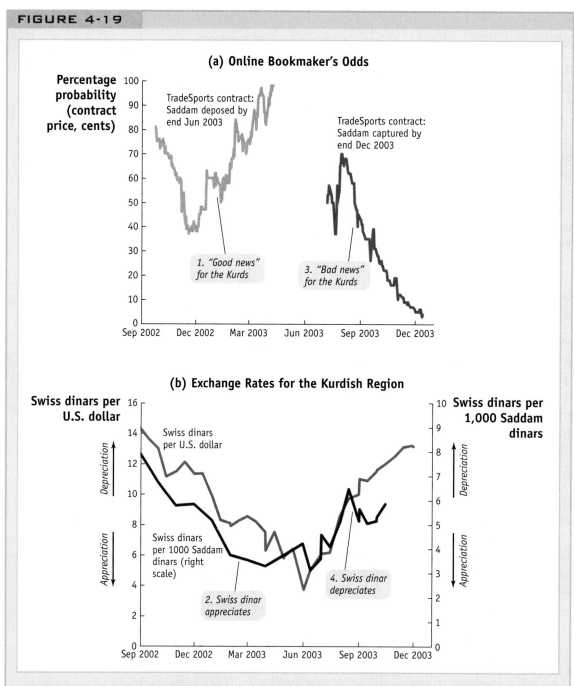

(a) Online Bookmaker's Odds

Percentage probability (contract price, cents)

TradeSports contract: Saddam deposed by end Jun 2003

TradeSports contract: Saddam captured by end Dec 2003

1. "Good news" for the Kurds

3. "Bad news" for the Kurds

(b) Exchange Rates for the Kurdish Region

Swiss dinars per U.S. dollar

Swiss dinars per 1,000 Saddam dinars

Depreciation

Appreciation

Swiss dinars per U.S. dollar

Swiss dinars per 1000 Saddam dinars (right scale)

2. Swiss dinar appreciates

4. Swiss dinar depreciates

Exchange Rates and News in the Iraq War As regime change looked more likely in 2002 to 2003, as reflected in panel (a), the Swiss dinar, the currency used by the Kurds, appreciated against the U.S. dollar and the Saddam dinar, the currency used in the south, as shown in panel (b). When the invasion ended, the difficult postwar transition began. Insurgencies and the failure to find Saddam Hussein became a cause for concern, as reflected in panel (a). The Swiss dinar depreciated against the dollar until December 2003, as shown in panel (b).

Notes: Panel (a) shows two contract prices: the value in cents of a TradeSports contract that paid 100¢ if Saddam were deposed by the end of June 2003 and 0 otherwise and the value in cents of a contract that paid 100¢ if Saddam were captured by the end of December 2003, and 0 otherwise.

Source: From Mervyn King, 2004, The Institutions of Monetary Policy," *American Economic Review, 94(2), 1–13.*

affair would end badly for them and their currency. (However, when Saddam Hussein was captured on December 14, 2003, the Swiss dinar appreciated again.)

We can also track related movements in the Swiss dinar against the Saddam or print dinar. Before and during the war, while the Swiss dinar was appreciating against the U.S. dollar, it was also appreciating against the Saddam dinar. It strengthened from around 10 Swiss dinars per 1,000 Saddam in early 2002 to about 3 Swiss dinars per 1,000 Saddam in mid-2003. Then, as the postwar operations dragged on, this trend was reversed. By late 2003, the market rate was about 6 Swiss dinars per 1,000 Saddam. Again, we can see how the Kurds' fortunes appeared to the market to rise and fall.

What became of all these dinars? Iraqis fared better than the holders of Confederate dollars. A new dinar was created under a currency reform announced in July 2003 and implemented from October 15, 2003, to January 15, 2004.[12] Exchange rate expectations soon moved into line with the increasingly credible official conversion rates and U.S. dollar exchange rates for the new dinar. ■

Courtesy of the Federal Reserve Bank of Richmond

Courtesy Neil Shafer

Courtesy Neil Shafer

Courtesy Neil Shafer

Currencies in wartime: A Confederate 2 dollar note of 1864 issued in Richmond; an Iraqi "Swiss" 25 dinar from the Kurdish region; a widely forged post-1991 Iraqi "Saddam" 25 dinar note; a post-2003 250 new Iraqi dinar note.

KEY POINTS

1. Our theory of exchange rates builds on two ideas: arbitrage and expectations. We developed the theory first for the case of floating exchange rates.

2. In the short run, we assume prices are sticky and the asset approach to exchange rates is valid (Chapter 2). Interest-bearing accounts in different currencies may offer different rates of nominal interest. In addition, currencies may be expected to depreciate or appreciate against one another. There is an incentive for arbitrage: investors will shift funds from one country to another until the expected rate of return (measured in a common currency) is equalized. Arbitrage in the foreign exchange (FX) market determines today's spot exchange rate, and the FX market is in equilibrium when the uncovered interest parity condition holds. To apply the UIP condition, we need the expected exchange rate in the long run, so a forecast is needed.

---

[12] Under this reform, all the Swiss and Saddam notes were retired and a newly designed, secure currency for Iraq was brought into circulation nationally. As long as this currency reform was seen as credible, and the market believed it would successfully take place, the market rate would have to converge to the fixed rate set in advance by the authorities for note replacement. As the reform date approached, this convergence occurred, except for what appears to be a small "forgery risk premium" on the Saddam notes—detecting a fake among these notes was by no means simple.

3. In the long run, we assume prices are flexible and the monetary approach to exchange rates is valid (Chapter 3). This approach states that in the long run, purchasing power parity (PPP) holds so that the exchange rate must equal the ratio of the price levels in the two countries. Each price level in turn depends on the ratio of money supply to money demand in each country. The monetary approach can be used to forecast the long-run future expected exchange rate, which in turn feeds back into short-run exchange rate determination via the UIP equation.

4. Putting all of these ingredients together yields a complete theory of how exchange rates are determined in the short run and the long run (this chapter).

5. This model can be used to analyze the impact of changes to monetary policy as well as other shocks to the economy.

6. A temporary home monetary expansion causes home interest rates to fall and the home exchange rate to depreciate. It can be consistent with a nominal anchor in the long run.

7. A permanent home monetary expansion causes home interest rates to fall and the home exchange rate to depreciate and, in the short run, overshoot what will eventually be its long-run level. This policy is inconsistent with a nominal anchor in the long run.

8. The case of fixed exchange rates can also be studied using this theory. Under capital mobility, interest parity becomes very simple. In this case, the home interest rate equals the foreign interest rate. Home monetary policy loses all autonomy compared with the floating case. The only way to recover it is to impose capital controls. This is the essence of the trilemma.

KEY TERMS

asset approach to exchange rates, p. 118

fundamental equation of the asset approach to exchange rates, p. 119

FX market diagram, p. 121

nominal rigidity, p. 125

overshooting, p. 145

trilemma, p. 153

PROBLEMS

1. Use the money market and foreign exchange (FX) diagrams to answer the following questions about the relationship between the British pound ($£$) and the U.S. dollar ($\$$). Let the exchange rate be defined as U.S. dollars per British pound $E_{\$/£}$. We want to consider how a change in the U.S. money supply affects interest rates and exchange rates. On all graphs, label the initial equilibrium point A.

   a. Illustrate how a *temporary* decrease in the U.S. money supply affects the money and FX markets. Label your short-run equilibrium point B and your long-run equilibrium point C.

   b. Using your diagram from (a), state how each of the following variables changes in the *short run* (increase/decrease/no change): U.S. interest rate, British interest rate, $E_{\$/£}$, $E_{\$/£}^e$, and U.S. price level.

   c. Using your diagram from (a), state how each of the following variables changes in the *long run* (increase/decrease/no change relative to their initial values at point A): U.S. interest rate, British interest rate, $E_{\$/£}$, $E_{\$/£}^e$, and U.S. price level.

2. Use the money market and foreign exchange (FX) diagrams to answer the following questions. This question considers the relationship between the Indian rupee (Rs) and the U.S. dollar ($\$$). Let the exchange rate be defined as rupees per dollar $E_{Rs/\$}$. On all graphs, label the initial equilibrium point A.

   a. Illustrate how a *permanent* increase in India's money supply affects the money and FX markets. Label your short-run equilibrium point B and your long-run equilibrium point C.

b. By plotting them on a chart with time on the horizontal axis, illustrate how each of the following variables changes over time (for India): nominal money supply M_{IN}, price level P_{IN}, real money supply M_{IN}/P_{IN}, India's interest rate i_{Rs}, and the exchange rate $E_{Rs/\$}$.

c. Using your previous analysis, state how each of the following variables changes in the *short run* (increase/decrease/no change): India's interest rate, $E_{Rs/\$}$, $E^e_{Rs/\$}$, and India's price level.

d. Using your previous analysis, state how each of the following variables changes in the *long run* (increase/decrease/no change relative to their initial values at point A): India's interest rate, $E_{Rs/\$}$, $E^e_{Rs/\$}$, and India's price level.

e. Explain how overshooting applies to this situation.

3. Is overshooting (in theory and in practice) consistent with purchasing power parity? Consider the reasons for the usefulness of PPP in the short run versus the long run and the assumption we've used in the asset approach (in the short run versus the long run). How does overshooting help to resolve the empirical behavior of exchange rates in the short run versus the long run?

4. Use the money market and foreign exchange (FX) diagrams to answer the following questions. This question considers the relationship between the euro (€) and the U.S. dollar ($). Let the exchange rate be defined as U.S. dollars per euro, $E_{\$/€}$. On all graphs, label the initial equilibrium point A. Suppose that with financial innovation in the United States, real money demand in the United States decreases.

a. Assume this change in U.S. real money demand is temporary. Using the FX/money market diagrams, illustrate how this change affects the money and FX markets. Label your short-run equilibrium point B and your long-run equilibrium point C.

b. Assume this change in U.S. real money demand is permanent. Using a new diagram, illustrate how this change affects the money and FX markets. Label your short-run equilibrium point B and your long-run equilibrium point C.

c. Illustrate how each of the following variables changes over time in response to a perma-

nent reduction in real money demand: nominal money supply M_{US}, price level P_{US}, real money supply M_{US}/P_{US}, U.S. interest rate $i_\$$, and the exchange rate $E_{\$/€}$.

5. This question considers how the foreign exchange (FX) market will respond to changes in monetary policy. For these questions, define the exchange rate as Korean won per Japanese yen, $E_{W/¥}$. Use the FX and money market diagrams to answer the following questions.

a. Suppose the Bank of Korea permanently decreases its money supply. Illustrate the short-run (label equilibrium point B) and long-run effects (label equilibrium point C) of this policy.

b. Now, suppose the Bank of Korea announces it plans to permanently decrease its money supply but doesn't actually implement this policy. How will this affect the FX market in the short run if investors believe the Bank of Korea's announcement?

c. Finally, suppose the Bank of Korea permanently decreases its money supply, but this change is not anticipated. When the Bank of Korea implements this policy, how will this affect the FX market in the short run?

d. Using your previous answers, evaluate the following statements:

- If a country wants to increase the value of its currency, it can do so (temporarily) without raising domestic interest rates.
- The central bank can reduce both the domestic price level and value of its currency in the long run.
- The most effective way to increase the value of a currency is through surprising investors.

6. In the late 1990s, several East Asian countries used limited flexibility or currency pegs in managing their exchange rates relative to the U.S. dollar. This question considers how different countries responded to the East Asian currency crisis (1997–1998). For the following questions, treat the East Asian country as the home country and the United States as the foreign country. Also, for the diagrams, you may assume these countries maintained a currency peg (fixed rate) relative to the U.S. dollar. Also, for the following questions, you need consider only the short-run effects.

a. In July 1997, investors expected that the Thai baht would depreciate. That is, they expected that Thailand's central bank would be unable to maintain the currency peg with the U.S. dollar. Illustrate how this change in investors' expectations affects the Thai money market and FX market, with the exchange rate defined as baht (B) per U.S. dollar, denoted $E_{B/\$}$. Assume the Thai central bank wants to maintain capital mobility and preserve the level of its interest rate and abandons the currency peg in favor of a floating exchange rate regime.

b. Indonesia faced the same constraints as Thailand—investors feared Indonesia would be forced to abandon its currency peg. Illustrate how this change in investors' expectations affects the Indonesian money market and FX market, with the exchange rate defined as rupiahs (Rp) per U.S. dollar, denoted $E_{Rp/\$}$. Assume the Indonesian central bank wants to maintain capital mobility and the currency peg.

c. Malaysia had a similar experience, except that it used capital controls to maintain its currency peg and preserve the level of its interest rate. Illustrate how this change in investors' expectations affects the Malaysian money market and FX market, with the exchange rate defined as ringgit (RM) per U.S. dollar, denoted $E_{RM/\$}$. You need show only the short-run effects of this change in investors' expectations.

d. Compare and contrast the three approaches just outlined. As a policy maker, which would you favor? Explain.

7. Several countries have opted to join currency unions. Examples include the Euro area, the CFA franc union in West Africa, and the Caribbean currency union. This involves sacrificing the domestic currency in favor of using a single currency unit in multiple countries. Assuming that once a country joins a currency union, it will not leave, do these countries face the policy trilemma discussed in the text? Explain.

8. During the Great Depression, the United States remained on the international gold standard longer than other countries. This effectively meant that the United States was committed to maintaining a fixed exchange rate at the onset of the Great Depression. The U.S. dollar was pegged to the value of gold, along with other major currencies, including the British pound, French franc, and so on. Many researchers have blamed the severity of the Great Depression on the Federal Reserve and its failure to react to economic conditions in 1929 and 1930. Discuss how the policy trilemma applies to this situation.

9. On June 20, 2007, John Authers, investment editor of the *Financial Times,* wrote the following in his column "The Short View":

> The Bank of England published minutes showing that only the narrowest possible margin, 5–4, voted down [an interest] rate hike last month. Nobody foresaw this.... The news took sterling back above $1.99, and to a 15-year high against the yen.

Can you explain the logic of this statement? Interest rates in the United Kingdom had remained unchanged since the vote and were still unchanged after the minutes were released. What was contained in the news that caused traders to react? Use the asset approach.

10. We can use the asset approach to both make predictions about how the market will react to current events and understand how important these events are to investors. Consider the behavior of the Union/Confederate exchange rate during the Civil War. How would each of the following events affect the exchange rate, defined as Confederate dollars per Union dollar, $E_{C\$/\$}$?

a. The Confederacy increases the money supply by 2,900% between July and December of 1861.

b. The Union Army suffers a defeat in Battle of Chickamauga in September 1863.

c. The Confederate Army suffers a major defeat with Sherman's March in the autumn of 1864.

5

National and International Accounts: Income, Wealth, and the Balance of Payments

Money is sent from one country to another for various purposes: such as the payment of tributes or subsidies; remittances of revenue to or from dependencies, or of rents or other incomes to their absent owners; emigration of capital, or transmission of it for foreign investment. The most usual purpose, however, is that of payment for goods. To show in what circumstances money actually passes from country to country for this or any of the other purposes mentioned, it is necessary briefly to state the nature of the mechanism by which international trade is carried on, when it takes place not by barter but through the medium of money.

John Stuart Mill, 1848

In the next three chapters, we study economic transactions between countries, how they are undertaken, and what impact they have on the macroeconomy. In this chapter, we explore the international system of trade and payments and discover that international trade in *goods and services* is complemented by a parallel trade in *assets*.

In Chapter 1, we encountered George, the hypothetical American tourist in Paris. We learned about his use of exchange rate conversion—but how did he pay for his expenses? He traded some of his assets (such as dollar cash converted into euros, or charges on his debit card against his bank account) for goods and services (hotel, food, wine, and so on). This type of transaction is not unusual—each and every day households and firms routinely trade assets for goods and services within the economy. But when these transactions cross borders, they shape the relationship between the national economy and the rest of the world.

In a closed economy, it is one of the basic tasks of a macroeconomist to know how to measure economic transactions within the domestic economy because the collection and analysis of such data can help researchers to better model how the economy works and policy makers to better formulate effective policies. To this end, a macroeconomist examines important aggregate flows such as national output, consumption, investment, saving, and so on. The task of an international macroeconomist carries all the same responsibilities, and a few more besides: there are a host of additional economic transactions that take place across borders in an open economy, and in today's world economy these international flows of trade and finance have reached unprecedented levels and play an ever-growing role in research and policy formulation.

Cross-border flows can be measured in various ways—say, by trade imbalances or by the flows of international borrowing and lending—and data on all these flows are increasingly important subjects of discussion for economists and policy makers, for businesses, and even for the well-educated citizen. A glance at the media shows that a constant argument rumbles on about the size of the U.S. trade deficit (approaching a record $800 billion in 2006). There are also disputes about the corresponding trade surpluses in emerging economies like China and India, not to mention worries about the growing indebtedness of the United States to the rest of the world, and how these outcomes are related to trends in national saving and the government's budget. There are also concerns about how all of these flows relate to exchange rates. And in all these areas, there is often controversy over what policy intervention governments can or should take.

To understand what is at stake in such debates, and to try to find the right answers, we must first know what is being talked about. What do all these measures mean and how are they related? How does the global economy actually function? The goal of this chapter is to explain how trade and payments take place in the world economy and how they affect national income and wealth. In the remainder of the book, we use these essential tools, coupled with our understanding of exchange rates from the previous chapters, to understand the macroeconomic linkages between nations.

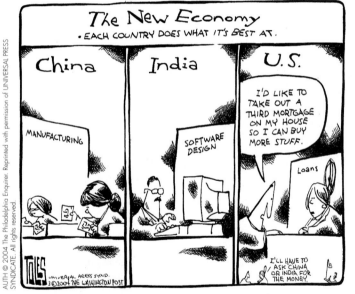

Beyond barter: International transactions involve not just goods and services but also financial assets.

1 Measuring Macroeconomic Activity: An Overview

To understand macroeconomic accounting in an open economy, we build on the accounting principles used to track payments in a closed economy. As you may know from previous courses in macroeconomics, a closed economy is characterized by a *circular flow of payments,* which shows how economic resources are exchanged for payments as they move through the economy. At various points in the flow, economic activity can be measured and these different measures are recorded in the **national income and product accounts.** In an open economy, however, such measurements are more complicated because there are cross-border flows to take into account. Such cross-border flows are recorded in the **balance of payments accounts.**

In this section, we avoid notation, formal definitions, and equations that describe the relationships among the various elements in these accounts so that we can develop some intuition about them. We start by recapping the closed economy case and then exploring how the principles are adapted and extended in an open economy. In later sections, we then move on to formal definitions and applications.

The Flow of Payments in a Closed Economy: Introducing the National Income and Product Accounts

The circular flow in a closed economy is shown in Figure 5-1. At the top is total expenditure on final goods and services, which is known as **gross national expenditure (GNE).** It is made up of three parts:

■ *Personal consumption expenditures* (usually called "consumption") equal total spending by private households on final goods and services,

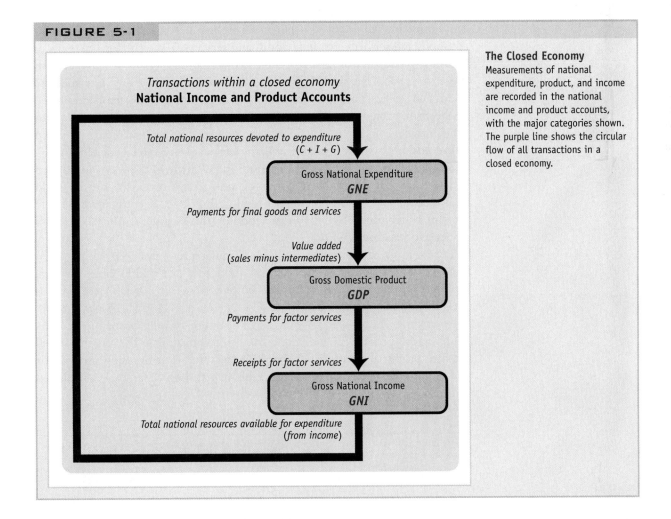

FIGURE 5-1

Transactions within a closed economy
National Income and Product Accounts

Total national resources devoted to expenditure
(C + I + G)

Gross National Expenditure
GNE

Payments for final goods and services

Value added
(sales minus intermediates)

Gross Domestic Product
GDP

Payments for factor services

Receipts for factor services

Gross National Income
GNI

Total national resources available for expenditure
(from income)

The Closed Economy
Measurements of national expenditure, product, and income are recorded in the national income and product accounts, with the major categories shown. The purple line shows the circular flow of all transactions in a closed economy.

including nondurable goods such as food, durable goods such as a television, and services such as window cleaning or gardening.

■ *Gross private domestic investment* (usually called "investment") equals total spending by firms or households on final goods and services to make additions to the stock of capital. Investment includes construction of a new house or a new factory, the purchase of new equipment, and net increases in inventories of goods held by firms.

■ *Government consumption expenditures and gross investment* (often called "government consumption") equal spending by the public sector on final goods and services, including spending on public works, national defense, the police, and the civil service. It does *not* include any transfer payments or income redistributions, such as Social Security or unemployment insurance payments—these are *not* purchases of goods or services, just rearrangements of private spending power.

All of this spending constitutes total demand in the market, that is, all payments for final goods and services. Because the economy is closed, it must also equal supply in that market. Hence, expenditure also equals total receipts by firms from sales of final goods and services.

What happens next to this expenditure? Is it the entire revenue of firms? No. Firms also sell goods to other firms for use as inputs: these are *intermediate* goods and services, not final goods and services. Thus, the total receipts of firms equal the sales of final and intermediate goods. What do firms do with those receipts? They make payments of two sorts. They buy intermediate goods and services for use as inputs, and they pay income to factors employed in the firm, such as wages to the owners of labor, dividends and interest to capital owners, and rent to landowners. The income paid to factors is called **value added;** by definition, it is what is left over once intermediate purchases are deducted from total sales. One important virtue of the way value added is defined is that intermediate goods are not double counted, as they would be if total sales were computed. As a result, value added is considered the true measure of productive activity in an economy; this measure is also called **gross domestic product (GDP).**

For example, suppose firm B, a table manufacturer, buys a $100 input from firm A, a lumber company harvesting wood, to make a $200 table, the final product. Suppose also that both firms employ labor and capital. Here GDP is total sales minus intermediates purchases, or ($200 + $100) − $100 = $200. This example shows that GDP is also a measure of *value added:* firm A has made a $100 product (wood) using labor and capital; firm B takes this intermediate product and adds a further $100 of value to it by using more labor and capital to make a final product (a table) worth $200. The total value added in the economy is $100 + $100 = $200.[1]

---

[1] Note that total sales of the two firms are $300, but this is a misleading measure of economic activity. After all, if firms A and B were to merge, then the input would be produced within the merged firm and total sales would then be only $200. Yet economic activity hasn't changed in this example, only firm ownership. GDP avoids double counting and is a measure of economic activity that does not change if firms reorganize.

As we have defined it, value added or GDP equals sales of final goods and services, plus intermediate sales, minus intermediate purchases. Because this is a closed economy, the last two items cancel out (demand equals supply for intermediates), and we are left with the result that in a closed economy, GNE (the expenditure on final goods and services) equals GDP (the sales of final goods and services, value added). In a closed economy, then, GDP equals GNE: expenditure is the same as production.

What happens next to value added? All value added is paid as income to the domestic entities that own the factors used in production. These entities may be households, government, or firms, but in the aggregate such distinctions are not important. All such income (wages, rents, interest, and so on) is considered to be part of the total income resources of the economy, as measured by **gross national income (GNI).** Hence, in a closed economy, the expenditure on total goods and services (GNE) equals value added (GDP), which is paid as income to productive factors (GNI). Expenditure is the same as product, which is the same as income.

Lastly, there is no way for a closed economy to finance expenditure except out of its own income, so GNI is, in turn, spent and must be the same as expenditure (GNE). Now we see that GNE equals GNI, which equals GDP, which equals GNE.

We can sum up the circular flow with reference to Figure 5-1. We start with consumption, investment, and government consumption. These make up GNE, which is total payments to firms for final goods and services, which becomes value added or GDP, which is then paid as income or GNI, which is then spent as consumption, investment, and government consumption, which make up GNE, and we are back to square one. The circular flow is complete. Ensure you understand this recap: the accounting is about to get more complicated.

The Flow of Payments in an Open Economy: Incorporating the Balance of Payments Accounts

The circular flow of Figure 5-1 is neat and tidy in a closed economy. But the preceding logic doesn't apply in an open economy because we ignored payments flows to and from the rest of the world, the items that are recorded in a nation's *balance of payments accounts.* Figure 5-2 incorporates these flows schematically.

If you can understand Figure 5-2, then the remainder of this chapter will follow easily. The circulating purple arrows on the left side of the figure represent the circular flow in a closed economy as we have just discussed. They are wholly within the purple box, which represents the home country, and they do not cross the edge of that box, which represents the international border.

In an open economy, there are cross-border flows represented by green arrows. We now examine the five key points on the figure where these flows appear:

1. At point 1, we see how international flows of goods and services affect the net receipts of domestic firms (sales minus intermediate

FIGURE 5-2

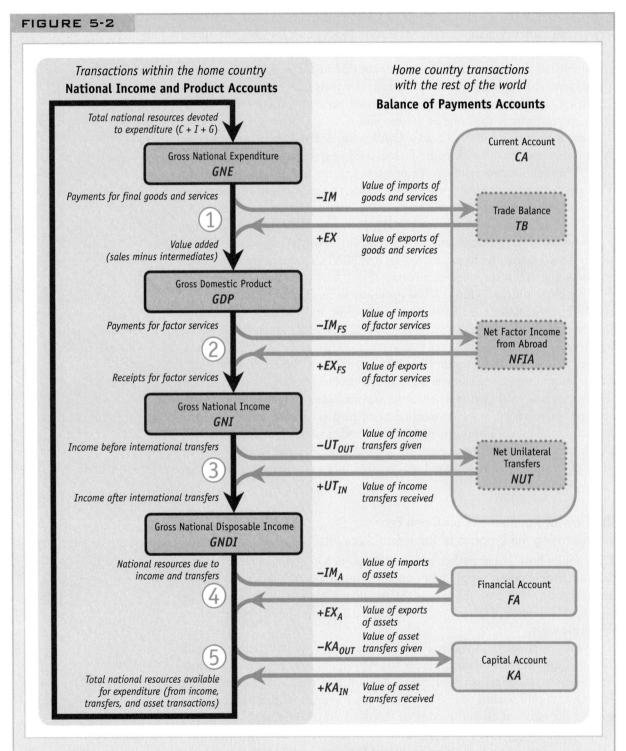

Transactions within the home country
National Income and Product Accounts

Home country transactions
with the rest of the world
Balance of Payments Accounts

Total national resources devoted to expenditure (C + I + G)

Gross National Expenditure
GNE

Payments for final goods and services

①

−IM | Value of imports of goods and services

+EX | Value of exports of goods and services

Value added (sales minus intermediates)

Gross Domestic Product
GDP

Payments for factor services

②

−IM_{FS} | Value of imports of factor services

+EX_{FS} | Value of exports of factor services

Receipts for factor services

Gross National Income
GNI

Income before international transfers

③

−UT_{OUT} | Value of income transfers given

+UT_{IN} | Value of income transfers received

Income after international transfers

Gross National Disposable Income
GNDI

National resources due to income and transfers

④

−IM_A | Value of imports of assets

+EX_A | Value of exports of assets

⑤

−KA_{OUT} | Value of asset transfers given

Total national resources available for expenditure (from income, transfers, and asset transactions)

+KA_{IN} | Value of asset transfers received

Current Account
CA

Trade Balance
TB

Net Factor Income from Abroad
NFIA

Net Unilateral Transfers
NUT

Financial Account
FA

Capital Account
KA

The Open Economy Measurements of national expenditure, product, and income are recorded in the national income and product accounts, with the major categories shown on the left. Measurements of international transactions are recorded in the balance of payments accounts, with the major categories shown on the right. The purple line shows the flow of transactions within the home economy, and the green lines show all the cross-border transactions.

purchases), which make up value added or GDP for the home country. In an open economy, some expenditure is used to purchase foreign goods. These **imports** must be subtracted from GNE because those payments never reach domestic firms. In addition, some foreign expenditure is used to purchase domestic goods. These **exports** must be added to GDP because payments for exports are paid to domestic firms. The difference between payments made for imports and payments received for exports is called the **trade balance,** and it equals net payments to domestic firms due to trade. Allowing for the trade balance, GNE plus the trade balance equals GDP or total value added.

2. At point 2, we see how international flows of factor services and corresponding income payments affect national income, GNI, for the home country. In an open economy, some domestic payments to capital, labor, and land may be owned by (and paid to) foreign entities, and similarly some foreign payments to capital, labor, and land may be owned by (and paid to) domestic entities. For example, if a foreign company builds an automobile factory in the United States, then it will receive payments of profits each year; these are considered payments by the United States for imported capital services (in the form of the factory that the foreigners have built); and if any foreign employees work at the plant, their wages would not be counted as part of U.S. income and are considered instead as payments for imported labor services. Hence, some home GDP may be remitted to foreign entities as payment for factor services, and these **factor service imports** are income payments that never reach domestic entities. Similarly, some foreign GDP may be remitted to domestic entities as payment for their factor services. These **factor service exports** are income payments made to domestic entities. The difference is the **net factor income from abroad (NFIA),** which equals factor service exports minus factor service imports. We see that GDP plus net factor income from abroad equals GNI, the total income earned by domestic entities.

3. At point 3, we see that the home country may not retain all of its earned income GNI. Why? Domestic entities might give some of it away—for example, as foreign aid or remittances by migrants to families back home. Gifts are examples of *unilateral transfers.* **Net unilateral transfers (NUT)** equal the amount of unilateral transfers the country receives from the rest of the world minus the amount it gives to the rest of the world. These net transfers have to be added to GNI to calculate the total income resources available to the home country, which is called **gross national disposable income (GNDI),** hence GNI plus net unilateral transfers equals GNDI. On the balance of payments accounts side of the figure, the sum of the trade balance, net factor income from abroad, and net unilateral transfers is called the **current account.**

4. At point 4, we see that an open economy can increase or decrease the resources it has to spend by trading assets internationally. By trade in assets, we mean the cross-border movement in ownership of a financial claim: for example, if foreigners buy some domestic stocks, bonds, or real estate, they pay the domestic seller of those assets. When foreign entities acquire assets from home entities, the value of these **asset exports** must be added to GNDI. In this way, we measure the total resources available for home expenditure. Conversely, if domestic entities acquire assets from the rest of the world, there are fewer resources available for spending at home. These **asset imports** must be subtracted from GNDI. The difference of asset exports minus asset imports is called the **financial account.**

5. Finally, at point 5, we see that a country may not simply buy and sell assets when trading assets with the rest of the world. It might also transfer assets as gifts. As with income transfers, these must be accounted for. The **capital account** equals capital transfers from the rest of the world minus capital transfers to the rest of the world. These net asset transfers are added to home GNDI when calculating resources available for expenditure in the home country. It is these resources that become total spending, GNE. With all of these adjustments, the flow of Figure 5-2 is fully modified to account for international transactions.[2]

Summary

We conclude our discussion of Figure 5-2 with two key points. First, it shows a clear breakdown between two different sets of transactions. On the left side, in the purple box, are all transactions within the home economy, the key elements of the *national income and product accounts.* On the right side, the green arrows and boxes show all of the international transactions that affect the home economy. These transactions are the key elements of the *balance of payments accounts.* The rest of this chapter explores these two accounts in more detail, moving from the intuitive, schematic description in Figure 5-2 to more formal definitions and accounting identities that we can put to practical use when analyzing macroeconomic data and developing macroeconomic models.

Second, there is one more key insight that jumps out from Figure 5-2 after a moment's thought. The modifications to the circular flow tell us something very important about the balance of payments. We start at the top with GNE, and we first add the three current account terms: we add the trade balance to get GDP, we add net factor income from abroad to get GNI, and then we add net unilateral transfers received to get GNDI. Next we add net asset exports measured by the financial account and net capital transfers measured by the capital account. And we finally get back to GNE. In other words, we started

---

[2] In the past, both the financial and capital accounts were jointly known as "the capital account." This should be kept in mind not only when consulting older documents but also when listening to contemporary discussion because not everyone cares for the new (and somewhat confusing) nomenclature.

with GNE, added in *everything* that goes in the balance of payments accounts, and still ended up back with GNE. Hence, the sum of all the items in the balance of payments account, the net sum of all those cross-border flows, must amount to zero! The balance of payments *does* balance—an important result we explore in more detail later in this chapter.

2 National Accounts: Product, Expenditure, and Income

In the last section, and particularly in Figure 5-2, we informally sketched out all the important national and international transactions. With that overview in mind, we can now more quickly and effectively define the key accounting concepts in the two sets of accounts before putting them to use. We start with the national income and product accounts in this section and continue with the balance of payments accounts in the next section.

Three Approaches

There are three main approaches to the measurement of aggregate economic activity:

- The **expenditure approach** looks at the demand for goods: it examines how much is spent on demand for final goods and services. The key measure is gross national expenditure, *GNE,* the value of all expenditures on final goods and services in the economy.

- The **product approach** looks at the supply of goods: it measures the net value of all goods and services produced by the private sector, where "double counting" is ruled out by excluding the value of intermediate inputs. The key measure is *GDP,* or value added, the value of all goods and services produced by firms in the economy minus the value of all the intermediate goods purchased by firms.

- The **income approach** focuses on payments to factors: it tracks the amount of income received by domestic entities. One key measure is *GNI,* the value of all income payments earned by all factors resident in the economy. The other key measure is *GNDI,* a measure that becomes important when the economy opens. *GNDI* equals *GNI* plus the value of net transfers received from the rest of the world.

The three approaches generate the same answer in the closed economy but not in an open economy. Having gained some intuition in Figure 5-2, we can now explore the accounting in more formal detail.

From GNE to GDP: Accounting for Trade in Goods and Services

For notation, we let GNE consist of consumption, denoted C; investment denoted I; and government consumption, denoted G. Let total exports of goods and services be denoted EX and imports IM; $EX - IM$ is the trade balance, as defined previously.

The difference between *GNE* and *GDP* arises from trade in goods and services. To see how, we use the fact that in the market for *all* goods and services, demand equals supply, allowing for trade with the rest of the world (ROW), so that the following expression must be true in the home market for all goods and services:

$$\underbrace{\left(\begin{array}{c} \text{Total sales} \\ \text{by home firms} \end{array}\right) + IM}_{\substack{\text{All goods} \\ \text{sold} \\ \text{by ROW}}} = \underbrace{[C + I + G]}_{\substack{\text{Final goods} \\ \text{purchased} \\ \text{by home}}} + \underbrace{\left(\begin{array}{c} \text{Intermediate purchases} \\ \text{by home firms} \end{array}\right) + EX.}_{\substack{\text{All goods} \\ \text{purchased} \\ \text{by ROW}}}$$

$$\underbrace{}_{\substack{\text{Total value of goods and services} \\ \text{sold (final and intermediate)}}} \qquad \underbrace{}_{\text{Total value of goods and services purchased (final and intermediate)}}$$

The left-hand side is the value of everything sold in the home market, the right-hand side, the value of everything purchased in the home market. These must be equal.

We can rearrange the previous equation and use the definition of *GDP* as value added, to write *GDP* as follows:

(5-1)
$$\underbrace{GDP}_{\substack{\text{Gross domestic} \\ \text{product}}} = \underbrace{\left(\begin{array}{c} \text{Total sales} \\ \text{by home firms} \end{array}\right) - \left(\begin{array}{c} \text{Intermediate purchases} \\ \text{by home firms} \end{array}\right)}_{\text{Definition of value added}}$$

$$= \underbrace{[C + I + G]}_{\substack{\text{Gross national} \\ \text{expenditure } GNE}} + \underbrace{[EX - IM]}_{\text{Trade balance } TB}.$$

This important expression is called the **GDP identity.** The GDP identity says that *gross domestic product is equal to gross national expenditure (GNE) plus the trade balance (TB)*.

We may note in passing that the expression just given makes due allowance for trade in intermediate goods, a factor that is often ignored. An intermediate export adds to home *GDP* because it is sold by a home firm but not bought by a home firm, so it does not cancel out in the computation of value added. Conversely, an intermediate import is subtracted from home *GDP* because it is bought by a home firm but not sold by a home firm. It is important to understand and account for these transactions properly because, due to globalization and outsourcing, trade in intermediate goods has taken on increasing importance in recent years (see **Headlines: Who Makes the iPod?**).

The trade balance, *TB,* is also often referred to as *net exports.* Because it is the net value of exports minus imports, it may be positive or negative.

If *TB* > 0, we say a country has a *trade surplus.*
If *TB* < 0, we say a country has a *trade deficit.*

For example, in 2006 in the United States, *GNE* was $14,010 billion and the trade balance, *TB,* was −$763 billion. Adding these figures, we find that gross domestic product, *GDP,* for 2006 was $13,247 billion.

HEADLINES

Who Makes the iPod?

Properly accounting for trade in intermediate goods is easier said than done.

Who makes the Apple iPod? Here's a hint: It is not Apple. The company outsources the entire manufacture of the device to a number of Asian enterprises, among them Asustek, Inventec Appliances and Foxconn.

But this list of companies isn't a satisfactory answer either: They only do final assembly. What about the 451 parts that go into the iPod? Where are they made and by whom?

Three researchers at the University of California, Irvine—Greg Linden, Kenneth L. Kraemer and Jason Dedrick—applied some investigative cost accounting to this question, using a report from Portelligent Inc. that examined all the parts that went into the iPod.

Their study, sponsored by the Sloan Foundation, offers a fascinating illustration of the complexity of the global economy, and how difficult it is to understand that complexity by using only conventional trade statistics.

The retail value of the 30-gigabyte video iPod that the authors examined was $299. The most expensive component in it was the hard drive, which was manufactured by Toshiba and costs about $73. The next most costly components were the display module (about $20), the video/multimedia processor chip ($8) and the controller chip ($5). They estimated that the final assembly, done in China, cost only about $4 a unit.

One approach to tracing supply chain geography might be to attribute the cost of each component to the country of origin of its maker. So $73 of the cost of the iPod would be attributed to Japan since Toshiba is a Japanese company, and the $13 cost of the two chips would be attributed to the United States, since the suppliers, Broadcom and PortalPlayer, are American companies, and so on.

But this method hides some of the most important details. Toshiba may be a Japanese company, but it makes most of its hard drives in the Philippines and China. So perhaps we should also allocate part of the cost of that hard drive to one of those countries. The same problem arises regarding the Broadcom chips, with most of them manufactured in Taiwan. So how can one distribute the costs of the iPod components across the countries where they are manufactured in a meaningful way?

To answer this question, let us look at the production process as a sequence of steps, each possibly performed by a different company operating in a different country. At each step, inputs like computer chips and a bare circuit board are converted into outputs like an assembled circuit board. The difference between the cost of the inputs and the value of the outputs is the "value added" at that step, which can then be attributed to the country where that value was added.

The profit margin on generic parts like nuts and bolts is very low, since these items are produced in intensely competitive industries and can be manufactured anywhere. Hence, they add little to the final value of the iPod. More specialized parts, like the hard drives and controller chips, have much higher value added.

According to the authors' estimates, the $73 Toshiba hard drive in the iPod contains about $54 in parts and labor. So the value that Toshiba added to the hard drive was $19 plus its own direct labor costs. This $19 is attributed to Japan since Toshiba is a Japanese company.

Continuing in this way, the researchers examined the major components of the iPod and tried to calculate the value

Who is making it?

added at different stages of the production process and then assigned that value added to the country where the value was created. This isn't an easy task, but even based on their initial examination, it is quite clear that the largest share of the value added in the iPod goes to enterprises in the United States, particularly for units sold here.

The researchers estimated that $163 of the iPod's $299 retail value in the United States was captured by American companies and workers, breaking it down to $75 for distribution and retail costs, $80 to Apple, and $8 to various domestic component makers. Japan contributed about $26 to the value added (mostly via the Toshiba disk drive), while Korea contributed less than $1.

The unaccounted-for parts and labor costs involved in making the iPod came to about $110. The authors hope to assign those labor costs to the appropriate countries, but as the hard drive example illustrates, that's not so easy to do.

This value added calculation illustrates the futility of summarizing such a complex manufacturing process by using conventional trade statistics. Even though Chinese workers contribute only about 1 percent of the value of the iPod,

Continued on next page.

the export of a finished iPod to the United States directly contributes about $150 to our bilateral trade deficit with the Chinese.

Ultimately, there is no simple answer to who makes the iPod or where it is made. The iPod, like many other products, is made in several countries by dozens of companies, with each stage of production contributing a different amount to the final value.

The real value of the iPod doesn't lie in its parts or even in putting those parts together. The bulk of the iPod's value is in the conception and design of the iPod. That is why Apple gets $80 for each of these video iPods it sells, which is by far the largest piece of value added in the entire supply chain.

Those clever folks at Apple figured out how to combine 451 mostly generic parts into a valuable product. They may not make the iPod, but they created it. In the end, that's what really matters.

Source: Hal R. Varian, "An iPod Has Global Value. Ask the (Many) Countries That Make It," New York Times, June 28, 2007.

From GDP to GNI: Accounting for Trade in Factor Services

Trade in factor services occurs when, say, the home country is paid income by a foreign country as compensation for the labor, capital, and land owned by home entities but in service in the foreign country. We say the home country is exporting factor services to the foreign country and receiving factor income in return.

Factor income includes payments for labor services (such as income paid to workers posted overseas who remain home nationals) and payments on income from assets (such as investment income in the form of dividends or interest payments from overseas assets such as debt, equity, or land owned by home entities). A good example of a labor service export would be a home country professional temporarily working overseas, say a U.S. architect freelancing in London. But note that the architect's income would not be considered a labor service export if he is working in London for a U.S. firm and is paid by a U.S. head office; in this case, the United States is exporting architectural services, a service export that is part of the trade balance; in the current account, much hangs on such picky distinctions.

A clear example of trade in capital services is *foreign direct investment,* such as U.S.-owned factories in Ireland (or Japanese-owned factories in the United States). These domestically located factories are overseas *physical* assets that yield income to the foreign owners each period. Other examples of trade in capital services include overseas *financial* assets such as loans to foreign governments, firms, and households; purchases of foreign securities or real estate generating interest or rents; and so on. Conceptually, these items are all similar: overseas assets generate streams of service income for the home country, income that represents payment for the capital advanced by the home country to the foreign country at some time in the past. Similarly, and symmetrically, the home country will make service payments to the rest of the world.

How can these service income payments be accounted for? As we have seen, by definition, *GDP* is paid as income. Some of this income is paid to foreigners as *income payments,* denoted IM_{FS}, for factor services imported by the home country. The remainder is paid to domestic entities. In addition, domestic entities receive income payments from foreign entities as *income receipts,* denoted EX_{FS}, for factor services exported by the home country.

Thus, gross national income (GNI), the total income earned by domestic entities, is[3]

$$GNI = GDP \quad + \quad \underbrace{EX_{FS}}_{\substack{\text{Foreign income payments} \\ \text{to domestic factors}}} \quad - \quad \underbrace{IM_{FS}}_{\substack{\text{Domestic income payments} \\ \text{to foreign factors}}}.$$

This is the **GNI identity.** The last two terms, income receipts minus income payments, are the home country's *net factor income from abroad,* denoted by $NFIA = EX_{FS} - IM_{FS}$. This may be a positive or a negative number, depending on whether income receipts are larger or smaller than income payments. The GNI identity says that *gross national income is equal to gross domestic product (GDP) plus net factor income from abroad (NFIA).*

From the previous equation and the GDP identity, Equation (5-1), we find that

$$(5\text{-}2) \quad GNI = \underbrace{C + I + G}_{\substack{\text{Gross national expenditure} \\ GNE}} \underbrace{\;+\; \underbrace{(EX - IM)}_{\substack{\text{Trade balance} \\ TB}}}_{GDP} + \underbrace{(EX_{FS} - IM_{FS})}_{\substack{\text{Net factor income from abroad} \\ NFIA}}.$$

For example, in 2006 the United States received income payments from foreigners EX_{FS} of \$666 billion and made income payments to foreigners IM_{FS} of \$636 billion, so net factor income from abroad, $NFIA$, was +\$30 billion. Earlier in this chapter, we computed U.S. GDP to be \$13,247 billion; because of net factor income from abroad, however, U.S. GNI was a little higher at \$13,277 billion.

APPLICATION

Celtic Tiger or Tortoise?

International trade in factor services can generate a difference in the national accounts between product and income measures. In the United States, this difference is typically small, but at times $NFIA$ can play a major role in a country's national accounts.

In the 1970s, Ireland was one of the poorer countries in Europe, but it was soon to experience three decades of speedy economic growth with an accompanying investment boom now known as the Irish Miracle. From 1975 to 2005, Irish real GDP per person grew at a phenomenal rate of 4.4% per year—not as rapid as in some developing countries but extremely rapid by the standards of the rich countries of the European Union (EU) or the Organization for Economic Cooperation and Development (OECD). Comparisons with fast-growing Asian economies—the "Asian Tigers"—soon had people speaking of the "Celtic Tiger" when referring to Ireland.

---

[3] GNI is the accounting concept formerly known as GNP, or *gross national product.* The term GNP is still often used, but GNI is technically more accurate because the concept is a measurement of income rather than product. Note that in cases in which there are taxes (or subsidies) on production and imports, they will be counted in GDP (for production taxes) and in GNE (for both). Those taxes are also added to GNI, in addition to factor incomes. This treatment of taxes ensures that GNI is computed on a similar basis to GDP and that the tax income to the home country is properly counted as a part of home income. We avoid these complexities in the simple case studied here.

Did Irish citizens enjoy all of these gains? No. Figure 5-3 shows that in the 1970s Ireland's annual net factor income from abroad was virtually nil—about €10 per person (in 2000 real euros) or 0.1% of *GDP.* Yet by 2002–03, nearly 20% of Irish *GDP* was being shipped overseas to make net factor income payments to foreigners. What explained this dramatic change? The boom was heavily dependent on investment by foreigners. The computer factories built by Apple in Cork and by Intel in County Kildare are just two examples, but the pattern was widespread. By some estimates, 75% of Ireland's industrial-sector *GDP* originated in foreign-owned plants in 2004. And those foreigners expected their big Irish investments to generate income, and so they did, in the form of net factor payments abroad amounting to almost one fifth of Irish *GDP.* This meant that Irish *GNI* was a lot smaller than Irish *GDP*—and the latter might have been inflated anyway as a result of various accounting problems.[4]

FIGURE 5-3

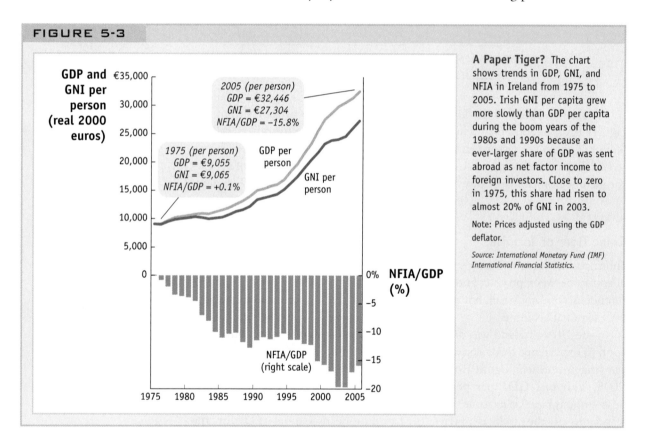

A Paper Tiger? The chart shows trends in GDP, GNI, and NFIA in Ireland from 1975 to 2005. Irish GNI per capita grew more slowly than GDP per capita during the boom years of the 1980s and 1990s because an ever-larger share of GDP was sent abroad as net factor income to foreign investors. Close to zero in 1975, this share had risen to almost 20% of GNI in 2003.

Note: Prices adjusted using the GDP deflator.

Source: International Monetary Fund (IMF) International Financial Statistics.

---

[4] See, for example, Antoin E. Murphy, 1994, *The Irish Economy: Celtic Tiger or Tortoise?* (Dublin: Money Markets International), or, more recently, Rossa White, "How Irish GDP Is Inflated," Davy, *Weekly Market Comment,* Bank of Ireland Group, March 7, 2005. Some special factors exacerbated the difference between GDP and GNI in Ireland such as special tax incentives that encouraged foreign firms to keep their accounts in a way that generated high profits "on paper" (that is, high reported value added) at their Irish subsidiaries rather than in their (high tax) home country. A common technique would be transfer pricing, in which, say, a U.S. multinational underinvoices its imports into Ireland by €10 million and generates a correspondingly larger Irish profit (and a smaller U.S. profit). This accounting device understates Irish imports and hence raises GDP by €10 million while adding €10 million to Irish NFIA, leaving zero impact on GNI. If one could undo these accounting devices, Irish GDP would be corrected downward, but Irish GNI would not be affected. For these reasons, too, many economists believe that Irish GNI, as well as being more conservative, might also be a truer measure of the economy's performance.

This example shows how *GDP* can be a misleading measure of economic performance. In 2004, Ireland was the 4th richest OECD economy ranked by *GDP* per capita but was ranked only 17th in *GNI* per capita.[5] The Irish outflow of net factor payments is certainly an extreme case, but it serves to underscore an important point about income measurement in open economies. Any country that relies heavily on foreign investment to generate economic growth is not getting a free lunch. Irish *GNI* per person grew at "only" 3.7% from 1975 to 2005 to arrive at €27,304; this was 0.7% per year less than the growth rate of *GDP* per person, which rose to €32,446 (both income figures are inflation adjusted and expressed in 2000 real euros). Living standards grew impressively, but the more humble *GNI* figures may give a more accurate measure of what the Irish Miracle has meant for the Irish. ■

The Intel Ireland campus: This plant at Collinstown Industrial Park, Leixlip, County Kildare is Intel's fourth largest manufacturing site overall and the largest outside of the United States. The site represents a €4.5 billion investment and employs 4,700 direct employees and indirect long-term contractors.

From GNI to GNDI: Accounting for Transfers of Income

Our derivations so far fully describe economic activity in the market. However, nonmarket transactions also need to be accounted for if our accounts are to be complete and accurate. International nonmarket transfers of goods, services, and income include such things as foreign aid by governments (official development assistance—ODA—and other help), private charitable gifts to foreign recipients (i.e., philanthropy), and income remittances by individuals (for example, to relatives or friends in other countries). These transfers are "gifts" and may take the form of goods and services (food aid, volunteer medical services) or income transfers.

Suppose a country receives transfers worth UT_{IN} and gives transfers worth UT_{OUT}; then its net unilateral transfers, denoted *NUT*, are given by $NUT = UT_{IN} - UT_{OUT}$. Because this is a net amount, it may be positive or negative.

In general, net unilateral transfers play a small role in the income and product accounts for most high-income countries (net outgoing transfers are typically no more than 5% of *GNI*). But they can be important for some low-income countries that receive a great deal of foreign aid or migrant remittances, as seen in Figure 5-4.

You might think that net unilateral transfers are a better measure of a country's generosity toward foreigners than official development assistance, which is but one component. For example, in the United States, where private gifts to charity are substantial, the difference between the two measures can be very large, as shown in Table 5-1. Still, measuring national generosity is highly controversial and a recurring theme of

NET WORK

Go to the UN website and find out what the Millennium Development Goals are (http://www.un.org/millenniumgoals). Go to the Gleneagles summit website and examine the promises made (http://www.g8.gov.uk/). Use the Web to check up on how well these G8 promises are being kept, such as the UN goal of 0.7% of GDP in official development assistance, the promise to eradicate export subsidies, and the aim to double aid by 2010. (Hint: Google sites such as Oxfam or the Jubilee Debt Campaign, or look for the World Bank Tools for Monitoring the Millennium Development Goals.)

---

[5] Joe Cullen, "There's Lies, Damned Lies, and Wealth Statistics," *Irish Times,* May 1, 2004.

FIGURE 5-4

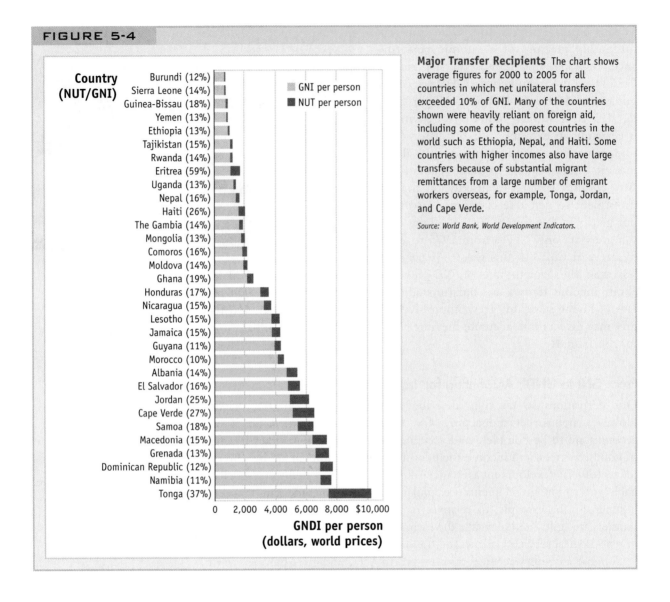

Major Transfer Recipients The chart shows average figures for 2000 to 2005 for all countries in which net unilateral transfers exceeded 10% of GNI. Many of the countries shown were heavily reliant on foreign aid, including some of the poorest countries in the world such as Ethiopia, Nepal, and Haiti. Some countries with higher incomes also have large transfers because of substantial migrant remittances from a large number of emigrant workers overseas, for example, Tonga, Jordan, and Cape Verde.

Source: World Bank, World Development Indicators.

current affairs (see **Headlines: Are Rich Countries "Stingy" with Foreign Aid?**).

To include the impact of aid and all other transfers in the overall calculation of a country's income resources, we must add net unilateral transfers to gross national income. We thus obtain a full measure of national income in the open economy, known as gross national disposable income (*GNDI*), henceforth denoted *Y*. This is summarized in the **GNDI identity:**

$$(5\text{-}3) \qquad Y = GNDI = GNI + NUT.$$

In general, we will use *GNDI* as our measure of national income *Y* henceforth. Why? We frequently see reference to *GDP* and other measures of

TABLE 5-1

More Assistance Than Meets the Eye? This table presents USAID's estimates of total "U.S. international assistance" to developing countries in 2000. This includes far more than official development assistance (ODA, $9.9 billion in 2000). Other government assistance amounted to $12.7 billion (e.g., USAID transfers to Israel, Eastern Europe, and the Baltics, and Newly Independent States; the State Department's educational, cultural, and peacekeeping operations; antiterrorism, nonproliferation, military education, and training activities by the Department of Defense). The table also includes the substantial U.S. gifts of private philanthropy by various entities, such as foundations, corporations, and religious groups. Lastly, the table includes remittances, whereby foreign workers send often large sums of money back to their extended family in their country of origin. The table shows that ODA is but one component of total transfers, and, at 18%, it is a very small share for the United States.

Category	2000, U.S. $ (billions)	Share of Total (%)
U.S. official development assistance	9.9	18
All other U.S. government assistance	12.7	22
U.S. private assistance	33.6	60
Of which: Foundations	1.5	
Corporations	2.8	
Private voluntary organizations*	6.6	
Universities and colleges	1.3	
Religious congregations	3.4	
Individual remittances	18	
Total U.S. international assistance	56.2	100

* Including the value of volunteer time.

Source: U.S. Agency for International Development, 2003, Foreign Aid in the National Interest: Promoting Freedom, Security, and Opportunity, Table 6.1.

national economic activity. But we have already seen that *GDP* is not a true measure of income because, unlike *GNI*, it does not include net factor income from abroad. But *GNI* is not a perfect measure either: it still leaves out international transfers. *GNDI* is a preferred measure because it most closely corresponds to the resources available to the nation's households, and national welfare depends most closely on this accounting measure.

What the National Economic Aggregates Tell Us

Building on the intuition in Figure 5-2, we have arrived at the key mathematical implications of the international flows we have studied. The three key equations—Equations (5-1), (5-2), and (5-3)—define the important national economic aggregates in an open economy:

$$GDP = GNE + TB;$$
$$GNI = GDP + NFIA;$$
$$GNDI = GNI + NUT.$$

HEADLINES

Are Rich Countries "Stingy" with Foreign Aid?

The Asian tsunami on December 26, 2004, was one of the worst natural disasters of modern times. Some aftershocks were felt in international politics. Jan Egeland, UN undersecretary general for humanitarian affairs and emergency relief, declared, "It is beyond me why we are so stingy." His comments rocked the boat in many rich countries, especially in the United States where ODA fell short of the UN goal of 0.7% of GNI. But the United States gives in other ways, making judgments about stinginess far from straightforward.

Can Its Value Be Counted? An Indonesian soldier thanks two U.S. airmen after a U.S. Navy helicopter delivered fresh water to tsunami victims 30 miles southwest of Banda Aceh, Indonesia, Saturday, January 8, 2005. The Pentagon reported that there were nearly 16,000 U.S. military personnel in the region, supported by 26 ships, 58 helicopters, and 43 fixed-wing aircraft. They delivered more than 10 million pounds of food and supplies, provided more than 400,000 gallons of fresh water, and treated 2,000 patients. As a matter of bookkeeping, the normal operating costs of military assets used for humanitarian purposes are not fully counted as part of official development assistance, nor even included in other government assistance as part of unilateral transfers.

Is the United States stingy when it comes to foreign aid? . . . The answer depends on how you measure. . . .

In terms of traditional foreign aid, the United States gave $16.25 billion in 2003, as measured by the Organization of Economic Cooperation and Development (OECD), the club of the world's rich industrial nations. That was almost double the aid by the next biggest net spender, Japan ($8.8 billion). Other big donors were France ($7.2 billion) and Germany ($6.8 billion).

But critics point out that the United States is much bigger than those individual nations. As a group, member nations of the European Union have a bit larger population than the United States and give a great deal more money in foreign aid—$49.2 billion altogether in 2003.

In relation to affluence, the United States lies at the bottom of the list of rich donor nations. It gave 0.15% of gross national income to official development assistance in 2003. By this measure, Norway at 0.92% was the most generous, with Denmark next at 0.84%.

Bring those numbers down to an everyday level and the average American gave 13 cents a day in government aid, according to David Roodman, a researcher at the Center for Global Development (CGD) in Washington. Throw in another nickel a day from private giving. That private giving is high by international standards, yet not enough to close the gap with Norway, whose citizens average $1.02 per day in government aid and 24 cents per day in private aid. . . .

But the administration sees that count as too restrictive. Andrew Natsios, head of the U.S. Agency for International Development, claimed on television last week that U.S. foreign aid was $24 billion in 2003, up from $10.6 billion when President Clinton took office. Some experts say that number, bigger than the OECD count, is a bit mysterious. It probably includes some debt forgiveness, such as $1 billion for the Congo. Last month, the United States forgave $4 billion in Iraqi debt, which may get counted in 2004 numbers for foreign aid. . . .

Moreover, the United States has a huge defense budget, some of which benefits developing countries. Making a judgment call, the CGD includes the cost of UN peacekeeping activities and other military assistance approved by a multilateral institution, such as NATO. So the United States gets credit for its spending in Kosovo, Australia for its intervention in East Timor, and Britain for military money spent to bring more stability to Sierra Leone. . . .

"Not to belittle what we are doing, we shouldn't get too self-congratulatory," says Frederick Barton, an economist at the Center for Strategic and International Studies in Washington.

Source: "Foreign Aid: Is the U.S. Stingy?" Christian Science Monitor/MSN Money, January 6, 2005.

Combining these three equations, we obtain our preferred measure of national income, Y:

$$Y = GNDI = GNE + TB + NFIA + NUT.$$

And if we expand all terms on the right-hand side using their definitions, we find that

$$(5\text{-}4) \quad Y = \underbrace{\underbrace{C + I + G}_{GNE} + \{\underbrace{(EX - IM)}_{\substack{\text{Trade balance} \\ (TB)}} + \underbrace{(EX_{FS} - IM_{FS})}_{\substack{\text{Net factor income from} \\ \text{abroad } (NFIA)}} + \underbrace{(UT_{IN} - UT_{OUT})}_{\substack{\text{Net unilateral transfers} \\ (NUT)}}\}}_{\substack{\text{Current account} \\ (CA)}}}_{GNDI}.$$

On the left is gross national disposable income. The first term on the right is gross national expenditure. The other terms on the right measure the difference between the two. This term consists of all international transactions of goods, services, and income. It is so important that it has a special name. It is called the current account (CA).

The key lesson is that in a closed economy, there are no international transactions: $TB = NFIA = NUT = 0$ (and thus the CA is zero), so the four main aggregates are the same: $GNDI = GNI = GDP = GNE$. In an open economy, all four of these aggregates can be different.

Understanding the Data for the National Economic Aggregates

Now that we've learned how a nation's principal economic aggregates are affected by international transactions in theory, let's see how this works in practice. In this section, we take a look at some data from the real world to see how they are recorded and presented in official statistics.

Table 5-2 shows data for the United States in 2006 reported by the Bureau of Economic Analysis in the official national income and product accounts.

Lines 1 to 3 of the table show the components of gross national expenditure, GNE. Personal consumption expenditures C were $9,269 billion, gross

TABLE 5-2

U.S. Economic Aggregates in 2006 The table shows the computation of GDP, GNI, and GNDI using the components of gross national expenditure, the trade balance, international income payments, and unilateral transfers.

Line	Category	Symbol	$ billions
1	Consumption (personal consumption expenditures)	C	9,269
2	+ Investment (gross private domestic investment)	I	2,213
3	+ Government consumption (government expenditures)	G	2,528
4	= Gross national expenditure	GNE	14,010
5	+ Trade balance	TB	−763
6	= Gross domestic product	GDP	13,247
7	+ Net factor income from abroad	$NFIA$	+30
8	= Gross national income	GNI	13,277
9	+ Net unilateral transfers	NUT	−80
10	= Gross national disposable income	$GNDI$	13,197

Note: Details may not add to totals because of rounding.

Source: U.S. Bureau of Economic Analysis, NIPA Tables 1.1.5 and 4.1, using the NIPA definition of the United States.

private domestic investment *I* was \$2,213 billion, and government consumption *G* was \$2,528 billion. Summing up, *GNE* was equal to \$14,010 billion, which is shown on line 4.

On line 5 appears the trade balance, *TB,* which was the net export of goods and services, in the amount −\$763 billion. (That net exports are negative means that the United States imported more goods and services than it exported.) Adding this to *GNE* gives gross domestic product *GDP* on line 6, which amounted to \$13,247 billion.

Next we account for net factor income from abroad, *NFIA,* equal to +\$30 billion on line 7, and adding this to *GDP* gives gross national income, *GNI,* equal to \$13,277 billion as shown on line 8.

Finally, to get to the bottom line, we account for the fact that the United States receives net unilateral transfers from the rest of the world of −\$80 billion (that is, the United States makes net transfers to the rest of the world of \$80 billion) on line 9. Adding these negative transfers to *GNI* results in a gross national disposable income, *GNDI,* of \$13,197 billion on line 10.

Some Recent Trends Figures 5-5 and 5-6 show recent trends in various components of U.S. national income. The identity we derived in Equation (5-4) says that national income can be broken down into two parts: *GNE* and *CA.* These can then be broken down into additional parts. Examining these breakdowns gives us a sense of the relative magnitude and economic significance of each component.

In Figure 5-5, *GNE* is shown as the sum of consumption *C,* investment *I,* and government consumption *G.* Consumption accounts for about 70% of *GNE,* while government consumption *G* accounts for about 15%. Both of

FIGURE 5-5

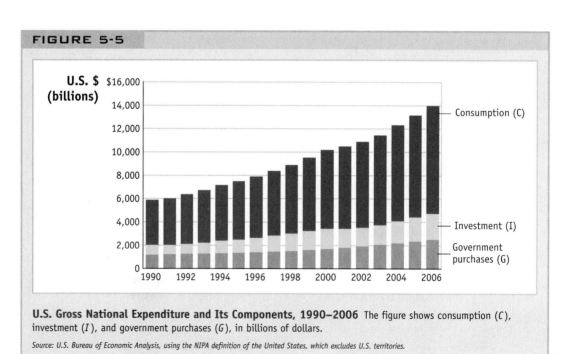

U.S. Gross National Expenditure and Its Components, 1990–2006 The figure shows consumption (*C*), investment (*I*), and government purchases (*G*), in billions of dollars.

Source: U.S. Bureau of Economic Analysis, using the NIPA definition of the United States, which excludes U.S. territories.

FIGURE 5-6

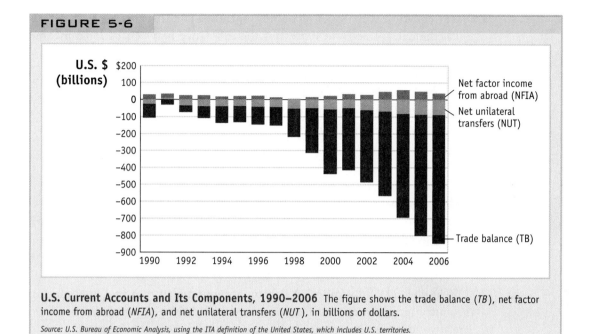

U.S. Current Accounts and Its Components, 1990–2006 The figure shows the trade balance (*TB*), net factor income from abroad (*NFIA*), and net unilateral transfers (*NUT*), in billions of dollars.

Source: U.S. Bureau of Economic Analysis, using the ITA definition of the United States, which includes U.S. territories.

these components are relatively stable. Investment accounts for the rest (about 15% of *GNE*), but investment tends to fluctuate more than *C* and *G* (for example, it fell after the year 2000 during a recession period). Over the period shown, *GNE* grew from $6,000 billion to about $14,000 billion in dollar terms.

In Figure 5-6, *CA* is shown as the sum of the trade balance (*TB*), net factor income from abroad (*NFIA*), and net unilateral transfers (*NUT*). The trade balance in the United States has been in deficit for the entire period shown, and the deficit grew larger over time. It is the dominant component in the current account and is fast approaching –$1,000 billion. In 2006 it was about –6% of gross national income. Net factor income from abroad is a much smaller figure and positive in all years shown, typically less than +$100 billion (less than 1% of national income). In a typical year, net unilateral transfers were of a similar magnitude but with the opposite sign, no larger than –$100 billion.[6]

NET WORK

Use the Web to locate the official macroeconomic statistics for your country. (In the United States, go to http://www.bea.gov.) Find the latest annual data corresponding to the measures discussed in this section. Was your country's GDP higher or lower than its GNE? Why? Was your country's GNI higher or lower than its GDP? Why? What about GNDI—was your country a net giver or receiver of transfers?

What the Current Account Tells Us

The current account plays a central role in this and subsequent chapters. In particular, it is important to remember that Equation (5-4) can be conveniently and concisely written as

(5-5)
$$Y = C + I + G + CA.$$

---

[6] In 1991 the United States was a net recipient of unilateral transfers, as a result of transfer payments from other countries in support of U.S. military expenses in the first Gulf War.

This equation is the open-economy **national income identity.** It tells us that the current account represents the difference between national income ($Y = GNDI$) and gross national expenditure ($GNE = C + I + G$). Hence:

> GNDI is greater than GNE if and only if CA is positive, or in surplus.
> GNDI is less than GNE if and only if CA is negative, or in deficit.

Subtracting $C + G$ from both sides of the last identity, we can see that the current account is also the difference between **national saving** (S) and investment:

$$(5\text{-}6) \qquad \underset{Y-C-G}{\underbrace{S}} = I + CA.$$

where national saving is defined as income minus consumption minus government consumption. This equation is called the **current account identity** even though it is just a rearrangement of the national income identity. Thus:

> S is greater than I if and only if CA is positive, or in surplus.
> S is less than I if and only if CA is negative, or in deficit.

What does all of this mean? A current account deficit measures how much a country spends in excess of income or—equivalently—how it saves too little relative to its investment needs. (Surpluses would mean the opposite.)

We can now understand the widespread use of the current account deficit in the press and elsewhere as a measure of how a country is "spending more than it earns" or "saving too little" or "living beyond its means"—a depiction often given a negative connotation. But can we use the current account to gauge a nation's economic health? What really drives the current account? How is it possible for a country to spend more or less than it earns? Is this a good thing? How long can it go on? These are some of the questions that we will answer in the remainder of this chapter and the chapters that follow.

We know current account imbalances are possible, for example, if assets are used to make payments for goods and services. Thus, to understand international transactions fully, we must understand the asset flows that take place alongside all the current account flows we have studied so far. This is our next task in this chapter. We will see that current account imbalances have implications for a country's level of wealth, and in the next chapter we will see why such imbalances cannot go on forever. In the long run, a country must still, in some precise sense, "live within its means."

APPLICATION

Global Imbalances

Our accounting tool kit allows us to understand in greater detail some remarkable quantitative features of financial globalization in recent years, including the explosion in *global imbalances,* the large current account surpluses and deficits seen in various countries and regions that are of great concern to policy makers and are much talked about in the media.

We now examine some of these trends in some detail. Figure 5-7 shows trends since 1970 in saving, investment, and the current account for four groups of industrial countries. All flows are expressed as ratios relative to each

FIGURE 5-7

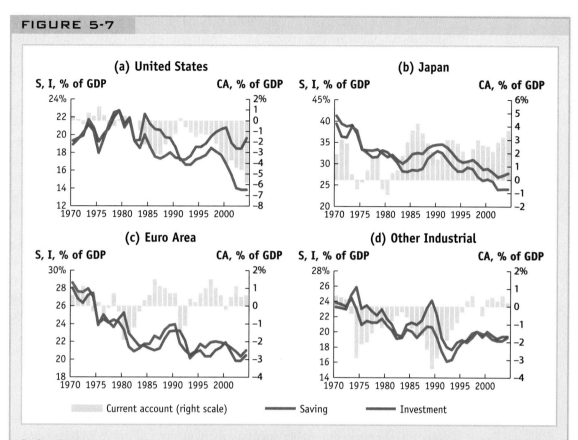

Saving, Investment, and Current Account Trends: Industrial Countries The charts show saving, investment, and the current account as a percent of GDP for four groups of industrial countries. The United States has seen both saving and investment fall since the 1970s, but saving has fallen further than investment, opening up a large current account deficit approaching 6% of GDP in 2004. Japan's experience is the opposite: investment fell further than savings, opening up a large current account surplus of about 3% to 4% of GDP. The Euro area has also seen saving and investment fall but has been closer to balance and has recently run a small surplus of about 0.5% of GDP. Other industrial countries (e.g., non-Euro area EU countries, Canada, Australia, and so on) ran large current account deficits in the 1970s and 1980s but have recently moved toward surplus. They too have seen a decline in both saving and investment.

Source: IMF, World Economic Outlook, *September 2005.*

region's GDP. Some trends stand out. First, in all regions, saving and investment have been on a marked downward trend for the past 30 years. From its peak, the ratio of saving to GDP fell by about 8 percentage points in the United States, about 15 percentage points in Japan, and about 6 percentage points in the Eurozone and other countries. Investment ratios typically followed a downward path in all regions, too—but this decline was steeper than the savings drop in Japan (a fall of about 15 percentage points), and there was hardly any decline in investment in the United States.

On some level, these trends accord with the recent history of the industrialized countries. The U.S. economy grew rapidly since 1990 and the Japanese economy grew very slowly, with other countries in between. The fast-growing U.S. economy generated high investment demand, while in slumping Japan investment collapsed; other regions maintained middling levels of growth and investment. Concerning saving, all the countries shown have suffered from aging populations with fewer workers for each elderly person, a trend commonly associated with decreased saving as the "demographic burden" of the unproductive retirees raises consumption relative to income.

As we would expect from a look at the current account identity ($CA = S - I$), the investment and saving trends have had a predictable impact on the current accounts of industrial countries. Because saving fell faster than investment in the United States, the current account moved sharply into deficit, a trend that was only briefly arrested in the early 1990s. By 2003 the U.S. current account was at a record deficit level close to −6% of U.S. GDP. In Japan, saving fell less than investment, so the opposite happened: a very big current account surplus opened up in the 1980s and 1990s, and it is currently near 4% of Japanese GDP. In the other industrial regions, saving and investment did not diverge so much, so the current account has recently remained closer to balance.

To uncover the sources of the trends in total saving, Figure 5-8 examines two of its components, public and private saving. We define **private saving** as that part of after-tax private sector disposable income that is *not* devoted to private consumption C. After-tax private sector disposable income, in turn, is defined as national income Y minus the net taxes T paid by households to the government. Hence, private saving S_p is

(5-7) $$S_p = Y - T - C.$$

Private saving can be a positive number, but if the private sector consumption exceeds after-tax disposable income, then private saving will be negative.

FIGURE 5-8

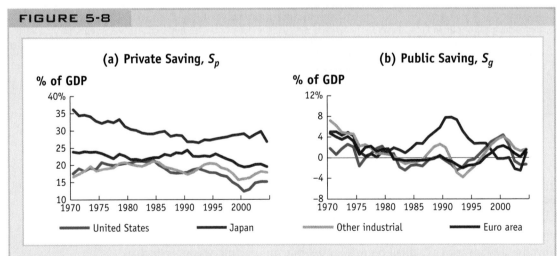

Private and Public Saving Trends: Industrial Countries The chart on the left shows private saving and the chart on the right public saving, both as a percent of GDP. Private saving has been declining in the industrial countries, especially in Japan (since the 1970s) and in the United States (since the 1980s). Private saving has been more stable in the Euro area and other countries. Public saving is clearly more volatile than private saving. Japan has been mostly in surplus and massively so in the late 1980s and early 1990s. The United States briefly ran a government surplus in the late 1990s but has now returned to a deficit position.

Source: IMF, World Economic Outlook, September 2005.

(Here, the private sector includes households and private firms, which are ultimately owned by households.)

Similarly, we define **government saving** as the difference between tax revenue T received by the government and government purchases G.[7] Hence, government saving S_g equals

(5-8) $$S_g = T - G.$$

Government saving can be a positive number equal to the government surplus, when the government runs a *budget surplus* with tax revenue in excess of government consumption ($T > G$). If the government runs a *budget deficit,* however, government consumption exceeds tax revenue ($G > T$), and public saving will be negative.

If we add these last two equations, we see that private saving plus government saving equals total national saving:

(5-9) $$S_p + S_g = \underbrace{(Y - T - C)}_{\text{Private saving}} + \underbrace{(T - G)}_{\text{Government saving}} = Y - C - G = S.$$

In this last equation, taxes cancel out and do not affect saving in the aggregate because they are simply a transfer from the private sector to the public sector.

One striking feature of the charts in Figure 5-8 is the fairly smooth downward path of private saving compared with the volatile path of public saving. Public saving is government tax revenue minus spending, and it varies greatly as economic conditions change and as tax and spending policies vary. We see that over the years private saving (by firms and households) has dropped the most in Japan, with a smaller drop seen in the United States. In other countries, the trend has been a little steadier. As for public saving, the most noticeable feature is the very large surpluses run up in Japan in the boom of the 1980s and early 1990s that subsequently disappeared during the long slump in the mid-to-late 1990s and early 2000s. In other regions, surpluses in the 1970s soon gave way to deficits in the 1980s, and despite occasional improvements in the fiscal balance (as in the late 1990s), deficits have been the norm in the public sector. The United States witnessed a particularly sharp move from surplus to deficit after the year 2000.

Do government deficits cause current account deficits? In the popular press, these "twin deficits" are often spoken of as if they were inextricably linked. But in theory they need not be. All else equal, government deficits do cause current account deficits, since we can use the equation just given and the current account identity to write

(5-10) $$CA = S_p + S_g - I.$$

But all else may not be equal. One reason is that private saving may change. Suppose the government lowers your taxes by $100 this year and borrows to finance the resulting deficit but also says you will be taxed by an extra $100

[7] Here, the government includes all levels of government: national/federal, state/regional, local/municipal, and so on.

plus interest next year to pay off the debt. The theory of *Ricardian equivalence* asserts that you and other households will save the tax cut to pay next year's tax increase—so a fall in public saving is perfectly offset by a rise in private saving. However, only partial empirical support can be found for this theory. The private sector may offset lower government saving with higher private saving, but the offset is not complete or one for one.

How large is the effect of a government deficit on the current account deficit? Research suggests that a change of 1% of GDP in the government deficit (or surplus) coincides with a 0.2% to 0.4% of GDP change in the current account deficit (or surplus), a result consistent with a partial Ricardian offset.[8] In practice, this is the typical response embedded in most macroeconomic models used by agencies such as the International Monetary Fund (IMF) and OECD.

A second reason why the current account might move independently of saving (public or private) is that there might be changes in the level of investment. A comparison of Figures 5-7 and 5-8 shows that changes in investment can break the link between government deficits and current account deficits. For example, we can see from Figure 5-7 that the large U.S. current account deficits of the early to mid-1990s were driven by an investment boom, even as total saving rose slightly driven by an increase in public saving seen in Figure 5-8. Here there was no correlation between government deficit (falling) and current account deficit (rising).

Typically, however, government deficits and current account deficits do coincide (and similarly for surpluses). Figure 5-8 shows that after 2000 the U.S. government went into deficit and there was a large increase in the current account deficit seen in Figure 5-7, even though other factors were pulling in the opposite direction—U.S. investment was falling in Figure 5-7 and private saving was on the rise in Figure 5-8.

Finally, Figure 5-9 shows global trends in saving, investment, and the current account for industrial countries, developing countries that are most financially integrated into the world economy (emerging markets and oil exporters), and all countries. The large weight of the U.S. economy means that in aggregate, the industrial countries have shifted into current account deficit over this period, a trend that has been offset by a shift toward surplus in the developing countries. The industrialized countries all followed a trend of declining investment and saving ratios, but the developing countries saw the opposite trend: rising investment and saving ratios. For the developing countries, however, the saving increase was larger than the investment increase, allowing a current account surplus to open up. For the world as a whole, however, the industrial country trend dominates—because the GDP weight of those countries is still so large. Globally, saving and investment ratios have fallen in the past 30 years.

---

[8] Menzie D. Chinn and Hiro Ito, 2005, "Current Account Balances, Financial Development and Institutions: Assaying the World 'Savings Glut.'" National Bureau of Economic Research (NBER) Working Paper No. 11761.

FIGURE 5-9

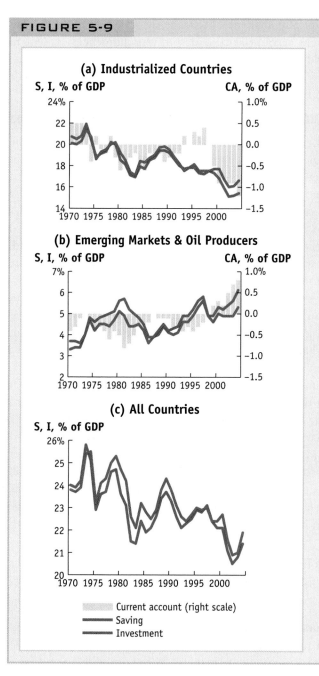

(a) Industrialized Countries

S, I, % of GDP   CA, % of GDP

(b) Emerging Markets & Oil Producers

S, I, % of GDP   CA, % of GDP

(c) All Countries

S, I, % of GDP

- ▨ Current account (right scale)
- ▬ Saving
- ▬ Investment

Global Imbalances The charts show saving (blue), investment (red), and the current account (yellow) as a percent of GDP. In the 1990s, emerging markets moved into current account surplus and this financed the overall trend toward current account deficit of the industrial countries. For the world as a whole since the 1970s, global investment and saving rates have declined as a percent of GDP, falling from a high of near 26% to lows near 20%.

Notes: Oil producers include Norway. The world data in panel (c) are affected by a statistical discrepancy: saving does not equal investment exactly, although in reality it must. For this reason, the global current account is shown as zero on the final chart.

Source: IMF, World Economic Outlook, *September 2005.*

Note that there are no current account data in the final chart. This is to be expected. Because we have no trade with aliens from other planets, the global current account should be zero, with world saving exactly equal to world investment. However, real-world data are subject to measurement error, and the data say that world saving does not exactly equal world investment. (For most of the past 30 years, the world has been running a small current account deficit according to the data, though the error has never been more than 1%

of world GDP and is typically smaller.) The final chart ignores this finding and reports the world current account as zero, despite the differences evident in the actual data on world saving and investment. ■

3 Balance of Payments Accounts: International Transactions

We have shown that for a given period the current account summarizes the flow of all international transactions composed of goods, services, and factor services plus nonmarket transfers. Hence, the current account is frequently a part of political and popular discussions, as you may have noticed from a glance at the financial pages of the newspapers, because it is of critical importance for economists, economic statisticians, and policy makers who want to understand the links between their home economies and the rest of the world.

However, flows involving goods, services, and factor services are not the only types of international transactions. There are also international transactions in financial assets such as stocks, debt, bonds, direct investments in plant and equipment, and so on. In this section, we learn that the trade in assets is also of great importance because it tells us how the current account is financed and, hence, whether a country is becoming more or less indebted to the rest of the world.

All countries maintain a more complete set of accounts that measures not just the transactions in the current account but also the financial transactions that make up the trade in assets between countries. The complete set of a country's international transaction accounts is commonly known as the *balance of payments accounts,* and this consists of the current account plus two other accounts, the capital account and the financial account.[9] We have already dealt with the current account. To understand how the capital and financial accounts work, we have to learn how to account for transactions in assets, once again building on the intuition developed in Figure 5-2.

Accounting for Asset Transactions

We begin our look at the balance of payments accounts with some new definitions that apply to the measurement of international transactions involving assets.

The Financial Account The financial account (*FA*) records transactions between residents and nonresidents that involve financial assets. We refer to the total value of financial assets that are received by the rest of the world from the home country as the home country's *export of assets,* denoted EX_A (the subscript "A" is for asset). We refer to the total value of financial assets that are received by the home country from the rest of the world in all transactions as the home country's *import of assets,* denoted IM_A.

---

[9] Officially, following the 1993 revision to the System of National Accounts by the U.N. Statistical Office, the place where international transactions are recorded should be called "rest of the world account" or the "external transactions account." The United States calls it the "international transactions account." However, the older terminology was the "balance of payments account," and this usage persists.

The financial account measures all "movement" of financial assets across the international border. By this, we mean a movement from home to foreign ownership, or vice versa, even if the assets do not physically move. This definition also covers all types of assets: real assets such as land or structures and financial assets such as debt or equity. The financial account also includes assets issued by any entity (firms, governments, households) in any country (home or overseas). And it includes market transactions as well as transfers, or gifts of assets, with the latter being considered in just a moment.

Subtracting asset imports from asset exports yields the home country's net overall balance on asset transactions, which is known as the financial account where $FA = EX_A - IM_A$. A negative FA means that the country has imported more assets than it has exported; a positive FA means the country has exported more assets than it has imported. The financial account therefore measures how the country accumulates or decumulates assets through international transactions.

The Capital Account The capital account (KA) covers two remaining areas of asset movement of minor quantitative significance. One is the acquisition and disposal of nonfinancial, nonproduced assets (e.g., patents, copyrights, trademarks, franchises, and so on). They have to be included here because such nonfinancial assets do not appear in the financial account, although like financial assets they can be bought and sold with resulting payments flows. The other important item in the capital account is capital transfers, notably the forgiveness of debt.[10]

As with unilateral income transfers, capital transfers must be accounted for properly. For example, the giver of an asset must deduct the value of the gift in the capital account to offset the export of the asset, which is recorded in the financial account, since in the case of a gift the export generates no associated payment. Similarly, recipients of capital transfers need to record them to offset the import of the asset recorded in the financial account.

Using similar notation to that employed with unilateral transfers of income, we can denote capital transfers received from the rest of the world by the home country as KA_{IN} and capital transfers received by the rest of the world from the home country as KA_{OUT}. Hence, $KA = KA_{IN} - KA_{OUT}$ denotes net capital transfers received. A negative KA indicates that more capital transfers were made by the home country than it received; positive KA indicates that the home country received more capital transfers than it made.

The capital account is usually a minor and technical accounting item for most developed countries, although some intra-firm debt write-offs by multinationals can be significant. However, in some developing countries, the capital account can play an important role because for some very poor countries, nonmarket debt forgiveness can be large whereas market-based international financial transactions may be small.

---

[10] The capital account does *not* include involuntary debt cancellation, such as results from unilateral defaults. Changes in assets and liabilities due to defaults are counted as capital losses, or valuation effects, which are discussed later in this chapter.

Accounting for Home and Foreign Assets

Asset trades in the financial account can be broken down into more detailed categories. The most important such decomposition divides assets into two types: assets issued by home entities (home assets) and assets issued by foreign entities (foreign assets). This breakdown of the asset trade is useful because it makes clear the distinction between the location of the asset issuer and the location of the asset owner.

By definition, from the home perspective, a foreign asset is a claim on a foreign country. When a home entity holds such an asset, it is called an **external asset** of the home country because it represents an obligation owed to the home country by the rest of the world. For example, when a U.S. firm invests overseas and acquires a computer factory located in Ireland, the acquisition is an external asset for the United States.

Conversely, from the home country's perspective, a home asset is a claim on the home country. When a foreign entity holds such an asset, it is called an **external liability** of the home country because it represents an obligation owed by the home country to the rest of the world. When a Japanese firm acquires an automobile plant in the United States, the acquisition is an external liability for the United States.

If we use superscripts "H" and "F" to denote home and foreign assets, we can write the financial account as the sum of the net exports of each type of asset:

(5-11)
$$FA = \underbrace{EX_A - IM_A}_{\text{Net export of assets}}$$

$$= \underbrace{(EX_A^H - IM_A^H)}_{\text{Net export of home assets}} + \underbrace{(EX_A^F - IM_A^F)}_{\text{Net export of foreign assets}}$$

$$= \underbrace{\underbrace{(EX_A^H - IM_A^H)}_{\text{Net export of home assets}}}_{\substack{= \\ \text{Net additions to} \\ \text{external liabilities}}} - \underbrace{\underbrace{(IM_A^F - EX_A^F)}_{\text{Net import of foreign assets}}}_{\substack{= \\ \text{Net additions to} \\ \text{external assets}}}.$$

What does this expression say? The first row is the definition of *FA* and the second row decomposes the measure of net exports into two types of assets, home and foreign. To get to the third row, we use the fact that net imports of foreign assets are just *minus* net exports of foreign assets.

The third row of this formula relates to our definitions of external assets and liabilities. It says that *FA* is equal to *the additions to external liabilities* (the home-owned assets moving into foreign ownership, net) *minus the additions to external assets* (the foreign-owned assets moving into home ownership, net). This is our first indication as to how flows of assets have implications for changes in wealth, a topic we return to shortly.

How the Balance of Payments Accounts Work

To make further progress in our quest to understand the links between flows of goods, services, income, and assets, we have to understand how the current account, capital account, and financial account are related. The first step is to show why it is that the balance of payments accounts must, indeed, balance.

A Macroeconomic View of the Balance of Payments The macroeconomic view of the balance of payments proceeds on the basis of the intuition presented in Figure 5-2, which set out the circular flow of payments. We use the definitions of the current account developed in the last section and expand on them further to allow for the asset trade. Recall, as in Equation (5-4), we start with gross national expenditure, which becomes gross domestic product once allowance is made for the trade balance, which becomes gross national income once net factor income from abroad is added, which then becomes gross national disposable income once net unilateral transfers are added:

$$Y = GNDI = GNE + TB + NFIA + NUT = \underbrace{GNE + CA}_{\substack{\text{Resources available to home} \\ \text{country due to income}}}.$$

Does this expression represent all of the resources that are available to the home economy to finance expenditure? No. It represents only the income resources. The home economy can free up (or use up) resources in another way: by engaging in net sales (or purchases) of assets. To account completely for the resources, we must add to the previous term the value of the net sales of assets by home to the rest of the world. We can calculate this value using our previous definitions:[11]

$$\underbrace{[\underbrace{EX_A}_{\substack{\text{Value of} \\ \text{all assets} \\ \text{exported}}} - \underbrace{KA_{OUT}}_{\substack{\text{Value of} \\ \text{all assets} \\ \text{exported} \\ \text{as gifts}}}]}_{\substack{\text{Value of all assets} \\ \text{exported via sales}}} - \underbrace{[\underbrace{IM_A}_{\substack{\text{Value of} \\ \text{all assets} \\ \text{imported}}} - \underbrace{KA_{IN}}_{\substack{\text{Value of} \\ \text{all assets} \\ \text{imported} \\ \text{as gifts}}}]}_{\substack{\text{Value of all assets} \\ \text{imported via purchases}}} = EX_A - IM_A + KA_{IN} - KA_{OUT}$$

$$= \underbrace{FA + KA}_{\substack{\text{Resources available to the} \\ \text{home country due to asset trades}}}.$$

Adding the last two expressions, we arrive at the value of the total resources available to the home country for expenditure purposes. This total value must equal the total value of home expenditure on final goods and services, GNE:

$$\underbrace{GNE + CA}_{\substack{\text{Resources available} \\ \text{to home country} \\ \text{due to income}}} + \underbrace{FA + KA}_{\substack{\text{Resources available} \\ \text{to the home country} \\ \text{due to asset trades}}} = GNE.$$

We can cancel GNE from both sides of this expression to obtain the important result known as the balance of payments identity or **BOP identity**:

(5-12) $$\underbrace{CA}_{\text{Current account}} + \underbrace{KA}_{\text{Capital account}} + \underbrace{FA}_{\text{Financial account}} = 0.$$

---

[11] Note that the KA terms also account for any net payments arising from transactions involving nonproduced, nonfinancial assets. This is typically a minor element. It is omitted from the equation for clarity.

This result is the formal expression of what we saw in Figure 5-2. There is still a circular flow in that we start and end with *GNE*. The difference is that along the way we have to account for transactions with the rest of the world. But all of those transactions serve to either expand or contract the resources available for expenditure in the home economy, and by the time we get back full circle, the total sum of the value of all those transactions must be zero.

A Microeconomic View of the Balance of Payments The last expression can be written in more expanded form as

$$
(5\text{-}13) \qquad \underbrace{(EX - IM)}_{TB} + \underbrace{(EX_{FS} - IM_{FS})}_{NFIA} + \underbrace{(UT_{IN} - UT_{OUT})}_{NUT}
$$

$$
\underbrace{\phantom{(EX-IM)+(EX_{FS}-IM_{FS})+(UT_{IN}-UT_{OUT})}}_{\substack{CA \\ \text{Current account}}}
$$

$$
+ \underbrace{(KA_{IN} - KA_{OUT})}_{\substack{KA \\ \text{Capital account}}} + \underbrace{(EX_A^H - IM_A^H) + (EX_A^F - IM_A^F)}_{\substack{FA \\ \text{Financial account}}} = 0.
$$

where we have drawn on the definitions of the current account, capital account, and financial account. Written this way, the BOP identity will allow us to see why the accounts must balance from a microeconomic standpoint. How?

Consider the work of national statisticians. To keep proper track of all international transactions, these statisticians follow simple rules summed up by the last equation. There are 12 transaction types (each preceded by either a plus or minus sign) and three accounts that they can appear in. If an item has a plus sign, it is called a balance of payments credit or **BOP credit.** The following 6 types of transactions receive a plus (+) sign and appear in the following accounts:

Current account (CA):   Exports of goods and services ($+EX$);
                        Exports of factor services ($+EX_{FS}$);
                        Unilateral transfers received ($+UT_{IN}$);
Capital account (KA):   Capital transfers received ($+KA_{IN}$);
Financial account (FA): Exports of home and foreign assets ($+EX_A^H$, $+EX_A^F$).

If an item has a minus sign, it is called a balance of payments debit or **BOP debit.** The following six types of transactions receive a minus (−) sign:

Current account (CA):   Imports of goods and services ($-IM$);
                        Imports of factor services ($-IM_{FS}$);
                        Unilateral transfers given ($-UT_{OUT}$);
Capital account (KA):   Capital transfers given ($-KA_{OUT}$);
Financial account (FA): Imports of home and foreign assets ($-IM_A^H$, $-IM_A^F$).

To see why these rules for each transaction ensure that the BOP accounts balance in aggregate, we have to understand only one simple principle:

Every market transaction has two parts. If party A engages in a transaction with a counterparty B, then A receives from B an item of a given value, and in return B receives from A an item of equal value. In general, the items may be goods, services, factor services, or assets.

The BOP accounts are just the same idea writ large, that is, applied to a nation as a whole. For example, suppose I export goods worth $100 and receive $100 in assets from a foreigner as payment. The former is a credit of +$100 for the export of goods in the current account, and the latter is a −$100 debit for the import of assets in the financial account. For every thing given by one party, something is received from the counterparty. The two cancel out. Understood this way, the BOP accounts are nothing more than a gigantic exercise in double-entry bookkeeping.

The only slight difficulty is that this principle applies only to market transactions, but statisticians also collect data on all transactions between countries, including nonmarket transactions such as gifts. In the BOP accounts, the value of such transfers appears in the net unilateral transfer (NUT) and capital account (KA) entries. These provide the necessary adjustments to ensure that nonmarket gifts, for which nothing is offered in return, are properly recorded and yet leave the BOP accounts in balance. For example, if my +$100 export is food aid, it isn't a market transaction, although it does appear as a credit item in total exports; however, it is offset in the BOP accounts by a −$100 debit in net unilateral transfers, corresponding to the value of my gift to the foreign country.

Examples: The Double-Entry Principle at Work We can make the double-entry principle more concrete by looking at some (mostly) hypothetical international transactions and figuring out how they would have been recorded in the U.S. BOP accounts.

1. Recall from Chapter 2 that in 2003 our friend George was in Paris for his vacation. Suppose he spent $110 (€100) on French wine one evening. An American tourist drinking in a foreign wine bar is engaging in the U.S. import of a foreign service. George pays with his American Express card. The bar is owed a total of $110 (or €100) by American Express (and Amex is owed by George). The United States has exported an asset to France: the bar now has a claim against American Express. From the U.S. perspective, this is an increase in U.S. assets owned by foreigners. The double entries in the U.S. BOP appear in the current account and the financial account:

CA: Drinks in Paris bar	$-IM$	−$110
FA: Bar's claim on AMEX	$+EX_A^H$	+$110

2. George was in the Paris bar to meet up with his Danish cousin Georg. They both work as wine merchants and consider themselves connoisseurs. In an ebullient mood after a few bottles of Bordeaux, George enthuses about Arkansas chardonnay and insists Georg give it a try. Georg counters by telling George he should really try some Jutland rosé. Both wines sell for $3 a bottle. Each cousin returns home and asks his firm to ship a case of each wine (worth $36) to the other. This barter transaction (involving no financial activity) would appear solely as two entries in the U.S. current account:

CA: Arkansas wine exported to Denmark	EX	+$36
CA: Jutland wine imported to United States	$-IM$	−$36

3. Later that night, George met a French entrepreneur in a smoky corner of the bar. George vaguely remembers the story: the entrepreneur's French tech company was poised for unbelievable success with an upcoming share issue. George returns to the United States and decides to invest $10,000 of his savings to buy the French stock; he is importing a French asset. When the stock is sold by the French bank BNP, George sends them a U.S. dollar check. BNP then has a claim against George's account at Citibank in New York, which amounts to the export of a home asset to France. The double entries fall within the U.S. financial account:

FA: George's French tech stocks	$-IM_A^F$	$-\$10,000$
FA: BNP claim against Citibank	$+EX_A^H$	$+\$10,000$

4. Rather surprisingly, George's French stocks do quite well. By December 2003, they have doubled in value. Feeling richer, George sets out to do some last-minute holiday shopping, but he also makes a $5,000 donation to charity. His charity purchases U.S. relief supplies that will be exported to Bam, Iran, following a devastating earthquake in that city. The two entries here are entirely in the U.S. current account. The supplies are a nonmarket export of goods offset by the value of the unilateral transfer:

CA: Relief supplies exported to Bam	EX	$+\$5,000$
CA: George's charitable gift	$-UT_{OUT}$	$-\$5,000$

5. George was also pleased to see that some poor countries are benefiting from another kind of foreign assistance, debt forgiveness. In June 2003, the U.S. secretary of state announced that as part of a large assistance package the United States would forgive $1 billion of debt owed by the government of Pakistan. This would decrease U.S.-owned assets overseas. The United States was exporting Pakistani assets: it hands the canceled debts back to Pakistan, a credit in the financial account. The two matching transactions would be seen in the U.S. BOP in the capital and financial accounts:

KA: U.S. grant of debt relief	$-KA_{OUT}$	$-\$1,000,000,000$
FA: Decline in U.S. external assets	$+EX_A^F$	$+\$1,000,000,000$

We could go on and on with such examples, but the key point is that every purchase of a good, service, factor service, or asset by a home country must be offset by a corresponding purchase of a good, service, or asset by the rest of the world, or by a nonmarket transfer. We may draw the following conclusion:

> *Whenever a transaction generates a credit somewhere in the BOP account, it must also generate a corresponding debit somewhere else in the BOP account. Similarly, every debit generates a corresponding credit.*

It might not be obvious where the offsetting item is, but it must exist somewhere *if* the accounts have been measured properly. (This is a big if, and we will see the consequences of mismeasurement shortly.)

Understanding the Data for the Balance of Payments Account

To illustrate all the principles we've learned, let's look at the United States' balance of payments account.[12] Table 5-3 shows an extract of the U.S. BOP accounts for 2006.

In the current account, in the top part of the table, we look first at the trade in goods and services on lines 1 and 3. Overall exports, *EX*, were a credit of

TABLE 5-3

The U.S. Balance of Payments in 2006 The table shows U.S. international transactions for 2006 in billions of dollars. Major categories are in bold type.

Major Account	Line	Category or Subcategory	Symbol	$ billions
Current Account	**1**	**Exports of goods and services**	$+EX$	**+1,446**
	1a	Of which: Goods		+1,023
	1b	Services		+423
	2	**Income receipts** [= exports of factor services]	$+EX_{FS}$	**+650**
	3	**Imports of goods and services** (−)	$-IM$	**−2,204**
	3a	Of which: Goods (−)		−1,861
	3b	Services (−)		−343
	4	**Income payments** [= imports of factor services] (−)	$-IM_{FS}$	**−614**
	5	**Net unilateral transfers**	NUT	**−90**
Capital and Financial Account	**6**	**Capital account** net	KA	**−4**
	7	**U.S.-owned assets abroad** net increase (−)	$+EX_A^F - IM_A^F$	**−1,055**
		[= net imports of ROW assets or financial outflow (−)]		
	7a	Of which: U.S. official reserve assets		+2
	7b	Other assets		−1,057
	8	**Foreign-owned assets in U.S.** net increase (+)	$+EX_A^H - IM_A^H$	**+1,860**
		[= net exports of U.S. assets or financial inflow (+)]		
	8a	Of which: Foreign official assets		+440
	8b	Other assets		+1,419
Statistical Discrepancy	**9**	**Statistical discrepancy** (sum of 1 to 8, sign reversed)	SD	**+11**
Summary Items		**Balance on current account** (lines 1, 2, 3, 4, and 5)	CA	**−811**
		Of which: Balance on goods and services (lines 1 and 3)	TB	−759
		Balance on income (lines 2 and 4)	$NFIA$	+37
		Balance on financial account (lines 7 and 8)	FA	**+804**
		Of which: Official settlements balance (lines 7a and 8a)		+443
		Nonreserve financial account (lines 7b and 8b)		+362

Notes: Details may not add to totals because of rounding. The statistical discrepancy shown here includes financial derivatives.

Source: U.S. Bureau of Economic Analysis, ITA Table 1, using the ITA definition of the United States. This includes U.S. territories, so these figures are slightly different from those in Table 5-2.

---

[12] This is published each year as the so-called international transactions account (ITA) by the BEA. The ITA uses a different definition of the U.S. territory than the national income and product accounts (NIPA), so these figures do not exactly match those in Table 5-2.

+$1,446 billion (line 1), and imports, *IM,* were a debit of −$2,204 billion (line 3). In the summary items, we see the balance on goods and services, the trade balance, *TB,* was −$759 billion (line 1 minus line 3). Exports and imports and the trade balance are also broken down even further into goods and service components (lines 1ab and 3ab).

The next part of the current account on lines 2 and 4 deals with trade in factor services, also known as the income account (referring to the income paid to those factors). Income receipts for factor service exports, EX_{FS}, generated a credit of +$650 billion and income payments for factor service imports, IM_{FS}, generated a debit of −$614 billion. Adding these two items resulted in net factor income from abroad *NFIA* equal to +$37 billion (line 2 minus line 4), a net credit.

Lastly, we see that net unilateral transfers *NUT* were −$90 billion, a net debit (line 5); the United States was a net donor as measured by the net transfer of goods, services, and income to the rest of the world. (Typically, in summary tables like these, unilateral transfers are shown only in net form.)

Overall, summing lines 1 through 5, the 2004 U.S. current account balance *CA* was −$811 billion, that is, a deficit of $811 billion, as shown in the summary items at the foot of the table.

A country that has a current account surplus is called a **(net) lender.** By the BOP identity, we know that it must have a deficit in its asset accounts, so like any lender it is, on net, buying assets (acquiring IOUs from borrowers). For example, China is a large net lender.

A country that has a current account deficit is called a **(net) borrower.** By the BOP identity, we know that it must have a surplus in its asset accounts, so like any lender it is, on net, selling assets (issuing IOUs to lenders). As we can see, the United States is a large net borrower.

Now we move to the capital and financial accounts. The United States had a small capital account *KA* of −$4 billion (line 6), meaning that it was making net transfers of assets to the rest of the world in 2004. (Typically, in summary tables like these, the capital account is shown only in net form.)

Lastly, we move to the financial account. As explained, this account can be broken down not just in terms of imports and exports of total assets, but in terms of the exports and imports of two types of assets: U.S. assets (U.S. external liabilities) and rest of the world assets (U.S. external assets). In this summary table, this route is taken, but only the net trades are shown for each kind of asset.

We see that the United States was engaged in the net import of foreign assets, so that external assets (U.S.-owned assets abroad) increased by $1,055 billion: this net import of foreign assets is recorded as a debit of −$1,055 billion (line 7). Note that the minus sign maintains the convention that imports are debits.

At the same time, the United States was engaged in net export of U.S. assets to the rest of the world so that external liabilities (foreign-owned assets in the United States) increased by $1,860 billion; the net export of U.S. assets is duly recorded as a credit of +$1,860 billion (line 8).

The sum of lines 7 and 8 gives the financial account balance of +$804 billion, recorded in the summary items.

In passing we note some important terminology commonly used in the financial account. The net import of $1,055 billion in foreign assets is also referred to as a **financial outflow** or *capital outflow* because these are financial purchases by U.S. entities of foreign assets (that is, the United States is lending to foreigners, so financing is going out). The net export of $1,860 billion of U.S. assets is also referred to as a **financial inflow** or *capital inflow* because these are financial purchases by foreign entities of U.S. assets (that is, the rest of the world is lending to the United States, so financing is coming in).

For further information on interventions by central banks, financial account transactions are often also broken down into reserve and nonreserve components. The changes in reserves arise from official intervention in the forex market—that is, from the purchases and sales by home and foreign monetary authorities. For example, if China's central bank purchases $50 billion in U.S. government bonds, this export of a U.S. asset appears as a credit in the reserve part of the U.S. financial account (part of line 8a). The balance on reserve transaction is called the **official settlements balance,** and the balance on all other asset trades is called the **nonreserve financial account.** We see here that U.S. authorities intervened very little: a net export of +$2 billion of U.S. reserves (line 7a) means that the Federal Reserve sold $2 billion in foreign (i.e., nondollar) exchange reserves to foreigners. In contrast, foreign central banks intervened a lot: U.S. entities sold them $440 billion in U.S. dollar reserve assets, and these sales accounted for about a quarter of all U.S. financial inflows. We shall investigate official reserve transactions in more detail when we study the mechanics of fixed exchange rates in Chapter 9.

Adding up the current account, capital account, and financial account (lines 1 through 8), we find the total of the three accounts was −$11 billion (−811 − 4 + 804 = −11). The BOP accounts are supposed to balance by adding to zero; −$11 billion is not zero. So in the actual data collected by the BEA, the BOP identity fails. This is not because the identity is incorrect (an identity must hold because of how the terms in the identity are defined). The failure results from the fact that, in reality, the statistical agencies find it impossible to track every single international transaction.

Some of these discrepancies, especially on the trade side, probably reflect simple measurement error. There may also be problems associated with the smuggling of goods (such as narcotics and other contraband) or trade tax evasion. However, more important errors are likely due to the mismeasurement, concealment, or illicit movement of financial income flows and assets movements (that is, money laundering and capital tax evasion). Many of these flows can move across borders without detection and lead to errors in income flows (errors in NFIA) and in asset flows (errors in FA).

To "account" for this error, statistical agencies create an accounting item, the *statistical discrepancy* (SD) equal to minus the error $SD = -(CA + KA + FA)$. By construction $CA + KA + FA + SD = 0$ and with that "correction," the amended version of the BOP identity will hold true in practice, sweeping away the real-world measurement problems. In the table, the statistical discrepancy is shown on line 9.[13]

Some Recent Trends Figure 5-10 shows recent trends in various components of the U.S. balance of payments. The sharp downward trend of the current account is as previously shown in Figure 5-6, so for the balance of payments identity to hold there must be an offsetting upward trend in other parts of the BOP accounts. This is indeed the case. Although the capital account has remained rather small, and despite the occasional blip in the statistical discrepancy, we can see that the United States has been financing its growing deficit on the current account by running an expanding surplus on the financial account. In the mid-1990s, there was close to a $100 billion current account deficit and a comparable financial account surplus. A decade later, the figures were more than five times bigger, in the region of $800 billion, and records were being broken every year.

FIGURE 5-10

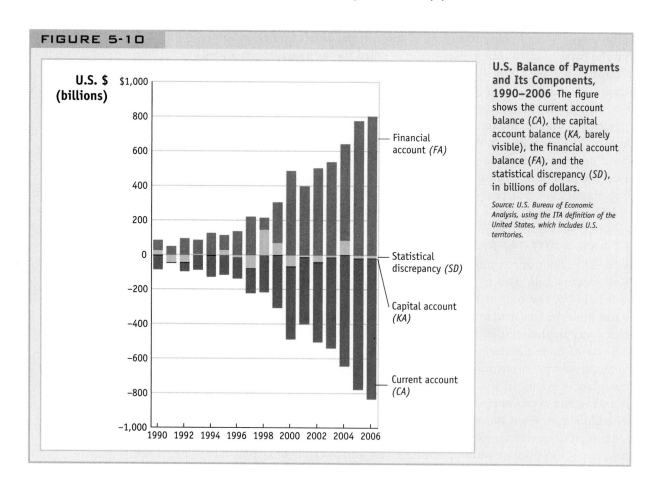

U.S. Balance of Payments and Its Components, 1990–2006 The figure shows the current account balance (*CA*), the capital account balance (*KA*, barely visible), the financial account balance (*FA*), and the statistical discrepancy (*SD*), in billions of dollars.

Source: U.S. Bureau of Economic Analysis, using the ITA definition of the United States, which includes U.S. territories.

---

[13] Prior to 2007, the U.S. statistical discrepancy included unmeasured financial derivatives transactions. Starting in 2007, the BEA estimates these transactions, but they are not as yet broken down in detail into home and foreign assets. For clarity, they are not reported here and are included in the statistical discrepancy in Table 5-3.

What the Balance of Payments Account Tells Us

In the previous section, we studied the current account, which measures a country's external imbalances in trades involving goods, services, factor services, and unilateral transfers. In the balance of payments accounts, we extended the coverage to include asset trades, and using the principle that market transactions must consist of two items traded of equal value—illustrated by double-entry bookkeeping—we found that the balance of payments accounts really do balance.

Surpluses in the current account must be offset by deficits in the asset part of the balance of payments accounts. Similarly, deficits in the current account must be offset by surpluses in asset accounts. What does this mean? How is it consistent with the idea that a current account surplus (or deficit) measures the extent to which a country is living within (or beyond) its means?

Suppose the capital account is zero, so that current account imbalances are not financed by asset gifts. A current account deficit of $1 billion must be balanced by a financial account surplus of $1 billion. In other words, the country must have net exports of $1 billion worth of assets to the rest of the world. As with a household, a country that is a net exporter of assets is called a borrower: overall, it is asking the rest of the world to accept promises of future payment (exports of assets) in return for current resources (imports of goods and services). We would also say that its net export of assets constitutes an increase in the country's (or household's) level of debt. A country with fewer assets (or more debt) would be said to be a country with less wealth.

Thus, by telling us how current account imbalances are financed, the balance of payments makes the connection between a country's income and spending decisions and the evolution of that country's wealth, an important connection we develop further in the final section of this chapter.

4 External Wealth

The measurement of a nation's income is not the only important economic variable that must be adapted to the open-economy environment. Economists and policy makers, and the general public, also care about *wealth*. And so, probably, do you.

For example, Anne has income and expenditures of $40,000 each year and savings in the bank of $10,000. But she has run her credit card balance up to $20,000. Beth's life is identical to Anne's in almost every respect, and she also has income and expenditures of $40,000 each year and savings of $10,000, but she has no credit card debt. Financially speaking, who is better off? Clearly it's Beth. Her income is the same as Anne's. But Anne's wealth or "net worth" is −$10,000 (savings of $10,000 minus debt of $20,000), whereas Beth has a net worth of +$10,000. Anne's wealth is −20% of her income; Beth's wealth is +20% of her income. These net worth figures are what is owed each person (here, by the bank) minus what they owe others (here, the credit card company). Would you rather be in Anne's shoes or Beth's?

Just as a household is better off with higher wealth, all else equal, so is a country. We can calculate a home country's "net worth" or **external wealth** with respect to the rest of the world by adding up all of the home assets owned by ROW (foreigners' claims against home) and subtracting all of the ROW assets owned by the home country (home claims against foreigners). Doing this for the United States at the end of year 2006, we would find that the United States had an external wealth of about −$2,600 billion. This made the United States the world's biggest debtor in history at the time of this writing. The United States' net debt to the rest of the world was about $9,000 for every American. Because GDP per person in the United States was about $45,000 in 2006, the external wealth of the U.S. was about −20% of GDP.

How did U.S. external wealth reach this level? Where will it go next? We can begin to address such questions only if we understand how the wealth levels of countries evolve. And, as we did for the national income and balance of payments accounts, we look first at some basic wealth accounting.

The Level of External Wealth

First, we give a definition of the level of a country's external wealth (W):

$$(5\text{-}14) \qquad \underbrace{\text{External wealth}}_{W} = \underbrace{\left(\begin{array}{c} \text{ROW assets} \\ \text{owned by home} \end{array}\right)}_{A} - \underbrace{\left(\begin{array}{c} \text{Home assets} \\ \text{owned by ROW} \end{array}\right)}_{L}.$$

External wealth equals the value of total external assets (A) minus the value of total external liabilities (L). The former is what is owed to the home country by the rest of the world, and the latter what is owed to the rest of the world by the home country. A country's level of external wealth is also referred to as its *net international investment position* or *net foreign assets*.

If $W > 0$, home is a **net creditor** *country: external assets exceed external liabilities.*

If $W < 0$, home is a **net debtor** *country: external liabilities exceed external assets.*

External wealth is only one part of a nation's total wealth. The other part of a nation's wealth is internal wealth, which corresponds to the total value of all nonfinancial assets in the home country. (The links between external wealth and total wealth are explored further in the appendix to this chapter.)

Because we are focusing on international economic relationships, our main emphasis is on external wealth. External wealth is of great importance because it measures the outstanding obligations of one country to another. Those obligations, and when and how they are paid, can be the source of great economic and political stress. Moreover, the net debts of nations, like those of individuals, ultimately carry a cost. To understand external wealth, let's look at how it is measured and how it evolves.

Changes in External Wealth

There are two reasons a country's level of external wealth changes over time.

1. *Financial flows:* As a result of asset trades, the country can increase or decrease its external assets and liabilities. How? Net exports of foreign assets cause an equal decrease in the level of external assets and hence a

corresponding decrease in external wealth. Net exports of home assets cause an equal increase in the level of external liabilities and hence a corresponding decrease in external wealth. For example, if net exports of assets (whether home or foreign) are +$1 billion, then the change in external wealth is −$1 billion. The net export of assets of all kinds is measured by the financial account (*FA*), and this has a negative effect on external wealth in any period.

2. *Valuation effects:* The value of existing external assets and liabilities may change over time because of capital gains or losses. In the case of external wealth, this change in value could be due to price effects or exchange rate effects. For example, suppose a U.S. citizen buys 100 shares of British Petroleum on the London Stock Exchange at £7 each. Suppose the exchange rate is $1.8 per pound. These U.S. external assets are worth $12.60 each (1.8 times 7), for a total of $1,260. Suppose the price of these shares then falls to £6, and the exchange rate stays the same. Each share is now worth $10.80 (1.8 times 6) and the 100 shares are valued at $1,080. Their value has fallen in dollar terms by $180 (£1 times 1.8 times 100), which is a capital loss. This is an example of a price effect. Now suppose the exchange rate rises to $2 per pound. Each share is still worth £6 in U.K. currency but $12 in U.S. currency (2 times 6), so the total value of the shares rises to $1,200, which, relative to the $1,080 they were previously worth, implies a capital gain of $120. This is an example of an exchange rate effect. Similar effects can change the value of external liabilities (see **Side Bar: The Nokia Economy**).

Adding up these two contributions to the change in external wealth (ΔW), we find

(5-15)
$$\underbrace{\left(\begin{array}{c}\text{Change in}\\ \text{external wealth}\end{array}\right)}_{\Delta W} = \underbrace{\left(\begin{array}{c}\text{Capital gains on}\\ \text{external wealth}\end{array}\right)}_{\substack{\text{Valuation effects}\\ =\\ \text{Capital gains minus capital losses}}} - \underbrace{\left(\begin{array}{c}\text{Financial}\\ \text{account}\end{array}\right)}_{\substack{\text{Net export of assets}\\ =\\ FA}}.$$

We gain a deeper understanding of this expression if we recall the BOP identity: the current account plus the capital account plus the financial account equals zero, $CA + FA + KA = 0$. Hence, minus the financial account equals the current account plus the capital account, $-FA = CA + KA$. Substituting this identity into Equation (5-15)

(5-16)
$$\underbrace{\left(\begin{array}{c}\text{Change in}\\ \text{external wealth}\end{array}\right)}_{\Delta W} = \underbrace{\left(\begin{array}{c}\text{Capital gains on}\\ \text{external wealth}\end{array}\right)}_{\substack{\text{Valuation effects}\\ =\\ \text{Capital gains minus capital losses}}} + \underbrace{\left(\begin{array}{c}\text{Current}\\ \text{account}\end{array}\right)}_{\substack{CA\\ =\\ \text{Net lending}}} + \underbrace{\left(\begin{array}{c}\text{Capital}\\ \text{account}\end{array}\right)}_{\substack{KA\\ =\\ \text{Net capital transfers received}}}.$$

This equation is a fundamental formula for changes in wealth in an open economy. Intuitively, it says that a country can increase external wealth in one of only three ways:

SIDE BAR

The Nokia Economy

Finland is a small Scandinavian country that is very open to international trade. Traditionally, for much of its history, the country exported products based on its natural resources and imported many manufactures, but the country also invested heavily in education and had a workforce and research staff capable of working with new technology. By the 1990s, this mix of capabilities set the stage for a remarkable revolution in the Finnish economy that was to lead to a rapid growth of income and wealth—but which was also to have striking international consequences.

Figure 5-11, panel (a), shows the very unusual path of Finnish external wealth from 1990 to 2003. Until 1997 not much happened and external wealth was stable: Finland was a net debtor to the tune of about minus $50 billion. Then in 1998 this net debt doubled to about $100 billion. The following year, 1999, it doubled *again* to $200 billion. In 1999 Finland's GDP was about $128 billion, so this meant that in the

course of just one year, in wealth terms, the Finns saw the equivalent of about one year's income go up in smoke.

What was going on? Was there cause to worry? Had the Finns engaged in a sudden consumption splurge financed by reckless new borrowing? No, nothing of the sort took place. To understand these events, we have to remember the role of valuation effects in national wealth, and the peculiar story of how the 1990s information technology boom hit Finland. That story was, more than anything else, a story of one company: Nokia. Nokia made cell phones and related products, and its competitive lead in that industry had much to do with the nature of Finland's investments in research and education in the past, as well as with a decision by the Finns to construct one of the world's first national wireless networks. By the mid-1990s, the tech boom in world stock markets was under way, and Nokia was one of the hottest stocks once investors realized its huge potential and

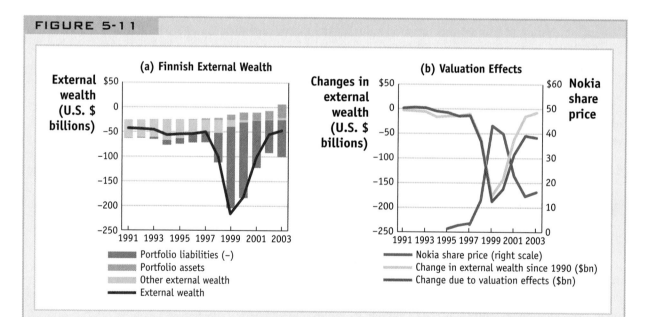

FIGURE 5-11

Finland's External Wealth, 1991–2003 The line in panel (a) shows the evolution of Finland's external wealth. From 1998 to 1999, a massive shift toward net debt occurred, which was reversed from 2000 to 2002. The columns in panel (a) show that this reversal was driven by a sudden increase in external portfolio liabilities at a time when all other components were shifting toward net credit. Panel (b) shows that the temporary explosion in external liabilities was almost entirely a result of valuation effects. And most of it was due to the impact of changes in the stock price of just one company: Nokia. This stock was a large part of Finland's external liabilities, especially after it had appreciated 40-fold in four years. The cumulative valuation effects mirror the movements in the Nokia stock price.

Sources: Wealth data from Gian Maria Milesi-Ferretti and Philip R. Lane, 2006, "The External Wealth of Nations Mark II: Revised and Extended Estimates of Foreign Assets and Liabilities, 1970–2004," IMF Working Paper No. 06/69. Nokia ADR price from Yahoo! Finance.

Continued on next page.

early lead in wireless communication technology. In the mid-1990s, foreign investors bought heaps of Nokia stock at (then) low prices.

Then the fun started. Nokia's stock price (like that of many information technology and dot.com firms) started to climb stratospherically. Soon the company was worth a fortune. From a macroeconomic perspective, it accounted for a large share of all Finnish assets and, because foreigners owned a big chunk of it, Nokia also constituted a vast and growing share of Finnish external liabilities. As Nokia's stock price rose by a factor of 40 from 1995 to 1999, the Nokia-related share of Finnish external liabilities also ballooned by a factor of 40 (or more, allowing for new purchases along the way). This asset price change for one Finnish stock—a valuation effect—almost by itself explained the sudden explosion in Finnish external portfolio liabilities (traded stocks and bonds) seen in Figure 5-11, panel (a). The strong correlation between valuation effects and changes in external wealth is evident in panel (b), which also plots the similar (but inverse) path of Nokia's U.S. dollar stock price.

Then, in 2000, the bubble burst. The years from 2000 to 2002 saw a massive collapse in stock markets worldwide, especially in tech stocks. Nokia was not immune (and also suffered from a stubborn adherence to candybar phone designs), and its stock price fell by two-thirds, putting the valuation effects into reverse. The earlier capital gains by foreigners on Nokia (a loss on the Finnish national balance sheet) were now replaced by capital losses (a capital gain for the Finns). By the end of this period, external wealth was back where it started—around minus $50 billion, as seen in panel (a).

What are the lessons of this odd story? It is testament to the potential power of valuation effects. In the unusual Finnish case, these effects were as large as 100% of GDP in one year. Another important lesson is to understand that external wealth can fluc-

Nokia: world-beating candybar phones and a driving force of Finnish external wealth.

tuate for reasons that have nothing to do with residents' behavior. In this period, Finns were extremely prudent, with high enough saving to run a current account surplus. (They were less keen on holding tech stocks than some foreigners, which explains why their external asset portfolio didn't explode like their external liabilities; on the other hand, maybe that was shown to be a wise diversification choice in the longer run.) The Finnish current account surplus meant that the Finns were purchasing additional external wealth, and these financial flows alone increased Finnish external wealth. These flows mattered relatively little, however; the surges of capital gains and losses were simply so large that, for a time, they became virtually the entire story.

- With the help of windfalls (enjoying positive capital gains)

- Through its own thrift (running a *CA* surplus, so expenditure is less than income)

- By the charity of others (running a *KA* surplus, by receiving gifts of wealth)

Similarly, it can reduce its external wealth by doing any of the opposites.

Understanding the Data on External Wealth

To track external wealth accurately, statisticians apply Equation (5-15). They face the challenge of not only of keeping tabs on every trade in assets but also correctly assessing the impact of changing financial market conditions around the world on the value of the country's external assets and liabilities.

Measures of levels and change in national external wealth are tabulated in an account known as the net international investment position. To illustrate with an example, a simplified version of this account for the United States appears in Table 5-4. The data in the table show a clear distinction between the contribution of financial flows to changes in external wealth—net trade in assets, in column (a)—and the impact of various kinds of valuation effects—columns (b), (c), and (d).

Table 5-4, line 3, column (a), shows that in 2006 the United States experienced a net financial inflow of $804 billion of capital, meaning that the United States, on net, exported $804 billion in assets (exports of $1,860 billion on line 1, minus imports of $1,055 billion on line 2). On their own, these financial flows would have reduced U.S. external wealth by $804 billion in just one year. Yet nothing of the sort happened because offsetting valuation effects of +$502 billion—columns (b), (c), and (d)—boosted U.S. external wealth over the same period. These valuation effects were driven by +$348 billion in

TABLE 5-4

U.S. External Wealth in 2005–2006 The table shows changes in the U.S. net international investment position in billions of dollars.

Category	Position, 2005 ($ billions)	Financial Flows (a)	Price Changes (b)	Exchange Rate Changes (c)	Other Changes (d)	Total (a + b + c + d)	Position, 2006 ($ billions)
			Of Which Valuation Effects				
1. External Assets	**10,386**	**1,055**	**676**	**269**	**131**	**2,131**	**12,517**
= U.S.-owned assets abroad, of which:							
U.S. official reserve assets	188	−2	31	3	0	32	220
U.S. government assets, other	78	−5	..	..	0	−5	72
U.S. private assets	10,121	1,063	645	266	131	2,105	12,225
2. External Liabilities	**12,683**	**1,860**	**328**	**48**	**198**	**2,433**	**15,116**
= Foreign-owned assets in the United States, of which:							
Foreign official assets in the United States	2,306	440	21	..	3	464	2,770
Other foreign assets	10,376	1,419	307	48	195	1,970	12,346
3. External Wealth							
= (1) minus (2)	**−2,296**	**−804**	**348**	**221**	**−66**	**−302**	**−2,599**
= Net international investment position of the United States							
Symbol	W (end 2005)	−FA	Capital gains			ΔW	W (end 2006)

Note: Details may not add to totals because of rounding. Financial derivatives are excluded.

Source: U.S. Bureau of Economic Analysis.

price change effects and $221 billion in exchange rate effects. The United States enjoyed massive capital gains sufficient to almost offset more than half of the capital inflow. The United States borrowed an additional $804 billion from various nations in 2003, but its external wealth fell by "only" $302 billion as shown on line 3. Talk about a free lunch.

These U.S. capital gains in 2006 were qualitatively fairly large. The valuation effects of +$302 billion amounted to approximately 2.5% of U.S. GDP. This amount was almost sufficient on its own to offset more than half of the large U.S. current account deficit that year. It was also a lot larger than the rate of U.S. real economic growth!

So what happened in 2006? Two main factors were at work. First, equity values rose worldwide. But U.S. external assets include a larger share of equities than U.S. external liabilities, which consist of a great deal of U.S. debt. This compositional difference in the two portfolios means that rising equity markets boost the values of U.S. external assets much more than U.S. external liabilities. Second, about 95% of U.S. external liabilities were denominated in U.S. dollars, including vast foreign holdings of U.S. Treasury bills, held either as foreign official assets in central banks or as low-risk assets by foreign investors. These assets tended to have a stable value in dollar terms and would not experience any exchange rate valuation effects because they are denominated in dollars. In contrast, about 65% of U.S. external assets (foreign direct investment, bank loans, government debt) were denominated in foreign currencies, such as the euro, that were appreciating against the dollar.

A back-of-the-envelope calculation explains what happened. Total U.S. external assets amounted to $10,386 billion at year's end 2005, as the table shows (line 1). According to Federal Reserve data in 2006, the dollar depreciated by about 4% against a trade-weighted basket of major currencies (the main currencies in which U.S. external assets are denominated). Rough estimates suggest that about 65% or approximately $6,800 billion of U.S. external assets were nondollar denominated and if their currencies saw an average 4% appreciation against the dollar, then we can guess that the United States would enjoy 4% of $6,800 billion, or +$272 billion in capital gains. Allowing for offsetting 4% capital losses on the 5% of liabilities not in dollars (4% of 5% of the $12,683 billion in line 2) would knock $25 billion off that for a net capital gain of about $247 billion, a figure fairly close to the $221 billion reported by the BEA (in line 3, column c).[14]

Some Recent Trends Over the longer run, the changes in external wealth in Equation (5-16) gradually cumulate. In the case of the United States, for the past three decades, the financial account has been almost always in surplus, reflecting a net export of assets to the rest of the world to pay

---

[14] Data on the currency composition of U.S. external wealth from Cedric Tille, 2005, "Financial Integration and the Wealth Effect of Exchange Rate Fluctuations," *Staff Reports* 226, Federal Reserve Bank of New York.

for chronic current account deficits (the capital account has been negligibly small).

If there were no valuation effects, then Equation (5-15) would make a simple prediction. The change in the level of external wealth between two dates should equal the cumulative net import of assets (minus the financial account) over the intervening period. If we take the U.S. external wealth level in 1989 and add to that level all subsequent financial inflows, we would estimate U.S. external wealth in 2003 at minus $5,489 billion. The officially reported 2003 figure was a lot smaller: minus $2,599 billion.

Why? Have we mislaid 3 trillion dollars? Valuation effects or capital gains generated the difference of $2,890 billion in external wealth over the period, and from 1989 to 2003 these effects reduced U.S. net external indebtedness in 2004 by more than half compared with the level that financial flows alone would have predicted. The flip side of these valuation effects is that the rest of the world outside the United States suffered an equal and opposite capital loss over the same period. Why? Capital gains always have a "zero sum" property—by symmetry, an increase in the dollar value of the home country's external assets is simultaneously an increase in the dollar value of the rest of the world's external liabilities.

These official statistics show that valuation effects can be significant and must be properly accounted for if we are to understand the evolution of external wealth. Still, it is puzzling that the United States, in contrast to most other countries, has been so adept at reaping such gains year after year. Is this a free lunch? Can it continue? We return to the mysterious long-run behavior of the United States' external wealth in the next chapter.

What External Wealth Tells Us

External wealth data tell us the net credit or debit position of a country with respect to the rest of the world. They include data on external assets (foreign assets owned by the home country) and external liabilities (home assets owned by foreigners). A creditor country has positive external wealth, a debtor country negative external wealth.

What drives external wealth? The current account told us about the imbalances in a country's external flows of goods, services, factor services, and income. The balance of payments accounts told us how these imbalances require offsetting financial flows of assets between countries. Countries with a current account surplus (deficit) must be net buyers (sellers) of assets. This buying and selling of assets has implications for external wealth. An increase in a country's external wealth results from every net import of assets; conversely, a decrease in external wealth results from every net export of assets. In addition, countries can experience capital gains or losses on their external assets and liabilities that cause changes in external wealth. All of these changes are summarized in the statement of a country's net international investment position.

5 Conclusions

The science of macroeconomics would be impossible without data, and the vast majority of the data we employ emerge from the efforts of official statisticians around the world. Notwithstanding the inevitable statistical discrepancies, and even the occasional errors of omission and commission (see **Headlines: Lies, Damned Lies . . .**), we would be lost without these measures of macroeconomic activity.

This chapter has illustrated some important accounting concepts and has highlighted some unusual and intriguing features of the current international economic system. We have seen how a consistent system of national income and product accounts allows for international trade flows (including trade in intermediate goods), cross-border factor income flows, and unilateral transfers. We have also seen how these net resource flows of goods and services can be matched against a parallel set of net payment activities involving assets in the balance of payments accounts. Finally, we have seen how trades in assets can be combined with capital gains and losses to track the evolution of a nation's external wealth, an important part of its

HEADLINES

Lies, Damned Lies . . .

In November 2004, after it had been allowed to join the Eurozone (which involved meeting a 3% budget deficit limit), Greece admitted its 2003 budget deficit was really 3.4% and twice as large as it had previously claimed. And the budget deficit had never been below 3% since 1999. The EU was not amused. But this is nothing new: manipulating statistics is one of the oldest professions.

As a newspaper, the *Financial Times* pays a good deal of attention to statistics. Imagine our perplexity, therefore, when Britain's Office for National Statistics said it had overestimated the growth in cash value of national output for the second quarter by 25 per cent, and Greece said it had underestimated its gross domestic product by 25 per cent. Is there nothing we can count on?

The little local error at the ONS seems to have been a computer programming glitch and, phew, makes a new interest rate rise less likely. As for Greece, its government has been caught fiddling the budget deficit figures before. Greeks, one surmises, are unlikely to feel 25 per cent wealthier simply because their statisticians have decided to "capture" black economy activities such as prostitution (which in better organised Ancient Greece, moreover, was formally taxed).

Revisions of GDP are common though rarely this big. If Greece gets its new wealth accepted, furthermore, it may end up paying in more and taking less out of the EU budget. That was what happened to Italy after it suddenly announced in 1987 that its economy was 15 per cent bigger and in one sorpasso had outstripped Britain's.

It is hard to know whether all this is economics or a party trick. If we were all to do each other's housework and invoice for it, economists joke, the recorded transactions would double our economies overnight. An ONS experiment at estimating household capital formation (aka DIY) and production (from childcare to needlework) would have added an imputed two thirds to UK output in 2000. So there you have it: the secret of high growth is to spend more time with your families (and in Greece with, ahem, friends).

Sources: "Leader: Inputs and Output," Financial Times, September 30, 2006. On the 2004 fiasco, see George Parker and Ralph Atkins, "Greece escapes expulsion from single currency," Financial Times, November 16, 2004.

total wealth, as recorded in the statement of the net international invest-ment position.

Examples from around the world revealed the potential importance of these international flows, and we presented a fuller exposition using as an example the United States' accounts of income, balance of payments, and external wealth. In the remainder of the book, we make extensive use of the concepts introduced in this chapter to develop theories that explore the global macroeconomic linkages between nations.

KEY POINTS

1. National flows of expenditure, product, income, and wealth, and international flows of goods, services, income, and assets, together measure important aspects of the performance of an economy and its relationship to the rest of the world economy. The records kept in the national income and product accounts, the balance of payments account, and the net international investment position track these data.

2. Gross national expenditure (GNE) measures an economy's expenditure (total spending on final goods). It is the sum of consumption, invest-ment, and government consumption: $GNE = C + I + G$.

3. Gross domestic product (GDP) measures an economy's product defined as value added (firm sales net of intermediate usage).

4. Gross national income (GNI) measures an econo-my's income (total payments to domestic factors).

5. Gross national disposable income (GNDI, also denoted Y) measures an economy's disposable income (including transfers).

6. In a closed economy, $GNE = GDP = GNI = GNDI$.

7. In an open economy, GDP need not equal GNE because imports and exports of goods and ser-vices (measured by the trade balance or TB) imply that the sum of goods and services demanded by domestic residents need not be the same as the sum of goods and services supplied by domestic firms. Thus, $GDP = GNE + TB$.

8. In an open economy, GDP need not equal GNI because imports and exports of factor services (measured by net factor income from abroad or NFIA) imply that factor income received by domestic residents need not be the same as fac-tor payments made by domestic firms. Thus, $GNI = GDP + NFIA$.

9. In an open economy, the true level of disposable income is best measured by gross national dispos-able income or $Y = GNDI$. GNDI need not equal GNI because net unilateral transfers (NUT) to foreigners may be nonzero, due to foreign aid and other nonmarket gifts. Thus, $Y = GNDI = GNI + NUT$.

10. The sum of all the aforementioned international transactions, $TB + NFIA + NUT$, is called the current account (CA).

11. From the relationships just outlined, we find that $Y = C + I + G + CA$. This expression is known as the *national income identity*.

12. National saving S is defined as $Y - C - G$. So from the national income identity, we can derive the *current account identity*: $S = I + CA$.

13. The current account equals investment minus saving. Movements in investment or saving, all else equal, feed directly into the current account. Saving can be broken down into public and pri-vate saving.

14. All international trades in goods and services and in assets are recorded in an account known as the balance of payments (BOP). As a result of dou-ble-entry bookkeeping, and allowing for gifts and transfers, the BOP must sum to zero.

15. The BOP contains the following:
    • Net exports of goods and services, TB, called the trade balance

- Net exports of factor services, *NFIA,* called the net factor income from abroad
- Net unilateral transfers received, *NUT,* called the net unilateral transfers
- Net transfers of assets received, *KA,* called the capital account
- Net exports of assets, *FA,* called the financial account

16. The first three items are the current account, *CA*. Since the BOP accounts sum to zero, this implies the *balance of payments identity: CA + FA + KA = 0.*

17. External wealth is a measure of a country's credit or debt position versus the rest of the world. It equals external assets—rest of world (ROW) assets owned by home—minus external liabilities (home assets owned by ROW). The net export (import) of assets lowers (raises) a country's external wealth. External wealth is one part of a country's total wealth.

18. External wealth can change for one of two reasons: the export or import of assets (called financial flows) or changes in the value of existing assets due to capital gains or losses (called valuation effects). Both of these channels affect net external wealth.

KEY TERMS

national income and product accounts, p. 167

balance of payments accounts, p. 167

gross national expenditure (GNE), p. 167

value added, p. 168

gross domestic product (GDP), p. 168

gross national income (GNI), p. 169

imports, p. 171

exports, p. 171

trade balance, p. 171

factor service imports, p. 171

factor service exports, p. 171

net factor income from abroad (NFIA), p. 171

net unilateral transfers (NUT), p. 171

gross national disposable income (GNDI), p. 171

current account, p. 171

asset exports, p. 172

asset imports, p. 172

financial account, p. 172

capital account, p. 172

expenditure approach, p. 173

product approach, p. 173

income approach, p. 173

GDP identity, p. 174

GNI identity, p. 177

GNDI identity, p. 180

national income identity, p. 186

national saving, p. 186

current account identity, p. 186

private saving, p. 188

government saving, p. 189

external asset, p. 194

external liability, p. 194

BOP identity, p. 195

BOP credit, p. 196

BOP debit, p. 196

(net) lender, p. 200

(net) borrower, p. 200

financial outflow, p. 201

financial inflow, p. 201

official settlements balance, p. 201

nonreserve financial account, p. 201

external wealth, p. 204

net creditor, p. 204

net debtor, p. 204

PROBLEMS

1. The table shows the OECD's 2004 ranking of member countries based on their GDP per person. Compute the ratio of GNI to GDP in each case. What does this imply about net factor income from abroad in each country? Compute the GNI per person rankings of these countries. Are there any major differences between the GDP and GNI per person rankings?

		GDP per Person	GNI per Person
1	Luxembourg	$64,843	$53,299
2	Norway	$41,880	$42,062
3	United States	$39,660	$39,590
4	Ireland	$36,536	$31,151
5	Switzerland	$34,740	$37,638
6	Netherlands	$33,571	$34,527
7	Iceland	$33,271	$31,897
8	Austria	$33,235	$32,843
9	Australia	$32,643	$31,462
10	Canada	$32,413	$31,751
11	Denmark	$32,335	$32,232
12	Belgium	$31,985	$31,675
13	United Kingdom	$31,780	$32,470
14	Sweden	$31,072	$31,007
15	Germany	$29,916	$28,732
16	Finland	$29,833	$30,361
17	Japan	$29,173	$29,739
18	France	$29,006	$29,287
19	Italy	$27,744	$27,586
20	Greece	$27,691	$27,412
21	Spain	$26,018	$25,672
22	New Zealand	$24,834	$23,205
23	Slovenia	$21,527	$21,268
24	Korea	$20,723	$20,771
25	Czech Republic	$19,426	$18,314
26	Portugal	$19,324	$19,029
27	Hungary	$16,519	$15,548
28	Slovak Republic	$14,651	$14,708
29	Poland	$13,089	$12,511
30	Mexico	$10,145	$9,989
31	Turkey	$7,212	$7,186

2. Note the following accounting identity for gross national income (*GNI*):

$$GNI = C + I + G + TB + NFIA.$$

Using this expression, show that in a closed economy, gross domestic product (*GDP*), gross national income (*GNI*), and gross national expenditures (*GNE*) are the same. Show that domestic investment is equal to domestic savings.

3. Show how each of the following would affect the U.S. balance of payments. Include a description of the debit and credit items, and in each case say which specific account is affected (e.g., imports of goods and services, *IM;* exports of assets, EX_A; and so on).

a. A California computer manufacturer purchases a $50 hard disk from a Malaysian company, paying the funds from a bank account in Malaysia.

b. A U.S. tourist to Japan sells his iPod to a local resident for yen worth $100.

c. The U.S. central bank sells $500 million of its holdings of U.S. Treasury bonds to a British financial firm and purchases pound sterling foreign reserves.

d. A foreign owner of Apple shares receives $10,000 in dividend payments, which are paid into a New York bank.

e. The central bank of China purchases $1 million of export earnings from a firm that has sold $1 million worth of toys to the United States, and the central bank holds these dollars as reserves.

f. The U.S. government forgives a $50 million debt owed by a developing country.

4. In 2007 the country of Ikonomia has a current account deficit of $1 billion and a nonreserve financial account surplus of $750 million. Ikonomia's capital account is in a $100 million surplus. In addition, Ikonomian factors located in foreign countries earn $700 million. Ikonomia has a trade deficit of $800 million. Assume Ikonomia neither gives nor receives unilateral transfers. Ikonomia's *GDP* is $9 billion.

a. What happened to Ikonomia's net foreign assets during 2007? Did it acquire or lose foreign assets during the year?

b. Compute the official settlements balance (*OSB*). Based on this number, what happened to the central bank's (foreign) reserves?

c. How much income did foreign factors of production earn in Ikonomia during 2007?

d. Compute net factor income from abroad (*NFIA*).

e. Using the identity *BOP = CA + FA + KA,* show that *BOP* = 0.

f. Compute Ikonomia's gross national expenditure (*GNE*), gross national income (*GNI*), and gross national disposable income (*GNDI*).

5. To answer this question, you must obtain data from the Bureau of Economic Analysis (BEA), http://www.bea.gov, on the U.S. balance of payments (BOP) tables. Go to interactive tables to obtain *annual* data for 2006 (the default setting is for quarterly data). It may take you some time to get familiar with how to navigate the website. *You need only refer to Table 1 on the BOP accounts.* Using the BOP data, compute the following for the United States:

   a. Trade balance (*TB*), net factor income from abroad (*NFIA*), net unilateral transfers (*NUT*), and current account (*CA*)
   b. Financial account (*FA*)
   c. Official settlements balance (*OSB*), referred to as "U.S. official reserve assets" and "Foreign official assets in the U.S."
   d. Nonreserve financial account (*NRFA*)
   e. Balance of payments (*BOP*). Note this may not equal zero because of statistical discrepancy. Verify that the discrepancy is the same as the one reported by the BEA.

6. Continuing from the previous question, find nominal GDP for the United States in 2006 (you can find it elsewhere on the BEA site). Use this information along with your previous calculations to compute the following:

   a. Gross national expenditure (*GNE*), gross national income (*GNI*), and gross national disposable income (*GNDI*)
   b. In macroeconomics, we often assume the U.S. economy is a closed economy when building models that describe how changes in policy and shocks affect the economy. Based on the previous data (BOP and GDP), do you think this is a reasonable assumption to make? Do international transactions account for a large share of total transactions (involving goods and services, or income) involving the United States?

7. During the 1980s, the United States experienced "twin deficits" in the current account and government budget. Since 1998 the U.S. current account deficit has grown steadily along with rising government budget deficits. Do government budget deficits lead to current account deficits? Identify other possible sources of the current account deficits. Do current account deficits necessarily indicate problems in the economy?

8. Consider the economy of Opulenza. In Opulenza, domestic investment was $400 million, and there was $20 million in capital gains or domestic wealth during 2007. Opulenzans purchased $120 million in new foreign assets during the year; foreigners purchased $160 million in Opulenzan assets. Assume the valuation effects total $1 million in capital gains or external wealth. (Note: Read the Appendix before answering this question.)

   a. Compute the change in domestic wealth in Opulenza.
   b. Compute the change in external wealth for Opulenza.
   c. Compute the change in total wealth for Opulenza.
   d. Compute domestic savings for Opulenza.
   e. Compute Opulenza's current account. Is the *CA* in deficit or surplus?
   f. Explain the intuition for the *CA* deficit/surplus in terms of savings in Opulenza, financial flows, and its domestic/external wealth position.
   g. How would a depreciation in Opulenza's currency affect its domestic, external, and total wealth? Assume that foreign assets owned by Opulenzans are denominated in foreign currency.

9. This question asks you to compute valuation effects for the United States in 2004, using the same methods mentioned in this chapter. Use the bea.gov website to collect the data needed for this question: look under the "International" heading.

   Visit the BEA's balance of payments data page and obtain the U.S. balance of payments for 2004 in billions of dollars. Be sure to get the annual data, not quarterly.

   Visit the BEA's net international investment position data page and obtain the U.S. net international investment position for end 2003 to end 2004.

   a. What was the U.S. current account for 2004?
   b. What was the U.S. financial account for 2004?
   c. What was the U.S. change in external wealth for 2004?

d. What was the U.S. total (net) valuation effect for 2004?

e. Does the answer to part (d) equal the answer to part (b) minus the answer to part (c)? Why?

f. What do the BEA data say was the U.S. valuation effect due to exchange rate changes for 2004?

   You may now assume that the U.S. dollar depreciated by 10% against major currencies in 2004, and use this average to estimate valuation effects.

g. What were end-2003 U.S. external liabilities? If 5% of these liabilities were in foreign currency and were subject to a 10% exchange rate appreciation against the dollar, what decrease in U.S. external wealth resulted?

h. What were end-2003 U.S. external assets? If 65% of these assets were subject to a 10% exchange rate appreciation against the dollar, what increase in U.S. external wealth resulted?

i. Using the answers to parts (g) and (h), what was the 2004 U.S. valuation effect due to exchange rate changes according to your rough calculation? Is it close to the BEA figure in part (f)?

10. Read **Side Bar: The Nokia Economy** again. At the height of the tech boom in 1999 to 2000, the external portfolio liabilities of Finland, most of them shares of Nokia, were worth in excess of $200 billion. Did this mean that the Finns were facing trouble with their foreign creditors? Suppose that in the year 2000 the many U.S. owners of these Finnish equities had wanted to cash them in. Could they have done so? Would the Finns have had to pay up, lowering their net external debt? If not, and had the U.S. sellers sold to non-Finns, would Finnish external wealth have changed at all? Now suppose the Finns had had $200 billion in debt claims against them coming due in 2000. Would that have been more troubling? Does your answer reveal an important difference between foreign investments that take the form of debt versus those that take the form of equity?

External Wealth and Total Wealth

In this chapter, we studied external wealth. But individuals and countries care about their total wealth. How does external wealth relate to total wealth?

A country's *total wealth* is the sum of the home capital stock (all nonfinancial assets in the home economy, denoted K) plus amounts owed to home by foreigners (A) minus amounts owed foreigners by home (L). That is, it is domestic wealth plus external wealth:

$$\text{Total wealth} = \underbrace{K}_{\text{Domestic wealth}} + \underbrace{(A - L)}_{\text{External wealth}}.$$

In this definition, note that we deliberately exclude financial assets owed by one home entity to another home entity because in the aggregate these cancel out and form no part of a country's total wealth.

Changes in the value of total wealth can then be written as follows:

$$\begin{pmatrix}\text{Change in}\\\text{total wealth}\end{pmatrix} = \underbrace{\begin{pmatrix}\text{Additions}\\\text{to } K\end{pmatrix} + \begin{pmatrix}\text{Additions}\\\text{to } A - L\end{pmatrix}}_{\text{Additions (acquisitions minus disposals)}} + \underbrace{\begin{pmatrix}\text{Capital}\\\text{gains on } K\end{pmatrix} + \begin{pmatrix}\text{Capital gains}\\\text{on } A - L\end{pmatrix}}_{\text{Valuation effects (gains minus losses)}}.$$

There are two kinds of terms in this expression. The total value of wealth (of a person or a country) may change due to *net additions* of assets (such as purchases, sales, or net gifts) or due to *valuation effects* (capital gains—or, if they are negative, capital losses—arising from changes in the prices of assets).

The previous equation can be simplified by two observations. First, additions to the domestic capital stock K have a simpler expression: they are known as investment, denoted I. (Strictly, this is the gross addition to the capital stock; the net addition would require the subtraction of depreciation, and in the previous notation that would be accounted for under valuation effects since depreciating assets fall in value.)

Second, additions to external wealth, $A - L$, also have a simpler expression: they are equal to net additions to external assets minus net additions to external liabilities, and as we saw in the main chapter, these are equal to *minus* the financial account, $-FA$.

Substituting, we can rewrite the last equations as

$$\begin{pmatrix}\text{Change in}\\\text{total wealth}\end{pmatrix} = \underbrace{I}_{\substack{\text{Additions to } K\\=\\\text{Additions to assets in}\\\text{the home economy}}} + \underbrace{(-FA)}_{\substack{\text{Additions to } A - L\\=\\\text{Net import of assets}\\\text{into the home}\\\text{economy}}} + \underbrace{\begin{pmatrix}\text{Capital}\\\text{gains on } K\end{pmatrix} + \begin{pmatrix}\text{Capital gains}\\\text{on } A - L\end{pmatrix}}_{\text{Valuation effects (gains minus losses)}}.$$

Now, using the BOP identity, we know that $CA + KA + FA = 0$ so that minus the financial account $-FA$ must equal $CA + KA$, hence we can write

$$\begin{pmatrix} \text{Change in} \\ \text{total wealth} \end{pmatrix} = I + CA + KA + \underbrace{\begin{pmatrix} \text{Capital} \\ \text{gains on } K \end{pmatrix} + \begin{pmatrix} \text{Capital gains} \\ \text{on } A - L \end{pmatrix}}_{\text{Valuation effects (gains minus losses)}}.$$

Notice what has happened here. The BOP identity makes the connection between external asset trade and activity in the current account. We take the connection one step further using the current account identity, $S = I + CA$, which allows us to write

$$\begin{pmatrix} \text{Change in} \\ \text{total wealth} \end{pmatrix} = S + KA + \underbrace{\begin{pmatrix} \text{Capital} \\ \text{gains on } K \end{pmatrix} + \begin{pmatrix} \text{Capital gains} \\ \text{on } A - L \end{pmatrix}}_{\text{Valuation effects (gains minus losses)}}.$$

The message of this expression is clear. As we all probably know from personal experience, there are only three ways to get more (or less) wealthy: do more (or less) saving (S), receive (or give) gifts of assets (KA), or enjoy the good (bad) fortune of capital gains (losses) on your portfolio. What is true about individuals' wealth is also true for the wealth of a nation in the aggregate.

Balance of Payments I: The Gains from Financial Globalization

Save for a rainy day.

Make hay while the sun shines.

Don't put all your eggs in one basket.

How does your household cope with economic shocks and the financial challenges they pose? Let's take an extreme example. Suppose you are self-employed and own a business. A severe storm appears and a flood overwhelms your town (think of Hurricane Katrina and New Orleans). This is bad news on several fronts. Business is down as people struggle to recover from the natural disaster, so you have almost no income for a while. Maybe your business premises are damaged and you will have to rebuild, so you must also plan to make new investment.

If you have no financial dealings with anyone, your household, as a little closed economy, faces a difficult trade-off as your income falls. Your household income has to equal its consumption plus investment. So would you try to maintain your level of consumption, and neglect the need to invest? Or would you invest, and let your household suffer as you cut back drastically on consumption to fund your investment? Faced with an emergency like this, most of us look beyond our own household, if we can. Outside help can get us through the hard times: we might hope for transfers (gifts from friends and family, or the government), or we might rely on financial markets (dip into savings, apply for a loan, or rely on an insurance payout, and so on).

What does this story have to do with international economics? If we redraw the boundaries of this experiment, expanding from the household unit, up to the local, regional, and finally national level, then the same logic applies. Countries face shocks all the time, and how they cope with them depends on whether they are open or closed.

To expand our parable from the household to the national level, let's look at some data from Caribbean and Central American countries that periodically face the same kind of shock as the hypothetical household we just described. Every year many tropical storms, some of them of hurricane strength, sweep through this region. The storms are large in size—hundreds of miles across—and most countries in the region are much smaller in size, some no more than little islets. For them, a hurricane is the town flood blown up to a national scale. The worst storms cause widespread destruction and loss of life.

Hurricanes are tragic human events, but they provide an opportunity for research. Scientists track them to understand the ocean and the environment. Economists can study a hurricane as an exogenous shock to see how an economy responds. Such an "act of God"—in economics jargon, a "natural experiment"—provides a laboratory-like test of economic theory. Figure 6-1 shows the average macroeconomic response in these countries after they are hit by a hurricane.

In dire straits, these countries do some of the things we expect households to do: accept nonmarket gifts (transfers from foreign countries) and borrow (by running a current account deficit). If we subtract the effect of the nonmarket transfers, we can examine market behavior alone, and the patterns in

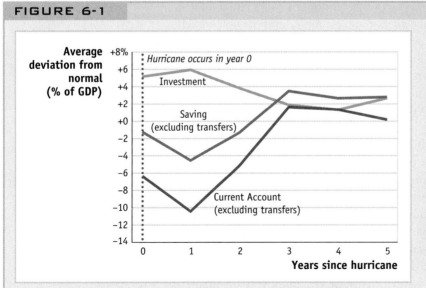

FIGURE 6-1

The Macroeconomics of Hurricanes The figure shows the average response (holding fixed transfers) of investment, saving, and the current account in a sample of Caribbean and Central American countries in the years during and after severe hurricane damage. The responses are as expected: investment rises (to rebuild), and saving falls (to limit the fall in consumption); hence, the current account moves sharply toward deficit.

Note: Transfers are excluded from saving and the current account, and the saving measure is calculated as $S - NUT = I + CA - NUT$.

Source: John C. Bluedorn, 2005, "Hurricanes: Intertemporal Trade and Capital Shocks," Oxford Economics Working Paper No. 2005-241.

the data are striking. As a fraction of GDP, investment is typically 3% to 6% higher than normal in the three years after a hurricane, and saving is 1% to 5% lower (holding fixed transfers). Combining the two, the current account (saving minus investment) falls dramatically and is 6% to 10% more in deficit than normal.

Hurricanes are extreme examples of economic shocks. They are not representative of the normal fluctuations that countries experience, but their very size and randomness expose important macroeconomic responses. They illustrate some of the important financial mechanisms that help open economies cope with all types of shocks, large and small.

In this chapter, we see how financially open economies can, in theory, use these financial mechanisms to reap gains from financial globalization. We first look at the role of international debt and show how countries may wish to save and borrow internationally for two purposes: consumption smoothing (the desire to save less when income falls so that consumption doesn't have to fall drastically) and efficient investment (the need to create productive capital stock). We also consider the role of equity markets in financial globalization and show how international portfolio diversification (such as the trading of stocks between countries) can also deliver benefits. Along the way, we discover how well these theoretical gains translate into reality, an area of some dispute among economists, and we show that many of these gains are yet to be realized. In the advanced countries, the gains can be large and somewhat more attainable, but in poorer countries the gains may be smaller and harder to realize through financial globalization—which, as we see in later chapters, may carry other risks.

Hurricane Mitch battered Central America from October 22, 1998, to November 5, 1998. It was the deadliest hurricane in more than 200 years and the second deadliest ever recorded.

1 Intertemporal Macroeconomics

Our introductory examples illustrated the importance of borrowing and lending as a way for countries (like households) to better cope with shocks. But as we saw in the last chapter, borrowing and lending activity also has implications for wealth, and the extent to which we can borrow and lend therefore depends on the limits placed on our debit and credit accumulation. Understanding these constraints is our first task in this chapter and is essential to understanding how financial globalization can have profound effects by affecting the choices available to a country.

We ended Chapter 5 by accounting for the change in external wealth from one period to the next. When we study an economy as it evolves over time, we are following a dynamic approach to macroeconomics rather than a static approach. The dynamic approach is also known as the *intertemporal approach* to macroeconomics.

In this section, we see how the intertemporal approach highlights a key constraint for an open economy in the long run: the long-run budget constraint, which tells us in a very precise way how and why a country must, in the long run, "live within its means." A country's ability to adjust its external wealth through borrowing and lending provides a buffer against economic shocks, but the long-run budget constraint shows there are limits to how the buffer can be used.

To see how, let's look at a simple household analogy. This year (year 0) you borrow $100,000 from the bank at an interest rate of 10% annually. You have no other wealth and inflation is zero. Consider two cases:

Case 1 *A debt that is serviced.* Every year you pay the 10% interest due on the principal amount of the loan, $10,000, but you never pay any principal. At the end of each year, the bank renews the loan (a *rollover*), so your wealth remains constant at −$100,000.

Case 2 *A debt that is not serviced.* You pay neither interest nor principal but ask the bank to roll over the principal *and* the interest due on it each year. In year 1, the overdue interest is $10,000, and your debt grows by 10% to $110,000. In year 2, the overdue interest is 10% of $110,000, or $11,000, and your debt grows by 10% again to $121,000. Assuming this process goes on and on, your level of debt grows by 10% every year.

Case 2 is not sustainable in the real world. Your debt level explodes to infinity—it grows by 10% every year forever. This case is sometimes called a rollover scheme, a pyramid scheme, or a "Ponzi game."[1] It illustrates the limits to the use of external wealth as a buffer against negative economic shocks—in the long run, the parties involved in the loan would simply not allow the debt to grow beyond a certain point. Debts must be paid off eventually. This requirement is the essence of the long-run budget constraint.

The Long-Run Budget Constraint

To see what it means for a country to service its debts, we have to understand how external wealth changes. To do so, we now develop a basic model that makes a number of simplifying assumptions, although the lessons of this model can be extended to other more complex cases.

- Prices are perfectly flexible. Under this assumption, all analysis in this chapter can be conducted in terms of real variables, and all monetary aspects of the economy can be ignored. (To convert to real terms, all quantities are simply inflation adjusted and expressed in fixed base-year prices.)

- The country is a **small open economy.** By this definition, the country cannot influence prices in world markets. It trades goods and services with the rest of the world through exports and imports. It can also lend or borrow overseas, but only using debt financing. There are no capital controls.

---

[1] This type of borrowing strategy is called a "Ponzi game" after the infamous swindler Charles Ponzi who engaged in a "pyramid" or "chain letter" operation of this type in Boston in the years 1919 to 1920, borrowing new money from an expanding base of creditors to pay off past debt.

- All debts carry a real interest rate r^*, the **world real interest rate,** which we assume to be constant. Because the country is small, it has to take the world real interest rate as given.

- The country pays a real interest rate r^* on its start-of-period debt liabilities L and is paid the same interest rate r^* on its start-of-period debt assets A. In any period, the country earns net interest income payments equal to $r^* A$ minus $r^* L$, or, more simply, $r^* W$ where W is external wealth $(A - L)$ at the start of the period. External wealth may vary over time.

- There are no unilateral transfers ($NUT = 0$), no capital transfers ($KA = 0$), and no capital gains on external wealth. Under this assumption, we know from the last chapter that, apart from the trade balance, the only other nonzero item in the current account is net factor income from abroad that takes the form of net interest paid (if the country is a debtor, with negative external wealth) or earned (if the country is a creditor with positive external wealth).

Calculating the Change in Wealth Each Period In Chapter 5, we saw that the change in external wealth equals the sum of three terms: the current account, the capital account, and capital gains on external wealth. In this special case, given the final assumption just listed, the last two terms are zero, and the current account equals the sum of two terms: the trade balance plus any net interest payments at the world interest rate on the external wealth held at the end of the last period. Thus, mathematically, we can write the change in external wealth from end of year $N-1$ to end of year N as

$$\Delta W_N = \underbrace{W_N - W_{N-1}}_{\substack{\text{Change in external} \\ \text{wealth this period}}} = \underbrace{TB_N}_{\substack{\text{Trade balance} \\ \text{this period}}} + \underbrace{r^* W_{N-1}}_{\substack{\text{Interest paid/received on} \\ \text{last period's external wealth}}},$$

where subscripts denote years. In this simplified world, external wealth can change for only two reasons: surpluses or deficits on the trade balance in the current period, or surpluses and deficits on net factor income arising from interest received or due on the level of external wealth last period.

Calculating Future Wealth Levels Now that we have a formula for wealth changes, and assuming we know the initial level of wealth in year $N-1$, we can compute the level of wealth at any time in the future by repeated application of the formula.

To find wealth at the end of year N, we rearrange the preceding equation:

$$\underbrace{W_N}_{\substack{\text{External wealth at} \\ \text{the end of this period}}} = \underbrace{TB_N}_{\substack{\text{Trade balance} \\ \text{this period}}} + \underbrace{(1 + r^*)W_{N-1}}_{\substack{\text{Last period's external wealth} \\ \text{plus interest paid/received}}}.$$

This is an important and intuitive result: wealth at the end of a period is the sum of two terms. The trade balance this period captures an addition to wealth due to net exports (exports minus imports). Wealth at the end of last period times $(1 + r^*)$ captures the wealth from last period plus the interest earned on that wealth.

The Two-Period Case To see this formula at work, let's examine a two-period example. We start in year 0, so $N = 0$. We suppose a country has some initial external wealth from the previous year −1 (an inheritance from the past) and can borrow or lend in the present period (year 0). We also impose the following limits: By the end of year 1, the country must end all external borrowing and lending. All debts owed or owing must be paid off, and thus the country ends the year with zero external wealth.

By the formula given earlier, $W_0 = (1 + r^*)W_{-1} + TB_0$. At the end of year 0, the country carries over from the last period (year −1) its initial wealth level, plus any interest accumulated on it. If the country runs a trade deficit, it runs its external wealth down by adding liabilities or cashing in external assets; conversely, if it runs a trade surplus, it lends that amount to the rest of the world.

What happens at the end of year 1 when the country must have zero external wealth? Applying the preceding formula again to year 1, we know that $W_1 = (1 + r^*)W_0 + TB_1$. We can substitute $W_0 = (1 + r^*)W_{-1} + TB_0$ to obtain

$$W_1 = (1 + r^*)^2 W_{-1} + (1 + r^*)TB_0 + TB_1.$$

In addition to its initial level of external wealth, two years later at the end of year 1 the country has accumulated wealth equal to the trade balance in years 0 and 1 plus the one year of interest earned (or paid) on the year 0 trade balance, plus the two years of interest earned (or paid) on its initial wealth.

Looking forward from year 0, if we require the left-hand side W_1 to be zero, then the right-hand side must be zero, too: to get to zero wealth at the end of period 1, the present and future trade balances (and accumulated interest on those balances) must be equal and opposite to initial wealth (and accumulated interest on that). Hence we require

$$-(1 + r^*)^2 W_{-1} = (1 + r^*)TB_0 + TB_1.$$

This is the two-period budget constraint.

Present Value Form If we divide the previous equation by $(1 + r^*)$ and rearrange, we find a much more intuitive and possibly familiar expression:

$$\underbrace{-(1 + r^*)W_{-1}}_{\substack{\text{Minus the present value of} \\ \text{wealth from last period}}} = \underbrace{TB_0 + \frac{TB_1}{(1 + r^*)}}_{\substack{\text{Present value of all present and} \\ \text{future trade balances}}}.$$

Every element in this rearrangement of the two-period budget constraint represents a quantity expressed in present value terms. It says that the present value of the two present and future trade balances (from years 0 and 1) must equal *minus* the present value of initial external wealth carried forward from the past (year −1).

By definition, a **present value** expresses a value X accruing N periods from now in terms of an equivalent lump sum today, taking into account any interest that accrues over the intervening period. If the interest rate is r^*, then the present value of X is $X/(1 + r^*)^N$. For example, if you are told that you will receive $121 at the end of year 2 and the interest rate is 10%, then the present value of that $121 now, in year 0, would be $100 because $100 × 1.1 (adding interest earned in year 1) × 1.1 (adding interest earned in year 2) = $121.

A Two-Period Example Let's put some numbers into the last equation. Suppose the country starts with a debt level of −$100 million at the end of year −1. Thus, W_{-1} = −$100 million. At a real interest rate of 10%, how can the country satisfy the two-period budget constraint and have a zero external balance at the end of year 1? The left-hand side is +$110 million, the present value (in period 0 terms) of minus external wealth (the initial debt in period −1 with one year's accrued interest). To pay off this $110 million at the end of period 1, the country must ensure that the present value of future trade balances adds up to +$110 million.

The country has many ways to do this. It could run a trade surplus of $110 million in period 0, pay off up front at the end of period 0, and then have balanced trade in period 1; or it could wait to pay off the debt until the end of period 1, which would require the country to run a trade surplus of $121 million in period 1 after having balanced trade in period 0. Or it could have any other combination of trade balances in periods 0 and 1 that allows it to pay off the debt and accumulated interest so that external wealth at the end of period 1 is zero and the budget constraint is satisfied.

The Long-Run Case By extending the two-period model to N periods, where N can run to infinity, the two-period budget constraint becomes the **long-run budget constraint (LRBC).** Repeating the two-period logic N times, external wealth after N periods is given by initial wealth (and accumulated interest on that wealth whether it is positive or negative) plus all the trade balances (and accumulated interest on those positive or negative balances). If external wealth is to be zero at the end of N periods, then the present value of the sum of N present and future trade balances must equal *minus* the present value of external wealth. If N runs to infinity, we get an infinite sum and arrive at the equation of the LRBC:[2]

$$(6\text{-}1) \quad \text{LRBC: } \underbrace{-(1+r^*)W_{-1}}_{\substack{\text{Minus the} \\ \text{Present value of wealth} \\ \text{from last period}}} = \underbrace{TB_0 + \frac{TB_1}{(1+r^*)} + \frac{TB_2}{(1+r^*)^2} + \frac{TB_3}{(1+r^*)^3} + \cdots.}_{\text{Present value of all present and future trade balances}}$$

---

[2] We can take the basic equation for the change in external wealth, $W_0 = (1 + r^*)W_{-1} + TB_0$, and apply it N times with repeated substitution to obtain wealth at the end of period N:

$$W_N = (1 + r^*)^{N+1}W_{-1} + (1 + r^*)^N TB_0 + (1 + r^*)^{N-1}TB_1 + (1 + r^*)^{N-2}TB_2 + \cdots + (1 + r^*)TB_{N-1} + TB_N$$

If we divide the previous equation by $(1 + r^*)^N$, we get

$$\frac{W_N}{(1+r^*)^N} = (1 + r^*)W_{-1} + TB_0 + \frac{TB_1}{(1+r^*)} + \frac{TB_2}{(1+r^*)^2} + \cdots + \frac{TB_N}{(1+r^*)^N}.$$

As we saw earlier, in a Ponzi game, external wealth W_N explodes, growing by a factor $(1 + r^*)$ every period. To prevent this, external wealth W_N (whether positive or negative) must grow more slowly in the long run than the factor $(1 + r^*)^N$. If that is this case, then as N approaches infinity, the left-hand side of the equation will approach zero. This in turn would imply that the right-hand side of the last equation must also approach zero. This leads directly to the LRBC Equation (6–1) in the text.

The LRBC ensures that any initial debt or credit is balanced by offsetting trade surpluses or deficits in present value terms. It rules out exploding external wealth.

A Long-Run Example: The Perpetual Loan

An example helps us understand and apply the long-run budget constraint and allows us to explore an important case that we use extensively in the rest of the chapter. Suppose today is year 0 and a country is to pay a constant amount X every year starting next year, year 1. What is the present value of that sequence of payments, which we shall denote $PV(X)$?

$$PV(X) = \frac{X}{(1 + r^*)} + \frac{X}{(1 + r^*)^2} + \frac{X}{(1 + r^*)^3} + \cdots.$$

This expression for $PV(X)$ is an infinite sum, but a simpler solution can be found. We multiply this equation by $(1 + r^*)$:

$$PV(X)(1 + r^*) = X + \frac{X}{(1 + r^*)} + \frac{X}{(1 + r^*)^2} + \frac{X}{(1 + r^*)^3} + \cdots.$$

If we subtract the first equation from the second, all of the terms on the right cancel out except X, so we get $r^* PV(X) = X$, and hence

(6-2)
$$\underbrace{\frac{X}{(1 + r^*)} + \frac{X}{(1 + r^*)^2} + \frac{X}{(1 + r^*)^3} + \cdots}_{PV(X)} = \frac{X}{r^*}.$$

For example, suppose the constant payment is $X = 100$ and the interest rate is 5% ($r^* = 0.05$). Equation (6-2) says that the present value of a stream of payments of 100 starting in year 1 is $100/0.05 = 2,000$:

$$\frac{100}{(1 + 0.05)} + \frac{100}{(1 + 0.05)^2} + \frac{100}{(1 + 0.05)^3} + \cdots \frac{100}{0.05} = 2,000.$$

This example, which has been chosen because it recurs later in this chapter, shows the stream of interest payments on a **perpetual loan** (i.e., an interest-only loan or, equivalently, a sequence of loans for which the principal is refinanced or *rolled over* every year). If the amount loaned by the creditor is $2,000 in year 0, and this principal amount is outstanding forever, then the interest that must be paid each year to service the debt is 5% of $2,000, or $100. Under these conditions, the present value of the future interest payments equals the value of the amount loaned in year 0. The LRBC is satisfied.

Implications of the LRBC for Gross National Expenditure and Gross Domestic Product

Finally, let's step back from all the equations and remind ourselves why the LRBC is a type of budget constraint. A budget constraint in economics always tells us something about the limits to expenditure, whether for a person, firm, government, or country, and the LRBC is no different—it relates national product to national expenditure.

Recall from Chapter 5 that the trade balance is the difference between gross domestic product and gross national expenditure, $TB = GDP - GNE$. If we insert this expression into the LRBC Equation (6-1) and collect terms, we see that

(6-3)

$$\underbrace{\underbrace{(1 + r^*)W_{-1}}_{\substack{\text{Present value} \\ \text{of wealth from} \\ \text{last period}}} + \underbrace{GDP_0 + \frac{GDP_1}{(1 + r^*)} + \frac{GDP_2}{(1 + r^*)^2} + \cdots}_{\text{Present value of present and future } GDP}}_{\text{Present value of the country's resources}}$$

$$= \underbrace{GNE_0 + \frac{GNE_1}{(1 + r^*)} + \frac{GNE_2}{(1 + r^*)^2} + \cdots}_{\substack{\text{Present value of present and future } GNE \\ = \\ \text{Present value of the country's spending}}}$$

The left side of this equation is the present value of the long-run resources of the country: the present value of any inherited wealth plus the present value of all present and future product as measured by *GDP*. The right side is the present value of all present and future spending ($C + I + G$) as measured by *GNE*.

Thus, the long-run budget constraint says that *in the long run, in present value terms, a country's expenditures (GNE) must equal its production (GDP) plus any initial wealth*. The LRBC shows how an economy must live within its means in the long run.

Summary

The key lesson of our simple intertemporal model is that a closed economy is subject to a tighter constraint than an open economy. In a closed economy, "living within your means" requires a country to have a zero trade balance every year; in an open economy, "living within your means" requires only that a country must maintain a balance between its trade deficits and surpluses that satisfies the long-run budget constraint.

This conclusion implies that an open economy ought to be able to do better (or no worse) than a closed economy in achieving its desired patterns of expenditure. This is the essence of the theoretical argument that there are gains from financial globalization.

We now examine this argument in greater detail and consider whether it is valid in the real world. To begin, we first consider the assumptions of the model and look at situations in which adjustments to these assumptions might be needed.

APPLICATION

The Favorable Situation of the United States

Two special assumptions greatly simplified our intertemporal model. We assumed that the same real rate of interest r^* applied to income received on assets and income paid on liabilities, and we assumed that there were no capital gains on external wealth. However, these assumptions are very clearly not satisfied for one country: the United States.

"Exorbitant Privilege" The United States has for many years since the 1980s been a net debtor (with $W = A - L < 0$). Under the model's simple assumptions, negative external wealth would lead to a deficit on net factor income from abroad, with $r^* W = r^* (A - L) < 0$. Yet U.S. net factor income from abroad has been positive in all that period, a pattern we saw in Chapter 5 (though this may be about to change). How can this be?

The only way a net debtor can earn positive net interest income is if it receives a higher rate of interest on its assets than it pays on its liabilities. The data show this to have been true for the United States consistently since the 1960s: the difference has been about 1.5 to 2 percentage points per year on average in this period, with a slight downtrend.

For example, suppose the United States receives interest at the world real interest rate r^* on its external assets but pays interest at a lower rate r^0 on its liabilities. Then its net factor income from abroad is now $r^* A - r^0 L = r^* W + (r^* - r^0)L$. The final term, the interest rate difference times total liabilities, is an extra income bonus that the United States earns by acting like a "banker to the world": borrowing low and lending high.

Understandably—like the customers in a bank—the rest of the world may from time to time resent this state of affairs. In the 1960s, French officials complained about the United States' "exorbitant privilege" of being able to borrow cheaply by issuing external liabilities in the form of reserve assets (Treasury debt) while earning higher returns on U.S. external assets such as foreign equity and foreign direct investment. Today, a look at the official U.S. Bureau of Economic Analysis (BEA) data suggests that most of the difference takes the form of a low interest rate on U.S. equity liabilities (low profits on foreign investment in the United States).[3]

"Manna from Heaven" But this isn't the only deviation from our simple model working in the United States' favor. The U.S. official statistics reveal that the country has long enjoyed systematic positive capital gains, *KG*, on its external wealth. This gain goes back to the 1980s and takes the form of an additional 2 percentage point differential between capital gains on external assets and capital losses on external liabilities, with differences spread out over several asset classes.

It is much harder to pin down where the capital gains are coming from because the BEA data suggest that these effects are due to neither price nor exchange rate effects, leading to some skepticism about what one economist described as "statistical manna from heaven." As with the "exorbitant privilege," this extra financial gain for the United States is also a loss for the rest of the world and has led some economists to describe the United States as becoming more like a "venture capitalist to the

[3] John Kitchen, 2007, "Sharecroppers or Shrewd Capitalists? Projections of the U.S. Current Account, International Income Flows, and Net International Debt," *Review of International Economics,* 15(5), 1036–1061; Barry Bosworth, Susan M. Collins, and Gabriel Chodorow Reich, "Returns on FDI: Does the US Really Do Better?" *Brookings Trade Forum 2007,* forthcoming.

world" given the large contribution of differential profits and capital gains on equity.[4]

Summary Adding the 2% capital gain differential to the 1.5% interest differential, we end up with a U.S. total return differential (interest plus capital gains) of about 3.5% per year since the 1980s. For comparison, in every other G7 country the figure is close to (and not statistically different from) 0 in the same period.

For the United States, these effects are too big to ignore. To augment our model for these effects, we would have to change the equation for the change in external wealth to reflect these extra bonuses or offsets that accrue in addition to the conventional terms reflecting the trade balance and interest payments:

$$\underbrace{\Delta W_N}_{\substack{\text{Change in}\\\text{external wealth}\\\text{this period}}} = \underbrace{W_N - W_{N-1}}_{} = \underbrace{TB_N}_{\substack{\text{Trade}\\\text{balance}\\\text{this period}}} + \underbrace{r^* W_{N-1}}_{\substack{\text{Interest paid/received}\\\text{on last period's}\\\text{external wealth}}} + \underbrace{(r^* - r^0)L}_{\substack{\text{Income due}\\\text{to interest rate}\\\text{differential}}} + \underbrace{KG.}_{\substack{\text{Capital gains}\\\text{on external}\\\text{wealth}}}$$

Conventional effects   Additional effects

Too Good to Be True? Now the implications of the final two terms become clearer for the U.S. economy. When positive, they offset wealth losses due to trade deficits. Thus, say, if these terms increase by 1% of GDP in value, then the U.S. could run an additional 1% of trade deficit forever and still satisfy the LRBC.

As Figure 6-2 shows, the United States has seen these offsets increase markedly in recent years, rising from 1% of GDP in the late 1980s to 2.8% of GDP in the early 2000s. This has led some economists to take a relaxed view of the swollen U.S. trade deficit because the large offsets mean that a large chunk of the trade deficit can simply be financed by the two offsets—and, with luck, in perpetuity.[5] However, we may not be able to count on that: longer-run evidence suggests that these offsets are certainly not stable and may be diminishing over time.[6]

Others warn that, given the fragility of these statistics, we really have no idea what is going on, and there may well have been no such differential returns all along, meaning that the U.S. external wealth position is really much worse than the official data suggest. Economist Daniel Gros calculated in 2006 that the United States had borrowed $5,500 billion over 20 years, but external wealth had fallen by "only" $2,800 billion. Have $2.7 trillion dollars been mislaid? Gros argues that most of this difference can be attributed to failures by the BEA to adequately measure foreign investor activity in the United States, both in terms of the assets that foreigners own and the investment earnings that they receive. Correcting for these problems would make all of the additional offset terms disappear—and double the estimated level of U.S. net indebtedness to the rest of the world.[7] ■

NET WORK

Go to the BEA website (bea.gov). Find the latest annual balance of payments data for the United States. Compute (a) income earned on external assets and (b) income paid on external liabilities. Find the latest net international investment position data for the United States. Compute (c) external assets and (d) external liabilities for the end of the prior year. Divide (a) by (c) and then divide (b) by (d) to find the implied rates of interest on external assets and liabilities. Is the United States still privileged?

---

[4] William R. Cline, 2005, *The United States as a Debtor Nation*, Washington, DC: Institute for International Economics and Center for Global Development. Pierre-Olivier Gourinchas and Hélène Rey, 2007, "From World Banker to World Venture Capitalist: US External Adjustment and the Exorbitant Privilege," in Richard Clarida, ed., *G7 Current Account Imbalances: Sustainability and Adjustment*, Chicago: University of Chicago Press.
[5] Ricardo Hausmann and Federico Sturzenegger, "'Dark Matter' Makes the US Deficit Disappear," *Financial Times*, December 7, 2005.
[6] Christopher M. Meissner and Alan M. Taylor, 2006, "Losing Our Marbles in the New Century? The Great Rebalancing in Historical Perspective," National Bureau of Economic Research (NBER) Working Paper No. 12580.
[7] Daniel Gross, "Discrepancies in US Accounts Hide Black Hole," *Financial Times*, June 14, 2006.

FIGURE 6-2

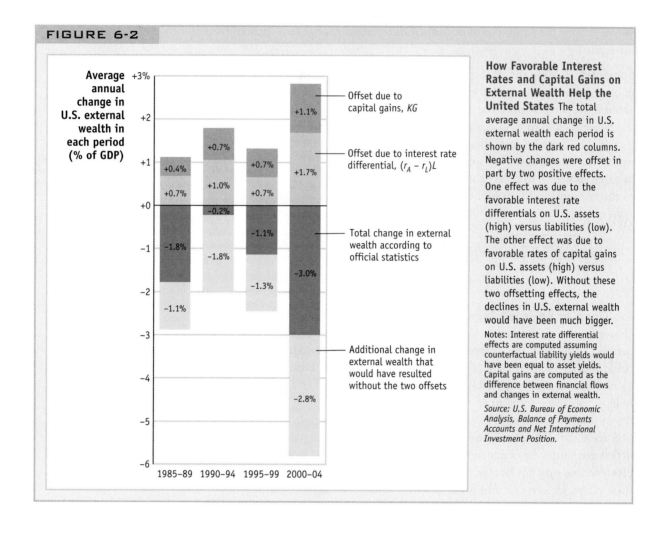

Average annual change in U.S. external wealth in each period (% of GDP)

Offset due to capital gains, KG

Offset due to interest rate differential, $(r_A - r_L)L$

Total change in external wealth according to official statistics

Additional change in external wealth that would have resulted without the two offsets

1985–89 1990–94 1995–99 2000–04

How Favorable Interest Rates and Capital Gains on External Wealth Help the United States The total average annual change in U.S. external wealth each period is shown by the dark red columns. Negative changes were offset in part by two positive effects. One effect was due to the favorable interest rate differentials on U.S. assets (high) versus liabilities (low). The other effect was due to favorable rates of capital gains on U.S. assets (high) versus liabilities (low). Without these two offsetting effects, the declines in U.S. external wealth would have been much bigger.

Notes: Interest rate differential effects are computed assuming counterfactual liability yields would have been equal to asset yields. Capital gains are computed as the difference between financial flows and changes in external wealth.

Source: U.S. Bureau of Economic Analysis, Balance of Payments Accounts and Net International Investment Position.

APPLICATION

The Difficult Situation of the Emerging Markets

The simple intertemporal model may not work for the United States. But it also makes assumptions that may not always work in emerging markets and developing countries.

The first assumption we might question is the one just discussed, that the country has the same real interest rate on assets as liabilities. For example, the United States borrows low and lends high. But for most poorer countries, the opposite is true, largely as a result of country risk—the risk premiums that investors expect before they will buy assets issued by these countries, whether government debt, private equity, or FDI profits.

Figure 6-3 plots government credit ratings (from Standard & Poor's) against public debt levels for a large sample of countries. Bond ratings are highly correlated with *risk premiums*. At the top of the figure are the advanced countries, and their bonds are all rated AA or better. Such bonds

FIGURE 6-3

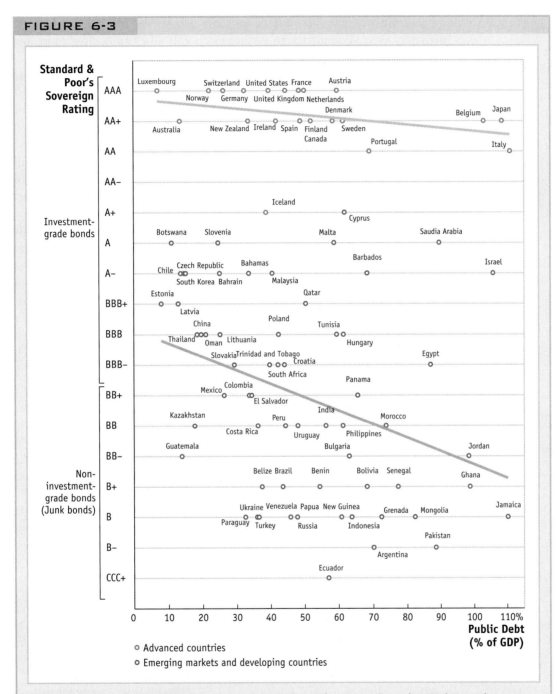

Sovereign Ratings and Public Debt Levels: Advanced Countries versus Emerging Markets and Developing Countries The data shown are for the period from 1995 to 2005. The advanced countries (green) are at the top of the chart. Their credit ratings (vertical axis) do not drop very much in response to an increase in debt levels (horizontal axis). And ratings are always high investment grade. The emerging markets and developing countries (orange) are at the bottom of the graph. Their ratings are low or junk, and their ratings deteriorate as debt levels rise.

Source: "How to Live with Debt," Ideas for Development in the Americas, Inter-American Development Bank, Research Department, Volume 11, September–December 2006, Figure 2.

carry miniscule risk premiums, and the risk premiums do not increase markedly even as countries go further into debt: they can borrow more and more without any great penalty.

In the bottom half of Figure 6-3, we see that the emerging markets and developing countries inhabit a very different world. They have worse credit ratings and correspondingly higher risk premiums. Only about half of the government bonds issued by these countries are considered investment grade, BBB– and above; the rest are considered junk bonds. Investors today are simply very worried about the risk of investing in these countries (in this case, lending to governments, but the idea carries over to private sector investments, too). They demand extra profit as compensation for the perceived risks.

Figure 6-3 also shows that ratings deteriorate as debt rises in poorer countries, something that is not true in the advanced countries. This observation shows the limits to borrowing for poorer countries: at some stage, the cost of borrowing gets prohibitive, if it is possible at all.

This example brings us to the other assumption of the simple model that sometimes fails to hold in poorer countries, the assumption that the country can borrow or lend as much as it wants at the prevailing world real interest rate. Obviously, on the lending side, it usually isn't a problem to save as much as you want (although, as we discuss later, some creditors are now facing some constraints on what assets they can buy). But on the borrowing side, lenders will often tell borrowers that they have reached a *debt limit* and can borrow no more. When that happens, access to external credit ceases, and anything additional a country wants to consume or invest now has to be taken out of its own domestic output.

Figure 6-4 illustrates the remarkable frequency with which emerging market countries experience this kind of isolation from global capital markets. Research by economists Guillermo Calvo and Carmen Reinhart has focused attention on **sudden stops** in the flow of external finance, especially in

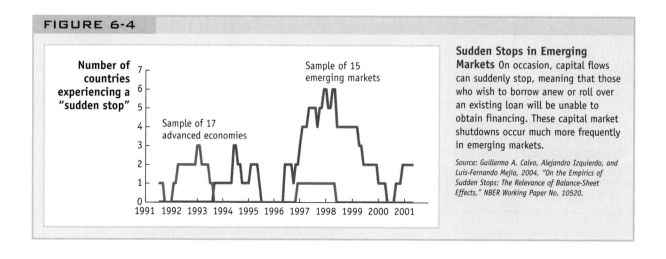

FIGURE 6-4

Sudden Stops in Emerging Markets On occasion, capital flows can suddenly stop, meaning that those who wish to borrow anew or roll over an existing loan will be unable to obtain financing. These capital market shutdowns occur much more frequently in emerging markets.

Source: Guillermo A. Calvo, Alejandro Izquierdo, and Luis-Fernando Mejía, 2004, "On the Empirics of Sudden Stops: The Relevance of Balance-Sheet Effects," NBER Working Paper No. 10520.

emerging markets.[8] In one of these events, a borrower country sees its financial account surplus rapidly shrink (suddenly nobody wants to buy any more of its domestic assets) and so the current account deficit also has to shrink (because there is no way to finance a trade imbalance). This limitation can be a jolting macroeconomic shock for any economy, requiring sudden adjustments to expenditure, and with potential adverse consequences for output if domestic investment is adversely affected by the credit crunch. As these constraints bite, the upside of financial globalization recedes, and the downside of instability may take its place. In later chapters, we examine why these credit market disruptions happen by looking in more detail at financial problems, crises, and default. ■

2 Gains from Consumption Smoothing

In the next two sections of this chapter, we bring together the long-run budget constraint and a simplified model of an economy to see how gains from financial globalization can be achieved in theory. In this section, we focus on the gains that result when an open economy uses external borrowing and lending to eliminate an important kind of risk, namely, undesirable fluctuations in aggregate consumption.

The Basic Model

We retain all of our earlier assumptions from the discussion of the long-run budget constraint. For example, there are no international transfers of income or capital, and the price level is perfectly flexible, so all nominal values are also real values, and so on. We also set out some new assumptions that will hold whether the economy is closed or open.

- Value added or GDP in the economy equals Q, and it is produced each period using only a labor input. This output may be subject to shocks.

- Consumption takes places in identical representative households, so we can use the terms "household" and "country" interchangeably. The country/household prefers to have a *smooth* level of consumption C at a constant value that is consistent with the long-run budget constraint.

- To keep the rest of the model simple—for now—we assume there are no other sources of demand, so investment I and government spending G are both equal to zero. Under these assumptions, when $I = G = 0$,

[8] On the disruptions and costs caused by sudden stops, see Guillermo Calvo and Carmen M. Reinhart, 2000, "When Capital Inflows Suddenly Stop: Consequences and Policy Options," in *Reforming the International Monetary and Financial System*, edited by Peter B. Kenen and Alexander K. Swoboda, Washington, D.C.: International Monetary Fund, pp. 175–201; Pablo E. Guidotti, Federico Sturzenegger and Agustín Villar, 2004, "On the Consequences of Sudden Stops," *Economía*, 4(2), 171–214. Michael M. Hutchison and Ilan Noy, 2006, "Sudden Stops and the Mexican Wave: Currency Crises, Capital Flow Reversals and Output Loss in Emerging Markets," *Journal of Development Economics*, 79(1), 225–248.

spending *GNE* equals personal consumption expenditures *C*. Hence, if the country is open, the trade balance, which is *GDP* minus *GNE*, equals *Q* minus *C* in this simple case. The trade balance is positive if *Q*, output, is greater than consumption *C;* if consumption is greater than output, then the trade balance is negative.

■ Our analysis begins at time 0, and we assume that the country begins with zero initial wealth inherited from the past, so that W_{-1} is equal to zero.

■ When the economy is open, we look at its interaction with the rest of the world (ROW). We assume that the country is small and ROW is large and the prevailing world real interest rate is constant at r^*. In the numerical examples that follow, we assume $r^* = 0.05 = 5\%$ per year.

Given these assumptions, in this special case the LRBC requires that the present value of future trade balances equals zero (since initial wealth is zero)

$$\underbrace{0}_{\text{Initial wealth is zero}} = \text{Present value of } TB = \underbrace{\text{Present value of } Q}_{\text{Present value of } GDP} - \underbrace{\text{Present value of } C,}_{\text{Present value of } GNE}$$

or equivalently,

(6-4) $$\underbrace{\text{Present value of } Q}_{\text{Present value of } GDP} = \underbrace{\text{Present value of } C.}_{\text{Present value of } GNE}$$

Remember, this equation says that the LRBC will hold, and the present value of TB will be zero, if and only if the present value of Q equals the present value of C.

Consumption Smoothing: A Numerical Example and Generalization

Now that we've clarified the assumptions for our two-country model, we can explore how countries smooth consumption by examining two cases:

■ A closed economy, in which $TB = 0$ in all periods, external borrowing and lending are shut down, and the LRBC is automatically satisfied

■ An open economy, in which TB can be nonzero, borrowing and lending are possible, and we must verify that the LRBC is satisfied

Let's first examine a numerical example that illustrates the gains from consumption smoothing. We will generalize the result later.

Closed versus Open, No Shocks Table 6-1 provides a numerical example for our model economy when it is closed and experiences no shocks. Output is 100 units in each period, and all output is devoted to consumption. The present value of 100 in each period starting in year 0 equals the present value of 100 in year 0, which equals 100, plus the present value of 100 in every subsequent year, which equals $100/0.05 = 2,000$, as we saw in the case of the perpetual loan, at Equation (6-2). Thus the present value of present and future output is $100 + 100/0.05 = 100 + 2,000 = 2,100$.

TABLE 6-1

A Closed or Open Economy with No Shocks Output equals consumption. Trade balance is zero. Consumption is smooth.

		Period							Present Value
		0	1	2	3	4	5	...	($r^* = 0.05$)
Output *GDP*	*Q*	100	100	100	100	100	100	...	2,100
Expenditure *GNE*	*C*	100	100	100	100	100	100	...	2,100
Trade balance	*TB*	0	0	0	0	0	0	...	0

Note: All variables take the same values from period 1 onward.

If an economy is open, nothing changes. The LRBC is satisfied because there is a zero trade balance at all times. Consumption is also perfectly smooth, so this is also the country's preferred consumption path even in an open economy. There are no gains from financial globalization here. Whether open or closed, the economy satisfies the requirements of consumption smoothing: in each period, household consumption equals the constant level of output.

Closed versus Open, Shocks This smooth outcome for the closed economy does not endure if it suffers shocks, such as one of the hurricanes discussed at the start of the chapter. Suppose there is a *temporary* unanticipated output shock of −21 units in year 0. Output falls to 79 and returns thereafter to a level of 100 forever. The change in the present value of output is the −21 lost in year 0, with no change in future years: the present value of output falls from 2,100 to 2,079, a drop of 1% (that is, 79 + 100/0.05 = 79 + 2,000 = 2,079).

What happens to output and consumption in a closed economy compared with an open economy? In the closed economy, there is no doubt what happens. Because all output is consumed and there is no possibility of a trade imbalance, consumption falls to 79 in year 0 and then rises back to 100 in year 1 and stays there forever. The path of consumption is no longer smooth, as shown in Table 6-2.

TABLE 6-2

A Closed Economy with Temporary Shocks Output equals consumption. Trade balance is zero. Consumption is volatile.

		Period							Present Value
		0	1	2	3	4	5	...	($r^* = 0.05$)
Output *GDP*	*Q*	79	100	100	100	100	100	...	2,079
Expenditure *GNE*	*C*	79	100	100	100	100	100	...	2,079
Trade balance	*TB*	0	0	0	0	0	0	...	0

Note: All variables take the same values from period 1 onward.

In the open economy, however, we can show how a smooth consumption path is still attainable. It can't be the original smooth consumption path of 100 every period. The country cannot afford that path anymore because the present value of output has now fallen. What smooth consumption path can it afford?

The key to solving this problem is to use the LRBC at Equation (6-4). Once we know the present value of output, we know the present value of consumption must be the same, and from there we can figure out the smooth consumption path. In this case, the present value of output has fallen 1% (from 2,100 to 2,079), so the LRBC Equation (6-3) tells us that the present value of consumption must also fall by 1%. How will this be achieved? Consumption can remain smooth, *and satisfy the LRBC,* if it falls by 1% in every year, from 100 to 99. Is this right? To double-check, we can compute the present value of C: using the perpetual loan formula again, this present value is $99 + 99/0.05 = 99 + 1,980 = 2,079$, which equals the present value of Q. The LRBC is satisfied.

Table 6-3 shows the path of all the important macroeconomic aggregates in this case. In year 0, if output Q is 79 and consumption C is 99, then the country runs a trade balance of $TB = -20$ (a deficit). In subsequent years, the country keeps consumption at 99, and with output equal to 100, it has a trade balance of $TB = +1$ (a surplus) and makes net factor payments of $NFIA = -1$ in the form of interest. The country must borrow 20 in year 0, and then makes 5% interest payments of 1 unit on the 20 units borrowed ever after. As we have seen, this is a standard perpetual loan, so this is yet another way of checking that the LRBC is satisfied.

In year 0, the current account, CA (equals $TB + NFIA$), is −20. In future years, the country's net factor income from abroad of −1 and trade balance of +1 imply that the current account is 0 in all future years, with no further borrowing. The country's external wealth W is therefore −20 in all periods, cor-

TABLE 6-3

An Open Economy with Temporary Shocks A trade deficit is run when output is temporarily low. Consumption is smooth.

		Period							Present Value
		0	1	2	3	4	5	...	($r^* = 0.05$)
Output *GDP*	Q	79	100	100	100	100	100	...	2,079
Expenditure *GNE*	C	99	99	99	99	99	99	...	2,079
Trade balance	*TB*	−20	+1	+1	+1	+1	+1	...	0
Net factor income from abroad	*NFIA*	0	−1	−1	−1	−1	−1	...	—
Current account	*CA*	−20	0	0	0	0	0	...	—
External wealth	*W*	−20	−20	−20	−20	−20	−20	...	—

Note: All variables take the same values from period 1 onward.

responding to the perpetual loan taken out in year 0. External wealth is constant at −20; it does not explode because interest payments are made in full each period and no further borrowing (e.g., rollover) is required.

The lesson is clear. When output fluctuates, a closed economy cannot smooth consumption, but an open one can.

Generalizing Suppose, more generally, that output Q and consumption C are initially stable at some value with $Q = C$ and external wealth is zero. The LRBC is satisfied if this situation persists because the trade balance is zero at all times.

Now suppose output unexpectedly falls in year 0 by an amount ΔQ, and then returns to its prior value for all future periods. This loss of output in year 0 reduces the present value of output (*GDP*) by an amount ΔQ. To meet the LRBC, the country must lower the present value of consumption. In the closed economy, it does this automatically by lowering consumption in year 0 by ΔQ. In the open economy, however, it lowers consumption uniformly by a smaller amount, $\Delta C < \Delta Q$, in *all* years. But how big a reduction is needed to meet the LRBC?

Because consumption falls less than output in year 0, the country will run a trade balance of $\Delta Q - \Delta C < 0$ (i.e., in deficit) in year 0, and an amount equal to this trade deficit must be borrowed and external wealth falls by the amount of this debt. In subsequent years, output returns to its normal level but consumption stays at a reduced level, so trade surpluses of ΔC are run in all subsequent years.

The LRBC requires that these surpluses be sufficient to service the debt, and this tells us how large the consumption reduction must be. A loan of $\Delta Q - \Delta C$ in year 0 requires interest payments of $r^*(\Delta Q - \Delta C)$ in later years. If the subsequent trade surpluses of ΔC are to cover these interest payments, then ΔC must be chosen so that

$$r^* \times \underbrace{(\Delta Q - \Delta C)}_{\substack{\text{Amount borrowed} \\ \text{in year 0}}} = \underbrace{\Delta C.}_{\substack{\text{Trade surplus in} \\ \text{subsequent years}}}$$

Interest due in subsequent years

To find out how big a cut in consumption is necessary, we rearrange and find

$$\Delta C = \frac{r^*}{1 + r^*} \Delta Q.$$

Our numerical example is thus generalizable: this result applies for any temporary shock ΔQ. In our example, we had $\Delta Q = 21$ and hence $\Delta C = (0.05/1.05) \times (21) = 1$. Hence, the country borrowed $\Delta Q - \Delta C = 20$ units in year 0 and cut its consumption by 1 unit in all periods.

Permanent Shocks? The previous examples considered a temporary shock to output and showed how consumption smoothing is possible, but the same argument does not hold for a permanent shock. If the shock is permanent, output will be lower by ΔQ in all years and not just in year 0. The only way a closed or open economy can satisfy the LRBC and keep consumption smooth in this case is to cut consumption by $\Delta C = \Delta Q$ in all years. This is optimal, even in an open economy, because consumption remains smooth, although at a reduced level.

This result contains important intuition: *consumers can smooth out temporary shocks, but they must adjust to permanent shocks.* For example, if your income drops by 50% just this month, you might borrow to make it through this month with minimal adjustment in spending; but if your income is going to remain 50% lower in every subsequent month, then you need to cut your spending.

Summary: Save for a Rainy Day

Financial openness allows countries to "save for a rainy day." This section's lesson has a simple household analogy. If you cannot use financial institutions to lend (save) or borrow (dissave), you have to spend what you earn each period. If you have unusually low income, you will have to consume little. If you have a windfall, you will have to spend it all. Using financial transactions to smooth consumption fluctuations makes a household better off. The same applies to countries.

In a closed economy, consumption equals output in every period, so output fluctuations immediately generate consumption fluctuations. In an open economy, the desired smooth consumption path can be achieved by running a trade deficit during bad times and a trade surplus during good times. By extension, deficits and surpluses can also be used to finance extraordinary and temporary (nonsmooth) emergency spending needs, such as the costs of war (see **Side Bar: Wars and the Current Account**).

SIDE BAR

Wars and the Current Account

In addition to considering temporary output shocks, we could also extend our theory to take into account the impact of temporary (yet "desirable") consumption shocks. Why would a country want to have the unsmooth consumption implied by such a shock? The most obvious example of such a shock is war.

Although we assumed zero government spending above, in reality countries' consumption includes private consumption C and public consumption G. It is simple to augment the model to include G as well as C. The constraint would still turn out to be that the present value of GNE (now equal to $C + G$) has to equal the present value of GDP. A war usually means a temporary increase in G.

Borrowing internationally to finance war-related costs goes back centuries. Historians have long argued about the importance of the creation of the British public debt market as a factor in the country's rise to global leadership compared with powerful continental rivals like France. From the early 1700s (thanks to rapid financial development led by major financiers like the Rothschilds) to the end of the Napoleonic Wars in 1815, the British were able to maintain good credit: they could cheaply and easily borrow domestically *and* externally (often from the Dutch) to finance the simultaneous needs of capital formation for the Industrial Revolution and high levels of military spending.

In the nineteenth century, borrowing to finance war-related costs became more commonplace. In the 1870s, the defeated French issued bonds in London to finance a reparation payment to the triumphant Germans. World Wars I and II saw massive lending by the United States to other allied countries. And more recently, when the United States went to war in Afghanistan (2001) and Iraq (2003), there was a sharp increase in the U.S. current account deficit and in external debt due in part to war-related borrowing.

Better at raising armies than finance, the French fought with one hand tied behind their back.

Consumption Volatility and Financial Openness

Does the evidence show that countries can avoid consumption volatility by embracing financial globalization? A simple test might be to compute the volatility of a country's consumption divided by the volatility of its output. As more consumption smoothing is achieved, the computed ratio ought to fall. In fact, in our simple model of a small, open economy that can borrow or lend without limit, this ratio should fall to zero when the gains from financial liberalization are realized. In practice, this will not be true to the extent that all countries share some common global shocks. For example, if every country suffers a negative shock, every country will want to borrow, but that is simply infeasible. Still, in practice not all shocks are global, so countries ought to be able to achieve *some* reduction in consumption volatility through external finance. (We shall consider the importance of local and global shocks later in this chapter.)

With this in mind, Figure 6-5 presents some discouraging evidence. On the horizontal axis, countries are sorted into ten groups (deciles) from least to most financially liberalized. On the left are more closed countries with tight capital controls (generally poorer countries), on the right the more open

FIGURE 6-5

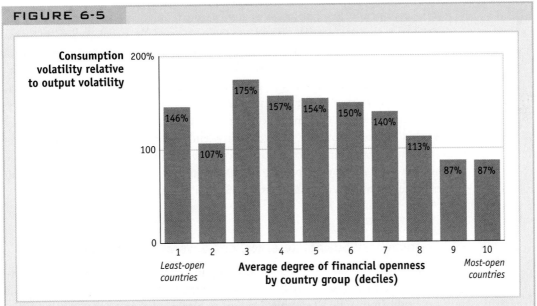

Consumption Volatility Relative to Output Volatility For a very large sample of 170 countries over the period 1995 to 2004, we compute the ratio of consumption volatility to output volatility, expressed as a percentage. A ratio less than 100% indicates that some consumption smoothing has been achieved. Countries are then grouped into ten groups (deciles), ordered from least financially open (1) to most financially open (10). The average volatility in each group is shown. Only the most financially open countries have volatility ratios less than 100%. The high ratios in groups 1 to 8 show, perversely, that consumption is even more volatile than output in these countries.

Note: Volatility is measured by the standard deviation of real output or consumption growth according to the Penn World Tables.

Source: Index of financial openness from Sebastian Edwards, "Capital Controls, Sudden Stops and Current Account Reversals," in Sebastian Edwards, ed., 2007, International Capital Flows, *Chicago: University of Chicago Press.*

countries permitting free movement of capital (mostly advanced countries). For all these countries, we assess their ability to smooth total consumption $(C + G)$ in the period from 1995 to 2004 using annual data. In closed countries, we would expect that the volatility of consumption would be similar to the volatility of output (GDP); the ratio of the two would be close to 100%. But if an open country were able to smooth consumption in line with our simple model, this ratio ought to be lower than 100%.

The figure shows that most groups of countries have an average consumption-to-output volatility ratio well above 100%. Moreover, as financial liberalization increases, this ratio shows little sign of decrease until fairly high levels of liberalization are reached (around the seventh or eighth decile). Indeed, until we get to the ninth and tenth deciles, all of these ratios are above 100%. Similar findings have been found using a variety of tests, and it appears to be only at a very high threshold that financial globalization delivers any consumption-smoothing benefits.[9]

What could be going on? In poorer countries, some of the relatively high consumption volatility must be unrelated to financial globalization—it is there even in closed countries. In the real world, households are not identical and global capital markets do not reach every person. Some people and firms do not or cannot participate in even domestic financial markets, perhaps due to backward financial systems. Other problems may stem from the way financial markets operate (e.g., poor transparency and regulation) in emerging market countries that are partially open and/or have partially developed their financial systems. There is also evidence that borrowing and lending alone (using debt) may not always be the most effective way to achieve a reduction in consumption risk, a topic we return to later when we consider diversification as an alternative strategy for coping with risk.

In sum, the evidence may not imply a failure of financial globalization per se, but it does not provide a ringing endorsement either. Consumption-smoothing gains may prove elusive for emerging markets until they advance further—by improving poor governance and weak institutions, developing their financial systems, and pursuing further financial liberalization. ■

APPLICATION

Precautionary Saving, Reserves, and Sovereign Wealth Funds

One obstacle to consumption smoothing in poorer countries is the phenomenon of sudden stops, which we noted earlier. If poorer countries can't count on credit lines when they need them, an alternative strategy is to engage in **precautionary saving** whereby the government acquires a buffer of external assets, a "rainy day" fund. That is, rather than allowing external wealth to fluctuate around an average of zero—sometimes in debt or sometimes in credit—the country maintains a higher positive "average balance" in its

---

[9] M. Ayhan Kose, Eswar S. Prasad, and Marco E. Terrones, 2007, "How Does Financial Globalization Affect Risk Sharing? Patterns and Channels," IZA Discussion Papers 2903, Institute for the Study of Labor (IZA).

external wealth account to reduce or even eliminate the need to go into a net debt position. This approach may provide a more reliable cushion than waiting to see whether borrowing is possible, although it is costly in that more consumption sacrifice is needed to establish the buffer.

In the world economy today, precautionary saving is on the rise and takes two forms. The first is the accumulation of **foreign reserves** by central banks. These reserves may be needed for other reasons, such as to maintain a fixed exchange rate (a topic we cover in Chapter 9), so there may be a possible conflict of goals if they are used for other objectives. But as external assets on the nation's balance sheet, these reserves can also be deployed during a sudden stop to cushion the domestic economy. Many economists argue that some part or even the greater part of reserve accumulation in recent years in emerging markets is driven by this precautionary motive.[10]

The second form of precautionary saving by governments is through what are called **sovereign wealth funds,** state-owned asset management companies that can take some government savings (including even central bank reserves) and invest them overseas, possibly in safe assets like reserves but also increasingly in riskier high-return assets such as equity and FDI. Some countries, like Norway, use such funds as a way to save natural resource windfalls for the future (Norway had an oil boom in the 1970s). Many newer funds have appeared in emerging markets and developing countries (such as Singapore, China, Malaysia, and Taiwan), but these funds have been driven more by precautionary saving than resource booms.

In 2005 a Chinese bid to acquire the Union Oil Company of California met fierce political opposition in the United States and was eventually dropped.

As of 2007, the biggest funds were in the United Arab Emirates ($875 billion), Singapore ($440 billion), Norway ($315 billion), China ($300 billion), and Saudi Arabia ($300 billion), with other large funds in Kuwait, Australia, Qatar, and Russia.[11]

Sovereign wealth funds seem likely to continue to grow in size and spread to other countries (see **Headlines: Copper-Bottomed Insurance**). However, despite having a legitimate economic rationale, it also seems likely that these funds will continue to generate international tensions as they seek to acquire more politically sensitive equity and FDI assets from the advanced countries (see **Headlines: The Next Globalization Backlash?**). ■

---

[10] Joshua Aizenman and Jaewoo Lee, 2005, "International Reserves: Precautionary versus Mercantilist Views, Theory and Evidence," NBER Working Paper No. 11366; Romain Ranciere and Olivier Jeanne, 2006, "The Optimal Level of International Reserves for Emerging Market Countries: Formulas and Applications," IMF Working Paper No. 06/229; Ceyhun Bora Durdu, Enrique G. Mendoza, and Marco E. Terrones, 2007, "Precautionary Demand for Foreign Assets in Sudden Stop Economies: An Assessment of the New Mercantilism," NBER Working Paper No. 13123.

[11] Reuters, "FACTBOX-Sovereign wealth funds brim with money," July 11, 2007.

HEADLINES

Copper-Bottomed Insurance

Many developing countries experience GDP volatility as a result of fluctuations in the price of some major commodity export. Sovereign wealth funds can buffer these shocks, and not just for oil exporters.

With copper prices soaring, Chile is flush with cash. That may not sound like a problem, but for a commodity-rich country, it can be a big one. . . . the government is saving what it calculates as windfall profits from its state-owned copper company and windfall taxes from privately owned mines. It is investing the money abroad in bonds and is also considering buying foreign stock funds. The idea is that when Chile's economy inevitably falters, the government can tap this "economic and social stabilization fund" for revenue.

"The question that plagues Latin America and other emerging markets is: How do you avoid the booms and busts from commodity cycles?" says Chile's fi-nance minister, Andrés Velasco. "In Chile we have a simple answer: spend that which is permanent and save that which is transitory."

So far, Chile has set aside about $6 billion for the stabilization fund and expects to add another $6 billion or so by the end of the year. The sum would be equivalent to about 10% of the country's gross domestic product, the total value of goods and services it produces in a year. . . .

In 1990, oil-rich Norway started a stabilization fund, which now has a portfolio of around $300 billion, a startling sum for a nation of 4.6 million. Chile copied Norway's approach, but its fund didn't begin to pile up assets until the past few years, as the price of copper soared to more than $3 a pound, triple its 2004 level. Banking part of that windfall requires far greater sacrifice by Chile, where the per-capita income in 2005 was $7,100, about one-seventh of Norway's. . . .

Setting aside so much money "is a crime," says Chilean Sen. Fernando Flores, who was once finance minister in the Marxist government of Salvador Allende and later made a fortune as a software entrepreneur in California. "We need a model of investment and education to create new industries."

But Chilean economic officials say it is critical to limit the effect of the copper boom so the country doesn't become too dependent on riches that can vanish quickly, resulting in budget shortfalls.

Excerpted from Bob Davis, "Can Copper-Rich Chile Avoid Surplus-Cash Pitfalls?" Wall Street Journal, May 14, 2007.

HEADLINES

The Next Globalization Backlash?

Sovereign wealth funds may not be welcomed by everyone.

The rise of government investment funds suddenly preoccupies financiers. . . . Five years ago, governments were sitting on $1.9 trillion in foreign currency reserves, which was roughly what they needed to stave off financial crises. Now they have $5.4 trillion, way beyond their prudential needs and more than triple the amount in the world's hedge funds. Increasingly, this cash is being moved into "sovereign wealth funds," which have come from obscurity to manage assets worth an additional $1.6 trillion. . . .

When central banks amass reserves, they park them in U.S. Treasury bills and risk-free bonds issued by other rich govern-ments. But the buzz about sovereign wealth funds signals that this is changing. The newly wealthy governments are following forebears that grew rich a generation back—the Gulf states, Singapore, Norway. They want a better return on their savings than they can get from Treasury bills, so they are going to invest in companies. . . .

But the political backlash is already beginning. China just bought a $3 billion stake in Blackstone Group, the American private-equity firm. . . . Sen. Jim Webb (D-Va.) raised the predictable red flag. Blackstone may own firms with sensitive national-security information, the senator maintained; therefore, the Chinese investment in Blackstone should have been delayed by regulators.

Imagine Webb's protests if the Chinese do what they say they will do: emulate one of Singapore's national wealth funds, Temasek Holdings, which buys direct stakes in foreign companies without going through a middleman such as Blackstone. Chunks of corporate America could be bought by Beijing's government—or, for that matter, by the Kremlin. Given the Chinese and Russian tendency to treat corporations as tools of government policy, you don't have to be paranoid to ask whether these would be purely commercial holdings.

Excerpted from Sebastian Mallaby, "The Next Globalization Backlash: Wait Till the Kremlin Starts Buying Our Stocks," Washington Post, June 25, 2007.

3 Gains from Efficient Investment

Suppose an economy has become open and has taken full advantage of the gains from consumption smoothing. Has it completely exploited all the benefits of financial globalization? The answer is no because openness delivers gains not only on the consumption side but also on the investment side by creating better ways for a country to augment its capital stock to take advantage of new production opportunities.

The Basic Model

To illustrate these gains, we must now refine the model we have been using and abandon the assumption that output can be produced without capital. Instead, we now assume that producing the output requires capital, which is created by making investments.

However, when we make this change, the LRBC (6-4) must be modified to include investment I (no longer zero) as part of GNE, although government consumption G is still assumed to be zero. So now, in this case, the LRBC is

$$0 = \underbrace{\text{Present value of } TB,}_{\text{Initial wealth is zero}}$$

or equivalently,

(6–5) $\quad \underbrace{\text{Present value of } Q}_{\text{Present value of } GDP} = \underbrace{\text{Present value of } C + \text{Present value of } I.}_{\text{Present value of } GNE}$

The LRBC will hold, and the present value of TB will be zero, if and only if the present value output Q equals the present value of expenditure $C + I$.

We can now study investment and consumption decisions using this modified LRBC, and again we examine two cases:

■ A closed economy, in which $TB = 0$ in all periods, external borrowing and lending are shut down, and the LRBC is automatically satisfied.

■ An open economy, in which TB can be nonzero, borrowing and lending are possible, and we must verify that the LRBC is satisfied.

Efficient Investment: A Numerical Example and Generalization

We now add investment possibilities to extend our previous example. Again, the country starts out with output Q equal to 100 and equal to consumption C, a zero trade balance, and zero external wealth. If that state persisted, the LRBC would be satisfied, as in the previous case. This describes life in both the closed and open economies when there are no shocks.

But now suppose there is a *shock* in year 0 that takes the form of a new investment opportunity. For example, it could be that in year 0 engineers discover that by building a new factory with a new machine, the country can produce a certain good much more cheaply than current technology allows. Or perhaps there is a resource discovery, but a mine must first be built to extract the minerals from the earth. What happens next? Again, we turn first to a numerical example and then supply a more general answer.

We assume that to make the investment (in machines or factories or mines) would require an investment expenditure of 16 units, but the investment will pay off in future years and would increase the country's output by 5 units in year 1 and all future years (but not in year 0).

The country now has to face some choices. First, should it undertake this investment? Second, is it better off when it is an open or closed economy? We find the answers to these questions (it should invest and it is better off when open) by looking at how an open economy would make the choice and then showing why the closed economy situation is suboptimal.

As in the previous example, the key to solving this problem is to look at the LRBC and how it changes as circumstances change. Before the shock, output and consumption were 100 in each year and had a present value of 2,100. Investment was 0 in every year, so the LRBC at Equation (6-5) is satisfied. If the economy decides to not proceed with the investment opportunity, this situation continues to prevail—whether the economy is closed or open.

What happens if the open economy undertakes the investment? First we must calculate the difference this would make to the country's resources as measured by the present value of output. It will be 100 today and then 105 in every subsequent year starting in year 1. The 100 today is worth 100 in present value terms; the 105 in every subsequent year is worth $105/0.05 = 2,100$. Thus, the present value of output when the investment is made rises to $100 + 2,100 = 2,200$. This is an increase of 100 over the old present value of output, which was just 2,100.

Can all of this extra output be devoted to consumption? No: to get it, the country has to make some investments, 16 units in the current period. So the present value of investment, previously 0, rises to 16. Now we can use the modified LRBC at Equation (6-5), which says the present value of output Q (equal to 2,200) must equal the present value of consumption C (as yet unknown) plus the present value of investment I (equal to 16). The present value of C must be the present value of Q minus the present value of I, namely, 2,200 minus 16, or 2,184. Thus, allowing for the fact that some expenditure has to be devoted to year 0 investment, the total resources left for consumption have risen by 4% in present value terms (from 2,100 without the investment to 2,184 with the investment).

We can now find the new level of consumption each period that satisfies the LRBC: because the present value of C has risen by 4% from 2,100 to 2,184, the country can afford to raise consumption C by 4% in all periods, from 100 to 104. (As a check, note that $104 + 104/0.05 = 2,184$.) Is the country better off if it makes the investment? The answer is clear: yes. Its consumption remains smooth, but it is 4% higher in all periods.

Table 6-4 lays out the details of this case. In year 0, consumption C is 104, and investment I is 16, *GNE* is 120 units, and there is a trade balance of −20 because output Q is only 100. The country has to borrow 20 units in year 0 to fund the investment of 16 plus 4 extra units of consumption. In all future years, consumption C is 104 with zero investment, so *GNE* is also 104, and with output Q at 105 the trade balance is +1.

The initial trade deficit of 20 in year 0 (which equals the current account in year 0) causes an external debt of 20 to appear. As a perpetual loan, with an interest rate of 5%, this debt of 20 must be serviced by net interest payments of −1 in each subsequent year for the LRBC to be satisfied. These interest payments of −1 offset the future trade surpluses of +1 forever. Hence, the current account is 0 in all future years, with no further borrowing, and the country's external wealth is −20 in all periods and does not explode.

This outcome is preferable to anything the closed economy can achieve. To attain the output level of 105 in all later years, the closed economy would have to cut consumption back to 84 in year 0 to free up 16 units for investment; it would then enjoy consumption of 105 in all subsequent years. But this is a volatile consumption path, not a smooth one. The open economy could also pursue this path, which would satisfy the LRBC (because *TB* is 0). But the economy will choose not to do so! The open economy is better off making the investment *and* consumption smoothing, two goals that the closed economy cannot simultaneously achieve.

Generalizing While the numbers in our example are invented, the lesson of the analysis applies to any situation in which a country confronts new

---

TABLE 6-4

An Open Economy with Investment and a Permanent Shock The economy runs a trade deficit to finance investment and consumption in period 0 and runs a trade surplus when output is higher in later periods. Consumption is smooth.

		Period							Present Value
		0	1	2	3	4	5	...	$(r^* = 0.05)$
Output *GDP*	Q	100	105	105	105	105	105	...	2,200
Expenditure *GNE*	C	104	104	104	104	104	104	...	2,184
	I	16	0	0	0	0	0	...	16
Trade balance	*TB*	−20	+1	+1	+1	+1	+1	...	0
Net factor income from abroad	*NFIA*	0	−1	−1	−1	−1	−1	...	—
Current account	*CA*	−20	0	0	0	0	0	...	—
External wealth	W	−20	−20	−20	−20	−20	−20	...	—

Note: All variables take the same values from period 1 onward.

investment opportunities. Suppose that a country starts with output Q equal to consumption C and zero external wealth. A new project appears requiring ΔK units of capital in year 0, generating an extra ΔQ units of output in year 1 and all later years (but not in year 0).

Ultimately consumers care about consumption C. In an open economy, as we have seen, they can smooth their consumption at a constant level C, given future output. The constant level of C is then limited only by the present value of consumption permissible under the LRBC. To maximize C, the consumer must maximize the present value of C. How?

Equation (6-5), the LRBC equation, says the present value of output must equal the present value of spending on consumption and investment. Rearranging, the present value of consumption must equal the present value of output minus the present value of investment. How is this maximized?

The increase in the present value of output $PV(Q)$ comes from extra output in every year but year 0, and the present value of these additions to output is, using Equation (6-2),

$$\text{Change in present value of output} = \frac{\Delta Q}{(1 + r^*)} + \frac{\Delta Q}{(1 + r^*)^2} + \frac{\Delta Q}{(1 + r^*)^3} + \cdots = \frac{\Delta Q}{r^*}.$$

The increase in the present value of investment $PV(I)$ arises from the new investment needed in year 0 to do the project:

$$\text{Change in present value of investment} = \Delta K.$$

So the project will increase the present value of consumption (or break even) if and only if the increase in the present value of output is greater than (or equal to) the increase in the present value of investment. Comparing the last two equations, this outcome occurs if and only if $\Delta Q / r^*$ $\geq \Delta K$. There are two ways to look at this. Rearranging, investment happens when

$$\underbrace{\Delta Q}_{\substack{\text{Output increase in} \\ \text{subsequent periods}}} \geq \underbrace{r^* \times \Delta K.}_{\substack{\text{Interest payment due in} \\ \text{subsequent periods to finance} \\ \text{initial investment}}}$$

The intuition is that investment occurs up to the point at which the annual benefit from the marginal unit of capital (the extra ΔQ) exceeds the annual cost of borrowing that capital (the interest payments $r^* \Delta K$). Put another way, investment happens when

$$\underbrace{\frac{\Delta Q}{\Delta K}}_{\text{Marginal product of capital}} \geq \underbrace{r^*.}_{\text{World real interest rate}}$$

This is a standard formula for the optimal or efficient level of investment and may look familiar from other courses in economics. Firms will take on investment projects as long as the **marginal product of capital,** or *MPK,* is equal to or exceeds the real interest rate.

Again, we see that a result first illustrated by a numerical example can be applied more generally.

Summary: Make Hay while the Sun Shines

After all this work, a remarkable result is revealed. In an open economy, consumption and investment decisions are separable—firms and households save or borrow in the world capital market. Yet there is a deeper connection. Firms maximize profits, and profits accrue to households as factor income. Investment behavior of firms on the production side maximizes the present value of resources available on the consumption side. Investment efficiency matters because—in the end—it leads to consumption gains.

An open economy can address the investment problem by setting *MPK* equal to the world real rate of interest. If conditions are unusually good (high productivity), it makes sense to invest more capital and produce more output. Conversely, when conditions turn bad (low productivity), it makes sense to lower capital inputs and produce less output. As we have seen, this strategy maximizes the present value of output minus investment, which equals the present value of consumption. The economy can then address the separate problem of how to smooth the path of consumption. As we know from the previous section, this is possible in an open economy because households can lend to or borrow from the rest of the world.

A closed economy has to be self-sufficient. Any resources invested are resources not consumed. Thus, all else equal, more investment implies less consumption. This creates a nasty trade-off. When investment opportunities are good, the country wants to invest to generate higher output in the future; also, anticipating that higher output, the country wants to consume more today. It cannot do both.

Proverbially, financial openness helps countries to "make hay while the sun shines"—and, in particular, to do so without having to engage in a trade-off against the important objective of consumption smoothing. The lesson here has a simple household analogy. Suppose you find a great investment opportunity. If you have no financial dealings with the outside world, you would have to save—you would have to sacrifice consumption to finance the investment.

APPLICATION

Delinking Saving from Investment

The story of the Norwegian oil boom provides a good illustration of our theory. North Sea oil was discovered in the 1960s, but the mass exploitation of this resource was unprofitable as long as cheap and plentiful supplies of oil were being produced elsewhere, primarily in the Persian Gulf. Then came the first "oil shock" in the early 1970s, when the cartel of Oil Producing and Exporting Countries (OPEC) colluded to dramatically raise world oil prices. The Norwegians, the British, and most other people took the view that this event was a permanent geopolitical shock that would, along with other trends like global economic growth, permanently raise the real price of oil—a view that turned out to be largely correct. At the higher oil prices, it suddenly made sense to exploit North Sea oil. Starting in the early 1970s, oil platforms, pipelines, refineries, and terminals were sprouting offshore and along the coast of Norway, causing its capital stock to permanently increase in response to a new productive investment opportunity.

Figure 6-6 shows the path of saving (S) and investment (I) measured as ratios of GDP in Norway from 1965 to 1990. The oil boom is clearly visible in the investment share of GDP, which in the 1970s rose about 10 percentage points above its typical level. Had Norway been a closed economy, this additional investment would have been financed by a decrease in the share of output devoted to public or private consumption. As you can see, no such sacrifice was necessary. Norway's saving rate was flat in this period or even fell slightly. In Norway's open economy, saving and investment were delinked and the difference was made up by the current account $CA = S - I$, which moved sharply into deficit, approaching minus 15% of GDP at one point. Thus, all of the short-run increase in investment was financed by foreign investment in Norway, much of it by multinational oil companies.

FIGURE 6-6

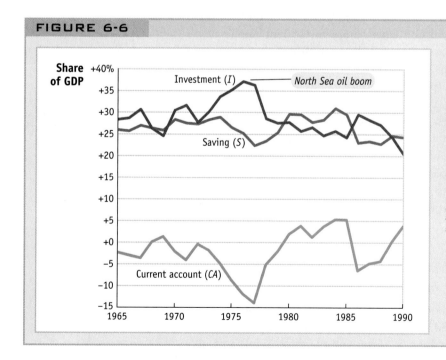

The Oil Boom in Norway Following a large increase in oil prices in the early 1970s, Norway invested heavily to exploit oil fields in the North Sea. Norway took advantage of openness to finance a temporary increase in investment by running a very large current account deficit, thus increasing its indebtedness to the rest of the world. At its peak, the current account deficit was more than 10% of GDP.

Source: Alan M. Taylor, 2002, "A Century of Current Account Dynamics," Journal of International Money and Finance, 21(6), November, 725–748.

Is Norway a special case? Economists have examined large international data sets to see whether there is general evidence that countries can delink investment decisions from saving decisions just as the Norwegians did. One approach follows the pioneering work of Martin Feldstein and Charles Horioka.[12] They estimated what fraction β of each additional dollar saved tended to be invested in the same country. In other words, in their model, if saving rose by an amount ΔS, they estimated that investment would rise by an amount $\Delta I = \beta \Delta S$. In a closed economy, the "savings retention" measure β would equal 1, but they argued that increasing financial openness would tend to push β below 1.

For example, suppose one were to estimate β for the period 1980 to 2000 for three groups of countries with differing degrees of financial integration: in a sample of countries in the European Union, where international financial integration had advanced furthest, the estimated value of β is 0.26; in a sample of all developed countries with a somewhat lower level of financial integration, the estimate of β is 0.39; and in a sample of emerging markets, where financial integration was lower still, the estimate of β is 0.67.[13] Financially open countries seem to have a greater ability to delink saving and investment, in that they have a much lower "savings retention" measure β. ■

How could they affjord it? An oil platform under construction in Norway.

Can Poor Countries Gain from Financial Globalization?

Our analysis shows that if the world real interest rate is r^* and a country has investment projects for which the marginal product of capital MPK exceeds r^*, then the country should borrow from the rest of the world because the pecuniary benefits from the project will exceed the costs of financing. We now apply this idea to examine an enduring question in international macroeconomics: Why doesn't capital flow to poor countries?

Production Function Approach To look more deeply into this question, economists have to take a stand on what they think determines a country's marginal product of capital. For this analysis, they usually employ a model based on a **production function** that describes production in any economy by mapping available capital per worker, $k = K/L$, and the prevailing level of **productivity**, A (sometimes called the level of technology), to the resulting level of output per worker, $q = Q/L$, where Q is GDP.

---

[12] Martin Feldstein and Charles Horioka, 1980, "Domestic Saving and International Capital Flows," *Economic Journal,* 90(358), 314–329.
[13] Calculations are based on data from International Monetary Fund (IMF), International Financial Statistics, with investment and saving measured as a share of GDP.

A simple and widely used production function takes the form

$$q = A \times k^{\theta},$$

q: Output per worker
A: Productivity level
k^{θ}: Capital per worker

where the exponent θ is a number between 0 and 1 that measures the contribution of capital to production.[14] Specifically, θ is the elasticity of output with respect to capital: a 1% increase in capital per worker generates a $\theta\%$ increase in output per worker. In the real world, θ has been estimated to be approximately one-third, and this is the value we employ here.[15] An illustration is given in the top part of Figure 6-7, panel (a), which graphs the production function for the case in which $\theta = 1/3$ and the productivity level is set at a reference level of 1, so $A = 1$.

With this production function, what is the marginal product of capital, *MPK*? The incremental change in output per worker Δq divided by the incremental change in capital per worker Δk is the slope of the production function. As we can see from the figure, the slope *MPK* decreases as k increases because there are *diminishing returns* to the use of increasing k, a standard property in most simple macroeconomic models.

From the preceding formula, we find that the slope of the production function is

$$MPK = \frac{\Delta q}{\Delta k} = \underbrace{\theta A k^{\theta-1}}_{\text{Slope of the production function}} = \theta \times \frac{q}{k}.$$

Thus, in this case, the marginal product of capital is proportional to output per worker divided by capital per worker (also known as the output-capital ratio, or the average product of capital). The *MPK* for the case $\theta = 1/3$ and $A = 1$ is shown in the bottom part of Figure 6-7, panel (a).

A Naive Model: When Countries Have Identical Productivity Levels
To see how a country responds to the investment possibilities opened up by financial globalization, let's look at what happens in a small open economy for which the production function is as given previously with $A = 1$ so that per-worker output is $q = k^{1/3}$. The naive aspect is that, for the time being, we will assume that every country in the world shares the same productivity level.

To understand whether and how this country will invest, we need to understand how its *MPK* varies as k varies. For example, suppose the country considers increasing k by a factor of 8. Because $q = k^{1/3}$, q increases by a factor 2 (the cube root of 8). We shall suppose this brings the country up to the U.S. level of output per worker. Because $MPK = \theta q/k$, and because q has risen by a factor of 2 and k has risen by a factor of 8, *MPK* would change by a factor of $\frac{1}{4}$; that is, it would fall to $\frac{1}{4}$ its previous level.

---

[14] This is called the Cobb-Douglas production function.
[15] Douglas Gollin, 2002, "Getting Income Shares Right," *Journal of Political Economy,* 110(2), April, 458–474.

FIGURE 6-7

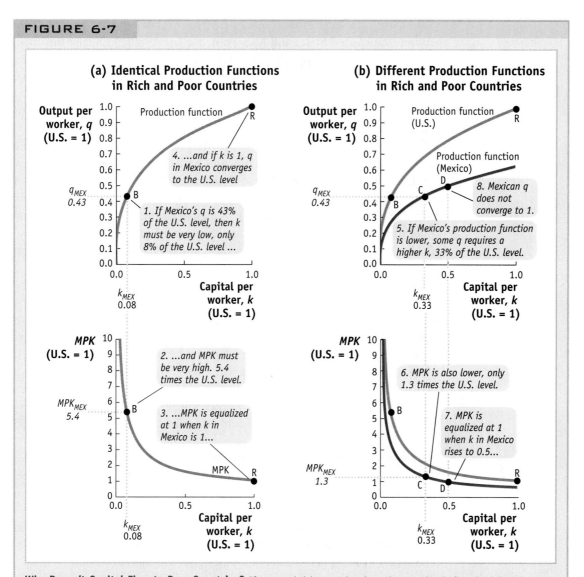

(a) Identical Production Functions in Rich and Poor Countries

Output per worker, q (U.S. = 1)

Production function

4. ...and if k is 1, q in Mexico converges to the U.S. level

q_{MEX} 0.43

B

1. If Mexico's q is 43% of the U.S. level, then k must be very low, only 8% of the U.S. level ...

Capital per worker, k (U.S. = 1)

k_{MEX} 0.08

MPK (U.S. = 1)

2. ...and MPK must be very high. 5.4 times the U.S. level.

MPK_{MEX} 5.4

B

3. ...MPK is equalized at 1 when k in Mexico is 1...

MPK

R

Capital per worker, k (U.S. = 1)

k_{MEX} 0.08

(b) Different Production Functions in Rich and Poor Countries

Output per worker, q (U.S. = 1)

Production function (U.S.)

R

Production function (Mexico)

D

8. Mexican q does not converge to 1.

q_{MEX} 0.43

B

C

5. If Mexico's production function is lower, some q requires a higher k, 33% of the U.S. level.

Capital per worker, k (U.S. = 1)

k_{MEX} 0.33

MPK (U.S. = 1)

6. MPK is also lower, only 1.3 times the U.S. level.

B

7. MPK is equalized at 1 when k in Mexico rises to 0.5...

MPK_{MEX} 1.3

C D

R

Capital per worker, k (U.S. = 1)

k_{MEX} 0.33

Why Doesn't Capital Flow to Poor Countries? If poor and rich countries share the same level of productivity (a common production function), then *MPK* must be very high in poor countries, as shown in panel (a). For example, if B represents Mexico and R the United States, we would expect to see large flows of capital to poor countries, until their capital per worker *k* and, hence, output per worker *q* rise to levels seen in the rich world (movement from point B to point R). The result is convergence. This doesn't happen in reality. Poor and rich countries have different levels of productivity (different production functions) and so *MPK* may not be much higher in poor countries than it is in rich countries, as shown in panel (b). The poor country (Mexico) is now at C and not at B. Now investment occurs only until *MPK* falls to the rest of the world level at point D. The result is divergence. Capital per worker *k* and output per worker *q* do not converge to the levels seen in the rich country.

The naive model says that poor countries with an output per worker at $\frac{1}{2}$ the U.S. level have an MPK at 4 times the U.S level. By extension, countries with one-quarter the U.S. per-worker output level ought to have an MPK at 16 times the U.S level. And so on.

To make this experiment more concrete, let us look at the situation between the United States and Mexico in the late 1980s.[16] During this time, the United States had approximately twice the *GDP* per worker of Mexico. Now we will choose units and measure all quantities using a scale such that the U.S. variables take the value 1, so q and k are equal to 1 in the United States; at that time, q was 0.43 in Mexico (that is, output per worker was 43% of the U.S. level; in what follows, all data are rounded).

Now suppose that the economies of Mexico and the United States were described by the same production function with a common productivity level $A = 1$ in both countries. In Figure 6-7, panel (a), the United States is at point R (for rich) and Mexico is at point B, with a capital per worker k that is only 8% of the U.S. level. What is Mexico's marginal product of capital? According to the naive model, it is 5.4 times the U.S. marginal product of capital. Why? *MPK* is θ (a constant) times q/k. In the United States, $q/k = 1$; in Mexico $q/k = 0.43/0.08 = 5.4$.

We can think of the United States and other rich countries as representing the rest of the world—a large financially integrated region, from Mexico's point of view. The world real interest rate r^* would be the opportunity cost of capital to the rest of the world, that is, the rich world's *MPK*. If that real interest rate r^* is, say, 10% in rich countries like the United States, then their *MPK* is 10%, and our naive model implies that Mexico has an *MPK* of 54%!

To take an extreme example, look at India, a much poorer country than Mexico. In India's case, output per worker was just 8.6% of the U.S. level in 1988. Using the naive model, we would infer that the *MPK* in India was 135 times the U.S. level![17]

To sum up, the naive model says that the poorer the country, the higher its *MPK,* due to the twin assumptions of diminishing returns and a common productivity level. Investment ought to have been very profitable in Mexico (and India and all other poor countries). Investment in Mexico should continue up until Mexico ends up at point R, an outcome economists would describe as **convergence,** whereby poor countries invest until they reach the same level of capital per worker and output per worker as the rich country.

The Lucas Paradox: Why Doesn't Capital Flow from Rich to Poor Countries? Prior to the past decade or two, a widespread view among economists was that poor countries had access to exactly the same technologies as rich countries, given the flow of ideas and knowledge around a globalizing world. Economists also assumed that if policies shifted to allow greater movement of capital, foreign investment would flood in because the very poverty

---

[16] In 1985, levels of GDP per worker were \$23,256 in Mexico and \$48,164 in the United States (in 1996 international dollars), according to the reference source for such data, the Penn World Tables. By 1995 this gap had widened a little. The data in this example are based on Robert E. Hall and Charles I. Jones, 1999, "Why Do Some Countries Produce So Much More Output Per Worker Than Others?" *Quarterly Journal of Economics,* 114(1), 83–116.

[17] First solve for the relative level of capital per worker in India: $k_{IND}/k_{US} = [q_{IND}/q_{US}]^{1/\theta} = [0.086]^3 = 0.000636$. The relative *MPK* in India would then equal $[q_{IND}/q_{US}]/[k_{IND}/k_{US}] = [0.086]/[0.086]^3 = 1/[0.086]^2 = 135$.

of these countries seemed to imply that capital was scarce and had a high marginal product, according to the naive model.

As Nobel laureate Robert Lucas wrote in his widely cited article "Why Doesn't Capital Flow from Rich to Poor Countries?":

> If this model were anywhere close to being accurate, and if world capital markets were anywhere close to being free and complete, it is clear that, in the face of return differentials of this magnitude, investment goods would flow rapidly from the United States and other wealthy countries to India and other poor countries. Indeed, one would expect no investment to occur in the wealthy countries.... The assumptions on technology and trade conditions that give rise to this example must be drastically wrong, but exactly what is wrong with them, and what assumptions should replace them?[18]

What is wrong, in short, is that the assumption of identical productivity levels *A,* as represented by the single production function in Figure 6-7, panel (a), though often invoked, is completely invalid. Can we do better?

An Augmented Model: When Countries Have Different Productivity Levels To see why capital does not flow to poor countries, we now suppose that the same model still applies except that *A,* the productivity level, is different in the United States and Mexico, as denoted by differing subscripts:

$$\underbrace{q_{US}}_{\substack{\text{Output per worker}\\\text{in the United States}}} = \underbrace{A_{US}k_{US}{}^{\theta}}_{\text{U.S. production function}} \quad \text{and} \quad \underbrace{q_{MEX}}_{\substack{\text{Output per worker}\\\text{in Mexico}}} = \underbrace{A_{MEX}k_{MEX}{}^{\theta}}_{\text{Mexican production function}}.$$

Now countries can have different production functions and different *MPK* curves, depending on their level of productivity, as shown in Figure 6-7, panel (b). The Mexican curves are shown here lower than the U.S. curves, and we now show that this is the way they are in reality.

The earlier *MPK* equation still holds for each country, so we can compute the *MPK* ratio as

$$\frac{MPK_{MEX}}{MPK_{US}} = \frac{[\theta q_{MEX}/k_{MEX}]}{[\theta q_{US}/k_{US}]} = \frac{q_{MEX}/q_{US}}{k_{MEX}/k_{US}}.$$

Using this equation, we can see why the naive model isn't true. We know that $q_{MEX}/q_{US} = 0.43$, but data on capital per worker show that $k_{MEX}/k_{US} = 0.33$. Plugging these numbers into the formula just given says that *MPK* in Mexico is not 5.4 times the U.S. level but only about 1.3 times (0.43/0.33). In our model, this difference can be explained by only one thing—a lower productivity level in Mexico.

Put another way, in reality the data show that Mexico has about one-third the capital per worker of the United States. Thus, if the naive model were true, Mexico would have an output level per worker only $(1/3)^{1/3} = 0.69$ or 69% of the U.S. level. As we know, however, Mexico's output per worker was

---

[18] Robert E. Lucas Jr., 1990, "Why Doesn't Capital Flow from Rich to Poor Countries?" *American Economic Review,* 80(2), May, 92–96. Lucas presented the India example with the assumption that capital's share was 0.4 rather than one-third and that India's output per worker was one-fifteenth of the U.S. level. In that case, India's MPK is "only" 58 times the U.S. level, an equally absurd result.

much less, only 0.43 or 43% of the U.S. level. Again, this difference can be explained by only one thing—a lower productivity level in Mexico. A in Mexico must be equal to only $0.43/0.69 = 0.63$ as compared with A equal to 1 in the United States. This lower productivity level means that Mexico's production function and MPK curves are lower than the same curves in the United States.

This more accurate representation of reality is shown in Figure 6-7, panel (b). Mexico is not at point B, as was assumed in panel (a); it is really at point C on a different (lower) production function and a different (lower) MPK curve. This means that the MPK gap between Mexico and the United States (where MPK equals 1) is much smaller and this in turn means that very little capital is likely to migrate to Mexico from the United States.

The measured MPK differentials in the augmented model do not seem to indicate a major failure of global capital markets to allocate capital efficiently. But it has implications for convergence. Mexico would borrow only enough to move from point C to point D, at which points its MPK is equal to r^*. This would raise its output per worker a little, but it would still be a long way behind the United States.

APPLICATION

A versus k

In our previous calculations, we found that Mexico did not have a high level of MPK relative to the United States. Hence, large flows of capital into Mexico would not be expected, and Mexico would remain relatively poor even with access to global financial markets.

What about other developing countries? Table 6-5 repeats the exercise for many developing countries, including Mexico. In all cases, GDP gains from financial globalization are large with the naive model but disappointingly small with the more realistic model augmented to allow for productivity differences. Moreover, if we were to allow for the fact that gross national income (GNI) gains are less than GDP gains as a result of the payments to foreign capital that would be due on any of the hypothetical foreign investments, then we would find that the net GNI gains would be smaller still.

This is a profound result. Once we allow for productivity differences, investment will not cause poor countries to reach the same level of capital per worker or output per worker as rich countries. Economists describe this outcome as one of long-run **divergence** between rich and poor countries. Unless poor countries can lift their levels of productivity (raise A), access to international financial markets is of limited use. They may be able to borrow capital (and so raise k), but there isn't that much for it to be productively invested in.

We may conclude that on average in the developing world, the global capital market is not failing. Rather, low levels of productivity A in developing countries make investment unprofitable.

TABLE 6-5

Why Capital Doesn't Flow to Poor Countries The table shows data on actual output and capital per worker (columns 1 and 2). Column 3 shows the level of productivity relative to the United States that is implied by the data on output and capital per worker. Productivity differences are large for poor countries. If these differences are assumed away, then the gains from financial globalization in poor countries could be large (columns 4, 5). But if they remain, the gains will be small (columns 6, 7).

| | | | | Outcomes with Financial Globalization | | | |
| | Data | | Implied Productivity (U.S. = 1) | With U.S. Productivity Level, A_{us} Increase in: | | With Actual Productivity, A Increase in: | |
Country, Group, or Region	$\dfrac{q}{q_{us}}$ (1)	$\dfrac{k}{k_{us}}$ (2)	$\dfrac{A}{A_{us}}$ (3)	Capital k (4)	Output q (5)	Capital k (6)	Output q (7)
Latin America							
Argentina	0.42	0.38	0.58	+163%	+139%	+15%	+5%
Brazil	0.32	0.24	0.51	+311	+214	+50	+15
Chile	0.26	0.26	0.41	+289	+280	+4	+1
Mexico	0.43	0.33	0.63	+207	+131	+53	+15
Asia							
China	0.06	0.05	0.17	+2,001	+1,569	+41	+12
India	0.09	0.04	0.24	+2,213	+1,064	+180	+41
Indonesia	0.11	0.09	0.24	+980	+805	+30	+9
Pakistan	0.13	0.04	0.37	+2,202	+679	+408	+72
Africa							
Congo	0.12	0.06	0.32	+1,677	+722	+218	+47
Kenya	0.06	0.03	0.18	+3,078	+1,674	+140	+34
Nigeria	0.05	0.04	0.14	+2,259	+1,970	+22	+7
South Africa	0.25	0.23	0.41	+334	+300	+13	+4
Per Capita Income Quintiles							
1st (Poorest 20% of countries)	0.04	0.02	0.15	+5,371	+2,474	+210	+46
2nd (2nd Poorest 20%)	0.10	0.07	0.25	+1,426	+907	+86	+23
3rd (Middle 20%)	0.21	0.18	0.38	+463	+368	+32	+10
4th (2nd Richest 20%)	0.40	0.37	0.56	+167	+148	+12	+4
5th (Richest 20%)	0.75	0.85	0.80	+17	+32	−17	−6
Major Groups							
Developing	0.15	0.11	0.31	+836	+572	+65	+18
Emerging	0.29	0.23	0.48	+329	+241	+41	+12

Source: Robert E. Hall and Charles I. Jones, 1999, "Why Do Some Countries Produce So Much More Output Per Worker Than Others?" Quarterly Journal of Economics, 114(1), February, 83–116.

But what is A? An older school of thought focused on A as reflecting a country's *technical efficiency,* construed narrowly as a function of its technology and management capabilities. Today, many economists believe there is very little obstacle to the flow of such knowledge between countries, and so the problem must really be one of implementation. Hence the level of A may primarily reflect a country's *social efficiency,* construed broadly to include institutions, public policies, and even cultural conditions such as the levels of trust or labor quality. Low productivity might then follow from low levels of human capital (poor education policies) or poor quality institutions (bad governance, poor provision of public goods including infrastructure, corruption, and red tape). And indeed there is some evidence that, among poorer countries, more capital does tend to flow to the countries with better institutions.[19]

More Bad News? The augmented model presents a more accurate description of reality. Productivity levels differ enormously across countries and explain why the same inputs (capital per worker) do not generate the same outputs (GDP per worker) in different countries. As long as these productivity gaps remain, capital is less inclined to migrate and convergence will not occur. But it could be argued that by extending the model and its interpretation even further, we might arrive at even gloomier conclusions:

- *The model makes no allowance for risk premiums.* Suppose the *MPK* is 10% in the United States and 13% in Mexico. The differential may be a risk premium to compensate investors for the risk of investing in an emerging market (e.g., risks of regulatory changes, tax changes, expropriation, and other political risks). In that case, no capital flows happen. In Figure 6-7, panel (b), Mexico stays at point C and gets no richer.

- *Risk premiums may be large enough to cause capital to flow "uphill" from poor to rich.* If world capital markets imposed a risk premium higher than 3%, say 7%, then capital would actually *leave* Mexico for the United States, moving to the lower *MPK* region, not because of higher profits but in search of a *safe haven* or shelter from risks. In Figure 6-7, panel (b), Mexico would move left of point C as capital declined, and would get poorer. Is this a relevant case? Yes. Bond market data in Figure 6-8 show that risk premiums can be substantial in emerging markets, including Mexico. And U.S. Treasury securities data indicate that from 1994 to 2006, U.S. holdings of Mexican assets rose from $50 billion to $65 billion, but Mexican holdings of U.S. assets rose from $5 billion to $95 billion. On net, capital moved north.

- *The model assumes that investment goods can be acquired at the same relative price in output terms everywhere.* In fact, the model treats one unit of investment as the same as one unit of output. But in developing countries, it often costs much more than one unit of output to purchase one unit of capital goods. Poor countries have often been ill equipped to produce cheap nontraded capital goods (such as buildings or

[19] Laura Alfaro, Sebnem Kalemli-Ozcan and Vadym Volosovych, 2005, "Why Doesn't Capital Flow from Rich to Poor Countries? An Empirical Investigation," NBER Working Paper No. 11901; James R. Lothian, 2006, "Institutions, Capital Flows and Financial Integration," *Journal of International Money and Finance,* 25(3), April, 358–369.

FIGURE 6-8

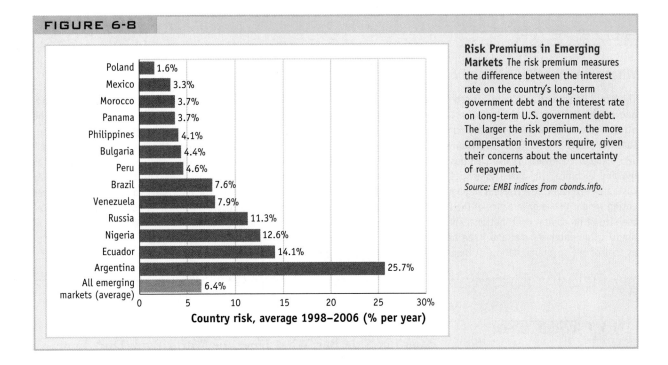

Risk Premiums in Emerging Markets The risk premium measures the difference between the interest rate on the country's long-term government debt and the interest rate on long-term U.S. government debt. The larger the risk premium, the more compensation investors require, given their concerns about the uncertainty of repayment.

Source: EMBI indices from cbonds.info.

bridges), and their imported capital goods (such as machines) have often been quite expensive because of trade costs (such as tariffs and transport costs).[20]

■ *The model assumes that the contribution of capital to production is equal across countries.* In our estimates, we used a reasonable estimate that the elasticity of output with respect to capital was one-third. But recent research suggests that capital's share may be much lower in many developing countries where a large part of *GDP* is derived from natural resources with little use of produced capital inputs.[21]

■ *The model suggests that foreign aid may do no better than foreign investors in promoting growth.* The model doesn't care where additional capital comes from. Investments paid for by transfers (aid or debt relief) rather than private investments face the same low *MPK* and the same divergence result holds. This observation is at the center of a major dispute over whether **foreign aid** can make a difference to long-term development and growth or if it is only an act of charity to prop up the poor (or even a total waste of money). The argument also extends to nonmarket and preferential lending offered to poor

---

[20] Alan M. Taylor, 1998, "On the Costs of Inward-Looking Development: Price Distortions, Growth, and Divergence in Latin America," *Journal of Economic History,* 58(1), March, 1–28; Jonathan Eaton and Samuel Kortum, 2001, "Trade in Capital Goods," *European Economic Review,* 45(7), 1195–1235.
[21] Francesco Caselli and James Feyrer, 2007, "The Marginal Product of Capital," *Quarterly Journal of Economics,* 122(2), 535–568.

SIDE BAR

What Does the World Bank Do?

The World Bank (worldbank.org), based in Washington, D.C., is one of the Bretton Woods "twins" established in 1944 (the other is the International Monetary Fund). Its main arm, the International Bank for Reconstruction and Development, has 185 member countries. Its main purpose is to provide financing and technical assistance to reduce poverty and promote sustained economic development in poor countries. A country's voting weight in the governance of the World Bank is based on the size of its capital contributions. The World Bank can raise funds at low interest rates and issue AAA-rated debt as good as that of any sovereign nation. It then lends to poor borrow-ers at low rates. Because the borrower nations could not ob-tain loans on these terms (or even any terms) elsewhere, the loans are a form of aid or transfer. In return for the preferen-tial rate, the bank may approve a loan for a particular devel-opment purpose (building infrastructure, for example) or to support a policy reform package. Controversially, conditions may also be imposed on the borrowing nation, such as changes in trade or fiscal policy. As a result of sovereignty, the imple-mentation of the conditions and the use of the loans have in some cases not turned out as intended, although outright de-fault on these preferential loans is almost unheard of.

NETWORK

To learn more about the aid debate, download some of the conflicting arguments made by two prominent figures: Jeffrey Sachs and William Easterly (Google: sachs easterly). See, for example, their "Foreign Aid Face Off" in the *Los Angeles Times* (latimes.com, April 30, 2006, and May 7, 2006). For some impartial views, down-load and read two articles: one by Nicholas Kristof ("Aid: Can It Work?" *New York Review of Books,* October 5, 2006) and one by Martin Wolf ("Aid Is Well Worth Trying," *Financial Times,* July 5, 2005); neither should require a sub-scription. After weighing up all these arguments, do you feel more or less optimistic about what aid can achieve?

countries by international financial institutions such as the **World Bank** (see **Side Bar: What Does the World Bank Do?**). In sup-port of the case that aid can make a difference, aid proponents argue that aid can finance public goods that can jolt a poor country out of a bad equilibrium or "poverty trap"—goods that private markets can-not provide (such as infrastructure, public health, and education). Aid skeptics reply that the evidence for such effects is weak, either because the links are not there or because in practice aid is so bureaucratized and subject to so many diversions and misappropria-tions that very little of it actually gets spent wisely, and hence much of it doesn't end up fulfilling even a charitable function (see **Headlines: A Brief History of Foreign Aid**).

Some efforts are now being made to ensure more aid is directed toward countries with better institutional environments: the U.S. Millennium Challenge Corporation has pursued this goal, as has the World Bank. But not only is it too soon to see if these goals are being achieved, it is also unclear whether they will succeed. Past evidence is not encouraging: a recent exhaustive study of aid and growth by economists Raghuram Rajan and Arvind Subramanian concluded: "We find little robust evidence of a positive (or negative) relationship between aid inflows into a country and its economic growth. We also find no evidence that aid works better in better policy or geographical environments, or that certain forms of aid work bet-ter than others. Our findings suggest that for aid to be effective in the future, the aid apparatus will have to be rethought."[22] ■

---

[22] Raghuram G. Rajan and Arvind Subramanian, 2008, "Aid and Growth: What Does the Cross-Country Evidence Really Show?" *Review of Economics and Statistics,* forthcoming.

HEADLINES

A Brief History of Foreign Aid

Foreign aid is frequently on the political agenda. But can it make any difference?

In 1985, when Bob Geldof organized the rock spectacular Live Aid to fight poverty in Africa, he kept things simple. "Give us your fucking money" was his famous (if apocryphal) command to an affluent Western audience—words that embodied Geldof's conviction that charity alone could save Africa. He had no patience for complexity: we were rich, they were poor, let's fix it. As he once said to a luckless official in the Sudan, after seeing a starving person, "I'm not interested in the bloody system! Why has he no food?"

Whatever Live Aid accomplished, it did not save Africa. Twenty years later, most of the continent is still mired in poverty. So when, earlier this month, Geldof put together Live 8, another rock spectacular, the utopian rhetoric was ditched. In its place was talk about the sort of stuff that Geldof once despised—debt-cancellation schemes and the need for "accountability and transparency" on the part of African governments—and, instead of fund-raising, a call for the leaders of the G-8 economies to step up their commitment to Africa. (In other words, don't give us your fucking money; get interested in the bloody system.) Even after the G-8 leaders agreed to double aid to Africa, the prevailing mood was one of cautious optimism rather than euphoria.

That did not matter to the many critics of foreign aid, who mounted a lively backlash against both Live 8 and the G-8 summit. For them, continuing to give money to Africa is simply "pouring billions more down the same old ratholes," as the columnist Max Boot put it. At best, these critics say, it's money wasted; at worst, it turns countries into aid junkies, clinging to the World Bank for their next fix. Instead of looking for help, African countries need to follow the so-called Asian Tigers (countries like South Korea and Taiwan), which overcame poverty by pursuing what Boot called "superior economic policies."

Skepticism about the usefulness of alms to the Third World is certainly in order. Billions of dollars have ended up in the pockets of kleptocratic rulers—in Zaire alone, Mobutu Sese Soko stole at least four billion—and still more has been misspent on massive infrastructure boondoggles, like the twelve-billion-dollar Yacyreta Dam, between Argentina and Paraguay, which Argentina's former President called "a monument to corruption." And historically there has been little correlation between aid and economic growth.

This checkered record notwithstanding, it's a myth that aid is doomed to failure. Foreign aid funded the campaign to eradicate smallpox, and in the sixties it brought the Green Revolution in agriculture to countries like India and Pakistan, lifting living standards and life expectancies for hundreds of millions of people. As for the Asian nations that Africa is being told to emulate, they may have pulled themselves up by their bootstraps, but at least they were provided with boots. In the postwar years, South Korea and Taiwan had the good fortune to become, effectively, client states of the U.S. Between 1946 and 1978, in fact, South Korea received nearly as much U.S. aid as the whole of Africa. Meanwhile, the billions that Taiwan got allowed it to fund a vast land-reform program and to eradicate malaria. And the U.S. gave the Asian Tigers more than money; it provided technical assistance and some military defense, and it offered preferential access to American markets.

Coincidence? Perhaps. But the two Middle Eastern countries that have shown relatively steady and substantial economic growth—Israel and Turkey—have also received tens of billions of dollars in U.S. aid. The few sub-Saharan African countries that have enjoyed any economic success at all of late—including Botswana, Mozambique, and Uganda—have been major aid recipients, as has Costa Rica, which has the best economy in Central America. Ireland (which is often called the Celtic Tiger), has enjoyed sizable subsidies from the European Union. China was the World Bank's largest borrower for much of the past decade.

Nobody doubts that vast amounts of aid have been squandered, but there are

Continued on next page.

© Signe Wilkinson/Cartoonistgroup

reasons to think that we can improve on that record. In the first place, during the Cold War aid was more often a geopolitical tool than a well-considered economic strategy, so it's not surprising that much of the money was wasted. And we now understand that the kind of aid you give, and the policies of the countries you give it to, makes a real difference. A recent study by three scholars at the Center for Global Development found that, on average, foreign aid that was targeted at stimulating immediate economic growth (as opposed to, say, dealing with immi-

nent crises) has had a significantly beneficial effect, even in Africa.

There's still a lot wrong with the way that foreign aid is administered. Too little attention is paid to figuring out which programs work and which don't, and aid still takes too little advantage of market mechanisms, which are essential to making improvements last. There's plenty we don't know about what makes one country succeed and another fail, and, as the former World Bank economist William Easterly points out, the foreign-aid establishment has

often promised in the past that things would be different. So we should approach the problem of aid with humility. Yet humility is no excuse for paralysis. In 2002, President Bush created the Millennium Challenge Account, which is designed to target assistance to countries that adopt smart policies, and said that the U.S. would give five billion dollars in aid by 2006. Three years later, a grand total of $117,500 has been handed out. By all means, let's be tough-minded about aid. But let's not be hardheaded about it.

Source: James Surowiecki, "A Farewell to Alms?" New Yorker, July 25, 2005.

4 Gains from Diversification of Risk

In the second section of this chapter, we studied consumption smoothing. Simplifications were made. We used a borrowing and lending approach, we considered a small open economy, we assumed that countries owned their own output, and we treated output shocks as given. We then saw how debt could be used to smooth out the output shocks, leaving consumption volatility lower than output volatility.

However, we also saw that in practice countries are unable to eliminate the effects of output volatility. The problems seem especially difficult in emerging markets and developing countries. We also saw that a reliance on debt to borrow and lend may be part of the problem because there may be limits to borrowing, risk premiums, and sudden stops in the availability of credit.

Are there other ways for a country to cope with shocks to output? Yes. In this section, we show how **diversification,** another facet of financial globalization, can help smooth shocks by promoting risk sharing. With diversification, countries not only own the right to income from their own output but also may own rights to income from the output of other countries as well. We see how, by using financial openness to trade such rights—for example, in the form of capital equity claims like stocks and shares—countries may be able to reduce the volatility of their incomes (and hence their consumption levels) without *any* net lending or borrowing.

Diversification: A Numerical Example and Generalization

To keep things simple and focus only on diversification, we assume that there is no borrowing, so the current account must be zero at all times. To illustrate the gains from diversification, we examine the special case of two countries, A and B, which are identical except that their outputs always fluctuate in opposite directions, that is, with a perfect inverse correlation.

We now explore how this world economy performs in response to the output shocks. We examine a special case in which there are two possible random outcomes for the shocks, state 1 and state 2, and each "state of the world" is assumed to have an equal (50%) probability of happening. In terms of output levels, state 1 is a bad state for A and a good state for B; state 2 is a good state for A and a bad state for B.

We will assume that all output is consumed and there is no investment or government spending. As we know from Chapter 5, output is then distributed to factors in the form of income. We will assume output is divided 60-40 between labor income and capital income in each country. But the key question for us will be, who owns this income? Domestic residents or foreigners?

Home Portfolios At first each country is closed, and the households in each country own the capital stock of their own country and own no foreign assets. Thus, A owns 100% A capital, and B owns 100% B capital. Under these assumptions, output (as measured by gross domestic product, GDP) is the same as income (as measured by gross national income, GNI) in A and B.

Although we can generalize later, we begin our analysis with the numerical example given in Table 6-6, panel (a). In state 1, A's output is 90, of which 54 units are payments to labor and 36 units are payments to capital; in state 2, A's output rises to 110, and factor payments rise to 66 for labor and 44 units for capital. The opposite is true in B: in state 1, B's output is higher than it is in state 2. Using our national accounting definitions from Chapter 5, we know that in each closed economy consumption C equals income GNI equals output GDP. In both A and B, all of these quantities are volatile and so GNI, and hence consumption, flips randomly between 90 and 110 in each country. The variation of GNI about its mean of 100 is plus or minus 10 in each country, an undesirable risk.

World Portfolios When the countries are in different states, notice what happens to their capital incomes (the sum of which equals world capital income). When one country's income is up, the other's is down. The shocks in the two countries are, in this special case, opposite and equal. Thus world GDP equals world GNI and is always 200 in state 1 or 2; it is the sum of outputs or GDP in A and B (200 = 90 + 110). Similarly, world labor income is always 120 and world capital income is always 80.

Even as the A and B payments to capital vary in panel (a), the world portfolio pays 80 to capital in either state of the world, as illustrated in Figure 6-9. It is now apparent that the two countries can achieve partial income smoothing if they diversify their portfolios of capital assets and hold a half share of the *world portfolio* that consists of 50% A capital and 50% B capital. Indeed, this is what standard portfolio theory says that investors should try to do. If they do, then the result would be as shown in Table 6-6, panel (b).

Now each country owns one-half of its own capital stock but sells the other half to the other country in exchange for half of the other country's capital stock.[23] Each country's output or GDP is still as it was described in panel (a). But now country incomes or GNI can differ from their outputs or

---

[23] Note that this financial transaction would balance in the financial account, as a pure asset trade, so no borrowing or lending is needed and the current account remains zero, as we have assumed.

TABLE 6-6

Portfolio Diversification Choices: Diversifiable Risks In countries A and B, *GDP* is allocated 60% to labor income and 40% to capital income. There are two "states of the world": State 1 is bad for A and good for B; state 2 is the opposite. On average, *GDP* equals 100, but in the good state, *GDP* is 110, and in the bad state it is only 90. Thus, world *GDP* and *GNI* always equal 200, world labor income is always 120, and world capital income is always 80. When each country holds only its own assets as in panel (a), *GNI* equals *GDP* and is very volatile. When each country holds a 50% share of the world portfolio as in panel (b), *GNI* volatility decreases because capital income is now smoothed. When each country holds a portfolio made up only of the other country's capital as in panel (c), *GNI* volatility falls even further by making capital income vary inversely with labor income.

(a) When Countries Hold 100% Home Portfolios
Each Country Owns 100% of Its Own Capital

	COUNTRY A			COUNTRY B			WORLD		
	Capital Income	Labor Income	*GDP* = *GNI*	Capital Income	Labor Income	*GDP* = *GNI*	Capital Income	Labor Income	*GDP* = *GNI*
State 1	36	54	90	44	66	110	80	120	200
State 2	44	66	110	36	54	90	80	120	200
Variation about mean	∓4	∓6	∓10	±4	±6	±10	0	0	0

(b) When Countries Hold World Portfolios
Each Country Owns 50% A Capital and 50% B Capital with Payoffs as in Panel (a)

	COUNTRY A			COUNTRY B			WORLD		
	Capital Income	Labor Income	*GNI*	Capital Income	Labor Income	*GNI*	Capital Income	Labor Income	*GDP* = *GNI*
State 1	40	54	94	40	66	106	80	120	200
State 2	40	66	106	40	54	94	80	120	200
Variation about mean	0	∓6	∓6	0	±6	±6	0	0	0

(c) When Countries Hold 100% Foreign Portfolios
Each Country Owns 100% of the Other Country's Capital with Payoffs as in Panel (a)

	COUNTRY A			COUNTRY B			WORLD		
	Capital Income	Labor Income	*GNI*	Capital Income	Labor Income	*GNI*	Capital Income	Labor Income	*GDP* = *GNI*
State 1	44	54	98	36	66	102	80	120	200
State 2	36	66	102	44	54	98	80	120	200
Variation about mean	±4	∓6	∓2	∓4	±6	±2	0	0	0

GDP. Owning 50% of the world portfolio means that each country has a capital income of 40 every period. Labor income risk in A and B does not change: labor income still varies between 54 and 66 in the bad and good states, so total income (and hence consumption) varies between 94 and 106. Thus, as Table 6-6, panel (b), shows, capital income for each country is

FIGURE 6-9

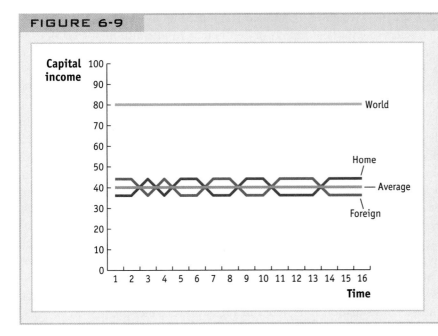

Portfolio Diversification and Capital Income: Diversifiable Risks The figure shows fluctuations in capital income over time for different portfolios, based on the data in Table 6-6. Countries trade claims to capital income by trading capital assets. When countries hold the world portfolio, they each earn a 50-50 split (or average) of world capital income. World capital income is constant if shocks in the two countries are asymmetrical and cancel out. All capital income risk is then fully diversifiable.

smoothed at 40 units, the average of A and B capital income in panel (a), as also illustrated in Figure 6-9.

How does the balance of payments work when countries hold the world portfolio? Consider country A. In state 1 (bad for A, good for B), A's income or *GNI* exceeds A's output, *GDP*, by 4 (94 − 90 = +4). Where does the extra income come from? The extra is net factor income from abroad of +4. Why is it +4? This is precisely equal to the difference between the income earned on A's external assets (50% of B's payments to capital of 44 = 22) and the income paid on A's external liabilities (50% of A's payments to capital of 36 = 18). What does A do with that net factor income? A runs a trade balance of −4, which means that A can consume 94, even when A's output is only 90. The trade balance is the difference between output and consumption. Adding the trade balance of −4 to net factor income from abroad of +4 means that the current account is 0, and there is still no need for any net borrowing or lending, as assumed. These flows are reversed in state 2 (good for A, bad for B).

Note that after diversification, income or *GNI* varies in A and B by plus or minus 6 (around a mean of 100), which is less than the range of plus or minus 10 seen in Table 6-6, panel (a). This is because 40% of income is capital income and so 40% of the A income fluctuation of 10 can be smoothed by the portfolio diversification.

Generalizing For a moment, let us try to generalize the concept of capital income smoothing through diversification. Consider the volatility of just capital income in the example we have just studied. Each country's payments to capital are volatile. A portfolio of 100% A capital or 100% B capital has capital income that varies by plus or minus 4 (between 36 and 44). But a 50-50 mix of the two leaves the investor with a portfolio of minimum, zero volatility (it always pays 40).

The situation we have just studied is summed up in Figure 6-10, panel (a), which refers to either country, A or B. There is an identical high level of capital income volatility when the country holds either a 100% home portfolio or a 100% foreign portfolio. However, holding a mix of the two reduces capital income volatility and a minimum volatility of zero can be achieved by holding the 50-50 mix of the world capital income portfolio.

But to generalize, we need to recognize that the world is not so simple. In reality, not all shocks are asymmetric. The outputs of A and B may not have a perfect inverse or negative correlation (a correlation of −1) as we have assumed here. In general, there will be *common shocks,* identical or symmetric shocks that occur to both countries that cannot be diminished by any form of asset trade. For example, suppose we added a new shock with two new states, A and B; in state A, the new shock adds five units to each country's output; in state B output, it subtracts five units. There is no way to avoid this shock by portfolio diversification. The shocks in each country are perfectly positively correlated (correlation +1). If this were the only shock, the countries' outputs would move up and down together and diversification would be pointless. This situation is depicted in Figure 6-10, panel (b).

FIGURE 6-10

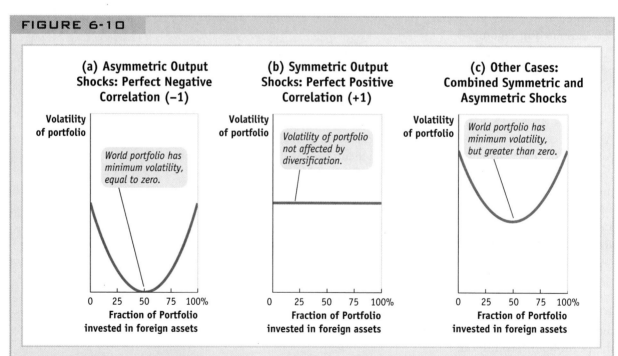

Return Correlations and Gains from Diversification The charts plot the volatility of capital income against the share of the portfolio devoted to foreign capital. The two countries are identical in size and experience shocks of similar amplitude. In panel (a), shocks are perfectly asymmetric (correlation = −1), capital income in the two countries is perfectly *negatively* correlated. Risk can be eliminated by holding the world portfolio, and there are large gains from diversification. In panel (b), shocks are perfectly symmetric (correlation = +1), capital income in the two countries is perfectly *positively* correlated. Risk cannot be reduced, and there are no gains from diversification. In panel (c), when both types of shock are present, the correlation is neither perfectly negative nor positive. Risk can be partially eliminated by holding the world portfolio, and there are still some gains from diversification.

Still, in the real world, not all shocks are symmetric or common, either. As long as there are *some* shocks that are asymmetric, or country specific, and not common between the home and foreign country, then the two countries will have some gains from the diversification of risk. In this more general case in which symmetric and asymmetric shocks are combined, as depicted in Figure 6-10, panel (c), holding a 100% portfolio of domestic (or foreign) assets generates a volatile income. But holding the 50-50 world portfolio will lower the volatility of income, albeit not all the way to zero (see the Appendix at the end of the chapter).

Limits to Diversification: Capital versus Labor Income As we saw in Table 6-6, panel (b), elimination of total income risk cannot be achieved by holding the world portfolio, even in the case of purely asymmetric shocks of capital assets. Why? Because labor income risk is not being shared. Admittedly, the same theory would apply if one could trade labor like an asset, but this is impossible because ownership rights to labor cannot be legally traded in the same way as one can trade capital or other property (that would be slavery).

Yet while it is true that labor income risk (and hence *GDP* risk) may not be diversifiable through the trading of claims to labor assets or *GDP*, this is not quite the end of our story—in theory at least. We saw in Table 6-6, panel (a), that capital and labor income in each country are perfectly correlated in this example: a good state raises both capital and labor income, and a bad state lowers both. This is not implausible—in reality shocks to production do tend to raise and lower incomes of capital and labor simultaneously. This means that, as a risk-sharing device, trading claims to capital income can substitute for trading claims to labor income.

To illustrate this substitution potential, imagine an unreal scenario in which the residents of each country own *no* capital stock of their own country but own the entire capital stock of the other country. As shown in Table 6-6, panel (c), owning only the other country's portfolio achieves more risk sharing than holding 50% of the world portfolio.

For example, when A is in the good state (state 2), A's labor income is 66 but A's capital income is 36 (assumed now to be 100% from B, which is in the bad state). This adds up to a *GNI* of 102. In the bad state for A (state 1), A's labor income is 54, but A's capital income is 44 (from B, which is in a good state), for a total *GNI* of 98. So A's income (and consumption) vary by plus or minus 2, between 98 and 102 in panel (c). Compare this fluctuation of ±2 around the mean of 100 to the fluctuations of ±10 (home portfolio) and ±6 (the world portfolio) in panels (a) and (b).

You can see how additional risk reduction has been achieved. A would like to own claims to 50% of B's *total* income. It could achieve this by owning 50% of B's capital and 50% of B's labor. But labor can't be owned, so A tries to get around the restriction of owning 0% of B's labor by acquiring much more than 50% of B's capital. Because labor's share of income in both countries is more than half in this example—a realistic ratio—this strategy allows for the elimination of some, but not all, risk.

The Home Bias Puzzle

So much for theory. In practice, we do not observe countries owning foreign-biased portfolios or even the world portfolio. Countries tend to own portfolios that suffer from a strong **home bias:** a tendency of investors to devote a disproportionate fraction of their wealth to assets from their own home country, when a more globally diversified portfolio might protect them better from risk.

To illustrate this, economist Karen Lewis compared the risk and return for sample portfolios that U.S. investors could have chosen from for the period 1970 to 1996. She imagined an experiment in which some assets are allocated to a domestic portfolio (the S&P 500) and the remainder to an overseas portfolio (Morgan Stanley's EAFE fund). In this stylized problem, the question is what weight to put on each portfolio, when the weights must sum to 100%. In reality, U.S. investors picked a weight of about 8% on foreign assets. Was this a smart choice?

Figure 6-11 shows the risk and return for every possible weight between 0% and 100%. Return is measured by the mean rate of return (annualized percent per year); risk is measured by the standard deviation of the return (its root mean square deviation from its mean).

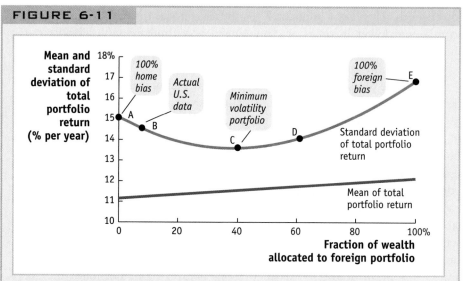

FIGURE 6-11

Portfolio Diversification in the United States The figure shows the return (mean of monthly return) and risk (standard deviation of monthly return) for a hypothetical portfolio made up from a mix of a pure home U.S. portfolio (the S&P 500) and a pure foreign portfolio (the Morgan Stanley EAFE) using data from the period 1970 to 1996. U.S. investors with a 0% weight on the overseas portfolio (point A) could have raised that weight as high as 39% (point C) and still raised the return and lowered risk. Even moving to the right of C (toward D) would make sense, though how far would depend on how the investor viewed the risk-return trade-off. The actual weight seen was extremely low at just 8% (point B) and was considered a puzzle.

Source: Karen K. Lewis, 1999, "Trying to Explain Home Bias in Equities and Consumption," Journal of Economic Literature, 37(2), 571–608.

With regard to returns, the foreign portfolio had a slightly higher average return than the home portfolio in this period, so increasing the weight on the foreign portfolio would have increased the returns: the mean return line slopes up slightly from left to right. What about risk? A 100% foreign portfolio (point E) would have generated higher risk than the home U.S. portfolio (point A); thus E is above A. However, we know that some mix of the two portfolios ought to produce a lower volatility than either extreme because the two returns are not perfectly correlated. This minimum volatility will not be zero because there are some undiversifiable, symmetric shocks, but it will be lower than the volatility of the 100% home and 100% foreign portfolios: overseas and domestic returns are not perfectly correlated, implying that substantial country-specific diversifiable risks exist.

In fact, Lewis showed that a U.S. investor with a 0% weight on the overseas portfolio (point A) could have raised that weight to as much as 39% (point C), while simultaneously raising the average of her total return *and* lowering its risk. Even moving to the right of C (toward D) would make sense, though how far would depend on how the investor viewed the risk-return trade-off. Choosing a weight as low as 8% (point B) would seem to be a puzzle.

Broadly speaking, economists have had one of two reactions to the emergence of the "home bias puzzle" in the 1990s. One is to propose many different theories to explain away the home bias puzzle: Perhaps it is costly to acquire foreign assets, or get information about them? Perhaps there are asymmetries between home and foreign countries' consumption patterns (due to nontraded goods or trade frictions or even tastes) that make domestic assets a better hedge against domestic consumption risk? Perhaps home investors worry about regulatory barriers and the problems of corporate governance in foreign markets? These and many other solutions have been tried in extremely complex economic models, but none has been judged a complete success.

The other reaction of economists has been to look at the evidence of home bias in the period from the 1970s to the 1990s (the period of the Lewis study) as a legacy of the pronounced deglobalization of financial markets in the postwar period that might slowly disappear. Recent evidence suggests that this might be happening to some degree. Table 6-7 reveals a dramatic increase in overseas equity investments in a sample of advanced countries from 1970 to 2003, with a very strong upward trend after 1985. For example, in the United States, the foreign share of the U.S. portfolio has risen from 5.6% in 1990 to 12.7% in 2003. Over the same period, the U.K. portfolio saw its foreign share rise from 33.1% to 52.4%. Figure 6-12 shows the extent of cross-border holdings of assets in today's global economy.

Furthermore, these figures might understate the true extent to which residents have diversified away from home capital because many large multinational firms have capital income streams that flow from operations in many countries. For example, an American purchasing a share of Intel or Ford, or a Briton purchasing a share of BP, or a Japanese purchasing a share of Sony, is really purchasing shares of income streams from the globally diversified operations of these companies. Technically, Intel is recorded in the data as a 100% U.S. "home" stock, but this makes the home bias puzzle look much worse than

TABLE 6-7

Financial Globalization and the Reduction in Home Bias In a sample of advanced countries we can see that investors have gradually devoted a larger share of their portfolios to overseas investments since the 1970s.

		Overseas Investment (% of Domestic Market Capitalization)							
		1970	1975	1980	1985	1990	1995	2000	2003
Canada	All investments	2%	1.9%	2.1%	2.4%	6%	12.9%	18.7%	14.3%
	Equity	3.1	3.2	3.6	3.5	9.6	25.4	29.3	21.2
Germany	All investments	4.9	2.4	2.7	5.8	10.2	14.5	30	31.1
	Equity	—	—	—	—	—	16.9	37.8	42.1
Japan	All investments	—	1.3	2	6.9	10.7	12.1	13.6	16.7
	Equity	—	—	—	—	2.2	4	8.3	9.9
United Kingdom	All investments	9.5	8.6	11.4	27.5	34	37.1	42.6	48.1
	Equity	—	—	—	—	33.1	33.5	40.9	52.4
United States	All investments	1.5	2.1	2.3	2.2	3.5	6.4	7.8	7.4
	Equity	0.8	1.1	1.3	2	5.6	9.3	10.5	12.7

Source: International Monetary Fund (IMF), World Economic Outlook, April 2005, Table 3.2.

it really is because investors do seem to overweight firms such as these that provide an indirect foreign exposure.[24]

Recent trends in diversification within portfolios and within companies may mean that even if the puzzle cannot be explained away, perhaps it will gradually go away. ■

Summary: Don't Put All Your Eggs in One Basket

If countries were able to borrow and lend without limit or restrictions in an efficient market, our discussions of consumption smoothing and efficient investment would seem to suggest that they should be able to cope with all possible shocks and attain a smooth level of consumption, regardless of the disturbances to output and investment. In reality, as the evidence shows, countries are not able to fully exploit the intertemporal borrowing mechanism.

In this environment, diversification of income risk through the international trading of assets can deliver substantial benefits. In theory, if countries were able to pool their income streams and take shares from that common pool of income, all country-specific shocks would be averaged out, leaving countries exposed only to common global shocks to income, the sole remaining undiversifiable shocks that cannot be avoided.

---

[24] Fang Cai and Francis E. Warnock, 2006, "International Diversification at Home and Abroad," NBER Working Paper No. 12220.

FIGURE 6-12

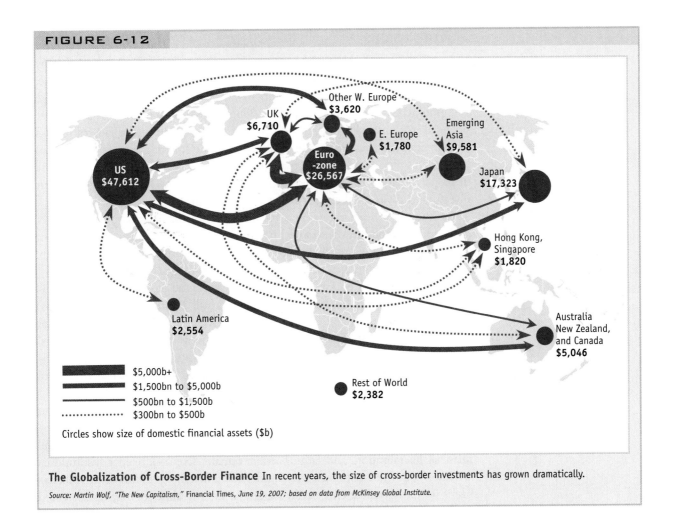

The Globalization of Cross-Border Finance In recent years, the size of cross-border investments has grown dramatically.

Source: Martin Wolf, "The New Capitalism," Financial Times, June 19, 2007; based on data from McKinsey Global Institute.

Financial openness allows countries—like households—to follow the old adage "Don't put all your eggs in one basket." The lesson here has a simple household analogy. Think of a self-employed person who owns a ski shop. If the only capital she owns is her own business capital, then her capital income and labor income move together, and go up in good times (winter) and down in bad times (summer). Her total income could be smoothed if she sold some stock in her company and used the proceeds to buy stock in another company that faced asymmetric shocks (a surf shop, perhaps).

In practice, however, risk sharing through asset trade is limited. For one thing, the number of assets is limited. The market for claims to capital income is incomplete because not all capital assets are traded (for example, many firms are privately held and are not listed on stock markets), and the trade in labor assets is legally prohibited. Moreover, even with the traded assets available, investors have shown very little inclination to invest their wealth outside their own country, although that may be slowly changing in an environment of ongoing financial globalization.

5 Conclusions

If a firm or household were to retreat from the national financial market by keeping its money in a bag in a closet, paying cash for *all* its purchases (house, cars, appliances, toothpaste, gum, and so on), we would regard it as a strange and potentially costly move. By allowing households to save and borrow, financial markets help households smooth consumption in the face of shocks to their income (such as a debilitating illness, the loss of a job, destruction of property by floods or other acts of nature). Likewise, financial markets allow firms to borrow to invest efficiently in productive projects and permit investors to diversify their portfolios across a wide range of assets.

On the global scale, the same principles apply in theory to countries, subject to the long-run budget constraint. They, too, face income shocks, new investment opportunities, and country-specific risks. We have seen how they can similarly benefit from access to an external capital market—the global capital market.

Theory proves to be far from reality, however: the extent to which countries make use of global financial markets is still limited. Even in the most financially open advanced countries, consumption shocks remain, investment is often financed out of domestic saving, and a home bias persists in investors' portfolios. In poorer countries, we see no consumption smoothing gains realized, and there is little scope for development based on external finance until current low productivity levels are improved.

Are global capital markets failing? To the criticism that financial globalization doesn't work, one could respond that it hasn't really been fully tried yet. Many emerging markets and most developing countries are still on the road to full financial liberalization, and large barriers remain. Even so, deeper institutional weaknesses in these countries may hinder the efficient operation of the mechanisms we have studied. One could argue that such weaknesses may be corrected or diminished by the stimulus to competition, transparency, accountability, and stability that financial openness may provide.[25] But absent further institutional improvements, the benefits of financial globalization are likely to be much smaller for these countries, and they must also be weighed against potential offsetting costs, such as the risk of crises, which will be discussed in Chapters 9 and 11.

KEY POINTS

1. Countries can use their external wealth as a buffer to smooth consumption in the face of fluctuations in output or investment. However, this process is not without its limits. The country must service its debts and must not allow debts to roll over and grow without limit at the real rate of interest.

2. The condition that guarantees that debts are serviced is the *long-run budget constraint,* or LRBC: the present value of future trade deficits must equal minus the present value of initial wealth.

3. The long-run budget constraint can be put another way: the present value of *GDP* plus the present value of initial wealth (the country's

---

[25] M. Ayhan Kose, Eswar Prasad, Kenneth S. Rogoff, and Shang-Jin Wei, 2006, "Financial Globalization: A Reappraisal," NBER Working Paper No. 12484.

resources) must equal the present value of *GNE* (the country's spending).

4. In a closed economy, the country must satisfy $TB = 0$ in *every* period as there is no external trade in goods or assets. In an open economy, the economy has to satisfy only the long-run budget constraint, which states that *TB* equals minus the present value of initial wealth. The former is a tighter constraint than the latter—implying that there can be gains from financial globalization.

5. The current account may be lower than normal in any period when there is unusually high private or public consumption (during a war for example), unusually low output (such as occurs after a natural disaster), or unusually high investment (such as that following a natural resource discovery). Numerical examples can illustrate these phenomena and how external wealth adjusts.

6. If poor countries had the same productivity as rich countries, there would be substantial gains from investing in poor countries where the marginal product of capital, or *MPK,* would be much higher. However, this is not the case, and there is little evidence of investment inefficiency at the global level as measured by *MPK* gaps between countries. What gaps there are may be due to risk premiums. Consequently, large-scale investment (and foreign aid) in poor countries may not accelerate economic growth.

7. In addition to lending and borrowing, a country can reduce its risk by the international diversification of income claims. In practice, only capital income claims (capital assets) are tradable. Labor is not a tradable asset.

8. When assets are traded internationally, two countries can eliminate the income risk arising from country-specific or idiosyncratic shocks; such risk is called diversifiable risk. However, they can do nothing to eliminate the global risk, the shock common to both countries, called undiversifiable risk.

9. In practice, the use of the current account as a buffer and the extent of diversification fall far short of theory's prediction even in advanced countries. Consumption volatility persists, domestic investment is mostly financed from domestic saving, and portfolios display pronounced home bias.

10. In emerging markets and developing countries, financial openness has progressed more slowly and access to global capital markets is more limited and often on worse terms. The gains from financial openness appear weaker, and there is the downside risk of sudden stops and other crises. For gains to be realized, countries may require deeper institutional changes and further liberalization.

KEY TERMS

small open economy, p. 222
world real interest rate, p. 223
present value, p. 224
long-run budget constraint (LRBC), p. 225
perpetual loan, p. 226
sudden stops, p. 232

precautionary saving, p. 240
foreign reserves, p. 241
sovereign wealth funds, p. 241
marginal product of capital (*MPK*), p. 247
production function, p. 249
productivity, p. 249

convergence, p. 252
divergence, p. 254
foreign aid, p. 257
World Bank, p. 258
diversification, p. 260
home bias, p. 266

PROBLEMS

1. Using the notation from the text, answer the following questions. You may assume that net labor income from abroad is zero, there are no capital gains on external wealth, and there are no unilateral transfers.

a. Express the change in external wealth (ΔW_0) at the end of period 0 as a function of the economy's trade balance (TB_0), the real interest rate (a constant, r^*), and initial external wealth (W_{-1}).

b. Using (a), write an expression for the stock of external wealth at the end of period 0 (W_0). This should be written as a function of the economy's trade balance (TB_0), the real interest rate, and initial external wealth (W_{-1}).

c. Using (a) and (b), write an expression for the stock of external wealth at the end of period 1 (W_1). This should be written as a function of the economy's trade balance (TB) each period, the real interest rate, and initial external wealth (W_{-1}).

d. Using your answers from (a), (b), and (c), write an expression for the stock of external wealth at the end of period 2 (W_2). This should be written as a function of the economy's trade balance (TB) each period, the real interest rate, and initial external wealth (W_{-1}).

e. Suppose we require that W_2 equal zero. Write down the condition that the three trade balances (in periods 0, 1, and 2) must satisfy. Arrange the terms in present value form.

2. Using the assumptions and answers from the previous question, complete the following:

a. Write an expression for the *future value* of the stock of external wealth in period N (W_N). This should be written as a function of the economy's trade balance (TB) each period, the real interest rate r^*, and initial external wealth.

b. Using the answer from (a), write an expression for the *present value* of the stock of external wealth in period N (W_N).

c. The "no Ponzi game" conditions force the present value of W_N to tend to zero as N gets large. Explain why this implies that the economy's initial external wealth is equal to the present value of future trade deficits.

d. How would the expressions in parts (a) and (b) change if the economy had net labor income (positive or negative) to/from abroad or net unilateral transfers? Explain briefly.

3. *In this question assume all dollar units are real dollars in billions, e.g., $150 means $150 billion.* It is year 0. Argentina thinks it can find $150 of domestic investment projects with an *MPK* of 10% (each $1 invested pays off $0.10 in every later year). Argentina invests $84 in year 0 by borrowing $84 from the rest of the world at a world real interest rate r^* of 5%. There is no further borrowing or investment after this.

Use the standard assumptions: Assume initial external wealth W (W in year −1) is 0. Assume $G = 0$ always; and assume $I = 0$ except in year 0. Also, assume $NUT = KA = 0$ and that there is no net labor income so that $NFIA = r^*W$.

The projects start to pay off in year 1 and continue to pay off all years thereafter. Interest is paid in perpetuity, in year 1 and every year thereafter. In addition, assume that if the projects are not done, then $GDP = Q = C = \$200$ in all years, so that $PV(Q) = PV(C) = 200 + 200/0.05 = 4,200$.

a. Should Argentina fund the $84 worth of projects? Explain your answer.

b. Why might Argentina be able to borrow only $84 and not $150?

c. From this point forward, assume the projects totaling $84 are funded and completed in year 0. If the MPK is 10%, what is the total payoff from the projects in future years?

d. Assume this is added to the $200 of GDP in all years starting in year 1. In dollars, what is Argentina's $Q = GDP$ in year 0, year 1, and later years?

e. At year 0, if Argentina makes the investment, what is the new $PV(Q)$ in dollars? Hint: To ease computation, calculate the value of the increment in $PV(Q)$ due to the extra output in later years.

f. At year 0, if Argentina makes the investment, what is the new $PV(I)$ in dollars? Therefore, what does the LRBC say is the new $PV(C)$ in dollars?

g. Assume that Argentina is trying to achieve consumption smoothing. What is the percent change in $PV(C)$? What is the new level of C in all years? Is Argentina better off?

h. For the year the projects go ahead, year 0, explain Argentina's balance of payments as follows: State the levels of $CA, TB, NFIA,$ and FA.

i. What happens in later years? State the levels of $CA, TB, NFIA,$ and FA in year 1 and every later year.

4. Continuing from the previous question, we now consider Argentina's external wealth position.

a. What is Argentina's external wealth W in year 0 and later?

b. Suppose Argentina has a one-year debt (i.e., not a perpetual loan) that must be rolled over every year. After a few years, in year N, the world interest rate rises to 15%. Can Argentina stick to its original plan? What are the interest payments due on the debt if $r^* = 15\%$? If $I = G = 0$, what must Argentina do to meet those payments?

c. Suppose Argentina decides to unilaterally default on its debt. Why might Argentina do this? State the levels of $CA, TB, NFIA,$ and FA in year N and all subsequent years. What happens to the Argentine level of C in this case?

d. When the default occurs, what is the change in Argentina's external wealth W? What happens to the rest of the world's (ROW's) external wealth?

e. External wealth data for Argentina and ROW are recorded in the account known as the net international investment position. Is this change in wealth recorded as a financial flow, a price effect, or an exchange rate effect?

5. Using production function and MPK diagrams, answer the following questions. For simplicity, assume there are two countries: a poor country (with low living standards) and a rich country (with high living standards).

a. Assuming that poor and rich countries have the same production function, illustrate how the poor country will converge with the rich country. Describe how this mechanism works.

b. In the data, countries with low living standards have capital-to-worker ratios that are too high to be consistent with the model used in (a). Describe and illustrate how we can modify the model used in (a) to be consistent with the data.

c. Given your assumptions from (b), what does this suggest about the ability of poor countries to converge with rich countries? What do we expect to happen to the gap between rich and poor countries over time? Explain.

Using the model from (b), explain and illustrate how convergence works in the following cases.

d. The poor country has a marginal product of capital that is higher than that of the rich country.

e. The marginal products in each country are equal. Then, the poor country experiences an increase in human capital through government funding of education.

f. The marginal products in each country are equal. Then, the poor country experiences political instability such that investors require a risk premium to invest in the poor country.

6. Assume that Brazil and the United States have different production functions $q = f(k)$ where q is output per worker and k is capital per worker. Let $q = Ak^{1/3}$. You are told that relative to the U.S. = 1, Brazil has an output per worker of 0.32 and capital per worker of 0.24. Can A be the same in Brazil as in the United States? If not, compute the level of A for Brazil. What is Brazil's MPK relative to the United States?

7. Use production function and MPK diagrams to examine Turkey and the EU. Assume that Turkey and the EU have different production functions $q = f(k)$ where q is output per worker and k is capital per worker. Let $q = Ak^{1/3}$. Assume that the productivity level A in Turkey is lower than A in the EU.

a. Draw a production function diagram (with output per worker, q, as a function of capital per worker, k) and MPK diagram (MPK versus k) for the EU. (Hint: Be sure to draw the two diagrams with the production function directly above the MPK diagram so that the level of capital per worker, k, is consistent on your two diagrams.)

b. For now, assume capital cannot flow freely in and out of Turkey. On the same diagrams, plot Turkish production function and MPK curves, assuming that the productivity level A in Turkey is half the EU level and that Turkish MPK exceeds EU MPK. Label the EU position in each chart EU and the label the Turkish position T1.

c. Assume capital can now flow freely between Turkey and the EU and the rest of the world and that EU is already at the point where $MPK = r^*$. Label r^* on the vertical axis of the MPK diagram. Assume no risk premium. What will be Turkey's capital per worker level k? Label this outcome point T2 in each diagram. Will Turkey converge to the EU level of q? Explain.

8. This question continues from the previous problem, focusing on how risk premiums explain the gaps in living standards across countries.

   a. Investors worry about the rule of law in Turkey and also about the potential for hyperinflation and other bad macroeconomic policies. Because of these worries, the initial gap between MPK in Turkey and r^* is a risk premium, RP. Label RP on the vertical axis of the MPK diagram. Now where does Turkey end up in terms of k and q?

   b. In light of (a), why might Turkey be keen to join the EU?

   c. Some EU countries are keen to exclude Turkey from the EU. What might be the *economic* arguments for that position?

9. In this chapter, we saw that financial market integration is necessary for countries to smooth consumption through borrowing and lending. Consider two economies: Czech Republic and France. For each of the following shocks, explain how and to what extent each country can trade capital to better smooth consumption.

   a. The Czech Republic and France each experience an EU-wide recession.

   b. A strike in France leads to a reduction in French income.

   c. Floods destroy a portion of the Czech capital stock, lowering Czech income.

10. Assume that a country produces an output Q of 50 every year. The world interest rate is 10%. Consumption C is 50 every year, and $I = G = 0$. There is an unexpected drop in output in year 0, so output falls to 39 and is then expected to return to 50 in every future year. If the country desires to smooth consumption, how much should it borrow in period 0? What will the new level of consumption be from then on?

11. Assume that a country produces an output Q of 50 every year. The world interest rate is 10%. Consumption C is 50 every year, and $I = G = 0$. There is an unexpected war in year 0, which costs 11 units and is predicted to last one year. If the country desires to smooth consumption, how much should it borrow in period 0? What will the new level of consumption be from then on?

The country wakes up in year 1 and discovers that the war is still going on and will eat up another 11 units of expenditure in year 1. If the country still desires to smooth consumption looking forward from year 1, how much should it borrow in period 1? What will be the new level of consumption from then on?

12. Consider a world of two countries, Highland (H) and Lowland (L). Each country has an average output of 9 and desires to smooth consumption. All income takes the form of capital income and is fully consumed each period.

   a. Initially there are two states of the world, Pestilence (P) and Flood (F). Each happens with 50% probability. Pestilence affects Highland and lowers the output there to 8, leaving Lowland unaffected with an output of 10. Flood affects Lowland and lowers the output there to 8, leaving Highland unaffected with an output of 10. Devise a table with two rows corresponding to each state (rows marked P, F). In three columns, show income to three portfolios: the portfolio of 100% H capital, the portfolio of 100% L capital, and the portfolio of 50% H + 50% L capital.

   b. Two more states of world appear: Armageddon (A) and Utopia (U). Each happens with 50% probability but is uncorrelated with the P-F state. Armageddon affects both countries equally and lowers income in each country by a further 4 units, whatever the P-F state. Utopia leaves each country unaffected. Devise a table with four rows corresponding to each state (rows marked PA, PU, FA, FU). In three columns, show income to three portfolios: the portfolio of 100% H capital, the portfolio of 100% L capital, and the portfolio of 50% H + 50% L capital.

Compare your answers to parts (a) and (b) and consider the optimal portfolio choices. Does diversification eliminate consumption risk in each case? Explain.

APPENDIX TO CHAPTER 6

Common versus Idiosyncratic Shocks

In reality, home and foreign incomes will not have a perfect inverse correlation as we have assumed in the text. Let us generalize a bit more for our two countries, and focus on capital income.

A More General Case Suppose the shocks to capital income are a and b, for countries A and B, respectively, and that these take a random value each period. The common shock is the *average shock* in the two countries: $\frac{1}{2}(a + b)$. In the chapter, we assumed the average shock was zero, so the shocks were equal and opposite. In the real world, however, this need not be the case.

We can define the A-specific shock as the shock a minus the average shock: $a - \frac{1}{2}(a + b) = \frac{1}{2}(a - b)$. Similarly, the B-specific shock is b minus the average shock: $b - \frac{1}{2}(a + b) = \frac{1}{2}(b - a)$. These *idiosyncratic shocks* are nonzero as long as the A shock is not the same as the B shock, that is, as long as a is not equal to b.

By doing this algebraic manipulation, the A shock can be written as the common shock plus the A-specific shock:

$$a = \underbrace{\frac{1}{2}(a + b)}_{\text{Common shock}} + \underbrace{\frac{1}{2}(a - b)}_{\text{A-specific shock}}.$$

Similarly, the B shock can be written as the common shock plus the B-specific shock:

$$b = \underbrace{\frac{1}{2}(a + b)}_{\text{Common shock}} + \underbrace{\frac{1}{2}(b - a)}_{\text{B-specific shock}}.$$

We see that the country-specific shocks are the exact opposites of each other: $\frac{1}{2}(a - b)$ and $\frac{1}{2}(b - a)$. The good news is that country-specific shocks are a *diversifiable* risk and satisfy the conditions of the simple case examined in the chapter. So the income risk they generate can be eliminated by diversification: in the world portfolio, the country-specific shocks cancel out, as we can see by adding up the last two equations.

But the common shock is $\frac{1}{2}(a + b)$. As long as this is nonzero, these shocks matter, that is, as long as the shocks are not equal and opposite, pure asymmetric country-specific shocks. The bad news is, the global shocks are an *undiversifiable* risk—no matter which assets you own, you get hit with the global shock, so asset trade offers no escape from these risks.

Numerical Example Figure 6-A1 (an extension of Figure 6-9) provides an illustration of the partial reduction in risk that can be achieved in this case. In

Figure 6-9, each country owned 50% of the world portfolio. Thus, capital incomes in each state were as follows: in state 1, A = 36, B = 44; in state 2, A = 44, B = 36. The occurrence of states 1 and 2 was random with 50-50 odds. If A and B diversified by each holding 50% of the world portfolio, they had stable capital income of 40 every period.

In Figure 6-A1, we add an extra "global" shock, which has two states, X and Y, that occur at random with 50-50 odds. However, the random X-Y shock is *independent* of the 1-2 shock. We suppose that when the global shock is in state X, both countries receive an extra five units of capital income. When the global shock is in state Y, both countries receive five units less of capital income.

There are now four possible states of the world: 1X, 1Y, 2X, and 2Y. Each has a 25% chance of occurring. For the four states, the capital incomes of the portfolios are as follows:

1X	Home = 41	Foreign = 49	World = 90	Average = 45
2X	Home = 49	Foreign = 41	World = 90	Average = 45
1Y	Home = 31	Foreign = 39	World = 70	Average = 35
2Y	Home = 39	Foreign = 31	World = 70	Average = 35

From this table, and the example shown in Figure 6-A1, we see as expected, that in this world, holding half of the world portfolio eliminates the risk associated with fluctuations between states 1 and 2. The best that each country can do is to have an income that fluctuates between 45 (half of 90, state X) and 35 (half of 70, state Y). In state X, all income risk associated with states 1 and 2 is gone. And in state Y, all income risk associated with states 1 and 2 is gone. But nothing can be done to eliminate the risk associated with fluctuations between states X and Y.

This more general result does not overturn our basic findings. Holding a 100% home portfolio generates a volatile capital income. So does holding a 100% foreign portfolio. Holding a mix of the two lowers the volatility of capital income, at least when some of the shocks are country-specific shocks, which is always the case in the real world.

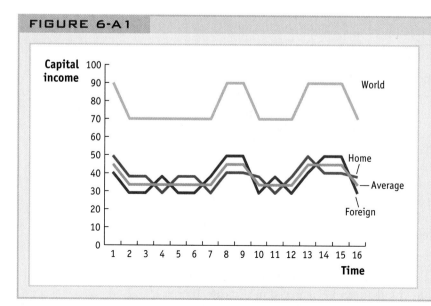

FIGURE 6-A1

Portfolio Diversification and Capital Income: Undiversifiable Risks We take the example from Table 6-6 and Figure 6-9 and we add a common "global" shock to each country. With probability 50%, each country experiences a five-unit increase in capital income, and with probability 50% experiences a five-unit decrease in capital income. Holding half of the world portfolio reduces *but does not eliminate* capital income risk entirely because the global shock is an undiversifiable risk for the world as a whole.

Balance of Payments II: Output, Exchange Rates, and Macroeconomic Policies in the Short Run

If demand shifts from the products of country B to the products of country A, a depreciation by country B or an appreciation by country A would correct the external imbalance and also relieve unemployment in country B and restrain inflation in country A. This is the most favorable case for flexible exchange rates based on national currencies.

Robert Mundell, 1961

It is easy to understand the dislike . . . for a [fixed exchange rate] system which dictated that a slump must be aggravated by monetary reactions, although, doubtless, [people] had forgotten that the same system served to enhance booms.

Alec Ford, 1962

In November 2004, the president of the European Central Bank, Jean-Claude Trichet, declared that the movements in the euro–dollar exchange rate were "not welcome from the standpoint of the ECB." He also called the movements "brutal," repeating the same term he had used in January 2004. However, later the same month, Alan Greenspan, then chairman of the U.S. Federal Reserve, seemed perfectly at ease as he hinted that movements in the dollar's exchange rate were most likely to continue as an acceptable means of macroeconomic adjustment for the U.S. economy. Why was the ECB president so fretful? Why was his American counterpart so relaxed? Clearly—in the view of at least one of the central bankers—the exchange rate must matter for the economy as a whole.

Thus far our study of exchange rates has been largely disconnected from the rest of the economy. In Chapters 2 through 4, we were able to develop a simple and coherent theory of exchange rates, but we treated the economy's level of output as given. To arrive at a more complete macroeconomic model, we now need to take an important step forward, extending our theory to address the more relevant case in which both exchange rates and output can fluctuate in the short run. To do this, we must also make use of Chapter 5, which provided us with an accounting framework in which to understand how macroeconomic aggregates (including output, income, consumption, investment, and the trade balance) fit together in the open economy.

The model we study is an open-economy variant of the well-known IS-LM model that is widely used in the study of closed-economy macroeconomics. The key assumption of this type of Keynesian model is that prices are "sticky" in the short run so that output is determined by shifts in demand in the goods market. When we are finished, we will have a model that explains the relationships among all the major macroeconomic variables in an open economy in the short run.

Naturally, such a model can shed light on many issues of concern to policy makers. To see how monetary and fiscal policy affect the economy, we put the model to use and discuss how such policies can be used to stabilize the economy, maintain full employment, and avoid booms and busts. One key lesson of this chapter is that the feasibility and effectiveness of macroeconomic policies depend crucially on the type of exchange rate regime in operation.

1 Demand in the Open Economy

To understand short-run macroeconomic fluctuations, we need to understand how short-run disturbances affect three important markets in an economy: the goods market, the money market, and the forex market. In Chapters 2 through 4, we studied the forex market and the money market. As we build this new model, we will recap and apply what we learned in those chapters. What about the goods market? In earlier chapters, we assumed that output was fixed at a level $\overline{Y}$. We took this to be the full-employment level of output that would be expected to prevail in the long run, when all factor market prices adjust to ensure that all factors like labor and capital are employed. But these assumptions are valid only in the long run. We must now develop a short-run model of the goods market. We construct a Keynesian model in which prices are sticky in the short run, and we then show how fluctuations in demand can create fluctuations in real economic activity.

To start building this model, in this section we first have to make our assumptions clear and then understand how demand is defined and why it fluctuates. Then, drawing on the expenditure accounting we learned in Chapter 5, we build a model of aggregate demand based on its constituent parts: private consumption demand (C), investment demand (I), government purchases (G), and the trade balance (TB). Once we understand the various factors that influence these components of demand, we then describe the short-run goods market equilibrium.

Preliminaries and Assumptions

Our interest in this chapter is to study short-run fluctuations in a simplified, abstract world of two countries. Our main focus is the home economy. We use an asterisk to denote foreign variables when we need them. For our purposes, the foreign economy can be thought of as "the rest of the world" (ROW). The key assumptions we make are as follows:

- Because we are examining the short run, we assume that home and foreign price levels, $\overline{P}$ and $\overline{P^*}$, are fixed due to price stickiness. As a result of price stickiness, expected inflation is fixed at zero, $\overline{\pi^e} = 0$. If prices are fixed in this way, all quantities can be treated as both real and nominal quantities in the short run because there is no inflation in the short run.

- We also assume that government spending $\overline{G}$ and taxes $\overline{T}$ are fixed at some constant level, which may be subject to policy change.

- We also assume that conditions in the foreign economy such as foreign output $\overline{Y^*}$ and the foreign interest rate $\overline{i^*}$ are fixed and taken as given. Our main interest is in the home economy—its equilibrium and its fluctuations.

- We also simplify by treating output and income as equivalent, so that Q equals Y; that is, gross domestic product (GDP) equals gross national disposable income $(GNDI)$. From Chapter 5, we know that the difference between the two equals net factor income from abroad plus net unilateral transfers. The analysis in this chapter could easily be extended to include these additional sources of income, but this adds additional complexity without offering any further insights. So for now, we ignore those issues.

- We assume that net factor income from abroad $(NFIA)$ and net unilateral transfers (NUT) are zero, which also implies that the current account (CA) equals the trade balance (TB), so for the rest of this chapter, we shall just refer to the trade balance.

Our main objective is to understand the determination of output (income) in the home economy. As we learned in Chapter 5, output (supply of goods) must equal total expenditure (demand for goods). In turn, the demand for goods and services is made up of four components: consumption, investment, government consumption, and the trade balance. We next examine each component of demand in turn and seek to understand its short-run determinants.

Consumption

The simplest model of aggregate private consumption relates household **consumption** C to **disposable income** Y^d. As we learned in Chapter 5, disposable income is the level of total pretax income Y received by households minus the taxes paid by households $\overline{T}$, so that $Y^d = Y - \overline{T}$. Consumers tend to consume more as their disposable income rises, a relationship that can be represented by an increasing function, called the consumption function:

$$\text{Consumption} = C = C(Y - \overline{T})$$

A typical consumption function of this form is shown in Figure 7-1; it slopes upward because consumption increases when disposable income increases.

This is known as the *Keynesian consumption function,* and it is based on very different assumptions about consumer behavior than the ones we employed in the last chapter. In Chapter 6, we studied how countries might engage in consumption smoothing so that consumption in any given year did not depend on income in that year, at least in theory. In contrast, the Keynesian consumption function seen here assumes that private consumption expenditure *is* sensitive to changes in current income. This assumption seems to be a reasonable match with reality, at least in the short run, given the empirical finding that there is very little consumption smoothing seen in practice.

Marginal Effects The slope of the consumption function is called the **marginal propensity to consume (MPC),** and it tells us how much of every extra $1 of disposable income received by households is spent on consumption. We generally assume that *MPC* is between 0 and 1: when consumers receive an extra unit of disposable income (whether it's a euro, dollar, or yen), they will consume only a fraction of it and save the remainder. For example, if you elect to spend $0.75 of every extra $1 of disposable income you receive, your *MPC* is 0.75. We can also define the *marginal propensity to save (MPS)* as $1 - MPC$, so in this example $MPS = 0.25$, meaning that $0.25 of every extra $1 of disposable income is saved.

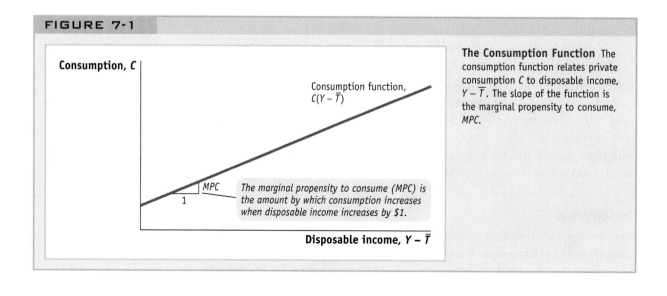

FIGURE 7-1

The Consumption Function The consumption function relates private consumption C to disposable income, $Y - \overline{T}$. The slope of the function is the marginal propensity to consume, *MPC*.

Investment

The simplest model of aggregate investment acknowledges that firms face an array of possible investment projects with differing real returns and states that a firm will invest capital in a project only if the real returns exceed the firm's cost of borrowing capital. The firm's borrowing cost is the **expected real interest rate** r^e, which equals the nominal interest rate i minus the expected rate of inflation π^e, so that $r^e = i - \pi^e$. It is important to note that in general the expected real interest rate depends not only on the nominal interest rate but also on expected inflation. However, under the simplifying assumption we made previously that expected inflation is zero, the expected real interest rate equals the nominal interest rate, $r^e = i$.

When the expected real interest rate in the economy falls, we expect more investment projects to be undertaken. For example, at a real interest rate of 10%, there may be only $1 billion worth of profitable investment projects that firms wish to undertake; but if the real interest rate falls to 5%, there may now be $2 billion worth of profitable projects. Hence, our model assumes that investment I is a decreasing function of the real interest rate; that is, investment falls as the real interest rate rises.

$$\text{Investment} = I = I(i)$$

Remember that this is true only because when expected inflation is zero, the real interest rate equals the nominal interest rate. Figure 7-2 shows a typical investment function of this type. It slopes downward because as the real interest rate falls, the quantity of investment rises.

The Government

The functions of the government in this model are simple. It collects an amount T of **taxes** from private households and spends an amount G on **government consumption** of goods and services.

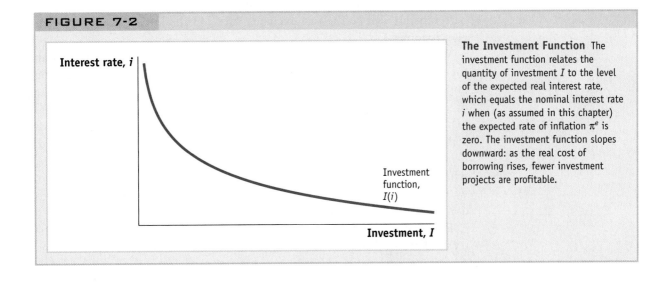

FIGURE 7-2

Interest rate, i

Investment function, $I(i)$

Investment, I

The Investment Function The investment function relates the quantity of investment I to the level of the expected real interest rate, which equals the nominal interest rate i when (as assumed in this chapter) the expected rate of inflation π^e is zero. The investment function slopes downward: as the real cost of borrowing rises, fewer investment projects are profitable.

Note that the latter includes only actual spending on actual goods and services bought by the public sector at all levels. For example, G includes military equipment and personnel, transport and infrastructure, public universities and schools, and so forth. Excluded from this concept are the often-huge sums involved in government **transfer programs,** programs that redistribute income between households, such as social security, medical care, or unemployment benefit systems. Such transfers are excluded because we assume that *in the aggregate* they do not generate any change in the total expenditure on goods and services; they merely change who gets to engage in the act of spending.

In the unlikely event that $G = T$ exactly, government spending exactly equals taxes and we say that the government has a *balanced budget*. If $T > G$, the government is said to be running a *budget surplus* (of size $T - G$); if $G > T$, a *budget deficit* (of size $G - T$ or, equivalently, a negative surplus of $T - G$).

Fiscal policy is concerned with the levels of taxes T and spending G set by the government. In this chapter, we do not study in detail why or how governments make such policy choices; we make the simple assumption that the levels of taxes and spending are set exogenously, at least in the short run, at some fixed levels, denoted by an overbar:

$$\text{Government purchases} = G = \overline{G};$$
$$\text{Taxes} = T = \overline{T}.$$

Policy makers may change these levels of taxes and spending at any time. We analyze the impact of such changes on the economy later in this chapter.

The Trade Balance

In Chapter 5, we saw from an accounting standpoint that the trade balance, equal to exports minus imports, measures the impact of foreign trade on the demand for domestic output. We now move beyond accounting and develop a model of what determines imports and exports. The key determinants will be the real exchange rate and the level of home and foreign incomes.

What is the role of the exchange rate? Recall George, the American tourist we met at the start of Chapter 2, who was faced with a depreciating dollar-euro exchange rate during his repeated visits to Paris over the course of several years. If U.S. and French prices are sticky (constant in euros and U.S. dollar terms), then as the U.S. exchange rate depreciates, French goods and services became more and more expensive in dollar terms. In the end, George was ready to take a vacation in California instead. In the aggregate, when spending patterns change in response to changes in the exchange rate, we say that there is **expenditure switching** from foreign purchases to domestic purchases.

Expenditure switching is a major factor in determining the level of a country's exports and imports. In Chapter 3, we learned that the real exchange rate is the price of goods and services in a foreign economy relative to the price of goods and services in the home economy. If the home country's exchange rate is E, the home price level is $\overline{P}$ (fixed in the short run), and the foreign price level is $\overline{P}^*$ (also fixed in the short run), then the real exchange rate q of the home country is defined as $q = E\overline{P}^*/\overline{P}$.

For example, suppose that the home country is the United States, and the reference basket of goods costs \$100; suppose that in Canada the same basket costs C\$120 and the exchange rate is \$0.90 per Canadian dollar. In the expression $q = E\overline{P}^*/\overline{P}$, the numerator $E\overline{P}^*$ is the price of foreign goods converted into home currency terms, $\$108 = 120 \times 0.90$; the denominator $\overline{P}$ is the home currency price of home goods, \$100; the ratio of the two is the real exchange rate, $q = \$108/\$100 = 1.08$. This is the relative price of foreign goods in terms of home goods. In this case, U.S. goods are cheaper than Canadian goods.

A rise in the real exchange rate (a depreciation) signifies that foreign goods have become more expensive relative to home goods. As the real exchange rate rises, both home and foreign consumers will respond by *expenditure switching*: the home country will import less (as *home* consumers switch to buying home goods) and export more (as *foreign* consumers switch to buying home goods). For example, in the preceding example, we would expect Canadians to switch to buying U.S. goods as U.S. goods get cheaper relative to Canadian goods (see **Headlines: Soaring Loonie Drives Canadian Shoppers South**). These arguments provide a first insight:

■ *We expect the trade balance of the home country to be an increasing function of the home country's real exchange rate.*

The other determinant of the trade balance we might wish to consider is the income level in each country. As we argued earlier in our discussion of the consumption function, when domestic disposable income increases, consumers tend to spend more on all forms of consumption, including consumption of foreign goods. These arguments provide a second insight:

■ *We expect an increase in home income to be associated with an increase in home imports and a fall in the home country's trade balance.*

Symmetrically, from the rest of the world's standpoint, an increase in rest of the world income ought to be associated with an increase in rest of the world spending on home goods, resulting in an increase in home exports. This is our third insight:

■ *We expect an increase in rest of the world income to be associated with an increase in home exports and a rise in the home country's trade balance.*

Combining the three lessons, we can write the trade balance as a function of three variables, namely, the real exchange rate, home disposable income, and rest of the world disposable income:

$$TB = TB(\underbrace{E\overline{P}^*/\overline{P}}_{\substack{\text{Increasing} \\ \text{function}}}, \underbrace{Y - T}_{\substack{\text{Decreasing} \\ \text{function}}}, \underbrace{Y^* - T^*}_{\substack{\text{Increasing} \\ \text{function}}}).$$

HEADLINES

Soaring Loonie Drives Canadian Shoppers South

Following exchange rate appreciations, Canadians traditionally head south to shop, and they still do so despite the increased hassles and delays at the border.

Bellingham is a small city just an hour's drive from Vancouver, excluding what can be lengthy delays to clear the border, but the shopping experience is light years distant from Canada. There are more brands, greater variety—and best of all, far lower prices for many goods.

With the rise of the Canadian dollar toward parity with the U.S. greenback for the first time in three decades, more and more Canadians are headed to Bellingham, where staff in many of the stores say half their business comes from north of the border, and other U.S. border towns. Business is booming, too, for Canadian customs officials, where lineups can grow to several hours at peak weekend times.

Al Weber, hopping across the border from Surrey, B.C., rattles off the value of the Canadian dollar—to two decimal places—as he prepares to plunge into the shopping bliss of Bellis Fair, where virtually every store is advertising deep discounts and even regularly priced items are far below the cost of comparable Canadian goods.

Two hours later, Mr. Weber re-emerges with a pair of shorts and a shirt that cost him $30, but would have set him back as much as $100 (Canadian) in Surrey, he says. But the savings won't be spent in Canada. "Now, he's taking me out for lunch," his wife, Gale Weber, said with a grin.

That one purchase sums up the challenge for Canada's retail sector: A yawning discrepancy in prices threatens to draw consumers south of the border, now that the currency gap has dramatically narrowed. . . .

The story is the same across the northern United States, including New York, where the parking lot of Buffalo's Walden Galleria is awash in Ontario licence plates, even on a weekday.

Buoyed by the strong Canadian dollar, Debbie Gresko and her teenaged daughter, Brooke, made the trek to Buffalo this week to do some shopping. And shop they did: two pairs of jeans for $22 (U.S.); five T-shirts for $5.99 each; a picture frame for $12.99; a pair of shoes for $40; a shirt at Hollister for $40; and $155 worth of merchandise at Target. . . .

"If it [the dollar] was extremely low, we wouldn't have come. We're not silly," said Ms. Gresko, resting her bags. But, she added, lower taxes and the huge sales are an added inducement. Delays at the border, even the $71 in duties and taxes that the Greskos had to pay, aren't much of a worry. So long as the dollar remains strong,

she plans to do another round of cross-border shopping before Christmas. . . .

The rise in the dollar has removed the biggest barrier to cross-border shopping, but others remain. Duties are a factor. Even though goods made within the NAFTA zone of Canada, the U.S. and Mexico are free of such surcharges, there is still an abundance of products from other countries that will have added costs.

And there is the cost of the trip itself, both in money and time. Waiting times at busy border crossings can soar on weekends; even midweek, those using the Pacific Gate crossing to return to Canada faced an 80-minute delay. . . .

But the biggest danger for domestic retailers is that a taste of the U.S. shopping experience may prove addictive for Canadians, whatever the technical hindrances and irritations. . . .

Source: Excerpted from Patrick Brethour and Caroline Alphonso, "Soaring Loonie Drives Canadian Shoppers South," Toronto Globe and Mail, July 28, 2007.

We show the relationship between the trade balance and the real exchange rate in Figure 7-3, for the home country, all else equal—that is, holding home and foreign disposable income fixed. The trade balance is an *increasing* function of the real exchange rate $E\bar{P}^{*}/\bar{P}$. Thus, the relationship shown in Figure 7-3 is upward sloping. The reason is that an increase in the real

FIGURE 7-3

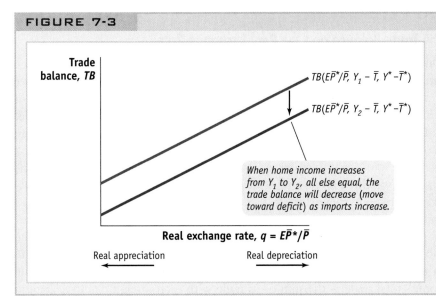

The Trade Balance and the Real Exchange Rate The trade balance is an increasing function of the real exchange rate $E\overline{P}^*/\overline{P}$. When there is a real depreciation (a rise in q), foreign goods become more expensive relative to home goods, and we expect the trade balance to increase as exports rise and imports fall (a rise in TB). The trade balance may also depend on income. If home income levels rise, then some of the increase in income may be spent on the consumption of imports. For example, if home income rises from Y_1 to Y_2, then the trade balance will decrease, whatever the level of the real exchange rate, and the trade balance function will shift down.

exchange rate (a real depreciation) increases TB by raising exports and lowering imports, implying a movement along the curve drawn.

The effect of the real exchange rate on the trade balance is now clear. What about the effects of changes in output? An illustration of the impact of an increase in home output on the trade balance is shown in Figure 7-3. At any level of the real exchange rate, an increase in home output leads to more spending on imports, lowering the trade balance. This would be represented as a downward shift in the trade balance curve, that is, a reduction in TB for a given level of Y.

Marginal Effects The impact of changes in output on the trade balance can also be thought of in terms of the marginal propensity to consume. Suppose home output (which equals home income here) rises by an amount $\Delta Y = \$1$ and that, all else equal, this leads to an increase in home imports of $\Delta IM = \$MPC_F$, where $MPC_F > 0$. We refer to MPC_F as the *marginal propensity to consume foreign imports*. For example, if $MPC_F = 0.1$, this means that out of every additional $\$1$ of income, $\$0.10 = 10$ cents are spent on imports.

How does MPC_F relate to the MPC seen earlier? After a $\$1$ rise in income, any additional goods consumed have to come from somewhere, home or abroad. The fraction $\$MPC$ of the $\$1$ increment spent on all consumption must equal the sum of the incremental spending on home goods plus incremental spending on foreign goods. Let $MPC_H > 0$ be the *marginal propensity to consume home goods*. By assumption, $MPC = MPC_H + MPC_F$. For example, if $MPC_F = 0.10$ and $MPC_H = 0.65$, then $MPC = 0.75$; for every extra dollar of disposable income, home consumers spend 75 cents, 10 cents on imported foreign goods and 65 cents on home goods.[1]

---

[1] A similar calculation can be applied to the export function, where exports will depend on the marginal propensity to consume imports in the foreign country.

APPLICATION

The Trade Balance and the Real Exchange Rate

Our theory assumes that the trade balance increases when the real exchange rate rises. Is there evidence to support this proposition? In Figure 7-4, we examine the evolution of the U.S. trade balance (as a share of GDP) in recent years as compared with the U.S. real exchange rate with the rest of the world.

By considering the home country to be the United States and the foreign "country" to be the rest of the world, we cannot use data on the bilateral real exchange rate q available for any individual foreign country. We need a composite or weighted average measure of the price of goods in all foreign countries relative to the price of U.S. goods. To accomplish this, economists construct *multilateral* measures of real exchange rate movement.

As with multilateral nominal exchange rates discussed in Chapter 2, the most common weighting scheme uses a weight equal to that country's share in the home country's trade. If there are N foreign countries, we can write home's total trade as the sum of its trade with each foreign country: Trade = $\text{Trade}_1 + \text{Trade}_2 + ... + \text{Trade}_N$. Applying a trade weight to each bilateral exchange rate change, we can obtain the percentage change in home's multilateral real exchange rate or **real effective exchange rate:**

$$\frac{\Delta q_{\text{effective}}}{q_{\text{effective}}} = \underbrace{\left(\frac{\text{Trade}_1}{\text{Trade}}\frac{\Delta q_1}{q_1}\right) + \left(\frac{\text{Trade}_2}{\text{Trade}}\frac{\Delta q_2}{q_2}\right) + ... + \left(\frac{\text{Trade}_N}{\text{Trade}}\frac{\Delta q_N}{q_N}\right)}_{\text{Trade-weighted average of bilateral real exchange rate changes}}.$$

FIGURE 7-4

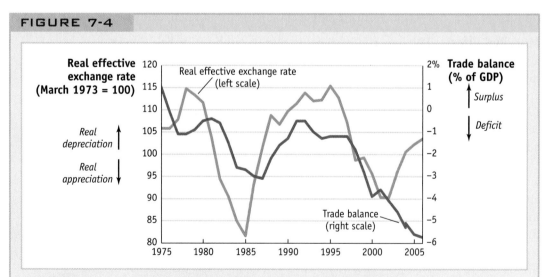

The Real Exchange Rate and the Trade Balance: United States, 1975-2006 Does the real exchange rate affect the trade balance in the way we have assumed? The data show that the U.S. trade balance is correlated with the U.S. real effective exchange rate index. Because the trade balance also depends on changes in U.S. and rest of the world disposable income (and other factors), it may respond with a lag to changes in the real exchange rate, so the correlation is not perfect (as seen in the years 2000 to 2006).

Sources: U.S. Federal Reserve; Bureau of Economic Analysis NIPA.

For example, if we trade 40% with country 1 and 60% with country 2, and we have a real appreciation of 10% against 1 but a real depreciation of 30% against 2, then the change in our real effective exchange rate is (40% × −10%) + (60% × 30%) = (0.4 × −0.1) + (0.6 × 0.3) = −0.04 + 0.18 = 0.14 = + 14%. That is, we have experienced an effective trade-weighted real depreciation of 14%.

Figure 7-4 shows that the U.S. multilateral real exchange rate and the U.S. trade balance are positively correlated, as predicted by our model. In periods when the United States has experienced a real depreciation (a rise in the real effective exchange rate), the U.S. trade balance has tended to increase. Conversely, real appreciations (periods when the real exchange rate falls) have usually been associated with a fall in the trade balance.

However, you may also notice from the figure that the correlation between changes in the real exchange rate and changes in the trade balance is not perfect. Indeed, there appears to be lag between, say, a real depreciation and a rise in the trade balance (as seen in the mid-1980s). This is not surprising. Our approach provides a simple model of the trade balance, but we should bear in mind that the variables do not always behave in the ways we've predicted. It is possible that the trade balance, and its underlying import and export orders, may react only slowly or weakly to changes in the real exchange rate and that the trade balance may react in unexpected ways (see **Side Bar: Barriers to Expenditure Switching: Pass-Through and the J Curve** and also the appendix to this chapter). We can also see that the U.S. trade balance and the real exchange rate move in opposite directions in the years 2000 to 2006. As we saw in Chapter 5, other factors, such as tax cuts and wartime spending, affected the U.S. current account in this period. ■

SIDE BAR

Barriers to Expenditure Switching: Pass-Through and the J Curve

The basic analysis in the text assumes that two key mechanisms are operating. First, we assume that a nominal depreciation causes a real depreciation and raises the price of foreign imports relative to home exports. Second, we assume that such a change in relative prices will lower imports, raise exports, and increase the trade balance. In reality, there are reasons why both mechanisms operate weakly or with a lag.

Trade Dollarization, Distribution, and Pass-Through

One assumption we made was that prices are sticky in local currency. But what if some *home* goods prices are set in *foreign* currency?

For example, let the foreign country be the United States and suppose a share d of the home-produced basket of goods is priced in U.S. dollars at a sticky *dollar* price $\overline{P}_1$. Suppose the remaining share, $1 - d$, is priced, as before, in local currency at a sticky *local currency* price, $\overline{P}_2$. Thus

$$\left.\begin{array}{l}\text{Price of foreign goods}\\\text{relative to dollar-priced}\\\text{home goods}\end{array}\right\} = \frac{E \times \overline{P}^*}{E \times \overline{P}_1} = \frac{\overline{P}^*}{\overline{P}_1} \text{ has a weight} = d$$

$$\left.\begin{array}{l}\text{Price of foreign goods}\\\text{relative to local-currency-priced}\\\text{home goods}\end{array}\right\} = \frac{E \times \overline{P}^*}{\overline{P}_2} \text{ has a weight} = 1 - d$$

What now is the price of all foreign-produced goods relative to all home-produced goods (the real exchange rate)? It is the weighted sum of the prices of the two parts of the basket. Hence, we find

$$q = \text{Home real exchange rate} = d\frac{\overline{P}^*}{\overline{P}_1} + (1 - d)\frac{E\overline{P}^*}{\overline{P}_2}.$$

The first term with a weight d does not contain E because both numerator and denominator are dollar prices (already

Continued on next page.

expressed in a common currency). Only the second term with a weight $(1 - d)$ contains E, since the prices are in different currencies. Thus, a 1% increase in E will lead to only a $(1 - d)$% increase in the real exchange rate.

When d is 0, all home goods are priced in local currency and we have our basic model. A 1% rise in E causes a 1% rise in q. There is full *pass-through* from changes in the nominal exchange rate to changes in the real exchange rate because changes in the *nominal* exchange rate "pass through" one to one into changes in the *real* exchange rate. But as d rises, pass-through falls. If d is 0.5, then a 1% rise in E causes just a 0.5% rise in q. The real exchange rate becomes less responsive to changes in the nominal exchange rate, and this means that expenditure switching effects will be muted.

So what? It turns out that many countries around the world conduct a large fraction of their trade in a currency other than their own, such as U.S. dollars. The most obvious examples of goods with dollar prices are the major commodities: oil, copper, wheat, and so on. For example, in a country in which exports are, say, more than 90% oil as they are in some Persian Gulf economies, a nominal depreciation of the exchange rate does almost nothing to change the price of exports (more than 90% of which are priced in dollars) relative to the price of imports (again, overwhelmingly priced in dollars).

But the phenomenon of dollar invoicing—and in Greater Europe, euro invoicing—extends to a much wider range of traded goods, as shown in Table 7-1. For example, 93% of U.S. imports are priced in dollars: if these prices are sticky, then a U.S. depreciation will hardly change the prices of these imports at all. The table also shows that some Asian countries have trade flows that are 70% to 90% dollarized. Much of this is intra-Asian trade itself; if, say, a Korean supplier sells to a Japanese manufacturer, very often they conduct the trade not in yen or won, but entirely in U.S. dollars, which is the currency of neither the exporter nor the importer! Finally, the table also shows that the phenomenon of foreign currency pricing extends to Europe: many Eurozone countries have large export shares denominated in dollars, and most "new accession" EU member states in Eastern Europe have export shares largely denominated in euros.

Trade dollarization is not the only factor limiting pass-through in the real world. There is also the problem that even after an import has arrived at the port, it still has to pass through various intermediaries before it reaches the final customer. The retail, wholesale, and other distribution activities all add a local currency cost or markup to the final price when the import is sold to the ultimate buyer. Suppose the markup is $100 on an import that costs $100 at the port, so the good retails for $200 in shops. Suppose a 10% devaluation of the dollar raises the port price to $110. All else

TABLE 7-1

Trade Dollarization The table shows the extent to which the dollar and the euro were used in the invoicing of payments for exports and imports of different countries. In the United States, for example, 100% of exports are invoiced and paid in U.S. dollars but so, too, are 93% of imports. In Asia, U.S. dollar invoicing is very common, accounting for 48% of Japanese exports and more than 75% of exports and imports in Korea, Malaysia, and Thailand. In Europe the euro figures more prominently as the currency used for trade, but the U.S. dollar is still used in a sizable share of transactions.

	Exports Denominated in		Imports Denominated in	
	U.S. Dollar	Euro	U.S. Dollar	Euro
United States	100%	—	93%	—
United Kingdom	26	21%	37	27%
Australia	70	1	50	9
Asia				
Japan	48	10	9	5
Korea	83	7	80	5
Malaysia	90	—	90	—
Thailand	85	3	76	4
Eurozone				
Belgium	32	55	33	57
France	34	52	47	45
Germany	24	63	34	55
Italy	18	75	25	70
Greece	46	47	55	40
Luxembourg	25	53	37	42
Portugal	28	55	33	60
Spain	30	61	36	60
EU new accession countries				
Bulgaria	35	62	34	64
Cyprus	45	22	35	46
Czech Rep.	13	70	18	66
Estonia	70	9	22	62
Hungary	12	83	19	73
Latvia	27	57	—	49
Poland	26	64	28	59
Slovakia	12	74	21	60
Slovenia	10	87	13	83

Source: Linda Goldberg and Cédric Tille, "The Internationalization of the Dollar and Trade Balance Adjustment," Federal Reserve Bank of New York Staff Report 255, August 2006.

equal, the retail price will rise to just $210, only a 5% increase at the point of final sale, so again the expenditure switching by final users will be muted by the limited pass-through from port prices to final prices. For example, a recent study of 76 developed and developing countries found that, over the period of one year, a 10% exchange rate depreciation resulted in a 6.5% rise in imported goods prices at the port of arrival but perhaps only a 4% rise in the retail prices of imported goods.*

The J Curve

Our model of the trade balance assumes that a real depreciation improves a country's trade balance by increasing exports and reducing imports. In reality, however, these effects may be slow to appear because orders for export and import goods are placed several months in advance, with payment made much later at the time of delivery. In this case, at the moment of depreciation there will be no instantaneous change in export and import volumes. Even after the typical lead time for orders has elapsed, it might still be the case that exports and imports respond sluggishly due to other frictions as firms and intermediaries try to cope with the changing demands of consumers in each country by expanding or contracting their capacity.

What does this slow adjustment imply? Exports will continue to sell for a time in the same quantity and at the same domestic price. Therefore, total export earnings remain fixed in the immediate aftermath of the depreciation. What will change is the domestic price paid for the import goods. They will have become more expensive in domestic currency terms—a little or a lot, depending on the extent of pass-through. If the same quantity of imports flows in but costs more per unit, then the home country's total import bill will have risen. As a result, with export earnings fixed but import expenditures rising, the trade balance will initially *fall* rather than rise, as shown in Figure 7-5. Only after time passes, and export and import orders adjust to the new relative prices, will the trade balance improve and shift in the positive direction we have assumed.

Because of its distinctive shape, the curve traced out by the trade balance over time in Figure 7-5 is called the *J Curve*. Some empirical studies find that the effects of the J Curve last up to a year after the initial depreciation. Hence, the assumption that a depreciation boosts spending on the home country's goods may not hold in the very short run.

FIGURE 7-5

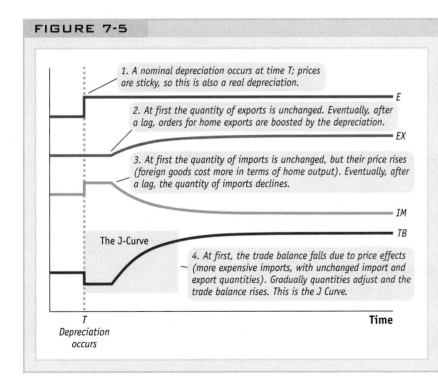

1. A nominal depreciation occurs at time T; prices are sticky, so this is also a real depreciation.

2. At first the quantity of exports is unchanged. Eventually, after a lag, orders for home exports are boosted by the depreciation.

3. At first the quantity of imports is unchanged, but their price rises (foreign goods cost more in terms of home output). Eventually, after a lag, the quantity of imports declines.

The J-Curve

4. At first, the trade balance falls due to price effects (more expensive imports, with unchanged import and export quantities). Gradually quantities adjust and the trade balance rises. This is the J Curve.

T
Depreciation occurs

Time

The J Curve When prices are sticky and there is a nominal and real depreciation of the home currency, it may take time for the trade balance to move toward surplus. In fact, the initial impact may be toward deficit. If firms and households place orders in advance, then import and export quantities may react sluggishly to changes in the relative price of home and foreign goods. Hence, just after the depreciation, the value of home exports *EX* will be unchanged. However, home imports now cost more due to the depreciation. Thus, the value of imports *IM* would actually *rise* after a depreciation, causing the trade balance $TB = EX - IM$ to fall. Only after some time would exports rise and imports fall, allowing the trade balance to rise relative to its predepreciation level. The path traced by the trade balance during this process looks vaguely like a letter J.

---

* Jeffrey A. Frankel, David C. Parsley, and Shang-Jin Wei, 2005, "Slow Passthrough around the World: A New Import for Developing Countries?" National Bureau of Economic Research (NBER) Working Paper No. 11199.

Exogenous Changes in Demand

We have already treated as given, or exogenous, the changes or *shocks* in demand that originate in changes to government purchases or taxes. However, other exogenous changes in demand can affect consumption, investment, or the trade balance, and it is important to know how to analyze these, too. Examples of such changes are illustrated in Figure 7-6.

■ *An exogenous change in consumption.* Suppose that at any given level of disposable income, consumers decide to spend more on consumption

FIGURE 7-6

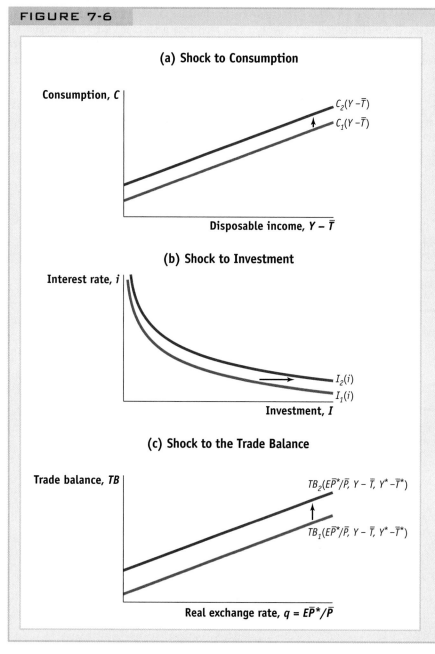

Exogenous Shocks to Consumption, Investment, and the Trade Balance (a) When households decide to consume more at any given level of disposable income, the consumption function shifts up. (b) When firms decide to invest more at any given level of the interest rate, the investment function shifts right. (c) When the trade balance increases at any given level of the real exchange rate, the trade balance function shifts up.

purchases. After this shock, the curve depicting the consumption function would shift up as in Figure 7-6, panel (a). For example, a sudden increase in household wealth following a stock market or housing market boom could lead to a shift in consumption of this sort, an effect that some economists consider an important factor in demand in many countries in recent years. This increase in wealth is a change in consumption demand unconnected to disposable income.

■ *An exogenous change in investment.* Suppose that at any given level of the interest rate, firms decide to invest more. After this shock, the curve depicting the investment function would shift up as in Figure 7-6, panel (b). For example, a belief that high-technology companies had great prospects for success led to a large surge in investment in this sector in many countries in the 1990s. This represented a change in investment demand unconnected to the interest rate.

■ *An exogenous change in the trade balance.* Suppose that at any given level of the real exchange rate, export demand rises and/or import demand falls. After one of these shocks, the curve depicting the trade balance function would shift up as in Figure 7-6, panel (c). Such a change happened in the 1980s in Japan when U.S. consumers' tastes shifted away from the large, domestic automobiles made in Detroit toward smaller, fuel-efficient, imported cars made in Japan. This represented a switch in demand away from U.S. and toward Japanese products unconnected with the real exchange rate.

2 Goods Market Equilibrium: The Keynesian Cross

We have now studied the determinants of each component of demand. We next put all the components together and show that the goods market is in equilibrium when total demand from all these components is equal to total supply.

Supply and Demand

The total aggregate *supply* of final goods and services is equal to total national output measured by *GDP*. Given our assumption that the current account equals the trade balance, gross national income Y equals *GDP*:

$$\text{Supply} = GDP = Y.$$

Aggregate demand, or just demand, consists of all the possible sources of demand for this real output. In Chapter 5, we studied the expenditure side of the national income accounts and identified several possible sources of demand: consumption, investment, government purchases, and the trade balance. In the previous section, we presented simple mathematical expressions for each of these components of demand, so we can now aggregate them and establish the conditions for an equilibrium in which demand is equal to supply.

In the national accounts, total output (Y) is allocated across all uses according to the national income identity. This accounting identity *always* holds true. But an identity is not an economic model. A model must explain how, in equilibrium, the observed demands take on their desired or planned values and still satisfy the accounting identity. How can we construct such a model?

We may write total demand for *GDP* as

$$\text{Demand} = D = C + I + G + TB.$$

We can substitute the formulae for consumption, investment, and the trade balance presented in the first section of this chapter into this total demand equation to obtain

$$D = C(Y - \overline{T}) + I(i) + \overline{G} + TB(E\overline{P}^*/\overline{P}, Y - \overline{T}, Y^* - \overline{T}^*).$$

In an equilibrium, demand D must equal supply Y, so from the preceding two equations we can see that the **goods market equilibrium condition** is simply

$$(7\text{-}1) \qquad Y = \underbrace{C(Y - \overline{T}) + I(i) + \overline{G} + TB(E\overline{P}^*/\overline{P}, Y - \overline{T}, Y^* - \overline{T}^*).}_{\text{Demand } D}$$

Determinants of Demand

The right-hand side of Equation (7-1) shows that many factors can affect demand: home and foreign output (Y and Y^*), home and foreign taxes (T and T^*), the home nominal interest rate (i), and the real exchange rate ($E\overline{P}^*/\overline{P}$). Let us examine each of these in turn. We start with home output Y, and assume that all other factors remain fixed.

A rise in output Y (all else equal) will cause the right-hand side to increase. For example, suppose there is an increase in output of $\Delta Y = \$1$. This change causes consumption spending C to increase by $+\$MPC$. The change in imports will be $+\$MPC_F$, causing the trade balance to change by $-\$MPC_F$. So the total change in D will be $\$(MPC - MPC_F) = \$MPC_H > 0$, a positive number. This is an intuitive result: an extra $\$1$ of output generates some spending on home goods (an amount $\$MPC_H$), with the remainder either spent on foreign goods (an amount $\$MPC_F$) or saved (an amount $\$MPS$).

Using this result, Figure 7-7 panel (a) plots demand D, the right-hand side of Equation (7-1), as a function of income or output Y only. For the moment, we hold fixed all other determinants of D. Because D increases as Y increases, the demand function has a positive slope MPC_H, a number between 0 and 1.

Also drawn is the 45-degree line, which represents Y, the left-hand side of Equation (7-1). The 45-degree line has a slope of 1, so it is steeper than the demand function.

This diagram is often called the *Keynesian cross*. It depicts the goods market equilibrium: the goods market is in equilibrium at point 1 where the two lines intersect, for that is the unique point where $D = Y$. This corresponds to an income or output level of Y_1.

Why does the goods market adjust to an equilibrium at this point? To the right of point 1, output tends to fall; to the left of point 1, output tends to rise. Why? At point 2, the output level is Y_2 and demand D exceeds supply Y; as inventories fall, firms expand production and output rises toward Y_1. At point 3, the output level is Y_3 and supply Y exceeds demand; as

FIGURE 7-7

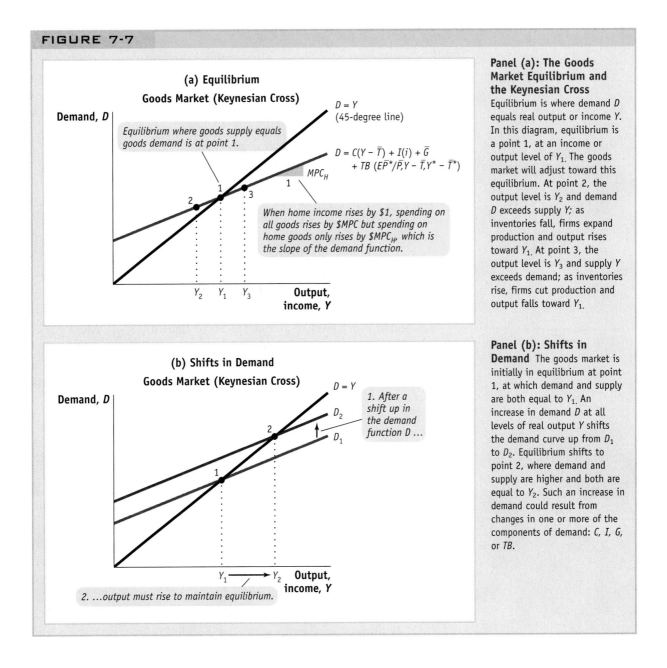

(a) Equilibrium
Goods Market (Keynesian Cross)

Demand, *D*

$D = Y$
(45-degree line)

Equilibrium where goods supply equals goods demand is at point 1.

$D = C(Y - \bar{T}) + I(i) + \bar{G}$
$+ TB (E\bar{P}^*/\bar{P}, Y - \bar{T}, Y^* - \bar{T}^*)$

MPC_H

When home income rises by $1, spending on all goods rises by $MPC but spending on home goods only rises by MPC_H, which is the slope of the demand function.

Y_2 Y_1 Y_3 **Output, income, Y**

(b) Shifts in Demand
Goods Market (Keynesian Cross)

Demand, *D*

$D = Y$

D_2

D_1

1. After a shift up in the demand function *D* ...

Y_1 ⟶ Y_2 **Output, income, Y**

2. ...output must rise to maintain equilibrium.

Panel (a): The Goods Market Equilibrium and the Keynesian Cross Equilibrium is where demand *D* equals real output or income *Y*. In this diagram, equilibrium is a point 1, at an income or output level of Y_1. The goods market will adjust toward this equilibrium. At point 2, the output level is Y_2 and demand *D* exceeds supply *Y*; as inventories fall, firms expand production and output rises toward Y_1. At point 3, the output level is Y_3 and supply *Y* exceeds demand; as inventories rise, firms cut production and output falls toward Y_1.

Panel (b): Shifts in Demand The goods market is initially in equilibrium at point 1, at which demand and supply are both equal to Y_1. An increase in demand *D* at all levels of real output *Y* shifts the demand curve up from D_1 to D_2. Equilibrium shifts to point 2, where demand and supply are higher and both are equal to Y_2. Such an increase in demand could result from changes in one or more of the components of demand: *C, I, G,* or *TB*.

inventories rise, firms cut production and output falls toward Y_1. Only at point 1 are firms in an equilibrium in which production levels are stable in the short run.

Note the crucial assumptions in this model are that prices are fixed and firms are willing to adjust their production and employment to meet whatever the desired level of demand happens to be. These assumptions may be plausible in the short run, but they will not apply in the long run, when prices can adjust and output and employment will be determined by the economy's ability to fully employ its technology and resources.

Factors That Shift the Demand Curve

The Keynesian cross also allows us to examine the impact of the other factors in Equation (7-1) on goods market equilibrium. Let's look at four important cases:

- A fall in taxes $\overline{T}$ (all else equal) increases disposable income. When consumers have more disposable income, they spend more on consumption. The increase in disposable income, through its effects on consumption C, raises demand at every level of output Y because C is increasing in disposable income. This is seen in Equation (7-1) and in Figure 7-7 panel (a). Thus, a fall in taxes can be depicted as an upward shift in the demand function from D_1 to D_2, as shown in Figure 7-7 panel (b). The increase in demand causes goods market equilibrium shifts from point 1 to point 2, to an output level Y_2. The lesson: any exogenous change in C (due to changes in taxes, tastes, and so on) will cause the demand curve to shift.

- An exogenous rise in government purchases $\overline{G}$ (all else equal) increases demand at every level of output as seen in Equation (7-1). More government purchases directly add to the total demand in the economy. This change results in an upward shift in the demand function D, again as in Figure 7-7 panel (b). The increase in demand causes goods market equilibrium shifts from point 1 to point 2, to an output level Y_2. The lesson: any exogenous change in G (due to changes in the government budget) will cause the demand curve to shift.

- A fall in the interest rate i (all else equal) will lead to an increase in I, as in Figure 7-6 panel (b). When firms face a lower interest rate, they find it profitable to engage in more investment projects, so they spend more. This leads to an increase in demand D, at every level of output Y. This change can be depicted as an upward shift in the demand function D, as seen in Equation (7-1) and Figure 7-7, panel (b). The increase in demand causes goods market equilibrium shifts from point 1 to point 2, to an output level Y_2. The lesson: any exogenous change in I (due to changes in interest rates, the expected profitability of investment, changes in tax policy, and so on) will cause the demand curve to shift.

- A rise in the nominal exchange rate E (all else equal) implies a rise in the real exchange rate EP^*/P (due to sticky prices). This is a real depreciation, and through its effects on TB via expenditure switching, it will increase demand D at any given level of home output Y. For example, Americans switch their spending from foreign goods to American goods when the dollar depreciates. This change can be depicted yet again as an upward shift in the demand function D, and yet again as in Figure 7-7 panel (b). The lesson: any change in the real exchange rate will cause the demand curve to shift (see **Headlines: Expenditure Switching and the Dollar Devaluation**).

HEADLINES

Expenditure Switching and the Dollar Devaluation

From 2001 to 2004, the U.S. dollar began a sustained depreciation against many currencies. The economic impacts were reflected in the following string of pronouncements—in the space of just one week—from all corners of the globe and found in the Financial Times.

Dollar's dive set to delight exporters as well as tourists *January 9, 2004.* Listen carefully to the crowds shuffling down New York's Fifth Avenue, and the more immediate effects of the plummeting dollar are obvious in the voices of European shoppers enjoying dramatic increases in purchasing power. One couple from London caused a stir at Saks department store by walking in and spending $25,000 on a single diamond necklace. . . . By the fourth quarter of this year, the National Association of Manufacturers expects exports to be up by 12 per cent, with its members also benefiting from falling imports as rivals abroad struggle

with the other side of the exchange rate coin.

Euro's rapid rise worries ECB *January 9, 2004.* The European Central Bank yesterday signaled its growing unease over the rapid rise of the euro against the dollar. . . . Jean Claude Trichet, bank president, said repeatedly the bank did not like "excessive volatility" in foreign exchange markets. . . . Pascal Lamy, the EU's trade commissioner, said the euro was approaching a level that could be worrying for the competitiveness of the eurozone's exporters.

Euro erodes Germany's role as an industrial powerhouse *January 13, 2004.* The currency's seemingly unstoppable

ascent against the dollar is speeding an industrial decline. . . . Economists expect even more jobs to go as German companies struggle to cut costs and boost productivity.

Strong currency hits Australians *January 13, 2004.* Almost one in five Australian manufacturers are considering moving production offshore because of the strengthening of the Australian dollar in the past two years, says a report. . . . The study, based on a survey of 800 manufacturers, found that lost sales due to import penetration were at least as significant as lower export returns. . . . "At this level exports struggle to compete on world markets," it said.

Summary

An increase in output Y causes a move along the demand curve. But any increase in demand that is *not* due to a change in output Y will instead cause the demand curve itself to shift upward in the Keynesian cross diagram, as in Figure 7-7 panel (b). Similarly, any contraction in demand not due to income changes will cause the demand function to shift downward.

To conclude, the main factors that shift the demand curve out can be summed up as follows:

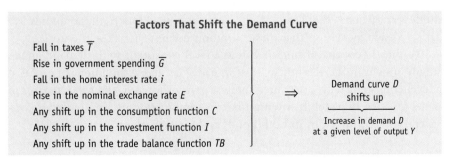

Factors That Shift the Demand Curve

Fall in taxes $\overline{T}$
Rise in government spending $\overline{G}$
Fall in the home interest rate i
Rise in the nominal exchange rate E
Any shift up in the consumption function C
Any shift up in the investment function I
Any shift up in the trade balance function TB

$\Rightarrow$

Demand curve D shifts up

Increase in demand D at a given level of output Y

The opposite changes will, of course, lead to a decrease in demand and shift the demand curve in.

3 Goods and Forex Market Equilibria: Deriving the IS Curve

We have made an important first step in our study of the short-run behavior of exchange rates and output. Our analysis of demand shows how the level of output in the economy adjusts to ensure a goods market equilibrium, given the levels of each component of demand. Each component in turn has its own particular determinants, and we have examined how shifts in these determinants or in other exogenous factors might shift the level of demand and hence the level of output required to ensure goods market equilibrium.

But there is more than one market in the economy, and a *general equilibrium* requires equilibrium in all markets—that is, equilibrium in the goods market, the money market, and the forex market. We need to bring these last two markets into the analysis, and we do that next by developing a tool of macroeconomic analysis known as the IS-LM diagram. A version of this may be familiar to you from the study of closed-economy macroeconomics, but in this chapter we develop a variant of this approach applicable to the open economy.

Analyzing equilibria in three markets simultaneously may seem like a tall order, but we shall proceed one step at a time. Our first step builds on the depiction of goods market equilibrium developed in the last section using the Keynesian cross and adds on the depiction of forex market equilibrium that we developed in Chapters 2 and 4.

Equilibrium in Two Markets

We begin by defining the **IS curve,** which is one part of the IS–LM diagram.

The IS curve shows combinations of output Y and the interest rate i where the goods and forex markets are in equilibrium.

We need to derive what the IS curve looks like. We do this in Figure 7-8. In panel (b), the *IS* curve will be derived. In panel (a), we use the Keynesian cross to analyze goods market equilibrium, and in panel (c) we impose the uncovered interest parity relationship to ensure that the forex market is in equilibrium. The peculiar orientation of this figure may not be obvious, but it can be briefly explained.

The Keynesian cross in panel (a) and the IS diagram in panel (b) share a common horizontal axis, the level of output or income. Hence, these figures are arranged one above the other so that these common output axes line up.

The forex market in panel (c) and the IS diagram in panel (b) share a common vertical axis, the level of the interest rate. Hence, these figures are arranged side by side so that these common interest rate axes line up.

We thus know that if output Y is at a level consistent with demand equals supply, shown in the Keynesian cross in panel (a), and if the interest rate i is at a level consistent with uncovered interest parity, shown in the forex market in panel (c), then in panel (b) we must have a combination of Y and i that is consistent with equilibrium in both goods and forex markets.

Forex Market Recap

If a forex market refresher is needed, we can recall from Chapters 2 and 4 that the forex market is in equilibrium when the expected returns expressed in domestic currency are the same on foreign and domestic interest-bearing

FIGURE 7-8

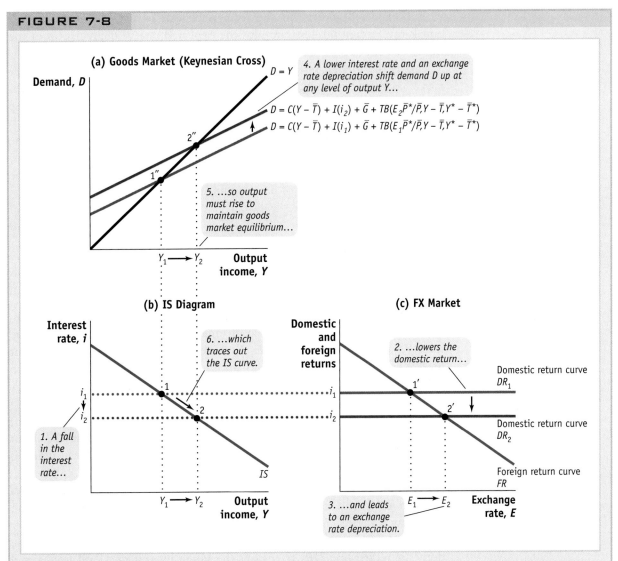

Deriving the IS Curve The Keynesian cross is in panel (a), IS curve in panel (b), and forex (FX) market in panel (c). The economy starts in equilibrium with output Y_1, interest rate i_1, and exchange rate E_1. Consider the effect of a decrease in the interest rate from i_1 to i_2, all else equal. In panel (c), a lower interest rate causes a depreciation; equilibrium moves from 1' to 2'. A lower interest rate boosts investment and a depreciation boosts the trade balance. In panel (a), demand shifts up from D_1 to D_2, equilibrium from 1" to 2", output from Y_1 to Y_2. In panel (b), we go from point 1 to point 2. The IS curve is thus traced out, a downward-sloping relationship between the interest rate and output. When the interest rate falls from i_1 to i_2, output rises from Y_1 to Y_2. The IS curve describes all combinations of i and Y consistent with goods and FX market equilibria in panels (a) and (c).

(money market) bank deposits. We saw at Equation (2-3) that this condition, known as uncovered interest parity (UIP), can be usefully approximated as

$$\underbrace{i}_{\substack{\text{Domestic} \\ \text{interest rate}}} = \underbrace{\underbrace{i^*}_{\substack{\text{Foreign} \\ \text{interest rate}}} + \underbrace{\left(\frac{E^e}{E} - 1\right)}_{\substack{\text{Expected rate of depreciation} \\ \text{of the domestic currency}}}}_{\text{Expected foreign return}}.$$

$\underbrace{}_{\text{Domestic return}}$

The expected return on the foreign deposit *measured in home currency* equals the foreign interest rate plus the expected rate of depreciation of the home currency.

Taking the foreign interest rate i^* and expectations of the future exchange rate E^e as given, we know that the right-hand side of this expression decreases as E increases; the intuition for this is that the more expensive it is to purchase foreign currency today, the lower the expected return must be, all else equal.

The inverse relationship between E and the expected foreign return on the right-hand side of the previous equation is shown by the FR (foreign returns) line in panel (b) of Figure 7-8. The domestic return DR is the horizontal line corresponding to the level of the domestic interest rate i.

Deriving the IS Curve

Using the setup in Figure 7-8, we can now derive the shape of the IS curve by considering how changes in the interest rate must affect output if the goods and forex markets are to remain in equilibrium.

Initial Equilibrium Let us suppose that the goods market and forex markets are initially in equilibrium at an interest rate i_1, an output or income level Y_1, and an exchange rate E_1. In panel (a) by assumption, at an output level Y_1, demand equals supply, so the output level Y_1 must correspond to the point $1''$, which is at the intersection of the Keynesian cross, and the figure is drawn accordingly.

In panel (c) by assumption, at an interest rate i_1 and an exchange rate E_1, the domestic and foreign returns must be equal, so this must be the point $1'$, which is at the intersection of the DR_1 and FR curves, and the figure is drawn accordingly.

Finally, in panel (b) by assumption, at an interest rate i_1 and an output level Y_1, both goods and forex markets are in equilibrium. Thus, the point 1 is on the IS curve, *by definition*.

Lines are drawn joining the equal output levels Y_1 in panels (a) and (b). The domestic return line DR_1 traces out the home interest rate level from panel (b) across to panel (c).

A Fall in the Interest Rate Now in Figure 7-8, let us suppose that the home interest rate falls from i_1 to i_2. What happens to equilibria in the two markets?

We first look at the forex market in panel (c). We know from our analysis of UIP in earlier chapters what happens when the home interest rate falls. Domestic deposits have a lower return and look less attractive to investors. The exchange rate faces depreciation pressure, and UIP tells us that to maintain forex market equilibrium, the exchange rate must rise from E_1 to E_2, which is at point $2'$, where FR is now equal to DR_2.

Now what happens to demand? In panel (a), demand must shift up, for two reasons, as discussed earlier.

First, the domestic interest rate has fallen. Firms are willing to engage in more investment projects, and their increased investment augments demand.

The increase in investment, all else equal, *directly* increases demand D at any level of output Y.

Second, the exchange rate E has risen or depreciated. Because we are assuming that prices are sticky in the short run, this rise in the nominal exchange rate E also causes a rise in the real exchange rate $E\overline{P}^*/\overline{P}$. That is, the nominal depreciation causes a real depreciation, and we know that this will also increase demand D via the trade balance TB due to expenditure switching, at any level of output Y. Consumers switch some of their expenditure from relatively more expensive foreign goods to relatively less expensive domestic goods, boosting demand. Thus, the fall in the interest rate *indirectly* boosts demand through the exchange rate and the trade balance.

One important observation is in order: in an open economy, the phenomenon of expenditure switching operates as an additional element in demand that is not present in the closed economy. *In the open economy, lower interest rates stimulate demand not only via the traditional closed-economy investment channel but also via the trade balance because lower interest rates cause a nominal exchange rate depreciation, which in the short run is also a real depreciation, which stimulates external demand via the trade balance.*

So, what now happens to output? Panel (a) supplies a clear answer: demand has shifted up, so in the Keynesian cross equilibrium in the goods market will be restored by a rise in output to Y_2, which corresponds to the point $2''$.

In panel (b), we can now derive the shape of the *IS* curve. By the previous reasoning, at an interest rate i_2 and an output or income level Y_2, both goods and forex markets are in equilibrium. Thus the point 2 is also on the *IS* curve, by definition.

We have now derived the shape of the IS curve, which describes goods and forex market equilibrium. When the interest rate falls from i_1 to i_2, output rises from Y_1 to Y_2. The IS curve is a downward-sloping relationship between the interest rate i and output Y.

Factors That Shift the IS Curve

In deriving the IS curve, we treated various demand factors as exogenous, including fiscal policy, price levels, and the exchange rate. If any factors other than the interest rate and income change, the position of the IS curve would have to change. These effects are central in any analysis of changes in an economy's equilibrium. We now explore several changes of this sort, which result in an increase in demand, that is, an upward shift in the demand curve in Figure 7-9 panel (a). (A decrease in demand would result from changes in the opposite direction.)

■ *A change in government spending.* If demand shifts up because of a *rise* in $\overline{G}$, a fiscal expansion, all else equal, what happens to the IS curve? The initial equilibrium point (Y_1, i_1) would no longer be a goods market equilibrium: if the interest rate is unchanged at i_1, then I is unchanged as are the exchange rate E and hence TB. Yet demand has risen due to the change in G. That demand has to be satisfied somehow, so more output has to be produced. Some—but not all—

FIGURE 7-9

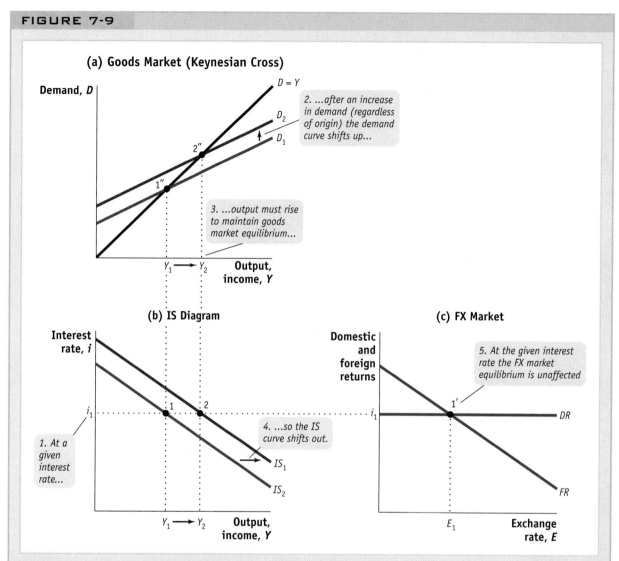

(a) Goods Market (Keynesian Cross)

Demand, *D*

D = Y

2. ...after an increase in demand (regardless of origin) the demand curve shifts up...

D_2

D_1

2″

1″

3. ...output must rise to maintain goods market equilibrium...

$Y_1 \longrightarrow Y_2$ **Output, income, Y**

(b) IS Diagram

Interest rate, *i*

i_1

1   2

1. At a given interest rate...

4. ...so the IS curve shifts out.

IS_1

IS_2

$Y_1 \longrightarrow Y_2$ **Output, income, Y**

(c) FX Market

Domestic and foreign returns

5. At the given interest rate the FX market equilibrium is unaffected

1′

i_1 DR

FR

E_1 **Exchange rate, E**

Exogenous Shifts in Demand Cause the IS Curve to Shift In the Keynesian cross in panel (a), when the interest rate is held constant at i_1, an exogenous increase in demand (due to other factors) causes the demand curve to shift up from D_1 to D_2 as shown, all else equal. This moves the equilibrium from 1″ to 2″, raising output from Y_1 to Y_2. In the IS diagram in panel (b), output has risen, with no change in the interest rate. The IS curve has therefore shifted right from IS_1 to IS_2. The nominal interest rate and hence the exchange rate are unchanged in this example, as seen in panel (c).

of that output will be consumed, but the rest can meet the extra demand generated by the rise in government spending. At the interest rate i_1, output must rise to Y_2 for the goods market to once again be in equilibrium. Thus, the IS curve must shift right as shown in Figure 7-9 panel (b).

■ *A change in taxes.* Suppose taxes were to decrease. With all other factors remaining unchanged, this tax cut makes demand shift up by boosting private consumption, all else equal. We assume that the interest rate i_1, the exchange rate E_1, and government's spending policy are all fixed. Thus, neither I nor TB nor G change. With an excess of demand, supply has to rise, so output must again increase to Y_2 and the IS curve shifts right.

- *A change in the foreign interest rate or expected future exchange rate.* A *rise* in the foreign interest rate i^* or a rise in the expected future exchange rate E^e causes a depreciation of the home currency, all else equal (recall that in the forex market, the FR curve shifts out because the return on foreign deposits has increased; if the home interest rate is unchanged, E must rise). A rise in E causes the real exchange rate to rise or depreciate, since prices are sticky, causing TB to rise. Thus, demand shifts up. Because C, I, and G do not change, there is an excess of demand, and supply has to rise to restore equilibrium. Output Y increases, and the IS curve shifts right.

- *A change in the home or foreign price level.* If prices are flexible, then a *rise* in foreign prices or a *fall* in domestic prices causes a home real depreciation, raising $q = E\overline{P}^*/\overline{P}$. This real depreciation causes TB to rise and, all else equal, causes demand to rise to a position like D_2. With an excess of demand, supply has to rise to restore equilibrium. Output Y must increase, and the IS curve shifts right.

Thus, the position of the IS curve is dependent on various factors that we treat as given (or exogenous), and we may write this using the notation

$$IS = IS(G, T, i^*, E^e, P^*, P).$$

There are many other exogenous shocks to the economy that can be analyzed in a similar fashion—for example, a sudden exogenous change in consumption, investment, or the trade balance. How will the IS curve react in each case? You may have detected a pattern from the preceding discussion.

The general rule is as follows: *Any type of shock that increases demand at a given level of output will shift the IS curve to the right; any shock that decreases demand will shift the IS curve down.*

Summing Up the IS Curve

When prices are sticky, the IS curve summarizes the relationship between output Y and interest rate i necessary to keep the goods and forex markets in short-run equilibrium. The IS curve is downward sloping. Why? Lower interest rates stimulate demand via the investment channel and, through depreciation, via the trade balance. Higher demand can be satisfied in the short run only by higher output. Thus, on the IS curve, when the interest rate falls, output rises, which implies a movement along the IS curve.

As for shifts in the IS curve, we have found that any factor that increases demand D at a given home interest rate i must cause the demand curve to shift up, leading to higher output Y and, as a result, an outward shift in the IS curve.

To conclude, the main factors that shift the IS curve out can be summed up as follows:

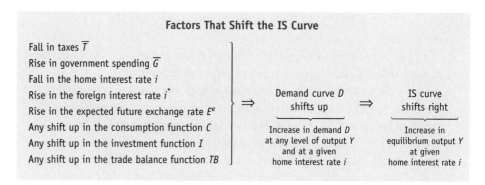

Remember that the two interest rate changes shown here have *indirect* effects on home demand via exchange rate depreciation of the home currency. In addition, changes in the *home* interest rate have a direct effect via investment demand.

The opposite changes will, of course, lead to a decrease in demand and shift the demand curve down and the IS curve to the left.

4 Money Market Equilibrium: Deriving the LM Curve

We have used the IS curve in combination with the forex market and the Keynesian cross to summarize equilibrium in the goods market as a set of combinations of Y and i that ensure goods demand equals goods supply in a way that is also consistent with forex market equilibrium. We have now taken care of equilibria in two out of three markets, so we have only one market left to worry about. In this section, we derive a set of combinations of Y and i that ensures equilibrium in the money market, a concept that can be represented graphically as the **LM curve.**

The LM curve is more straightforward to derive than the IS curve for a couple of reasons. First, the money market is something we have already studied in Chapters 3 and 4, so we will build up the LM curve from tools we already have at hand. Second, unlike the IS curve, the open-economy LM curve is no different from the closed-economy LM curve, so there will be no new material here if you have previously studied the closed-economy IS-LM model.

Money Market Recap

In our earlier study of the money market, we assumed that the level of output or income Y was given. In deriving the LM curve, we now face a new question: What happens in the money market when an economy's output changes?

In the short-run money-market equilibrium, the price level is assumed to be sticky at a level $\overline{P}$, and the money market is in equilibrium when the demand for real money balances, $L(i)Y$, equals the real money supply, $M/\overline{P}$:

(7-2)
$$\underbrace{\frac{M}{\overline{P}}}_{\substack{\text{Real} \\ \text{money} \\ \text{supply}}} = \underbrace{L(i)Y.}_{\substack{\text{Real} \\ \text{money} \\ \text{demand}}}$$

Figure 7-10, panel (a), shows how real money demand MD varies inversely with the nominal interest rate, with a demand curve for real money balances that is downward sloping. The real money supply MS is assumed fixed for now. Initially, the level of output is at Y_1 and the money market is in equilibrium at $1'$, where real money demand is on MD_1 at $M/\overline{P} = L(i_1)Y_1$.

However, if output changes, we know that the real money demand curve shifts. For example, if output rises to Y_2 and the real money supply $M/\overline{P}$ remains fixed, then real money demand increases because more output implies a larger amount of transactions in the economy for which money is needed. The real money demand curve shifts right to MD_2 and equilibrium requires $M/\overline{P} = L(i_2)Y_2$. Equilibrium moves from $1'$ to $2'$, and the interest rate rises from $i = i_1$ to $i = i_2$.

FIGURE 7-10

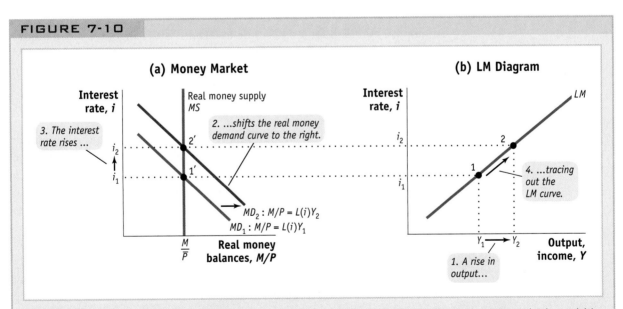

Deriving the LM Curve If there is an increase in real output from Y_1 to Y_2 in panel (b), the effect in the money market in panel (a) is to shift the demand for real money balances to the right, all else equal. If the real supply of money MS is held fixed at $M/\overline{P}$, then the interest rate rises from i_1 to i_2 and money market equilibrium moves from point $1'$ to point $2'$. The relationship thus described between the interest rate and output, all else equal, is known as the *LM* curve and is depicted in panel (b) by the shift from point 1 to point 2. The *LM* curve is upward sloping: when the output level rises from Y_1 to Y_2, the interest rate rises from i_1 to i_2. The *LM* curve in panel (b) describes all combinations of i and Y that are consistent with money market equilibrium in panel (a).

Deriving the LM Curve

This exercise can be repeated for any level of output Y. Doing so will generate a combination of interest rates i and outputs Y for which the money market is in equilibrium. This set of points is called the LM curve and is drawn in Figure 7-10, panel (b).

For example, if the real money supply is fixed at $M/\overline{P}$, an increase in output from Y_1 to Y_2 generates a rise in the nominal interest rate from i_1 to i_2 in panel (a), as we have just seen. But this can also be depicted as a move from point 1 to point 2 along the LM curve as shown in panel (b).

We have now derived the shape of the LM curve, which describes money market equilibrium. When output rises from Y_1 to Y_2, the interest rate rises from i_1 to i_2. The LM curve is an upward-sloping relationship between the interest rate i and output Y.

The two ways of depicting the money market equilibrium are entirely equivalent. The money market diagram shows the relationship between real money balances demanded and supplied at different interest rates, holding output fixed. The diagram with the LM curve shows the relationship between output and the interest rate holding real money balances fixed. Because the LM curve does *not* hold output fixed, it is important to developing our model of how output, interest rates, and exchange rates fluctuate in the short run.

Factors That Shift the LM Curve

An important reason for a shift in the LM curve is a change in the real money supply. (Changes in output result in a move *along* a given LM curve.) The LM curve tells us the interest rate i that equilibrates the money market at any given level of output Y. Given Y, we know that the equilibrium interest rate i depends on real money supply $M/\overline{P}$, and so the position of the LM curve depends on real money supply $M/\overline{P}$.

The effect of the real money supply on a nation's output is important because we are often interested in the impact of monetary policy changes on overall economic activity. To see how this operates via the LM curve, we can examine the money market diagram in Figure 7-11, panel (a). An increase in the nominal money supply with sticky prices raises real money supply from $M_1/\overline{P}$ to $M_2/\overline{P}$ and shifts the real money supply curve MS to the right.

What happens in the LM diagram if the exogenous real money supply $M/\overline{P}$ changes in this way? For a given level of output Y, the increased supply of real money drives the interest rate down to i_2, and equilibrium in the money market shifts from point $1'$ to point $2'$. A decrease in the interest rate to i_2 when the level of output is unchanged at Y means that we cannot be on the same LM curve as before. There must have been a downward shift of the LM curve from LM_1 to LM_2 in Figure 7-11, panel (b).

We have shown the following: *An increase in real money supply shifts the LM curve down or to the right; a decrease in the real money supply shifts the LM curve up or to the left.*

FIGURE 7-11

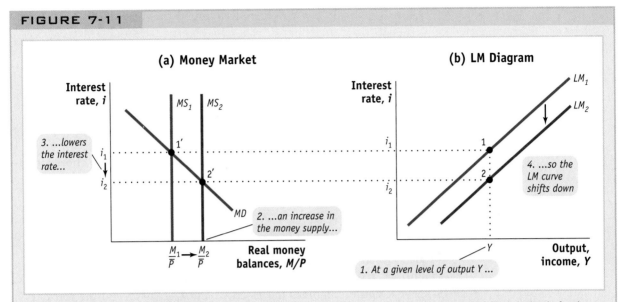

Change in the Money Supply Shifts the LM Curve In the money market, shown in panel (a), we hold fixed the level of real output Y, and hence real money demand MD. All else equal, we show the effect of an increase in money supply from M_1 to M_2. The real money supply curve moves out from MS_1 to MS_2. This moves the equilibrium from 1' to 2', lowering the interest rate from i_1 to i_2. In the LM diagram, shown in panel (b), the interest rate has fallen, with no change in the level of output, so the economy moves from point 1 to point 2. The LM curve has therefore shifted down from LM_1 to LM_2.

Thus, the position of the LM curve is a function of real money supply:

$$LM = LM(M/\overline{P})$$

Remember that prices are sticky and treated as given, so any change in the real money supply in the short run is caused by changes in the nominal money supply M, which for now we take as given or exogenous.

Other factors can influence the position of the LM curve. In addition to changes in the money supply, exogenous changes in real money demand will also cause the LM curve to shift. For example, for a given money supply, a decrease in the demand for real money balances (an increase in the L function) at a given level of output Y will tend to lower the interest rate, all else equal, which would be depicted as a shift down or to the right in the LM curve.

Summing Up the LM Curve

When prices are sticky, the LM curve summarizes the relationship between output Y and interest rate i necessary to keep the money market in short-run equilibrium for a given level of the real money supply. The LM curve is upward sloping. Why? In a money market equilibrium, if real money supply is constant, then real money demand must be also. If output rises, real money demand rises; a contraction in real money demand is then needed to maintain equilibrium, which is accomplished by a rise in the interest rate. Thus, on the LM curve, when output rises, so, too, does the interest rate.

As for shifts in the LM curve, we have found the following:

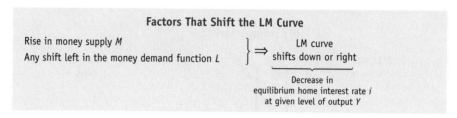

The opposite changes will, of course, lead to an increase in the home interest rate and shift the LM curve up or to the left.

5 The Short-Run IS-LM-FX Model of an Open Economy

We are now in a position to fully characterize an open economy that is in equilibrium in goods, money, and forex markets, as shown in Figure 7-12. This IS-LM-FX figure combines the *IS* curve, the *LM* curve, and the forex (FX) market diagram.

The *IS* and *LM* curves are both drawn in panel (a). The goods market is in equilibrium if and only if the economy is on the *IS* curve. The money market is in equilibrium if and only if the economy is on the *LM* curve. Thus, both markets are in equilibrium if and only if the economy is at point 1, the unique point of intersection of *IS* and *LM*.

FIGURE 7-12

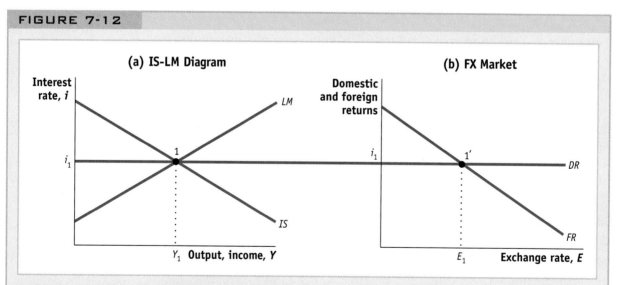

Equilibrium in the IS-LM-FX Model In panel (a), the IS and LM curves are both drawn. The goods and forex markets are in equilibrium when the economy is on the IS curve. The money market is in equilibrium when the economy is on the LM curve. Both markets are in equilibrium if and only if the economy is at point 1, the unique point of intersection of *IS* and *LM*. In panel (b), the forex (FX) market is shown. The domestic return *DR* in the forex market equals the money market interest rate. Equilibrium is at point 1′ where the foreign return *FR* equals domestic return *i*.

The forex market, or FX market, is drawn in panel (b). The domestic return DR in the forex market equals the money market interest rate. Equilibrium is at point 1' where the foreign return FR is equal to domestic return i.

In the remainder of this chapter, and in the rest of this book, we make extensive use of this graphical depiction of the open-economy equilibrium to analyze the short-run response of an open economy to various types of shocks. In particular, we will be interested in how government policies affect the economy and the extent to which they can be employed to enhance macroeconomic performance and stability.

Macroeconomic Policies in the Short Run

Now that we understand the open-economy IS-LM-FX model and all the factors that influence an economy's short-run equilibrium, we can use the model to look at how a nation's key macroeconomic variables (output, exchange rates, trade balance) are affected in the short run by changes in government macroeconomic policies.

We will focus on two main policy actions: changes in **monetary policy,** implemented through changes in the money supply, and changes in **fiscal policy,** involving changes in government spending or taxes. Of particular interest is the question of whether governments can use such policies to insulate the economy from fluctuations in output.

We will see that the impact of these policies is profoundly affected by a nation's choice of exchange rate regime, and we will consider the two polar cases of fixed and floating exchange rates. Many countries are on some kind of flexible exchange rate regime and many are on some kind of fixed regime, so considering policy effects under both fixed and floating systems is essential.

The key assumptions of this section are as follows. The economy begins in a state of long-run equilibrium. We then consider policy changes in the home economy, assuming that conditions in the foreign economy (i.e., the rest of the world) are unchanged. The home economy is subject to the usual short-run assumption of a sticky price level at home *and* abroad. Furthermore, we assume that the forex market operates freely and unrestricted by capital controls and the exchange rate is determined by market forces.

Temporary Policies, Unchanged Expectations Finally, we examine only *temporary* changes in policies. We will assume that long-run expectations about the future state of the economy are unaffected by the policy changes. In particular, the future expected exchange rate E^e is held fixed. The reason for studying temporary policies is that we are primarily interested in how governments use fiscal and monetary policies to handle temporary shocks and business cycles in the short run, and our model is applicable only in the short run.[3]

---

[3] Moreover, permanent changes may not be truly feasible given realistic constraints on governments. For example, a permanent increase in money supply, all else equal, would lead to a permanent increase in the price level, violating a money, exchange rate, or inflation target (the nominal anchor). A permanent increase in government spending, with no increase in taxes, would not be feasible given the government's long-run budget constraint.

The key lesson of this section is that policies matter and can have important macroeconomic effects in the short run. Moreover, their impacts depend in a big way on the type of exchange rate regime in place. Once we understand these linkages, we will better understand the contentious and ongoing debates about exchange rates and macroeconomic policies, including the never-ending arguments over the merits of fixed and floating exchange rates (a topic covered in detail in Chapter 8).

Monetary Policy under Floating Exchange Rates

In this policy experiment, we consider a temporary monetary expansion in the home country when the exchange rate is allowed to float. Because the expansion is not permanent, we assume there is no change in long-run expectations so that the expected future exchange rate remains steady at E^e. This means that there is no change in the expected foreign return curve in the forex market.

Figure 7-13 illustrates the predictions of the model. In panel (a) in the IS-LM diagram, the goods and money markets are initially in equilibrium at point 1. The interest rate in the money market is also the domestic return DR_1 that prevails in the forex market. In panel (b), the forex market is initially in equilibrium at point $1'$.

A temporary monetary expansion that increases the money supply from M_1 to M_2 would shift the LM curve to the right in panel (a) from LM_1 to LM_2, causing the interest rate to fall from i_1 to i_2. Domestic return falls from DR_1 to DR_2.

FIGURE 7-13

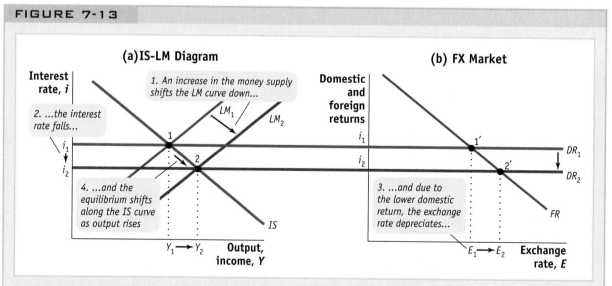

Monetary Policy under Floating Exchange Rates In panel (a) in the IS-LM diagram the goods and money markets are initially in equilibrium at point 1. The interest rate in the money market is also the domestic return DR_1 that prevails in the forex market. In panel (b), the forex market is initially in equilibrium at point $1'$. A temporary monetary expansion that increases the money supply from M_1 to M_2 would shift the LM curve down in panel (a) from LM_1 to LM_2, causing the interest rate to fall from i_1 to i_2. DR falls from DR_1 to DR_2. In panel (b), the lower interest rate implies that the exchange rate must depreciate, rising from E_1 to E_2. As the interest rate falls (increasing investment I) and the exchange rate depreciates (increasing the trade balance), demand increases, which corresponds to the move down the IS curve from point 1 to point 2. Output expands from Y_1 to Y_2. The new equilibrium corresponds to points 2 and $2'$.

In panel (b), the lower interest rate would imply that the exchange rate must depreciate, rising from E_1 to E_2. As the interest rate falls (increasing investment I) and the exchange rate depreciates (increasing the trade balance), demand increases, which corresponds to the move down the IS curve from point 1 to point 2. Output expands from Y_1 to Y_2. The new equilibrium corresponds to points 2 and 2′.

The intuition for this result is as follows: monetary expansion tends to lower the home interest rate, all else equal. A lower interest rate stimulates demand in two ways. First, directly in the goods market, it causes investment demand I to increase. Second, indirectly, it causes the exchange rate to depreciate in the forex market, which in turn causes expenditure switching in the goods market, which causes the trade balance TB to increase. Both I and TB are sources of demand and both increase.

To sum up: a temporary expansion of monetary policy under floating exchange rates is effective in combating economic downturns by boosting output. It raises output at home, lowers the interest rate, and causes a depreciation of the exchange rate. What happens to the trade balance cannot be predicted with certainty: increased home output will decrease the trade balance via import demand, but the real depreciation will increase the trade balance via expenditure switching. In practice, economists tend to assume that the latter outweighs the former, so the policy is usually predicted to increase the trade balance. (The case of a temporary contraction of monetary policy has opposite effects. As an exercise, work through this case using the same graphical apparatus.)

Monetary Policy under Fixed Exchange Rates

Now let's look at what happens when a temporary monetary expansion occurs in a home country that pegs its exchange rate with respect to the foreign country at $\bar{E}$. The key to understanding this experiment is to recall the uncovered interest parity condition: the home interest rate must equal the foreign interest rate under a fixed exchange rate.

Figure 7-14 puts the model to work. In panel (a) in the IS-LM diagram, the goods and money markets are initially in equilibrium at point 1. In panel (b), the forex market is initially in equilibrium at point 1′.

A temporary monetary expansion that increases the money supply from M_1 to M_2 would shift the LM curve down and to the right in panel (a), and the interest rate would tend to fall, as we have just seen. In panel (b), the lower interest rate would imply that the exchange rate would tend to rise or depreciate toward E_2. This is inconsistent with the pegged exchange rate $\bar{E}$, so the policy makers cannot alter monetary policy and shift the LM curve in this way. They must leave the money supply equal to M_1 and the economy cannot deviate from its initial equilibrium.

Implication: under a fixed exchange rate, autonomous monetary policy is not an option. What is going on? Remember that under a fixed exchange rate, the home interest rate must exactly equal the foreign interest rate, $i = i^*$, according to the uncovered interest parity condition. Any shift in the LM curve would violate this restriction and break the fixed exchange rate.

FIGURE 7-14

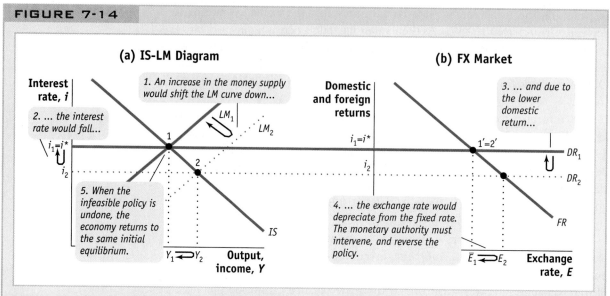

(a) IS-LM Diagram

Interest rate, i

1. An increase in the money supply would shift the LM curve down...

2. ... the interest rate would fall...

LM_1

LM_2

$i_1 = i^*$

1

i_2

2

5. When the infeasible policy is undone, the economy returns to the same initial equilibrium.

IS

$Y_1 \rightleftharpoons Y_2$ **Output, income, Y**

(b) FX Market

Domestic and foreign returns

3. ... and due to the lower domestic return...

$i_1 = i^*$

$1' = 2'$

DR_1

i_2

DR_2

4. ... the exchange rate would depreciate from the fixed rate. The monetary authority must intervene, and reverse the policy.

FR

$\bar{E}_1 \rightleftharpoons E_2$ **Exchange rate, E**

Monetary Policy under Fixed Exchange Rates In panel (a) in the IS-LM diagram the goods and money markets are initially in equilibrium at point 1. In panel (b), the forex market is initially in equilibrium at point 1′. A temporary monetary expansion that increases the money supply from M_1 to M_2 would shift the LM curve down in panel (a). In panel (b), the lower interest rate would imply that the exchange rate must depreciate, rising from $\bar{E}$ to E_2. This depreciation is inconsistent with the pegged exchange rate, so the policy makers cannot move LM in this way. They must leave the money supply equal to M_1. Implication: under a fixed exchange rate, autonomous monetary policy is not an option.

To sum up: monetary policy under fixed exchange rates is impossible to undertake. Fixing the exchange rate means giving up monetary policy autonomy. In Chapter 4, we learned about the trilemma: countries cannot simultaneously allow capital mobility, maintain fixed exchange rates, and pursue an autonomous monetary policy. We have now seen the trilemma at work in the IS-LM-FX framework. By illustrating a potential benefit of autonomous monetary policy (the ability to use monetary policy to increase output), the model clearly exposes one of the major costs of fixed exchange rates. Monetary policy, which in principle could be used to influence the economy in the short run, is ruled out by a fixed exchange rate.

Fiscal Policy under Floating Exchange Rates

We now turn to fiscal policy under a floating exchange rate. In this example, we consider a temporary increase in government spending from $\overline{G}_1$ to $\overline{G}_2$ in the home economy. Again, the effect is not permanent, so there are no changes in long-run expectations, and in particular the expected future exchange rate remains steady at $E^{e.}$

Figure 7-15 shows what happens in our model. In panel (a) in the IS-LM diagram, the goods and money markets are initially in equilibrium at point 1. The interest rate in the money market is also the domestic return DR_1 that prevails in the forex market. In panel (b), the forex market is initially in equilibrium at point 1′.

FIGURE 7-15

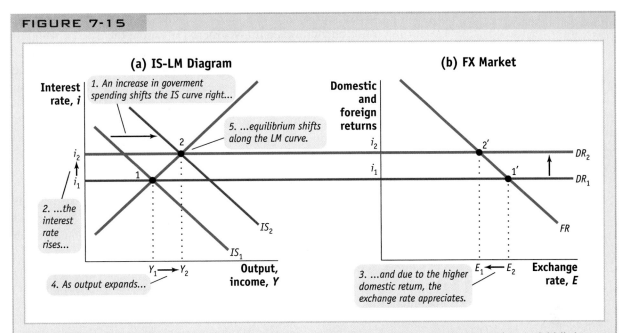

Fiscal Policy under Floating Exchange Rates In panel (a) in the IS-LM diagram the goods and money markets are initially in equilibrium at point 1. The interest rate in the money market is also the domestic return DR_1 that prevails in the forex market. In panel (b), the forex market is initially in equilibrium at point 1′. A temporary fiscal expansion that increases government spending from $\overline{G}_1$ to $\overline{G}_2$ would shift the IS curve to the right in panel (a) from IS_1 to IS_2, causing the interest rate to rise from i_1 to i_2. The domestic return shifts up from DR_1 to DR_2. In panel (b), the higher interest rate would imply that the exchange rate must appreciate, falling from E_1 to E_2. As the interest rate rises (decreasing investment I) and the exchange rate appreciates (decreasing the trade balance), demand falls, which corresponds to the move along the LM curve from point 1 to point 2. Output expands from Y_1 to Y_2. The new equilibrium corresponds to points 2 and 2′.

A temporary fiscal expansion that increases government spending from $\overline{G}_1$ to $\overline{G}_2$ would shift the IS curve to the right in panel (a) from IS_1 to IS_2, causing the interest rate to rise from i_1 to i_2. The domestic return rises from DR_1 to DR_2. In panel (b), the higher interest rate would imply that the exchange rate must appreciate, falling from E_1 to E_2. As the interest rate rises (decreasing investment I) and the exchange rate appreciates (decreasing the trade balance TB), demand falls, which corresponds to the move up the LM curve from point 1 to point 2. Output expands from Y_1 to Y_2. The new equilibrium is at points 2 and 2′.

What is happening here? The fiscal expansion raises output as the IS curve shifts right. But the increases in output will raise interest rates, all else equal, given a fixed money supply. The resulting higher interest rates will reduce the investment component of demand, and this limits the rise in demand to less than the increase in government spending. This impact of fiscal expansion on investment is often referred to as *crowding out* by economists.

The higher interest rate also causes the home currency to appreciate. As home consumers switch their consumption to now less expensive foreign goods, the trade balance will fall. Thus, the higher interest rate also (indirectly) leads to a *crowding out* of net exports, and this too limits the rise in output to less than the increase in government spending. Thus, in an open economy, fiscal expansion not only crowds out investment (by raising the interest rate) but also decreases net exports (by causing the exchange rate to appreciate).

To sum up: a temporary expansion of fiscal policy under floating exchange rates is effective. It raises output at home, raises the interest rate, causes an appreciation of the exchange rate, and decreases the trade balance. (A temporary contraction of fiscal policy has opposite effects. As an exercise, work through the contraction case using the same graphical apparatus.)

Fiscal Policy under Fixed Exchange Rates

Now let's see how the outcomes differ when the home country pegs its exchange rate with respect to the foreign country at E_1. The key is to recall the parity condition: the home interest rate must remain exactly equal to the foreign interest rate for the peg to hold.

Figure 7-16 shows what happens in this case. In panel (a) in the IS–LM diagram, the goods and money markets are initially in equilibrium at point 1. The interest rate in the money market is also the domestic return DR_1 that

FIGURE 7-16

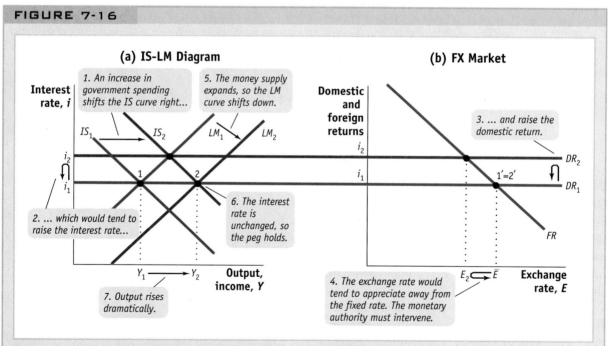

Fiscal Policy under Fixed Exchange Rates In panel (a) in the IS-LM diagram the goods and money markets are initially in equilibrium at point 1. The interest rate in the money market is also the domestic return DR_1 that prevails in the forex market. In panel (b), the forex market is initially in equilibrium at point 1′. A temporary fiscal expansion on its own increases government spending from $\overline{G}_1$ to $\overline{G}_2$ and would shift the IS curve to the right in panel (a) from IS_1 to IS_2, causing the interest rate to rise from i_1 to i_2. The domestic return would then rise from DR_1 to DR_2. In panel (b), the higher interest rate would imply that the exchange rate must appreciate, falling from $\overline{E}$ to E_2. To maintain the peg, the monetary authority must now intervene, shifting the LM curve down, from LM_1 to LM_2. The fiscal expansion thus prompts a monetary expansion. In the end, the interest rate and exchange rate are left unchanged, and output expands *dramatically* from Y_1 to Y_2. The new equilibrium corresponds to points 2 and 2′.

prevails in the forex market. In panel (b), the forex market is initially in equilibrium at point $1'$.

A temporary fiscal expansion that increases government spending from $\overline{G}_1$ to $\overline{G}_2$ would shift the IS curve to the right in panel (a) from IS_1 to IS_2, causing the interest rate to rise from i_1 to i_2. The domestic return would rise from DR_1 to DR_2. In panel (b), the higher interest rate would imply that the exchange rate must appreciate, falling from $\overline{E}$ to E_2. To maintain the peg, the monetary authority must intervene, shifting the LM curve to the right also, from LM_1 to LM_2. The fiscal expansion thus prompts a monetary expansion. In the end, the interest rate and exchange rate are left unchanged, and output expands *dramatically* from Y_1 to Y_2. The new equilibrium corresponds to points 2 and $2'$.

What is happening here? From the last example, we know that there is appreciation pressure associated with a fiscal expansion if the currency is allowed to float. To maintain the peg, the monetary authority must immediately alter its monetary policy at the very moment the fiscal expansion occurs so that the LM curve shifts from LM_1 to LM_2. The way to do this is to expand the money supply, and this generates pressure for depreciation, offsetting the appreciation pressure. If the monetary authority pulls this off, the market exchange rate will stay at the initial pegged level $\overline{E}$.

Thus, when a country is operating under a fixed exchange, fiscal policy is supereffective because any fiscal expansion by the government forces an immediate monetary expansion by the central bank to keep the exchange rate steady. The double, and simultaneous, expansion of demand by the fiscal and monetary authorities imposes a huge stimulus on the economy, and output rises from Y_1 to Y_2 (beyond the level achieved by the same fiscal expansion under a floating exchange rate).

To sum up: a temporary expansion of fiscal policy under fixed exchange rates raises output at home by a considerable amount. (The case of a temporary contraction of fiscal policy would have similar but opposite effects. As an exercise, work through this case using the same graphical apparatus.)

Summary

We have now examined the operation of fiscal and monetary policies under both fixed and flexible exchange rates and have seen how the impacts of these policies differ dramatically depending on the exchange rate regime. The outcomes can be summarized as follows:

Responses to Policy Shocks in the IS-LM-FX Model						
Exchange Rate Regime	Policy	Impact on:				
		i	E	I	TB	Y
Floating	Monetary expansion	↓	↑	↑	↑?	↑
	Fiscal expansion	↑	↓	↓	↓	↑
Floating	Monetary expansion	0	0	0	0	0
	Fiscal expansion	0	0	0	↓	↑

In this table, an up arrow ↑ indicates that the variable rises; a down arrow ↓ indicates that the variables falls; and a zero indicates no effect. The effects would be reversed for contractionary policies. The row of zeroes for monetary expansion under fixed rates results from the fact that the policy is actually infeasible.

In a floating exchange rate regime, autonomous monetary and fiscal policy is feasible. The power of monetary policy to expand demand comes from two forces in the short run: lower interest rates boost investment and a depreciated exchange rate boosts the trade balance, all else equal. In the end, though, the trade balance will experience downward pressure from an import rise due to the increase in home output. The net effect on output and investment is positive, and the net effect on the trade balance is unclear—but in practice it, too, is likely to be positive.

Expansionary fiscal policy is also effective under a floating regime, even though the impact of extra spending is offset by crowding out in two areas: investment is crowded out by higher interest rates, and the trade balance is crowded out by an appreciated exchange rate. Thus, on net, investment falls and the trade balance also falls, and the latter effect is unambiguously amplified by additional import demand arising from increased home output.

In a fixed exchange rate regime, monetary policy loses its power for two reasons. First, interest parity implies that the domestic interest rate cannot move independently of the foreign rate, so investment demand cannot be manipulated. Second, the peg means that there can be no movement in the exchange rate, so the trade balance cannot be manipulated by expenditure switching.

Only fiscal policy is feasible under a fixed regime. Tax cuts or spending increases by the government can generate additional demand. But a fiscal expansion then requires a monetary expansion to keep interest rates steady and maintain the peg. Fiscal policy becomes ultrapowerful in a fixed exchange rate setting—the reason for this is that if interest rates and exchange rates are held steady by the central bank, investment and the trade balance are never crowded out by fiscal policy. Monetary policy follows fiscal policy and amplifies it.

APPLICATION

The Rise and Fall of the Dollar in the 1980s

Do policies actually affect the economy in the way that our IS-LM-FX model predicts? The impacts of monetary and fiscal policy in the open economy are well illustrated by recent U.S. economic history.

At the end of the 1970s, the U.S. economy was wracked by high inflation. This phenomenon was deeply unpopular and the stage was set for a dramatic change in economic policies to tackle the problem. Federal Reserve Chairman Paul Volcker initiated a period of tight monetary policy from 1979 to 1982. The growth of the U.S. money supply was curtailed and nominal interest rates rose. In terms of our model, this policy change can be viewed as an upward shift of the LM curve. On its own, based on our analysis, this policy ought to have caused an appreciation of the U.S. dollar and a contraction in U.S. output (due to drops in investment demand and the trade balance).

At almost the same time, the administration of President Ronald Reagan, supported by Congress, implemented strongly expansionary fiscal policy, through a combination of tax cuts and increased spending (particularly military spending). In terms of our model, this policy change can be viewed as a sharp shift to the right of the IS curve. Based on our analysis, this policy alone would cause an appreciation of the U.S. dollar and an expansion in U.S. output that would offset the decrease in output caused by the monetary contraction (increased demand from private and public spending would offset the declines in investment and the trade balance).

The impact of the two policies together is shown in Figure 7-17. As the *LM* curve shifts to the left, output falls and interest rates rise, and the equilibrium in the economy shifts from point 1. As the *IS* curve moves up, interest rates rise

FIGURE 7-17

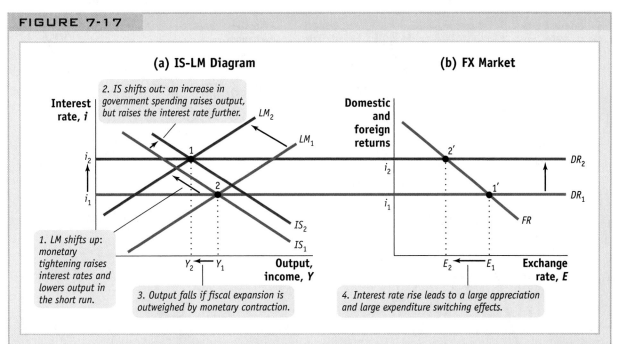

(a) IS-LM Diagram

2. IS shifts out: an increase in government spending raises output, but raises the interest rate further.

Interest rate, *i*

1. LM shifts up: monetary tightening raises interest rates and lowers output in the short run.

3. Output falls if fiscal expansion is outweighed by monetary contraction.

(b) FX Market

Domestic and foreign returns

4. Interest rate rise leads to a large appreciation and large expenditure switching effects.

U.S. Monetary and Fiscal Policy Shocks circa 1980 The years from 1979 to the mid-1980s saw a combination of contractionary monetary policy and expansionary fiscal policy in the United States, which was operating on a floating exchange rate. We can use our model to analyze the events as follows. In panel (a) in the IS-LM diagram, the goods and money markets are initially in equilibrium at point 1. The interest rate in the money market is also the domestic return DR_1 that prevails in the forex (FX) market. In panel (b), the forex market is initially in equilibrium at point 1′. In panel (a), suppose the *LM* curve shifts up and the *IS* curve shifts out. The new equilibrium corresponds to points 2 and 2′. Unambiguously, the interest rate rises from i_1 to i_2. The domestic return rises from DR_1 to DR_2. Output may rise or fall because the effects of the two policy changes work in opposite directions (as drawn output falls from Y_1 to Y_2). In the forex market, the increase in the interest rate causes the exchange rate to appreciate (fall) from E_1 to E_2. The model predicts a strong increase in interest rates and a large exchange rate appreciation; the effect on output is unclear.

further, output also starts to rise, and the equilibrium in the economy shifts to point 3.

This model predicts that interest rates would rise strongly and that output might fall or rise depending on the relative size and timing of the monetary and fiscal policy changes. As a result of the sharp rise in the home interest rate, investment would be predicted to fall, the dollar would be predicted to strengthen, and the trade balance would be predicted to move toward deficit.

The actual performance of the U.S. economy in this period is shown in Figure 7-18. The data match the predictions of the model quite well. Panel (a) shows the changes in macroeconomic policy. Monetary policy was tightening from 1978 to 1982 as the key interest rate set by the Federal Reserve (the federal funds rate) was raised from 5.5% to 16.4%. Starting slightly later, fiscal policy was eased, and the government deficit rose from 1.6% of GDP in 1979 to 5.9% of GDP in 1983.

FIGURE 7-18

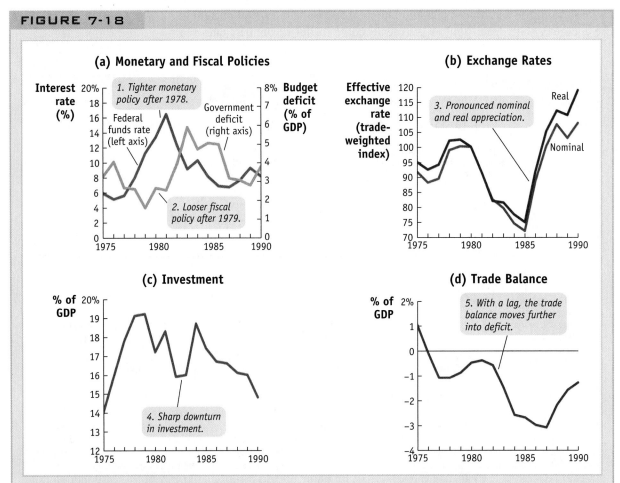

U.S. Monetary and Fiscal Policy, 1975–1990 As shown in panel (a), the early 1980s saw a combination of contractionary monetary policy and expansionary fiscal policy in the United States. As we saw in Figure 7-17, the IS-LM-FX model would predict a strong exchange rate appreciation, reduced investment, and a move toward deficit in the trade balance. Panels (b), (c), and (d) show that this is exactly what happened.

Sources: Federal Reserve; U.S. Bureau of Economic Analysis.

Panels (b), (c), and (d) show macroeconomic outcomes and allow us to see what happened in response to these policies. The dollar appreciated dramatically in both nominal and real terms. Investment fell as the nominal interest rate rose and the U.S. trade balance moved into a large deficit after a lag.

Our model gives no firm prediction of the net impact of this policy mix on output. In fact, output did fall sharply: in the United States, this was the worst recession of the postwar period—in fact it was a "double dip" recession with troughs in 1980 and 1982. This tells us that the effects of the fiscal expansion were either too little or too late to offset the effects of the collapse in investment and the trade balance. Still, although the fiscal expansion did not fully offset the monetary contraction, the U.S. economy of the early 1980s delivered higher output than it would have without any fiscal stimulus. ■

6 Stabilization Policy

We now have seen that macroeconomic policies can generate short-run effects on economic activity. These effects open up the possibility that the authorities can use changes in policies to try to keep the economy at or near its full-employment level of output. This is the essence of **stabilization policy.** If the economy is hit by a temporary adverse shock, policy makers could use expansionary monetary and fiscal policies to prevent a deep recession. Conversely, if the economy is pushed by a shock above its full employment level of output, contractionary policies could tame the boom.

For example, suppose a temporary adverse shock such as a sudden decline in investment, consumption, or export demand shifts the IS curve to the left. Or suppose an adverse shock such as a sudden increase in money demand suddenly moves the LM curve up. Either shock would cause home output to fall. In principle, the home policy makers could offset these shocks by using fiscal policy to shift either the IS curve or LM curve (or both) to cause an offsetting increase in output. When used judiciously, monetary and fiscal policies can thus be used to stabilize the economy and absorb shocks.

The policies must be used with care, however. If the economy is stable and growing, an additional temporary monetary or fiscal stimulus may cause an unsustainable boom that will, when the stimulus is withdrawn, turn into an undesirable bust. In their efforts to do good, policy makers must be careful not to destabilize the economy through the ill-timed, inappropriate, or excessive use of monetary and fiscal policies.

APPLICATION

Australia, New Zealand, and the Asian Crisis of 1997

At the end of 1997, many observers would have predicted economic difficulties for Australia and New Zealand in the short run. Both countries were very open to trade, and a large part of the demand for their exports was generated by a group of industrializing East Asian economies, including Korea, Thailand, and Indonesia. The problem was that all of these major trading partners suffered serious economic crises in 1997, which caused a large economic contraction in each country characterized by large declines in output and the demand for foreign goods. To some extent, the East Asian and Pacific region as a whole was likely to be dragged into recession by these events.

In our framework, the demand for Australia's and New Zealand's exports declined as a result of a contraction in foreign output Y^*. All else equal, they would have suffered an exogenous decline in their trade balance: at every real exchange rate, the demand for exports declined, and demand fell. These events would be represented by a leftward shift of Australia's and New Zealand's IS curves, which we can show in Figure 7-19.

Our model tells us that if the governments of Australia and New Zealand had chosen to ignore the Asian crisis, their economies would have contracted, home interest rates would have fallen, and the value of their currencies would have fallen. In Figure 7-19 panel (a), the IS–LM equilibrium shifts from point 1 to point 2, and the initial deterioration in trade balance would be only partially offset by the induced depreciation and increased investment. Forex market equilibrium would be at $2'$. In the end, demand would still be below its initial level and a recession would result.

However, this did not happen. The central banks of both Australia and New Zealand responded to the Asian crisis with expansionary monetary policy. This would be depicted in our model by a shift down or right in the LM

FIGURE 7-19

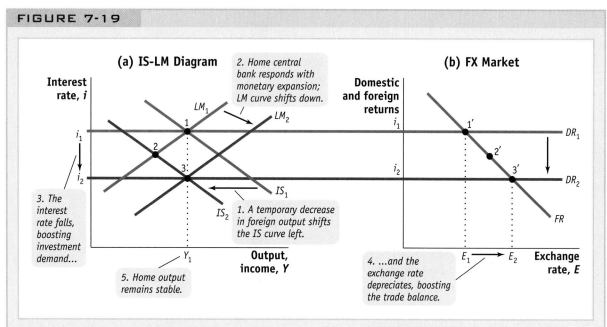

Stabilization Policy under Floating Exchange Rates In panel (a) in the IS-LM diagram, the goods and money markets are initially in equilibrium at point 1. The interest rate in the money market is also the domestic return DR_1 that prevails in the forex market. In panel (b), the forex market is initially in equilibrium at point $1'$. An exogenous negative shock to the trade balance (for example, due to a collapse in foreign output) causes the IS curve to shift in from IS_1 to IS_2. Without further action, output and interest rates would fall and the exchange rate would tend to depreciate as at points 2 and $2'$. The central bank can stabilize output at its former level by responding with a monetary policy expansion, increasing the money supply from M_1 to M_2. This causes the LM curve to shift down from LM_1 to LM_2. The new equilibrium corresponds to points 3 and $3'$. Output is now stabilized at the original level Y_1. The interest rate falls further. The domestic return falls from DR_1 to DR_2, and the exchange rate depreciates all the way from E_1 to E_2.

curve. The IS-LM equilibrium in the economy shifts from point 2 to point 3 in Figure 7-19 (panel a). At point 3, the further reduction in the home interest rate exacerbates the depreciation of the currency and stimulates demand through both the investment and expenditure-switching channels. Recession is avoided and output is sustained at its original level. The forex market in panel (b) ends up at 3′ with a large depreciation.

Figure 7-20 shows data for the Australian and New Zealand economies in this period. The home exchange rates were allowed to depreciate substantially, and as a result, the trade balances in both countries held up, partly due to export growth to non-Asian markets that was made possible by the temporary weakening of the real exchange rate.

FIGURE 7-20

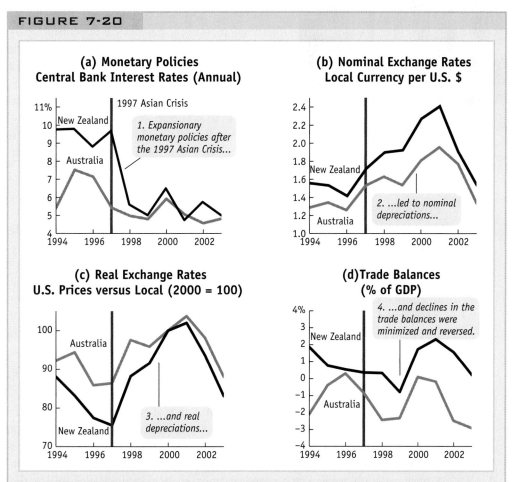

Demand Shocks Down Under Australian and New Zealand exports were likely to be badly hit after the 1997 Asian crisis as the outputs of their key trading partners contracted. Both countries were operating on floating exchange rates, however. To bolster demand, the central banks in both countries pursued expansionary monetary policies, lowering interest rates, as shown in panel (a), and allowing the domestic currency to depreciate about 30% in nominal terms, as shown in panel (b). This contributed to a real depreciation of about 20% to 30% in the short run, panel (c). As a result, the trade balances of both countries moved strongly toward surplus, illustrated in panel (d), and thus demand was higher than it would otherwise have been. In each country, a recession was avoided.

Sources: IMF, International Financial Statistics; World Bank, World Development Indicators.

This episode provides a good example of how policy makers can use a floating exchange rate to cushion the blows of external macroeconomic shocks. Policy makers in Australia and New Zealand knew that after the Asian crisis had passed—in a few years time—there would be renewed demand for their goods. In the short run, the problem was to manage a temporary drop in aggregate demand.

Christian Mushenko/Courtesy of Penfolds.

A case study: exports of wine and other Australian goods boomed after the real depreciation.

This response was widely praised in economic policy-making circles, as in the following quotation from the OECD's 1999 *Economic Survey of Australia*: "Australia has continued to grow above its trend rate over the past two years with the economy proving to be remarkably resilient in the face of significant weakness in many of its trading partners, especially in Asia. At the same time, inflation remained low and the rate of unemployment was reduced further. This performance was helped by dynamic growth of domestic demand at the time when the crisis broke out, and a credible mix of macro-policies which allowed the exchange rate to move freely, kept monetary conditions expansionary and maintained fiscal retrenchment." ■

Problems in Policy Design and Implementation

In this chapter, we have looked at open-economy macroeconomics in the short run and at the role that monetary and fiscal policies can play in determining economic outcomes. The simple models we used have clear consequences. On the face of it, if policy makers were really operating in such an uncomplicated environment, they would have the ability to exert substantial control and could always keep output steady at its full-employment level with no unemployed resources and no inflation pressure. In reality, life is more complicated for policy makers for a variety of reasons.

Policy Constraints Policy makers may not always be free to apply the policies they desire. A fixed exchange rate rules out any use of monetary policy. Other firm monetary or fiscal policy rules, such as interest rate rules or balanced-budget rules, place limits on policy. Even if policy makers decide to act, other constraints may bind them. While it is always feasible to print money, it may not be possible to raise the real resources necessary for a fiscal expansion. Countries with weak tax systems or poor creditworthiness—problems that afflict developing countries—may find themselves unable to tax or borrow to finance an expansion of spending even if they wish to do so.

Incomplete Information and the Inside Lag Our models assume that the policy makers have full knowledge of the state of the economy before they take corrective action: they observe the economy's IS and LM curves and know what shocks have hit. In reality, macroeconomic data are compiled slowly and it may take weeks or months for policy makers to fully understand the state of the economy today. Even then, it will take time to formulate a policy response (the lag between shock and policy actions is called the *inside lag*). On the monetary side, there may be a delay between policy meetings. On the fiscal side, it may take time to pass a bill through the legislature and then enable a real change in spending or taxing activity by the public sector.

Policy Response and the Outside Lag Even if they finally receive the correct information, policy makers then have to formulate the right response given by the model. In particular, they must not be distracted by other policies or agendas, nor subject to influence by interest groups that might wish to see different policies enacted. Finally, it takes time for whatever policies are enacted to have any effect on the economy, through the spending decisions of the public and private sectors (the lag between policy actions and effects is called the *outside lag*).

Long-Horizon Plans Other factors may make investment and the trade balance less sensitive to policy. If the private sector understands that a policy change is temporary, then there may be reasons not to change consumption or investment expenditure. Suppose a firm has to make a decision either to operate a plant for several years or else not to operate at all (e.g., the investment might be of an irreversible form). If the plant will sell to the domestic market, the firm may not be much deterred by a slightly higher real interest rate this year and may base its decision on the expected real interest rate that will affect its financing over the many years ahead. Similarly, if the plant is built for the export market, a temporary real appreciation may do little to affect the firm's calculation of whether it can break even in the long run in the foreign market. In circumstances like these, firms will be more interested in the long-run average level of the real interest rate and the real exchange rate, and less influenced by short-run fluctuations. As a result, the firms' investment and export activities may be less sensitive to short-run movements in interest and real exchange rates.

Weak Links from the Nominal Exchange Rate to the Real Exchange Rate Our discussion assumed that changes in the nominal exchange rate lead to real exchange rate changes. The reality is somewhat different. For example, according to carsdirect.com, the price of a BMW 325i rose from $27,100 in 2002 to $28,100 in 2004, a rise of $1,000 or just less than 4%. But the dollar depreciated 42% against the euro in those years, so why didn't the price of the BMW rise by 42%? There are a number of reasons for the weak or slow *pass-through* phenomenon. These include the dollarization of trade and the large distribution margins that separate retail prices from port prices (as we saw in **Side Bar: Barriers to Expenditure Switching: Pass-Through and the J Curve**). In addition, if markets for products are imperfectly competitive, firms can charge different prices in different locations. BMW sells through exclusive dealers and this foils arbitrage; government regulation also foils arbitrage by requiring that cars meet different standards in Europe versus the United States. With this insulation from arbitrage, a firm like BMW can charge a steady price in one country even if the exchange rate moves temporarily. It may wish to do so to avoid the volatile sales and alienated customers that would result from repeatedly changing its retail price list. This type of pricing strategy, called *pricing to market,* could potentially expose the firm to a risk of losses if the exchange rate moves unfavorably—but, as we know, the firm can hedge against such losses using currency derivatives and other financial products (see Chapter 2), and many multinational firms do just that.

Pegged Currency Blocs Our model's predictions are also affected by the fact that for some major countries in the real world, their exchange rate arrangements are characterized—often not as a result of their own choice—by a mix of floating and fixed exchange rate systems with different trading partners. In the years 2002 to 2004, the dollar depreciated markedly against the euro, pound, and several other floating currencies, but in the "Dollar Bloc" (Japan, China, India, and others), the monetary authorities ensured that the appreciation of their currencies against the dollar was small or zero. When a large bloc of other countries pegs to the U.S. dollar, this limits the ability of the United States to engineer a real effective depreciation.

Weak Links from the Real Exchange Rate to the Trade Balance Our discussion also assumed that real exchange rate changes lead to changes in the trade balance. There may be several reasons why these linkages are weak in reality. One major reason is the presence of substantial transaction costs in trade. Suppose the exchange rate is $1 per euro and an American is currently consuming a domestic good that costs $100 as opposed to a European good costing €100 = $100. If the dollar appreciates to $0.95 per euro, then the European good looks cheaper on paper, only $95. Should the American switch to the import? Yes, if the good can be moved without cost—but there are few such goods! If shipping costs $10, it still makes sense to consume the domestic good until the exchange rate falls below $0.90 per euro. In examples like this, the real exchange rate can move substantially within a *neutral band* (or *band of inaction*) where the existence of transaction costs breaks the link between price movements and shifts in demand. Practically, this means that expenditure switching may be a nonlinear phenomenon: it will be weak at first and then much stronger as the real exchange rate change grows larger. This phenomenon, coupled with the J Curve effects discussed earlier, may cause the response of the trade balance in the short run to be small or even in the wrong direction.

7 Conclusions

The analysis of macroeconomic policy is different in an open economy than in a closed economy. The trade balance generates an additional source of demand, and its fluctuations are driven by changes in output and the real exchange rate. Expenditure switching is a key mechanism at work here: as international relative prices change, demand shifts from foreign to home goods and vice versa.

The open economy IS-LM-FX framework is a workhorse model for analyzing the macroeconomic responses to shocks and to changes in monetary and fiscal policies. Exploring these responses, in turn, draws out some clear contrasts between the operation of fixed and flexible exchange rate regimes.

Under flexible exchange rates, monetary and fiscal policies can be used. Monetary expansions raise output and also lower the interest rate, which stimulates investment and causes a depreciation, which in turn stimulates the trade balance. Fiscal expansions raise output; raise the interest rate, which depresses investment; and cause an appreciation, which in turn lowers the trade balance.

With two policy tools available, the authorities have considerable flexibility. In particular, their ability to let the exchange rate adjust to absorb shocks makes a strong case for a floating exchange rate. Now we can understand the logic behind Robert Mundell's quote at the start of the chapter.

Under fixed exchange rates, monetary policy is unavailable because the home interest rate has to remain equal to the foreign interest rate, as spelled out by the trilemma. But fiscal policy has great power under a fixed exchange rate. Fiscal expansions raise output and force the monetary authority to expand the money supply to prevent any rise in the interest rate and any appreciation of the exchange rate. In contrast to the floating case, in which interest rate increases and exchange rate appreciation put downward pressure on investment and the trade balance, the demand stimulus is even greater.

With only one policy tool available, the authorities in fixed rate regimes have much less flexibility. They also expose the economy to more volatility because any demand shock will entail an immediate and reinforcing monetary shock. The tendency of fixed exchange rate systems to amplify demand shocks helps us understand the logic behind Alec Ford's quote at the start of the chapter.

Whatever the regime, fixed or floating, our findings suggest that macroeconomic policy can in principle be used to stabilize an open economy when it suffers from external shocks. Still, under floating exchange rates, more policy options are available (monetary and fiscal policy responses are feasible) than under fixed exchange rates (only a fiscal policy response is feasible).

Despite the simple lessons, however, real-world policy design is not straightforward. Policy makers face problems identifying shocks, devising the right response, and acting quickly enough to ensure their policy actions have a timely effect. Even then, under some conditions, the economy may respond in unusual ways.

KEY POINTS

1. In the short run, we assume prices are sticky at some preset level P. There is thus no inflation, and nominal and real quantities can be considered equivalent. We assume output GDP equals income Y and that the trade balance equals the current account (there are no transfers or factor income from abroad).

2. The Keynesian consumption function says that private consumption spending C is an increasing function of household disposable income $Y - T$.

3. The investment function says that total investment I is a decreasing function of the real or nominal interest rate i.

4. Government spending is assumed to be exogenously given at a level G.

5. The trade balance is assumed to be an increasing function of the real exchange rate EP^*/P, where P^* denotes the foreign price level.

6. The national income identity says that national output or income Y equals private consumption C, plus investment I, plus government spending G, plus the trade balance TB: $Y = C + I + G + TB$. The right-hand side of this expression is called *demand,* and its components depend on income, interest rates, and the real exchange rate. In equilibrium, demand must equal the left-hand side, supply, or total output Y.

7. If the interest rate falls in an open economy, demand is stimulated for two reasons. A lower interest rate directly stimulates investment. A lower interest rate also leads to an exchange rate depreciation, all else equal, which increases the trade balance. This demand must be satisfied in equilibrium: output rises. This is the basis of the IS curve: declines in interest rates must call forth extra output to keep the goods market in equilibrium. The IS curve is a line, a set of points Y and i where the goods market is in equilibrium, and it is downward sloping.

8. Real money demand is viewed as arising from transactions requirements. It increases when the volume of transactions (represented by national income Y) increases, and decreases when the opportunity cost of holding money, the nominal interest rate i, increases.

9. The money market equilibrium says that the demand for real money balances L must equal the real money supply: $M/P = L(i)Y$.

10. The money market equilibrium says that the demand for real money balances L must equal the supply M/P. This equation is the basis for the LM curve: increases in output must cause the interest rate to rise, all else equal. The LM curve is a line, a set of points Y and i where the money market is in equilibrium, and it is upward sloping.

11. The IS-LM diagram combines the IS and LM curves on one figure and shows the unique short-run equilibrium for output Y and the interest rate i. The IS-LM diagram can be coupled with the forex market diagram to summarize conditions in all three markets: goods, money, and forex. This combined IS-LM-FX diagram can then be used to assess the impact of various macroeconomic policies in the short run.

12. Under a floating exchange rate, the interest rate and exchange rate are free to adjust to maintain equilibrium. Thus, government policy is free to move either the IS or LM curves. The impacts are as follows:
   • Monetary expansion: LM shifts to the right, output rises, interest rate falls, exchange rate rises/depreciates.
   • Fiscal expansion: IS shifts to the right, output rises, interest rate rises, exchange rate falls/appreciates.

13. Under a fixed exchange rate, the interest rate is always equal to the foreign interest rates and the exchange rate is pegged. Thus, the government is not free to move the LM curve: monetary policy must be adjusted to ensure that LM is in such a position that these exchange rate and interest rate conditions hold. The impacts are as follows:
   • Monetary expansion: not feasible.
   • Fiscal expansion: IS shifts to the right, LM follows it and also shifts to the right, output rises strongly, interest rate and exchange rate are unchanged.

14. The ability to manipulate the IS and LM curves gives the government the capacity to engage in stabilization policies to offset shocks to the economy and to try to maintain a full-employment level of output. This is easier said than done: it is difficult to diagnose the correct policy response, and policies often take some time to have an impact, so that by the time the policy effects are felt they may be ineffective or even counterproductive.

KEY TERMS

consumption, p. 279

disposable income, p. 279

marginal propensity to consume (*MPC*), p. 280

expected real interest rate, p. 281

taxes, p. 281

government consumption, p. 281
transfer programs, p. 282
expenditure switching, p. 282
real effective exchange rate, p. 286
pass-through, p. 287

J Curve, p. 289
goods market equilibrium
    condition, p. 292
IS curve, p. 296

LM curve, p. 302
monetary policy, p. 307
fiscal policy, p. 307
stabilization policy, p. 317

PROBLEMS

1. In 2001 President George W. Bush and Federal Reserve Chairman Alan Greenspan were both concerned about a sluggish U.S. economy. They also were concerned about the large U.S. current account deficit. To help stimulate the economy, President Bush proposed a tax cut, while the Fed had been increasing U.S. money supply. Compare the effects of these two policies in terms of their implications for the current account. If policy makers are concerned about the current account deficit, discuss whether stimulatory fiscal policy or monetary policy makes more sense in this case.

2. Suppose that American firms become more optimistic and decide to increase investment expenditure today in new factories and office space.

   a. How will this increase in investment affect output, interest rates, and the current account?

   b. Now repeat part **a** assuming that domestic investment is *very* responsive to the interest rate so that U.S. firms will cancel most of their new investment plans if the interest rate rises. How will this affect the answer you gave previously?

3. For each of the following situations, use the IS–LM–FX model to illustrate the effects of the shock. For each case, state the effect of the shock on the following variables (increase, decrease, no change, or ambiguous): Y, i, E, C, I, TB. Assume the government allows the exchange rate to float and makes no policy response.

   a. Foreign output decreases.

   b. Investors expect a depreciation of the home currency.

   c. The money supply increases.

   d. Government spending increases.

4. How would a decrease in the money supply of Paraguay (currency unit is the "guaraní") affect its own output and its exchange rate with Brazil

(currency unit is the "real"). Do you think this policy in Paraguay might also affect output across the border in Brazil? Explain.

5. For each of the following situations, use the IS–LM–FX model to illustrate the effects of the shock and the policy response. Note: Assume the government responds by using monetary policy to stabilize output unlike Problem 3, and assume the exchange rate is floating. For each case, state the effect of the shock on the following variables (increase, decrease, no change, or ambiguous): Y, i, E, C, I, TB.

   a. Foreign income decreases.

   b. Investors expect a depreciation of the home currency.

   c. The money supply increases.

   d. Government spending increases.

6. Repeat the previous question, assuming the central bank responds in order to maintain a fixed exchange rate. In which case or cases will the government response be the same as in the previous question?

7. Toward the end of the year in 1999, consumers and businesses began to worry about "Y2K," the effect of switching over to a new dating system. There was concern that computers would be unable to process the switch from '99 to '00, creating potential problems in the receipt of regularly scheduled payments. In response, many individuals withdrew large sums of cash from their banking accounts, fearing they would be unable to access these funds. This would represent a positive shock to the money demand function (an increase in money demand for any given interest rate or output level). How would this shock affect U.S. output, interest rate, exchange rate, consumption, investment, and trade balance? How would your answer change if

the Fed used monetary policy to keep the interest rate fixed?

8. This question explores IS and FX equilibria in a numerical example.

 a. The consumption function is $C = 1.5 + 0.75(Y - T)$. What is the marginal propensity to consume, MPC? What is the marginal propensity to save, MPS?

 b. The trade balance is $TB = 5(1-[1/E]) - 0.25(Y - 8)$. What is the marginal propensity to consume foreign goods, MPC_F? What is the marginal propensity to consume home goods, MPC_H?

 c. The investment function is $I = 2 - 10i$. What is investment when the interest rate i is equal to $0.10 = 10\%$?

 d. Assume government spending is G. Add up the four components of demand and write down the expression for D.

 e. Assume forex market equilibrium is given by $i = ([1/E] -1) + 0.10$ where the two foreign return terms on the right are expected depreciation and the foreign interest rate. What is the foreign interest rate? What is the expected future exchange rate?

9. [Harder] Continuing the last question, solve for the IS curve: obtain an expression for Y in terms of i, G, and T (eliminate E).

10. Assume that initially the IS curve is given by

$$IS_1: Y = 12 - 1.5T - 30i + 2G,$$

and that the price level P is 1, and the LM curve is given by

$$LM_1: M = Y(1 - i).$$

The home central bank uses the interest rate as its policy instrument. Initially, the home interest rate equals the foreign interest rate of 10% or 0.1. Taxes and government spending both equal 2. Call this case 1.

 a. According to the IS_1 curve, what is the level of output Y? Assume this is the desired full-employment level of output.

 b. According to the LM_1 curve, at this level of output, what is the level of the home money supply?

 c. Plot the IS_1 and LM_1 curves for case 1 on a chart. Label the axes, and the equilibrium values.

 d. Assume that forex market equilibrium is given by $i = ([1/E] -1) + 0.10$ where the two foreign return terms on the right are expected depreciation and the foreign interest rate. The expected future exchange rate is 1. What is today's spot exchange rate?

 e. There is now a foreign demand shock, such that the IS curve shifts left by 1.5 units at all levels of the interest rate, and the new IS curve is given by

$$IS_2: Y = 10.5 - 1.5T - 30i + 2G.$$

The government asks the central bank to stabilize the economy at full employment. To stabilize and return output back to the desired level, according to this new IS curve, by how much must the interest rate be lowered from its initial level of 0.1? (Assume taxes and government spending remain at 2.) Call this case 2.

 f. At the new lower interest rate and at full employment, on the new LM curve (LM_2), what is the new level of the money supply?

 g. According to the forex market equilibrium, what is the new level of the spot exchange rate? How large is the depreciation of the home currency?

 h. Plot the new IS_2 and LM_2 curves for case 2 on a chart. Label the axes, and the equilibrium values.

 i. Return to part **e**. Now assume that the central bank refuses to change the interest rate from 10%. In this case, what is the new level of output? What is the money supply? And if the government decides to use fiscal policy instead to stabilize output, then, according to the new IS curve, by how much must government spending be increased to achieve this goal? Call this case 3.

 j. Plot the new IS_3 and LM_3 curves for case 3 on a chart. Label the axes, and the equilibrium values.

11. In this chapter, we've studied how policy responses affect economic variables in an open economy. Consider each of the problems in policy design and implementation discussed in this chapter. Compare and contrast each problem as it applies to monetary policy stabilization versus fiscal policy stabilization.

The Marshall-Lerner Condition

Our simple model assumed that a depreciation of a country's currency (a rise in q) will cause the trade balance to move toward surplus (a rise in TB). Is this assumption justified? Let's look at a simple example. Consider a hypothetical two-country world in which trade is initially balanced, so $TB = 0$ or $EX = IM$. The question of how the trade balance changes then simplifies to a question of whether the change in exports is greater or less than the change in imports. Let us consider a small percentage change in the real exchange rate, say $\Delta q/q = +1\%$, that is, a home real depreciation of 1%. Note that this is approximately a foreign real appreciation of 1%, since the foreign real exchange rate $q^* = 1/q$ is simply the inverse of the home real exchange rate, implying that $\Delta q^*/q^* = -1\%$.

As we have argued, when home exports look cheaper to foreigners, the real value of home exports expressed in home units of output will *unambiguously* rise. This effect is described by the elasticity of home exports with respect to the home real exchange rate, denoted η, where

$$\frac{\Delta EX}{EX} = \eta \times \frac{\Delta q}{q} = \eta\%.$$

That is, if the home country experiences a 1% real depreciation, its real exports (measured in home units) rise by $\eta\%$.

The same logic applies to the foreign country, with exports EX^*, real exchange rate $q^* = 1/q$, and elasticity η^*, so that

$$\frac{\Delta EX^*}{EX^*} = \eta^* \times \frac{\Delta q^*}{q^*} = \eta^*\%.$$

Our next step relies on the trade link between the two countries. Foreign exports must equal home imports, measured in any consistent units. In home real output units

Home imports in units of home output $= \underbrace{IM(q)}_{\substack{\text{Home imports} \\ \text{(real)}}};$

Foreign exports in units of home output $= \underbrace{(1/P)}_{\substack{\text{Divide by home} \\ \text{price level to} \\ \text{convert to home} \\ \text{output units}}} \times \underbrace{E}_{\substack{\text{Exchange rate} \\ \text{converts} \\ \text{foreign to} \\ \text{domestic} \\ \text{currency}}} \times \underbrace{P^*}_{\substack{\text{Price of} \\ \text{foreign} \\ \text{basket in} \\ \text{foreign} \\ \text{currency}}} \times \underbrace{EX^*(q^*)}_{\substack{\text{Foreign exports} \\ \text{(real)}}}.$

Value of foreign exports in foreign currency

Value of foreign exports in home currency

Equating these two terms, we find that $IM(q) = (EP^*/P) \times EX^* (q^*)$. Thus,

$$IM(q) = q \times EX^* (q^*).$$

This expression makes intuitive sense for the stylized two-country world that we are studying. It states that IM, the quantity of home imports (measured in *home* output units) must equal the quantity of foreign exports EX^* (measured in *foreign* output units) multiplied by a factor q that converts units of foreign goods to units of home goods (since q is the relative price of foreign goods, that is, home goods per unit of foreign goods).

For a small change, we may write the percentage change in the previous equation as follows. On the left is the percentage change in imports; on the right is the percentage change in q *times* EX^*, which equals the percentage change in q *plus* the percentage change in EX^*:

$$\frac{\Delta IM}{IM} = \frac{\Delta q}{q} + \frac{\Delta EX^*}{EX^*} = \frac{\Delta q}{q} + \left[\eta^* \times \frac{\Delta q^*}{q^*} \right] = 1\% + [\eta^* \times (-1\%)] = (1 - \eta^*)\%.$$

What is going on here? On the home import side, two effects come into play. Foreigners export a lower volume of their more expensive goods measured in foreign output units (a volume effect of $-\eta^*\%$), but those goods will cost more for home importers in terms of home output (a price effect of 1%). The price effect follows because the real exchange rate (the relative price of the foreign goods in terms of domestic goods) has increased (by 1%), and this makes every unit of imports cost more in real terms.

Starting from balanced trade with $EX = IM$, a 1% home real depreciation will cause EX to change by $\eta\%$ and IM to change by $1 - \eta^*\%$. The trade balance (initially zero) will increase (to become positive) if and only if the former impact on EX exceeds the latter impact on IM. This occurs if and only if $\eta > 1 - \eta^*$, or, equivalently

$$\eta + \eta^* > 1.$$

The last expression is known as the *Marshall-Lerner condition*: it says that the trade balance will increase only after a real depreciation if the responsiveness of trade volumes to real exchange rate changes is sufficiently large (or sufficiently elastic) to ensure that the volume effects exceed the price effects.

APPENDIX 2 TO CHAPTER 7

Multilateral Real Exchange Rates

How do the predictions of our model change when a country trades with multiple countries or regions? Can our theory be extended to this more realistic case? Can we make a sensible aggregation of trade flows, trade balances, and real exchange rates across, say, N different countries?

Suppose that for trade with any foreign country (say, country 1), the fractional change in home exports EX_1 and imports IM_1 given a small change in the real exchange rate q_1 is

$$\frac{\Delta EX_1}{EX_1} = \varepsilon \times \frac{\Delta q_1}{q_1}; \qquad \frac{\Delta IM_1}{IM_1} = -\varepsilon \times \frac{\Delta q_1}{q_1}.$$

The parameter $\varepsilon > 0$ is an *elasticity*. In this case, it is the elasticity of exports and imports with respect to the real exchange rate. When q rises by 1% (a real depreciation), exports rise by $\varepsilon\%$ and imports fall by $\varepsilon\%$. (A more complicated analysis is needed when the import and export elasticities differ; see the first appendix.)

From these relationships, we find the following by rearranging:

$$\Delta TB_1 = \Delta EX_1 - \Delta IM_1 = \varepsilon \frac{\Delta q_1}{q_1} EX_1 - \varepsilon \frac{\Delta q_1}{q_1} IM_1$$

$$= \varepsilon \times (EX_1 + IM_1) \times \frac{\Delta q_1}{q_1}$$

$$= \varepsilon \times \text{Trade}_i \times \frac{\Delta q_1}{q_1}$$

where $\text{Trade}_i = [EX_i + IM_i]$ is the total trade of the home country with country i.

Adding up this last equation across all countries, the change in the home trade balance is given by $\Delta TB = \Delta TB_1 + \Delta TB_2 + \ldots + \Delta TB_N$, which we can write

$$\Delta TB = \varepsilon \times \left[\text{Trade}_1 \frac{\Delta q_1}{q_1} + \text{Trade}_2 \frac{\Delta q_2}{q_2} + \ldots + \text{Trade}_N \frac{\Delta q_N}{q_N} \right].$$

We normalize by total trade, where $\text{Trade} = \text{Trade}_1 + \text{Trade}_2 + \ldots + \text{Trade}_N$, to obtain

$$\Delta TB = \varepsilon \times \text{Trade} \times \underbrace{\left[\frac{\text{Trade}_1}{\text{Trade}} \frac{\Delta q_1}{q_1} + \frac{\text{Trade}_1}{\text{Trade}} \frac{\Delta q_2}{q_2} + \ldots + \frac{\text{Trade}_1}{\text{Trade}} \frac{\Delta q_N}{q_N} \right]}_{\text{Trade-weighted average of bilateral real exchange rate changes}}.$$

The expression in brackets might look familiar. In Chapter 2, we introduced the concept of a *trade-weighted change in the nominal exchange rate*—the change in the value of a currency against a basket of currencies, where the change in each country-pair's nominal exchange rate was weighted by that particular country-pair's share of trade volume.

The preceding expression is very similar, only with nominal exchange rates replaced by real exchange rates, as seen in this chapter. The expression shows that (with some assumptions) our model can be extended to more realistic scenarios with many countries. We just have to use the change in a trade-weighted real exchange rate covering all trading partners.

Fixed versus Floating: International Monetary Experience

In truth, the gold standard is already a barbarous relic. All of us, from the Governor of the Bank of England downwards, are now primarily interested in preserving the stability of business, prices, and employment, and are not likely, when the choice is forced on us, deliberately to sacrifice these to the outworn dogma . . . Advocates of the ancient standard do not observe how remote it now is from the spirit and the requirements of the age.

John Maynard Keynes, 1923

How many more fiascoes will it take before responsible people are finally convinced that a system of pegged exchange rates is not a satisfactory financial arrangement for a group of large countries with independent political systems and independent national policies?

Milton Friedman, 1992

The gold standard in particular—and even pegged exchange rates in general—have a bad name. But the gold standard's having lost her name in the 1920s and 1930s should not lead one to forget her 19th century virtues. . . . Can these lost long-term virtues be retrieved without the world again being in thrall to the barbarous relic? . . . In an integrated world economy, the choice of an exchange rate regime—and thus the common price level—should not be left to an individual country. The spillover effects are so high that it should be a matter of collective choice.

Ronald McKinnon, 2002

A century ago, economists and policy makers may have had their differences of opinion, but—unlike today—they were virtually unanimous in their agreement about the ideal choice of exchange rate regime. Fixed exchange rates were viewed as the best choice. Even if some countries occasionally adopted a floating rate, it was usually with the expectation that they would soon return to a fixed or pegged rate.

The preferred method for fixing the exchange rate was also more or less agreed upon. It was the **gold standard,** a system in which the value of a country's currency was fixed relative to an ounce of gold and, hence, relative to all other currencies that were also pegged to gold. The requirements of the gold standard were strict: although monetary authorities could issue paper money, they were obliged to freely exchange paper currency for gold at the official fixed rate.

Figure 8-1 documents more than 100 years of exchange rate arrangements around the world. From 1870 to 1913, most of the world converged on the gold standard. At the peak in 1913, approximately 70% of countries were part of the gold standard system; very few floated (about 20%) or used other metallic standards (about 10%).

Since 1913 much has changed. Adherence to the gold standard weakened during World War I, waxed and waned in the 1920s and 1930s, then was never seen again. John Maynard Keynes and other policy makers designed a new system but one in which exchange rates were still fixed.

In the period after World War II, the figure shows that many currencies were pegged to the U.S. dollar. The British pound, the French franc, and the German mark were also somewhat popular peg choices. Yet because the pound, franc, and mark were all pegged to the dollar at this time, the vast

FIGURE 8-1

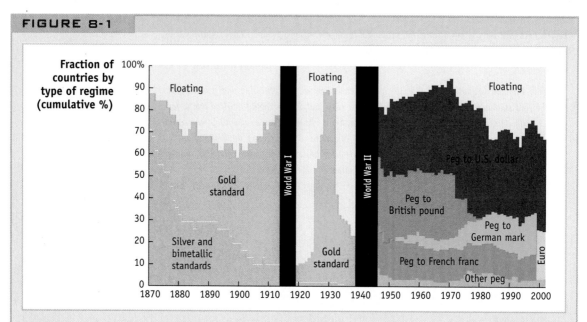

Exchange Rates Regimes of the World, 1870–2000 The shaded regions show the fraction of countries on each type of regime by year, and they add up to 100%. From 1870 to 1913, the gold standard became the dominant regime. During World War I (1914–1918), most countries suspended the gold standard, and resumptions in the late 1920s were brief. After further suspensions in World War II (1939–1945), most countries were fixed against the U.S. dollar (the pound, franc, and mark blocs were indirectly pegged to the dollar). Starting in the 1970s, more countries opted to float. In 1999 the euro replaced the franc and the mark as the base currency for many pegs.

Sources: Christopher M. Meissner, 2005, "A New World Order: Explaining the International Diffusion of the Gold Standard, 1870–1913," Journal of International Economics 66(2), July, 385–406; Christopher M. Meissner and Nienke Oomes, 2006, "Why Do Countries Peg the Way They Peg? The Determinants of Anchor Currency Choice," Cambridge Working Papers in Economics 0643, Faculty of Economics, University of Cambridge.

majority of the world's currencies ended up, directly or indirectly, on what amounted to a "dollar standard" system.

Like the gold standard, the dollar-based system didn't endure either. Beginning in the early 1970s, floating exchange rates became more common, and they now account for about 30% of all currency regimes. Remember that these data count all countries' currencies equally, without any weighting for economic size (measured by GDP). In the larger economies of the world, and especially among the major currencies, floating regimes are even more prevalent.

What has been going on? Why do some countries choose to fix and others to float? Why do they change their minds at different times? These are the main questions we confront in this chapter, and they are among the most enduring and controversial questions in international macroeconomics. They have been the cause of conflicts among economists, policy makers, and commentators for many years.

On one side of the debate are those like Milton Friedman (quoted at the start of this chapter) who in the 1950s, against the prevailing fixed rate orthodoxy, argued that floating rates are obviously to be preferred, have clear economic advantages, and are the only politically feasible solution. On the opposing side of the debate are figures like Ronald McKinnon (also quoted at the beginning of the chapter) who think that only a system of fixed rates can prevent noncooperative policy making, keep prices and output stable, and encourage international flows of trade and finance.

What are the pros and cons of different exchange rate regimes? Are the answers black and white? And why should we care?

NET WORK

Visit the International Monetary Fund's website (www.imf.org) and locate the latest classification of exchange rate regimes in all countries around the world. How many countries are fixing and how many are floating?

1 Exchange Rate Regime Choice: Key Issues

In previous chapters, we have examined the workings of the economy under fixed and floating exchange rates. One advantage of understanding the workings of these regimes in such detail is that we are now in a position to address a perennially important macroeconomic policy question: What is the best exchange rate regime choice for a given country at a given time? In this section, we explore the pros and cons of fixed and floating exchange rates by combining the models we have developed with additional theory and evidence.

APPLICATION

Britain and Europe: The Big Issues

One way to begin to understand the choice between fixed and floating regimes is to look at countries that have sometimes floated and sometimes fixed and to examine their reasons for switching. In this case study, we look behind the British decision to switch from an exchange rate peg to floating in September 1992.

We start by asking, why did Britain first adopt a peg? The answer derives from Britain's membership in the European Union (EU) since the 1970s and the steps being taken in the 1980s and 1990s by EU member states to move toward a common currency, the euro, which arrived in 1999. We discuss the euro in greater detail in Chapter 10. For now, we note that the push for a common currency was part of a larger program to create a single market across Europe. Fixed exchange rates, and ultimately a common currency, were seen as a means to promote trade and other forms of cross-border exchange by lowering transaction costs. In addition, it was also felt that an exchange rate anchor might help lower British inflation.

An important stepping-stone along the way to the euro was a fixed exchange rate system called the Exchange Rate Mechanism (ERM), which tied all member currencies together at fixed rates. The most important currency in the ERM was the German mark or deutsche mark (DM). Effectively, in the 1980s and 1990s, the German central bank, the Bundesbank, retained monetary autonomy and had the freedom to set its own money supply levels and nominal interest rates. For other countries, joining the ERM meant that, in effect, they had to *unilaterally* peg to the DM.[1] Thus, we would say that the DM was the **base currency** or **center currency** (or Germany was the *base country* or *center country*) in the fixed exchange rate system.

Britain joined the ERM in 1990. Based on our analysis of fixed exchange rates in Chapter 7, we can understand the implications of that choice using Figure 8-2. This figure shows the familiar one-country IS-LM-FX diagram for Britain and also shows another IS-LM diagram for the center country, Germany. We treat Britain as the home country and Germany as the foreign country, and we denote foreign variables with an asterisk.

Panel (a) shows an IS-LM diagram for Germany, with German output on the horizontal axis and the German DM interest rate on the vertical axis. Panel (b) shows the British IS-LM diagram, with British output on the horizontal axis. Panel (c) shows the British forex market, with the exchange rate in pounds per mark. The vertical axes of panels (b) and (c) show returns in pounds, the home currency.

Initially, we suppose the three diagrams are in equilibrium as follows. In panel (a), at point 1″, German output is Y_1^* and the DM interest rate i_1^*. In panel (b), at point 1, British output is Y_1 and the pound interest rate is i_1. In panel (c), at point 1′, the pound is pegged to the DM at the fixed rate $\overline{E}$ and expected depreciation is zero. The trilemma tells us that monetary policy autonomy is lost in Britain: the British interest rate must equal the German interest rate, so there is uncovered interest parity with $i_1 = i_1^*$.

A Shock in Germany With the scene set, our story begins with a threat to the ERM from an unexpected source. The countries of eastern Europe began their transition away from communism, a process that famously began with the fall of the Berlin Wall in 1989. After the wall fell, the reunification of East and West Germany was soon under way. Because the economically backward East Germany required significant public spending to support social services, pay unemployment benefits, modernize infrastructure, and so on, the reunification imposed large fiscal costs on Germany; but West Germans were willing to pay

---

[1] Officially, all currencies in the ERM pegged to a virtual basket of currencies called the ecu (European currency unit), the precursor of the euro. In practice, though, the DM served as the predominant reserve currency and the de facto base currency.

FIGURE 8-2

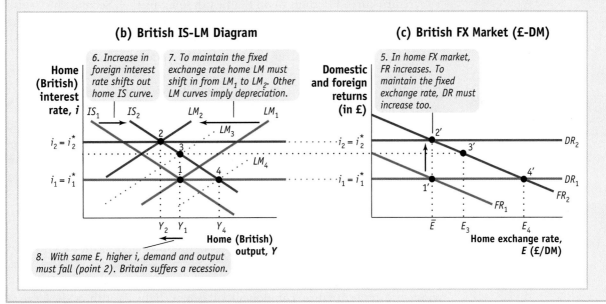

(a) German IS-LM Diagram

Foreign (German) interest rate, i^*

1. Government increases spending after reunification: IS^* curve shifts out.

2. Bundesbank tightens monetary policy to stabilize output: LM^* curve shifts in.

3. Large rise in interest rate i^*.

4. A boom is avoided: output stays at Y_1^*.

Foreign (German) output, Y^*

IS_1^* IS_2^* LM_2^* LM_1^*

i_2^* i_3^* i_1^*

2″ 3″ 1″

Y_1^* Y_3^*

Off the Mark: Britain's Departure from the ERM in 1992 In panel (a), German reunification raises German government spending and shifts IS^* out. The German central bank contracts monetary policy, LM^* shifts up, and German output stabilizes at Y_1^*. Equilibrium shifts from point 1″ to point 2″, and the German interest rate rises from i_1^* to i_2^*. In Britain, under a peg, panels (b) and (c) show that foreign returns FR rise and so the British domestic return DR must rise to $i_2 = i_2^*$. The German interest rate rise also shifts out Britain's IS curve slightly from IS_1 to IS_2. To maintain the peg, Britain's LM curve shifts up from LM_1 to LM_2. At the same exchange rate and a higher interest rate, demand falls and output drops from Y_1 to Y_2. Equilibrium moves from point 1 to point 2. If the British were to float, they could put the LM curve wherever they wanted. For example, at LM_4 the British interest rates holds at i_1 and output booms, but the forex market ends up at point 4 and there is a depreciation of the pound to E_4. The British could also select LM_3, stabilize output at the initial level Y_1, but the peg still has to break with E rising to E_3.

(b) British IS-LM Diagram

Home (British) interest rate, i

6. Increase in foreign interest rate shifts out home IS curve.

7. To maintain the fixed exchange rate home LM must shift in from LM_1 to LM_2. Other LM curves imply depreciation.

IS_1 IS_2 LM_2 LM_1

$i_2 = i_2^*$

$i_1 = i_1^*$

2 3 LM_3 1 4 LM_4

Y_2 Y_1 Y_4

Home (British) output, Y

8. With same E, higher i, demand and output must fall (point 2). Britain suffers a recession.

(c) British FX Market (£-DM)

Domestic and foreign returns (in £)

5. In home FX market, FR increases. To maintain the fixed exchange rate, DR must increase too.

$i_2 = i_2^*$

$i_1 = i_1^*$

2′ 3′ DR_2

1′ 4′ DR_1 FR_2

FR_1

$\bar{E}$ E_3 E_4

Home exchange rate, E (£/DM)

---

these costs to see their country united. As we know from Chapter 7, an increase in German government consumption G^* can be represented as a shift to the right in the German IS curve, from IS_1^* to IS_2^* in panel (a). This shift would have moved the German economy's equilibrium from point 1″ to point 3″. All else equal, the model predicts an increase in German interest rates from i_1^* to i_3^* and a boom in German output from Y_1^* to Y_3^*.[2] This was indeed what started to happen.

---

[2] All else would not have been equal under this shift, given the ERM; Germany's interest rate increase would have been matched by other ERM members to preserve their pegs. For Germany, those shifts would be increases in the foreign interest rate (from Germany's perspective), and those responses would, in turn, have shifted Germany's IS curve a tiny bit farther. These extra effects are minor and make no substantive difference to the analysis, so the extra shift is not shown here, for clarity.

The next chapter in the story involves the Bundesbank's response to the German government's expansionary fiscal policy. The central bank was deeply afraid that the boom in output might cause an increase in German rates of inflation, and it wished to take steps to head off that risk. Using its policy autonomy, the Bundesbank elected to tighten monetary policy: it contracted the money supply and raised interest rates. As we know from Chapter 7, this policy change can be represented as a shift up in the German LM curve, from LM_1^* to LM_2^* in panel (a). As drawn here, we suppose that the Bundesbank stabilizes German output at the initial level Y_1^* by raising German interest rates to the even higher level of i_2^*.[3]

Choices for the Other ERM Countries What happened in the countries of the ERM that were pegging to the DM? We examine what these events implied for Britain, but the other ERM members faced the same problems. From the IS-LM-FX model of Chapter 7, and as we recap here, we know that events in Germany would have had two implications for the British IS-LM-FX model. First, as the German interest rate i^* rises, the British foreign return curve FR shifts up in the British forex market. Second, the British IS curve will move out. Now we only have to figure out how much the British IS curve shifts, what the British LM curve is up to, and hence how the equilibrium outcome depends on British policy choices.

Float and Prosper? First, let us suppose that the Bank of England had left interest rates unchanged in Britain at i_1 and suppose British fiscal policy had also been left unchanged. In addition, then, we assume that Britain would allow the pound-DM exchange rate to float in the short run, but for simplicity we shall assume that the same expected exchange rate would prevail in the long run, so that the long-run future expected exchange rate E^e remained unchanged at $\overline{E}$. Think first about the investment component of demand: I in Britain would be unchanged at $I(i_1)$. But in the forex market in panel (c), with the domestic return DR_1 held at i_1 by the Bank of England and with the foreign return rising from FR_1 to FR_2, the new equilibrium is at 4′ and the exchange rate must rise to E_4: the pound would have to depreciate against the DM, implying an exit from the ERM system. But now think about the trade balance component of demand: the British trade balance would rise because a nominal depreciation is also a real depreciation in the short run, given sticky prices.[4] As we saw in Chapter 7, in the Keynesian cross the British demand curve shifts up and so does the British equilibrium output: that is, an increase in the foreign interest rate always shifts out the home IS curve, all else equal. In the figure, we see this in panel (b), with

---

[3] Interest rate responses in the ERM (described in footnote 2) would, in turn, have moved Germany's IS curve out yet farther, requiring a bit more tightening from the Bundesbank. Again, these indirect effects do not affect the analysis and are not shown, for clarity.

[4] This is true in a pure two-country model, and, from the British perspective, Germany is the "rest of the world." With many countries, however, the direction of change is still the same. All else equal, a British real depreciation against Germany will still imply a depreciation of the British real effective exchange rate against the rest of the world.

British interest rates still at i_1, and British output rising to Y_4, on the new IS curve IS_2. To keep the interest rate as low as i_1, as output rises, the Bank of England would expand the money supply and the British LM curve would shift out from LM_1 to LM_4. If Britain were to float and depreciate, Britain would experience a boom.

Peg and Suffer? Obviously, the course of action just described would not be compatible with Britain's continued ERM membership. If Britain's exchange rate were to stay pegged to the DM because of the ERM, the outcome for Britain would not be so rosy. In this scenario, the trilemma means that Britain would have to increase its interest rate and follow the lead of the center country, Germany. In panel (b), the pound interest rate would have to rise to the level $i_2 = i_2^*$ to maintain the peg, so that in panel (c) the domestic return rises from DR_1 to DR_2 in step with the foreign return's rise from FR_1 to FR_2, with a new FX market equilibrium at 2′. The Bank of England would accomplish this by tightening monetary policy and lowering the British money supply. In panel (b), under a peg, the new position of the IS curve at IS_2 would imply an upward shift in the British LM curve, as shown by the move from LM_1 to LM_2. So the British IS-LM equilibrium would now be at point 2, with output at Y_2. The adverse consequences for the British economy are apparent. At point 2, as compared with the initial point 1, British demand has fallen. Why? British interest rates have risen (depressing investment demand I), but the exchange rate has remained at its pegged level $\overline{E}$ (so there is no change in the trade balance). To sum up, in this scenario the IS curve may have moved right a bit, but the opposing shift in the LM curve is even larger. If Britain were to stay pegged, Britain would experience a recession. This is exactly what was happening in 1992.

As we have noted, if the British pound had been floating against the DM, then leaving interest rates unchanged would have been an option, and Britain could have achieved equilibrium at point 4 with a higher output, Y_4. Indeed, as we know, the whole range of monetary policy options would have been opened up by floating, including, for example, the choice of a mild monetary contraction, shifting the British LM curve from LM_1 to LM_3, moving equilibrium in panel (b) to point 3, stabilizing U.K. output at its initial level Y_1, with the FX market in panel (c) settling at point 3′ with a mild depreciation of the exchange rate to E_3.

What Happened Next? In 1992 the British Conservative government came to the conclusion that the gains of being in the ERM and the euro project were smaller than costs suffered due to a German interest rate hike that was a reaction to Germany-specific events. Two years after joining the ERM, Britain opted out.[5]

---

[5] This description of the British decision to exit the ERM is a little flattering; the precise circumstances of the exit were rather chaotic, a series of events we discuss in Chapter 9.

FIGURE 8-3

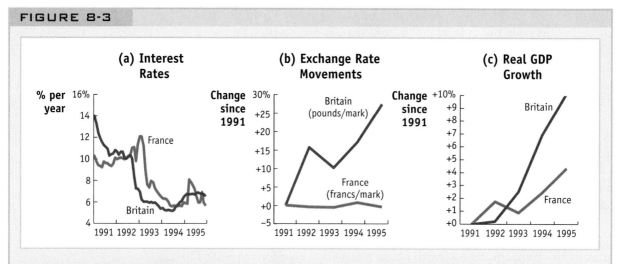

Floating Away: Britain versus France after 1992 Britain's decision to exit the ERM allowed for more expansionary British monetary policy after September 1992. In other ERM countries that remained pegged to the mark, such as France, monetary policy had to be kept tighter to maintain the peg. Consistent with the model, the data show lower interest rates, a more depreciated currency, and faster output growth in Britain compared with France after 1992.

Note: Interest rates are three-month LIBOR, annualized rates.

Sources: Data from Global Financial Data; econstats.com; IMF, International Financial Statistics.

Many Britons are opposed to the euro, some vehemently so.

Did Britain make the right choice? In Figure 8-3, we compare the economic performance of Britain with that of France, a large EU economy that maintained its ERM peg. Britain lowered interest rates in the short run after September 1992 and depreciated its exchange rate against the DM. In comparison, France never depreciated and had to maintain higher interest rates to keep the franc pegged to the DM until German monetary policy eased a year or two later, as shown in panels (a) and (b). As our model would predict, the British economy boomed in subsequent years. The French suffered slower growth, a fate shared by most of the other countries that stayed in the ERM.

The British choice still stands to this day. Although the option to rejoin the ERM has remained open since 1992, the British have not shown much interest. The idea of pegging to, much less joining, the euro, is deeply unpopular. All subsequent British governments have decided that the benefits of increased trade and economic integration with Europe were smaller than the associated costs of sacrificing British monetary autonomy. ■

Key Factors in Exchange Rate Regime Choice: Integration and Similarity

We started this chapter with a case study because such an example of a real-world policy choice brings into sharp focus the trade-offs that policy makers face as they choose between fixed exchange rates (pegs) and floating exchange rates (floats).

At different times and with differing degrees of enthusiasm, British authorities could see the potential benefits of participating fully in an economically integrated Europe with a single market, including the gains that would flow from being in the ERM fixed exchange rate system. The fixed exchange rate promised to lower the costs of economic transactions among the members of the ERM zone. But the British could also see—as the events of 1992 made clear—that there would be times when the monetary policy being pursued by authorities in Germany would be out of line with policy that was best for Britain. The fundamental source of this divergence between what Britain wanted and what Germany wanted was that each country faced different shocks. The fiscal shock that Germany experienced after reunification was not felt in Britain or any other ERM country.

To better understand these trade-offs, and hence the decision to fix or float, we now examine the core issues more closely: economic *integration* as measured by trade and other transactions, and economic *similarity,* as measured by the similarity of shocks.

Economic Integration and the Gains in Efficiency

The term "economic integration" refers to the growth of market linkages in goods, capital, and labor markets between regions and countries. We have argued that by lowering transaction costs a fixed exchange rate might promote integration and hence increase economic efficiency. Why?

Trade is the most obvious example of an activity that volatile exchange rates might discourage. Prices and exchange rates should be more stable once exchange rate volatility is removed, encouraging arbitrage and lowering the costs of trade. But trade is not the only type of international economic activity likely to be discouraged by exchange rate fluctuations. Currency-related transaction costs and uncertainty also act as a barrier to cross-border capital and labor flows and may also create welfare losses for countries. In Chapter 6, we saw that cross-border capital flows allow gains from financial globalization through consumption smoothing, investment efficiency, and risk sharing. Currency-related frictions may restrict such capital flows, thus lowering welfare. Similarly, currency uncertainty may deter cross-border flows of labor by affecting people's willingness to relocate. Such frictions will restrict migration to a lower level than would be seen in a hypothetical frictionless world, again lowering welfare.

We conclude: *If there is a greater degree of economic integration between markets in the home country and the base country (to which the home country's currency is pegged), then there will be a larger volume of transactions between the two, and the home country will benefit more from fixing its exchange rate with the base country. As integration rises, the efficiency benefits of a common currency increase.*

Economic Similarity and the Costs of Asymmetric Shocks

We have also argued that a fixed exchange rate can lead to costs. Our argument depended on the assumption that one country experienced a country-specific shock or **asymmetric shock** that was not shared by the other country: that is, the shocks were dissimilar.

Our case study showed why an *asymmetric* shock causes problems: it leads to a conflict between the policy goals of the two countries. In our example, German policy makers wanted to tighten monetary policy to offset a boom caused by a positive demand shock due to expansionary foreign fiscal policy. But British policy makers did not want to implement the same policy because they had not experienced the same shock.

Now we can begin to see why similar or *symmetric* shocks cause no problems. Imagine a different scenario in which both Britain and Germany experience an identical demand shock. Both monetary authorities would like to respond identically, raising interest rates in each country by the same amount to stabilize output. Fortunately, this desired symmetric increase in interest rates would not conflict with Britain's fixed exchange rate commitment. If interest rates were initially set at a low common level $i_1 = i_1^*$, they would just be raised to a new higher common level $i_2 = i_2^*$. Here, Britain can stabilize output *and* stay pegged because uncovered interest parity is still satisfied! The exchange rate $\overline{E}$ does not change, and even though Britain is pegging unilaterally to Germany, Britain has the interest rate it would choose even if it floated and were free to make an independent monetary policy choice.

The simple, general lesson we can draw is that for a home country that unilaterally pegs to a foreign country, asymmetric shocks generate costs in terms of lost output. Desired foreign and home monetary policies will sometimes differ, but the peg means that foreign's policy choice will be imposed on home. In contrast, symmetric shocks do not generate any costs because desired foreign and home monetary policies will be the same, and foreign's imposed choice will suit home perfectly.

In reality, the application of this idea is more complex. The countries may not be identical and the shocks may be a mix of symmetric and asymmetric shocks of different magnitudes. It is possible, although algebraically tedious, to account for these complexities in the same framework. At the end of the day, however, the main point holds true.

We conclude: *If there is a greater degree of economic similarity between the home country and the base country (to which the home country's currency is pegged), meaning that the countries face more symmetric shocks and fewer asymmetric shocks, then the economic stabilization costs to home of fixing its exchange rate with the base become smaller. As economic similarity rises, the stability costs of common currency decrease.*

Simple Criteria for a Fixed Exchange Rate

We are now in a position to set out a simple theory of exchange rate regime choice by considering the *net benefits* of pegging versus floating. The net benefits equal the benefits minus the costs. Our discussions about integration and similarity have shown the following:

- *As integration rises, the efficiency benefits of a common currency increase.*
- *As symmetry rises, the stability costs of a common currency decrease.*

Our theory says that if market integration or symmetry rises, the net benefits of a fixed exchange rate also rise. If the net benefits are negative, the home country ought to float if the decision is based solely on its economic interests. If the net benefits turn positive, the home country ought to fix.

Figure 8-4 illustrates the theory graphically in an **symmetry-integration diagram** in which the horizontal axis measures the degree of economic integration between a pair of locations, say A and B, and the vertical axis measures the symmetry of the shocks experienced by the pair A and B.

We use the figure to consider the question of whether A should peg unilaterally to B (or vice versa). Suppose conditions change and the pair moves up and to the right, for example, from point 1 toward point 6. Along this path, integration and symmetry are both increasing, so the net benefits of fixing are also increasing. At some critical point (point 2 in the graph), the net benefits turn positive. Before that point, floating is best. After that point, fixing is best.

FIGURE 8-4

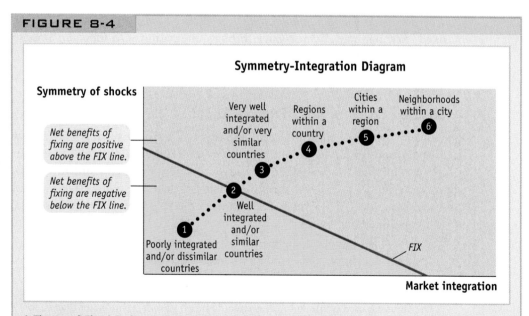

A Theory of Fixed Exchange Rates Points 1 to 6 in the figure represent a pair of locations. Suppose one location is considering pegging its exchange rate to its partner. If their markets become more integrated (a move to the right along the horizontal axis) or if the economic shocks they experience become more symmetric (a move up on the vertical axis), the net economic benefits of fixing increase. If the pair moves far enough up or to the right, then the benefits of fixing exceed costs (net benefits are positive), and the pair will cross the fixing threshold given by the *FIX* line. Above the line, it is optimal for the region to fix. Below the line, it is optimal for the region to float.

Our argument is more general: whatever the direction of the path, as long as it moves up and to the right, it must cross some threshold like point 2 beyond which benefits outweigh costs. Thus, there will exist a set of points—a downward-sloping line passing through point 2—that delineates this threshold. We refer to this as the *FIX* line, as shown in Figure 8-4. Points above the *FIX* line satisfy the economic criteria for a fixed exchange rate.

What might different points on this chart mean? To give an example, if we are at point 6, we might think of A and B as neighborhoods in a city—they are very well integrated and an economic shock is usually felt by all neighborhoods in the city. If A and B were at point 5, they might be two cities. If A and B were at point 4, they might be the regions of a country, still above the *FIX* line. If A and B were at point 3, they might be neighboring, well-integrated countries with few asymmetric shocks. Point 2 is right on the borderline. If A and B were at point 1, they might be less well-integrated countries with more asymmetric shocks and our theory says they ought to float.

The key prediction of our theory is this: *Pairs of countries above the FIX line (more integrated, more similar shocks) will gain economically from adopting a fixed exchange rate. Those below the FIX line (less integrated, less similar shocks) will not.*

In a moment, we develop and apply this theory further. But first, we ask whether there is evidence to support the theory's two main assumptions: Do fixed exchange rates deliver gains through integration? Do they also impose costs by obstructing stabilization policy?

APPLICATION

Do Fixed Exchange Rates Promote Trade?

Probably the single most powerful argument *for* a fixed exchange rate is that it might boost trade by eliminating trade-hindering frictions. The idea is an old one. In 1878 the United States had yet to rejoin the gold standard following the Civil War. Policy makers were debating whether going back on gold made sense, and J. S. Moore, a U.S. Treasury official testifying before Congress, was questioned on the subject:

> Question: Do you not think that the use of a common standard of value has a tendency to promote a free commercial interchange between the various countries using it?
>
> Answer: If two countries, be they ever so distant from each other, should have the same standard of money . . . there would be no greater harmonizer than such an exchange.

Benefits Measured by Trade Levels As we have noted, this was the conventional wisdom among policy makers in the late nineteenth and early twentieth centuries, and research by economic historians has found strong support for their views: all else equal, a pair of countries adopting the gold standard had bilateral trade levels 30% to 100% higher than comparable pairs of countries that were off the gold standard.[6] Thus, it appears that the gold standard *did* promote trade.

What about fixed exchange rates today? Do they promote trade? Economists have exhaustively tested this hypothesis using increasingly sophisticated statistical methods. Some recent evidence is reported in Figure 8-5, which classifies country pair A–B in four different ways:

a. The two countries are using a *common currency* (that is, A and B are in a currency union or A has unilaterally adopted B's currency).

b. The two countries are linked by a *direct* exchange rate peg (that is, A's currency is pegged to B's).

c. The two countries are linked by an *indirect* exchange rate peg, via a third currency (that is, A and B have currencies pegged to C but not directly to each other).

d. The two countries are not linked by any type of peg (that is, their currencies float against one another, even if one or both might be pegged to some other third currency).

Using this classification and trade data from 1973 to 1999, economists Jay Shambaugh and Michael Klein compared trade levels in the pegged

FIGURE 8-5

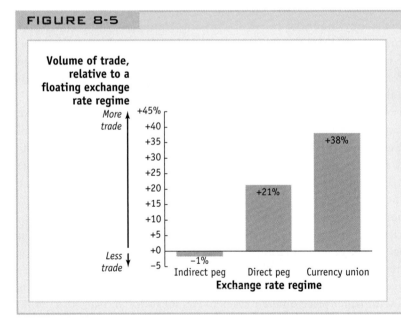

Do Fixed Exchange Rates Promote Trade?
The chart shows one study's estimates of the impact on trade of fixed exchange rates relative to floating. Indirect pegs were found to have a small but statistically insignificant impact on trade. A direct peg raises trade by 21%. A currency union raises trade by 38%.

Note: Based on a gravity model of trade with binary controls for each type of exchange rate regime using country-pair fixed effects.

Source: Michael W. Klein and Jay C. Shambaugh, 2006, "Fixed Exchange Rates and Trade," Journal of International Economics, 70(2), December, 359–383.

---

[6] J. Ernesto López Córdova and Christopher M. Meissner, 2003, "Exchange Rate Regimes and International Trade: Evidence from the Classical Gold Standard Era, 1870–1913," *American Economic Review,* 93(1), March, 344–353; Antoni Estevadeordal, Brian Frantz, and Alan M. Taylor, 2003, "The Rise and Fall of World Trade, 1870–1939," *Quarterly Journal of Economics,* 118(2), May, 359–407; Marc Flandreau and Mathilde Maurel, 2005, "Monetary Union, Trade Integration, and Business Cycles in 19th Century Europe," *Open Economies Review,* 16(2), January, 135–152. The quotation is cited in an earlier draft of the paper by López Córdova and Meissner.

regimes—(a) through (c)—with the benchmark level of trade under a floating regime (d). They also used careful statistical techniques to control for the problem of reverse causality, and found that their estimates were robust (the problem being that higher trade might have caused countries to fix their exchange rates).

The figure shows their key estimates, according to which currency unions increased levels of trade by 38%. They also found that just the adoption of a fixed exchange rate would promote trade, although only for the case of *direct* pegs. Adopting a direct peg increased trade levels by approximately 21% compared with trade levels seen under a floating exchange rate. Indirect pegs had a negligible and statistically insignificant impact on bilateral trade.[7]

Benefits Measured by Price Convergence Examining the effect of exchange rate regimes on trade levels is just one way to evaluate the impact of currency arrangements on international market integration, and it has been extensively researched. An alternative and growing empirical literature examines the relationship between exchange rate regimes and price convergence. These studies use the law of one price (LOOP) and purchasing power parity (PPP), which we saw first in Chapter 3, as their benchmark criteria for an integrated market.

If fixed exchange rates promote trade by lowering transaction costs, then we would expect to find that differences between prices (measured in a common currency) ought to be smaller among countries with pegged rates than among countries with floating rates. In other words, under a fixed exchange rate, we should find that LOOP and PPP are more likely to hold than under a floating regime. (Recall that it is convergence in prices that underlies the gains-from-trade argument.)

Statistical methods can be used to detect how large price differences have to be between two locations before arbitrage begins. Research on prices of baskets of goods shows that as exchange rate volatility increases, the price differences widen and the speed at which prices in the two markets converge decreases. These findings offer support for the hypothesis that fixed exchange rates promote arbitrage and price convergence.[8]

At a more microeconomic level, economists have also studied convergence in the prices of individual goods. For example, several studies focused on Europe have looked at the prices of various goods in different countries (for example, retail prices of cars and TV sets, and the prices of Marlboro cigarettes in duty-free shops) and have concluded that higher exchange rate volatility is associated with larger price differentials between locations. In particular, while price gaps still remain for many goods, the "in" countries that maintained

[7] Michael W. Klein and Jay C. Shambaugh, 2006, "Fixed Exchange Rates and Trade," *Journal of International Economics*, 70(2), December, 359–383.

[8] Maurice Obstfeld and Alan M. Taylor, 1997, "Nonlinear Aspects of Goods-Market Arbitrage and Adjustment: Heckscher's Commodity Points Revisited," *Journal of the Japanese and International Economies*, 11(4), December, 441–479.

membership in the ERM (and now the Eurozone) saw prices converge much more than the "out" countries that floated.[9] ■

Do Fixed Exchange Rates Diminish Monetary Autonomy and Stability?

Probably the single most powerful argument *against* a fixed exchange rate is provided by the trilemma. An economy that unilaterally pegs to a foreign currency sacrifices its monetary policy autonomy.

We have seen the result many times now. If capital markets are open, arbitrage in the forex market implies uncovered interest parity. If the exchange rate is fixed, expected depreciation is zero, and the home interest rate must equal the foreign interest rate. The stark implication is that when a country pegs, it relinquishes its independent monetary policy: it has to adjust the money supply M at all times to ensure that the home interest rate i equals the foreign interest rate i^*.

The preceding case study of Britain and the ERM is one more example. Britain wanted to decouple the British interest rate from the German interest rate. To do so, it had to stop pegging the pound to the deutsche mark. Once it had done that, instead of having to contract the British economy as a result of unrelated events in Germany, it could maintain whatever interest rate it thought was best suited to British economic interests.

The Trilemma, Policy Constraints, and Interest Rate Correlations Is the trilemma truly a binding constraint? Economist Jay Shambaugh tested this proposition, and Figure 8-6 shows some evidence using his data. As we have seen, there are three main solutions to the trilemma. A country can do the following:

1. Opt for open capital markets, with fixed exchange rates (an "open peg")
2. Opt to open its capital market but allow the currency to float (an "open nonpeg")
3. Opt to close its capital markets ("closed")

In case 1, changes in the country's interest rate should match changes in the interest rate of the base country to which it is pegging. In cases 2 and 3, there is no need for the country's interest rate to move in step with the base.

Figure 8-6 displays evidence for the trilemma. On the vertical axis is the annual change in the domestic interest rate; on the horizontal axis is the annual change in the base country interest rate. The trilemma says that in an open peg the two changes should be the same and the points should lie on

---

[9] Marcus Asplund and Richard Friberg, 2001, "The Law of One Price in Scandinavian Duty-Free Stores," *American Economic Review,* 91(4), September, 1072–1083; Pinelopi Koujianou Goldberg and Frank Verboven, 2004, "Cross-Country Price Dispersion in the Euro Era: A Case Study of the European Car Market," *Economic Policy,* 19(40), October, 483–521; Jean Imbs, Haroon Mumtaz, Morten O. Ravn and Hélène Rey, 2004, "Price Convergence: What's on TV?" Unpublished paper, London Business School, CEPR, Princeton University and National Bureau of Economic Research (NBER).

FIGURE 8-6

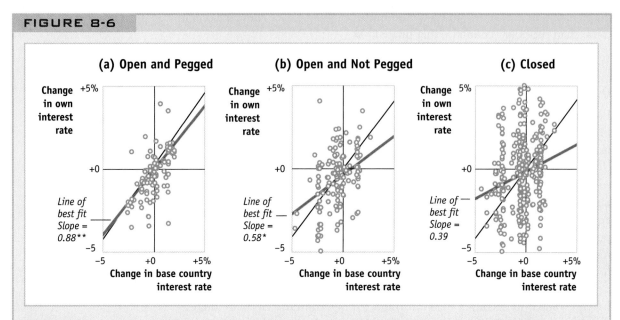

The Trilemma in Action The trilemma says that if the home country is an open peg, it sacrifices monetary policy autonomy because changes in its own interest rate must match changes in the interest rate of the base country. Panel (a) shows that this is the case. The trilemma also says that there are two ways to get that autonomy back: switch to a floating exchange rate or impose capital controls. Panels (b) and (c) show that either of these two policies permits home interest rates to move more independently of the base country.

Notes: ** Statistically significant at 1% level. * Statistically significant at 5% level. Hyperinflations excluded.

Source: Data from Jay C. Shambaugh, 2004, "The Effect of Fixed Exchange Rates on Monetary Policy," Quarterly Journal of Economics, 119(1), February, 300–351.

the 45-degree line. Indeed, for open pegs, shown in panel (a), the correlation of domestic and base interest rates is high and the line of best fit has a slope very close to 1. There are some deviations (possibly due to some pegs being more like bands), but these findings show that open pegs have very little monetary policy autonomy. In contrast, for the open nonpegs, shown in panel (b), and closed economies, shown in panel (c), domestic interest rates do not move as much in line with the base interest rate, the correlation is weak, and the slopes are much smaller than 1. These two regimes allow for some monetary policy autonomy.[10]

Costs Measured by Output Volatility
The preceding evidence suggests that open pegs have less monetary independence. But it does not tell us directly whether they suffer because their monetary authorities cannot engage in sta-

---

[10] The correlation isn't perfect for open pegs, nor is it zero for the other cases. This may not be surprising. Pegs are defined as de facto fixed within a ±2% band. The band allows central banks a little bit of flexibility with their exchange rates and interest rates that would be lacking in a strict peg (a band of zero width). As for nonpegs and closed countries, there may be reasons why their correlation with the base isn't zero. For example, they may have inflation targets or other guides to monetary policy that cause their interest rates to follow paths similar to those of the base country, or they may face some of the same (common) shocks as the base country. In other words, these countries have some room for maneuver that open pegs don't have, but how much they choose to use it is another matter.

bilization policy. To provide direct evidence of this effect, we would need to show that countries with fixed exchange rates suffered larger output fluctuations, all else equal.

Figure 8-7 shows results of a study by economists Atish Ghosh, Anne-Marie Gulde, Jonathan Ostry, and Holger Wolf. For the entire sample studied, they found that the volatility of output growth *is* much higher under fixed regimes. Once we split the sample into rich and poor countries, we can see that the result holds even more strongly for poorer countries.[11]

However, all else is certainly not equal among the sample countries. They differ in all kinds of characteristics that may affect output volatility, not just the exchange rate regime. When studies control for other factors (such as volatility in fiscal policy and in the terms of trade), they have found similar patterns, although the biggest impacts are generally found in the emerging market and developing countries.[12] It appears that one cost of adopting a fixed exchange rate regime is a more volatile level of output, a cost that is consistent with the theory we have developed. ■

FIGURE 8-7

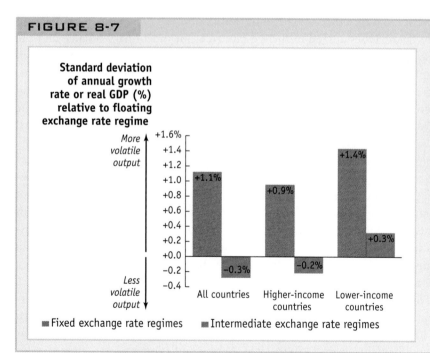

Exchange Rate Regimes and Output Volatility Based on annual data for a large sample of countries from 1960 to 1990, fixed exchange rate regimes were generally associated with higher output volatility than floating rate regimes, especially in poor countries. This finding is consistent with a key implication of the trilemma: only floating rate regimes can use monetary policy for stabilization purposes. By allowing some exchange rate flexibility, intermediate regimes appear to avoid stabilization costs, except in the poorest countries.

Source: Atish R. Ghosh, Anne-Marie Gulde, Jonathan D. Ostry and Holger C. Wolf, 1997, "Does the Nominal Exchange Rate Regime Matter?" NBER Working Paper No. 5874.

[11] Atish R. Ghosh, Anne-Marie Gulde, Jonathan D. Ostry, and Holger C. Wolf, 1997, "Does the Nominal Exchange Rate Regime Matter?" NBER Working Paper No. 5874.
[12] See, for example, Eduardo Levy-Yeyati and Federico Sturzenegger, 2003, "To Float or to Fix: Evidence on the Impact of Exchange Rate Regimes on Growth," *American Economic Review,* 93(4), September, 1173–1193; Kenneth Rogoff, Ashoka Mody, Nienke Oomes, Robin Brooks, and Aasim M. Husain, 2004, "Evolution and Performance of Exchange Rate Regimes," IMF Occasional Paper No. 229, International Monetary Fund.

2 Other Benefits of Fixing

In the previous section, we laid out the two most important factors affecting the economics of exchange rate regime choice: integration and similarity. In this section, we explore some other factors that affect the choice of exchange rate regime, factors that warrant particular attention in developing countries.

Fiscal Discipline, Seigniorage, and Inflation

One common argument in favor of fixed exchange rate regimes in developing countries is that an exchange rate peg prevents the government from using money printing as a way to finance government expenditure. Under such a financing scheme, the central bank is called upon to *monetize* a deficit (that is, hand over money to the government in exchange for debt). This leads to high inflation, and the source of the government's revenue is ultimately an inflation tax (called *seigniorage*) levied on the members of the public who hold money (see **Side Bar: The Inflation Tax**).

High inflation and hyperinflation (inflation in excess of 50% *per month*) are undesirable. Hence, if nothing else can prevent them, a fixed exchange rate may start to look more attractive. In this section, we explore this argument in more detail. Does a fixed exchange rate rule out inflationary finance and the abuse of seigniorage by the government? In principle, yes, but as we saw in Chapter 3, any nominal anchor will do the same. If a country's currency floats, its central bank can print a lot or a little money, with very different inflation outcomes. If a country's currency is pegged, the central bank might run the peg well, with fairly stable prices, or run the peg so badly that a crisis occurs, the exchange rate ends up in free fall, and inflation erupts.

Nominal anchors—whether money targets, exchange rate targets, or inflation targets—imply a "promise" by the government to ensure certain monetary policy outcomes in the long run. However, these promises do not guarantee that the country will achieve these outcomes. All policy announcements including a fixed exchange rate are to some extent "cheap talk." If pressure from the treasury to monetize deficits gets too strong, the commitment to any kind of anchor could fail. (As we shall see in the next chapter, fixed exchange rates fail all too frequently.)

The debate over whether fixed exchange rates improve inflation performance cannot be settled by theory alone—it is an empirical question. What has happened in reality? Table 8-1 lays out the evidence on the world inflation performance from 1970 to 1999. Average inflation rates are computed for the world as a whole and for subgroups of countries following the classification introduced in Chapter 1: advanced economies (rich countries), emerging markets (middle income countries integrated in world capital markets), and developing countries (other countries).

For all countries (column 1) we can see that average inflation performance appears to be largely unrelated to the exchange rate regime, whether the choice is a peg (17.4%), limited flexibility (11.1%), managed floating (14.0%), or freely floating (9.9%). Only the "freely falling" has astronomical rates of

TABLE 8-1

Inflation Performance and the Exchange Rate Regime Cross-country annual data from the period 1970 to 1999 can be used to explore the relationship, if any, between the exchange rate regime and the inflation performance of the economy. Floating is associated with slightly lower inflation in the world as a whole and in the advanced countries (columns 1 and 2). In emerging markets and developing countries a fixed regime eventually delivers lower inflation outcomes, but not right away (columns 3 and 4).

	Annual Inflation Rate (%)			
Regime Type	World	Advanced Countries	Emerging Markets and Developing Countries	Emerging Markets and Developing Countries (Excluding the Year after a Regime Change)
Fixed	17.4%	4.8%	19.6%	8.8%
Limited flexibility	11.1	8.3	12.4	10.8
Managed floating	14.0	7.8	15.1	14.7
Freely floating	9.9	3.5	21.2	15.8
Freely falling	387.8	47.9	396.1	482.9

Source: Author's calculations based on the dataset from Kenneth Rogoff, Ashoka Mody, Nienke Oomes, Robin Brooks, and Aasim M. Husain, 2004, "Evolution and Performance of Exchange Rate Regimes," IMF Occasional Paper No. 229, International Monetary Fund.

inflation (387.8%). Similar results hold for the advanced countries (column 2) and for the emerging markets and developing countries (column 3). Inflation rates are higher in the latter sample, but the first four regimes have similar inflation, with fixed and freely floating almost indistinguishable.

We may conclude that as long as monetary policy is guided by *some* kind of nominal anchor, the particular choice of fixed and floating may not matter that much.[13] Possibly the only place where the old conventional wisdom remains intact is in the developing countries, where fixed exchange rates can help to deliver lower inflation rates after high inflations or hyperinflations. Why? In those situations, people may need to see the government tie its own hands in a very open and verifiable way for expectations of perpetually high inflation to be lowered, and a peg is one way to do that. This can be seen in Table 8-1, column 4. If we exclude the first year after a change in the exchange rate regime we exclude chaotic periods after high inflations and hyperinflations when inflation (and inflationary expectations) may still persist even after the monetary and exchange rate policies have changed. But once things settle down in years two and later, fixed exchange rates generally do deliver lower (single-digit) inflation rates than other regimes.

■ *Bottom line: It appears that fixed exchange rates are neither necessary nor sufficient to ensure good inflation performance in many countries. The main exception appears to be in developing countries beset by high inflation, where an exchange rate peg may be the only credible anchor.*

---

[13] Kenneth Rogoff, Ashoka Mody, Nienke Oomes, Robin Brooks and Aasim M. Husain, 2004, "Evolution and Performance of Exchange Rate Regimes," IMF Occasional Paper No. 229, International Monetary Fund.

SIDE BAR

The Inflation Tax

How does the inflation tax work? Consider a situation in which a country with a floating exchange rate faces a constant budget deficit and is unable to finance it through domestic or foreign borrowing. To cover the deficit, the treasury department calls on the central bank to "monetize" the deficit by purchasing an amount of government bonds equal to the deficit.

For simplicity, suppose output is fixed at Y, prices are completely flexible, and inflation and the nominal interest rate are constant. At any instant, money grows at a rate $\Delta M/M = \Delta P/P = \pi$, so the price level rises at a rate of inflation π equal to the rate of money growth. The Fisher effect tells us that the nominal interest rate is $i = r^* + \pi$, where r^* is the world interest rate.

This ongoing inflation erodes the real value of money held by households. If a household holds M/P in real money balances, then a moment later when prices have increased by an amount $\Delta M/M = \Delta P/P = \pi$, a fraction π of the real value of the original M/P is lost to inflation. The cost of the inflation tax to the household is $\pi \times M/P$. For example, if I hold \$100, the price level is currently 1, and inflation is 1%, then after one period the initial \$100 is worth only \$99 in real (inflation-adjusted) terms, and the price level rises to 1.01.

What is the inflation tax worth to the government? It can spend the extra money printed ΔM to buy real goods and services

worth $\Delta M/P = (\Delta M/M) \times (M/P) = \pi \times (M/P)$. For the preceding example, the money supply expands from \$100 to \$101, and this would provide financing worth \$1 to the government. The real gain for the government equals the real loss to the households.

The amount that the inflation tax transfers from household to the government is called seigniorage, which can be written as

$$\underbrace{\text{seigniorage}}_{\text{Inflation tax}} = \underbrace{\pi}_{\text{Tax rate}} \times \underbrace{\frac{M}{P}}_{\text{Tax base}} = \pi \times L(r^* + \pi)Y.$$

The two terms are often viewed as the tax rate (here, inflation) and the tax base (the thing being taxed; here, money). The first term rises as inflation π rises, but, as we know from Chapter 3, the second term goes to zero as π gets large. People try to hold almost no money if inflation gets very high, and real money demand $L(r^* + \pi)Y$ falls to zero.

Because of these two offsetting effects, the inflation tax tends to hit diminishing returns as a source of real revenue: as inflation increases, the tax generates increasing real revenues at first, but eventually the rise in the first term is overwhelmed by the fall in the second term. Once a country is in a hyperinflation, the economy is usually well beyond the point at which real inflation tax revenues are maximized.

Liability Dollarization, National Wealth, and Contractionary Depreciations

As we saw in Chapter 5, exchange rate changes can have a big effect on national wealth. External assets and liabilities are never entirely denominated in local currency, so movements in the exchange rate can affect the value of a country's external assets and liabilities. For developing countries and emerging markets afflicted by the problem of *liability dollarization,* the wealth effects can be large and destabilizing, providing another argument for fixing the exchange rate, as we now show.

Suppose there are just two countries and two currencies, Home and Foreign. Home has external assets A_H denominated in Home currency (say, pesos) and A_F denominated in Foreign currency (say, U.S. dollars). Similarly, it has external liabilities L_H denominated in Home currency and L_F denominated in Foreign currency. The nominal exchange rate is E (with the units being Home currency per unit of Foreign currency—here, pesos per dollar).

The value of Home's dollar external assets and liabilities can be expressed in pesos as EA_F and EL_F, respectively, using an exchange rate conversion.

Hence, the Home country's total external wealth is the sum total of assets minus liabilities expressed in local currency:

$$W = \underbrace{(A_H + EA_F)}_{\text{Assets}} - \underbrace{(L_H + EL_F)}_{\text{Liabilities}}.$$

Now suppose there is a small change ΔE in the exchange rate, all else equal. This does not affect the values of A_H and L_H, but it *does* change the values of EA_F and EL_F expressed in pesos. We can express the resulting change in national wealth as

(8-1)
$$\Delta W = \underbrace{\Delta E}_{\substack{\text{Change in} \\ \text{exchange rate}}} \times \underbrace{[A_F - L_F]}_{\substack{\text{Net international} \\ \text{credit(+) or debit(−)} \\ \text{position in dollar assets}}}.$$

The expression is intuitive and revealing. After a depreciation ($\Delta E > 0$), the wealth effect is positive if Foreign currency assets exceed Foreign currency liabilities (the net dollar position in brackets is positive) and negative if Foreign currency liabilities exceed Foreign currency assets (the net dollar position in brackets is negative).

For example, consider first the case in which Home experiences a 10% depreciation, with assets of $100 billion and liabilities of $100 billion. External wealth is initially zero. What happens to Home wealth in pesos if it has half or $50 billion of assets in dollars and no liabilities in dollars? It has a net credit position in dollars, so it ought to gain. Half of assets and all liabilities are expressed in pesos, so their value does not change. But the value of the half of assets denominated in dollars will rise in peso terms by 10% times $50 billion. In this case, a 10% depreciation increases peso external wealth by $5 billion because it increases the value of a net foreign currency credit position.

Now look at the case in which Home experiences a 10% depreciation, as in the preceding example, but now Home has zero assets in dollars and half or $50 billion of liabilities in dollars. All assets and half of liabilities are expressed in pesos, so their value does not change. But the value of the half of liabilities denominated in dollars will rise in peso terms by 10% times $50 billion. In this case, a depreciation decreases peso external wealth by $5 billion because it increases the value of a net foreign currency debit position.

Destabilizing Wealth Shocks Why do these wealth effects have implications for stabilization policy? In Chapter 7, we saw that nominal exchange rate depreciation can be used as a short-run stabilization tool in the IS-LM-FX model. In the face of an adverse demand shock in the Home country, for example, a depreciation will boost Home aggregate demand by switching expenditure toward Home goods. Now we can see that exchange rate movements might also affect aggregate demand by affecting external wealth.

These impacts matter because it is easy to imagine more complex short-run models of the economy in which wealth affects the demand for goods.

For example:

- Consumers might spend more when they have more wealth. In this case, the consumption function of Chapter 7 would become $C(Y - T,$ Total wealth), and consumption would depend not just on after-tax income but also on wealth.

- Firms might find it easier to borrow if their wealth increases (for example, wealth increases will raise the net worth of firms, increasing the collateral available for loans). The investment function of Chapter 7 would then become $I(i,$ Total wealth), and investment would depend on both the interest rate and wealth.

We can now begin to understand the importance of the exchange rate valuation effects summarized in Equation (8-1). This equation says that countries have to satisfy a very special condition to avoid changes in external wealth whenever the exchange rate moves: the value of their foreign currency external assets must exactly equal foreign currency external liabilities. If foreign currency external assets do not equal foreign currency external liabilities, the country is said to have a *currency mismatch* on its external balance sheet, and exchange rate changes will affect national wealth.

If foreign currency assets exceed foreign currency liabilities, then the country experiences an increase in wealth when the exchange rate depreciates. From the point of view of stabilization, this is likely to be beneficial: additional wealth will complement the direct stimulus to aggregate demand caused by a depreciation, making the effect of the depreciation *even more* expansionary. This benign scenario applies to only a few countries, most notably the United States.

However, if foreign currency liabilities exceed foreign currency assets, then the country experiences a *decrease* in wealth when the exchange rate depreciates. From the point of view of stabilization policy (discussed in Chapter 7), this wealth effect is unhelpful because the fall in wealth will tend to offset the conventional stimulus to aggregate demand caused by a depreciation. In principle, if the valuation effects are large enough, the overall effect of a depreciation can be contractionary! For example, while an interest rate cut might boost investment, and the ensuing depreciation might also boost the trade balance, such upward pressure on aggregate demand may well be offset partially or fully (or even outweighed) by adverse wealth changes that put downward pressure on demand.

We now see that if a country has an adverse (i.e., negative) net position in foreign currency assets, then the conventional arguments for stabilization policy (and the need for floating) are at best weak and at worst invalid. For many emerging market and developing economies, this is a serious problem. Most of these poorer countries are net debtors, so their external wealth shows a net debit position overall. But their net position in foreign currency is often just as much in debit, or even more so, because their liabilities are often close to 100% dollarized.

Evidence Based on Changes in Wealth When emerging markets experience large depreciations, they often suffer serious collapses in external wealth. To illustrate the severity of this problem, Figure 8-8 shows the impact of

FIGURE 8-8

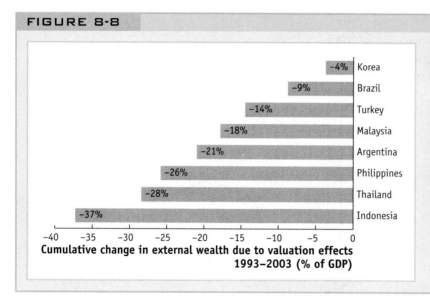

Cumulative change in external wealth due to valuation effects 1993–2003 (% of GDP)

Exchange Rate Depreciations and Changes in Wealth These countries experienced crises and large depreciations of between 50% and 75% against the U.S. dollar and other major currencies in the period from 1993 to 2003. Because they had large fractions of their external debt denominated in foreign currencies, they all suffered negative valuation effects causing external wealth to fall, in some cases quite dramatically.

Source: IMF, World Economic Outlook, April 2005, Figure 3.6.

exchange rate valuation effects on wealth in eight countries. All the countries witnessed exchange rate crises in the period in which the domestic currency lost much of its value relative to the U.S. dollar. Following the 1997 Asian crisis, Korea, the Philippines, and Thailand saw their currencies depreciate by about 50%; Indonesia's currency depreciated by 75%. In 1999 the Brazilian real depreciated by almost 50%. In 2001 Turkey's lira depreciated suddenly by about 50%, after a long slide. And in Argentina, the peso depreciated by about 75% in 2002.

All of these countries also had a problem of liability dollarization, with large levels of currency mismatch. In the case of the Asian countries, they had borrowed a great deal in yen and U.S. dollars. In the cases of Turkey, Brazil, and Argentina, they had borrowed extensively in U.S. dollars. We would predict, therefore, that all the countries ought to have seen large declines in external wealth as a result of the valuation effects, and indeed this was the case. Countries such as Brazil and Korea escaped pretty lightly, with wealth falling cumulatively by only 5% to 10% of GDP. Countries with larger exposure to foreign currency debt, or with larger depreciations, suffered much more: in Argentina, the Philippines, and Thailand, the losses were 20% to 30% of one year's GDP and in Indonesia almost 40% of one year's GDP.

Evidence Based on Output Contractions Figure 8-8 tells us that countries with large liability dollarization suffered large wealth effects. But do these wealth effects cause serious economic damage—serious enough to warrant consideration as a factor in exchange rate regime choice?

Figure 8-9 suggests that wealth effects are associated with contractions and that the damage is pretty serious. Economists Michele Cavallo, Kate Kisselev, Fabrizio Perri, and Nouriel Roubini looked at the correlation between an approximate measure of the wealth losses on net foreign currency liabilities suf-

FIGURE 8-9

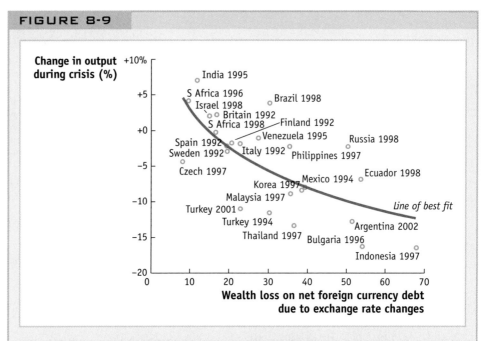

Foreign Currency Denominated Debt and the Costs of Crises This chart shows the correlation between a measure of the negative wealth impact of a real depreciation (horizontal axis) and the output costs (the extent of the contraction in real GDP) after an exchange rate crisis (a large depreciation). On the horizontal axis, the wealth impact is estimated by multiplying net debt denominated in foreign currency (as a fraction of GDP) by the size of the real depreciation (a log scale is used). The negative correlation shows that larger losses on foreign currency debt due to exchange rate changes are associated with larger output losses.

Source: Data from Michele Cavallo, Kate Kisselev, Fabrizio Perri, and Nouriel Roubini, "Exchange Rate Overshooting and the Costs of Floating," Federal Reserve Bank of San Francisco Working Paper Series, Working Paper 2005–07, May 2005.

fered during the large depreciations seen after an exchange rate crisis, and a measure of the subsequent fall in real output.[14] There is clearly a very strong correlation. For example, after 1992 Britain barely suffered any negative wealth effect and, as we noted earlier, did rather well in terms of subsequent economic performance: the case of Britain in 1992 sits in the upper left part of this scatter plot (very small wealth loss, no negative impact on GDP). At the other extreme are examples like Indonesia, where liability dollarization led to massive wealth losses after the 1997 crisis: the case of Indonesia in 1997 sits in the lower right part of this scatter plot (large wealth loss, large negative impact on GDP).

"Original Sin" Such findings have had a profound influence among professional international macroeconomists in recent years. Previously, external wealth effects were largely ignored and poorly understood. But now, especial-

---

[14] Michele Cavallo, Kate Kisselev, Fabrizio Perri, and Nouriel Roubini, 2005, "Exchange Rate Overshooting and the Costs of Floating," Federal Reserve Bank of San Francisco Working Paper Series, Working Paper 2005-07.

ly after the adverse consequences of recent large depreciations, it is universally recognized that the problem of currency mismatch, driven by liability dollarization, plays a profound role in many developing countries and is a legitimate factor to be considered during any debate over the choice of exchange rate regime.

It is an old problem. In the long history of international investment, one remarkably constant feature has been the inability of most countries—especially poor countries on the periphery of global capital markets—to borrow from abroad in their own currencies. In the late nineteenth century, such countries had to borrow in gold, or in a "hard currency" such as British pounds or U.S. dollars. The same is true today, as is apparent from Table 8-2. In the world's financial centers and the Eurozone, only a small fraction of external liabilities are denominated in foreign currency. In other countries, the fraction is much higher; in developing countries, it is close to 100%.

Economists Barry Eichengreen, Ricardo Hausmann, and Ugo Panizza used the term "original sin" to refer to a country's inability to borrow in its own currency.[15] As the provocative name suggests, a long-run perspective reveals that the "sin" is highly persistent and originates very deep in a country's historical past. Countries that have a weak record of macroeconomic

TABLE 8-2

Measures of "Original Sin" Only a few developed countries can issue external liabilities denominated in their own currency. In the financial centers and the Eurozone, the fraction of external liabilities denominated in foreign currency is less than 10%. In the remaining developed countries, it averages about 70%. In developing countries, external liabilities denominated in foreign currency are close to 100% on average.

	External Liabilities Denominated in Foreign Currency (average, %)
Financial centers (United States, United Kingdom, Switzerland, Japan)	8%
Eurozone countries	9
Other developed countries	72
Eastern European countries	84
Middle East and African countries	90
Developing countries	93
Asia/Pacific countries	94
Latin American and Caribbean countries	100

Source: Barry Eichengreen, Ricardo Hausmann, and Ugo Panizza, "The Pain of Original Sin," in Barry Eichengreen and Ricardo Hausmann, eds., 2005, *Other People's Money: Debt Denomination and Financial Instability in Emerging-Market Economies,* Chicago: University of Chicago Press.

---

[15] Barry Eichengreen, Ricardo Hausmann, and Ugo Panizza, 2005, "The Pain of Original Sin," in Barry Eichengreen and Ricardo Hausmann, eds., *Other People's Money: Debt Denomination and Financial Instability in Emerging-Market Economies,* Chicago: University of Chicago Press.

Two Russian bonds: a 100 ruble bond of 1915 and a 1,000 U.S. dollar bond of 1916. Creditors knew the dollar value of the ruble bond could be eroded by ruble depreciation. Only default could erode the value of the dollar bond.

management—often due to institutional or political weakness—have in the past been unable to follow prudent monetary and fiscal policies. Domestic currency debts were often diluted in real value by periods of high inflation. Creditors were then unwilling to hold such debt, obstructing the development of a domestic currency bond market. Creditors were then willing to lend only in foreign currency, that is, to hold debt that promised a more stable long-term value.

Still, sinners can find redemption. Another view argues that the problem is one of global capital market failure: for many small countries, the pool of their domestic currency liabilities may be too small to offer any significant risk diversification benefits to foreign investors. In this case, multinational institutions might step in to create markets for securities in the currencies of small countries, or in baskets of such currencies. An alternative view argues that as such countries reform—improve their institutional quality, design better policies, secure a low-inflation environment, and develop a better reputation—they will eventually free themselves from original sin and be able to issue external debt in their own currency. Many observers think this is already happening. Habitual "sinners" such as Mexico, Brazil, Colombia, and Uruguay have recently been able to issue some debt in their own currency (see **Headlines: The Last Temptation?**). In addition, many countries are also reducing currency mismatch by piling up large stocks of foreign currency assets in central bank reserves and sovereign wealth funds. The recent trends indicate substantial progress in reducing this problem as compared with the 1990s.[16]

Yet any optimism must be cautious. Only time will tell whether countries have really turned the corner and put their "sinful" ways behind them. Progress on government borrowing is still very slow in many countries, and this leaves the problem of mismatches in the private sector. While the private sector exposure could be insured by the government, that insurance could introduce the risk of abuse in the form of *moral hazard,* the risk that an insured entity will engage in excessive risk taking knowing that it will be bailed out. Finally, one might ask, why not simply hedge all the exchange rate risk? Ideally, this would be a great solution, but in many emerging markets and developing countries, currency derivative markets are underdeveloped. Many currencies cannot be

---

[16] Barry Eichengreen and Ricardo Hausmann, 2005, "Original Sin: The Road to Redemption," in Barry Eichengreen and Ricardo Hausmann, eds., *Other People's Money: Debt Denomination and Financial Instability in Emerging-Market Economies,* Chicago: University of Chicago Press; John D. Burger and Francis E. Warnock, 2003, "Diversification, Original Sin, and International Bond Portfolios," International Finance Discussion Paper 755, Board of Governors of the Federal Reserve System (U.S.); Camilo E. Tovar, 2005, "International Government Debt Denominated in Local Currency: Recent Developments in Latin America," *BIS Quarterly Review,* 109–118; Philip E. Lane and Jay C. Shambaugh, 2007, "Financial Exchange Rates and International Currency Exposures," NBER Working Paper No. 13433 (September).

HEADLINES

The Last Temptation?

Emerging markets are increasingly finding takers for their domestic currency debt.

Rafael Correa has brought a fresh face to Ecuador's presidency and some anachronistic habits to its treasury. Last week he quibbled over $135m of interest due on his country's foreign bonds, before coughing up at the last minute. Mr. Correa thinks Ecuador's debt is partly "illegitimate" and lacks a whole-hearted commitment to repaying on time and in full.

This kind of inconstancy is, however, quite out of season among Ecuador's neighbours and peers. . . . Retirement, not delinquency, is a more fashionable fate for emerging-market bonds these days. Many governments have tried to buy back nearly all of their external debt in an effort to impress creditors and reach investment grade. Indeed, the stock of external debt is so low, and spreads so thin, that JPMorgan is losing faith in its own benchmark. Spreads on the global EMBI [emerging-market bond index] do not "reflect the dynamics currently at play in emerging markets," the bank says.

The index's obsolescence reflects the decline in the dollar as the currency of emerging economies' borrowing. Dollar bonds now account for just 28% of their outstanding government debt. Securities issued in a country's own currency—pesos or zlotys, not dollars—are more worthy of investors' attention, JPMorgan says.

This is a welcome shift. After the Asian financial crisis, Barry Eichengreen of the University of California, Berkeley, and Ricardo Hausmann of Harvard University noted that crisis-hit emerging economies all suffered from the same "original sin": their governments could not borrow in their own currency. No amount of good works could save them. Even governments with sound policies, such as Chile's, shared this problem. As a result, currency crises automatically became debt crises. When the local currency fell, the burden of the country's dollar-denominated debt rose, often to unsustainable levels.

But since then, emerging economies have been undergoing a sort of redemption. Buoyant global commodity prices and healthy manufacturing exports have given them a collective trade surplus. And while the dollar was regarded as a safe haven in the 1990s, pessimism about its future has increased investor demand for currencies considered to be undervalued. As a result, even Argentina, which is still wrangling with jilted bondholders in the courts over its 2001 default, is issuing new debt in pesos and finding ready takers.

But there is more to this transformation than a standard swing of the business cycle. Many countries now float their currencies to some degree, and most have abandoned the boom-time deficit spending that paved the way for subsequent defaults. And even though issuing dollar-denominated bonds is cheaper, numerous finance ministers appear to think the safety of borrowing in one's own currency is worth the cost. It is always reassuring to know you can print the money you owe.

In addition, the more sovereign—and corporate—debt that is issued in local currencies, the deeper and more resilient local capital markets become. Even governments running healthy budget surpluses are issuing new securities, in an effort to add liquidity to their financial systems. Their securities provide a benchmark for corporate bonds, allowing companies to borrow for longer periods. With currencies under better control, markets for derivatives and the securitisation of products like mortgages are also beginning to sprout. Eventually, the middle classes in these nations may enjoy the kind of access to credit that rich-country consumers now take for granted.

But despite the explosive growth projected for these capital markets, it is too early entirely to write off original sin or the EMBI. Analysts still value it, as a snapshot indicator of the risk of investing in these countries. And it might take only one rogue central banker to send lenders scurrying back to the dollar. "The ability to borrow in your own currency is a great convenience," says Arijit Dutta, who covers emerging markets for Morningstar, an investment-research firm. "In the long term, it will be structural improvements that determine if they retain this privilege." The redeemed can always relapse.

Source: Excerpted from "Bye-Bye EMBI," Economist, February 22, 2007.

hedged at all, and for others the markets are poorly developed, and the costs high.

If developing countries are unable to avoid currency mismatches, they must try to cope with them. One option is to reduce or stop external borrowing, but for reasons discussed in Chapter 6, the gains from financial globalization mean that few countries want to pursue a policy of financial autarky. A more feasible—and perhaps only—alternative is for developing countries to seek to minimize or eliminate valuation effects by limiting the movement of the exchange rate. This is indeed what we observe, and evidence shows that the larger a country's stock of foreign currency liabilities relative to GDP, the more likely that country is to peg to the currency in which the external debt is issued.[17]

- *Bottom line: In countries that cannot borrow in their own currency, floating exchange rates are less useful as a stabilization tool and may be destabilizing. This applies particularly to developing countries, and these countries will prefer fixed exchange rates to floating exchange rates, all else equal.*

Summary

We began the chapter by emphasizing the two key factors that influence the choice of fixed versus floating rate regimes: economic integration (market linkages) and economic similarity (symmetry of shocks). But we now see that many other factors can affect the benefits of fixing relative to floating.

A fixed exchange rate may have some additional benefits in some situations. It may be the only transparent and credible way to attain and maintain a nominal anchor—which may be particularly important in emerging markets and developing countries with weak institutions, a lack of central bank independence, strong temptations to use the inflation tax, and poor reputations for monetary stability. A fixed exchange rate may also be the only way to avoid large fluctuations in external wealth, which can also be a problem in emerging markets and developing countries with high levels of liability dollarization. These may be powerful additional reasons to fix, and they seem to apply with extra force in poorer countries. Therefore, such countries may be less willing to allow their exchange rates to float—a situation that economists Guillermo Calvo and Carmen Reinhart have termed **fear of floating.**

To illustrate the influence of additional costs and benefits in our graphical representation, consider a Home country thinking of pegging to the U.S. dollar as a base currency. Such a Home country with a fear of floating would perceive additional benefits to a fixed exchange rate. So it would be willing to peg its exchange at lower levels of integration and similarity. We would represent this as in Figure 8-10 by an inward shift of the FIX line from FIX_1 to FIX_2. Without fear of floating, based on FIX_1, the Home country would float with symmetry-integration measures given by points 1 and 2, and fix at point 3. But if it had fear of floating, based on FIX_2, it would elect to fix at point 2 because the extra benefits of a fixed rate lower the threshold.

[17] Ricardo Hausmann, Ugo Panizza, and Ernesto Stein, 2001, "Why Do Countries Float the Way They Float?" *Journal of Development Economics*, 66(2), December, 387–414; Christopher M. Meissner and Nienke Oomes, 2006, "Why Do Countries Peg the Way They Peg? The Determinants of Anchor Currency Choice," Cambridge Working Papers in Economics 0643, Faculty of Economics, University of Cambridge.

FIGURE 8-10

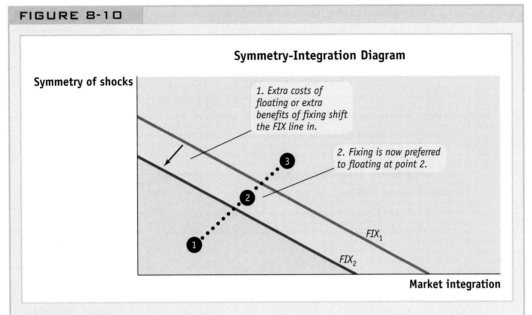

Symmetry-Integration Diagram

Symmetry of shocks

1. Extra costs of floating or extra benefits of fixing shift the FIX line in.

2. Fixing is now preferred to floating at point 2.

FIX_1

FIX_2

Market integration

A Shift in the FIX Line Additional benefits of fixing or higher costs of floating will lower the threshold for choosing a fixed exchange rate. The FIX line moves down. Choosing a fixed rate now makes sense, even at lower levels of symmetry or integration (e.g., at point 2).

3 Fixed Exchange Rate Systems

To provide a foundation, the discussion so far has considered only the simplest type of fixed exchange rate: a single home country unilaterally pegging to a foreign base country. In reality there are more complex arrangements, called **fixed exchange rate systems,** which involve multiple countries. Examples include the global *Bretton Woods system* in the 1950s and 1960s and the European *Exchange Rate Mechanism* (ERM) through which all potential euro members must pass.

These systems were based on a **reserve currency system** in which there are N countries $(1, 2, \ldots, N)$ participating. One of the countries, the center country (the Nth country), provides the reserve currency (the Nth currency), which is the base to which all the other noncenter countries peg. In the Bretton Woods system, for example, N was the U.S. dollar; in the ERM, N was the German mark until 1999, and is now the euro.

Throughout this chapter, we have assumed that a noncenter country pegs unilaterally to a center country, and we know that this leads to a fundamental asymmetry. The center country has monetary policy autonomy and can set its own interest rate i^* as it pleases. The noncenter country then has to adjust its own interest rate such that i is equal to i^* in order to maintain the peg. The noncenter country loses its ability to conduct stabilization policy, but the center country keeps that power. The asymmetry can be a recipe for political conflict and is known as the *Nth currency problem.*

Are these problems serious? And is there a better arrangement that can be devised? In this section, we show that **cooperative arrangements** may be the answer. We study two kinds of cooperation. One form of cooperation is based on mutual agreement and compromise between center and noncenter about the setting of interest rates. The other form of cooperation is based on mutual agreements about adjustments to the levels of the fixed exchange rates themselves. We now see how these two forms of cooperation work and what they mean for both the center and noncenter countries.

Cooperative and Noncooperative Adjustments to Interest Rates

Figure 8-11, panel (a), uses a now-familiar example to illustrate the possibility of policy conflict between center and noncenter countries. Suppose that Home, which is the noncenter country, experiences an adverse demand shock, but Foreign, the center country, does not. We have studied this case before: the Home IS curve shifts left and the Home LM curve then must shift up to maintain the peg and ensure the home interest rate i is unchanged and equal to i^*.

FIGURE 8-11

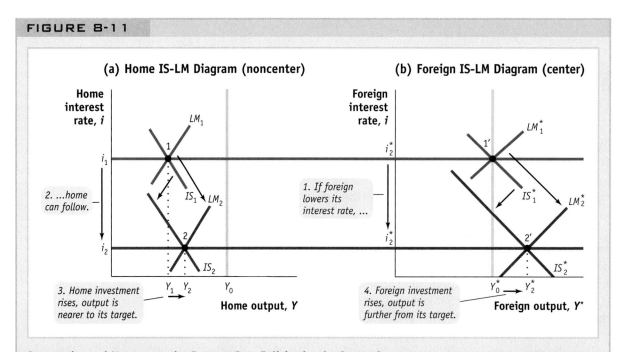

(a) Home IS-LM Diagram (noncenter)

(b) Foreign IS-LM Diagram (center)

Cooperative and Noncooperative Interest Rate Policies by the Center Country In panel (a), the noncenter home country is initially in equilibrium at point 1 with output at Y_1, which is lower than desired output Y_0. In panel (b), the center foreign country is in equilibrium at its preferred output level Y_0^* at point 1'. Home and foreign interest rates are equal, $i_1 = i_1^*$, and home is unilaterally pegged to foreign. Foreign has monetary policy autonomy. If the center country makes no policy concession, this is the noncooperative outcome.

With cooperation, center can make a policy concession and lower its interest rate and home can do the same and maintain the peg. Lower interest rates in the other country shift each country's IS curve in, but the easing of monetary policy in both countries shifts each country's LM curve down. The net effect is to boost output in both countries. The new equilibria at points 2 and 2' lie to the right of points 1 and 1'. Under this cooperative outcome, foreign accepts a rise in output away from its preferred level, from Y_0^* to Y_2^*. Meanwhile, home output gets closer to its preferred level, rising from Y_1 to Y_2.

We now assume that these shifts have already occurred, and we start the analysis with the home equilibrium at point 1 (where IS_1 and LM_1 intersect) in the home IS-LM diagram in panel (a). Home output is at Y_1, which is lower than Home's desired output Y_0. Foreign is in equilibrium at point 1′ (where IS_1^* and LM_1^* intersect) in the foreign IS-LM diagram in panel (b). Because it is the center country, Foreign is assumed to have used stabilization policy and is therefore at its preferred output level Y_0^*. The home interest rate equals the foreign interest rate, $i_1 = i_1^*$ since Home is pegged to Foreign, and this is the interest rate shown on both vertical axes.

Because this is a unilateral peg, only Foreign, the center country, has monetary policy autonomy and the freedom to set nominal interest rates. Home is in recession, but Foreign has its desired output. If the center country makes no policy concession to help Home out of its recession, this would be the noncooperative outcome. There would be no burden sharing between the two countries: Home is the only country to suffer.

Now suppose we shift to a cooperative outcome in which the center country makes a policy concession. How? Suppose Foreign lowers its interest rate from i_1^* to i_2^*. Home can now do the same, and indeed must do so to maintain the peg. How do the IS curves shift? As we know from Chapter 7, a lower Foreign interest rate implies that, *all else equal,* Home demand is lower, so the Home IS curve shifts in to IS_2; similarly, in panel (b), a lower Home interest rate implies that, *all else equal,* Foreign demand is lower, so the Foreign IS* curve shifts in to IS_2^* in panel (b). However, the easing of monetary policy in both countries means that the LM curves shift down in both countries to LM_2 and LM_2^*.

What is the net result of all these shifts? To figure out the extent of the shift in the IS curve, we can think back to the Keynesian cross and the elements of demand. The peg is being maintained. Because the nominal exchange rate is unchanged, the real exchange rate is unchanged, so neither country sees a shift in its Keynesian cross demand curve due to a change in the trade balance. But both countries do see a rise in the Keynesian cross demand curve, because investment demand rises thanks to lower interest rates. The rise in demand tells us that new equilibrium points 2 and 2′ lie to the right of points 1 and 1′: even though the IS curves have shifted in, the downward shifts in the LM curves dominate, and so output in each country will rise in equilibrium.

Compared with the noncooperative equilibrium outcome at points 1 and 1′, Foreign now accepts a rise in output away from its preferred stable level, as output booms from Y_0^* to Y_2^*. Meanwhile, Home is still in recession, but the recession is not as deep, and output is at a level Y_2 that is higher than Y_1. In the noncooperative case, Foreign achieves its ideal output level and Home suffers a deep recession. In the cooperative case, Foreign suffers a slightly higher output level than it would like and Home suffers a slightly lower output level than it would like. This is a cooperative outcome. The burden of the adverse shock to Home has been shared with Foreign.

Caveats Why would Home and Foreign agree to a cooperative arrangement in the first place? Cooperation might be possible in principle if neither country wants to suffer too much exchange rate volatility against the other—that is, if they are *close* to wanting to be in a fixed arrangement but neither wants to unilaterally peg to the other. A unilateral peg by either country gives all the benefits of fixing to both countries but imposes a stability cost on the pegger alone. Suppose neither country is willing to pay that price. This rules out a unilateral peg by either country. They could simply float, but they would then lose the efficiency gains from fixing. But if they can somehow set up a peg with a system of policy cooperation, then they could achieve a lower instability burden than under a unilateral peg and this could tip the scales enough to allow the gains from fixing to materialize.

Cooperation sounds great on paper. But the historical record casts doubt on the ability of countries to even get as far as announcing cooperation on fixed rates, let alone actually backing that up with true cooperative behavior. Indeed, it is rare to see credible cooperative announcements under *floating* rates, where much less is at stake. Why?

A major problem is that, at any given time, the shocks that hit a group of economies are typically asymmetric. A country at its ideal output level not suffering a shock may be unwilling to change its monetary policies just to help out a neighbor suffering a shock and keep a peg going. In theory, cooperation rests on the idea that my shock today could be your shock tomorrow, and we can all do better if we even out the burdens with the understanding that they will "average out" in the long run. But policy makers have to be able to make credible long-run commitments to make this work and suffer short-run pain for long-run gain. History shows that these abilities are often sadly lacking: shortsighted political calculations commonly trump longer-term economic considerations.

For example, consider the European Exchange Rate Mechanism (ERM), which was effectively a set of unilateral pegs to the German mark. The ERM was very clearly built around the idea of safeguarding gains from trade in Europe through fixed rates, but the designers knew that it had to incorporate some burden-sharing measures to ensure that the costs of absorbing shocks didn't fall on every country but Germany. The measures proved inadequate, however, and in the crisis of 1992 the German Bundesbank ignored pleas from Italy, Britain, and other countries for an easing of German monetary policy as recessions took hold in the bloc of countries pegging to the German mark. When the test of cooperation came along, Germany wanted to stabilize Germany's output, not anybody else's. Thus, even in a group of countries as geographically and politically united as the European Union, it was tremendously difficult to make this kind of cooperation work. (As we shall see in Chapter 10, this problem was alleviated by true monetary union, with the arrival of the euro and the creation of the European Central Bank.)

The lesson here is that the center country in a reserve currency system has tremendous autonomy, which it may be unwilling to give up lightly, thus making cooperative outcomes hard to achieve consistently.

Cooperative and Noncooperative Adjustments to Exchange Rates

We have studied interest rate cooperation. Is there scope for cooperation in other ways? Yes. Countries may decide to adjust the level of the fixed exchange rate. Such an adjustment is (supposedly) a "one-shot" jump or change in the exchange rate at a particular time, which for now we assume to be unanticipated by investors. Apart from that single jump, at all times before and after the change, the exchange rate is left fixed and Home and Foreign interest rates remain equal.

Suppose a country that was previously pegging at a rate $\overline{E}_1$ announces that it will henceforth peg at a different rate, $\overline{E}_2 \neq \overline{E}_1$. By definition, if $\overline{E}_2 > \overline{E}_1$, there is a **devaluation** of the home currency; if $\overline{E}_2 < \overline{E}_1$ there is a **revaluation** of the home currency.

These terms are similar to the terms "depreciation" and "appreciation" (defined in Chapter 2), which also define exchange rate changes. Strictly speaking, the terms "devaluation" and "revaluation" should be used only when pegs are being adjusted; "depreciation" and "appreciation" should be used to describe exchange rates that float up or down. Note, however, that these terms are often used loosely and interchangeably.

A framework for understanding peg adjustment is shown in Figure 8-12. We assume now that both Home and Foreign are noncenter countries in a

FIGURE 8-12

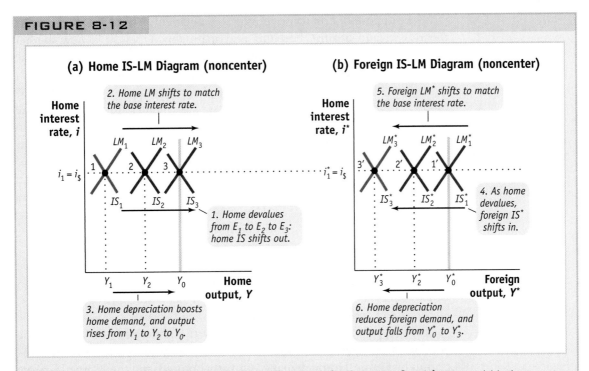

(a) Home IS-LM Diagram (noncenter)

(b) Foreign IS-LM Diagram (noncenter)

Cooperative and Noncooperative Exchange Rate Adjustments by Noncenter Countries In panel (a), the noncenter home country is initially in equilibrium at point 1 with output at Y_1, which is lower than desired output Y_0. In panel (b), the noncenter foreign country is in equilibrium at its preferred output level Y_0^* at point 1'. Home and foreign interest rates are equal to the base (dollar) interest rate and to each other, $i_1 = i_1^* = i_\$$, and home and foreign are unilaterally pegged to the base.

With cooperation, home devalues slightly against the dollar (and against foreign) and maintains a peg at a higher exchange rate. The home interest and foreign interest rates remain the same. But the home real depreciation causes home demand to increase: IS shifts out to IS_2. This is also a foreign real appreciation, so foreign demand decreases: IS* shifts in to IS_2^*. Under this cooperative outcome at points 2 and 2', foreign accepts a fall in output away from its preferred level, from Y_0^* to Y_2^*. Meanwhile, home output gets closer to its preferred level, rising from Y_1 to Y_2.

With noncooperation, home devalues more aggressively against the dollar. After a large home real depreciation, IS shifts out to IS_3 and IS* shifts in to IS_3^*. Under this noncooperative outcome at points 3 and 3', home gets its preferred output Y_0 by "exporting" the recession to foreign, where output falls all the way to Y_3^*.

pegged exchange rate system and that each is pegged to a third center currency, say the U.S. dollar.

(Why this change in the setup compared with the last section? Interest rate adjustment required us to study moves by the center country to help noncenter countries; with exchange rate adjustment, it is only noncenter countries who change their exchange rates vis-à-vis the center, so in this problem our focus shifts away from the center country.)

We assume that the center (the United States) is a large country with monetary policy autonomy that has set its interest rate at $i_\$$. Home is pegged to the U.S. dollar at $\overline{E}_{\text{home}/\$}$ and Foreign is pegged at $\overline{E}^*_{\text{foreign}/\$}$. In the home IS-LM diagram in panel (a), Home equilibrium is initially at point 1 (where IS_1 and LM_1 intersect). Again, due to a prior adverse demand shock, Home output is at Y_1 and is lower than Home's desired output Y_0. In the foreign IS-LM diagram in panel (b), Foreign is at its desired output level Y_0^* at point 1′ (where IS_1^* and LM_1^* intersect). Because Home and Foreign peg to the center currency (here the U.S. dollar), Home and Foreign interest rates are equal to the dollar interest rate, $i_1 = i_1^* = i_\$$.

Now suppose that in a cooperative arrangement, Home devalues against the dollar (and against Foreign) and maintains a peg at a new, higher exchange rate. That is, there is an unanticipated rise $\overline{E}_{\text{home}/\$}$. The Home and Foreign interest rates remain equal to the dollar interest rate, $i_1 = i_1^* = i_\$$, since Home and Foreign still peg. We can think back to the IS-LM model, or back to the Keynesian cross, if necessary, to figure out the impact of the change. Because the nominal depreciation by Home is also a real depreciation, Home sees demand increase: the Home IS curve shifts out to IS_2. Furthermore, the real depreciation for Home is also a real appreciation for Foreign, so Foreign demand *decreases:* the IS^* curve shifts in to IS_2^*. The outcome is cooperative because the burden of the adverse demand shock is being shared: Home output at Y_2 is lower than the ideal Y_0 but not as low as at Y_1; and Foreign has accepted output lower at Y_2^* than its ideal Y_0^*.

Why might this kind of cooperation work? Home and Foreign could agree that Home would devalue a little (but not too much) so that both countries would jointly feel the pain. Some other time, when Foreign has a nasty shock, Home would "repay" by feeling some of Foreign's pain.

Now suppose we shift to a noncooperative outcome in which Home devalues more aggressively against the dollar. Now after a large real depreciation by Home, Home demand is greatly boosted, and the Home IS curve shifts out a long way to IS_3. Home's real depreciation is also a large real appreciation for Foreign, where demand is greatly reduced, so the Foreign IS^* curve shifts in a long way to IS_3^*. The outcome is noncooperative: Home now gets its preferred outcome with output at its ideal level Y_0; it achieves this by "exporting" the recession to Foreign, where output falls all the way to Y_3^*.

There are two footnotes to this analysis. First, we have only considered a situation in which Home wishes to devalue to offset a negative demand shock.

But the same logic applies when Home's economy is "overheating" and policy makers fear that output is above the ideal level, perhaps creating a risk of inflationary pressures. In that case, Home may wish to revalue its currency, in which case it exports the overheating to Foreign.

Second, we have not considered the center country, here the United States. In reality, the center country also suffers some decrease in demand if Home devalues because the center will experience a real appreciation against Home. However, there is less to worry about here. After all, it is the center country, with policy autonomy, and can always use stabilization policy as a remedy. Thus, there may be a monetary easing in the center country, a secondary effect that we do not consider here. The key impacts of the devaluation—increased output for Home and reduced output for Foreign—are felt in the countries pegging to the center country.

Caveats We can now see that adjusting the peg is a policy that may be cooperative or noncooperative in nature. If noncooperative, it is usually referred to as a **beggar-thy-neighbor policy:** Home can improve its position at the expense of Foreign and without Foreign's agreement. When Home is in recession, and its policy makers choose to devalue and force a real depreciation, they are engineering a diversion of some of world demand toward Home goods and away from the rest of the world's goods.

This finding brings us to the main drawback of admitting noncooperative adjustments into a fixed exchange rate system. Two can play this game! If Home engages in such a policy, it is possible for Foreign to respond with a devaluation of its own in a tit-for-tat way. Down that road lies exchange rate mayhem, and the pretense of a fixed exchange rate system is over. The countries will no longer be pegging and will be playing a new noncooperative game against each other with floating exchange rates.

Cooperation may be most needed to sustain a fixed exchange rate system with adjustable pegs, so as to restrain beggar-thy-neighbor devaluations. But can it work? Consider continental Europe since World War II, under both the Bretton Woods system and the later European systems such as ERM (which predated the euro). A persistent concern of European policy makers in this period was the threat of beggar-thy-neighbor devaluations. For example, the British pound and the Italian lira devalued against the dollar and later the German mark on numerous occasions from the 1960s to the 1990s, and although some of these peg adjustments had the veneer of official multilateral decisions, some (like the 1992 ERM crisis) occurred when cooperation broke down.

APPLICATION

The Gold Standard

Our analysis in this section has focused on the problems of a reserve currency system in which there is one center country issuing a currency (for example, the dollar or euro) to which all other noncenter countries peg. As we know from Figure 8-1, this is an apt description of most fixed exchange rate arrangements at the present time and going back as far as World War II. A key issue in such systems is the asymmetry between the center country, which retains monetary autonomy, and the noncenter countries, which forsake it.

Are there symmetric fixed exchange rate systems, in which there is no center country and the asymmetry created by the Nth currency problem can be avoided? In theory the ERM system worked this way; but, as the 1992 crisis showed, there was, in practice, a marked asymmetry between Germany and the other ERM countries. Historically, the only true symmetric systems have been those in which countries fixed the value of their currency relative to some commodity. The most famous and important of these systems was the gold standard, and this system had no center country because countries did not peg the exchange rate at $\overline{E}$, the local currency price of a base currency, but instead they pegged $\overline{P_g}$ the local currency price of gold.

How did this system work? Under the gold standard, gold and money were seamlessly interchangeable, and the combined value of gold and money in the hands of the public was the relevant measure of money supply (M). For example, consider two countries, Britain pegging to gold at $\overline{P_g}$ (pounds per ounce of gold) and France pegging to gold at $\overline{P_g^*}$ (francs per ounce of gold). Under this system, one pound cost $1/\overline{P_g}$ ounces of gold, and each ounce of gold cost $\overline{P_g^*}$ francs, according to the fixed gold prices set by the central banks in each country. Thus one pound cost $E_{\text{par}} = \overline{P_g^*}/\overline{P_g}$ francs, and this ratio defined the *par* exchange rate implied by the gold prices in each country.

The gold standard rested on the principle of free convertibility. This meant that central banks in both countries stood ready to buy and sell gold in exchange for paper money at these mint prices, and the export and import of gold was unrestricted. This allowed arbitrage forces to stabilize the system. How?

Suppose the market exchange rate in Paris (the price of one pound in francs) was E francs per pound and deviated from the par level, with $E < E_{\text{par}}$ francs per pound. This would create an arbitrage opportunity. The franc has appreciated relative to pounds, and arbitrageurs could change one ounce of gold, into $\overline{P_g^*}$ francs at the French central bank, and then into $\overline{P_g^*}/E$ pounds in the market, which could be shipped to London and converted into $\overline{P_g^*}/(E\overline{P_g})$ ounces of gold, which could then be brought back to Paris. But we assumed that $E < E_{\text{par}}$, and so $\overline{P_g^*}/(E\overline{P_g}) = E_{\text{par}}/E > 1$, so the trader ends up with more than an ounce of gold and makes a profit.

As a result of this trade, gold would leave Britain and the British money supply would fall (pounds were being redeemed at the Bank of England by the French traders, and the gold exported back to France). At the same time, gold would enter France, expanding the French money supply (since the traders could leave it in gold form, or freely change it into franc notes at the Banque de France).

We can note how the result tends to stabilize the foreign exchange market in just the same way as interest arbitrage did in Chapter 4. Here, the pound was depreciated relative to par and the arbitrage mechanism caused the British money supply to contract and the French money supply to expand. The arbitrage mechanism depended on French investors buying "cheap" pounds. This would bid up the price of pounds in Paris, so E would rise toward E_{par}, stabilizing the exchange rate at its par level.

Four observations are worth noting. First, the process of arbitrage was not really costless, so if the exchange rate deviated only slightly from parity the profit from arbitrage might be zero or negative (i.e., a loss). Thus, there was a small band around the par rate in which the exchange rate might fluctuate without any arbitrage occurring. However, this band, delineated by limits known as the upper and lower "gold points," was typically small, permitting perhaps at most ±1% fluctuations in E on either side of E_{par}. The exchange rate was, therefore, very stable. For example, from 1879 to 1914, when Britain and the United States were pegged to gold at a par rate of $4.86 per pound, the daily dollar-pound market exchange rate in New York was within 1% of its par value 99.97% of the time (and within half a percent 77% of the time).[18]

Second, in our example we examined arbitrage in only one direction, but, naturally, there would have been a similar profitable arbitrage opportunity—subject to transaction costs—in the opposite direction if E had been above E_{par} and the franc had been depreciated relative to parity. (Working out how one makes a profit in that case, and what the net effect would be on each country's money supply, is left as an exercise.)

Third, gold arbitrage would enforce a fixed exchange rate at E_{par} (plus or minus small deviations within the gold points), thus setting expected depreciation to zero. Interest arbitrage between the two countries' money markets would equalize the interest rates in each country. So our earlier approach to the study of fixed exchange rates remains valid, including a central principle, the trilemma.

Fourth, and most important, we see the inherent symmetry of the gold standard system when operated according to these principles. Both countries share in the adjustment mechanism, with the money supply contracting in the gold outflow country (here Britain) and the money supply expanding in the gold inflow country (here France). In theory, if these principles were adhered to, neither country has the privileged position of being able to not change its monetary policy, in marked contrast to a center country in a reserve currency system. But in reality, the gold standard did not always operate quite so smoothly, as we see in the next section. ■

[18] Eugene Canjels, Gauri Prakash-Canjels, and Alan M. Taylor, 2004, "Measuring Market Integration: Foreign Exchange Arbitrage and the Gold Standard, 1879–1913," *Review of Economics and Statistics,* 86(4), 868–882.

NET WORK

Find the photo of the $20 gold coin on this page and the specifications in its caption. Calculate the U.S. dollar price of 1 ounce of gold under the pre-1913 gold standard. Now use the Internet to find details, including gold content, of a British gold sovereign coin worth £1 in the same era. Calculate the British pound price of 1 ounce of gold under the pre-1913 gold standard. Now compute the implied pound-dollar exchange rate. Check your answer against the value given in the text.

Courtesy of Blanchard Gold, Inc.

The U.S. gold parity was $20.67 per troy ounce from 1834 to 1933, so a $20 gold coin like this 1907 Saint Gaudens Double Eagle contained 20/20.67 = 0.9675 ounces of gold.

4 International Monetary Experience

A vast diversity of exchange rate arrangements have been used throughout history. In Chapter 2, we saw how different countries fix or float at present; at the start of this chapter, we saw how exchange rate arrangements have fluctuated over more than a century. These observations motivated us to study how countries choose to fix or float.

To try to better understand the international monetary experience and how we got to where we are today, we now apply what we have learned in the book so far. In particular we rely on the trilemma, first seen in Chapter 4, which tells us that countries cannot simultaneously meet the three policy goals of a fixed exchange rate, capital mobility, and monetary policy autonomy. With the feasible policy choices thus set out, we draw on the ideas of this chapter concerning the costs and benefits of fixed and floating regimes to try to understand why various countries have made the choices they have at different times.[19]

The Rise and Fall of the Gold Standard

As we saw in Figure 8-1, the history of international monetary arrangements from 1870 to 1939 was dominated by one story: the rise and fall of the gold standard regime. In 1870 about 15% of countries were on gold, rising to about 70% in 1913 and almost 90% during a brief period of resumption in the 1920s. But by 1939, only about 25% of the world was pegged to gold. What happened? The analysis in this chapter provides insights into one of the grand narratives of economic history.[20]

The period from 1870 to 1914 was the first era of globalization, with increasingly large flows of trade, capital, and people between countries. Depending on the countries in question, some of these developments were attributable to technological developments in transport and communications (such as steamships, the telegraph, and so on); some were a result of policy change (such as tariff reductions). Our model suggests that as the volume of trade and other economic transactions between nations increase, there will be more to gain from adopting a fixed exchange rate (as in Figure 8-4). Thus, as nineteenth-century globalization proceeded, it was likely that more countries crossed the FIX line and met the economic criteria for fixing.

There were also other forces at work encouraging a switch to the gold peg before 1914. The stabilization costs of pegging were either seen as insignificant—since the pace of economic growth was not that unstable—or else politically irrelevant—since the majority of those adversely affected by business cycles and unemployment were from the

---

[19] Barry Eichengreen, 1996, *Globalizing Capital: A History of the International Monetary System,* Princeton, NJ: Princeton University Press; Maurice Obstfeld and Alan M. Taylor, 2004, *Global Capital Markets: Integration, Crisis, and Growth,* Cambridge: Cambridge University Press.
[20] Lawrence Officer, October 1, 2001, "Gold Standard," *EH.Net Encyclopedia,* edited by Robert Whaples, http://eh.net/encyclopedia/article/officer.gold.standard.

mostly disenfranchised working classes. With the exception of some emerging markets, price stability was the major goal and the inflation tax was not seen as useful except in emergencies.

As for the question, why peg to gold? (as opposed to silver, or something else), note that once a gold peg became established in a few countries, the benefits of adoption in other countries would increase further. If you are the second country to go on the gold standard, it lowers your trade costs with one other country; if you are the 10th or 20th country to go on, it lowers your trade costs with 10 or 20 other countries; and so on. This can be thought of as a "snowball effect" (a *network externality,* as economists say) where only one standard can dominate in the end.[21]

This is not to say that all was plain sailing before 1914. Many countries joined gold, only to leave temporarily due to a crisis. Even in countries that stayed on gold, not everyone loved the gold standard. The benefits were often less palpable than the costs, particularly in times of deflation or in recessions. For example, in the United States, prices and output stagnated in the 1890s, drawing support to populists who wanted to leave the gold standard and escape its monetary strictures. The tensions reached a head at the 1896 Democratic Convention in Chicago, when presidential candidate William Jennings Bryan ended his speech saying: "Having behind us the producing masses of this nation and the world, supported by the commercial interests, the laboring interests and the toilers everywhere, we will answer their demand for a gold standard by saying to them: You shall not press down upon the brow of labor this crown of thorns, you shall not crucify mankind upon a cross of gold." (Bryan lost, the pro–gold McKinley became president, the Gold Standard Act of 1900 was passed to bury any doubts, and tensions defused as economic growth and gold discoveries raised output and prices.)

Bryan's "cross of gold"

These trends were upset by World War I. For belligerent countries, the war required financing. The inflation tax was heavily used, and this implied exit from the gold standard. In addition, once a war began in Europe (and later drew in the United States), the majority of global trade was affected by conflict: trade was almost 100% wiped out between belligerents, and fell by 50% between belligerents and neutrals. This effect persisted long after the war ended, and it was exacerbated by protectionism (higher tariffs and quotas) in the 1920s. By the 1930s, world trade had fallen to close to half of its 1914 level. All of these developments meant that the rationale for fixing based on gains from trade was being weakened.[22]

[21] Christopher M. Meissner, 2005, "A New World Order: Explaining the International Diffusion of the Gold Standard, 1870–1913," *Journal of International Economics,* 66(2), July, 385–406.

[22] Reuven Glick and Alan M. Taylor, 2005, "Collateral Damage: Trade Disruption and the Economic Impact of War," NBER Working Paper No. 11565; Antoni Estevadeordal, Brian Frantz, and Alan M. Taylor, 2003, "The Rise and Fall of World Trade, 1870–1939," *Quarterly Journal of Economics,* 118(2), May, 359–407.

Then, from 1929 on, the Great Depression undermined the stability argument for pegging to gold. The 1920s and 1930s featured much more violent economic fluctuations than had been seen prior to 1914, raising the costs of pegging. Moreover, politically speaking, these costs could no longer be ignored. The rise of labor movements and political parties of the left started to give voice and electoral weight to constituencies that cared much more about the instability costs of a fixed exchange rate.[23]

Other factors also played a role. The Great Depression was accompanied by severe deflation, so to stay on gold might have risked further deflation given the slow growth of gold supplies to which all money supplies were linked. Deflation linked to inadequate gold supplies therefore undermined the usefulness of gold as a nominal anchor.[24] Many countries had followed beggar-thy-neighbor policies in the 1920s, choosing to repeg their currencies to gold at devalued rates, making further devaluations tempting. Among developing countries, many economies were in recession before 1929 because of poor conditions in commodity markets, so they had another reason to devalue (as some did as early as 1929). The war had also left gold reserves distributed in a highly asymmetric fashion, leaving some countries with few reserves for intervention to support their pegs; as backup many countries now used major currencies as reserves, too, but the value of these reserves depended on everyone else's commitment to the gold peg, a commitment that was increasingly questionable.

All of these weaknesses undermined the confidence and credibility of the commitment to gold pegs in many countries, making the collapse of the pegs more likely. Currency traders would then speculate against various currencies, raising the risk of a crisis (a process we explore fully in Chapter 9). In the face of such speculation, in 1931 both Germany and Austria imposed capital controls, and Britain floated the pound against gold. The gold standard system then unraveled in a largely uncoordinated, uncooperative, and destructive fashion.

In the language of the trilemma, with its three solutions or "corners," the 1930s saw a movement by policy makers away from the "open capital market/fixed exchange rate" corner, and the other two corners came to dominate. Countries unwilling to close their capital markets by imposing controls opted to abandon the gold peg and moved to the "open capital market/floating exchange rate" solution, allowing them to regain monetary policy autonomy: Britain and the United States among others made this choice. Countries willing to adopt capital controls but unwilling to suffer the volatility of a floating rate moved to the "closed capital market/fixed exchange rate" solution, allowing them to regain monetary

---

[23] Barry Eichengreen, 1992, *Golden Fetters: The Gold Standard and the Great Depression,* New York: Oxford University Press.

[24] World gold production more or less kept pace with output growth in the nineteenth century, but output grew much faster than gold stocks in the twentieth century. If gold gets scarcer, its relative price must rise. But if the money price of gold is pegged, the only way for the relative price of gold to rise is for all other prices to fall—that is, by economy-wide price deflation.

policy autonomy in a different way: Germany and many countries in South America made this choice. Gaining monetary autonomy gave all of these countries the freedom to pursue more expansionary monetary policies to try to revive their economies, and most of them did just that. Finally, a few countries remained on the gold standard and did not devalue or impose controls, in part because they were not forced off gold (they had large reserves) and in part because they were worried about the inflationary consequences of floating. France was such a country. Countries that stuck with the gold standard paid a heavy price: compared with 1929, countries that floated had 26% higher output in 1935, and countries that adopted capital controls had 21% higher output, as compared with the countries that stayed on gold.[25]

Figure 8-13 shows these outcomes diagrammatically. To sum up: although many other factors were important, trade gains and an absence of (or political indifference to) stability costs helped bring the gold standard into being before

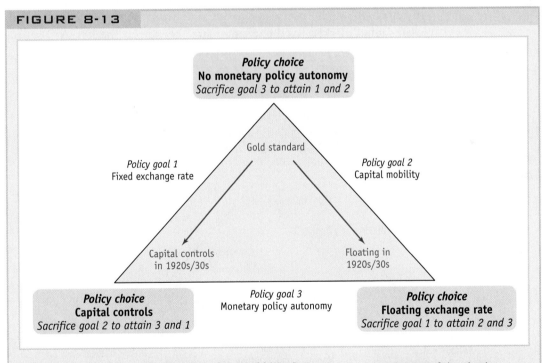

FIGURE 8-13

Solutions to the Trilemma before and after World War I As in Figure 4-16, each corner of the triangle represents a viable policy choice. The labels on the two adjacent edges of the triangle are the goals that can be attained; the label on the opposite edge is the goal that has to be sacrificed. Trade gains and an absence of (or political indifference to) stability costs help explain how the gold standard came into being before 1914 (top corner). Subsequently, reduced trade gains and higher actual (or politically relevant) stability costs help explain the ultimate demise of the gold standard in the 1920s and 1930s. Countries sought new solutions to the trilemma to achieve policy autonomy, either by floating (bottom right corner) or by adopting capital controls (bottom left corner).

---

[25] Maurice Obstfeld and Alan M. Taylor, 2004, *Global Capital Markets: Integration, Crisis, and Growth,* Cambridge: Cambridge University Press. The output cost estimates are from p. 143.

1914; reduced trade gains and stability costs that were higher (or more politically relevant) help explain the ultimate demise of the gold standard in the interwar period.

Bretton Woods to the Present

The international monetary system of the 1930s was utterly chaotic. Near the end of World War II, allied economic policy makers gathered in the United States, at Bretton Woods, New Hampshire, to try to ensure that the postwar economy fared better. The architects of the postwar order, notably Harry Dexter White and John Maynard Keynes, constructed a system that preserved one key tenet of the gold standard regime—by keeping fixed rates—but discarded the other by imposing capital controls. The trilemma was resolved in favor of exchange rate stability to encourage the rebuilding of trade in the postwar period. Countries would peg to a reserve currency, the U.S. dollar; this made the U.S. dollar the center or base currency and the United States the center or base country. The U.S. dollar was in turn pegged to gold at a fixed price, a last vestige of the gold standard.

In Figure 8-14, the postwar period starts with the world firmly in the "closed capital market/fixed exchange rate" corner on the left. At Bretton

FIGURE 8-14

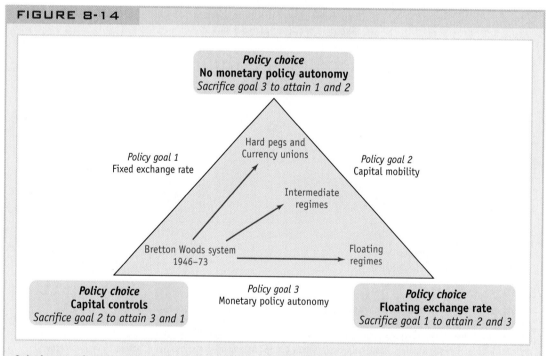

Solutions to the Trilemma since World War II In the 1960s, the Bretton Woods system became unsustainable because capital mobility could not be contained. Thus, countries could no longer have fixed rates and monetary autonomy (bottom left corner). In the advanced countries, the trilemma was resolved by a shift to floating rates, which preserved autonomy and allowed for the present era of capital mobility (bottom right corner). The main exception was the currency union of the Eurozone. In developing countries and emerging markets, the "fear of floating" was stronger; when capital markets were opened, monetary policy autonomy was more often sacrificed and fixed exchange rates were maintained (top corner).

Woods, the interests of international finance were seemingly dismissed, amid disdain for the speculators who had destabilized the gold standard in the 1920s and 1930s: U.S. Treasury Secretary Henry Morgenthau pronounced that the new institutions would "drive . . . the usurious money lenders from the temple of international finance." At the time, only the United States allowed full freedom of international capital movement, but this was soon to change.

It was obvious that to have trade one needed to have payments, so some kind of system for credit was needed, at least on a short-term basis. By the late 1950s, after getting by with half measures, many countries in Europe and elsewhere were ready to liberalize financial transactions related to current account transactions to free up the trade and payments system. At the same time, they sought to limit speculative financial transactions that were purely asset trades within the financial account (e.g., interest arbitrage by forex traders).

Unfortunately, in practice it proved difficult then (and has proved so ever since) to put watertight controls on financial transactions. Controls in the 1960s were very leaky and investors found ways to circumvent them and move money offshore from local currency deposits into foreign currency deposits. Some used accounting tricks such as over- or underinvoicing trade transactions to move money from one currency to another. Others took advantage of the largely unregulated offshore currency markets that had emerged in London and elsewhere in the late 1950s.

As capital mobility grew and controls failed to hold, the trilemma tells us that countries pegged to the dollar stood to lose their monetary policy autonomy. This was already a reason for them to think about exiting the dollar peg. With autonomy evaporating, the devaluation option came to be seen as the most important way of achieving policy compromise in a "fixed but adjustable" system. But increasingly frequent devaluations (and some revaluations) undermined the notion of a truly fixed rate system, made it more unstable, generated beggar-thy-neighbor policies, and—if anticipated—encouraged speculators.

The downsides became more and more apparent as the 1960s went on. Other factors included a growing unwillingness in many countries to peg to the U.S. dollar, after inflation in the Vietnam War era undermined the dollar's previously strong claim to be the best nominal anchor currency. It was also believed that this inflation would eventually conflict with the goal of fixing the dollar price of gold and that the United States would eventually abandon its commitment to convert dollars into gold, which happened in August 1971. By then it had become clear that U.S. policy was geared to U.S. interests, and if the rest of the world needed a reminder about asymmetry, they got it from U.S. Treasury Secretary John Connally, who in 1971 uttered the memorable words "the dollar is our currency, but it's your problem."

Figure 8-14 tells us what must happen in an international monetary system once capital mobility reasserts itself, as happened to the Bretton Woods system in the 1960s. The "closed capital market/fixed exchange rate" corner on the left is no longer an option. Countries must make a choice: they can stay fixed and have no monetary autonomy (move to the top corner), or they can float and recover monetary autonomy (move to the right corner).

These choices came to the fore after the Bretton Woods system collapsed in 1971 to 1973. How did the world react? There have been a variety of outcomes, and the tools developed in this chapter help us to understand them:

■ Most advanced countries have opted to float and preserve monetary policy autonomy. This group includes the United States, Japan, United Kingdom, Australia, and Canada. They account for the growing share of floating regimes in Figure 8-1. For these countries, stability costs outweigh integration benefits. They are at the bottom right corner of the trilemma diagram (although they do float against the rest of the world).

■ A group of European countries instead decided to try to preserve a fixed exchange rate system among themselves, first via the ERM and now "irrevocably" through the adoption of a common currency, the euro (they are fixed against each other, although they do float against the rest of the world). Integration gains in the closely integrated European market might, in part, explain this choice (a topic we discuss in more detail in Chapter 10). This group of countries is at the top corner of the trilemma diagram.

■ Some developing countries have maintained capital controls, but many of them (especially the emerging markets) have opened their capital markets. Given the "fear of floating" phenomenon, their desire to choose fixed rates (and sacrifice monetary autonomy) is much stronger than in the advanced countries, all else equal. These countries are also at the top corner of the trilemma diagram.

■ Some countries, both developed and developing, have camped in the middle ground: they have attempted to maintain intermediate regimes, such as "dirty floats" or pegs with "limited flexibility." India is often considered to be a case of an intermediate regime somewhere between floating or fixed. Such countries are somewhere in the middle on the right side of the trilemma diagram.

■ Finally, some countries still impose some capital controls rather than embrace globalization. China has been in this position, although change is afoot. These countries, mostly developing countries, are clinging to the bottom left corner of the trilemma diagram.

5 Conclusions

Exchange rate regimes have varied a great deal across countries and across time and continue to do so. Explaining why this is the case, and figuring out the optimal choice of exchange rate regime, is a major task in international macroeconomics.

We began this chapter by studying the main costs and benefits of fixed versus floating regimes. Fixing enhances the economic efficiency of international transactions. Floating allows the authorities to stabilize the economy with monetary policy. The clash between these two goals creates a trade-off. Only with enough economic integration (more gains on transactions) and sufficiently symmetric shocks (less need for policy autonomy) do fixed exchange rates make sense, as shown in the symmetry-integration diagram.

However, other factors can affect the trade-off, especially in emerging markets and developing countries: fixed exchange rates may provide the only credible nominal anchor after a high inflation, and they insulate countries with net foreign currency debt from the adverse wealth effects of depreciations.

Finally, we examined exchange rate systems in theory and in practice. Over the years, fixed rate systems such as the gold standard and the Bretton Woods system have come and gone, with collapses driven, at least in part, by failures of cooperation. That leaves us today with no real international monetary "system" at all, but rather many countries, and occasionally groups of countries, pursuing their own interests and trying to make the best choice of regime given their particular circumstances. But as this chapter has shown, there may be good reasons why "one size fits all" will never apply to exchange rate regimes.

KEY POINTS

1. There has been, and still is, a wide variety of exchange rate regimes in operation.

2. Countries will reap benefits from a fixed exchange rate to the extent that it lowers transaction costs and promotes trade, investment, and migration with the base country or region.

3. Countries will face costs from a fixed exchange rate to the extent that they encounter different economic shocks and hence desire to pursue monetary policies different from those of the base country or region.

4. The costs and benefits of fixing can be summed up on a symmetry-integration diagram. At high levels of symmetry and/or integration, above the FIX line, it makes sense to fix. At low levels of symmetry and/or integration, below the FIX line, it makes sense to float.

5. A fixed rate may confer extra benefits if it is the only viable nominal anchor in a high-inflation country and if it prevents adverse wealth shocks caused by depreciation in countries suffering from a currency mismatch.

6. Using these tools and the trilemma, we can better understand exchange rate regime choices in the past and in the present.

7. Before 1914 it appears the gold standard did promote integration, and political concern for the loss of stabilization policies was limited.

8. In the 1920s and 1930s, increased isolationism, economic instability, and political realignments undermined the gold standard.

9. After 1945 and up to the late 1960s, the Bretton Woods system of fixed dollar exchange rates was feasible, with strict controls on capital mobility, and was attractive as long as U.S. policies were not at odds with the rest of the world.

10. Since 1973, different countries and groups of countries have gone their own way, and exchange rate regimes reflect the sovereign choice of each country.

KEY TERMS

gold standard, p. 332
base currency, p. 334
center currency, p. 334
asymmetric shock, p. 340
symmetry-integration diagram,
  p. 341

fear of floating, p. 358
fixed exchange rate system, p. 359
reserve currency system, p. 359
cooperative arrangements, p. 360

devaluation, p. 363
revaluation, p. 363
beggar-thy-neighbor policy, p. 365

PROBLEMS

1. Using the IS-LM-FX model, illustrate how each of the following scenarios affects the Home country. Compare the outcomes when the Home country has a fixed exchange rate with the outcomes when the Home currency floats.

   a. The Foreign country increases the money supply.

   b. The Home country cuts taxes.

   c. Investors expect a future appreciation in the Home currency.

2. The Estonian kroon is currently (in 2007) pegged to the euro. Using the IS-LM-FX model for Home (Estonia) and Foreign (Eurozone), illustrate how each of the following scenarios affects Estonia:

   a. The Eurozone reduces its money supply.

   b. Estonia cuts government spending to reduce its budget deficit.

   c. The Eurozone countries increase their taxes.

3. Consider two countries that are currently pegged to the euro: Slovakia and Comoros.

Slovakia is currently a member of the European Union, allowing it to trade freely with other EU countries. Exports to the Eurozone account for the majority of Slovakia's trade, which mainly takes the form of manufacturing goods and equipment. In contrast, Comoros is an archipelago of islands off the eastern coast of southern Africa that exports food commodities primarily to the United States and France. The Comoros historically maintained a peg with the French franc, switching to the euro when France joined the Eurozone. Compare and contrast Slovakia and Comoros in terms of their likely degree of integration symmetry with the Eurozone. Plot Comoros, Eurozone, and Slovakia on a symmetry-integration diagram as in Figure 8-4.

4. Use the symmetry-integration diagram as in Figure 8-4 to explore the evolution of international monetary regimes from 1870 to 1939—that is, during the rise and fall of the gold standard.

a. From 1870 to 1913, world trade flows doubled in size relative to GDP, from about 10% to 20%. Many economic historians think this was driven by exogenous declines in transaction costs, some of which were caused by changes in transport technology. How would you depict this shift for a pair of countries in the symmetry-integration diagram that started off just below the FIX line in 1870? Use the letter A to label your starting point in 1870 and use B to label the end point in 1913.

b. From 1913 to 1939, world trade flows collapsed, falling in half relative to GDP, from about 20% back to 10%. Many economic historians think this was driven by exogenous increases in transaction costs from rising transport costs and increases in tariffs and quotas. How would you depict this shift for a pair of countries in the symmetry-integration diagram that started off just above the FIX line in 1913? Use the letter B to label your starting point in 1913 and use C to label the end point in 1939.

c. Other economic historians contend that these changes in transaction costs arose endogenously. When countries went on the gold standard, they lowered their transaction costs and boosted trade. When they left gold, costs increased. If this is true, then do points A, B, and C represent unique solutions to the problem of choosing an exchange rate regime?

d. Changes in other factors in the 1920s and 1930s had an impact on the sustainability of the gold standard. These included the following:
  i. An increase in country-specific shocks
  ii. An increase in democracy
  iii. Growth of world output relative to the supply of gold
  In each case, explain why these changes might have undermined commitment to the gold standard.

5. Many countries experiencing high and rising inflation, or even hyperinflation, will adopt a fixed exchange rate regime. Discuss the potential costs and benefits of a fixed exchange rate regime in this case. Comment on fiscal discipline, seigniorage, and expected future inflation.

6. In the late 1970s, several countries in Latin America, notably Mexico, Brazil, and Argentina, had accumulated large external debt burdens. A significant share of this debt was denominated in U.S. dollars. The United States pursued contractionary monetary policy from 1979 to 1982, raising dollar interest rates. How would this affect the value of the floating Latin American currencies relative to the U.S. dollar? How would this affect their external debt and interest payments in local currency terms? If these countries had wanted to prevent a change in the local currency value of their external debt, what would have been the appropriate policy response, and what would be the drawbacks?

7. The Home currency is the peso and trades at 1 peso per dollar. Home has external assets of $200 billion, all of which are denominated in dollars. It has external liabilities of $400 billion, 75% of which are denominated in dollars.

   a. Is Home a net creditor or debtor? What is Home's external wealth?
   b. What is Home's net position in dollar-denominated assets?
   c. If the peso depreciates to 1.2 pesos per dollar, what is the change in Home's external wealth in pesos?

8. Evaluate the empirical evidence on how currency depreciation affects wealth and output across countries. How does the decision of maintaining a fixed versus floating exchange rate regime depend on a country's external wealth position?

9. Home signs a free-trade agreement with Foreign, which lowers tariffs and other barriers

to trade. Both countries are very similar in terms of economic shocks, as they each produce very similar goods. Use a symmetry-integration diagram as in Figure 8-4 as part of your answer to the following questions.

a. Initially trade rises. Does the rise in trade make Home more or less likely to peg its currency to the Foreign currency? Why?

b. In the longer run, freer trade causes the countries to follow their comparative advantage and specialize in producing very different types of goods. Does the rise in specialization make Home more or less likely to peg its currency to the Foreign currency? Why?

Exchange Rate Crises: How Pegs Work and How They Break

Global capital markets pose the same kinds of problems that jet planes do. They are faster, more comfortable, and they get you where you are going better. But the crashes are much more spectacular.
Lawrence Summers, U.S. Secretary of the Treasury, 1999

Either extreme: a fixed exchange rate through a currency board, but no central bank, or a central bank plus truly floating exchange rates; either of those is a tenable arrangement. But a pegged exchange rate with a central bank is a recipe for trouble.
Milton Friedman, Nobel laureate, 1998

In the last chapter, we treated the question "fixed or floating?" as a one-time problem of exchange rate regime choice. We implicitly assumed that, once that choice was made, either option would be a stable and sustainable regime, if selected.

Unfortunately, the reality is different. The typical fixed exchange rate succeeds for a few years, only to break. A recent study found that the average duration of any peg was about five years, and the median duration was only two years.[1] When the break occurs, there is often a large and sudden depreciation and burdensome economic and political costs. Such a collapse is known as an *exchange rate crisis*.

---

[1] Michael W. Klein and Jay C. Shambaugh, 2006, "The Nature of Exchange Rate Regimes," NBER Working Paper No. 12729. Since 1970, with the exception of some peculiar countries (the few destined to join the euro, oil exporters like Saudi Arabia and Bahrain, and tiny microstates like Bhutan and Kiribati), only a handful of pegs have lasted longer than a decade, and only one, Hong Kong's peg to the U.S. dollar, was still surviving at the time of this writing. See also Maurice Obstfeld and Kenneth Rogoff, 1995, "The Mirage of Fixed Exchange Rates," *Journal of Economic Perspectives,* 9(4), Fall, 73–96.

Despite recurrent crises, fixed exchange rates are not extinct. Typically, after a crisis, a country that prefers to have a fixed exchange rate (for reasons discussed in Chapter 8) will try to peg again. Yet there is an important asymmetry in regime changes: the shift from floating to fixed is generally smooth and planned, but the shift from fixed to floating is typically unplanned and catastrophic.

Understanding exchange rate crises is a major goal of international macroeconomics because of the damage they do, not only to the country in which the crisis occurs but often to its neighbors and trading partners. Crises are thus an important issue for us to consider after a chapter looking at the pros and cons of fixed and floating regimes. Crises imply that there is one additional and significant cost associated with fixing.

1 Facts about Exchange Rate Crises

To understand the importance of exchange rate crises, we spend a few moments examining what crises look like and the costs associated with them.

What Is an Exchange Rate Crisis?

A simple definition of an **exchange rate crisis** would be a "big" depreciation.[2] How big is big enough to qualify as a crisis? This is inherently subjective. In practice, in an advanced country, a 10% to 15% depreciation might be considered large. In emerging markets, the bar might be set higher, say 20% to 25%.[3] Examples of such crises are shown in Figure 9-1.

Panel (a) shows the depreciation of six European currencies against the German mark after 1992. Four currencies (the escudo, lira, peseta, and pound) were part of the European Exchange Rate Mechanism (ERM); the other two (the markka and krona) were not in the ERM but were pegging to the German mark. All six currencies lost 15% to 25% of their value against the mark within a year.

In panel (b), we see the cumulative depreciation of seven emerging market currencies against the U.S. dollar in various crises that occurred from 1994 to 2002. These depreciations, while also very rapid, were much larger than those in panel (a). These currencies lost 50% to 75% of their value against the dollar in the year following the crisis.

The figure illustrates two important points. First, exchange rate crises can occur in advanced countries as well as in emerging markets and developing

---

[2] We will be focusing mostly on crises thus defined, when the peg actually breaks and there is a sizable depreciation. However, economists sometimes use a broader concept of a *currency crisis* based on other criteria such as reserve losses. See Barry Eichengreen, Andrew K. Rose and Charles Wyplosz, 1995, "Exchange Market Mayhem: The Antecedents and Aftermath of Speculative Attacks," *Economic Policy*, 10(21), 249–312.

[3] One widely used definition requires at least a 25% depreciation in one year to be sure that such a depreciation is beyond the limits of even a wide band, and a rate of depreciation that is at least 10% higher than in the previous year to ensure that the depreciation is not just part of a broken crawl. Jeffrey A. Frankel and Andrew K. Rose, 1996, "Currency Crashes in Emerging Markets: An Empirical Treatment," *Journal of International Economics*, 41(3–4), November, 351–366.

FIGURE 9-1

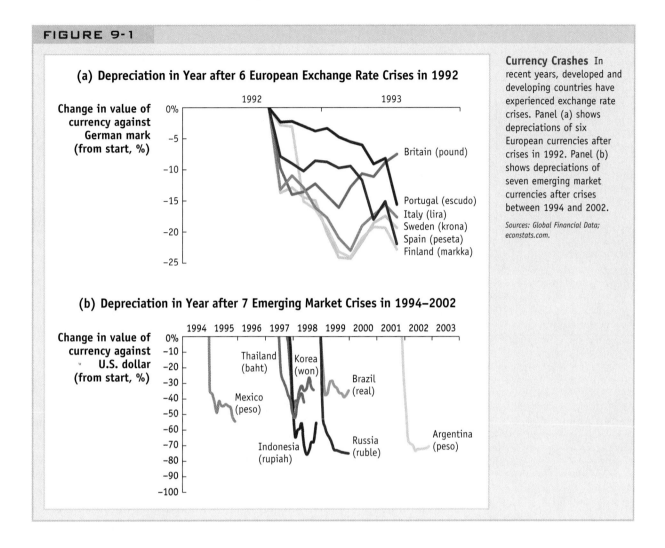

(a) Depreciation in Year after 6 European Exchange Rate Crises in 1992

Change in value of
currency against
German mark
(from start, %)

Britain (pound)

Portugal (escudo)
Italy (lira)
Sweden (krona)
Spain (peseta)
Finland (markka)

(b) Depreciation in Year after 7 Emerging Market Crises in 1994–2002

Change in value of
currency against
U.S. dollar
(from start, %)

Thailand (baht)
Korea (won)
Brazil (real)
Mexico (peso)
Indonesia (rupiah)
Russia (ruble)
Argentina (peso)

Currency Crashes In recent years, developed and developing countries have experienced exchange rate crises. Panel (a) shows depreciations of six European currencies after crises in 1992. Panel (b) shows depreciations of seven emerging market currencies after crises between 1994 and 2002.

Sources: Global Financial Data; econstats.com.

countries. Second, the magnitude of the crisis, as measured by the subsequent depreciation of the currency, is often much greater in emerging markets and developing countries.

How Costly Are Exchange Rate Crises?

A mass of evidence has accumulated concerning the potentially damaging effects of exchange rate crises. The economic costs are often significant. (So, too, are the political costs: see **Side Bar: The Political Costs of Crises.**)

Some evidence of this sort is presented in Figure 9-2. Annual rates of growth of GDP in years close to crises were compared with growth in other (i.e., "normal") years to obtain a measure of how growth differs during crisis periods. The figure shows that just before a crisis all countries have economic growth that is somewhat slower, between 0.5% and 1.0% below normal.

After a typical crisis, advanced countries and emerging markets react differently. In advanced countries, growth accelerates and is above normal by the second and third years after the crisis. Advanced countries tend to bounce back.

FIGURE 9-2

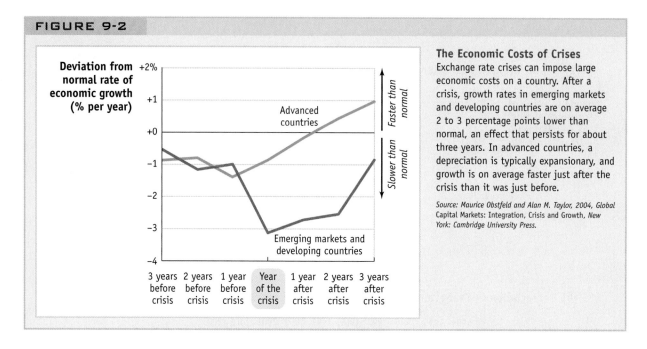

Deviation from normal rate of economic growth (% per year)

Advanced countries

Faster than normal

Slower than normal

Emerging markets and developing countries

3 years before crisis / 2 years before crisis / 1 year before crisis / Year of the crisis / 1 year after crisis / 2 years after crisis / 3 years after crisis

The Economic Costs of Crises
Exchange rate crises can impose large economic costs on a country. After a crisis, growth rates in emerging markets and developing countries are on average 2 to 3 percentage points lower than normal, an effect that persists for about three years. In advanced countries, a depreciation is typically expansionary, and growth is on average faster just after the crisis than it was just before.

Source: Maurice Obstfeld and Alan M. Taylor, 2004, Global Capital Markets: Integration, Crisis and Growth, New York: Cambridge University Press.

Emerging markets do not bounce back, and growth usually plummets: it is 2.5% to 3% below normal in the year of the crisis and the two subsequent years and is still 1% below normal in the third year. All those reductions in growth add up to about a 10% decline in GDP relative to its typical trend three years after the crisis—a major recession.[4]

The major downturns in emerging markets have serious economic and social consequences. For example, in the aftermath of the Argentina crisis of 2001 to 2002, news reports were filled with shocking tales of unemployment, financial ruin, rising poverty, hunger, and deprivation. After the Asian crisis of 1997, the recoveries were a little faster, but the economic misfortunes were still deep and painful.

Causes: Other Economic Crises Why are exchange rate crises sometimes so damaging? Drawing new lessons from the crises of the 1990s, economists now recognize that exchange rate crises usually go hand in hand with other types of economically harmful financial crises, especially in emerging markets. In the private sector, if banks and other financial institutions face adverse shocks, they may become insolvent, causing them to close or declare bankruptcy: this is known as a **banking crisis.** In the public sector, if the government faces adverse shocks, it may default and be unable or unwilling to pay the principal or interest on its debts: this is known as a **default crisis.** Both banking and default crises can have damaging effects on the economy because they disrupt the flow of credit within and between countries. (In Chapter 11, we examine default crises in more detail, including their links to banking and exchange rate crises.)

---

[4] If we were to cumulate these effects over the seven-year time span, we would deduce that advanced countries typically witness a cycle in which they fall perhaps at most 3% below their normal GDP trend but then recover, whereas emerging markets and developing countries typically suffer a deep downturn, with output at times more than 10% below its normal trend and permanently lower.

SIDE BAR

The Political Costs of Crises

Exchange rate crises don't simply have economic conse-quences—they often have political consequences, too. Figure 9-3 shows that exchange rate crises are often followed by per-sonnel changes at the central bank or finance ministry and not infrequently by a change at the top as well.

At first, this result might seem implausible. As the economist Jeffrey Frankel puts it, speaking of the Indonesian crisis of 1997: "What is it about devaluation that carries such big polit-ical costs? How is it that a strong ruler like Indonesia's Suharto can easily weather 32 years of political, military, ethnic, and en-vironmental challenges, only to succumb to a currency crisis?"[*]

In emerging markets, we know that the economic costs of exchange rate crises can be large, so this helps explain how a Suharto could be undermined. There are many other examples: the Radical Party is the oldest political party in Argentina, but after the exchange rate crisis in 2001 to 2002 under the lead-ership of President Fernando de la Rúa and Economy Minister Domingo Cavallo, the party faced extinction, polling just 2.3% in the 2003 presidential election.[†]

Still, why do exchange rate crises carry large political costs in advanced countries where the exit from an exchange rate peg often allows for a depreciation and favorable growth per-formance? A pertinent example is the decision by Britain's Conservative government to exit the ERM on "Black Wednes-day," September 16, 1992. Chancellor Norman Lamont left his job within a year, and Prime Minister John Major tasted defeat at the next general election in 1997, despite faster economic growth after 1992.

Before the crises: Domingo Cavallo, Fernando de la Rúa, Norman Lamont, David Cameron.

The legacy of "Black Wednesday" haunted the Conservatives for years. On the bellwether question of economic competence, the polls gave the new Labour government and its longtime chancellor, Gordon Brown, a massive lead for many years: this was a vital issue of trust that helped keep Labour in power for so long. It was not until late 2005 that the Conservatives had an overall lead in the opinion polls, under their fifth leader in eight years, David Cameron (who had been a junior minister working under Lamont at the Treasury on that fateful day in 1992).

Even when a depreciation turns out to be good for the econ-omy, the collapse of a peg typically destroys the reputations of politicians and policy makers for credibility and competence. Regaining the trust of the people can take a very long time.

[*] Jeffrey A. Frankel, "Mundell-Fleming Lecture: Contractionary Currency Crashes in Developing Countries," IMF Staff Papers 52(2), 149–192.
[†] Cavallo had previously served the rival Peronist Party as economy minister in the Menem administration and had presided over the creation of the fixed exchange rate regime, as well as its collapse.

FIGURE 9-3

Probability of change

- In a normal 12-month period
- In a 12-month period following an exchange rate crisis

Change in head of government: 21%, 29%

Change in Finance Minister and/or Central Bank Governor: 36%, 58%

The Political Costs of Crises
Exchange rate crises usually impose large political costs on those in power. Compared with what is likely to happen during normal, noncrisis times, it is 22% more likely that one of the two main officials with economic responsibilities (the finance minister and the central bank governor) will be out of a job the year following a crisis. It is also 8% more likely that the head of government (such as a president, prime minister, or premier) will have to depart for one reason or another.

Note: Data on heads of government are from 1971 to 2003, and data on finance ministers and central bank governors are from 1995 to 1999.

Source: Jeffrey A. Frankel, 2005, "Mundell-Fleming Lecture: Contractionary Currency Crashes in Developing Countries," IMF Staff Papers 52(2), 149–192.

Thus, in a broader context, international macroeconomists have three crisis types to consider: exchange rate crises, banking crises, and default crises. Evidence shows they are complementary to each other and hence are likely to occur simultaneously:

■ *The likelihood of a banking or default crisis increases significantly when a country is having an exchange rate crisis.* The evidence? One study found that the probability of a banking crisis was 1.6 times higher during an exchange rate crisis (16% versus 10% on average). Another study found that the probability of a default crisis was more than 3 times higher during an exchange rate crisis (39% versus 12% on average).[5] Explanations for these impacts focus on valuation effects. As we saw in Chapter 8, a big depreciation causes a sudden increase in the local currency value of dollar debts (principal and interest). Because this change in value can raise debt burdens to intolerable levels, it should come as no surprise that exchange rate crises are frequently accompanied by financial distress in both private and public sectors.

■ *The likelihood of an exchange rate crisis increases significantly when a country is having a banking or default crisis.* The evidence? The same two studies just noted found that the probability of an exchange rate crisis was 1.5 times higher during a banking crisis (46% versus 29% on average). The probability of an exchange rate crisis was more than 5 times higher during a default crisis (84% versus 17% on average). Explanations for these reverse effects center on the issuance of money by the central bank to bail out banks and governments. Banking crises can be horrendously costly. For example, as seen in Table 9-1, one study found that the fiscal costs of fixing a damaged banking sector (e.g., through recapitalization of insolvent institutions) exceeded 25% of GDP in 10 cases and was at least 10% of GDP in another 17 cases. If a country is having a banking crisis, the central bank will be under pressure to extend credit to weak banks to prop them up. If a country is having a default crisis, the government will lose access to foreign and domestic loans and may pressure the central bank to extend credit. Why does the extension of credit by the central bank threaten the peg? In this chapter, we show how a peg works and how, if the central bank issues money for costly bailout operations, it can place the peg at risk by causing a loss of reserves.

These findings show how crises are likely to happen in pairs, known as **twin crises,** or all three at once, known as **triple crises,** magnifying the costs of any one type of crisis.

Summary

Exchange rate crises have been recurring for more than 100 years, and we have not seen the last of them. They can generate significant economic costs, and policy makers and scholars are seriously concerned about how to prevent

[5] Graciela L. Kaminsky and Carmen M. Reinhart, 1999, "The Twin Crises: The Causes of Banking and Balance-of-Payments Problems," *American Economic Review,* 89(3), June, 473–500; Carmen M. Reinhart, 2002, "Default, Currency Crises, and Sovereign Credit Ratings," *World Bank Economic Review,* 16(2), August, 151–170.

TABLE 9-1

Costly Banking Crises The table shows the estimated costs of major banking crises since the 1970s, in the cases in which costs exceeded 5% of GDP.

Country and Year(s)	Cost (% of GDP)	Country and Year(s)	Cost (% of GDP)
Indonesia 1997	55%	Benin 1988–1990	17%
Argentina 1980–1982	55	Senegal 1988–1991	17
China 1990s	47	Malaysia 1997	16
Jamaica 1995–2000	44	Mauritania 1984–1993	15
Chile 1981–1986	42	Paraguay 1995–1999	13
Thailand 1997	35	Czech Republic 1991	12
Macedonia 1993–1994	32	Taiwan 1997–1998	12
Turkey 2000	31	Finland 1991–1994	11
Israel 1977–1983	30	Hungary 1991–1995	10
South Korea 1997	28	Tanzania 1980s and 1990s	10
Côte d'Ivoire 1988–1991	25	Norway 1987–1993	8
Japan 1991	24	Philippines 1998	7
Uruguay 1981–1985	24	Russia 1998–1999	6
Ecuador 1988	20	Ghana 1982–1989	6
Mexico 1994–1997	19	Colombia 1982–1987	5
Venezuela 1994–1995	18	Sri Lanka 1989–1993	5
Spain 1977–1985	17	Malaysia 1985–1988	5

Source: Gerard Caprio and Daniela Klingebiel, "Episodes of Systemic and Borderline Financial Crises," World Bank, January 2003. Data compiled by Martin Wolf, "Fixing Global Finance," SAIS Lectures, March 2006.

them. What is it about fixed exchange rate regimes that make them so fragile? Why and how do crises happen? These are the questions we address in the rest of this chapter.

2 How Pegs Work: The Mechanics of a Fixed Exchange Rate

To start, we must first understand how a pegged exchange rate works. Once we know what policy makers have to do to make a peg work, we will then be in a position to understand the factors that make a peg break.

To help us understand the economic mechanisms that operate in a fixed exchange rate system, we develop a simple model of what a central bank does. We then use the model to look at the demands placed on a central bank when a country adopts a fixed exchange rate.

Preliminaries and Assumptions

We consider a small open economy, in which the authorities are trying to peg to some foreign currency. We make the following assumptions, some of which may be relaxed in later analyses:

■ For convenience, and without implying that we are referring to any specific country, we assume that the home currency is called the peso.

The currency to which home pegs is the U.S. dollar. We assume the authorities have been maintaining a fixed exchange rate, with E fixed at $\overline{E} = 1$ (one peso per U.S. dollar).

■ The country's central bank controls the money supply M by buying and selling assets in exchange for cash. The central bank trades only two types of assets: domestic bonds, often government bonds, denominated in local currency (pesos), and foreign assets, denominated in foreign currency (dollars).

■ The central bank intervenes in the forex market to peg the exchange rate. It stands ready to buy and sell foreign exchange reserves at the fixed exchange rate $\overline{E}$. If it has no reserves, it cannot do this and the exchange rate is free to float: the peg is broken.

■ Unless stated otherwise, we assume that the peg is credible: everyone believes it will continue to hold. Uncovered interest parity then implies that the home and foreign interest rates are equal: $i = i^*$.

■ We also assume for now that the economy's level of output or income is assumed to be exogenous; that is, it is treated as given and denoted Y.

■ There is a stable foreign price level $P^* = 1$ at all times. In the short run, the home country's price is sticky and fixed at a level $P = 1$. In the long run, if the exchange rate is kept fixed at 1, then the home price level will be fixed at 1 as a result of purchasing power parity.

■ As in previous chapters, the home country's demand for real money balances M/P is determined by the level of output Y and the nominal interest rate i and takes the usual form, $M/P = L(i)Y$. The money market must be in equilibrium, so money demand is always equal to money supply.

■ We use the simplest model of a fixed exchange rate, where there is no financial system. The only money is currency, also known as M0 or the monetary base. The monetary base (M0) and broad money (M1) are then the same, so the money supply is denoted M. This assumption allows us to examine the operation of a fixed exchange rate system by considering only the effects of the actions of a central bank.

■ If there is no financial system, we do not need to worry about the role of private banks in creating broad money through checking deposits, loans, and so on. A simple generalization would allow for banks by letting broad money be a constant multiple of the currency.[6] Still, the existence of a banking system is important, and even without formal theory, we will see later in the chapter how it affects the operation of a fixed exchange rate.

The Central Bank Balance Sheet

The key problem we must understand is how the home central bank manages its assets in relation to its sole liability, the money in circulation.

---

[6] Allowing that multiple (the money multiplier) to vary is also possible, but detailed analysis of that mechanism is beyond the scope of this chapter.

Suppose the central bank has purchased a quantity B pesos of domestic bonds. By, in effect, loaning money to the domestic economy, the central bank's purchases are usually referred to as **domestic credit** created by the central bank. These purchases are also called the bank's *domestic assets.* Because the central bank purchases these assets with money, this purchase generates part of the money supply. The home money supply created as a result of the central bank's issuing of domestic credit is denoted B.

Now suppose the central bank has also purchased a quantity R dollars of foreign exchange reserves, usually referred to as **reserves** or *foreign assets,* and that the exchange rate is pegged at a level $\overline{E} = 1$. The central bank also purchases its reserves with money. Thus, given that the exchange rate has always been 1 (by assumption), the money supply created as a result of the central bank's purchase of foreign exchange reserves is $\overline{E}R = R$.[7]

Because the central bank holds only two types of assets, the last two expressions add up to the total money supply in the home economy:

$$(9\text{-}1) \qquad \underbrace{M}_{\text{Money supply}} = \underbrace{B}_{\text{Domestic credit}} + \underbrace{R.}_{\text{Reserves}}$$

This equation states that the money supply equals domestic credit plus reserves.

This expression is also useful when expressed not in levels but in changes:

$$(9\text{-}2) \qquad \underbrace{\Delta M}_{\substack{\text{Change in} \\ \text{money supply}}} = \underbrace{\Delta B}_{\substack{\text{Change in} \\ \text{domestic credit}}} + \underbrace{\Delta R.}_{\substack{\text{Change in} \\ \text{reserves}}}$$

This expression says that changes in the money supply must result from either changes in domestic credit or changes in reserves.

For example, if the central bank buys additional reserves $\Delta R = \$1{,}000$, the money it spends adds $\Delta M = \$1{,}000$ to the money in circulation. If the central bank creates additional domestic credit of $\Delta B = 1{,}000$ pesos, it buys 1,000 pesos of government debt, and this also adds $\Delta M = 1{,}000$ pesos to the money in circulation.

One common way of depicting Equation (9-1) is to write down each entry and construct the **central bank balance sheet.** The domestic debt and foreign reserves purchased by the central bank are its **assets,** $B + R$. The money supply issued by the central bank M is its **liabilities.**

Following is a hypothetical central bank balance sheet. The central bank has purchased 500 million pesos in domestic government bonds and 500 million pesos in foreign exchange reserves. The total money in circulation resulting from these purchases is 1,000 million pesos. As on any balance sheet, total assets equal total liabilities.

---

[7] In reality, central banks may have acquired reserves in the past at more or less favorable exchange rates, so the current peso value of reserves may be greater than or less than the peso value of the money spent to purchase them. In such cases, the central bank may have positive or negative net worth arising from capital gains or losses on previously purchased reserves (although whether such gains are recorded on the central bank's balance sheet depends on its accounting practices and whether it marks reserves at book value or market value). We ignore this problem because it does not greatly affect the analysis that follows.

SIMPLIFIED CENTRAL BANK BALANCE SHEET (MILLIONS OF PESOS)			
Assets		**Liabilities**	
Reserves *R* *Foreign assets (dollar reserves)*	500	**Money supply *M*** *Currency in circulation*	1,000
Domestic credit *B* *Domestic assets (peso bonds)*	500		

Fixing, Floating, and the Role of Reserves

The crucial assumption in our simple model is that the central bank maintains the peg by intervening in the foreign exchange market by buying and selling reserves at the fixed exchange rate. In other words, our model supposes that if the central bank wants to fix the exchange rate, it must have some reserves it can trade to achieve that goal. We also assume, for now, that it holds reserves only for this purpose. Thus:

We are assuming that the exchange rate is fixed if and only if the central bank holds reserves; and the exchange rate is floating if and only if the central bank has no reserves.

These assumptions simplify our analysis by giving us a clear correspondence between the central bank balance sheet and the exchange rate regime. In reality, the correspondence may be less clear, but the mechanisms in our model still play a dominant role.

For example, countries may adjust domestic credit as well as reserves. But in no cases does a country attempt to maintain a peg with zero reserves and rely *solely* on domestic credit adjustments. Why? In the very short run, forex market conditions can change so quickly that only direct intervention in that market through reserve trading can maintain the peg. Large adjustments to domestic credit may also pose problems in an emerging market by causing instability in the bond market.

Countries can also float and yet keep some reserves on hand for reasons that are ignored in our model. They may want reserves on hand for future emergencies, such as war; or as a savings buffer in the event of a sudden stop to financial flows (discussed in Chapter 6); or so they can peg at some later date.[8] Thus, the minimum level of reserves the central bank will tolerate on its balance sheet may not be at zero, but it would not affect our analysis if we adjusted everything that follows to allow for a higher threshold.

How Reserves Adjust to Maintain the Peg

We now turn to the key questions we need to answer to understand how a peg works. What level of reserves must the central bank have to maintain the peg? And how are reserves affected by changing macroeconomic conditions?

---

[8] Some of these functions may be provided by other reserve-holding agencies within the government (such as the Treasury or a sovereign wealth fund). But often all reserves are held by the central bank, which frequently serves as the financial agent of the country.

If the central bank can maintain a level of reserves above zero, we know the peg will hold. If not, the peg breaks.

We can rearrange Equation (9-1) to solve for the level of reserves, with $R = M - B$. Why do we do that? It is important to remember that reserves are the unknown variable here: by assumption, reserves change as a result of the central bank's interventions in the forex market, which it must undertake to maintain the peg.

Because (in nominal terms) money supply equals money demand, given by $M = \bar{P} L(i) Y$, we can restate and rearrange Equation (9-1) to solve for the level of reserves:

$$\text{(9-3)} \qquad \underbrace{R}_{\text{Reserves}} = \underbrace{\bar{P} L(i) Y}_{\text{Money demand}} - \underbrace{B.}_{\text{Domestic credit}}$$

By substituting money demand for money supply, we can investigate how shocks to money demand (say, due to changes in output or the interest rate) or shocks to domestic credit affect the level of reserves.

We can solve this equation. Under our current assumptions, every element on the right-hand side is exogenous and known. The home price level is fixed, the output level is exogenous, interest parity tells us that the home interest rate equals the foreign interest rate, and we can treat domestic credit as predetermined by the central bank's purchases of domestic government debt.

Why is this answer for the reserve level correct and unique? Recall from Chapter 4 how forex market equilibrium is attained. If the central bank bought more reserves than this, home money supply would expand and the home nominal interest rate would fall, the peso would depreciate, and the peg would break. To prevent this, the central bank would need to intervene in the forex market. The central bank would have to offset its initial purchase of reserves to keep the supply of pesos constant and keep the exchange rate holding steady. Similarly, if the central bank sells reserves for pesos, it would cause the peso to appreciate and would have to reverse course and buy the reserves back. The peg means that the central bank must keep the reserves at the level specified in Equation (9-3).

Graphical Analysis of the Central Bank Balance Sheet

Based on this tool kit, we show the mechanics of a pegged exchange rate in Figure 9-4, which illustrates the central bank balance sheet. On the horizontal axis is the money supply M and on the vertical axis is domestic credit B, both measured in pesos. Money demand is initially at the level M_1, and domestic credit is at B_1.

Two important lines appear in this figure. If reserves R are zero, then all of the money supply is due to domestic credit and Equation (9-1) tells us that $M = B$. The points where $M = B$ are on the 45-degree line. Points on this line, like point Z, correspond to cases in which the central bank balance sheet contains no reserves. By assumption, the country will then have a floating exchange rate, so we call this the **floating line.**

FIGURE 9-4

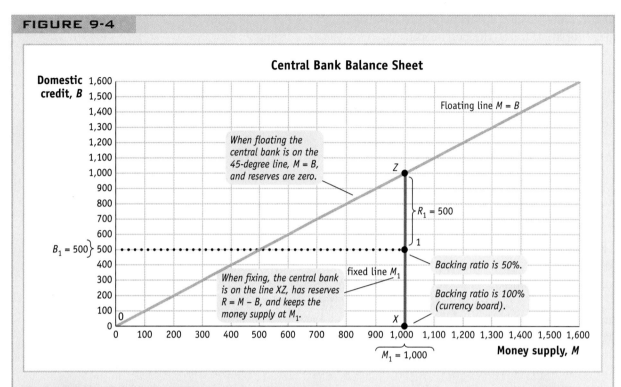

The Central Bank Balance Sheet Diagram On the 45-degree line, reserves are at zero, and the money supply M equals domestic credit B. Variations in the money supply along this line would cause the exchange rate to float. There is a unique level of the money supply M_1 (here assumed to be 1,000) that ensures that the exchange rate is at its chosen fixed value. To fix the money supply at this level, the central bank must choose a mix of assets on its balance sheet that corresponds to points on line XZ, points at which domestic credit B is less than money supply M. At point Z, reserves would be at zero; at point X, reserves would be 100% of the money supply. Any point in between on XZ is a feasible choice. At point 1, for example, domestic credit is $B_1 = 500$, reserves are $R_1 = 500$, and $B_1 + R_1 = M_1 = 1,000$.

When the assets of the central bank include both reserves and domestic credit, then B and R are both greater than zero and they add up to M. The state of the central bank balance sheet must correspond to a point such as point 1 in this diagram, somewhere on the vertical line XZ. We call this the **fixed line** because on this line the money supply is at the level M_1 necessary to maintain the peg.

If domestic credit is B_1, then reserves are $R_1 = M_1 - B_1$, the vertical (or horizontal) distance between point 1 and the 45-degree floating line. Hence, the distance to the floating line tells us how close to danger the peg is by showing how close we are to the point where reserves run out.[9] The point farthest

---

[9] It is important to remember that under our assumptions, all other points in the figure (representing other balance sheet configurations) are ruled out. Floating means having zero reserves and being on the 45-degree line. Other points below the 45-degree line are ruled out because we assume that reserves imply pegging, and these other points would imply a higher or lower level of the money supply and hence an exchange rate other than the pegged rate $\bar{E}$. Points above the 45-degree line are also ruled out: they imply $B > M$ and $R < 0$, which is impossible because reserves cannot be negative.

from danger is X, on the horizontal axis. At this point, domestic credit B is zero and reserves R equal the money supply M. A fixed exchange rate that always operates with reserves equal to 100% of the money supply is known as a **currency board** system.[10]

Summing up: *If the exchange rate is floating, the central bank balance sheet must correspond to points on the 45-degree floating line; if the exchange rate is fixed, the central bank balance sheet must correspond to points on the vertical fixed line.*

The model is now complete, and with the aid of our key tools—the tabular and graphical representations of the central bank balance sheet—we can see how a central bank that is trying to maintain a peg reacts to two types of shocks. We first look at shocks to the level of money demand and then shocks to the composition of money supply.

Defending the Peg I: Changes in the Level of Money Demand

We first look at shocks to money demand and how they affect reserves by altering the level of money supply M. As we saw in Equation (9-3), money supply is equal to money demand, as given by the equation $M = \bar{P}L(i)Y$. If the price level is fixed, then money demand will fluctuate only in response to shocks in output Y and the home interest rate i (which equals the foreign interest rate i^* if the peg is credible). For now, output is exogenous, and a rise in output will raise money demand. The foreign interest rate is also exogenous, and a rise in the foreign interest rate will raise the home interest rate and thus lower money demand. We assume all else is equal, so domestic credit is constant.

A Shock to Home Output or the Foreign Interest Rate Suppose output falls or the foreign interest rate rises. We treat either of these events as an exogenous shock for now, all else equal, and suppose it decreases money demand by, say, 10% at the current interest rate.

For example, suppose we start with a central bank balance sheet as given earlier. Initially, money supply is $M_1 = 1,000$ million pesos. Suppose money demand then falls by 10%. This would lower money demand by 10% to $M_2 = 900$ million pesos. A fall in the demand for money would lower the interest rate in the money market and put depreciation pressure on the exchange rate. A floating rate would depreciate in these circumstances. To maintain the peg, the central bank must keep the interest rate unchanged. To achieve this goal, it must sell 100 million pesos ($100 million) of reserves, in

---

[10] Strictly speaking, a currency board must satisfy certain other legal and procedural rules, such as it must own only low-risk interest-bearing foreign assets, not foreign liabilities. It must not perform any function except to exchange domestic currency for foreign currency at the fixed rate. It cannot lend to the domestic banking system to avert banking panics, for example. However, it may hold a bit more than 100% reserve backing, say 105% to 110%, to guard against fluctuations in the value of its foreign assets. See Kurt Schuler, "Introduction to Currency Boards" (http://users.erols.com/kurrency/intro.htm).

exchange for cash, so that money supply contracts as much as money demand. The central bank's balance sheet will then be as follows:

SIMPLIFIED CENTRAL BANK BALANCE SHEET AFTER MONEY DEMAND FALLS (MILLIONS OF PESOS)			
Assets		**Liabilities**	
Reserves R *Foreign assets (dollar reserves)*	400	**Money supply M** *Currency in circulation*	900
Domestic credit B *Domestic assets (peso bonds)*	500		

In Figure 9-5, we can trace the implications of the shock using our graphical apparatus. The demand for money has fallen, so the *fixed line* is still vertical, but it shifts from the initial money demand level $M_1 = 1,000$ to a new lower level $M_2 = 900$. There is no change to domestic credit, so it remains

FIGURE 9-5

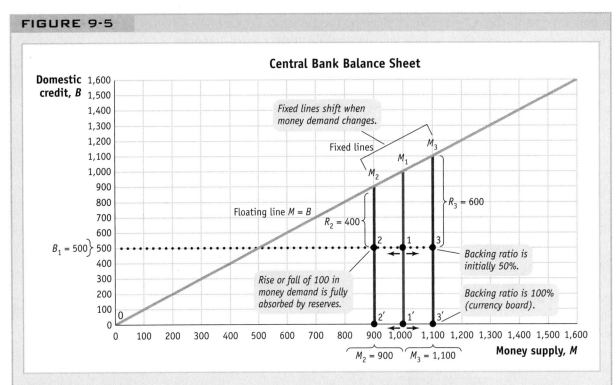

Shocks to Money Demand If money demand falls, interest rates tend to fall, leading to pressure for an exchange rate to depreciate. To prevent this, the central bank must intervene in the forex market and defend the peg by selling reserves and hence lowering the money supply to keep the interest rate fixed and ensure that money supply equals money demand. As shown here, the money supply declines from $M_1 = 1,000$ to $M_2 = 900$. If domestic credit is unchanged at $B_1 = 500$, the change in the central bank balance sheet is shown by a move from point 1 to point 2, and reserves absorb the money demand shock by falling from $R_1 = 500$ to $R_2 = 400$. An opposite positive shock is shown by the move from point 1 to point 3, where $M_3 = 1,100$ and $R_3 = 600$. In a currency board system, a country maintaining 100% reserves will be on the horizontal axis with zero domestic credit, $B = 0$. A currency board adjusts to money demand shocks by moving from point 1′ to point 2′ or 3′.

constant at the level $B_1 = 500$. Thus, the central bank's balance sheet position shifts from point 1 to point 2. This shift takes the balance sheet position closer to the floating line in the diagram: reserves are falling. At point 2, reserves have fallen from $R_1 = 500$ to $R_2 = 400$, as shown.

Figure 9-5 also shows what would happen with the opposite shock. If money demand increased by 10% from the initial money demand level $M_1 = 1,000$ to a new higher level $M_3 = 1,100$, the central bank would need to prevent an interest rate rise and an appreciation by expanding the money supply by 100 pesos. The central bank would need to intervene and increase the money supply by purchasing \$100 of reserves. The central bank's balance sheet position would then shift from point 1 to point 3, moving away from the floating line, with reserves rising from $R_1 = 500$ to $R_3 = 600$.

Equation (9-3) confirms these outcomes as a general result when domestic credit is constant (at B_1 in our example). We know that if the change in domestic credit is zero, $\Delta B = 0$, then any change in money supply must equal the change in reserves $\Delta R = \Delta M$. This is also clear from Equation (9-2).

We have shown the following: *Holding domestic credit constant, a change in money demand leads to an equal change in reserves.*

The Importance of the Backing Ratio In the first example above, money demand and money supply fell by 10% from 1,000 to 900, but reserves fell by 20% from 500 to 400. The proportional fall in reserves was greater than the proportional fall in money because reserves R were initially only 500 and just a fraction (one-half) of the money supply M, which was 1,000. When money demand fell by 100, reserves had to absorb all of the change, with domestic credit unchanged.

The ratio R/M is called the **backing ratio,** and it indicates the fraction of the money supply that is backed by reserves on the central bank balance sheet. It, therefore, tells us the size of the maximum negative money demand shock that the regime can withstand without running out of reserves *if* domestic credit remains unchanged. In our example, the backing ratio was 0.5 or 50% (reserves were 500 and money supply 1,000 initially), so the central bank could absorb up to a 50% decline in the money supply before all reserves run out. Because reserves were only 500 to start with, a shock of -500 to money demand would cause reserves to just run out.

In general, *for a given size of a shock to money demand, a higher backing ratio will better insulate an economy against running out of reserves, all else equal.*[11]

---

[11] To see this, recall that the change in money supply equals the change in reserves $\Delta M = \Delta R$; hence, for a given *proportional* size of money demand shock $\Delta M/M$, the proportional loss in reserves $\Delta R/R$ can be computed as

$$\% \text{ Change in reserves} = \frac{\Delta R}{R} = \frac{\Delta M}{R} = \frac{\Delta M/M}{R/M} = \frac{\% \text{ Change in money supply}}{\text{Backing ratio}}.$$

The higher the backing ratio, the smaller the proportional loss of reserves $\Delta R/R$ for a given size of money demand shock $\Delta M/M$. In our example, the backing ratio was 0.5, so a 10% drop in money supply implied a $10\%/0.5 = 20\%$ drop in reserves.

In Figure 9-5, the higher the backing ratio, the higher the level of reserves R and the lower the level of domestic credit B, for a given level of money supply M. In other words, the central bank balance sheet position on this figure would be closer to the horizontal axis and farther away from the floating line. This is the graphical representation of the idea that a high backing ratio makes a peg safer.

Currency Board Operation This maximum backing ratio of 100% is maintained at all times by a currency board. A 100% backing ratio puts the country exactly on the horizontal axis. In Figure 9-5, a currency board would start at point 1′, not point 1. Because reserves would then be 1,000 to start with, a shock of up to −1,000 to money demand could be accommodated without reserves running out. In the face of smaller shocks to money demand such as we have considered, of plus or minus 100, the central bank balance sheet would move to points 2′ or 3′, with reserves equal to money supply equal to money demand equal to 900 or 1,100. These points are as far away from the 45-degree floating line as one can get in this diagram, and they show how a currency board keeps reserves at a maximum 100%. A currency board can be thought of as the safest configuration of the central bank's balance sheet because with 100% backing, the central bank can cope with *any* shock to money demand without running out of reserves. Currency boards are considered a *hard peg* because their high backing ratio ought to confer on them greater resilience in the face of money demand shocks.

Why Does the Level of Money Demand Fluctuate? Our result tells us that to maintain the fixed exchange rate, the central bank must have enough reserves to endure a money demand shock without running out. A shock to money demand is not under the control of the authorities, but they must respond to it. Thus, it is important for policy makers to understand the sources and likely magnitudes of such shocks. Under our assumptions, money demand shocks originate either in shocks to home output Y or the foreign interest rate i^* (since we have assumed $i = i^*$).

We studied output fluctuations in Chapters 1 and 6, and one thing we observed was that output tends to be much more volatile in emerging markets and developing countries. Thus, the prudent level of reserves is likely to be much higher in these countries. Volatility in foreign interest rates can also be important, whether in U.S. dollars or in other currencies that form the base for pegs.

However, we must also confront a new possibility—that the peg is not fully credible and that simple interest parity fails to hold. In this case, the home interest rate will no longer equal the foreign interest rate, and additional disturbances to home money demand can be caused by the spread between the two. As we now see, this is a vital step toward understanding crises in emerging markets and developing countries.

APPLICATION

Risk Premiums in Advanced and Emerging Markets

So far in the book, we have assumed that uncovered interest parity (UIP) requires that the domestic return (the interest rate on home bank deposits) equal the foreign interest rate plus the expected rate of depreciation of the home currency. However, an important extension of UIP needs to be made when additional risks affect home bank deposits: a **risk premium** is then added to the foreign interest rate to compensate investors for the perceived risk of holding a home domestic currency deposit. This perceived risk is due to an aversion to exchange rate risk or a concern about default risk:

$$
(9\text{-}4) \quad \underbrace{i}_{\substack{\text{Peso} \\ \text{interest} \\ \text{rate}}} = \underbrace{i^*}_{\substack{\text{Dollar} \\ \text{interest} \\ \text{rate}}} + \underbrace{\frac{\Delta E^e_{\text{peso/\$}}}{E_{\text{peso/\$}}}}_{\substack{\text{Expected rate of} \\ \text{depreciation} \\ \text{of the peso}}} + \left(\begin{array}{c}\text{Exchange rate} \\ \text{risk premium}\end{array}\right) + \left(\begin{array}{c}\text{Default} \\ \text{risk premium}\end{array}\right).
$$

Interest rate spread
(equal to zero if peg is credible and there are no risk premiums)

The left-hand side is still the domestic return, but the right-hand side is now a *risk-adjusted foreign return*. The final three terms are the difference between home and foreign interest rates, and their sum total is known as the **interest rate spread.** What causes these spreads?

The first part of the interest rate spread is the **currency premium:**

$$
\text{Currency premium} = \frac{\Delta E^e_{\text{peso/\$}}}{E_{\text{peso/\$}}} + \left(\begin{array}{c}\text{Exchange rate} \\ \text{risk premium}\end{array}\right).
$$

The currency premium should be zero for a credibly pegged exchange rate: the peso is not expected to change in value relative to the dollar. But if a peg is not credible, and investors suspect that the peg may break, there could be a premium reflecting both the size of the expected depreciation and the currency's perceived riskiness. The currency premium therefore reflects the credibility of monetary policy.

The second part of the interest rate spread is known as the **country premium:**

$$
\text{Country premium} = \left(\begin{array}{c}\text{Default} \\ \text{risk premium}\end{array}\right).
$$

The country premium is compensation for perceived default risk (settlement or counterparty risk). It will be greater than zero if investors suspect a risk of losses when they attempt to convert a home (peso) asset back to foreign currency (dollars) in the future. Such a loss might occur because of expropriation, bank failure, surprise taxation, delays, capital controls, other regulations, and so on. The country premium therefore reflects the credibility of property rights.

Why does all this matter? Fluctuations in currency and country premiums have the same effect in Equation (20-4) as fluctuations in the foreign interest rate i^*. Sudden increases in the interest rate spread raise the risk-adjusted foreign return and imply sudden increases in the domestic return, here given by the (peso) interest rate i. In some countries, these spreads can be large and volatile—and even more volatile than the foreign interest rate.

Figure 9-6 presents interest rate spreads for two countries with fixed exchange rates. Panel (a) shows an advanced country, Denmark, which pegs to

FIGURE 9-6

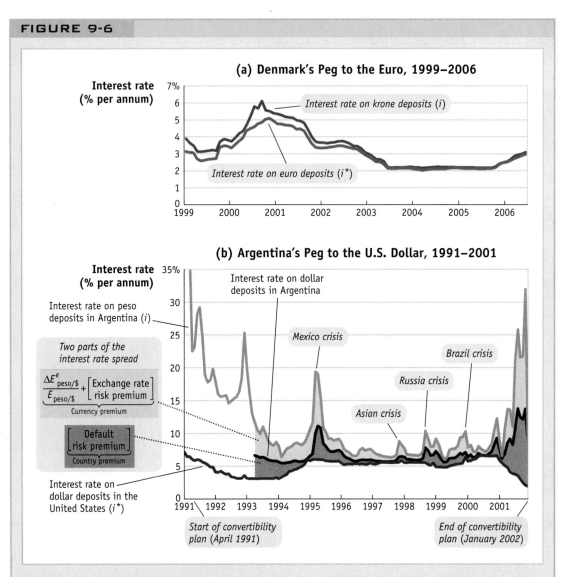

(a) Denmark's Peg to the Euro, 1999–2006

Interest rate (% per annum)

Interest rate on krone deposits (i)

Interest rate on euro deposits (i^*)

(b) Argentina's Peg to the U.S. Dollar, 1991–2001

Interest rate (% per annum)

Interest rate on peso deposits in Argentina (i)

Interest rate on dollar deposits in Argentina

Mexico crisis

Brazil crisis

Russia crisis

Asian crisis

Two parts of the interest rate spread

$$\underbrace{\frac{\Delta E^e_{peso/\$}}{E_{peso/\$}} + \left[\begin{array}{c}\text{Exchange rate}\\\text{risk premium}\end{array}\right]}_{\text{Currency premium}}$$

$$\underbrace{\left[\begin{array}{c}\text{Default}\\\text{risk premium}\end{array}\right]}_{\text{Country premium}}$$

Interest rate on dollar deposits in the United States (i^*)

Start of convertibility plan (April 1991)

End of convertibility plan (January 2002)

Interest Rate Spreads: Currency Premiums and Country Premiums When advanced countries peg, the interest rate spread is usually close to zero, and we can assume $i = i^*$. An example is Denmark's peg to the euro in panel (a), where the correlation between the krone and euro interest rates is 0.99. When emerging markets peg, interest rate spreads can be large and volatile, due to both currency and country premiums. An example is Argentina's peg to the U.S. dollar in panel (b), where the correlation between the peso interest rate and the U.S. interest rate is only 0.38.

Note: Three-month interest rates for krone-euro; two-month for peso-dollar.

Source: econstats.com.

the euro; panel (b) shows an emerging market, Argentina, which pegged to the dollar from 1991 to 2001.

In Denmark, there was some spread in the early years of the euro from 1999 to 2002 (up to about 0.5% per annum), perhaps reflecting a worry that the krone-euro peg might not endure. After 2003 the spread was almost imperceptible (less than 0.1% per annum). Overall, the simple correlation between the krone interest rate and the euro interest rate was very high, equal to 0.99. Investors came to see the peg as credible, eliminating the currency premium almost entirely. They also had no fear of default risk if they invested in Denmark, eliminating the country premium almost entirely. One could therefore make the simple assumption that i was equal to i^* with no spread.

In Argentina the spreads were large. The annual peso and dollar interest rates were far apart, often differing by 2 or 3 percentage points and sometimes differing by more than 10 percentage points. Most striking is that changes in the spread were usually more important in determining the Argentine interest rate than were changes in the actual foreign (U.S. dollar) interest rate. Overall, the correlation between the peso interest rate i and the dollar interest rate i^* was low, equal to only 0.38. What was going on?

We can separately track currency risk and country risk because Argentine banks offered interest-bearing bank deposits denominated in both U.S. dollars and Argentine pesos. The lower two lines in panel (b) show the interest rate on U.S. dollar deposits in the United States (i^*) and the interest rate on U.S. dollar deposits in Argentina. Because the rates are expressed in the same currency, the difference between these two interest rates cannot be the result of a currency premium. It represents a pure measure of country premium: investors required a higher interest rate on dollar deposits in Argentina than on dollar deposits in the United States because they perceived that Argentine deposits might be subject to a default risk. (Investors were eventually proved right: in the 2001–2002 crisis, many Argentine banks faced insolvency, some were closed for a time, and a "pesification" law turned many dollar assets into peso assets ex post, a form of expropriation and a contractual default.)

The upper line in panel (b) shows the interest rate on peso deposits in Argentina (i), which is even higher than the interest rate on U.S. dollar deposits in Argentina. Because these are interest rates on bank deposits in the same country, the difference between these two rates cannot be due to a country premium. It represents a pure measure of currency premium. Investors required a higher interest rate on peso deposits in Argentina than on dollar deposits in Argentina because they perceived that peso deposits might be subject to a risk of depreciation, that is, a collapse of the peg. (Investors were eventually proved right: in the 2001–2002 crisis, the peso depreciated by 75% from $1 to the peso to about $0.25 to the peso, or four pesos per U.S. dollar.)

Summary Pegs in emerging markets are different from those in advanced countries. Because of fluctuations in interest rate spreads, they are subject to even greater interest rate shocks than the pegs of advanced countries, as a result of **credibility** problems. Currency premiums may fluctuate due to changes in investors' beliefs about the durability of the peg, a problem of the credibility of monetary policy. Country premiums may fluctuate due to changes in investors' beliefs about the security of their investments, a problem of the credibility of property rights.

Still, not every movement in emerging market spreads is driven by economic fundamentals. For example, in Argentina the figure shows that investors revised their risk premiums sharply upward when other emerging market countries were experiencing crises in the 1990s: Mexico in 1994, Asia in 1997, and later Russia and Brazil. With the exception of Brazil (a major trade partner for Argentina), there were no major changes in Argentine fundamentals during these crises. Thus, many economists consider this to be evidence of **contagion** in global capital markets, possibly even a sign of market inefficiency or irrationality, where crises in some parts of the global capital markets trigger adverse changes in market sentiment in faraway places. ■

APPLICATION

The Argentine Convertibility Plan before the Tequila Crisis

The central bank balance sheet diagram helps us to see how a central bank manages a fixed exchange rate and what adjustments need to be made in response to a shock in money demand.

We can gain some familiarity and see the usefulness of this apparatus if we actually put it to use in a concrete example. We will look at the fixed exchange rate system in Argentina known as the Convertibility Plan, which began in 1991 and ended in 2002. In this plan, a peg was maintained as one peso per dollar. With the aid of Figure 9-7, we focus first on how the central bank managed its balance sheet during an early phase of the plan, in 1993 and 1994. (We will discuss later years shortly.)

Money Demand Shocks, 1993–1994 The evolution of money supply and reserves is shown in panel (a). From point 1 to point 2 (April 1993 to November/December 1994), all was going well. Argentina had recovered from its hyperinflation in 1989 to 1990, prices were stable, and the economy was growing—and so was money demand. But money demand equals money supply. The central bank kept domestic credit more or less unchanged in this period at 4 billion pesos, so reserves expanded (from 8 billion to 11 billion pesos) hand in hand with the base money supply expansion (from 12 billion to 15 billion pesos). The backing ratio rose from about 67% (8/12) to about 73% (11/15). In the central bank balance sheet diagram in panel (b), this is shown by the horizontal move from point 1 to point 2 as the money demand shock causes the fixed line to shift out from M_1 to M_2, so that higher levels of base money supply are now consistent with the peg.

Then a nasty shock happened: a risk premium shock, as we saw earlier. It came about as a result of the so-called Tequila crisis in Mexico in December 1994. Interest rate spreads widened for Argentina because of currency and country premiums, raising the home interest rate. Argentina's money demand fell. In panel (a), from point 2 to point 3 (November/December 1994 to January/February 1995), base money supply contracted by 1 billion pesos, and this was absorbed almost entirely by a contraction in reserves

FIGURE 9-7

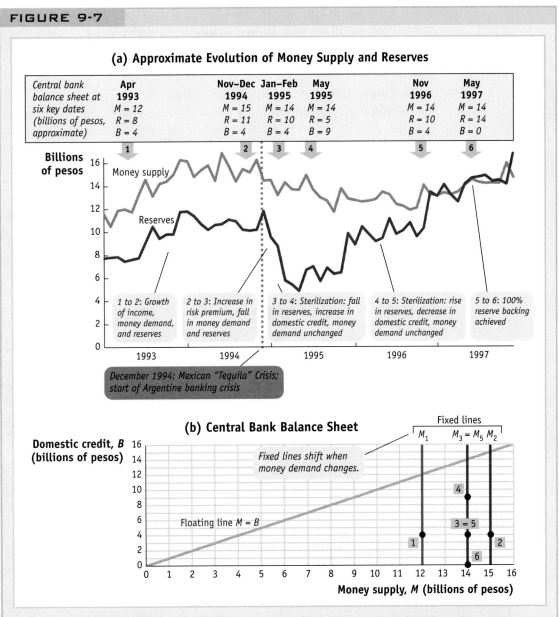

(a) Approximate Evolution of Money Supply and Reserves

Central bank balance sheet at six key dates (billions of pesos, approximate)	Apr 1993	Nov–Dec 1994	Jan–Feb 1995	May 1995	Nov 1996	May 1997
	M = 12	M = 15	M = 14	M = 14	M = 14	M = 14
	R = 8	R = 11	R = 10	R = 5	R = 10	R = 14
	B = 4	B = 4	B = 4	B = 9	B = 4	B = 0

1 to 2: Growth of income, money demand, and reserves

2 to 3: Increase in risk premium, fall in money demand and reserves

3 to 4: Sterilization: fall in reserves, increase in domestic credit, money demand unchanged

4 to 5: Sterilization: rise in reserves, decrease in domestic credit, money demand unchanged

5 to 6: 100% reserve backing achieved

December 1994: Mexican "Tequila" Crisis; start of Argentine banking crisis

(b) Central Bank Balance Sheet

Fixed lines shift when money demand changes.

Floating line M = B

Argentina's Central Bank Operations, 1993–1997 In this period, one peso was worth one U.S. dollar. Panel (a) shows the money supply and reserves. The difference between the two is domestic credit. Six key dates are highlighted before, during, and after the Mexican Tequila crisis. In panel (b), the balance sheet of the central bank at these key dates is shown. Prior to the crisis, domestic credit was essentially unchanged, and reserves grew from $8 billion to $11 billion as money demand grew from M_1 to M_2 in line with rapid growth in incomes (move from point 1 to 2). After the crisis hit in December 1994, interest rate spreads widened, money demand fell from M_2 to M_3, but domestic credit stood still (to point 3) and $1 billion in reserves were lost. In 1995 there was a run on banks and on the currency, and the central bank sterilized by expanding domestic credit by 5 billion pesos and selling $5 billion of reserves as money demand remained constant (to point 4). Reserves reached a low level of $5 billion. By 1996 the crisis had passed and the central bank now replenished its reserves, reversing the earlier sterilization. Domestic credit fell by 5 billion pesos and reserves increased by $5 billion (to point 5, same as point 3). Further sterilized purchases of $4 billion of reserves brought the backing ratio up to 100% in 1997 (to point 6).

Source: IMF, International Financial Statistics. Data compiled by Kurt Schuler.

from 11 billion to 10 billion pesos. The backing ratio fell to about 71% (10/14). In panel (b), this change is shown by the horizontal move from point 2 to point 3 as the money demand shock causes the fixed line to shift in from M_2 to M_3.

To Be Continued Through all of these events, the backing ratio remained high and domestic credit remained roughly steady at around 4 billion pesos, corresponding to our model's assumptions so far. People wanted to swap some pesos for dollars, but nothing catastrophic had happened. However, this was about to change. The shock to Argentina's interest rate proved damaging to the real economy and especially the banking sector. Argentines also became nervous about holding pesos. Foreigners stopped lending to Argentina as the economic situation looked riskier. The central bank stepped in to provide assistance to the ailing banks. But we have yet to work out how a central bank can do this and still maintain a peg. After we complete that task, we will return to the story and see how Argentina managed to survive the Tequila crisis. ■

Defending the Peg II: Changes in the Composition of Money Supply

So far we have examined changes to the level of money demand. We have assumed that the central bank's policy toward domestic credit was *passive,* and so B has been held constant up to now. In contrast, we now study shocks to domestic credit B, all else equal; and to isolate the effects of changes in domestic credit, we will assume money demand is constant.

If money demand is constant, then so is money supply. Therefore, the key lesson of this section will be that, on its own, a change in domestic credit cannot affect the level of the money supply, only its composition in terms of domestic credit and reserves. So we will also need to consider why such a policy is ever pursued.

A Shock to Domestic Credit Suppose that the central bank increases domestic credit by an amount $\Delta B > 0$ from B_1 to B_2. This could be the result of an *open market operation* by the bank's bond trading desk to purchase bonds from private parties. Or it could be the result of a demand by the country's economics ministry that the bank directly finance government borrowing. For now we do not concern ourselves with the cause of this policy decision, nor whether it makes any sense. We just ask what implications it has for a central bank trying to peg, all else equal. Domestic output is assumed to be unchanged and the foreign interest rate is also unchanged.

For example, suppose we go back again and start with a central bank balance sheet with money supply at its initial level of $M_1 = 1,000$ million pesos. The bank then expands domestic credit from 500 million pesos by buying $\Delta B = 100$ million pesos in bonds. All else equal, this action puts more money in circulation, which lowers the interest rate in the money market and puts depreciation pressure on the exchange rate. A floating rate would depreciate in these circumstances. The central bank must sell enough reserves to keep the interest rate unchanged. To achieve that, it must sell 100 million pesos ($100 million) of reserves, in exchange for cash, so that the money supply remains unchanged. The central bank's balance sheet will then be as follows:

SIMPLIFIED CENTRAL BANK BALANCE SHEET AFTER EXPANSION OF DOMESTIC CREDIT (MILLIONS OF PESOS)			
Assets		**Liabilities**	
Reserves *R* *Foreign assets (dollar reserves)*	400	**Money supply *M*** *Money in circulation*	1,000
Domestic credit *B* *Domestic assets (peso bonds)*	600		

What is the end result? Domestic credit B changes by +100 million pesos (rising to 600 million pesos), foreign exchange reserves R change by −100 million pesos (falling to 400 million pesos), and the money supply M remains unchanged (at 1,000 million pesos).

The bond purchases expand domestic credit but also cause the central bank to lose reserves as it is forced to intervene in the forex market. There is no change in monetary policy as measured by home money supply (or interest rates) because the sale and purchase actions by the central bank are perfectly offsetting. Accordingly, this type of central bank action is described as **sterilization** or a sterilized intervention, or a sterilized sale of reserves.

In Figure 9-8, we trace the implications of sterilization policies using our graphical apparatus. On the vertical axis, domestic credit rises from B_1 to B_2. The balance sheet position of the central bank therefore shifts up the fixed line from point 1 to point 2. Reserves fall by ΔB from $R_1 = 500$ to $R_2 = 400$. The central bank has moved closer to point Z, the danger point of zero reserves on the 45-degree line. The backing ratio falls from 50% to 40%.

Figure 9-8 also shows what would happen with the opposite shock. If domestic credit fell by 100 million pesos to 400 million pesos at B_3, with an unchanged money demand, then reserves would rise by 100 million pesos. The central bank's balance sheet ends up at point 3. Reserves rise from $R_1 = 500$ to $R_3 = 600$. The backing ratio now rises from 50% to 60%.

We also see in Figure 9-8 that sterilization is impossible in the case of a currency board because a currency board requires that domestic credit always be zero and that reserves be 100% of the money supply at all times.

Equation (9-3) confirms this as a general result. We know that if the change in money demand is zero, then so is the change in money supply, $\Delta M = 0$, hence the change in domestic credit $\Delta B > 0$ must be offset by an equal and opposite change in reserves $\Delta R = -\Delta B < 0$. This is also clear from Equation (9-2).

We have shown the following: *Holding money demand constant, a change in domestic credit leads to an equal and opposite change in reserves, which is called a sterilization.*

Why Does the Composition of the Money Supply Fluctuate? Our model

tells us that sterilization has no effect on the level of money supply and hence no effect on interest rates and the rest of the economy. This begs the question, why would central banks bother to do this? In the case of buying and selling

FIGURE 9-8

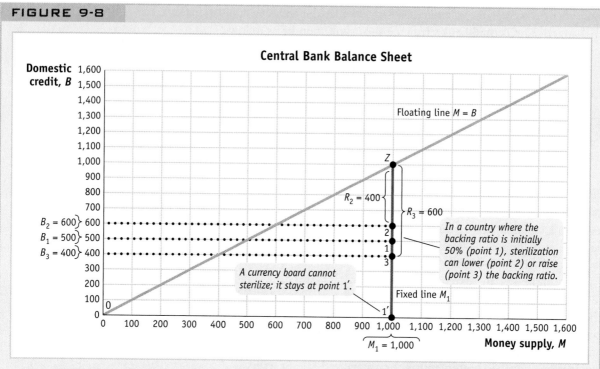

Central Bank Balance Sheet

Floating line $M = B$

Z

$R_2 = 400$

$R_3 = 600$

$B_2 = 600$ } 600
$B_1 = 500$ } 500
$B_3 = 400$ } 400

2
1
3

In a country where the backing ratio is initially 50% (point 1), sterilization can lower (point 2) or raise (point 3) the backing ratio.

A currency board cannot sterilize; it stays at point 1'.

Fixed line M_1

1'

$M_1 = 1,000$

Money supply, M

Domestic credit, B

Sterilization If domestic credit rises, money supply rises, all else equal, interest rates tend to fall, putting pressure on the exchange rate to depreciate. To prevent this depreciation, keep the peg, and stay on the fixed line, the central bank must intervene and defend the peg by selling reserves to keep the money supply fixed. As shown here, the money supply is $M_1 = 1,000$. If domestic credit increases from $B_1 = 500$ to $B_2 = 600$, the central bank balance sheet moves from point 1 to point 2, and reserves fall from $R_1 = 500$ to $R_2 = 400$. An opposite shock is shown by the move from point 1 to point 3, where $B_3 = 400$ and $R_3 = 600$. If the country maintains 100% reserves, it has to stay at point 1': a currency board cannot engage in sterilization.

government bonds, which is the predominant form of domestic credit, the effects are controversial but are generally thought to be small. The only possible effect would be indirect, via portfolio changes in the bond market. If the central bank absorbs some government debt, it leaves less peso debt for the private sector to hold, and this could change the risk premium on the domestic interest rate. But evidence for that type of effect is rather weak.[12]

However, there is another type of domestic credit that can have very important effects on the wider economy. This is domestic credit caused by a decision by the central bank to lend to private commercial banks in difficul-

---

[12] This argument (which applies also to sterilized interventions under floating rates, which do not alter the level of the money supply) supposes that the central bank trades a large enough amount of the country's government debt that it can affect the default premium. If that were true, then an expansion of domestic credit would lower the amount of government debt that the private sector would have to hold and might convince private investors to tolerate a lower risk premium. This might then filter through into long- and short-term interest rates in the home economy, with beneficial effects. However, while this line of argument is true in theory, the evidence is often weak and inconsistent and a source of ongoing controversy. See Maurice Obstfeld, 1982, "Can We Sterilize? Theory and Evidence," *American Economic Review,* 72(2), May, 45–50; Lucio Sarno and Mark P. Taylor, 2001, "Official Intervention in the Foreign Exchange Market: Is It Effective and, If So, How Does It Work?" *Journal of Economic Literature,* 39(3), September, 839–868.

ty. Here the central bank would be fulfilling one of its traditional responsibilities as the protector of the domestic financial system. This has real effects because a domestic banking crisis, if allowed to happen, can cause serious economic harm by damaging the economy's payments system and credit markets.

In theory, when it comes to banks that are having difficulties, economists distinguish between banks that are illiquid and those that are insolvent. Let's see how loans from the central bank to private commercial banks affect the central bank balance sheet for these two important cases, where we are careful to note that for this case we can no longer assume that M0 (currency or base money) is the same as M1 (narrow money, which includes checking deposits) or M2 (broad money, which includes saving deposits).

- *Insolvency and bailouts.* A private bank is **insolvent** if the value of its liabilities (e.g., customers' deposits) exceeds the value of its assets (e.g., loans, other securities, and cash on hand). Often, this happens when the bank's assets unexpectedly lose value (loans turn bad, stocks crash). In some circumstances, the government may offer a rescue or **bailout** to banks in such a damaged state, as it may be unwilling to see the bank fail (for political or even for economic reasons, if banks provide valuable intermediation services to the economy). This may happen in an incremental way, if the banks at first obtain a loan from the central bank, and then find their loans rolled over for a very long time, or even forgiven with some or all interest and principal unpaid. Suppose the central bank balance sheet was originally 500 reserves and 500 domestic credit, with base money supply of 1,000. The cash from a bailout (say 100) goes to the private bank and domestic credit rises (by 100) to 600 on the central bank's balance sheet. Because there has been no increase in base money demand, as more cash has gone into circulation, reserves must fall (by 100) to 400, as in Figure 9-9, panel (a). It is like (and indeed is equivalent to) the central bank buying bonds worth 100 directly from the government (clearly a sterilization, as we saw previously) and the government then bailing out the private bank with the proceeds. Bottom line: bailouts are very risky for the central bank because they cause reserves to drain, endangering the peg.

- *Illiquidity and bank runs.* A private bank may be solvent, but it can still be **illiquid:** it holds some cash, but its loans cannot be sold (liquidated) quickly at a high price and depositors can withdraw at any time. If too many depositors attempt to withdraw at once, the bank is in trouble if it has insufficient cash on hand: this is known as a **bank run.** In this situation, the central bank may lend money to commercial banks that are running out of cash. What is going on? Suppose the monetary base is M0 and equals 1,000 as in the last example, but broad money is M2 (including bank deposits) and equals 2,000. The difference of 1,000 is the value of bank checking and saving deposits. Now let there be a run at a bank. Customers rush in and demand 100 in cash, and the bank has to borrow 100

FIGURE 9-9

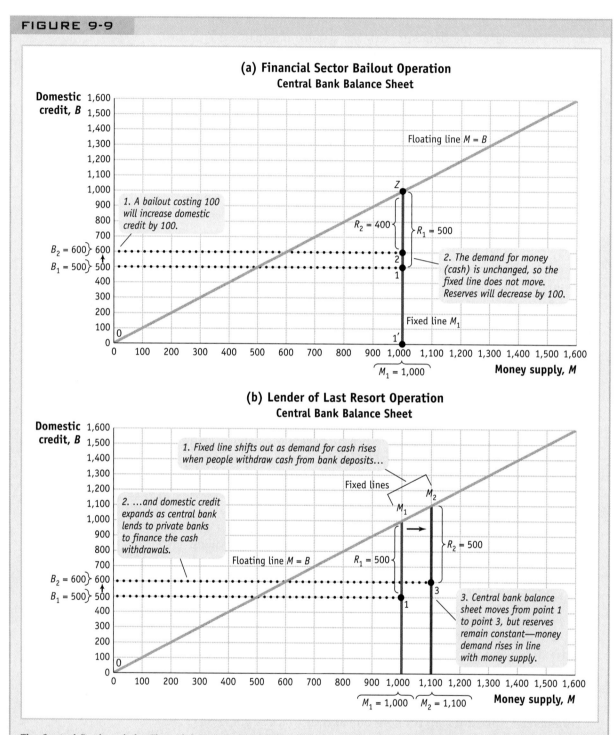

(a) Financial Sector Bailout Operation
Central Bank Balance Sheet

Domestic credit, B

Floating line $M = B$

1. A bailout costing 100 will increase domestic credit by 100.

$R_2 = 400$
$R_1 = 500$

$B_2 = 600$
$B_1 = 500$

2. The demand for money (cash) is unchanged, so the fixed line does not move. Reserves will decrease by 100.

Fixed line M_1

$M_1 = 1,000$

Money supply, M

(b) Lender of Last Resort Operation
Central Bank Balance Sheet

Domestic credit, B

1. Fixed line shifts out as demand for cash rises when people withdraw cash from bank deposits...

Fixed lines
M_1 M_2

2. ...and domestic credit expands as central bank lends to private banks to finance the cash withdrawals.

Floating line $M = B$

$R_1 = 500$
$R_2 = 500$

$B_2 = 600$
$B_1 = 500$

3. Central bank balance sheet moves from point 1 to point 3, but reserves remain constant—money demand rises in line with money supply.

$M_1 = 1,000$ $M_2 = 1,100$

Money supply, M

The Central Bank and the Financial Sector In panel (a), a bailout occurs when the central bank prints money and buys domestic assets—the bad assets of insolvent private banks. There is no change in demand for base money (cash), so the expansion of domestic credit leads to a decrease of reserves. In panel (b), private bank depositors want to shift from holding deposits to holding cash. If the central bank acts as a lender of last resort and temporarily lends the needed cash to illiquid private banks, both the demand and supply of base money (cash) rise, so the level of reserves is unchanged.

from the central bank to satisfy them. We suppose the bank is at zero cash or at the lowest level permitted by regulation—so it is constrained; and every other bank is likewise constrained, or fearful of lending to the troubled bank, or also in a run, so the problem cannot be solved by interbank lending. The central bank is then the **lender of last resort.** Crucially, as well as the central bank expanding domestic credit (by 100) to 600, we also have base money demand (demand for cash) rising (by 100) to 1,100. This means we have a combination of the two types of shocks we have studied: an increase in domestic credit *and* an increase in (base) money demand, as shown in Figure 9-9, panel (b). Now reserves do not change; they stay at 500. Why? The central bank is satisfying a demand for more cash, which absorbs the expansion of domestic credit. The situation will just revert to normal when the run ends and the private bank pays back its loan to the central bank. Bottom line: providing liquidity to solvent banks is not risky for the central bank because there is no reserve drain to threaten the peg.

This simple classification is useful but the reality is more complex. The difference between insolvency and illiquidity is unclear. If depositors fear that banks have either problem, and that the central bank may bail them out slowly or partially, they will seek to withdraw their deposits and put them in a safe place. If the problem is big, the fear may affect all depositors and all banks, and due to uncertainty nobody knows which banks are safe, which illiquid and which insolvent. In many emerging markets and developing countries, this kind of panic often

The Old Lady doth protest too much: In September 2007 the Bank of England assured Northern Rock depositors that the bank would not fail. The bank's balance sheet was widely believed to be healthy (solvency), but the bank had run short of cash to fund mortgages (illiquidity). Despite official assurances, depositors ran all the same, preferring cash in hand to government promises.

leads to a flight from deposits not into local currency but into foreign bank deposits, since the extent of any bailout may be unclear, and so the survival of the peg may be in doubt too. The beliefs can also be self-fulfilling. A bank that faces a run may have to sell illiquid assets in a hurry at a low price, damaging itself and magnifying the problem. As depositors demand foreign currency they drain reserves and make it more likely that devaluation will happen. A country at risk of devaluation faces a higher risk premium, worsening economic conditions and encouraging a flight from the currency. If a depreciation did happen, then banks and firms that have foreign currency liabilities will be in even worse shape, so running looks even better. And so the vicious circle continues (we develop these ideas further in Chapter 11).[13]

To get a sense of the challenges faced by a central bank when confronted with difficulties in the banking sector under a fixed exchange rate, let us return to the case of Argentina after the Mexican Tequila crisis.

---

[13] See Martin S. Feldstein, 1999, "A Self-Help Guide for Emerging Markets," *Foreign Affairs,* 78(2), 93–109.

The Argentine Convertibility Plan after the Tequila Crisis

When we left Argentina at the end of the last application, the Mexican Tequila crisis had just hit in December 1994, and base money supply had fallen by a billion pesos. This change was shown in Figure 9-7 by the move from point 2 to point 3. With domestic credit steady, this meant that reserves also fell by a billion pesos to a level of 10 billion in January/February 1995.

Banking Crisis, 1995 Higher interest rates were reducing output as the private sector struggled with the high cost of credit. The government's budget deficit grew as tax revenues fell. Commercial bank balance sheets were damaged by bad loans and depressed asset prices. The country now faced the threat of a banking crisis.[14]

The central bank began extending loans, even to banks of questionable solvency. The loans became more abundant and for a much longer duration. Concerns grew that the central bank had stepped up to, or over, the line between acting as a lender of last resort and bailing out.

People feared that banks would fail, but they could not easily tell the difference between a strong bank and a weak one. People withdrew checking and saving deposits, but the run made it only more likely that banks would fail. Contagion and uncertainty meant that the panic hit all banks, weak and strong alike. Dollar deposits caused an additional problem. If people wanted to withdraw pesos, the central bank's peso loans helped, but if they wanted to withdraw dollars, the peso loans would head right back to the central bank as the commercial banks demanded dollar reserves to satisfy the dollar claims.

Even as people started to run from bank deposits to cash, higher interest rates and lower output depressed the demand for cash. Reserves drained, casting more doubt on the viability of the fixed exchange rate, raising the currency premium, and draining more reserves. Given the fears of a banking crisis *and* exchange rate crisis, cash and bank deposits were switched into dollars and moved to banks in Montevideo, Miami, or other offshore locations. People were now starting to run from the currency, too.

The consequences for the central bank balance sheet were dramatic. Domestic credit expanded from 4 billion pesos to 9 billion pesos in the first half of 1995, as seen in Figure 9-7 at point 4 in panel (a), even as base money supply remained more or less steady near 14 billion pesos. Cash demand held up, but people were moving bank deposits into pesos and then offshore—and the central bank was providing the peso liquidity (to banks) and then the dollar liquidity (to people) to allow this capital flight to happen. As a result of this sterilization, reserves fell to a low of just 5 billion pesos, with the backing ratio collapsing to a low of about 36% (5/14). In the central bank balance sheet diagram in Figure 9-7, panel (b), the country was now moving vertically up to

---

[14] See Laura D'Amato, Elena Grubisic and Andrew Powell, 1997, "Contagion, Bank Fundamentals or Macroeconomic Shock? An Empirical Analysis of the Argentine 1995 Banking Problems," Working Paper No. 2, Central Bank of Argentina, Buenos Aires; Charles W. Calomiris and Andrew Powell, 2000, "Can Emerging Market Bank Regulators Establish Credible Discipline? The Case of Argentina, 1992–1999," NBER Working Paper No. 7715.

point 4 and getting perilously close to the floating line, the dangerous place where reserves run out.

Help from the IMF and Recovery In late 1994, Argentina was at the point of being cut off from further official lending by the International Monetary Fund as a result of its failure to reduce its fiscal deficit and pursue other reforms. With private credit markets screeching toward a sudden stop after the Tequila crisis, and the government running a large deficit, the situation looked bleak.

However, after the Tequila crisis, the United States advanced a large assistance package to Mexico, and the IMF took a more lenient view of the Argentine situation, fearing the possibility of a global financial crisis if Argentina crashed, too. IMF lending resumed. This was seen as "catalytic" in putting an end to the sudden stop, and a "Patriotic Bond" was issued in private capital markets. The loans provided desperately needed dollars. Some of the dollars could then be poured into the central bank. This replenished reserves, but it also revealed the scale of the bailing out. A substantial fund was set up to salvage insolvent commercial banks, a move that finally erased the stain of the bailouts from the central bank's balance sheet (bad commercial bank debt to the central bank was socialized and then turned into a government debt to foreigners).[15]

The Argentine authorities squeaked through a crisis, the economy recovered, capital flows resumed, and eventually the central bank's emergency loans were paid back. By 1996 economic growth had picked up, interest rate spreads eased, and confidence returned. The central bank reversed its earlier sterilization policies and replenished reserves by contracting domestic credit. By November 1996, domestic credit was back down to 4 billion pesos (its precrisis level), and by May 1997, the central bank had gone further and reduced domestic credit to zero. These steps are shown in the central bank balance sheet diagram in Figure 9-7, panel (b), by the moves from point 4 to point 5 to point 6.

Postscript Argentina's central bank ended up with a 100% backing ratio and was in a position to act as a strict currency board. However, it did not do so and in subsequent turbulent times continued to exercise discretion in its use of sterilization policies. The Convertibility Plan came to an end in 2001, however, when its room for maneuver finally ran out: the economy was in recession, the government was deeper in debt, the IMF and private creditors had reached their lending limits, and the government was reduced to raiding the banks and the central bank for resources. The details of that story, which are tied up with the Argentine 2001 default, are taken up in Chapter 11. ■

The Central Bank Balance Sheet and the Financial System

We can see from the experience of Argentina and many other countries that the existence of a financial system affects the operations and balance sheet of the central bank. In particular, whether as a result of its own policy choices, formal laws and regulations, or political pressure, the typical central bank takes on the responsibility for monitoring, regulating, and—in an emergency—protecting a country's commercial banking system.

---

[15] For a detailed account of Argentina's travails, see Paul Blustein, 2005, *And the Money Kept Rolling in (and Out): Wall Street, the IMF, and the Bankrupting of Argentina,* New York: Public Affairs.

A More General Balance Sheet As a result of its interactions with banks, the central bank's balance sheet is in reality more complicated than we have assumed in our simplified model. Typically it looks something like this, with some hypothetical values inserted:[16]

GENERAL CENTRAL BANK BALANCE (MILLIONS OF PESOS)			
Assets		**Liabilities**	
Foreign assets of which:	950	**Foreign liabilities** of which:	50
Foreign reserves (all currencies)	950	*Foreign currency debt issued by the*	50
Gold	0	*central bank*	
Domestic assets of which:	500	**Domestic liabilities** of which:	400
Domestic government bonds bought	300	*Domestic currency debt issued by the*	400
Loans to commercial banks	200	*central bank*	
		Money supply *M* of which:	1,000
		Currency in circulation	900
		Reserve liabilities to commercial banks	100

In the first row, the central bank's *net foreign assets* are worth 900, given by 950 minus 50. We see that foreign assets can include other currencies besides the anchor currency (the dollar) and may also include gold. There may also be off-setting foreign liabilities if the central bank chooses to borrow. In this example, gold happens to be 0, foreign reserves are 950, and foreign liabilities are 50.

In the second row, *net domestic assets* are worth 100, 500 minus 400. We see that domestic assets may be broken down into government bonds (here 300) and loans to commercial banks (here 200). All of these assets can be offset by domestic liabilities, such as debt issued in home currency by the central bank. In this example, the central bank has issued 400 in domestic debt, which we shall assume was used to finance the purchase of foreign reserves.

Finally, the money supply is a liability for the central bank worth 1,000, as before. However, not all of that currency is "in circulation" (i.e., outside the central bank, in the hands of the public or in commercial bank vaults). Typically, central banks place *reserve requirements* on commercial banks and force them to place some cash on deposit at the central bank. This is considered a prudent regulatory device. In this case, currency in circulation is 900, and 100 is in the central bank as part of reserve requirements.

Despite all these refinements, the lessons of our simple model carry over. For example, in the simple approach, money supply (*M*) equaled foreign assets (*R*) plus domestic assets (*B*). We now see that, in general, money supply is equal to *net foreign assets* plus *net domestic assets*. The only real difference is the ability of the central bank to borrow by issuing nonmonetary liabilities, whether domestic or foreign.

---

[16] For simplicity, we assume that the bank has zero net worth, so total assets equal total liabilities. In general, this will not be true from day to day as the central bank can make gains and losses on its assets and liabilities, and it may also have operating profits and losses. However, net worth is typically not very large and, over the longer run, any gains and losses are typically absorbed by the government treasury.

Sterilization Bonds Why do central banks expand their balance sheets by issuing such liabilities? To see what the central bank can achieve by borrowing, consider what the preceding balance sheet would look like if the central bank had not borrowed to fund the purchase of reserves.

Without issuing domestic liabilities of 400 and foreign liabilities of 50, reserves would be lower by 450. In other words, they would fall from 950 to their original level of 500 seen in the example at the start of this chapter. Domestic credit would then be 500, as it was in that earlier example, with money supply of 1,000. Thus, what borrowing to buy reserves achieves is not a change in monetary policy (money supply and interest rates are unchanged, given the peg) but an increase in the backing ratio. Instead of a 50% backing ratio (500/1,000), the borrowing takes the central bank up to a 95% backing ratio (950/1,000).

But why stop there? What if the central bank borrowed, say, another 300 by issuing domestic debt and used the proceeds to purchase more reserves? Its domestic liabilities would rise from 400 to 700 (net domestic assets would fall from +100 to −200), and on the other side of the balance sheet, reserves (foreign assets) would rise from 950 to 1,250. Money supply would still be 1,000, but the backing ratio would be 125%. This could go on and on. Borrow another 250, and the backing ratio would be 150%.

As we have seen, these hypothetical operations are all examples of changes in the *composition* of the money supply—in terms of net foreign assets and net domestic assets—holding fixed the *level* of money supply. In other words, this is just a more general form of sterilization. And *sterilization is just a way to change the backing ratio, all else equal.*

What is new here is that the central bank's *net* domestic assets (assets minus liabilities) can be less than zero because the central bank is now allowed to borrow. Many central banks do just this, by issuing bonds—or **sterilization bonds** as they are fittingly described. This allows the backing ratio to potentially exceed 100%.

Looking back at Figure 9-8, we could depict this by allowing reserves R to represent *net* foreign assets, credit B to represent *net* domestic assets, and by allowing B to be less than zero. The key equation $M = R + B$ still holds, and the fixed and floating lines work as before, as long as we interpret zero *net* foreign assets as the trigger for a switch from fixed to floating.[17] So we can imagine that the fixed line in Figure 9-8 can extend down below the horizontal axis.

Going below the horizontal axis means that net domestic credit is negative, and the backing ratio is more than 100%. Why might countries want backing that high? As we saw, Argentina had high backing of more than 70% on the eve of the Tequila crisis, but this would not have been enough for the peg to survive a major run from the financial system to dollars. In Figure 9-8, the zone below the horizontal axis would be an ultrasafe place, even farther from the floating line. Many countries have recently sought refuge in that direction (see **Side Bar: The Great Reserve Accumulation in Emerging Markets**).

---

[17] As we have argued, the precise level of that trigger may be arbitrary without affecting the insights from this analysis.

SIDE BAR

The Great Reserve Accumulation in Emerging Markets

An illustration of reserve buildup via sterilization is provided by the activities of the People's Bank of China, whose central bank balance sheet diagram is shown in Figure 9-10 in yuan (¥) units. The vertical distance to the 45-degree line represents net foreign assets *R*, which were essentially the same as foreign reserves because the Bank had close to zero foreign liabilities.*

From 1995 to 2003, net domestic credit in China grew very slowly, from ¥1,409 billion to ¥2,218 billion, but rapid economic growth and financial development caused base money demand to grow rapidly. It more than doubled, from ¥2,076 billion to ¥5,284 billion. Thus, most of the base money supply growth of ¥3,208 billion was absorbed by ¥2,399 billion of reserve accumulation. In this period, the backing ratio rose from 32% to 58%.

From 2003 to 2006, net domestic credit fell by ¥2,927 billion and eventually turned negative as the central bank sold large amounts of sterilization bonds. Money supply growth

continued, rising from ¥5,284 billion to ¥7,776 billion, an increase of ¥2,492 billion. But the sterilization caused reserves to rise by almost twice as much, by ¥5,419 billion. The backing ratio rose from 58% to 109%.

Given the country's economic (and political) importance, the Chinese case attracts a lot of attention—but it isn't the only example of this type of central bank behavior. Figure 9-11 shows the massive increase in reserves at central banks around the world in recent years: it started in about 1999, it mostly happened in Asia in countries pegging (more or less) to the dollar, and much of it was driven by large-scale sterilization. What was going on?

Causes of the Reserve Accumulation

Why are these countries, most of them poor emerging markets, accumulating massive hoards of reserves? There are various pos-

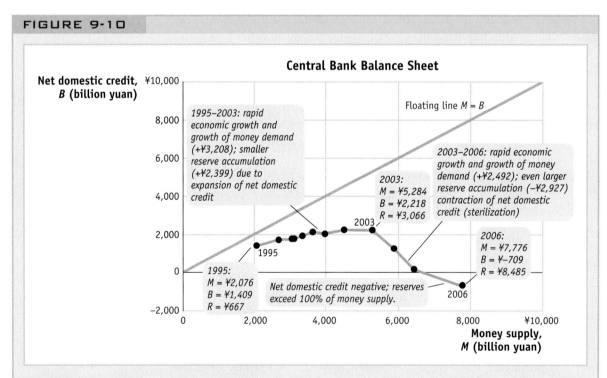

FIGURE 9-10

Central Bank Balance Sheet

Net domestic credit, *B* (billion yuan)

Floating line *M* = *B*

1995–2003: rapid economic growth and growth of money demand (+¥3,208); smaller reserve accumulation (+¥2,399) due to expansion of net domestic credit

2003–2006: rapid economic growth and growth of money demand (+¥2,492); even larger reserve accumulation (–¥2,927) contraction of net domestic credit (sterilization)

2003: M = ¥5,284 B = ¥2,218 R = ¥3,066

2003

1995

1995: M = ¥2,076 B = ¥1,409 R = ¥667

2006: M = ¥7,776 B = ¥–709 R = ¥8,485

Net domestic credit negative; reserves exceed 100% of money supply.

2006

Money supply, *M* (billion yuan)

Sterilization in China By issuing "sterilization bonds," central banks can borrow from domestic residents to buy more reserves. With sufficient borrowing of this kind, the central bank can end up with negative net domestic credit and reserves in excess of 100% of the money supply. The chart shows how this has happened in China in recent years: from 1995 to 2003, net domestic credit in China was steady, and so reserve growth was almost entirely driven by money demand growth (large movement to the right). From 2003 to 2006, extensive sterilization (large movement down) sent net domestic credit below zero, and, despite still-strong money demand growth, sterilization explains more than half of the reserve growth in the later period.

sible motivations for these reserve hoards, in addition to simply wanting greater backing ratios to absorb larger shocks to money demand.[†] For example, the countries may fear a sudden stop, when access to foreign capital markets dries up. Foreign creditors may cease to roll over short-term debt for a while, but if reserves are on hand the central bank can temporarily cover the shortfall. This precautionary motive leads to policy guidelines or rules suggesting that an adequate and prudent level of reserves should be some multiple either of foreign trade or of short-term debt. In practice, such ratios usually imply reserve levels less than 100% of M0, the narrow money supply.

An alternative view, illustrated by the case of Argentina that we studied, would tend to focus on a different risk, the fragility of the financial sector. If there is a major banking crisis with a flight from local deposits to foreign banks, then a central bank may need a far greater level of reserves, adequate to cover some or all of M2, the broader measure of money that includes deposits and other liquid commercial bank liabilities. Because M2 can be several times M0, the reserve levels adequate for these purposes could be much larger and well over 100% of M0. Because reserves now far exceed traditional guidelines based on trade or debt levels, fears of financial fragility might be an important part of the explanation for the scale of the reserve buildup with reserve backing in excess of 100% of M0. As economist Martin Feldstein pointed out after the Asian crisis, it is unrealistic to expect safe and crisis-free banking

sector operations in emerging markets (in 2007 we even saw bank runs in a developed country, the United Kingdom). But if countries are pegged, they then need to watch out for the peg: "...sufficient liquidity, either through foreign currency reserves or access to foreign credit, would let a government restructure and recapitalize its banks without experiencing a currency crisis. The more international liquidity a government has, the less depositors will feel that they must rush to convert their currency before the reserves are depleted. And preventing a currency decline can be the best way to protect bank solvency."[‡]

Thus, current reserve levels can be seen as a reaction, in part, to the financial crises of the recent past: policy makers have taken a "never again" stance, with a large war chest of reserves piled up to guard against any risk of exchange rate crises. Is this wise? The benefits may seem clear, but many economists think this "insurance policy" carries too heavy an economic cost as countries invest in low-interest reserves and forsake investments with higher returns (see **Headlines: Too Much of a Good Thing?**).

---

* In this period, foreign liabilities were just 1% of foreign assets.
† For a survey of the various possible explanations of the reserve buildup, see Joshua Aizenman, 2007, "Large Hoarding of International Reserves and the Emerging Global Economic Architecture," NBER Working Paper No. 13277; Olivier Jeanne, 2007, "International Reserves in Emerging Market Countries: Too Much of a Good Thing?" Brookings Papers on Economic Activity 1: forthcoming
‡ See Martin S. Feldstein, 1999, "A Self-Help Guide for Emerging Markets," Foreign Affairs, 78.2 (March 1999): 93(1).

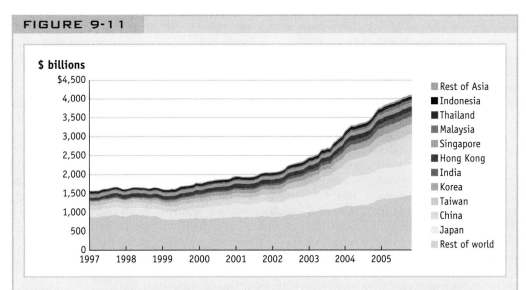

FIGURE 9-11

Reserve Accumulation, 1997–2005 By the end of 2005, reserve holdings worldwide exceeded $4,000 billion, more than double what they were in 1997. Most of the growth occurred in emerging markets, especially Asia. The bulk of these additional reserves were acquired through sterilization and have caused several countries' holdings of foreign exchange reserves to exceed 100% of the monetary base.

Source: IMF, International Financial Statistics. Data compiled by Martin Wolf, "Fixing Global Finance," SAIS Lectures, March 2006.

HEADLINES

Too Much of a Good Thing?

Large reserve holdings have a very high opportunity cost. Too high?

It's often argued that foreigners funnel their money into the United States because it is a great investment. But for many countries, plowing money into the United States these days is not all that compelling a deal.

Poor nations are financing much of the United States' current account deficit. They are losing money in the process, and as the losses mount, they will be tempted to do something better with their cash. Consider Russia. Over the last five years, its foreign currency reserves have multiplied by eight, to more than $200 billion. . . .

To accumulate reserves without stoking inflation, the central bank will typically get the necessary cash by selling ruble bonds, which are paying a return of about 12 percent a year. It will then buy dollars or euros to invest in American or European government securities, which offer yields around 5 percent or less.

Seven percentage points are a lot to give up. With the ruble stable on foreign exchange markets, the annual cost to the Russian government of maintaining $200 billion in reserves could amount to $14 billion a year or more, about three times what it spent on education in all of 2004. Russia's central bank is not the only one that is leaving a fortune on the table. China has amassed one of the largest stashes of reserves in history: more than $800 billion at the end of last year [2005]. Reserves of the African countries reached $162 billion at year-end.

Altogether, by the count of the International Monetary Fund, international reserves held by developing countries doubled in just three years, reaching $2.9 trillion at the end of 2005, equivalent to almost one-third of their total gross domestic product. Much of this money is languishing at low rates of return in American government bonds.

"It is an irony of our times that the majority of the world's poorest people now live in countries with vast international financial reserves," Lawrence H. Summers, the [then] president of Harvard and a former Treasury secretary, told an audience of Indian economists in Mumbai [in 2006]. . . .

There is a logic to this investment strategy, unprofitable as it is. . . . These reserves are simply insurance against financial disaster. A long list of developing countries have experienced devastating crises in the last 15 years: Mexico in 1994; Thailand, Indonesia and other Asian countries in 1997; Russia in 1998; Brazil in 1999; and Argentina in 2002. . . .

These crises exacted a heavy cost. . . . And they turned the developing world into a much more prudent place. As the dust settled over the ruins of many former "emerging" economies, a new creed took hold among policy makers in the developing world: Pile up as much foreign exchange as possible. . . .

Dani Rodrik, an economist at the John F. Kennedy School of Government at Harvard, calculated that if a country had a 10 percent chance of suffering a big reversal in capital inflows in any given year, and if a financial crisis would cost about 10 percent of its G.D.P., it would not be unreasonable for it to pay an insurance premium equivalent to 1 percent of G.D.P.

But developing countries seem to have been carried away by prudential excess. Many poor countries hold vastly more in reserves than recommended. . . . Russia has "excess reserves" equivalent to about a fifth of its G.D.P., Mr. Summers said. Malaysia's excess is equivalent to half its total output.

India, Mr. Summers told his Mumbai audience, has excess reserves of more than $100 billion. If it invested them better, he said, it could reasonably expect a return equivalent to 1 to 1.5 percent of its $785 billion gross domestic product; that share would be more than the Indian government spends on health care. . . .

There are cheaper forms of insurance: rather than accumulating reserves, poor countries could achieve the same level of financial security by limiting the accumulation of short-term debt, Mr. Rodrik said. Moreover, years have gone by without new financial disasters, and the memory of past crises is fading. If this continues, governments across the developing world will question the value of such costly insurance when there are so many other things to do with the money.

"People are going to start to re-evaluate the objectives of economic policy," Mr. Rodrik said. "They are likely to put more weight on employment and economic growth and a little less weight on avoiding a financial crisis."

Source: Extracted from Eduardo Porter, "Are Poor Nations Wasting Their Money on Dollars?" New York Times, April 30, 2006.

Summary

In this section, we examined the constraints on the operations of the central bank when a fixed exchange rate is in operation. We focused on the central bank balance sheet, which in its simplest form describes how the narrow money supply (monetary base) is backed by foreign assets (reserves) and domestic assets (domestic credit). We have seen how, in response to money demand shocks, the central bank buys or sells reserves, to defend the peg. The central bank can also change the composition of the money supply through sterilization operations, which keep the money supply constant.

Two Types of Exchange Rate Crises When reserves go to zero, the country is floating, changes in domestic credit cause changes in the money supply, and the peg breaks. The central bank balance sheet diagrams in Figure 9-12 show two ways in which pegs can break:

■ In panel (a), in the first type of crisis, domestic credit is constantly expanding, so the central bank is pushed up the fixed line until reserves run out. At this point, the currency floats, the money supply then grows without limit, and, in the long run, the exchange rate depreciates.

■ In panel (b), in the second type of crisis, there is no long-run tendency for the money supply to grow, but there is a short-run temptation to expand the money supply temporarily, leading to a temporarily lower interest rate and a temporarily depreciated exchange rate.

In the next two sections, we develop models of these two types of crisis. Although the descriptions just given appear simple, a deeper examination reveals some peculiar features that illustrate the powerful role played by market expectations in triggering crises.

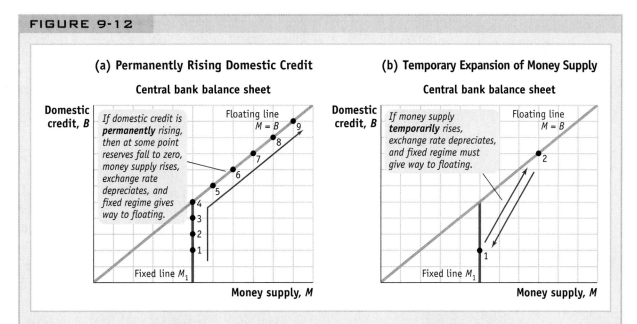

FIGURE 9-12

(a) Permanently Rising Domestic Credit

Central bank balance sheet

(b) Temporary Expansion of Money Supply

Central bank balance sheet

Two Types of Exchange Rate Crisis In our model, using the central bank balance sheet diagram, we can see what actions will cause the peg to break. Two types of crisis are highlighted here. In panel (a), a permanent and ongoing expansion of domestic credit is incompatible with a fixed exchange rate regime because, sooner or later, reserves will be reduced to zero, and then the money supply starts to expand. In panel (b), a temporary expansion of domestic credit and the money supply will lower interest rates and depreciate the exchange rate, even if a reversal of this policy is expected in the future. Both policies take the country off the fixed line and onto the floating line.

3 How Pegs Break I: Inconsistent Fiscal Policies

We begin with a so-called **first generation crisis model** of inconsistent fiscal policies in a country with a fixed exchange rate, a model proposed by the economist Paul Krugman.[18] This kind of crisis model has been successfully applied to many historical cases, including a series of Latin American crises in the 1980s.

The Basic Problem: Fiscal Dominance

In this model, the level of output plays no role, so we assume output is fixed at some level Y. However, the price level P plays an important role, and we allow the price level to be flexible and determined by purchasing power parity (PPP), as in the monetary model of Chapter 3. For now we keep all our earlier assumptions from this chapter.

We assume that the government is running a persistent deficit DEF because of insufficient tax revenue, and the government's situation is so dire it is unable to borrow from any creditor. It therefore turns to the central bank for financing. In this type of environment, economists speak of a situation of **fiscal dominance** in which the monetary authorities ultimately have no independence. The treasury hands over bonds in the amount DEF to the central bank, and receives cash in the amount DEF in return, and uses the cash to fund the government deficit. As a result, domestic credit B increases by an amount $\Delta B = DEF$ every period. For simplicity, we assume that domestic credit B is growing at a constant positive rate $\Delta B/B = \mu$. For example, if $\mu = 0.1$ then domestic credit B is growing at 10% per period.

Given our previous graphical analysis of the central bank balance sheet, we can see that the fixed exchange rate is doomed. As in Figure 9-12, panel (a), every change in the level of domestic credit leads to an equal and opposite change in the level of reserves. This process can't go on forever. Reserves must eventually run out. At that point, the peg breaks and the central bank shifts from a fixed exchange rate regime to a floating regime, in which the money supply equals domestic credit, $M = B$. We note a key point:

Once reserves run out, the money supply M, which was previously fixed, grows at the same rate as domestic credit, $\Delta M/M = \Delta B/B = \mu$.

The reason the peg breaks in this situation is simple. There is an inconsistency between the authorities' commitment to a monetary policy of a fixed exchange rate and a fiscal policy of continuously monetizing deficits through a limitless expansion of domestic credit. On the face of it, crisis results from elementary incompetence on the part of the authorities; to be more generous, we might say that the crisis happens because authorities are willing to let it happen because of overriding fiscal priorities.

A Simple Model

In many ways, this situation is familiar. We have already seen the implications of long-run money growth. In Chapter 3, we learned what will happen in

---

[18] Paul Krugman, 1979, "A Model of Balance-of-Payments Crises," *Journal of Money, Credit and Banking,* 11(3), August, 311–325.

response to such an *unexpected* increase in the rate of money supply growth: if prices can adjust flexibly, then, after the change, the economy ends up with all nominal values growing at the rate μ, the rate of growth of domestic credit. There will be inflation as prices P rise at a rate μ, and depreciation as the exchange rate E rises at a rate μ.

The Myopic Case Figure 3-14 (p. 105) described a case in which the rate of growth of the money supply unexpectedly increased by a fixed amount. We apply the same analysis here and assume that investors are *myopic* and do not see the crisis coming. (To be more realistic, we relax this assumption in a moment, but the myopic case provides useful insights.)

Drawing on what we know, Figure 9-13 uses an example to describe this kind of crisis scenario, assuming that prices are stable in the foreign country, that the foreign interest rate is $i^* = 5\%$, and that all variables evolve continuously through time. For simplicity, we start with $M = P = E = 1$, and at all times we assume the foreign price level is 1, $P^* = 1$.

Starting at time 1, in the fixed regime, domestic credit is less than the money supply, $B < M$, and reserves are positive $R > 0$. But because of the monetization of deficits, B is gradually rising, and, as a result, R is steadily falling. Eventually reserves run out, and thereafter $B = M$ and $R = 0$. We assume for now the regime change occurs at time 4. In the fixed regime, up to that point, money supply M is fixed, but when floating starts, M grows at a rate μ. This is shown in panel (a).

Because prices are flexible, the monetary model of Chapter 3 tells us that P will be fixed until time 4 and then it will grow at a rate μ. Thus, inflation rises by an amount μ at time 4. The Fisher effect tells us that an increase in the home inflation rate causes a one-for-one increase in the home interest rate. So the home interest rate i must rise by an amount μ as we move from the fixed to the floating regime. This is shown in panel (b).

An increase in the home interest rate i at time 4 lowers the demand for real money balances $M/P = L(i)Y$ because in the money demand function, L is a decreasing function of i. Thus M/P falls discontinuously (jumps) as we change from fixed to floating. Because the money supply M does not change at time 4, the discontinuous drop in M/P can be accommodated only by a jump in the flexible price level P at time 4. Because PPP holds continuously (and because $P^* = 1$), $E = P/P^* = P$, the discontinuous rise in P also means a discontinuous rise in E at time 4, and a depreciation of the home currency. Both E and P jump up and start to grow at rate μ at time 4, as shown in panel (c).

To sum up, in Figure 9-13, the exchange rate crisis is at time 4, but the exchange rate doesn't merely drift continuously away from its previous fixed level. It *jumps* away discontinuously. The new floating path of the exchange rate is a rising trend, with growth rate μ, which is above the old fixed rate at time 4.

For example, if the money growth rate is 10% after the crisis, as assumed, then there is a 10 percentage point increase in the interest rate from 5% to 15%. Now suppose this reduces real money demand by 20%, from 1.00 to 0.80. Because the nominal money supply M equals 1 just before and just after the crisis, it does not jump at time 4, so to get M/P to fall from 1.00 to 0.80, P must jump up, from 1.0 to $(1/0.80) = 1.25$, implying an instantaneous 25% increase in P. To maintain purchasing power parity, there must

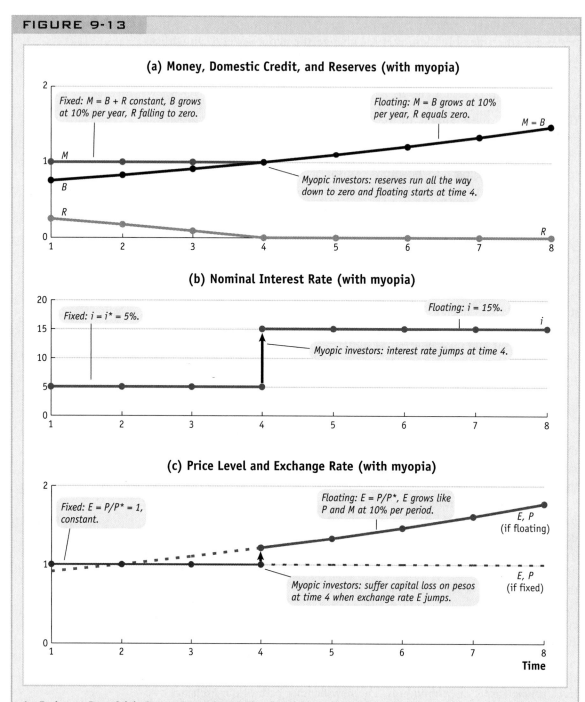

FIGURE 9-13

(a) Money, Domestic Credit, and Reserves (with myopia)

Fixed: M = B + R constant, B grows at 10% per year, R falling to zero.

Floating: M = B grows at 10% per year, R equals zero.

Myopic investors: reserves run all the way down to zero and floating starts at time 4.

(b) Nominal Interest Rate (with myopia)

Fixed: i = i* = 5%.

Floating: i = 15%.

Myopic investors: interest rate jumps at time 4.

(c) Price Level and Exchange Rate (with myopia)

Fixed: E = P/P* = 1, constant.

Floating: E = P/P*, E grows like P and M at 10% per period.

E, P (if floating)

E, P (if fixed)

Myopic investors: suffer capital loss on pesos at time 4 when exchange rate E jumps.

Time

An Exchange Rate Crisis Due to Inconsistent Fiscal Policies: Myopic Case In the fixed regime, money supply M is fixed, but expansion of domestic credit B implies that reserves R are falling to zero. Suppose the switch to floating occurs when reserves run out at time 4. Thereafter, the monetary model tells us that M, P, and E will all grow at a constant rate (here 10% per period). The expected rates of inflation and depreciation are now positive, and the Fisher effect tells us that the interest rate must jump up at period 4 (by 10 percentage points). The interest rate increase means that real money demand $M/P = L(i)Y$ falls instantly at time 4. The money supply does not adjust immediately, so this jump in M/P must be accommodated by a jump in prices P. To maintain purchasing power parity, E must also jump at the same time. Hence, myopic investors face a capital loss on pesos at time 4.

CHAPTER 9 ■ EXCHANGE RATE CRISES: HOW PEGS WORK AND HOW THEY BREAK **417**

also be a 25% increase in the exchange rate E, to 1.25, followed by growth at 10%.

One significant implication of the jump in nominal values is that anyone holding a peso that was worth 1 dollar will suddenly be left holding a peso that is worth only $1/1.25 = 0.8$ dollars. Investors holding pesos at the moment of crisis will suffer a capital loss (in dollar terms) if this model accurately describes their behavior.

The Forward-Looking Case There is good reason to believe that investors will not be as shortsighted as we have assumed. It is usually well known when a government has a deficit that is being monetized, even if the authorities try to conceal the problem.

Let us move to the other extreme, *forward-looking* behavior, which for now we take to mean *perfect foresight*. We now refer to Figure 9-14, which explains how this scenario departs from the myopic version we just saw in Figure 9-13. Suppose peso holders see that domestic credit is rising and reserves are falling. Knowledgeable people will speculate that the fixed rate is going to break in the near future. They will foresee that pesos will experience a sudden loss of dollar value if they hold them until the bitter end at time 4 when reserves would run out under myopia. They will therefore decide to dump pesos sooner. But when? And how?

All investors will want to dump pesos at the same time (in this model all investors are identical). When investors sell all their holdings of a particular currency, it is known as a **speculative attack.** When such an attack occurs, the economy must *immediately* switch to the floating regime we have already studied, since once it has zero reserves the money supply M will forever be equal to domestic credit B—which has been and will be growing at the constant rate μ. At that same moment in time, the nominal interest rate will also jump up, as the Fisher effect kicks in as before, and there will be a jump down in both money demand (as the interest rise hits) and in money supply (as the attack drains all remaining reserves).

In our example, the key lesson is that once an attack occurs, the economy completely switches over to the floating regime. Under myopia the switch was at time 4. But now, the switch happens well before time 4, and at the time of the attack the economy's inflation, exchange rates, prices, and interest rates all flip over to their new trajectories. This leaves one question: When does the speculative attack occur? From Figure 9-14, the answer must be: at time 2. In this case, the path of the price level P and the exchange rate E are continuous as we switch from fixed to floating. Only then can the switch occur without any expected dollar gains or losses on holding pesos.

How does this pin down the attack at time 2? Suppose the attack were at any time later than 2, such as time 3. As we can see from the diagram, this requires a jump up in the exchange rate, a *discontinuous depreciation*. If they wait to attack until time 3, peso holders suffer a capital loss and they have waited too long. What if the attack is before time 2, say, at time 1? An attack at time 1 implies a *discontinuous appreciation* of the peso. But if that were so, any individual peso holder would enjoy capital gains (in dollars) from holding on to pesos rather than

FIGURE 9-14

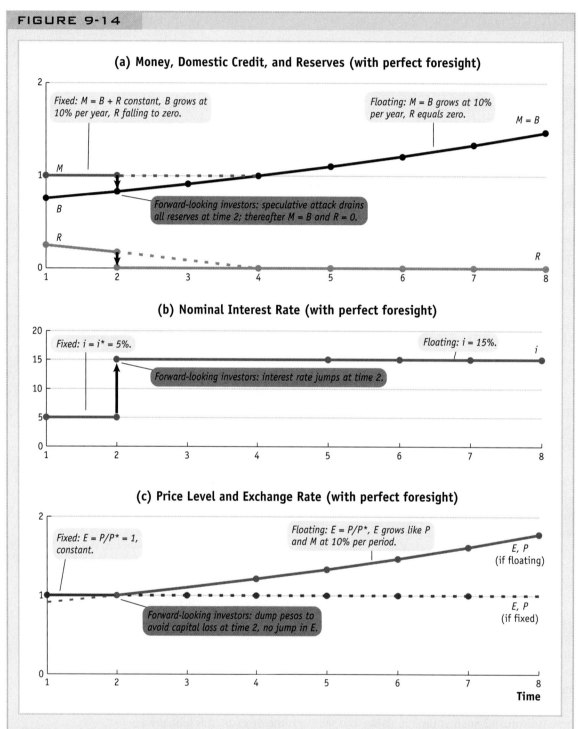

(a) Money, Domestic Credit, and Reserves (with perfect foresight)

Fixed: M = B + R constant, B grows at 10% per year, R falling to zero.

Floating: M = B grows at 10% per year, R equals zero.

M = B

M

B

Forward-looking investors: speculative attack drains all reserves at time 2; thereafter M = B and R = 0.

R

R

(b) Nominal Interest Rate (with perfect foresight)

Fixed: i = i* = 5%.

Floating: i = 15%.

i

Forward-looking investors: interest rate jumps at time 2.

(c) Price Level and Exchange Rate (with perfect foresight)

Fixed: E = P/P* = 1, constant.

Floating: E = P/P*, E grows like P and M at 10% per period.

E, P (if floating)

E, P (if fixed)

Forward-looking investors: dump pesos to avoid capital loss at time 2, no jump in E.

Time

An Exchange Rate Crisis Due to Inconsistent Fiscal Policies: Perfect Foresight Case Compare with Figure 9-13. If investors anticipate a crisis, they will seek to avoid losses by converting the pesos they are holding to dollars before period 4. The rational moment to attack is at time 2, the point at which the switch from fixed to floating is achieved without any jumps in E or P. Why? At time 2, the drop in money demand (due to the rise in the interest rate) exactly equals the decline in the money supply (the reserve loss), and money market equilibrium is maintained without the price level having to change.

exchanging them for reserves at the central bank at the prior fixed rate. They would then desire to wait and let everyone else attack and pocket the gains. But if one person thinks like that, all do, and the attack cannot materialize.

The speculative attack model teaches an important lesson. One moment, a central bank may have a pile of reserves on hand, draining away fairly slowly, giving the illusion that there is no imminent danger. The next moment, the reserves are all gone. The model can therefore explain why fixed exchange rates sometimes witness a sudden collapse rather than a long, lingering death.

APPLICATION

The Peruvian Crisis of 1986

An example of a crisis driven by inconsistent fiscal policies and excessive expansion of domestic credit is provided by the events in Peru from 1985 to 1986, illustrated in Figure 9-15.

In the early 1980s, Peru's political and economic conditions were highly unfavorable. The country had endured a period of social unrest and military rule in the 1970s, and the government had an enormous external debt burden. World commodity prices fell, exports and economic growth slowed, and government deficits grew. At the same time, world interest rates sharply increased.

The Peruvian government defaulted on its debt obligations and began negotiations with the IMF and other creditors. Denied fresh loans from world capital markets, and with low tax receipts that could not cover rising spending, government financing came to rely on money printing by the central bank—that is, the inflation tax. Domestic credit grew by 65% in 1982, 165% in 1983, and 93% in 1984—a rough doubling every year, on average. The dollar value of Peru's currency, the sol, rapidly sank.

As economic conditions deteriorated further and political violence by guerilla groups intensified, President Alan García Pérez was elected to office in 1985. One important economic measure he instituted immediately was a fixed exchange rate. This stopped the depreciation and was intended to give Peru a firm nominal anchor. But, as we now know, its durability would depend on whether García's administration could solve its fiscal problems and put an end to the monetization of government deficits.

Some fiscal reform was attempted, and the economy recovered slightly: the government budget improved at first. But the administration could not get the government budget out of the red for long. The deficit fell from 2%–3% of GDP to near zero in early 1986, but by mid-1986 it was growing again, averaging over 5% and peaking at 8%–9% of GDP in late 1986 and 1987. The printing presses of the central bank kept running, and domestic credit grew 84% in 1985, 77% in 1986, and 146% in 1987—still, on average, a rough doubling every year.

Only now, under a fixed exchange rate, something had to give. With domestic credit exploding, the central bank was continually selling reserves to defend the peg.[19] Reserves fell from a peak of $2,000 million in early 1986 to

---

[19] The peg spent most of its time close to 17,300 sol/$. Various realignments to 20,000 and then 33,000 sol/$ in late 1987 bought a little time at the end.

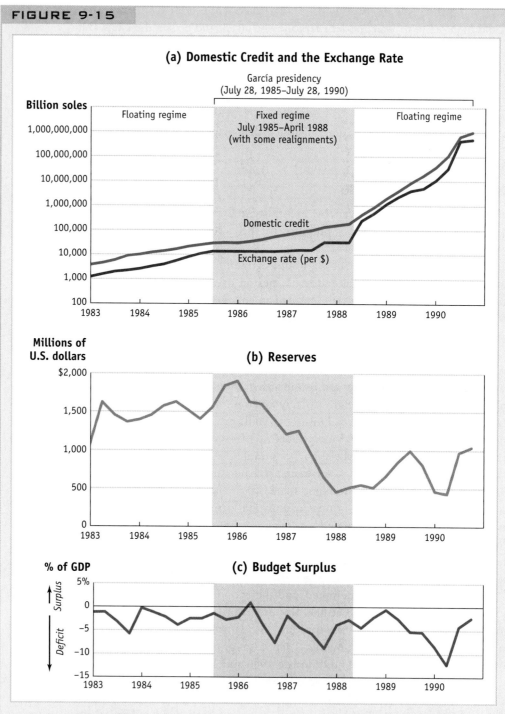

FIGURE 9-15

A Crisis in Peru: The Inconsistent Policies of the García Administration From 1985 to 1986, the Peruvian government implemented a fixed exchange rate regime, but government budget problems required significant monetization of budget deficits. Monetary and fiscal policies were inconsistent: a peg was in place, but domestic credit grew exponentially (note that the exchange rate and domestic credit are shown on logarithmic scales). The central bank lost three-quarters of its reserves in two years, and the peg had to be abandoned.

Source: IMF, International Financial Statistics.

$500 million in early 1988. The authorities finally threw in the towel in April 1988 before the attack was complete and so avoided losing all their dollar reserves. The sol began to float and depreciation was rapid: the sol hit 250,000 sol/$ in September, 500,000 in November, and 1,200,000 by March 1989, and Peru was heading into a hyperinflation.[20]

The data closely match the predictions of the model. Under the peg, reserves drain as domestic credit grows, and the exchange rate is stable. Under the float, reserves are stable, and the exchange rate grows hand in hand with the expansion of domestic credit.

By the time García left office, Peru was an economic shambles. García's popularity sank. The 1990 presidential election was won by a political newcomer, Alberto Fujimori, who would struggle with the problems created by his predecessor (and problems of his own). Yet, remarkably, in 2006 Alan García Pérez was elected president of Peru for a second time. Twenty years is a long time in politics. ■

Floating voter: Alan García in 2006.

Expectations and the Critical Level of Reserves What determines the *critical level of reserves* R_c at which the crisis occurs? In the speculative attack model, the size of the sudden reserve loss, and hence the timing of the crisis, depends critically on market expectations about the future growth rate of domestic credit. The reserves R_c lost at the moment of crisis will depend on how much money investors want to convert into reserves when they attack. This, in turn, depends on how much money demand shrinks as we move from fixed to floating, and that is driven by the change in the interest rate.

Let's assume that each percentage point increase in the interest rate causes a $\phi\%$ fall in real money balances.[21] At the moment of attack, the interest rate rises by an amount $\Delta i = \mu$, so the proportional fall in money demand is given by ϕ times that change. Thus, the change in money demand is given by $-\Delta M/M = \phi \times \mu$.

But we also know that the change in the money supply at the moment of attack $-\Delta M$ has to correspond exactly to the size of the reserve drain at the moment of attack, which equals the critical level of reserves R_c that are lost at that instant. Thus:

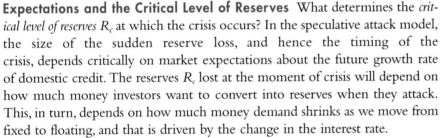

$$\underbrace{\frac{R_c}{M}}_{\substack{\text{Critical} \\ \text{backing ratio} \\ \text{when attack occurs}}} = \frac{-\Delta M}{M} = \underbrace{\phi}_{\substack{\text{Responsiveness} \\ \text{of money demand} \\ \text{to interest rate changes}}} \times \underbrace{\mu.}_{\substack{\text{Future} \\ \text{rate of growth of} \\ \text{domestic credit}}}$$

This expression tells us the ratio of the critical level of reserves R_c to the money supply M. It depends on the sensitivity of money demand to the interest rate and on the *expected future rate of growth* of domestic credit μ (remember, investors are *forward looking*).

---

[20] A common currency unit is used throughout this case study for consistency and commensurability. In reality, there were two currency reforms in Peru as a result of inflationary finance. The inti replaced the sol on February 1, 1985, at 1 inti per 1,000 soles, and on July 1, 1991, the nuevo sol replaced the inti at a rate of 1,000,000 nuevos soles per inti.

[21] This ϕ is called the interest semi-elasticity of money demand.

To illustrate, and continue our previous example, if the growth rate of domestic credit is expected to be $\mu = 10\%$, and if ϕ is 1.5, then the fall in money demand and money supply at the moment of attack is 10% times 1.5, or 15%. Thus, when reserves have drained so far that the backing ratio falls to 15%, the peg will break. But if μ rises to 20%, the critical backing ratio would be twice as large, at 30%.

We can now see that if people *expect* a fiscal problem to worsen (expect the deficit to increase, and thus domestic credit to grow faster to finance it) then reserves drain faster, and the crisis hits sooner, at a higher critical level of reserves R_c. An increase in the *expected* rate of deficit monetization shortens the length of time that the peg will survive.

This result emphasizes the importance of market beliefs. Suppose a country has a level of reserves well above the critical level. There is no imminent crisis. Then market beliefs change, perhaps because news or rumors emerge about a budget problem. Investors now expect a higher growth rate of domestic credit. Suppose that, as a result of this change in expectations, the critical level of reserves rises so much as to equal the current level of reserves. With the change in expectations, the time for a speculative attack is now. A crisis will happen immediately, *even though there has been no change in the economic situation as of today*!

Summary

The first generation crisis model tells us that inconsistent fiscal policies can destroy a fixed exchange rate. Yet it is not actual fiscal policy that matters, but *beliefs* and *expectations* about future fiscal policy. But beliefs about future deficits may or may not be justified, so the model opens up the possibility that countries will be punished for crimes they do not intend to commit.

For example, some economists have argued that expected future deficits were a factor in the Asian currency crisis of 1997: the countries were affected by "crony capitalism" and the banking sectors were insolvent because of bad loans to insiders. Once the scale of these problems became known, investors believed that the monetary authorities would bail out the banks. Fears of a rapid future expansion of domestic credit thus undermined the pegs.[22]

4 How Pegs Break II: Contingent Monetary Policies

In the previous section, we found that inconsistent fiscal policies under a fixed exchange rate regime eventually cause an exchange rate crisis. However, the crises of the 1990s often did not conform to a model based on deficit monetization because budget problems were absent in many cases. In particular, the ERM crisis of 1992 affected developed countries in Europe, most of which were unlikely to monetize deficits. In countries with apparently sound economic policies, foreign currency speculators went for the attack and pegs broke.[23]

---

[22] See, for example, the discussion of Korea's precrisis weaknesses in the operation and regulation of the banking sector, and the central bank's willingness to furtively channel dollar reserves to bail out the banks, in Frederic Mishkin, 2006, *The Next Great Globalization: How Disadvantaged Nations Can Harness Their Financial Systems to Get Rich,* Princeton, NJ: Princeton University Press. See also Craig Burnside, Martin Eichenbaum, and Sergio Rebelo, 2001, "Prospective Deficits and the Asian Currency Crisis," *Journal of Political Economy,* 109(6), December, 1155–1197.

[23] A helpful survey is provided by Sweta C. Saxena, 2004, "The Changing Nature of Currency Crises," *Journal of Economic Surveys,* 18(3), 321–350.

Economists therefore developed alternative models of crises, with the pioneering work on the **second generation crisis model** being done by Maurice Obstfeld. These types of models can explain how, even when policy making is rational and purposeful—rather than incompetent and inconsistent—there may still be situations in which pegs break for no apparent reason.[24]

The Basic Problem: Contingent Commitment

The essence of the model is that policy makers are not committed to the peg under all circumstances. Defending the peg is therefore a **contingent commitment** (a slight oxymoron): if things get "bad enough," the government will let the exchange rate float rather than put the country through serious economic pain. The problem is that everyone—notably investors in the forex market—knows it and they will adjust their expectations accordingly.

To develop some intuition, we return to Britain and Germany in 1992, the example we saw at the start of Chapter 8 (p. 331). Let's recap the basic story: the German central bank raised interest rates to deal with a domestic shock, the fiscal expansion arising from German unification after 1989. This left Britain with a higher interest rate and a lower output level than was desired. What would Britain do in response?

If German interest rates are fairly low, so too are British interest rates, output costs in Britain are low, and nobody expects Britain to leave the peg. The peg is *credible.* But if German interest rates rise to high levels, output in Britain falls to an intolerably low level, and nobody expects Britain to stay on the peg for long. Instead, everyone thinks Britain will float and use expansionary monetary policy to boost output and depreciate the pound. The peg is *not credible,* and the market now expects a depreciation in the future.

The problem for Britain is that an expected depreciation will introduce a *currency premium,* as we saw earlier in this chapter. Investors will demand even higher interest rates in Britain to compensate for the imminent depreciation—and this will mean even lower output and even higher pain for Britain!

This creates a gray area. How? It is quite possible that the German interest rate can be at some "intermediate" level at which pegging is tolerable with no expected depreciation: people would expect the peg to hold and the peg would hold. But if there is an expected depreciation and a currency premium, pegging might be intolerable: people would expect the peg to fail and the peg would fail. Crucially, in both scenarios, ex ante market expectations are validated ex post, and hence would be considered "rational."

Based on these insights from the Britain-Germany example we now develop an economic model with such *self-fulfilling expectations.* In this model we may not always find a single, unique equilibrium but rather **multiple equilibria.** Whether there is a crisis or not depends entirely on market sentiment, and not simply economic fundamentals.

---

[24] Maurice Obstfeld, 1986, "Rational and Self-Fulfilling Balance-of-Payments Crises," *American Economic Review,* 76(1), March, 72–81.

FIGURE 9-16

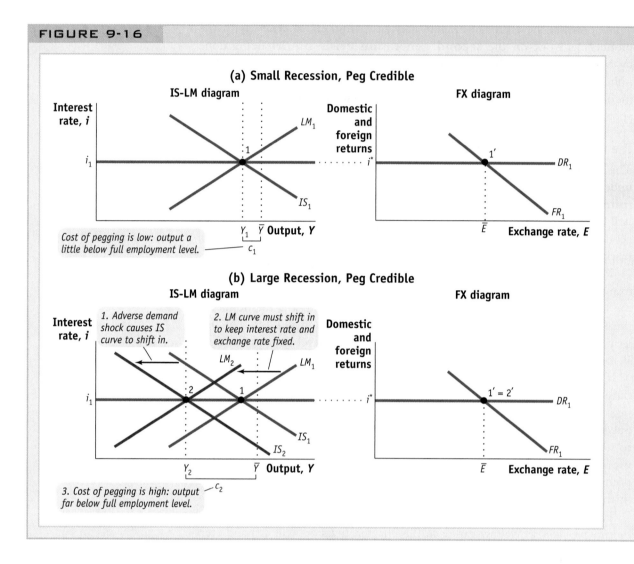

(a) Small Recession, Peg Credible

IS-LM diagram

Interest rate, i

LM_1

1

i_1 .... i^*

IS_1

Y_1 $\bar{Y}$ **Output, Y**

Cost of pegging is low: output a little below full employment level. — c_1

FX diagram

Domestic and foreign returns

1′

DR_1

FR_1

$\bar{E}$ **Exchange rate, E**

(b) Large Recession, Peg Credible

IS-LM diagram

Interest rate, i

1. Adverse demand shock causes IS curve to shift in.

2. LM curve must shift in to keep interest rate and exchange rate fixed.

LM_2 LM_1

2 1

i_1 .... i^*

IS_1

IS_2

Y_2 $\bar{Y}$ **Output, Y**

3. Cost of pegging is high: output far below full employment level. — c_2

FX diagram

Domestic and foreign returns

1′ = 2′

DR_1

FR_1

$\bar{E}$ **Exchange rate, E**

A Simple Model

In this type of model, we need a measure of the cost of maintaining the peg. The simplest cost measure is the deviation of output Y in the short run below its full employment level. To allow output to vary, we need to use the IS-LM-FX model introduced in Chapter 7, which means that we reverse some of the assumptions we made before. From now on, output Y will be variable rather than fixed, and it will be determined by the model. And from now on, prices will be sticky, not flexible, and treated as given.[25]

For simplicity, we assume there are *some* benefits from pegging, say, the gains from increased trade. Let these benefits be $b > 0$ and constant. Against the ben-

---

[25] The reason for this change in assumptions is that at the heart of this model the crisis is not driven by a set of policies that will ultimately break the nominal anchor—inflation plays no role here, so prices can be assumed steady; instead, the key mechanism in this model is the desire *in certain circumstances* to stabilize output by using temporary shifts in monetary policy, which means that the exchange rate must be allowed to float.

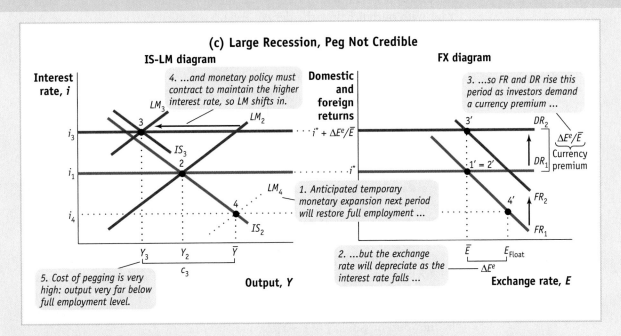

Contingent Commitments and the Cost of Maintaining a Peg This figure describes how the IS-LM-FX equilibrium changes as demand shocks occur and as the credibility of the peg weakens. The economy is pegging at a fixed exchange rate $\bar{E}$. In panel (a), the economy is at IS-LM equilibrium at point 1, with the FX market at point 1′. Output is a little below desired output, so the cost of pegging c_1 is small. In panel (b), there is an adverse shock to domestic demand, and the IS curve shifts in. LM shifts in, too, to maintain the peg. The new IS-LM equilibrium is at point 2, with FX market equilibrium at point 2′ (same as 1′). The cost of pegging c_2 is higher. Panel (c) shows that if the country wants to attain full employment output next period, it must move to point 4, shifting the LM curve out and allowing the FX market to settle at point 4′ with the exchange rate depreciating to E_{float}. The peg would still be in operation today, but, by definition, it would no longer be credible if such a policy change were anticipated. Because of the lack of credibility, investors would insist on receiving a positive currency premium *today*, and the home interest rate would rise to i_3, squeezing demand even more and moving the IS-LM equilibrium to point 3 and the FX market to point 3′. Now the cost of pegging c_3 is even higher: having a noncredible peg is more costly than having a credible peg.

efits of pegging, the government weighs costs c that equal the "output gap": full-employment $\bar{Y}$ output minus current output Y. If costs exceed benefits, we assume that the government will elect to float next period and use monetary policy to restore full employment output. For simplicity, we assume each period lasts one year. (Restricting attention to this type of rule keeps things simple while illustrating the key trade-offs.)

In Figure 9-16, we use the home IS–LM–FX diagram to look at how outcomes under the peg can depend on both economic fundamentals and market expectations. We assume foreign output is fixed at Y^*, and we also assume there is no fiscal policy change, so we can focus only on home monetary policy choices. Most important, we assume that investors are aware of the contingent commitment to the peg.

In this setup, it does not matter where adverse output shocks originate. They could result from increases in the foreign interest rate (as in the ERM example). Or they could be caused by a decline in the demand for home goods overseas. All that matters is that the home economy is in some kind of pain with output below the desired level.

Small Recession, Peg Credible Panel (a) shows a situation in which the pain is small. Initially, the IS_1 and LM_1 curves intersect at equilibrium point 1, and the home interest rate is $i_1 = i^*$ to maintain the peg. In the FX diagram, the domestic return is DR_1 and the foreign return FR_1. They intersect at point 1′ and the exchange rate is fixed at $E_1 = \overline{E}$. Home output is at Y_1, but we assume that the desired full employment level of home output is $\overline{Y}$, slightly higher than Y_1. In this situation, when the peg is credible, the economy suffers a small cost given by the "output gap": $c_1 = \overline{Y} - Y_1$.

Large Recession, Peg Credible Panel (b) shows a situation in which the adverse shock to output is large. The IS_2 and LM_2 curves now intersect at equilibrium point 2. The IS curve has moved left by assumption: it is the source of the adverse shock. The LM curve has moved in to maintain the peg and preserve interest parity, so that the home interest rate remains at $i_1 = i^*$. In the FX diagram, the domestic return is still DR_1 and the foreign return is still FR_1, and they intersect at point 2′, the same as point 1′, with $E_1 = \overline{E}$. Home output is now much lower at Y_2. Here, the economy suffers a larger cost given by the "output gap": $c_2 = \overline{Y} - Y_2$.

We obtain our first important result: *If the market believes that the peg is credible, the output gap (cost) increases as the size of the adverse shock increases.*

Large Recession, Peg Not Credible This is the most complex situation. Panel (c) assumes a large recession as in panel (b) but shows what happens if investors believe that the authorities will choose to depreciate next year to achieve desired output. We suppose exchange rate expectations are unchanged next year at the pegged rate. The IS curve will still be at IS_2, and the required monetary expansion next year will shift the LM curve to LM_4 so that the new equilibrium will be at point 4 with output at the desired level $\overline{Y}$, and a low interest rate of i_4. This will lead to a (temporary) depreciation next year, and the peg will break, and the exchange rate will rise from $\overline{E}$ to E_{float}. We can also see that to achieve full employment output, the lower that Y_2 is, the larger the required shift in the LM curve will be next year and the larger the resulting depreciation.

However, the government's response *next year* will be anticipated by investors. If they know that output is low enough to prompt a depreciation, they will expect a depreciation over the coming year of a size given by $\Delta E^e / \overline{E} = (E_{\text{float}} - \overline{E})/\overline{E} > 0$. This expected depreciation will appear as a currency premium *today* in the FX market of panel (c). The current period's (risk-adjusted) foreign return curve is shifted up by an amount equal to the currency premium as far as FR_2.

If the central bank wants to maintain the peg, despite it not being credible, it has to ensure forex market equilibrium at point 3′, so it must raise the home interest rate to i_3. At today's pegged rate $\overline{E}$, uncovered interest parity now requires a higher home interest rate $i_3 = i^* + \Delta E^e / \overline{E}$. Graphically, this means the domestic return curve must also shift up by an amount equal to the currency premium, as far as DR_2.

As we know from Chapters 7 and 8, this will depress home demand and lead to even lower home output today, which is shown at Y_3.

In more detail, today the IS curve moves out slightly to IS_3 due to expected depreciation, but the LM curve moves in a long way to to LM_3 to defend the peg. The latter effect dominates, because we know that demand and output have to be lower today given the combination of the same pegged exchange rate (no change in the trade balance) and a higher interest rate (lower investment demand). So the new IS-LM equilibrium is at point 3, to the *left* of point 2.

We also note that to achieve this monetary contraction, the central bank must sell reserves—and the drain can take the form of a speculative attack if the currency premium appears suddenly as a result of a switch in beliefs.

The loss of credibility makes a bad recession even worse. If the peg is not credible, a higher interest rate causes the costs of pegging to rise to $c_3 = \overline{Y} - Y_3$. Finally, we note that this cost will be higher when the output gap is higher, because a larger output gap implies a larger depreciation to restore full employment.

Our second important result: *If the forex market switches to believing that the peg is not credible, then reserves drain, the interest rate rises, and the output gap (cost) increases; also, the cost increases more if the output gap is larger to begin with.*

The Costs and Benefits of Pegging Our IS-LM-FX analysis is now complete, and all we need to do is consider the implications.

Figure 9-17 sums up the cost-benefit analysis. The horizontal axis measures the output gap, or the cost of pegging, *when the peg is credible*. We denote these costs $c(\overline{E})$. This notation indicates that this is the cost c when the exchange rate is expected to be at $\overline{E}$ next period. The first of our results showed that this cost rises, and we move right along the horizontal axis, whenever the country suffers an adverse shock under the peg.

The vertical axis measures and compares the costs and benefits of pegging. Benefits are constant at b. The costs when the peg is credible are equal to $c(\overline{E})$, so these will fall on the 45-degree line, since $c(\overline{E})$ is measured on the horizontal axis.

Finally, the cost of pegging when the peg is not credible is denoted $c(E_{float})$. This notation indicates that this is the cost c when the exchange rate is expected to be at E_{float} next period.

The second of our results showed that the costs of pegging when the peg is not credible are always greater than the costs when the peg is credible, due to the rise in the currency premium associated with an expected depreciation. In other words, the $c(E_{float})$ line is above the $c(\overline{E})$ line, as shown. We also saw that the difference gets larger as the costs get larger. In Figure 9-17, this means that the $c(E_{float})$ curve diverges from the $c(\overline{E})$ curve, as shown.

Corresponding to the previous analysis in Figure 9-16, point 1 (cost c_1) represents a small recession with a credible peg; point 2 (cost c_2) represents a large recession with a credible peg; point 3 (cost c_3) represents the same large recession with a noncredible peg.

With this basic apparatus, we can now analyze the "game" between the authorities and investors. To keep it simple, we suppose investors can choose from two beliefs about what the government will do: {peg, depreciate}. And

FIGURE 9-17

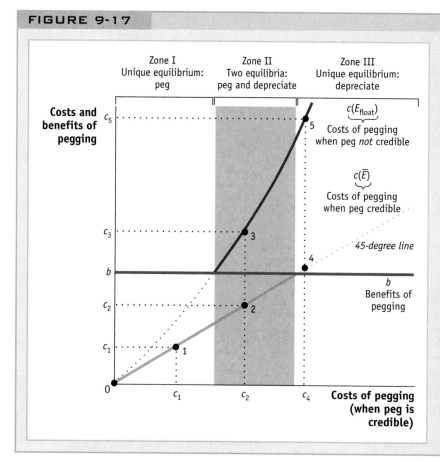

Zone I
Unique equilibrium:
peg

Zone II
Two equilibria:
peg and depreciate

Zone III
Unique equilibrium:
depreciate

Costs and benefits of pegging

c_5

$c(E_{float})$
Costs of pegging when peg *not* credible

5

$c(\overline{E})$
Costs of pegging when peg credible

c_3

3

4

45-degree line

b

b
Benefits of pegging

c_2

2

c_1

1

0

c_1 c_2 c_4

Costs of pegging (when peg is credible)

Contingent Policies and Multiple Equilibria Building on Figure 20-16, this figure shows how the costs of pegging depend on whether the peg is credible, and how that affects the game between the authorities and investors. The costs of pegging when the peg is credible are shown on the horizontal axis. To measure these costs on the vertical axis, we can read off from the 45-degree line. We know that the costs of pegging when the peg is not credible will be even higher. Costs rise when investors do not believe in the peg. We assume the government thinks the benefits of pegging (for example, lower trade costs) are fixed and equal to *B*. In this world, the peg is always credible in Zone I, where benefits always exceed costs: the government never wants to depreciate and investors know it. The peg is always noncredible in Zone III, where costs always exceed benefits: the government always wants to depreciate and investors know it. Zone II is the gray area: if investors believe the peg is credible, costs are low and the peg will hold; if investors believe the peg is noncredible, costs are higher and the peg will break.

we suppose the authorities then choose from two actions: {peg, depreciate}. Faced with this type of problem, economists search for what might be considered a rational outcome of the game. We look for a **self-confirming equilibrium,** that is, combinations of investor beliefs and government actions for which the ex post outcome validates the ex ante beliefs.

We can identify several such equilibria using Figure 9-17:

- In Zone I, $b > c(E_{float}) > c(\overline{E})$, so the benefits of pegging always outweigh both kinds of costs no matter what the market believes. The authorities will always choose to "peg." Anticipating this, the market belief will also be "peg," and this is the only ex ante belief that will be validated ex post. Benefits are always given by b, and costs are always those of a credible peg $c(\overline{E})$. There is a unique self-confirming equilibrium: peg, with costs corresponding to the solid portion of the line $c(\overline{E})$. (Example: point 1)

- In Zone III, $c(E_{float}) > c(\overline{E}) > b$, so both kinds of costs of pegging always outweigh the benefits no matter what the market believes. The authorities will always choose to "depreciate." Anticipating this, the market belief will also be "depreciate," and this is the only ex ante belief that will be validated ex post. Benefits are then always given by b, and the costs are always those of a noncredible peg $c(E_{float})$. There is a unique self-confirming equilibrium: depreciate, with costs corresponding to the solid portion of the line $c(E_{\text{float}})$. (Example: point 5)

- In Zone II, $c(E_{\text{float}}) > b > c(\overline{E})$. If the market belief is "depreciate," then the benefits b of pegging are less than the costs of the noncredible peg $c(E_{\text{float}})$; authorities will then choose "depreciate," and market beliefs are validated for this case. Conversely, if the market belief is "peg," then the benefits b of pegging are greater than the costs of a credible peg $c(\overline{E})$; authorities will then choose "peg," and the market beliefs are also validated for this case. There are two self-confirming equilibria in this zone. Zone II is shown as a gray area in the diagram. And appropriately so! In this range, there is no unique equilibrium, and depending on market beliefs, costs may correspond to the solid portions of either line $c(\overline{E})$ or line $c(E_{\text{float}})$. (Example: points 2 and 3)

APPLICATION

The Man Who Broke the Bank of England

Our analysis of contingent policies is highly simplified but advances our understanding of the potential for capricious outcomes driven by shifts in market sentiment. Changes in market sentiment, often called "animal spirits," emerge here from a model based on rational actors.

In some circumstances, the instability problem is much worse than we have suggested here, for a couple of reasons. First, we have assumed that the government does not exit the peg immediately when it suffers pain, so expectations of depreciation are slow. If a 10% devaluation is feared in one year, this causes a 10% currency premium. But if it is expected to happen in three months (next quarter), then the expected rate of depreciation on an *annualized* basis is much higher and is given by a fourfold compounding of a 10% increase: this is 46% (because 1.10 to the power 4 equals 1.46). So the currency premium would be approximately 46%, a heavy penalty. If the 10% devaluation were expected in one month, the premium would be more than 200% on an annualized basis.[26] As the time frame shrinks, the currency premium explodes!

For example, in 1992 Swedish interest rates climbed astronomically as investors speculated on the imminent demise of the krona's peg to the German mark. The annualized short-term (overnight) lending rate climbed to 75% on September 8 and 500% on September 19. Such an interest rate was not politically tenable for very long. Investors knew this, and they were proved right.

A second issue is how beliefs form in the first place. Suppose we are in Zone II at the "no crisis" self-confirming equilibrium, with beliefs and actions corresponding to "peg." A mass switch in beliefs to "depreciate" would also be

---

[26] In these cases, the rate of depreciation is not small, so the UIP approximation formula is not appropriate. For precision, the exact UIP formula should be used: $1 + i = (1 + i^*)E^e/E$. For example, to use this formula, if the foreign interest rate is 2%, but a 10% devaluation is expected after one quarter, then the formula says that on an annual basis the home interest rate will be given by $1 + i = (1.02) \times (1 + 0.10)^4 = 1.4934$. So the home interest rate is about 49.3%, and subtracting the foreign rate of 2%, we find a currency premium of 47.3%, still close to the 46% given by the approximation formula. In the case of a 10% depreciation expected after 1 week, with 52 weeks per year, the home interest rate will be given by $1 + i = (1.02) \times (1 + 0.10)^{12} = 3.2012$, so the home interest rate is 220% and the currency premium is 218%.

a self-confirming equilibrium. How does the market end up in one equilibrium or the other?

If traders are a group of many individuals, spread diffusely throughout the market, then it is unclear how they could all suddenly coordinate a switch to a new set of beliefs. And if each trader can place only a small bet, then it would be irrational for any trader to switch beliefs—unless all traders switch, and without coordination the switch is not going to happen and the peg stands a chance of holding.

But what if there are only a few traders? Or even just one very large trader who can make very big bets? If that single trader changes beliefs, the entire market goes from believing "peg" (no bets) to believing "depreciate" (making as big a bet against the home currency as possible). The coordination problem is solved. This is illustrated by the British ERM crisis of 1992. The large trader was the Quantum Fund, owned by the famous (to some, infamous) investor George Soros, who likes to use the term "reflexivity" to describe how markets shape events, as well as vice versa.

Soros's firm placed one big bet after another, until he had borrowed billions of pounds and parked all the money in German mark deposits. "It was an obvious bet, a one-way bet," he later recalled.[27] If the pound held, he could convert his marks back to pounds having paid a small interest cost (the difference between pound and mark interest rates for a few days); if the peg broke, he made billions as the pound fell. And who sold him the marks in exchange for pounds? The Bank of England, under orders from the U.K. Treasury, was intervening furiously, selling marks to prop up the pound at the limits of the ERM band.

The sudden increase in the currency premium was inducing a massive reserve drain. On the morning of September 16, 1992, the pressure on the pound became intense. The government made a feeble defense, raising the Bank's interest rates too little, too late, from 10% to 12% and, at the last gasp, to 15%. The bears were unimpressed. With market sentiment so strong, reserve outflow was unlikely to halt without stronger measures, such as the Swedes had taken the week before. But with the British economy performing weakly, the government had little stomach for triple-digit interest rates—something investors well knew.

It was all over by lunchtime, with the bulk of the reserves lost, and an estimated £4 billion spent in a futile defense. The event has gone down in history as one more legendary British exchange rate fiasco. ■

George Soros: "Reflexivity is, in effect, a two-way feedback mechanism in which reality helps shape the participants' thinking and the participants' thinking helps shape reality."

Summary

Our results are striking. If government policies are contingent, then they will depend on market sentiment. But market sentiment in turn depends on what the market thinks the government will do. If costs of pegging are "low," then pegs hold when they "should"—when the government has no desire to exit. If costs of pegging are "high," then crises happen when they "should"—when the government clearly wants to exit. But in between these extremes, an ambiguity arises in the form of multiple equilibria because for some "medium" range of costs, a crisis occurs if and only if the market expects a crisis.

---

[27] Ashley Seager, "Black Wednesday Still Haunts Britain," Reuters, September 16, 2002.

5 Conclusions

Fixed exchange rates show no signs of disappearing. Despite all their potential benefits, however, history shows another persistent feature—the recurrent crises that mark the collapse of fixed regimes.

In this chapter, we studied two kinds of crises. Adverse fiscal conditions can send the money supply out of control. And changes in the real economy can weaken the commitment to a peg. Expectations matter in each case—shifts in investor sentiment can make the crises occur "sooner" (that is, when economic fundamentals are better), leading to worries that some crises are an unnecessary and undeserved punishment.

Can We Prevent Crises?

With these insights, we can now confront the major policy problem: How can these crises be prevented? A number of solutions have been proposed that merit mention:

- *The case for capital controls.* Crises occur in the forex market. Shut down that market, and the risk of crisis should be lower. However, experience shows that capital controls are hard to implement and are never watertight. Empirically, there seems to be no consistent evidence that controls work (in terms of various measures such as crisis frequency, growth, monetary autonomy). In addition, countries tend to want to maintain financial openness as a way to obtain some of the gains from financial globalization noted in Chapter 6. Controls could be slapped on as a temporary device, but, given the speed with which crises can unfold, the door often ends up being shut after the reserves have bolted. For some examples (Malaysia after 1997, Spain after 1992), a case can be made that controls made a positive difference in a time of crisis, but in large samples, the effects are weak or negative.[28]

- *The case against intermediate regimes.* One lesson of the models presented in this chapter is that a change in market expectations can trigger "unnecessary" crises, with no deterioration in fundamentals today. After the experience of the 1990s, many leading economists came around to the view that intermediate regimes, the so-called dirty floats and soft pegs, were very risky in this regard. Under such regimes, the extent of the authorities' commitment to the exchange rate target would be seen as questionable, meaning that departures from the target to monetize deficits or pursue monetary autonomy might be suspected, leading to self-fulfilling crises. Solution: in the trilemma diagram, countries should get out of the

---

[28] See, for example, Sebastian Edwards and Jeffrey A. Frankel, eds., 2002, *Preventing Currency Crises in Emerging Markets,* National Bureau of Economic Research Conference Report, Chicago: University of Chicago Press; Sebastian Edwards, ed., 2007, *Capital Controls and Capital Flows in Emerging Economies: Policies, Practices, and Consequences,* National Bureau of Economic Research Conference Report, Chicago: University of Chicago Press; Reuven Glick, Xueyan Guo and Michael Hutchison, 2006, "Currency Crises, Capital-Account Liberalization, and Selection Bias," *Review of Economics and Statistics,* 88(4), November, 698–714; Rawi Abdelal and Laura Alfaro, 2003, "Capital and Control: Lessons from Malaysia, *Challenge,* 46(4), July, 36–53.

middle and move to the corners. This view came to be known as the **corners hypothesis** or the *missing middle*. Given the prevailing view that controls were not a viable option, this reduced the trilemma to a dilemma: in this "bipolar" view, only the two extremes of a hard peg or a true float were recommended (an idea dating back to Milton Friedman, quoted at the start of this chapter). Evidence has mounted that intermediate regimes have been more crisis prone in the past (up to five times as likely to have a crisis as a hard peg, according to one study), but the move away from such regimes appears to be very slow.[29]

■ *The case for floating.* In a crisis, a peg breaks. If there isn't a peg, there is nothing to break. It might be desirable for all countries to float from that perspective. However, in Chapter 8, we saw that there can be powerful reasons to peg, especially in emerging market and developing countries with *fear of floating*. And empirically, there is no overwhelming trend toward floating regimes in recent years. Thus, the floating corner has not attracted all that many countries in practice.

■ *The case for hard pegs.* If floating is out, then the "bipolar view" suggests that (short of dollarizing) countries should go the other way and adopt a really hard peg like a currency board. According to the IMF classification, only a few countries have taken this route, such as Estonia, Hong Kong, and—until its 2001–02 crisis—Argentina. Not all of these regimes were *strict* currency boards, but they could all be considered hard pegs, with high reserve ratios and some rules to try to limit domestic credit. Did they work? Some worked very well. It may seem pedantic to point out that the Hong Kong Monetary Authority wasn't following the strict rules; the system has worked, and the massive reserves kept the peg alive even in times of financial market turmoil. But hard pegs can also break like any other kind of government commitment, if the authorities deem it necessary, as in Argentina. Lesson: all fixed exchange rates can end up being cheap talk, no matter how much armor they appear to have.[30]

■ *The case for improving the institutions of macroeconomic policy and financial markets.* If hard pegs are not a panacea, then risks to pegged regimes might be minimized if the rest of the macroeconomic and financial structure in a country could be endowed with greater strength, increased stability, and enhanced transparency. Admittedly, these goals

---

[29] After Friedman, the corners hypothesis gained new life in the 1990s and became influential in the minds of leading international economists and policy makers, such as Andrew Crockett, Barry Eichengreen, Stanley Fischer, and Lawrence Summers. For surveys of the intellectual history and arguments for and against the bipolar views, see Morris Goldstein, 2002, *Managed Floating Plus*, Policy Analyses in International Economics, No. 66, Washington, D.C.: Peterson Institute for International Economics; Thomas D. Willett, 2007, "Why the Middle Is Unstable: The Political Economy of Exchange Rate Regimes and Currency Crises," *World Economy*, 30(5), 709–732. On crisis frequency and evidence for a trend away from the middle, see Andrea Bubula and Inci Otker-Robe, *The Continuing Bipolar Conundrum*, IMF Finance and Development, March 2004. Evidence of no such trend is given by Kenneth Rogoff, Ashoka Mody, Nienke Oomes, Robin Brooks and Aasim M. Husain, 2004, "Evolution and Performance of Exchange Rate Regimes," IMF Occasional Paper No. 229.

[30] With the exception of Bosnia and Estonia, most modern "currency boards" have violated the strict rule against using domestic credit and have not kept the backing ratio close to 100%. See "Measures of Activism in Monetary Policy for Currency Board-Like Systems," by Kurt Schuler, June 2005 (http://www.dollarization.org/), based on data from the IMF, International Financial Statistics.

are always desirable no matter what the exchange rate regime, but they take on added importance when a country is pegging because fiscal and banking problems have emerged as the root cause of so many crises. The steps involved may be slow, incremental, bureaucratic, and unglamorous. But their defenders would claim that, although they lack the magic-bullet quality of currency boards and other schemes tried by mercurial finance ministers, these improvements are the foundations on which any successful fixed exchange rate regime must be built.

■ *The case for an international lender of last resort.* We have seen that the adequate level of reserves to avert a crisis can depend on market sentiment. Why not borrow more reserves? This solution is not possible if lenders worry about an imminent crisis and you face a sudden stop. This is where the **International Monetary Fund (IMF)** can help. The IMF may lend to countries in difficulty if it thinks they can restore stability in a timely fashion with the help of a loan. But making the right judgments is far from easy. The IMF may impose unwelcome loan conditions that require policy change, including, for example, stricter control of budget deficits. These conditions are sometimes ignored (possibly leading to a suspension of the loan program). They have also been criticized on occasion for being too hard (Korea in 1997) or too soft (Argentina in 2001). Moreover, the capacity of the IMF to lend is limited and is increasingly dwarfed by private capital flows, causing concerns that future attacks may be too large for any IMF program to contain. Not that larger rescue capacity is necessarily good—at a basic level, many worry that the prospect of IMF bailouts, like any kind of insurance, may encourage lax behavior (*moral hazard*), which could worsen the crisis problem. Not surprisingly, the role of the IMF has been constantly under question in the current era of globalization.[31]

■ *The case for self-insurance.* What if a country wants to peg, but none of the above ideas offers much comfort? What if controls are unattractive, floating too risky, and currency boards too much of a straightjacket? What if a country knows that its domestic macroeconomic and financial architecture is still in a state of remodeling? What if the country looks back at the 1990s and worries that IMF programs will be too small, too late, too full of conditions, or not available at crunch time? In some ways, this describes many of the Asian countries, and other emerging markets, in the 2000s. The vast reserve buildup of recent years may be seen as a giant exercise in saving for a rainy day to protect these countries against the vicissitudes of global finance.

After what happened in 1997 some Asian countries may not turn to the IMF again—and with their reserve accumulation, they may not need to.

N E T W O R K

Was the IMF response to the 1990s crises satisfactory? You can hear both sides of the argument in a famous exchange that took place in 2002 between two leading scholars and policy makers, Joseph Stiglitz and Kenneth Rogoff. Visit the World Bank's B-Span online video site and watch the famous confrontation on video (Google: Stiglitz Rogoff video).

---

[31] For a critical and nontechnical appraisal of IMF actions in the period from 1994 to 2002, see Paul Blustein, 2001, *The Chastening: Inside the Crisis That Rocked the Global Financial System and Humbled the IMF,* New York: Public Affairs; and Paul Blustein, 2005, *And the Money Kept Rolling in (and Out): Wall Street, the IMF, and the Bankrupting of Argentina,* New York: Public Affairs.

KEY POINTS

1. An exchange rate crisis is a large and sudden depreciation that brings to an end a fixed exchange rate regime.

2. Such crises are common. The typical fixed exchange rate lasts only a few years. History shows that crises can affect all types of countries—advanced, emerging, and developing.

3. Crises have economic costs that tend to be very large in emerging markets and developing countries. Political costs are also large.

4. To avoid a crisis, the central bank in a country with a fixed exchange rate regime must have the ability to peg the exchange rate. In practice, this means the central bank needs foreign currency reserves, which can be bought or sold in the forex market at the fixed rate.

5. In a simple model of a central bank, the money supply consists of domestic credit and foreign reserves. Money demand is exogenous and is determined by interest rates and output levels that we assume are beyond the control of the authorities when the exchange rate is pegged. In this model, reserves are simply money demand minus domestic credit.

6. If money demand rises (falls), holding domestic credit fixed, reserves rise (fall) by the same amount.

7. If domestic credit rises (falls), holding money demand fixed, reserves fall (rise) by the same amount and the money supply is unchanged. The combined result is called sterilization.

8. When the central bank gives assistance to the financial sector, it expands domestic credit. If it is

a bailout, money demand is unchanged, and reserves drain. If it is a loan to satisfy depositors' demand for cash, then reserves stay constant.

9. A first generation crisis occurs when domestic credit grows at a constant rate forever, usually due to the monetization of a chronic fiscal deficit. Eventually reserves drain and the money supply grows at the same rate, causing inflation and depreciation. Myopic investors do not anticipate the drain, and when reserves run out, they see a sudden jump (depreciation) in the exchange rate. Investors with foresight will try to sell domestic currency before that jump happens and by doing so will cause a speculative attack and a sudden drain of reserves.

10. A second generation attack occurs when the authorities' commitment to the peg is contingent. If the domestic economy is suffering too high a cost from pegging, the authorities will consider floating and using expansionary monetary policy to boost output by allowing the currency to depreciate, thus breaking the peg. If investors anticipate that the government will break the peg, they will demand a currency premium, making interest even higher under the peg and raising the costs of pegging still further. In this setup, at some intermediate costs, the authorities will maintain the peg as long as investors find the peg credible, but they will allow their currency to depreciate if investors find the peg not credible. This creates multiple equilibria and self-fulfilling crises.

KEY TERMS

PROBLEMS

1. The economic costs of currency crises appear to be larger in emerging markets and developing countries than they are in advanced countries. Discuss why this is the case, citing the interaction between the currency crisis and the financial sector. In what ways do currency crises lead to banking crises in these countries? In what ways do banking crises spark currency crises?

2. Using the central bank balance sheet diagrams, evaluate how each of the following shocks affects a country's ability to defend a fixed exchange rate.
   a. The central bank buys government bonds.
   b. Currency traders expect an appreciation in the home currency in the future.
   c. An economic expansion leads to a change in home money demand.
   d. The foreign interest rate increases.

3. Consider the central bank balance sheet for the country of Riqueza. Riqueza currently has $1,800 million escudos in its money supply, $1,100 million of which is backed by domestic government bonds; the rest is backed by foreign exchange reserves. Assume that Riqueza maintains a fixed exchange rate of 1 escudo per dollar, the foreign interest rate remains unchanged, and money demand takes the usual form, $M/P = L(i)Y$. Assume prices are sticky.
   a. Show Riqueza's central bank balance sheet, assuming there are no private banks. What is the backing ratio?
   b. Suppose that Riqueza's central bank sells $200 million in government bonds. Show how this affects the central bank balance sheet. Does this change affect Riqueza's money supply? Explain why or why not. What is the backing ratio now?
   c. Now, starting from this new position, suppose that there is an economic downturn in Riqueza, so that real income contracts by 10%. How will this affect money demand in Riqueza? How will forex traders respond to this change? Explain the responses in the money market and the forex market.

   d. Using a new balance sheet, show how the change described in **c** affects Riqueza's central bank. What happens to domestic credit? What happens to Riqueza's foreign exchange reserves? Explain the responses in the money market and the forex market.
   e. How will the change above affect the central bank's ability to defend the fixed exchange rate? What is the backing ratio now? Describe how this situation differs from one in which the central bank buys government bonds in part b.

4. What is a currency board? Describe the strict rules about the composition of reserves and domestic credit that apply to this type of monetary arrangement.

5. What is a Lender of Last Resort and what does it do? If a central bank acts as a Lender of Last Resort under a fixed exchange rate regime, why are reserves at risk?

6. Suppose that a country's money supply is $1,200 million and its domestic credit is equal to $800 million in the year 2005. The country maintains a fixed exchange rate, the central bank monetizes any government budget deficit, and prices are sticky.
   a. Compute total reserves for the year 2005. Illustrate this situation on a central bank balance sheet diagram.
   b. Now, suppose the government unexpectedly runs a $100 million deficit in the year 2006 and the money supply is unchanged. Illustrate this change on your diagram. What is the new level of reserves?
   c. If the deficit is unexpected, will the central bank be able to defend the fixed exchange rate?
   d. Suppose the government runs a deficit of $100 million each year from this point forward. What will eventually happen to the central bank's reserves?
   e. In what year will the central bank be forced to abandon its exchange rate peg and why?
   f. What if the future deficits are anticipated? How does your answer to part **e** change? Explain briefly.

7. Consider two countries with fixed exchange rate regimes. In one country, government authorities exert fiscal dominance. In the other they do not. Describe how this affects the central bank's ability to defend the exchange rate peg. How might this difference in fiscal dominance affect the central bank's credibility?

8. The government of the Republic of Andea is currently pegging the Andean peso to the dollar at $E = 1$ peso per dollar. Assume the following: In year 1 the money supply M is 2,250 pesos, reserves R are 1,250 pesos and domestic credit B is 1,000 pesos. To finance spending, B is growing at 50% per year. Inflation is currently zero, prices are flexible, PPP holds at all times, and initially $P = 1$. Assume also that the foreign price level is $P^* = 1$, so PPP holds. The government will float the peso if and only if it runs out of reserves. The U.S. nominal interest rate is 5%. Real output is fixed at $Y = 2,250$ at all times. Real money balances are $M/P = 2,250 = L(i)Y$, and L is initially equal to 1.

   a. Assume that Andean investors are myopic and do not foresee the reserves running out. Compute domestic credit in years 1, 2, 3, 4, and 5. At each date, also compute reserves, money supply, and the growth rate of money supply since the previous period (in percent).

   b. Continue to assume myopia. When do reserves run out? Call this time T. Assume inflation is constant after time T. What will that new inflation rate be? What will the rate of depreciation be? What will the new domestic interest rate be? (Hint: use PPP and Fisher effect.)

   c. Continue to assume myopia. Suppose that at time T, when the home interest rate i increases, then $L(i)$ drops from 1 to 2/3. Recall that Y remains fixed. What is M/P before time T? What will be the new level of M/P after time T, once reserves have run out and inflation has started?

   d. Continue to assume myopia. At time T, what is the price level going to be right before reserves run out? Right after? What is the percentage increase in the price level? In the

exchange rate? (Hint: Use the answer to part c, and use PPP.)

   e. Suppose investors know the rate at which domestic credit is growing. Is the path described above consistent with rational behavior? What would rational investors want to do instead?

   f. Given the above data, when do you think a speculative attack would occur? At what level of reserves will such an attack occur? Explain your answer.

9. A peg is not credible when investors fear depreciation in the future, despite official announcements. Why is the home interest rate always higher under a noncredible peg than under a credible peg? Why does that make it more costly to maintain a noncredible peg than a credible peg? Explain why nothing more than a shift in investor beliefs can cause a peg to break.

10. You are the economic advisor to Sir Bufton Tufton, the Prime Minister of Perfidia. The Bank of Perfidia is pegging the exchange rate of the local currency, the Perfidian albion. The albion is pegged to the wotan, which is the currency of the neighboring country of Wagneria. Until this week both countries have been at full employment. This morning, new data showed that Perfidia was in a mild recession, 1% below desired output. Tufton believes a downturn of 1% or less is economically and politically acceptable but a larger downturn is not. He must face the press in 15 minutes and is considering making one of three statements:

   a. "We will abandon the peg to the wotan immediately."

   b. "Our policies will not change unless economic conditions deteriorate further."

   c. "We shall never surrender our peg to the wotan."

   What would you say to Tufton concerning the merits of each statement?

11. What steps have been proposed to prevent exchange rate crises? Discuss their pros and cons.

10

The Euro

There is no future for the people of Europe other than in union.

Jean Monnet, a "founding father" of the European Union

This Treaty marks a new stage in the process of creating an ever closer union among the peoples of Europe, in which decisions are taken as closely as possible to the citizen.

Maastricht Treaty (Treaty on European Union), 1992, Title 1, Article A

Political unity can pave the way for monetary unity. Monetary unity imposed under unfavorable conditions will prove a barrier to the achievement of political unity.

Milton Friedman, Nobel laureate, 1997

In 1961 the economist Robert Mundell wrote a paper discussing the idea of a *currency area,* also known as a **currency union** or *monetary union,* in which states or nations replace their national monies with a single currency, a common money.

At the time, almost every country was a separate currency area, so Mundell had doubts as to whether his research would have any practical relevance: "What is the appropriate domain of a currency area? It might seem at first that the question is purely academic since it hardly appears within the realm of political feasibility that national currencies would ever be abandoned in favor of any other arrangement."[1]

Almost forty years later, in 1999, 11 nations in Europe elected to form such a currency area, now known as the *Euro area,* or **Eurozone.** Later that year, Mundell found himself the recipient of a Nobel Prize.

---

[1] Robert Mundell, 1961, "A Theory of Optimum Currency Areas," *American Economic Review,* 51, September, 657–665.

The Eurozone has since expanded and continues to expand. By 2008 there will be 15 member countries. They will all be using the new notes and coins bearing the name **euro** and the symbol €, which have taken the place of old national currencies (the francs, marks, liras, and others).

The euro remains one of the boldest experiments in the history of the international monetary system, a new currency that is used by more than 300 million people in one of the world's most prosperous economic regions. The euro is having enormous economic impacts that will be felt for many years to come and is an essential object of study for those interested in today's global macroeconomy.

The goal of this chapter is to understand as fully as possible the logic of the euro project. We first examine the euro's economic logic, by exploring and applying theories, developed by Mundell and others, that seek to explain when it makes economic sense for different economic units (nations, regions, states) to adopt a common currency and when it makes economic sense for them to have distinct monies. To spoil the surprise: based on the current evidence, most economists judge that the Eurozone may not make sense from a purely economic standpoint, at least for now.

We then turn to the historical and political logic of the euro and discuss its distant origins and recent evolution within the larger political project of the European Union. Looking at the euro from these perspectives, we can see how the euro project unfolded as part of a larger enterprise. In this context, the success of the euro depends on assumptions that the EU functions smoothly as a political union and adequately as an economic union—assumptions that are constantly under question.

The Ins and Outs of the Eurozone Before we begin our discussion of the euro, we need to familiarize ourselves with the EU and the Eurozone. At the start, policy makers imagined that the euro would end up as the currency of the **European Union (EU).** The EU is a mainly economic, but increasingly political, union of countries that is in the process of extending across—and some might argue beyond—the geographical boundaries of Europe. The main impetus for the euro project came in 1992 with the signing of the Treaty on European Union, at Maastricht, in the Netherlands. Under the **Maastricht Treaty,** the EU initiated a grand project of *Economic and Monetary Union (EMU).* A major goal of the EMU was the establishment of a currency union in the EU whose monetary affairs would be managed cooperatively by members through a new European Central Bank (ECB).[2]

The map in Figure 10-1 shows the state of play at the time of this writing in 2007. The map depicts some of the EU's main political and mone-

---

[2] Some small non-EU, non-Eurozone states also use the euro: Monaco, San Marino, Vatican City, and Andorra have legal agreements allowing them to use the euro as their de jure legal tender (they had previously used the national currencies of their neighbors). All of these countries except Andorra can mint their own euro coins. Some other peoples use the euro as their de facto currency, notably the Montenegrins and Kosovars, who are keen to assert their autonomy from Serbia and its currency, the Serbian dinar (they had previously used the German mark as their currency).

FIGURE 10-1

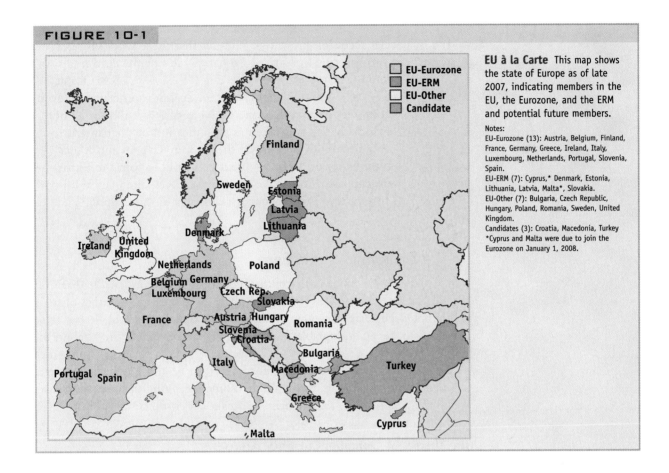

EU-Eurozone
EU-ERM
EU-Other
Candidate

EU à la Carte This map shows the state of Europe as of late 2007, indicating members in the EU, the Eurozone, and the ERM and potential future members.

Notes:
EU-Eurozone (13): Austria, Belgium, Finland, France, Germany, Greece, Ireland, Italy, Luxembourg, Netherlands, Portugal, Slovenia, Spain.
EU-ERM (7): Cyprus,* Denmark, Estonia, Lithuania, Latvia, Malta*, Slovakia.
EU-Other (7): Bulgaria, Czech Republic, Hungary, Poland, Romania, Sweden, United Kingdom.
Candidates (3): Croatia, Macedonia, Turkey
*Cyprus and Malta were due to join the Eurozone on January 1, 2008.

tary alignments. The two are not the same: different countries choose to participate in different aspects of economic and monetary integration, a curious feature of the EU project known as *variable geometry*.

■ As of 2007, the EU comprised 25 countries (EU-25). Ten of these had joined as recently as 2004, and Romania and Bulgaria had joined in 2007. Three more candidate countries were formally seeking to join—Croatia, Macedonia, and Turkey.[3]

■ A country can be in the EU but not in the Eurozone. It is important to remember who's "in" and who's "out." In 1999 three EU members opted to stay out of the Eurozone and keep their national currencies: these "out" countries were Denmark, Sweden, and the United Kingdom. In addition, all new EU entrants, like the 12 countries that joined the EU since 2004, started in the "out" group. On January 1, 2007, the first of these, Slovenia, became a member of the Eurozone.

NETWORK

Do some research on the Internet to construct an updated version of the map in Figure 10-1. You can find membership information on the websites of the European Union (europa.eu.int) and the European Central Bank (www.ecb.int). Since this book was written, have any new countries joined the EU, or applied to join? Have any countries entered the ERM, or exited from it? Have any new countries adopted the euro?

---

[3] Until a naming dispute with Greece is resolved, Macedonia is often referred to in official communications as "the Former Yugoslav Republic of Macedonia" or, if you prefer acronyms, FYROM.

Euro notes and coins.

■ As we shall see, most of the "outs" want to be "in." The official accession procedure requires that those who wish get "in" must first peg their exchange rates to the euro in a system known as the *Exchange Rate Mechanism* (ERM) for at least two years and satisfy certain qualification criteria. Seven countries were part of the ERM as of 2007, and for all but Denmark, this was taken as an indication of their intent to adopt the euro shortly. Of these seven, Cyprus and Malta were expected to be the next countries to join the Eurozone on January 1, 2008. We discuss the ERM, the qualification criteria, and other peculiar rules later in this chapter.

1 The Economics of the Euro

John Stuart Mill, a nineteenth-century economist, thought it a "barbarism" that all countries insisted on "having, to their inconvenience and that of their neighbors, a peculiar currency of their own." Barbaric or not, it has long appeared to be an immutable law that national currencies are the norm. Currency unions are quite rare.[4] Economists presume that such outcomes reflect a deeper logic. A common currency may be more convenient—put another way, it has benefits. But it also has some costs. And the costs must outweigh the benefits for the "barbarism" of national currencies to persist.

The Theory of Optimum Currency Areas

How does a country decide whether to join a currency union? To answer this question, let's see if one country, Home, should join a currency union with another country, Foreign. (Our analysis can be generalized to a case in which Foreign consists of multiple members of a larger currency union.)

If countries make a decision that best serves their self-interest—that is, an optimizing decision—when they form a currency union, then economists use the term **optimum currency area (OCA)** to refer to the resulting monetary union. How can such a decision be made?

To decide whether joining the currency union serves its economic interests, Home must evaluate whether the benefits outweigh the costs. This decision is similar to the decision as to whether to select a fixed or floating exchange rate, which we discussed in Chapter 8, so two familiar ideas from that previous discussion can be applied and extended in what follows.

Market Integration and Efficiency Benefits Adopting a common currency implies that the two regions will henceforth have a fixed exchange rate—in particular, it will be fixed at 1. Hence, the same market integration criterion

---

[4] Many currency unions are unilateral—cases of "dollarization" (defined in Chapter 2) involving the adoption of a foreign currency by a country that plays no role in managing the common currency (e.g., Panama's use of the U.S. dollar). In only a few cases are currency unions multilateral—cases in which all countries have shared participation in the monetary affairs of the union, the Eurozone being the most notable example.

we used to discriminate between fixed and floating regimes can be applied to the case of an OCA:

If there is a greater the degree of economic integration between the home region (A) and the other parts of the common currency zone (B), then there will be a larger volume of transactions between the two, and the larger will be the economic benefits of adopting a common currency due to lowered transaction costs and reduced uncertainty.

Economic Symmetry and Stability Costs Adopting a common currency implies that the two regions will henceforth have the same monetary policy—each region will lose its monetary autonomy, and the monetary authorities who have control of the common currency will decide upon a common interest rate for all members. Hence, the same similarity criterion we used to discriminate between fixed and floating regimes can be applied to the case of an OCA:

If a home country and its potential currency union partners are more economically similar or "symmetric" (they face more symmetric shocks and fewer asymmetric shocks), then it is less costly for the home country to join the currency union.

Simple Optimum Currency Area Criteria

We are now in a position to set out a theory of an optimum currency area by considering the *net benefits* of adopting a common currency. The net benefits equal the benefits minus the costs. The two main lessons we have just encountered suggest the following:

- *As market integration rises, the efficiency benefits of a common currency increase.*

- *As symmetry rises, the stability costs of a common currency decrease.*

Summing up, the OCA theory says that if either market integration or symmetry increases, the net benefits of a common currency will rise. If the net benefits are negative, the home country would stay out based on its economic interests. If the net benefits turn positive, the home country would join based on its economic interests.

Figure 10-2 illustrates the OCA theory graphically, using the same symmetry-integration diagrams used in Chapter 8. On the horizontal axis is a measure of market integration for the Home-Foreign pair. On the vertical axis is a measure of the symmetry of the shocks experienced by the Home-Foreign pair. If the Home-Foreign pair moves up and to the right in the diagram, then the benefits increase, the costs fall, and so the net benefit of a currency union rises. At some point, the pair crosses a threshold, the OCA line, and enters a region in which it will be optimal for them to form a currency union based on their economic interests.

The figure looks familiar. The derivation of the OCA line here is identical to the derivation of the FIX line in Chapter 8, which raises an important question.

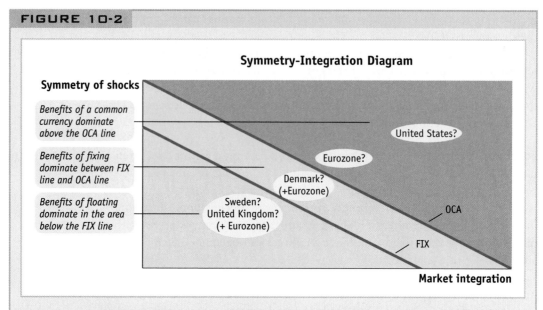

FIGURE 10-2

Symmetry-Integration Diagram

Symmetry of shocks

Benefits of a common currency dominate above the OCA line

Benefits of fixing dominate between FIX line and OCA line

Benefits of floating dominate in the area below the FIX line

United States?

Eurozone?

Denmark? (+Eurozone)

Sweden? United Kingdom? (+ Eurozone)

OCA

FIX

Market integration

Stylized OCA Criteria Two regions are considering a currency union. If markets become more integrated (a move right on the horizontal axis), the net economic benefits of a currency union increase. If the economic shocks they experience become more symmetric (a move up the vertical axis), the net economic benefits of a currency union also increase. If the parts of the region move far enough up or to the right, benefits exceed costs, net benefits are positive, and they cross the OCA threshold. In the shaded region above the line, it is optimal for the parts of the region to form a currency union. In practice, the OCA line is likely to be above and to the right of the FIX line.

What's the Difference between a Fix and a Currency Union?

If choosing to fix and choosing to form a currency union were identical decisions, then the FIX and OCA lines would be one and the same. In reality, we think they are likely to differ—and that the OCA line is likely to be above the FIX line, as drawn in Figure 10-2. Thus, when countries consider forming a currency union, the economic tests (based on symmetry and integration) will set a higher bar than they would set for judging whether it is merely optimal to fix.

Why might this be so? To give a concrete example, let's consider the case of Denmark, which we studied in Chapter 4 as an example of the trilemma in Europe. The Danes are in the ERM, so the krone is pegged to the euro. But Denmark has spent a long time in the ERM and shows no signs of taking the next step into the Eurozone. This preference has been democratically expressed—proposals to join the Eurozone have been defeated by referendum. The Danish position looks slightly odd at first glance. Denmark appears to have ceded monetary autonomy to the ECB because its interest rate tracks the euro interest rate closely. Yet the Danes do not gain the full benefits of a currency union because transactions between Denmark and the Eurozone still require a change of currency.

Still, one can make a logical case for Denmark to keep its own currency. By doing so, it better preserves the *option* to exercise monetary autonomy at some future date, even if the option is not being used currently. For one thing, even under the ERM, although the krone is pegged very tightly to the euro within ±2% by choice, the Danes could employ the full ±15% band allowed by ERM and give themselves much more exchange rate flexibility. (A ±15% band isn't a very hard peg—recall that the standard de facto threshold for a peg is no more than ±2% variation in one year.) And because they have only gone so far as pegging to—and not joining—the euro, the Danes are always free to leave the ERM at some future date (as Sweden and the United Kingdom have done) if they want the even greater flexibility of a more freely floating exchange rate.

Now, contrast the position of Denmark with that of Italy, the country in which rumors of departure from the Eurozone have been strongest. Compared with a Danish exit from the ERM, an Italian exit from the euro would be messy, complicated, and costly. The actual process of retiring euros and reprinting and reintroducing new lira as money would be difficult enough. But more seriously, all Italian contracts were switched from the lira to the euro, in particular the private and public debt contracts. So there would be a monumental legal battle over the implicit defaults that would follow from the "lirification" of such euro contracts. Some countries have tried these kinds of strategies, but the examples are not too encouraging. In the 1980s, Liberia de-dollarized (and descended into economic crisis) and in 2002 Argentina legislated the "pesification" of its dollar contracts (and descended into economic crisis).

Because the future cannot be known with certainty, countries may value the option to change their monetary and exchange rate regime in the future. Exit from a peg is easy—some might say too easy—and happens all the time. Exit from a common currency is much more tricky (the Eurozone has *no* exit procedure) and is expected to be costly. We conclude that because a country's options are more limited after joining a common currency than after joining a peg, the country will set tougher conditions for the former; thus, the optimal OCA region will be smaller than the optimal fixing region, as shown in Figure 10-2.

Other Optimum Currency Area Criteria

Our simple model in Figure 10-2 illustrated two basic motives for joining a currency union, but there could be many other forces at work. These other considerations can still be examined using the same framework, which allows us to consider several additional arguments for joining a currency union.

Labor Market Integration In the analysis so far (as in Chapter 8), the home and foreign countries trade goods and services, but labor is immobile between the two countries. But what if we suppose instead that Home and Foreign have an integrated labor market, so that labor is free to move between them? This allows for an alternative adjustment mechanism in the event of asymmetric shocks.

For example, suppose there is a negative shock in Home. If output falls and unemployment rises in Home, then labor will start to migrate to Foreign, where unemployment is lower. The more fluid this migration response, the less painful the impact of the negative shock on Home, and the less need there will be for an independent monetary policy response in Home for stabilization purposes. With an excess supply of labor in one region and excess demand in the other region, adjustment will occur through migration.

This reasoning suggests that the cost to Home of forming a currency union with Foreign, due to the loss of monetary policy autonomy, will be lower when the degree of labor market integration between Home and Foreign is higher, because labor mobility provides an alternative adjustment mechanism. All else equal, the possibility of gains of this sort would lower the OCA threshold, as reflected in the shift down of the OCA line from OCA_1 to OCA_2 in Figure 10-3. This shift expands the shaded zone where currency union is preferred: countries are more likely to want to form a currency union the greater the labor market integration between them.

Fiscal Transfers We have now examined two possible mechanisms through which countries in an OCA can cope with asymmetric shocks: monetary policy and labor markets. We have ignored fiscal policy. All else equal, one might argue that a country's fiscal policy is autonomous and largely independent of whether a country is inside or outside a currency union. But there is one important exception: fiscal policy will not be independent when a currency union is built on top of a federal political structure with fiscal mechanisms that permit interstate transfers—a system known as *fiscal federalism*.

FIGURE 10-3

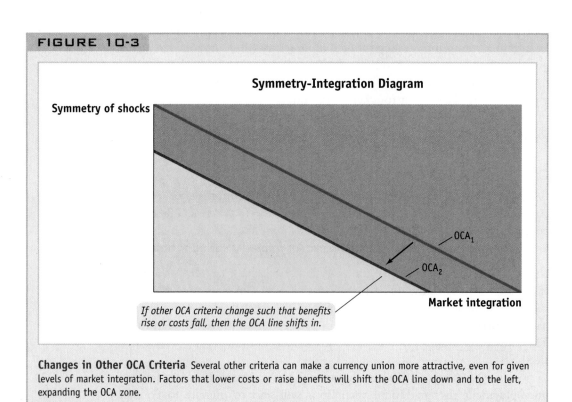

Symmetry-Integration Diagram

Symmetry of shocks

OCA_1

OCA_2

Market integration

If other OCA criteria change such that benefits rise or costs fall, then the OCA line shifts in.

Changes in Other OCA Criteria Several other criteria can make a currency union more attractive, even for given levels of market integration. Factors that lower costs or raise benefits will shift the OCA line down and to the left, expanding the OCA zone.

If a region has fiscal federalism, then a third adjustment channel is available: when Home suffers a negative shock, the effects of the shock can be cushioned by fiscal transfers from Foreign, allowing more expansionary fiscal policy in Home than might otherwise be the case. For this argument to be compelling, however, the fiscal transfers must be large enough to make a difference. They must also help overcome some limit on the exercise of fiscal policy, so as to finance policies that could not be financed in some other way (for example, by government borrowing).

If these conditions are satisfied, then the presence of fiscal transfers will lower the costs of joining a currency union. We could represent the possibility of gains of this sort in Figure 10-3, where, all else equal, enhanced fiscal transfers would mean a lower OCA threshold, so the OCA line shifts down from OCA_1 to OCA_2. This shift expands the shaded zone where currency union is preferred: the better the fiscal transfer mechanisms, the more countries are likely to want to join the currency union.

Monetary Policy and Nominal Anchoring One important aspect of Home joining a currency union is that Home's central bank ceases to manage monetary policy (or ceases to exist altogether). Monetary policy is then carried out by a common central bank, whose policies and actions may be subject to different designs, objectives, and political oversight. This may or may not be a good thing, depending on whether the overall monetary policy performance of Home's central bank is (or is expected to be) as good as that of the common central bank.

For example, suppose that Home suffers from chronic high inflation that results from an **inflation bias** of Home policy makers—the inability to resist the political pressure to use expansionary monetary policy for short-term gains. In the long run, on average, inflation bias leads to a higher level of expected inflation and actual inflation. But average levels of unemployment and output are unchanged because higher inflation is expected and inflation has no real effects in the long run.

Suppose that the common central bank of the currency union would be a more politically independent central bank that can resist political pressures to use expansionary monetary policy for short-term gains. It performs better by delivering low inflation on average, and no worse levels of unemployment or output. In this case, joining the currency union improves economic performance for Home by giving it a better nominal anchor: in this scenario, loss of monetary autonomy can be a good thing.

There is a possibility that this criterion was important for several Eurozone member states that historically have been subject to high inflation—for example, Italy, Greece, and Portugal. We can represent the possibility of monetary policy gains of this sort in Figure 10-3, where, all else equal, a worsening in the home nominal anchor (or an improvement in the currency union's nominal anchor) shifts the OCA line down. For countries with a record of high and variable inflation, the OCA threshold will fall, so again the OCA line moves down from OCA_1 to OCA_2. This shift also expands the shaded zone where currency union is preferred: given levels of market integration and symmetry, high-inflation countries are more likely to want to join the currency union the larger are the monetary policy gains of this sort. (Later on we will consider the concerns of the low-inflation countries in this scenario.)

Political Objectives Finally, we turn to noneconomic gains and the possibility that countries will join a currency union even if it makes no pure economic sense for them to do so. For instance, one can imagine that Home's "political welfare" may go up, even if pure economic welfare goes down. How?

Suppose a state or group of states is in a situation in which forming a currency union has value for political, security, strategic, or other reasons. For example, when the United States expanded westward in the nineteenth century, it was accepted, without question, that new territories and states would adopt the U.S. dollar. In recent times, eastward expansion of the EU comes with an assumption that, in the end, accession to the union will culminate in monetary union. These beliefs, assumptions, and accords did not rest very much, if at all, on any of the OCA criteria we have discussed so far. Instead, they were an act of political faith, of a belief in the states' common political future, a statement about destiny.

Political benefits can also be represented in Figure 10-3 by the OCA line shifting down from OCA_1 to OCA_2. In this scenario, for countries between OCA_1 and OCA_2, there are *economic costs* to forming a currency union, but these are outweighed by the *political benefits*. The political dimension of the European Union has played a significant role in EU and Eurozone history, a topic we discuss later in the chapter.

APPLICATION

Optimum Currency Areas: Europe versus the United States

On first glance, the theory of optimum currency areas helpfully sets out the important criteria by which we can judge whether it is in a country's interest to join a currency union. But while the OCA criteria work well in theory, in reality the costs and benefits of a currency union cannot be measured with any great accuracy.

Recognizing this, we can try an alternative approach and use comparative analysis to shed some light on the issue by answering a slightly different question: How does Europe compare with the United States on each of the OCA criteria? Clearly, if one took the view that the United States works well as a common currency zone, and if we find that Europe performs as well as or better than the United States on the OCA criteria, then these findings would lend indirect support to the economic logic of the euro.

Goods Market Integration within the EU European countries trade a lot with each other. But as far as we can tell (the available data are not entirely comparable), the individual states within the United States trade even more with each other. For the large census regions of the United States shown in Figure 10-4, panel (a), manufacturing trade ranges from 30% to 70% of gross state product. The figure for EU countries is typically much

FIGURE 10-4

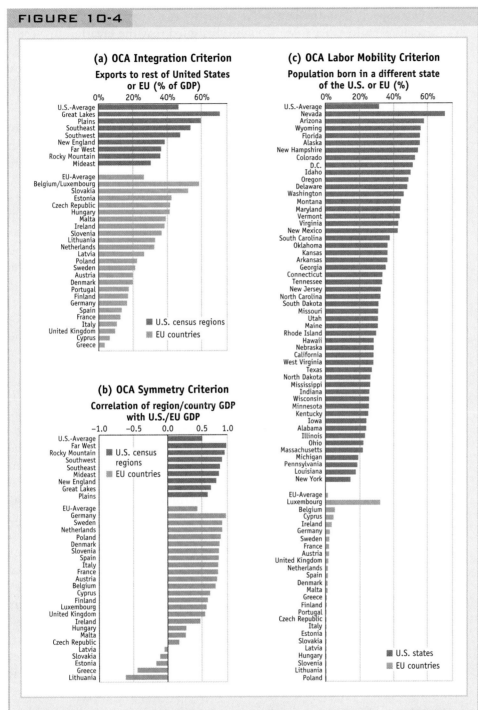

OCA Criteria for Europe and the United States Most economists think the United States is much more likely to satisfy the OCA criteria than the EU is. Why? Data in panel (a) show that interregional trade in the United States rises to levels much higher than those seen among EU countries. Data in panel (b) show that U.S. and EU shocks are comparably symmetric. Data in panel (c) show that U.S. labor markets are very integrated compared with the EU.

Sources: HM Treasury, 2003, The United States as a Monetary Union, *London: HMSO; Paul de Grauwe, 2003,* Economics of Monetary Union, *6th ed., Oxford, England: Oxford University Press; Eurostat; bea.gov.*

smaller, especially in the larger EU countries that are comparable in size to the census regions. At best, it might be argued that the creation of a "single market" in the EU is still a work in progress (as we shall see in the next section), and so it might well be that these intra-EU trade flows will rise further as the EU's internal market becomes more integrated. On this test, Europe is probably behind the United States for now.

Symmetry of Shocks within the EU A direct way to look at symmetry of shocks is to compare the correlation of a state's GDP annual growth rate with the annual GDP growth of the entire zone. These data are shown in Figure 10-4, panel (b), and most EU countries compare quite favorably with the U.S. states on this test: in both cases, the average correlation with the entire zone's GDP growth rate is close to 0.5. (Although there are some distinct outliers in the EU case, they are small countries and we would find some outliers at the state level in the U.S. data as well.) This result is not too surprising: there is no strong consensus that EU countries are more exposed to local shocks than the regions of the United States. However, as we shall see in a moment, one potential problem for the EU is what happens in the future: one effect of deeper EU goods market integration could be that EU countries start to specialize more. In that case, the risk of asymmetric shocks will increase and the EU will be less likely to satisfy the OCA criteria.

Labor Mobility within the EU The data in Figure 10-4, panel (c), show what is well known: labor in Europe is much less mobile between states than it is in the United States. More than 30% of U.S. residents were born in a different U.S. state than the one in which they live. In the EU, only 1.5% of people were born in a different EU country from the one in which they live. The same is true, as one would expect, of the year-to-year flow of people between regions: it is also an order of magnitude larger in the United States than in the EU. There are obvious explanations for this: differences in culture and language present obstacles to intra-EU migration that are largely absent in the United States. In addition, although the EU is working to ease such frictions, the local regulatory environment and red tape make it burdensome for Europeans to live and work in another EU country, even if they have a legal right to do so. Finally, labor markets in Europe are generally less flexible, making it harder to hire and fire workers, something that may dissuade workers from moving from one place to another in search of better opportunities. Economists have found that differences in unemployment across EU regions tend to be larger and more persistent than they are across the individual states of the United States. In short, the labor market adjustment mechanism is weaker in Europe. On this test, Europe is far behind the United States.

Fiscal Transfers A survey of the literature suggests that when a U.S. state goes into a recession, for every $1 drop in that state's government revenue, the federal government compensates with an offsetting transfer of about 15 cents.[5]

---

[5] HM Treasury, 2003, *The United States as a Monetary Union,* London: HMSO.

Stabilizing transfers of this kind are possible only when states agree to engage in fiscal federalism, whereby substantial taxing and spending authority is given to the central authority. The United States has such stabilizing transfers, but the EU does not. Although individual states in the EU achieve similar results within their own borders, at the level of the EU as a whole, the fiscal transfer mechanism is nonexistent: the EU budget is little more than 1% of EU GDP and is devoted to other purposes, notably agricultural subsidies.

Summary On the simple OCA criteria, the EU falls short of the United States as a successful optimum currency area, as shown in Figure 10-5. Goods market integration is a little bit weaker, fiscal transfers are negligible, and labor mobility is very low. At best, one can note that economic shocks in the EU are fairly symmetric, but this fact alone gives only limited support for a currency union given the shortcomings in other areas.

Some economists argue that the economic stability costs are exaggerated: they have doubts about stabilization policy in theory (e.g., the Keynesian view that prices are sticky in the short run) or in practice (e.g., the caveats about policy activism noted in Chapter 7). But most economists think there are still costs involved when a country sacrifices monetary autonomy. They worry that some or all Eurozone countries now have an inappropriate one-size-fits-all monetary policy, and that there are additional risks such as the absence of a well-defined lender of last resort mechanism in the Eurozone.

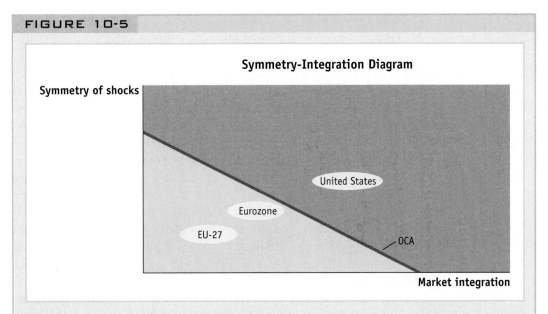

FIGURE 10-5

Symmetry-Integration Diagram

Symmetry of shocks

United States

Eurozone

EU-27

OCA

Market integration

Stylized OCA View of the EU and the United States Most economists consider that the Eurozone and EU countries do not satisfy the OCA criteria—they have too little market integration and their shocks are too asymmetric. The Eurozone may be closer to the OCA line since integration runs deeper there, but it is still far behind the United States on the OCA criteria. If we expand to the EU of 27, it is likely that this larger zone fails to meet OCA criteria by an even larger margin, with lower integration and higher asymmetry than the current Eurozone.

On balance, economists tend to believe that the EU, and the current Eurozone within it, was not an optimum currency area in the 1990s when the EMU project took shape and that nothing much has happened yet to alter that judgment. ■

Are the OCA Criteria Self-Fulfilling?

Our discussion so far has taken a fairly static view of the OCA criteria. Countries treat all of the conditions just discussed as given, and, assuming they have adequate information, they can then judge whether the costs of forming a currency union outweigh the benefits. However, another school of thought argues that some of the OCA criteria are not given (i.e., exogenous) and fixed in stone, but rather they are economic outcomes (i.e., endogenous) determined by, among other things, the creation of the currency union itself. In other words, even if the Eurozone isn't an OCA now, by adopting a common currency it might become an OCA in the future.

Consider goods market integration, for example. The very act of joining a currency union might be expected to promote more trade, by lowering transaction costs. Indeed, that is one of the main supposed benefits. In that case, if the OCA criteria were applied *ex ante* (before the currency union forms), then many countries might exhibit low trade volumes. Their low integration might mean that the OCA criteria are not met, and the currency union might not be formed based on those characteristics. However, if the currency union went ahead anyway, then it might be the case that *ex post* (after the currency union is up and running) countries would trade so much more that in the end the OCA criteria would indeed be satisfied.

This kind of argument is favored by euro-optimists, who see the EU single market project as an ongoing process and the single currency as one of its crucial elements. This logic suggests that the OCA criteria can be self-fulfilling, at least for a group of countries that are ex ante close to—but not quite—fulfilling the OCA requirements. For example, suppose the EU started out at point 1 in Figure 10-6, just below the OCA line. If the EU countries would only "just do it" and form a monetary union, then they would wake up and discover that they had jumped to point 2 once the common currency had boosted trade among them, and, hey presto: while monetary union didn't make sense beforehand, it does after the fact. Thus, even if the EU or the Eurozone does not look like an OCA now, it might turn out to be an OCA once it is fully operational. However, Euro-pessimists doubt that this self-fulfilling effect will amount to much. Evidence is mixed, and the exact magnitude of this effect is subject to considerable dispute (see **Headlines: Currency Unions and Trade**).[6]

A further argument made by optimists is that greater integration under the EU project might also enhance other OCA criteria. For example, if goods

---

[6] Some believe a common currency will have other effects, perhaps also encouraging labor and capital mobility within the Eurozone as well. These might also change the OCA calculus, but significant evidence on these effects has not been found as yet.

FIGURE 10-6

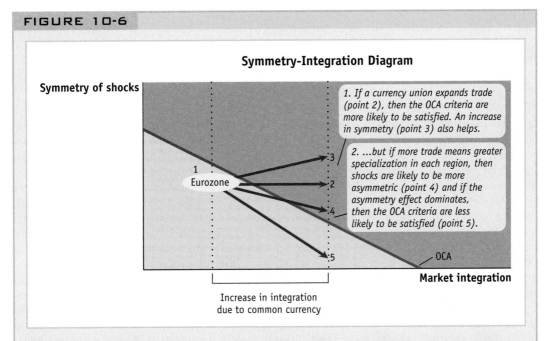

Symmetry-Integration Diagram

Symmetry of shocks

1. If a currency union expands trade (point 2), then the OCA criteria are more likely to be satisfied. An increase in symmetry (point 3) also helps.

2. ...but if more trade means greater specialization in each region, then shocks are likely to be more asymmetric (point 4) and if the asymmetry effect dominates, then the OCA criteria are less likely to be satisfied (point 5).

Eurozone

1

3

2

4

5

OCA

Market integration

Increase in integration
due to common currency

Self-Fulfilling OCA Criteria Euro-optimists think that the OCA criteria can be self-fulfilling. Suppose the Eurozone is initially at point 1, but then the effects of EMU start to be felt. Eventually there will be an increase in market integration (more trade, capital flows, migration) moving the zone to point 2. There may also be a greater synchronization of shocks in the Eurozone, moving the zone to point 3. However, euro-pessimists note that market integration and more trade might also lead to more specialization by each country in the EU. In that case, the shocks to each country are likely to become more *asymmetric*, implying a move toward point 4 or point 5. In the case of point 5, the case for an OCA grows weaker, not stronger, after the long-run effects of the currency union have been worked out.

markets are better connected, a case can be made that shocks will be more rapidly transmitted within the EU and will be felt more symmetrically. Thus, creating the Eurozone will not only boost trade but also increase the symmetry of shocks, corresponding to a shift from point 1 to point 3 in Figure 10-6. Such a process would strengthen the OCA argument even more.

Set against this optimistic view is the worrying prospect that further goods market integration might also lead to more specialization in production. According to this argument, once individual firms can easily serve the whole EU market, and not just their national market, they will exploit economies of scale and concentrate production. Some sectors in the EU might end up being concentrated in a few locations. Whereas in the past, trade barriers and other frictions allowed every EU country to produce a wide range of goods, in the future we might see more clustering (the United States provides many examples, such as the auto industry in Detroit or high technology in Silicon Valley). If specialization increases, each country will be less diversified and will face more asymmetric shocks. In Figure 10-6, this might correspond to a move from point 1 to point 4, where the case for OCA would strengthen, though not by much; or even a move to point 5, where the costs of asymmetric shocks

HEADLINES

....

Currency Unions and Trade

Will Eurozone trade rise as a result of the adoption of the euro?
The effects seen so far do not appear to be very large.

In the continuing controversies about Europe's bold experiment in monetary union, there has at least been some agreement about where the costs and benefits lie. The costs are macroeconomic, caused by forgoing the right to set interest rates to suit the specific economic conditions of a member state. The benefits are microeconomic, consisting of potential gains in trade and growth as the costs of changing currencies and exchange-rate uncertainty are removed.

A new study[*] by Richard Baldwin, a trade economist at the Graduate Institute of International Studies in Geneva, scythes through [previous] estimates. He works out that the boost to trade within the euro area from the single currency is much smaller: between 5% and 15%, with a best estimate of 9%. Furthermore, the gain does not build up over time but has already occurred. And the three European Union countries that stayed out—Britain, Sweden and Denmark—have gained almost as much as founder members, since the single currency has raised their exports to the euro zone by 7%.

Interest in the potential trade gains from the euro was primed . . . by a startling result from research into previous currency unions. In 2000 Andrew Rose, an economist at the University of California, Berkeley, reported that sharing a currency boosts trade by 235%.[**] Such a number looked too big to be true. It clashed with earlier research that found exchange-rate volatility reduced trade only marginally. . . .

Despite such worries, researchers continued to find large trade effects from currency unions. Mr. Baldwin explains why these estimates are unreliable. The main problem is that most of the countries involved are an odd bunch of small, poor economies that are in unions because of former colonial arrangements. Such is their diversity that it is impossible to model the full range of possible influences on their trade. But if some of the omitted factors are correlated with membership of a monetary union, the estimate of its impact on trade is exaggerated. And causality is also likely to run the other way: small, open economies, which would in any case trade heavily, are especially likely to share a currency. . . .

The intractable difficulties in working out the trade effect from previous currency unions means that previous estimates are fatally flawed. But the euro has now been in existence since the start of 1999, with notes and coins circulating since January 2002, so there is an increasing body of evidence based on its experience. That has certainly highlighted the macroeconomic disadvantages for its 12 member states. The loss of monetary sovereignty has hobbled first Germany and, more recently, Italy.

Despite these drawbacks, some studies have pointed to a substantial increase in trade within the euro area arising from monetary union, for example by 20–25% in the first four years. As with the previous currency unions, however, many other explanatory influences might have come into play. Fortunately, unlike those earlier unions, there is a "control" group: the three countries that stayed out. This is particularly useful because they have shared other relevant aspects of membership of the EU, such as trade policy. It is on the basis of this that Mr. Baldwin reaches his best estimate of a 9% increase in trade within the euro area because of monetary union.

As important, he establishes that the boost to trade did not occur, as expected, by lowering the transaction costs for trade within the euro area. Had it done so, the stimulus would have been a fall in the prices of goods traded between eurozone members relative to those traded with countries outside the currency union. However, Mr. Baldwin fails to find either this expected relative decline or the trade diversion it would have generated from the three countries that stayed out. He argues that another mechanism was at work. The introduction of the euro has in effect brought down the fixed cost of trading in the euro area. This has made it possible for companies selling products to just a few of the 12 member states to expand their market across more or all of them. This explains why the boost to trade has essentially been a one-off adjustment; and why countries that stayed out have benefited almost as much as those that joined.

[T]here is also an important lesson for the 12 members of the euro area. Even if their economies were insufficiently aligned to be best suited for a currency union, one hope has been that the euro would make them converge as they trade much more intensively with one another. The message from Mr. Baldwin's report is that this is too optimistic. Countries in the euro area will have to undertake more reforms, such as making their labour markets more flexible, if they are to make the best of life with a single monetary policy.

[*]Richard Baldwin, In or Out: Does it Matter? An Evidence-based Analysis of the Euro's Trade Effects, London: Centre for Economic Policy Research, 2006.
[**]Andrew K. Rose, 2000, "One Money, One Market: The Effect of Common Currencies on Trade," Economic Policy, 30, April, 7–45.
Source: Excerpted from "Economics Focus: The Euro and Trade," Economist, June 22, 2006.

....

are so large that they dominate the gains from market integration, so that the case for an OCA is weakened.

Some speculate that certain other OCA criteria could be affected by the adoption of the euro: Maybe the common currency will encourage greater labor and capital mobility? Maybe it will encourage more fiscal federalism? As with the arguments about the effects on trade creation and specialization, evidence for these claims is quite sketchy. We cannot make a definitive judgment until the Eurozone experiment has run for a few more years and there are sufficient data to make reliable statistical inferences.

Summary

We have seen how a calculation of economic costs and benefits can help us decide whether a common currency makes sense. But it appears that the EU is almost certainly not an optimum currency area. Admittedly, this conclusion does not apply with equal force to the entire EU. Some subgroups of countries may have satisfied the OCA criteria. For decades Luxembourg has, in fact, used the Belgian franc as a currency; and the Dutch guilder has been closely tied to the German mark. The BeNeLux countries, and maybe Austria too, were always well integrated with Germany and therefore stronger candidates for a currency union. Other countries also had some very strong criteria for joining: for Italy, perhaps, where monetary policy was often more erratic, a better nominal anchor might have outweighed other negatives.

So if the EU is not an OCA, then why does the euro exist? The euro project was seen as something bigger. This was a currency designed to unify a whole continent of disparate economies, to include France and Germany, Italy and the United Kingdom, to run from west to east, from Scandinavia to the Mediterranean—and it developed with very little reference to the OCA criteria. To understand why the euro happened, we need to study political logic, which is the topic of the next section.

2 The History and Politics of the Euro

The political origins of the European Union and the euro project can be found in the past. As long ago as 1861, the eminent French writer and statesman Victor Hugo could imagine that "a day will come in which markets open to commerce and minds open to ideas will be the sole battlefields." The time line in Table 10-1 provides a summary of some of the most important events that have shaped European economic history since 1870. The course of events reveals a European project guided by politics as well as economics.

A Brief History of Europe

The table shows major political and economic events since 1870 and highlights the most important developments affecting monetary policy over the same time period. The table is divided into two periods: panel (a) sketches the more distant history that shaped the creation of the EU and progress

TABLE 10-1

(a) European Integration 1870–1992

	Major Political and Economic Events	Monetary Developments
1870–1914	Largely peaceful era; economic growth and stability.	The **gold standard** system of fixed exchange rates prevails.
1914–1945	World Wars I and II; economic malaise, Great Depression.	Collapse of gold standard, floating exchange rates with instability; capital controls widespread.
1946		The **Bretton Woods system** of fixed exchange rates established.
1947–1951	**Marshall Plan** reconstruction financed by United States and overseen by the **European High Authority.**	**European Payments Union** (EPU) is created to free up the European payments system and facilitate trade.
1954–1965	In 1954, France, West Germany, Italy, Belgium, Netherlands, Luxembourg form **European Coal and Steel Community** (ECSC). In 1957 they sign **Treaty of Rome** to form **European Economic Community** (EEC). In 1967 the **European Communities** (EC) merges EEC, ECSC, and Euratom; **Council of Ministers** and **European Commission** established.	
1971–1973	**1st enlargement:** Denmark, Ireland, and United Kingdom join (1973) to form an EC of 9 countries.	The **Bretton Woods system** of fixed exchange rates collapses.
1973–1979	**European Parliament** directly elected (1979).	**European Monetary System** (EMS) of monetary cooperation creates a currency basket called the **ecu** (a precursor of the euro) and the **Exchange Rate Mechanism** (ERM), a system of quasi-fixed exchange rates (1979). Belgium, Luxembourg, Denmark, Germany, France, Ireland, Italy, and Netherlands join EMS/ERM; United Kingdom joins EMS only.
1981–1986	**2nd and 3rd enlargements:** Greece (1981), Portugal and Spain (1986) expand EC to 12 countries.	Greece, Portugal, and Spain join EMS but not ERM.
1987–1990	**Single European Act** (1987) has goal of EC "single market" by 1992.	Spain (1989) and United Kingdom (1990) join ERM.
1990	**German reunification** in 1990 creates new unified German state, adding former East Germany to the EC.	Capital controls abolished in EC.
1991	**Maastricht Treaty** transforms EC into **European Union** (EU); to take effect in 1993. EU citizenship and EU enlargement process established. Plan for **Economic and Monetary Union** (EMU) adopted.	Plan for EMU includes a common currency (Britain and Denmark retain right to opt out), with ERM seen as an entry route. Rules for membership and **convergence criteria** established.
1992		Portugal joins ERM. **ERM crisis:** Britain exits ERM; ERM bands eventually widened.

toward EMU, culminating in the Maastricht Treaty of 1991; panel (b) supplies more detail on important recent events affecting the EU and the EMU project.

The EU project emerged as a cooperative response to a history of noncooperation among nations on the continent, which twice in the twentieth century spilled over into violent military conflict, in World War I (1914–1919) and World War II (1939–1945). Even during the interwar years, political tensions ran high and economic cooperation suffered. The situation was not

(b) European Integration 1993–2007

	Major Political and Economic Events	Monetary Developments
1993	EU sets out **Copenhagen Criteria,** the political and economic conditions that future EU applicants must satisfy.	Applicants are expected to enter ERM/EMS and achieve the requirements for monetary union within a given period of time.
1995	**4th enlargement:** Austria, Finland, and Sweden expand EU to 15 countries. **Treaty of Schengen** will create common border system and immigration policies and free travel zone (Ireland and United Kingdom opt out; non-EU countries Iceland, Norway, and Switzerland opt in.)	Austria, Finland, and Sweden join EMS. Austria (1995) and Finland (1996) join ERM.
1997	**Treaty of Amsterdam** addresses EU citizenship, rights, powers of European Parliament, employment, and common foreign and security policy.	**Stability and Growth Pact** (SGP) is adopted to further enforce the Maastricht budgetary rules.
1998	11 countries say they will adopt the euro: France, Germany, Italy, Belgium, Netherlands, Luxembourg, Ireland, Portugal, Spain, Austria, Finland	The **European Central Bank** (ECB) is created. The 11 euro countries freeze their bilateral exchange rates on December 31.
1999		The **euro** is introduced as a unit of account on January 1. Euro notes and coins will appear in 2002 and replace national currencies. Greece, Denmark join ERM.
2000		In Denmark voters reject euro adoption in a referendum.
2001	**Treaty of Nice** addresses EU expansion, amends and consolidates Rome and Maastricht treaties, and modifies voting procedures.	Greece becomes the 12th country to join the Eurozone.
2004	**5th enlargement:** Cyprus, the Czech Republic, Estonia, Hungary, Latvia, Lithuania, Malta, Poland, Slovakia, and Slovenia expand EU to 25 countries.	Estonia, Lithuania, and Slovenia join ERM.
2003		In Sweden voters reject euro adoption in a referendum.
2005	Ratification of EU **Constitutional Treaty** postponed indefinitely following rejection by voters in French and Dutch referenda. Controversial accession negotiations start for Turkey (an EU candidate since 1999 and an associate member of EEC/EC/EU since 1963).	Cyprus, Latvia, Malta, and Slovakia join ERM. 12 out of 25 Eurozone members are in violation of the Stability and Growth Pact rules.
2007	**6th enlargement:** Bulgaria and Romania expand EU to 27 countries.	Slovenia becomes the 13th country to join the Eurozone.

helped by the punishing economic burdens placed on Germany by the allied powers after World War I.[7] Matters only became worse during the severe economic downturn that was the Great Depression of the 1930s: protectionism surged again and the gold standard collapsed amid beggar-thy-neighbor devaluations (as discussed in Chapter 8).

---

[7] John Maynard Keynes, 1919, *The Economic Consequences of the Peace,* London: Macmillan.

In 1945, as a weak Europe emerged from the devastation of World War II, many feared that peace would only bring about a return to dire economic conditions. More economic suffering might also sow the seeds of more conflict in the future. At an extreme, some feared it would undermine the legitimacy of European capitalism, with the neighboring Soviet bloc all too eager to spread its alternative communist model.

What could be done? In a speech in Zurich, on September 19, 1946, Winston Churchill presented his vision:

> And what is the plight to which Europe has been reduced? . . . Over wide areas a vast quivering mass of tormented, hungry, care-worn and bewildered human beings gape at the ruins of their cities and their homes, and scan the dark horizons for the approach of some new peril, tyranny or terror. . . . That is all that Europeans, grouped in so many ancient states and nations . . . have got by tearing each other to pieces and spreading havoc far and wide. Yet all the while there is a remedy. . . . It is to recreate the European family, or as much of it as we can, and to provide it with a structure under which it can dwell in peace, in safety and in freedom. We must build a kind of United States of Europe.

Back from the Brink: Marshall Plan to Maastricht, 1945–1991 Into this crisis stepped the United States, to offer what has gone down in history as the most generous and successful reconstruction plan ever undertaken, the **Marshall Plan.**[8] From 1947 to 1951, the Americans poured billions of dollars worth of aid into the war-torn regions of Western Europe to rebuild economic infrastructure (the Soviet bloc refused to take part in the plan).

A poster created by the Economic Cooperation Administration, an agency of the U.S. government, to promote the Marshall Plan in Europe.

The Marshall Plan required that the funds be allocated and administered by a European High Authority, composed of representatives of all countries, which encouraged collective action to solve common problems. Many cooperative arrangements were soon established: to smooth international payments and help trade (European Payments Union, or EPU, 1950); to encourage trade and diminish rivalries in key goods like coal and steel (European Coal and Steel Community, or ECSC, in 1954); and to promote atomic and nuclear science without military rivalry (Euratom, in 1957).

In 1957 the **Treaty of Rome** was signed by six countries—France, West Germany, Italy, Belgium, Netherlands, and Luxembourg. They agreed to create the *European Economic Community,* or EEC, with plans for deeper economic cooperation and integration. In 1967 they went further and merged the EEC, the ECSC, and Euratom to create a new organization referred to as the *European Communities,* or EC. Two supranational bodies were created: the Council of Ministers, a decision-making body formed of national ministers, and an administrative body, the European Commission.

The dropping of the word "economic" (in the move from EEC to EC) was significant. By the 1960s, two future paths had emerged. Would the EC create

---

[8] George C. Marshall (1880–1959), American military leader in World War II and named U.S. Secretary of State in 1947, proposed the postwar reconstruction effort for Europe in a speech at Harvard University, Thursday, June 5, 1947.

just a zone of economic integration? Or would it go further and aspire to a political union or a federal system of states—and if so, how far? The question has been hotly debated ever since.

In the 1970s, two major challenges to the EC project emerged: problems of expansion and problems of monetary affairs. The expansion problem involved deciding when and how to admit new members. By 1973 the first enlargement added Denmark, Ireland, and the United Kingdom. The EC (i.e., the Council of Ministers) viewed these states as the right type to gain entry— they had solid credentials in terms of economic development and stability, and all were established democracies. In contrast, the second and third enlargements included countries with weaker economic and political claims—but all the same Greece (1981), Portugal (1986), and Spain (1986) were soon admitted to the growing club.

The problem of monetary affairs was precipitated by the collapse of the Bretton Woods system of fixed exchange rates in the early 1970s. As we saw in Chapter 8, the world had been operating since 1946 under a system of fixed dollar exchange rates with monetary autonomy, with the trilemma being resolved through the imposition of capital controls. In the 1970s, this system broke down and floating exchange rates became the norm in the advanced economies. At that time, except for wars and crises, Europe had spent roughly a century under some form of fixed exchange rate system, and European policy makers worried that floating exchange rates might compromise their goals for economic union. They announced they would create essentially a new mini-Bretton Woods of their own, and after muddling through for a few years, they officially did so with the creation of the *European Monetary System,* or EMS, in 1979.

The centerpiece of the EMS was the **Exchange Rate Mechanism (ERM),** a fixed exchange rate regime based on bands. The ERM defined each currency's central parity against a basket of currencies, the so-called *ecu* (European currency unit), the precursor to the euro. In practice, the non-German currencies ended up being pegged to the German mark, the central reserve currency in the system (just as the U.S. dollar had been the central reserve currency in the Bretton Woods system).

The ERM permitted a range of fluctuation on either side of the central value or *parity:* a narrow band of ±2.25% for most currencies (the escudo, lira, peseta, and pound were at times permitted a wider band of ±6%). In 1979 all EC countries except the United Kingdom joined the ERM; later, Spain joined in 1989, the United Kingdom in 1990, and Portugal in 1992. In principle, it was a "fixed but adjustable" system and the central parities could be changed, giving potential encouragement to speculators (also like Bretton Woods).

Crises and Opportunities: EMU and Other Projects, 1991–1999 The EC entered the 1990s with the drive for further integration still going strong. Since 1979 a directly elected European parliament had been at work. In 1987 the Single European Act was passed with the goal of reducing further the barriers between countries through the creation of a "single market" by 1992.

If, within the EC, the political momentum was still strong, it was soon given another push by the end of the Cold War in 1989. The Soviet Union disintegrated and communist rule in Eastern Europe came to an end, symbolized by the fall of the Berlin Wall. What was the EC going to do in response? The Germans had no doubts—East and West Germany would be reunited quickly, to form Germany again. German reunification was formally completed on October 3, 1990. For the EC as a whole, though, there was the question of how to react to the new states on their eastern flank.

Eastern Europe was keen to move quickly and decisively away from communism and autocracy and toward capitalism and democracy, and they saw joining the EC as a natural means to that end. From a political and security standpoint, the EC could hardly say no to the former communist countries, and so plans for further eastern enlargement had to be made. Other countries also waited in the wings. In the early 1990s, wars broke out in the Balkans, forcing the EC to confront the big hole in its map between Italy and Greece. Did the former Yugoslav states and Albania belong in "Europe," too? And discussion of the eastern frontier of the EC soon brought to the fore the question of Turkey, a country that has had EC Associate Member status since 1963 and yet had to wait until 2005 for formal admission talks to begin.

In the face of these political challenges, the EC needed to act with purpose, and the grandest treaty to date, the 1991 Treaty on European Union, or the Maastricht Treaty, was the response, reasserting more than ever the goal of creating an "ever closer union among the peoples of Europe." Adding more federal flavor, the treaty gave the EC a new name, the European Union, or EU, and created a notion of EU citizenship. The treaty also laid down the process for enlargement that would eventually take the EU, via three further enlargements in 1995, 2004, and 2007, from 12 countries to 15, 25, and 27.

Later political developments in the 1990s built on Maastricht. The 1993 Copenhagen Criteria provided formal conditions for new members wanting admission, such as rule of law, human rights, democracy, and so on. The 1995 Schengen Treaty established a zone for the free movement of people (though Ireland and the United Kingdom opted out). A fourth enlargement in 1995 brought Austria, Finland, and Sweden into the EU (Norway had signed up, but the people said no in a referendum). The 1997 Amsterdam Treaty forged ahead in EU foreign and security policy and strengthened the rights of EU citizenship and the powers of the European parliament.

The most ambitious part of the Maastricht Treaty was its economic element: the EU-wide goal of **Economic and Monetary Union (EMU).** The economic union would take the idea of a single market even further—to all goods and services, to capital markets, to labor markets—and would call on the European Commission to ensure that national laws and regulations did not stand in the way. But more than this, monetary union would propose a new currency (soon given the name "euro") for the entire EU. Under the plan for the euro, countries would transition from their pegged rates within the ERM into an irrevocable peg with the euro at an appointed date. But this plan almost immediately came into doubt.

The ERM proved to be a fragile fixed exchange rate system like any other. As we saw in the last chapter, its worst moment came in 1992. In the **ERM crisis,** several ERM countries suffered exchange rate crises and their pegs broke: the British pound, Italian lira, Portuguese escudo, and Spanish peseta. (Other non-ERM currencies such as the Swedish krona and the Finnish markka pegged to the mark also experienced crises and broken pegs). Even the currencies that stayed within the ERM had to have their bands widened so much as to make the peg look more like a float for a while. The whole system was reduced to a near shambles.

As we saw in the past two chapters, the fundamental cause of these crises was a tension between the macroeconomic objectives of the center country, Germany (tight monetary policy to prevent overheating after a large fiscal shock caused by reunification), and the objectives of the pegging countries (whose authorities wanted to use expansionary monetary policy to boost output).

The ghosts of the 1992 crisis still roam today. Many countries rejoined the ERM, some at a new rate or with a wider band: Spain, Italy, and Portugal all regrouped, reentered the ERM, and ultimately adopted the euro. But Britain permanently left the ERM and turned its back on the common currency. Sweden, officially committed to the euro, has never shown any interest in joining even the ERM. Today, in both Britain and Sweden, public opposition to the euro remains high. And there is always the fear that another ERM crisis could erupt in new EU members that are pegging to the euro as part of their preparation for joining the common currency.

Still, despite the exchange rate crisis in 1992, the ERM was patched up, and most countries remained committed to the plan to launch the euro. The ERM bands were widened in 1993 to a very slack ±15%, and most were happy to live within those limits and get ready for euro admission.

Where Are We Now? The EU and the Eurozone, 1999 and Beyond The euro was launched in 11 countries on January 1, 1999, and administered by a newly created central bank, the **European Central Bank (ECB).**[9] The ECB took control of monetary policy in all Eurozone countries on that date from each national central bank.[10] The national central banks still have responsibilities. They represent their country on the ECB Council and still supervise and regulate their own country's financial system. The euro immediately became the unit of account in the Eurozone, and a gradual transition took place as euros began to enter circulation and national currencies were withdrawn.

Officials launch euro trading, Frankfurt, January 4, 1999.

---

[9] The European Central Bank was established on June 1, 1998. It succeeded a prototype monetary authority, the European Monetary Institute (EMI), which for four and a half years had undertaken much of the groundwork for the euro project.

[10] All EU central banks cooperate as a group in the European System of Central Banks (ESCB). Within that group, the central banks of Eurozone member states (known, confusingly, as the Eurosystem banks) have a much closer relationship with the ECB. Only Eurosystem banks have representation on the ECB's Council.

Table 10-2 shows the history and current state of play in the EU at the time of this writing in late 2007. The table shows the dates of membership in the EU, the ERM, and the Eurozone. Also shown are the fixed exchange rate parities of all ERM and euro members—for the latter, these were frozen upon euro entry and became obsolete once the national currencies were retired.[11]

TABLE 10-2

The EU-27 and the Euro Project in 2007 This table shows the progress of each country through EU membership, ERM membership, and adoption of the euro, as of late 2007. The euro parities of Eurozone members and ERM members are also shown, although the former have now abolished their national currencies. Dates for future euro adoption are also given, although these are in many cases uncertain or unknown (shown by a question mark).

		YEAR THAT COUNTRY JOINED				
		EU	ERM	Eurozone	Euro Parity (€1 =)	National Currency (current or former)
Countries in the Eurozone	Austria	1995	1995	1999	13.7603	schilling
	Belgium	1959	1979	1999	40.3399	frank
	Finland	1995	1996	1999	5.94573	markka
	France	1959	1979	1999	6.55957	franc
	Germany	1959	1979	1999	1.95583	mark
	Greece	1981	1999	2001	340.75	drachma
	Ireland	1973	1979	1999	0.787564	pound
	Italy	1959	1979	1999	1936.27	lira
	Luxembourg	1959	1979	1999	40.3399	franc
	Netherlands	1959	1979	1999	2.20371	guilder
	Portugal	1986	1992	1999	200.482	escudo
	Slovenia	2004	2004	2007	239.64	tolar
	Spain	1986	1989	1999	166.386	peseta
Countries in the ERM	Cyprus	2004	2005	2008	0.585274	pound
	Denmark*	1973	1999	?	7.46038	krone
	Estonia	2004	2004	2009?	15.6466	kroon
	Latvia	2004	2005	2009?	0.702804	lat
	Lithuania	2004	2004	2009?	3.4528	litas
	Malta	2004	2005	2008	0.4293	lira
	Slovakia	2004	2005	2009?	35.4424	koruna
Other EU Countries	Bulgaria	2007	?	?	?	lev
	Czech Republic	2004	?	?	?	koruna
	Hungary	2004	?	?	?	forint
	Poland	2004	?	?	?	zloty
	Romania	2007	?	?	?	leu
	Sweden*	1995	?	?	?	krona
	United Kingdom*	1973	1990–92	?	?	pound

* The United Kingdom and Denmark can legally opt out of the euro. Sweden is opting out de facto by not joining the ERM. All other countries are expected to join at some point.

[11] Since 1999 the original ERM has been replaced with a modified ERM II, with the euro replacing its predecessor, the ecu, as the base currency for pegging. Notwithstanding the Maastricht Treaty, all ERM members now operate in a de jure ±15% band (although Denmark sticks to the old, narrow ±2.25% band).

As of 2007, the Eurozone contains 13 "in" countries. Eleven made the switch to the euro in 1999, Greece entered in 2001, and Slovenia joined in 2007. There are 14 "out" countries. In the ERM "waiting room," there are 7 countries, and one of them, Denmark, has been waiting a long time. There are 7 countries not in the ERM, although all except the United Kingdom and Sweden are expected to join the ERM and the euro in the medium term of five to ten years. Of the "out" countries, only Denmark and the United Kingdom can legally opt out of the euro indefinitely, although Sweden is acting as if it can, too; all three countries have significant popular opposition to the euro and are not expected to adopt the euro any time soon.

Summary

History shows that the countries of Europe have some deep tendency to prefer fixed exchange rates to floating rates. Apart from brief crisis episodes in times of turmoil (during wars, the Great Depression, and the early 1970s), most European countries have maintained pegged exchange rates against each other since the 1870s. They have now taken the additional step of adopting a common currency.

There have certainly been some economic changes in Europe that make it more likely to satisfy the OCA criteria now than at any time in the past. The EU project has pushed forward a process of deep economic integration, with major steps such as EMU and the Schengen Treaty bringing Europe closer to the ideal of a single market. But integration is still very much a work in progress, and the OCA criteria are unlikely to be met soon. Instead, European history suggests that the common currency fits as part of a political project rather than as a purely economic choice.

3 The ECB and the Eurozone in Theory and Practice

Suppose some German economists from the 1950s or 1960s could travel forward in time 40 or 50 years to the present day; they happen to pop up next to you on a Frankfurt street corner, and say "take me to the central bank," and they are then quite surprised when you lead them to the gleaming glass and steel Eurotower at Kaiserstrasse instead of the old Bundesbank building.

That the European Central Bank is located in Frankfurt is no coincidence, however. It is a testament to the strong influence of German monetary policy makers and politicians in the design of the euro project, an influence they earned on account of the exemplary performance of the German economy, and especially monetary policy, from the 1950s to the 1990s. To see how German influence has left its mark on the euro, we first examine how the ECB operates and then try to explain its peculiar goals and governance.

The European Central Bank

For economists, central banks have a few key features. To sum these up, we may ask: What policy instrument does the bank use? What is it supposed to do (goals) and not do (forbidden activities)? How are decisions on these policies made given the bank's governance structure? To whom is the bank

NETWORK

In October 1997 the British Labour government adopted its own criteria for euro membership. These are called the *five tests* and must be satisfied before the government will propose entry into the Eurozone. Use the Web to find out more about these tests. Who invented the five tests? When? Where? What, if anything, do they have to do with the OCA criteria? The Maastricht criteria? Do you think Britain will ever satisfy all five tests at once?

accountable, and, subject to that, how much independence does the bank have? For the ECB, the brief answers are as follows:

- *Instrument and goals.* The instrument used by the ECB is the interest rate at which banks can borrow funds. According to its charter, the ECB's primary objective is to "maintain price stability" in the euro area. Its secondary goal is to "support the general economic policies in the Community with a view to contributing to the achievement of the objectives of the Community." (Many central banks have similar instruments and goals, but the ECB has a relatively strong focus on inflation.)

- *Forbidden activities.* To prevent the use of monetary policy for other goals, the ECB may not directly finance member states' fiscal deficits or provide bailouts to member governments or national public bodies. In addition, the ECB has no mandate to act as a lender of last resort by extending credit to financial institutions in the Eurozone in the event of a banking crisis. (Most central banks are not so constrained, and they typically can act as a lender of last resort.)

- *Governance and decision making.* Monetary policy decisions are made at meetings of the ECB's Governing Council, which consists of the central bank governors of the Eurozone national central banks and six members of the ECB's executive board. In practice, policy decisions are made by consensus rather than by majority voting. Meetings are usually held twice each month.

- *Accountability and independence.* No monetary policy powers are given to any other EU institution. No EU institution has any formal oversight of the ECB, and the ECB does not have to report to any political body, elected or otherwise. The ECB does not release the minutes of its meetings. The ECB has independence not only with respect to its instrument (it sets interest rates) but also with respect to its goal (it gets to define what "price stability" means). (A small but growing number of central banks around the world has achieved some independence, but the ECB has more than most.)

On all three points, the working of the ECB has been subject to strong criticisms.

Criticisms of the ECB There is controversy over the price stability goal. The ECB chooses to define price stability as a Eurozone consumer price inflation rate of less than but "close to" 2% per year over the medium term. This target is asymmetrical (there is no lower bound to guard against deflation); it is also vague (the notions of "close to" and "medium term" are not defined).

There is controversy over having only price stability as a goal. On paper, the ECB technically has a secondary goal of supporting and stabilizing the Eurozone economy. But in practice, the ECB has acted as if it places little weight on economic performance, growth and unemployment, and where the real economy is in the business cycle. In this area, the ECB's policy preferences are different from, say, those of the U.S. Federal Reserve, which has a mandate from Congress not only to ensure price stability but also to achieve full employment. The ECB also differs from the Bank of England, whose Governor Mervyn King famously used the term "inflation nutter" to describe a policy maker with an excessive focus on price stability. The ECB's early obsessive focus on money and prices objectives was thought to reflect a combination of its Germanic heritage and its relative lack of long-term reputation, but this may change with time.

There is controversy over the ECB's way of conducting policy to achieve its goal. In addition to the "first pillar," which uses an economic analysis of expected price inflation to guide interest rate decisions, the bank has a "second pillar" in the form of a reference value for money supply growth (4.5% per annum). As we saw in Chapter 3, however, a fixed money growth rate can be consistent with an inflation target only by chance. For example, in the quantity theory model, which assumes a stable level of nominal interest rates in the long run, inflation equals the money growth rate minus the growth rate of real output. So the ECB's twin pillars will make sense only if real output just happens to grow at less than 2.5% per year, for only then will inflation be, at most, $4.5 - 2.5 = 2\%$ per year. Perhaps aware of the inconsistency of using two nominal anchors, the ECB has given the impression that most of the time it ignores the second pillar; nonetheless, concern about money supply growth is occasionally expressed (see **Headlines: The ECB Is from Mars, the Fed Is from Venus**).

There is controversy over the "forbidden activities." What happens in the event of a large banking crisis in the Eurozone? Most central banks are expected to extend credit to banks in case of such rare events, and they can print money to do so. In the Eurozone, the ECB can print the money but cannot do the lending; the national central banks can do the lending but can't print the money. National central banks can devise limited, local credit facilities or arrange private consortia to manage a small crisis, or they can hope for fiscal help from their national treasuries. Big crises could therefore prove more difficult to prevent or contain.

There is controversy over the decision-making process. Consensus decisions may favor the status quo, causing policy to lag when it ought to move. Insistence on having all central bank governors on the Council leads to a very large body in which consensus is harder to achieve. This design will become even more cumbersome as more countries join the euro, but the structure of the Council is set in the Maastricht Treaty and would be impossible to change without revising the treaty.

There is controversy over the ECB's lack of accountability. Because it answers to no political masters, some fear that people in the Eurozone will conclude that the ECB lacks legitimacy. Although the EU is a collection of democratic states, many of its decisions are made in places that are far from close to the people, notwithstanding the Maastricht Treaty's lofty language. Many EU bodies suffer a perceived "democratic deficit," including the work of the unelected Commission and the treaties pursued at the intragovernmental level with no popular ratification and little consultation. The ECB can appear to be even further removed at a supra-governmental level. There is nothing akin to the U.S. requirement that the Federal Reserve chairman

HEADLINES

The ECB Is from Mars, the Fed Is from Venus

The ECB's monetarist leanings have been questioned, even within the ECB itself.

Transatlantic differences over monetary strategy erupted into the open on Friday as the European Central Bank sought to modernise its policy of relying on money supply measures as an inflation early-warning system.

Jean-Claude Trichet, ECB president, used a Frankfurt conference to stress the importance of indicators such as M3, the broad money supply measure. But in contrast, Ben Bernanke, US Federal Reserve chairman, said a heavy reliance on money supply measures "would seem to be unwise in the US context," although money growth data might still offer important signals about future economic developments.

Mr. Trichet refused to comment on whether differences between the US and European economies justified a different approach to the use of money supply data. But he acknowledged the need for monetary analysis to become more sophisticated, taking into account financial innovation. . . .

The ECB's "monetary pillar," largely inherited from Germany's Bundesbank, is controversial among economists because of confusion about the implications of money supply for inflation. At the ECB-hosted conference, prominent officials from the Frankfurt institution made clear that they saw significant scope for refinements. . . . ECB research presented at the conference was open about the shortcomings of the bank's monetary analysis in its eight-year history.

Mr. Trichet said the monetary analysis had been instrumental in the ECB's decision to start raising interest rates in December 2005. At the time many economists and politicians feared its actions were premature given the uncertainties then about the Eurozone's economic outlook. "Without our thorough monetary analysis, we could have been in danger of falling behind the curve," he said.

Mr. Bernanke pointed to larger methodological problems in the US. "The rapid pace of financial innovation in the US has been an important reason for the instability of the relationships between monetary aggregates and other macroeconomic variables."

Changes in payment technologies and individuals' behaviour had meant usage of different kinds of accounts "have at times shifted rapidly and unpredictably."

Source: Excerpted from Ralph Atkins, "Trichet and Bernanke Differ on Strategy," *Financial Times*, November 10, 2006.

regularly answer questions from Congress. Rather, the ECB has a more informal dialogue and consultations with the Council, Commission, and Parliament. In response, the finance ministers of the Eurozone have ganged up to form the *Eurogroup,* which meets and opines about what is happening in the Eurozone and what the ECB is (or should be) doing. Occasionally, national heads of governments weigh in to attack the ECB's policy choices (as French President Nicolas Sarkozy did in 2007) or to defend them (as German Chancellor Angela Merkel did in response). Along with the EU's commissioner for economic and monetary affairs, they can make pronouncements and lobby, but they can do little more unless a treaty revision places the ECB under more scrutiny.

The German Model Some of these criticisms are valid and undisputed, but others are fiercely contested. Supporters of the ECB say that strong independence and freedom from political interference are exactly what are needed in a young institution that is still struggling to achieve credibility and that the dominant problem in the Eurozone in recent years has been inflation and not deflation. For many of these supporters, the ECB is set up the right way—almost a copy of the Bundesbank, with a strong focus on low inflation to the exclusion of other criteria and a complete separation of

monetary policy from the politics. Here, German preferences and German economic performance had been very
different from the rest of the Eurozone, yet they pre-
vailed. How can this be understood?

The ECB Tower and euro logo, Frankfurt.

German preferences for a low-inflation environment
have been extremely strong ever since the costly and
chaotic interwar hyperinflation, which we discussed in
Chapter 3. It was clear that the hyperinflation had been
driven by reckless fiscal policy, which had led politicians to
take over monetary policy and run the printing presses.
After that fiasco, strong anti-inflation preferences, translat-
ed from the people via the political process, were reflected
in the conduct of monetary policy by the Bundesbank
from 1958 until the arrival of the euro in 1999. To ensure that the
Bundesbank could deliver a firm nominal anchor, it was carefully insulated
from political interference.

Today, as we saw in Chapter 3, a popular recipe for sound monetary policy is a combination of central bank independence and an inflation target.
Sometimes, the inflation target is set by the government, the so-called *New
Zealand model*. But the so-called *German model* went further and faster: the
Bundesbank was not only the first central bank to be granted full independence, it was given both *instrument independence* (freedom to use interest rate
policy in the short run) and *goal independence* (the power to decide what the
inflation target should be in the long run). This became the model for the
ECB, when Germany set most of the conditions for entering a monetary
union with other countries where the traditions of central bank independence
were weaker or nonexistent.

Monetary Union with Inflation Bias We can see where Germany's preferences came from. But how did it get its way? A deep problem in modern macroeconomics concerns the *time inconsistency* of policies.[12] According to this view, all
countries have a problem with inflation bias under discretionary monetary policy. Policy makers would like to commit to low inflation, but without a credible
commitment to low inflation, a politically controlled central bank has a temptation to use "surprise" monetary policy expansions to boost output. Eventually,
this bias will be anticipated, built into inflation expectations, and hence, in the
long run, real outcomes—such as output, unemployment—will be the same
whatever the extent of the inflation bias. Long-run money neutrality means that
printing money can't make an economy more productive or create jobs.

The inflation bias problem can be solved if we can separate the central bank
from politics and install a "conservative central banker" who cares about inflation and nothing else. This separation was strong in Germany, but not elsewhere.
Hence, a historically low-inflation country (e.g., Germany) might be worried

---

[12] Finn E. Kydland and Edward C. Prescott, 1977, "Rules Rather Than Discretion: The Inconsistency of
Optimal Plans," *Journal of Political Economy*, 85, 473–492; Robert J. Barro and David B. Gordon, 1983, "Rules,
Discretion and Reputation in a Model of Monetary Policy," *Journal of Monetary Economics*, 12, 101–121.

that a monetary union with a high-inflation country (e.g., Italy) would lead to a monetary union with on average a tendency for middling levels of inflation— that is, looser monetary policies on average for Germany and tighter on average for Italy. In the long run, Germany and Italy would still get the same real outcomes (though in the short run, Germany might have a monetary-led boom and Italy a recession). But, while Italy might gain in the long run from lower inflation, Germany would lose from the shift to a high-inflation environment. Germany would need assurances that this would not happen, and because Germany was such a large and pivotal country in the EU, a Eurozone without Germany was unimaginable (based on simple OCA logic or on political logic). So Germany had a lot of bargaining power.

Essentially, the bargaining over the design of the ECB and the Eurozone boiled down to this: other countries were content to accept that in the long run their real outcomes would not be any different even if they switched to monetary policy run by the ECB under the German model, and thus had to settle for less political manipulation of monetary policy.

Or so they said at the time. But how could one be sure that these countries did in fact mean what they said? One could take countries' word for it— trust them. Or one could make them prove it—test them. In a world of inflation bias, trust in monetary authorities is weak, so the Maastricht Treaty established some tests—that is, some rules for admission.

The Rules of the Club

The Maastricht Treaty established five rules for admission to the euro zone, shown in Table 10-3. All five of these **convergence criteria** need to be satisfied for entry. Two of the five rules also serve as ongoing requirements for mem-

TABLE 10-3

Rules of Euro Membership The Maastricht Treaty of 1991 established five conditions that aspiring members of the Eurozone must satisfy prior to entry. The last two fiscal rules are also supposed to be obeyed by members even after entry.

Rule (* prior to entry only)	Criterion
Exchange rate*	Two consecutive years in ERM band with no devaluation (no change in central parity)
Inflation rate*	No more than 1.5 percentage points above the level in the three member states with the lowest inflation in the previous year
Long-term nominal interest rate*	No more than 2 percentage points above the level in the three member states with the lowest inflation in the previous year
Government deficit	No more than 3% of GDP in previous financial year[1]
Government debt	No more than 60% of GDP in previous financial year[2]

Notes:
The ERM bands in effect at the time of the Maastricht Treaty were *narrow* (±2.25% or ±6%); since 1993 they have been *wide* (±15%). The first rule is now applied using the wide bands. Escape clauses are included in the last two fiscal rules, as follows:
[1] Or "the ratio must have declined substantially and continuously and reached a level close to 3% or, alternatively, must remain close to 3% while representing only an exceptional and temporary excess."
[2] Or "the ratio must have sufficiently diminished and must be approaching the reference value at a satisfactory pace."

bership. The rules can be divided into two parts: three rules requiring convergence in nominal measures closely related to inflation and two rules requiring fiscal discipline to clamp down on the deeper determinants of inflation.

Nominal Convergence In Chapters 3 and 4, we explored some of the central implications of a fixed exchange rate, implications that also apply when two countries adopt a common currency (i.e., a fixed exchange rate of 1). Let's consider three implications:

- Under a peg, the exchange rate must be fixed or not vary beyond tight limits.
- PPP then implies that the two countries' inflation rates must be very close.
- UIP then implies that the two countries' long-term nominal interest rates must be very close.

In fact, we may recall that the Fisher effect says that the inflation differential must equal the nominal interest rate differential—so if one is small, the other has to be small, too.

These three conditions all relate to the nominal anchoring provided by a peg, and they roughly correspond to the first three Maastricht criteria in Table 10-3.

The rules say that a country must stay in its ERM band (with no realignment) for two years to satisfy the peg rule.[13] It must have an inflation rate "close to" that of the three lowest-inflation countries in the zone to satisfy the inflation rule. And it must have a long-term interest rate "close to" that in the three low-inflation countries.[14] All three tests must be met for a country to satisfy the admission criteria.

What is the economic sense for these rules? They appear, in some ways, superfluous because if a country credibly pegged to (or has adopted) the euro, theory says that these conditions would have to be satisfied in the long run anyway. For that reason they are also hard to criticize—except to say that, if the rules are going to be met anyway, why not "just do it" and let countries join the euro without such conditions? The answer relates to our earlier discussion about inflation bias. If two countries with different inflation rates adopt a common currency, their inflation rates must converge—but to what level, high or low?

The way the rules were written forces countries to converge on the lowest inflation rates in the zone. We have argued that this outcome is needed for

---

[13] The two-year requirement for the ERM means a country can't cheat by stabilizing its currency at the last minute, possibly in an opportunistic way to get in at a favorable (depreciated) rate that boosts demand for the country's output. Still, as currently interpreted, the ERM rule means that a currency only has to stay within the wide (post-1993) ±15% ERM bands, so the constraint is not all that tight. Also, following the exchange rate crises of 1992 in the United Kingdom and Sweden that gave the ERM a bad name, the two-year ERM membership rule might be waived if either of these two countries wishes to adopt the euro.
[14] The interest rate rule relates to the long-term interest rate for government borrowing, not the short-term rate that is central to UIP. Over the long run, the two move together and on average are generally separated by a positive *term premium*. Under a peg, then, countries will share identical *long-term* interest rates if and only if (i) there is no risk premium difference between them and (ii) there is no term premium difference, either. In practice, risk premiums and term premiums are higher for riskier borrowers, so in some ways this rule is also related to fiscal discipline (discussed in the next section).

low-inflation countries to sign up, although it will require possibly painful policy change in the high-inflation countries. The Maastricht criteria ensure that high-inflation countries go through this pain and attain credibility by demonstrating their commitment to low inflation before they are allowed in. This process supposedly prevents governments with a preference for high inflation from entering the Eurozone and then trying to persuade the ECB to go soft on inflation. These three rules can thus be seen as addressing the credibility problem in a world of inflation bias. All current euro members successfully satisfied these rules to gain membership, and the end result was marked inflation convergence as shown in Figure 10-7. Current ERM members are now going through the same test.

Fiscal Discipline The Maastricht Treaty wasn't just tough on inflation, it was tough on the causes of inflation, and it saw the fundamental and deep causes of inflation as being not monetary, but fiscal. The other two Maastricht rules are openly aimed at constraining fiscal policy. They are applied not just as a condition for admission but also to all member states once they are in. The rules say that government debts and deficits cannot be above certain reference levels (although the treaty allows some exceptions). These levels were chosen somewhat arbitrarily: a deficit level of 3% of GDP and a debt level of 60% of GDP. However arbitrary these reference levels are, there still exist economic rationales for having some kinds of fiscal rules in a monetary union in which the member states maintain fiscal sovereignty.

FIGURE 10-7

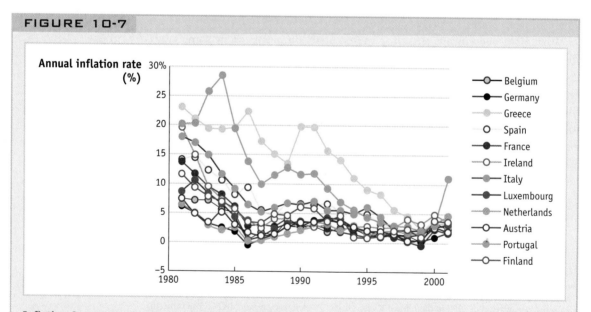

Inflation Convergence To meet the Maastricht Treaty's convergence criteria, the first 12 members of the Eurozone had to reduce their inflation level below a moving target. This target was equal to average inflation in the three lowest-inflation countries in the bloc plus 1.5 percentage points. This process ensured that the Eurozone began with a low inflation rate. The countries currently in the ERM must pass the same test before they can adopt the euro.

Source: European Economy, Statistical Annex, Autumn 2005.

Why might inflation ultimately be a fiscal problem? Consider two countries negotiating the treaty, one with low debt levels (e.g., Germany) and one with high debt levels (e.g., Italy). Germany has several possible fears in this case. One is that if Italy has high nominal debt (measured in lira, but soon to be measured in euros), Italy will lobby for high inflation once in the union (because inflation destroys the real value of the government's debt). Another fear is that Italy has a higher default risk, which might result in political pressure for the ECB to break its own rules and bail out Italy in a crisis, which the ECB can do only by printing euros and, again, generating more inflation.

The main arguments for the fiscal rules are that any deal to form a currency union will require fiscally weak countries to tighten their belts and meet criteria set by fiscally strong countries in order to further ensure against inflation.

Criticism of the Convergence Criteria Because these rules constitute the main gatekeeping mechanism for the Eurozone, they have been carefully scrutinized and have generated much controversy.

First, these rules involve asymmetric adjustments that take a long time. In the 1980s and 1990s, they mostly involved German preferences on inflation and fiscal policy being imposed at great cost on other countries. Germany had lower inflation and larger surpluses than most countries, and the criteria were set close to the German levels, not surprisingly. To converge on these levels, tighter fiscal and monetary policies had to be adopted in countries like France, Italy, Portugal, and Spain while they tried to maintain the peg (to obey rule 1: staying in their ERM bands). As we saw in Chapter 7, fiscal contractions are even more contractionary under a peg than under a float. Such policies are politically costly, and hence the peg may not be fully credible. As we saw in Chapter 9, foreign exchange traders often have doubts about the resolve of the authorities to stick with contractionary policies, and these doubts can increase the risk of self-fulfilling exchange rate crises, as happened in 1992. The same costs and risks now weigh on current Eurozone applicants seeking to pass these tests.

Second, the fiscal rules are seen as inflexible and arbitrary. The numerical targets have little justification: why 3% for the deficit and not 4%? Why 60% and not 70% for the debt level? As for flexibility, the rules in particular pay no attention to the stage of the business cycle in a particular applicant country. A country in a recession may have a very large deficit even if on average the country has a government budget that is pretty balanced across the whole business cycle. In other words, the well-established arguments for the prudent use of countercyclical fiscal policy are totally ignored by the Maastricht criteria. This is an ongoing problem, as we shall see in a moment.

Third, whatever good might result from the painful convergence process, it might be only fleeting. For example, the Greek or French governments of the 1990s may have subjected themselves to budgetary discipline and monetary conservatism. Have their preferences really changed or did they just go along with the rules (or pretend to) merely as a way to get in? The same question applies to current Eurozone applicants.

The problems just noted do not disappear once countries are in the Eurozone. Countries continue to have their own fiscal policies as members of the Eurozone; and they all gain a share of influence on ECB policy through the governance structure of the central bank. Countries' incentives are different once the carrot of EMU membership has been eaten.

Sticking to the Rules

If "in" countries desire more monetary and fiscal flexibility than the rules allow, and being "in" means they no longer risk the punishment of being excluded from the Eurozone, then a skeptic would have to expect more severe budgetary problems and more lobbying for loose monetary policy to appear once countries had entered the Eurozone.

On this point, as we shall see, the skeptics were to some extent proved right, but the problems they identified were not entirely ignored in the Eurozone's design. On the monetary side, success (low and stable Eurozone inflation) would rest upon the design of the ECB as an institution that could withstand political pressure and act with independence to deliver low inflation while ignoring pleas from member governments. In that respect, we have already noted the formidable efforts to make the ECB as independent as possible. On the fiscal side, however, success (in the shape of adherence to the budgetary rules) would rest on the mechanisms established to enforce the Maastricht fiscal criteria. This did not turn out quite so well.

The Stability and Growth Pact Within a few years of the Maastricht Treaty, the EU suspected that greater powers of monitoring and enforcement would be needed. Thus, in 1997 at Amsterdam, the EU adopted the **Stability and Growth Pact (SGP),** which the EU website has described as "the concrete EU answer to concerns on the continuation of budgetary discipline in Economic and Monetary Union." In the end, this provided no answer whatsoever and even before the ink was dry, naysayers were unkind enough to term it the "stupidity pact."

Throwing another acronym into the mix, the SGP was aimed at enforcing the 3% deficit rule and proposed the following to keep states in line: a "budgetary surveillance" process that would check on what member states were doing; a requirement to submit economic data and policy statements as part of a periodic review of "stability and convergence programs"; an "early warning mechanism" to detect any "slippage"; a "political commitment" that "ensures that effective peer pressure is exerted on a Member State failing to live up to its commitments"; and an "excessive deficits procedure" with "dissuasive elements" in the event of failure to require "immediate corrective action and, if necessary, allow for the imposition of sanctions."[15]

The shortcomings of the SGP, which became clear over time, were as follows:

■ Surveillance failed because member states concealed the truth about their fiscal problems. Some hired private-sector accounting firms to

---

[15] European Commission, Directorate General for Economic and Financial Affairs, "The Stability and Growth Pact." Published online. For a copy of this document see http://www.eubusiness.com/Finance/eustability-growth-pact/.

make their deficits look smaller via accounting tricks (a suspiciously common deficit figure was 2.9%). In the case of Greece, the government simply falsified deficit figures for the purpose of gaining admission to the euro in 2001 and owned up once they were in.

■ Punishment was weak, so even when "excessive deficits" were detected, not much was done about it. Peer pressure was ineffective, perhaps because so many of the governments were guilty of breaking the pact that very few had a leg to stand on. Corrective action was rare and states "did their best," which was often not very much. Formal SGP disciplining processes often started but never resulted in actual sanctions because heads of government in Council proved very forgiving of each other and unwilling to dispense punishments.

■ Deficit limits rule out the use of active stabilization policy, but they also shut down the "automatic stabilizer" functions of fiscal policy. Recessions automatically lower government revenues and raise spending, and the resulting deficits help boost aggregate demand and offset the recession. This makes deficit limits tough to swallow, even if monetary policy autonomy is kept as a stabilization tool. In a monetary union, where states have also relinquished monetary policy to the ECB, the pain of hard fiscal rules is likely to be intolerable.

■ Once countries joined the euro, the main "carrot" enticing them to follow the SGP's budget rules (or to pretend to follow them) disappeared. Hence, surveillance, punishment, and commitment all quite predictably weakened once the euro was up and running.

These failures of the SGP came to light only gradually, but by 2003 the pact was in ruins, once it became clear that France and (ironically) Germany would be in breach of the pact and that no serious action would be taken against them. Fiscal problems in the Eurozone have only gotten worse, and other aspects of coordination and commitment have been made more difficult.

4 Conclusions: Assessing the Euro

The euro project must be understood at least as much in political terms as in economic terms. We have seen how the OCA criteria can be used to examine the logic of currency unions, but in the case of the EU these are not the whole story: Europe does not appear to satisfy the narrow definition of an optimum currency area. In contrast, some of the most important criteria for the survival of the euro may relate to the non-OCA criteria that were included in the Maastricht Treaty. So how well can the euro hold up in the future? At the risk of caricature, we will contrast the views at the extremes of the debate.

Euro-Optimists For true optimists, the euro is already something of a success: it has functioned in a perfectly adequate way for more than five years and can be expected to become only more successful as time goes by. More countries are lining up to join the Eurozone. Even if there are costs in the short run, the argument goes, in the long run the benefits will become clear.

Optimists tend to stress that the OCA criteria might be self-fulfilling. In the long run, they think the euro will create more trade in the Eurozone. It may also create more labor and capital mobility. They downplay the risk that shocks will become more asymmetric, or at least think this will be outweighed by greater market integration. This will enhance the Eurozone's claim to be an OCA. Since the euro is only a few years old, data are scarce, and these claims can be neither proved nor refuted decisively at present. However, the little evidence we have suggests that although labor mobility has not changed much, goods and services trade in the Eurozone is rising (even if no faster than outside) and that capital market integration has perhaps improved even more dramatically, as measured by the increase in cross-border asset trade and FDI flows in the Eurozone.[16]

Optimists also tend to believe that the ECB will prove to be a strong, credible, independent central bank that can resist political interference. On paper, the ECB certainly has such characteristics, with a very high degree of independence compared with other central banks. Again, the costs of a common currency may be large in the short run, but as long as the ECB can deliver on its low-inflation target, the optimists reckon it will, in the end, command the respect of the peoples and politicians of the Eurozone.

At a global level, optimists note that the euro is increasingly becoming a reserve currency for foreign central banks, a vehicle currency for trade, and is now the dominant currency used in international bond markets. These developments show the market's confidence in the currency and also augur well for the future, since trade and financing costs may be expected to fall as the euro becomes more widely used around the globe.

Finally, like the "father" of the European Union, Jean Monnet, the optimists think that the adoption of the euro, like entry to the EU itself, means "no going back": there is simply no imaginable political future for Europe apart from union. Neither the euro nor the EU has exit mechanisms. Perhaps such an idea was inconceivable to the institutional designers. For true believers, the EU project ultimately rests on a deep belief in the political logic of the process and in a presumed common destiny for the peoples of Europe.

Euro-Pessimists For true pessimists, the preceding arguments are not convincing. Market integration will not radically change because the impact of the euro on (already-high) intra-EU trade levels will be small. Because cultural and linguistic barriers will persist, labor migration will be limited and held back even more by inflexible labor market institutions in most countries. In all markets, regulatory and other frictions will remain.

Moreover, there is resistance to further economic integration. In 2005 an EU directive to liberalize services proved unpopular in many countries and contributed to the failure of referenda on the proposed EU Constitutional

---

[16] For an excellent recent survey see Philip R. Lane, 2006, "The Real Effects of European Monetary Union," *Journal of Economic Perspectives,* 20(4), 47–66.

Treaty in France and the Netherlands. In many countries, the implications of a single market in all dimensions (goods, services, labor, capital) are only now being dimly understood. Governments and the Commission disagree about how far the process should go.

If integration stops for lack of political support, a key economic rationale for the euro unravels. If political support for the EU stalls, then the political logic is weakened. If some countries press ahead with deeper federalism while others stand aside, the variable geometry of the EU may be stretched so much as to undermine any sense of a common destiny among all EU nations.

On the other key OCA criterion, pessimists note that there is wide divergence in growth rates and inflation rates in the countries of the Eurozone (Figure 10-8). Low-growth, low-inflation countries tend to want looser monetary policy. High-growth, high-inflation countries tend to want tighter monetary policy. If different countries desire very different policies from the ECB, tensions may rise and governments may lose respect for the ECB's independence.

The euro could also be threatened by fiscal problems. The rules say governments cannot lobby the ECB for low interest rates or high inflation to make their debt payments lower, or to reduce the real value of their debts. But as history has typically shown, governments tend to trump central banks and will

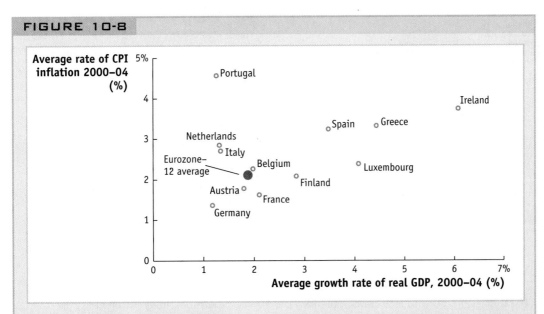

FIGURE 10-8

Eurozone Divergence, 2000–2004 The countries of the Eurozone have experienced very different growth and inflation rates. High-growth and high-inflation countries (top right on this chart) would typically consider adopting tighter monetary policy. Low-growth and low-inflation countries (bottom left on this chart) would typically consider adopting looser monetary policy. In the Eurozone, the ECB sets a common interest rate in all countries, so one size has to fit all.

Source: European Economy, Statistical Annex, Autumn 2005.

push them around if times get tough. Pessimists note that the Maastricht fiscal rules have evaporated and the Stability and Growth Pact has been emptied of meaning (Figure 10-9). If some states lobby for loose money, more fiscally prudent nations will object, and the resulting fight will cause uncertainty and undermine the credibility of the euro.

At worst, the tensions could be so great as to cause the breakup of the Eurozone into blocs or the reintroduction of the old national currencies. The ECB is continually voicing its concerns in this area but with seemingly little effect on member states' behavior. For example, in November 2005 the ECB asserted its power to deny Eurozone banks the right to use government bonds as collateral if those bonds' credit ratings fall too low; the power has yet to be put to the test.

Summary On the upside, the political dimension of the EU might yet carry the day in the long run, despite current setbacks; in the medium run, the OCA criteria might turn out better than one might think; and even if they don't in

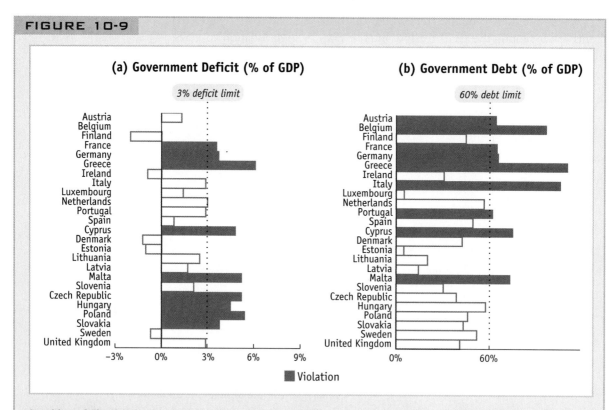

FIGURE 10-9

(a) Government Deficit (% of GDP)

(b) Government Debt (% of GDP)

Breaking of Fiscal Rules in 2005 The fiscal convergence criteria laid down by the Maastricht Treaty and affirmed by the Stability and Growth Pact have been widely ignored. Eurozone and ERM members should obey both rules, and all EU countries should obey the deficit rule. In panel (a), data for the EU-25 of 2005 show that 9 EU countries (3 Eurozone members and 2 ERM members) were violating the deficit rule. In panel (b), 9 countries (7 Eurozone members and 2 ERM members) were violating the debt rule. Overall, 13 EU countries (7 Eurozone members and 2 ERM members) were violating at least one rule.

Note: The deficit limit applies to all EU countries, not just Eurozone and ERM members.

Source: European Commission press releases.

the short run, the Eurozone can still survive and function as it does now, a workable albeit economically costly currency union.

On the downside, EU enlargement undercuts the OCA logic in the short run and could make the ECB's governance more cumbersome and make resolution of conflicts more difficult; in the long run, as the member states of the Eurozone encounter likely fiscal problems, there is a significant risk of a clash between fiscal goals of the governments and the monetary goals of the ECB.

What do the people think? The results of successive Eurobarometer polls indicate that only about 50%–60% of the citizens of the Eurozone think the euro has been beneficial. In some countries that figure is higher, in some lower. The euro remains an experiment—its arrival does not mark the end point of European monetary history, and its long-run fate is not entirely certain (see **Headlines: Whither the Euro?**).

A Romanian soldier raises the European Union flag in Bucharest, January 1, 2007.

HEADLINES

Whither the Euro?

In 2006, the Economist *newspaper discussed the state of the euro project.*

A Solid Currency, Maybe, But a Shame about the Economic Performance Next month, the European Union's innermost circle may embark on a new expansion, if tiny Slovenia gets the go-ahead to join the euro, in January 2007 [Author's note: it did]. At the same time, an even smaller place, Lithuania, is likely to be rebuffed [Author's note: it was], and told firmly that it is not ready for the single currency.

Elsewhere the euro is making its mark in a rather different way. Were Italy not a member, there would surely have been a run on the lira by now, given the troubles facing Romano Prodi's would-be centre-left coalition. And there actually has been a run on Iceland's currency—to the extent that some Icelanders have wondered whether they might perhaps be allowed to adopt the euro, please, to prevent further speculative attacks, even though Iceland is not a member of the EU.

In short, as it prepares to expand again, the euro seems to be working more or less as its founders intended. It has brought stability. . . . Countries are

queuing up to join (all EU countries bar Britain and Denmark, which have specially negotiated opt-outs, are supposed to become members one day). And the tests of readiness to enter the euro remain as they were agreed at Maastricht in 1991: low inflation, budgetary austerity and exchange-rate stability (the so-called "convergence criteria").

The reality is rather different. The euro is working, in that it is stable, has established itself as a currency and provides a monetary anchor. But it is not working as it was meant to. When it was dreamt up, the euro was supposed to bring about faster economic convergence. A single currency was the logical completion of the single market, it was said, and would encourage more integration. The end of exchange-rate risk would boost investment and bring economic cycles into line. The reduction in transaction costs would make economies more efficient, boosting growth.

Moreover, a single currency would, it was claimed, foster policy convergence. Because countries could no longer deval-

ue, they would be forced to undergo the hard grind of reform. Since reform would push all countries in a similar direction, the euro would produce convergence. True believers went further, arguing that currency union would, ultimately, bring about political union. Indeed, for them, that was the point. But even short of this, a single currency would still pull economies together. As a result, the perils of a one-size-fits-all monetary policy would not be so worrisome: eventually, one size would, indeed, fit all.

Seven years on, there has been convergence of a kind. The euro area's long-term interest rates are broadly the same: they have converged on Germany's. Some countries, such as Ireland and Spain, have played economic catch-up (convergence in income and wealth), though this may have little to do with the euro as such. Arguably, fiscal policy has converged too. That may sound odd when 13 of the 25 EU countries are being hauled over the coals for running "excessive" budget deficits. Yet euro governments have shown greater fiscal

Continued on next page.

restraint than their peers in America or Britain in the past few years.

There has, however, been less convergence of economic performance. Ireland has grown by an average of 6% a year since 1999, Germany by barely 1%. Spain's growth has been twice Portugal's. As a recent paper[*] from Bruegel, a think-tank in Brussels, points out, such divergences are no greater than among American states, but in America they usually result from states being at different points in the economic cycle; in Europe, growth differentials seem to be more persistent. There are few signs that economic cycles have become more closely aligned.

Even when countries have experienced similar pressures (loss of competitiveness, say), they have reacted differently. Ireland and Italy have both lost competitiveness (by running above-average inflation). But Irish exports have boomed, whereas Italy's have stagnated. Germany and France have both gained competitiveness (having below-average inflation), but French exports have been weak while Germany has regained its position as the world's biggest exporter of goods.

As a result, the risk of the euro's one-size-fits-all policy (that interest rates will be too loose for the hares, too tight for the tortoises) has been unpleasantly realised. And as for the broader ambitions for the euro, European countries have not noticeably converged upon economic reform, still less political union: witness the rejection of the draft EU constitution last year by French and Dutch voters.

In Search of Reality The euro, in short, has provided currency stability but has done little to promote growth, jobs or reform. That is a long way from branding the currency a complete failure. But it is clear that what matters most is the "real" side of the economy (growth, jobs, markets), not the nominal indicators of stability (inflation, budget deficits) that are used to decide both whether countries are ready to join, and how they are doing once they are in.

A key lesson is that flexible economies, such as Ireland's and Britain's, thrive, whether in or out of the euro. Inflexible ones can claw back lost competitiveness even inside the euro—but this takes a long time, and can come at a high price because they must keep growth in unit labour costs below average for years. Germany has done this. Italy and Portugal now face the same challenge, but without the German tradition of belt-tightening.

For countries now anxious to join the single currency, however, economic considerations hardly matter. They wanted to join the EU to show they were normal countries and now want to join the euro to show they are good Europeans. But being a good European can come at a cost—and it is not clear that all of the aspirants either understand this or are ready to pay.

[*]"The euro: only for the agile." By Alan Ahearne and Jean Pisani-Ferry.
Source: Excerpted from "Charlemagne: Euro Blues," Economist, April 29, 2006.

KEY POINTS

1. A currency union occurs when two or more sovereign nations share a common currency. Sometimes these arrangements are unilateral, such as when a country like Ecuador adopts the U.S. dollar. But some are multilateral, the most prominent example being the Eurozone.

2. The euro is (as of 2007) the currency of 13 European Union (EU) countries, and they manage it collectively by a common monetary authority, the European Central Bank (ECB). Most of the EU's 27 countries are expected to join the euro eventually.

3. According to the theory of optimum currency areas (OCAs), regions should employ a common currency only if they are well integrated and face fairly similar (symmetric) economic shocks. In that case, efficiency gains from trade should be large, and the costs of forgone monetary autonomy small.

4. A currency union is usually a more irreversible and costly step than simply fixing the exchange rate. The OCA threshold is therefore higher than the threshold for a fixed exchange rate (discussed in Chapter 8).

5. Additional economic factors can strengthen the case for an OCA. If regions have high labor mobility or large fiscal transfers, these mechanisms may make the costs of a currency union smaller for any given asymmetric shock. In addition, countries with a poor nominal anchor may be eager to join a currency union with a country with a better reputation for inflation performance.

6. Political considerations can drive monetary unions, as when countries feel they have a common destiny and wish to treat monetary union as part of a broader goal of political union.

7. The Eurozone has fairly high trade integration, although not quite as high as that of the United States. The Eurozone might or might not pass this OCA test.

8. The Eurozone has fairly symmetric shocks for most countries. The Eurozone probably does pass this OCA test.

9. The Eurozone has very low labor mobility between countries. The Eurozone almost certainly fails this OCA test.

10. The OCA criteria may fail ex ante, but they may be self-fulfilling: thanks to the common currency, after some years, trade and labor mobility may increase, tipping the balance in favor of an OCA ex post. But increasing specialization due to trade may cause more asymmetric shocks, which would push in the opposite direction.

11. The lack of compelling economic arguments for the euro leads us to study its historical and political origins. The EU must be understood as a political project, and the euro is an important part of the conception of the EU. Although many EU citizens have trust in this project, polls show it is only a bare majority.

12. The European Central Bank plays the pivotal role in securing the future of the euro. If it can deliver low inflation and economic stability comparable to the German central bank, after which it was designed, the euro is more likely to succeed as a currency in the EU and as a global currency. So far so good, but in many respects the ECB is untested—there has been no major monetary or fiscal crisis up to 2007.

13. Attempts to exert political influence on the ECB continue, and the Council of Ministers has often proved weak at punishing countries that break the rules of the Eurozone (the Maastricht criteria and the Stability and Growth Pact).

KEY TERMS

currency union, p. 437

Eurozone, p. 437

euro, p. 438

European Union (EU), p. 438

Maastricht Treaty, p. 438

optimum currency area (OCA), p. 440

inflation bias, p. 445

Marshall Plan, p. 456

Treaty of Rome, p. 456

Exchange Rate Mechanism (ERM), p. 457

Economic and Monetary Union (EMU), p. 458

ERM crisis, p. 459

European Central Bank (ECB), p. 459

convergence criteria, p. 466

Stability and Growth Pact (SGP), p. 470

PROBLEMS

1. One could view the United States as a currency union of 50 states. Compare and contrast the Eurozone and the United States in terms of the optimum currency area (OCA) criteria.

2. After German reunification and the disintegration of communist rule in Eastern Europe, several countries sought to join the European Union (EU) and later the Economic and Monetary Union (EMU). Why do you believe these countries were eager to integrate with Western Europe? Do you think policy makers in these countries believe that OCA criteria are self-fulfilling? Explain.

3. The Maastricht Treaty places strict requirements on government budgets and national debt. Why do you think the Maastricht Treaty called for fiscal discipline? If it is the central bank that is responsible for maintaining the fixed exchange rate, then why does fiscal discipline matter? How might this affect the gains/losses for joining a currency union?

4. The following figure shows hypothetical OCA criteria with the Eurozone for selected

countries *based solely on economic criteria*—that is, without reference to other political considerations. Refer to the diagram in responding to the questions that follow.

Symmetry-Integration Diagram

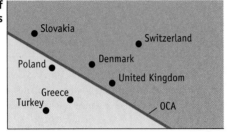

a. Which of the countries satisfies the OCA criteria for joining a monetary union?

b. Compare Poland and the United Kingdom in terms of the OCA criteria regarding *market integration* with the Eurozone. Discuss one possible source of differences in integration (with the EU) in the two countries.

c. Compare Poland and the United Kingdom in terms of the OCA criteria regarding *symmetric versus asymmetric shocks* (relative to the Eurozone). Discuss one possible source of differences in symmetry (with the EU) in the two countries.

d. Suppose that policy makers in both Poland and the United Kingdom care only about being able to use policy in response to shocks. Which is more likely to seek membership in the EMU and why?

e. What did the ERM crises reveal about the preferences of the United Kingdom? Why has the United Kingdom sought membership only in the EU without seeking membership in the Eurozone? Consider other costs and benefits not in the diagram, both economic and political.

f. What did membership of the Eurozone reveal about the preferences of Greece? Consider other costs and benefits not in the diagram, both economic and political.

5. Congress established the Federal Reserve System in 1914. Up to this point, the United States did not have a national currency; Federal Reserve notes are still the paper currency in circulation today. Earlier attempts at establishing a central bank were opposed on the grounds that a central bank would give the federal government monopoly over money. This was a reflection of the historic debate between maintaining states' rights versus establishing a strong centralized authority in the United States. That is, the creation of the Fed and a national currency would mean that states would no longer have the authority to control the money supply on a regional level. Discuss the debate between states' rights versus centralized authority in the context of the Economic and Monetary Union and the European Central Bank.

6. In 2002 there were reports that a group of six Gulf countries (Bahrain, Kuwait, Oman, Qatar, Saudi Arabia, and United Arab Emirates) were considering the introduction of a single currency. Currently, these countries use currencies that are effectively pegged to the U.S. dollar. These countries rely heavily on oil exports to the rest of the world, and political leaders in these countries are concerned about diversifying trade. Based on this information, discuss the OCA criteria for this group of countries. What are the greatest potential benefits? What are the potential costs?

7. Before taking office as the new Federal Reserve chairman, Ben Bernanke advocated for the adoption of an inflation target to promote price stability in the United States. Compare and contrast the Fed and European Central Bank in terms of their commitment to price stability and economic stability. Which central bank has more independence to pursue price stability as a primary objective? Explain.

8. Why do countries with less independent central banks tend to have higher inflation rates? Is it possible for the central bank to increase output and reduce unemployment in the long run? In the long run, is the German model a good one? Explain why or why not.

9. Compare the Maastricht Treaty convergence criteria with the OCA criteria. How are these convergence criteria related to the potential benefits and costs associated with joining a currency union? If you were a policy maker in a country seeking to join the EMU, which criterion would you eliminate and why?

Topics in International Macroeconomics

Economics is a science of thinking in terms of models joined to the art of choosing models which are relevant to the contemporary world.

John Maynard Keynes, 1938

Like other fields of economics, international macroeconomics is evolving continually. New empirical analyses are constantly appearing, deepening our understanding and bringing attention to new phenomena. New theoretical models are always being developed, to better explain long-standing puzzles or to confront new ones. The fast-changing global economic environment of recent years has pushed research forward faster than ever.

In the four stand-alone sections of this final chapter, we examine several important topics that have occupied the minds of researchers for many years and that remain at the cutting edge. In these "minichapters"—which can be read independently—we explore new issues as well as important extensions to the core models presented earlier in the book:

■ We ask whether purchasing power parity really works as a long-run theory of exchange rates. Evidence shows that a better theory has to explain why price levels are higher in richer countries. We develop such a theory and show how it can be applied to improve exchange rate forecasts.

■ We ask whether uncovered interest parity really works as a short-run theory of exchange rates. We show that forex traders often make massive profits (and also losses) and that such profits may even have a predictable component. If arbitrage operated to support uncovered interest parity in an efficient market, such profits ought to be eliminated. One explanation might be that there are limits to arbitrage, such as an aversion to the extreme riskiness of profits in the forex market.

■ We study more closely the recent phenomenon of global imbalances. We see how shifts in saving and investment can influence the world real interest rate and change the pattern of current account deficits and surpluses in different regions. We then look at what such patterns imply for the long run, and, in particular, how they will adjust to satisfy each country's long-run budget constraint.

■ We study the problem of defaults by governments on their debt. Some of the facts to be explained are why any lenders lend given the risk of default, why borrowers choose to default when they do, and what price they pay for defaulting. We develop a model in which adverse economic shocks (low output) make countries more likely to default. The bigger such shocks are, the more the countries default, and the less willing lenders are to lend, unless they receive a higher interest rate. The model fits various facts: poorer countries have more volatile output, are charged higher interest rates, and default more often even at lower levels of debt, and lenders don't make much profit.

1 Exchange Rates in the Long Run: Deviations from Purchasing Power Parity

According to the most recent data from the World Bank, in 2005 gross national income per capita in the United States was $43,560, but by converting incomes using the exchange rate, it was found that gross national income per capita in China was only $1,740, just 4% of the U.S. level. Were the Chinese really that poor in terms of material living standards? No.

When the calculations were repeated by comparing dollar incomes with the dollar prices of baskets of consumer goods, Chinese gross national income per capita was found to be about $7,000 in terms of U.S. consumer goods, so living standards were now seen to be four times as high, at 16% of the U.S. level. The reason: in dollar terms, most goods cost a lot less in China than in the United States. The dollar price level in China was lower than in the United States. The implication: PPP does not hold, and the real exchange rate is a long way from 1.

These adjustments have many implications: for example, they affect calculations of living standards, poverty, allocations of aid, and projections of growth, consumption, demographics, pollution, and so on. So we need to understand these deviations from PPP for many reasons, including the need to refine our theory of exchange rates. In Chapter 3, we showed that the expected future exchange rate could be predicted using the monetary approach to exchange rates, *if* purchasing power parity holds, that is, if baskets of goods sell for the same price in all locations. This provided a workable model of real exchange rates, but it was far from perfect. In this section, we address a major deficiency in PPP theory: its assumption that all goods are costlessly tradable.

Limits to Arbitrage

One way to set up a more realistic economic model would be to introduce costs of trading, which is now an important area of research in international economics.

To gain familiarity with trade costs and to see how they matter, let's assume that the cost of trading the good is equal to some fraction of the unit cost of the good at its source. For example, suppose there is one good, and it sells for $P = \$100$ in Home. It costs $10 to ship the good from Home to another country, Foreign. The **trade cost** is $c = 0.1 = 10\%$. The cost of the good on arrival in Foreign, including the trade cost, would be $P \times (1 + c) = \$110$.

How do trade costs affect arbitrage? If you were considering trying to make an arbitrage profit by shipping a $100 widget from Home to Foreign, then you wouldn't even think of doing it unless the Foreign price converted into dollars EP^* was at least $110 (where E is Home's exchange rate, and P^* is the Foreign price in Foreign currency). Otherwise, you make a loss once the trading costs are taken into account. Similarly, going from Foreign to Home, you wouldn't ship goods unless the Home price P was at least 10% above the foreign price EP^*.

More formally, the ratio of the prices in the two locations can be written in proportional terms as $q = EP^*/P$. As we learned in Chapter 3, for any basket of goods, q is also known as the *real exchange rate* of the home country. Thus, if $P = \$100$ and $EP^* = \$110$, then this relative price ratio would be $(110/100) = 1.1$.

As we have just seen, arbitrage from Home to Foreign is profitable only if the Foreign price is higher than the Home price adjusted for the trade cost, which requires $q = EP^*/P > 1 + c$. Conversely, arbitrage the other way is profitable only if the Home price is sufficiently higher than the Foreign price, with $1/q = P/(EP^*) > 1 + c$.

Thus, if q is below $1 + c$, there will be no arbitrage from Home to Foreign. And if q is above $1/(1 + c)$, there will be no arbitrage from Foreign to Home. So we have shown that, taking trade costs into account, the *no arbitrage condition* for market equilibrium is

$$\frac{1}{1 + c} \le \underbrace{\frac{EP^*}{P}}_{\substack{\text{Real exchange rate} \\ q}} \le 1 + c.$$

Let's look at what this condition implies for various levels of trading costs.

- *Zero costs.* With $c = 0$, the no arbitrage equilibrium condition reduces to an equality because both left- and right-hand sides equal 1, implying that $q = 1$. This equality is the condition for the law of one price (LOOP), which we expect to hold when arbitrage is costless. An illustration is shown in Figure 11-1, panel (a), which plots the hypothetical relative price q over time for Home and Foreign.

- *Low costs.* Suppose c is low, say, 10%, as in our example. If the price difference between source and destination is less than 10%, then

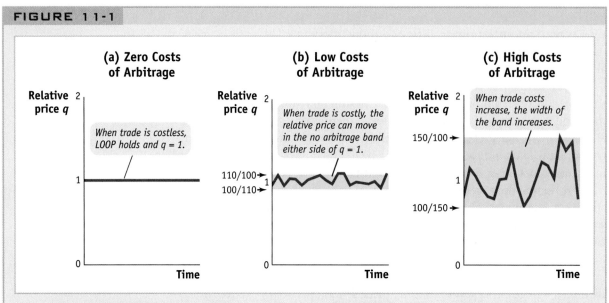

FIGURE 11-1

(a) Zero Costs of Arbitrage

Relative price *q*

When trade is costless, LOOP holds and q = 1.

(b) Low Costs of Arbitrage

Relative price *q*

When trade is costly, the relative price can move in the no arbitrage band either side of q = 1.

110/100
100/110

(c) High Costs of Arbitrage

Relative price *q*

When trade costs increase, the width of the band increases.

150/100

100/150

Time

No Arbitrage Bands The hypothetical relative price ratio *q* is shown in three cases. In panel (a), trade costs are zero, so the law of one price (LOOP) holds and *q* has to equal 1. In panel (b), trade costs are small, say 10%, so the prices in the two locations can differ. The high price can exceed the low price by up to 10%, so *q* can range between 100/110 (0.91) and 110/100 (1.1). In panel (c), trade costs are high, say 50%, so the high price may exceed the low price by up to 50%, so *q* can range between 150/100 and 100/150. Thus, as costs of arbitrage increase, deviations from simple LOOP and PPP become larger, and these "laws" become less useful.

there is no arbitrage. Hence, *q* is free to wander in what is called a **no-arbitrage band** between $1/(1 + c) = (100/110)$ and $1 + c = (110/100)$. For values of *q* between 0.91 and 1.1, then, the market is considered to be in equilibrium. This is shown in Figure 11-1, panel (b). Small deviations from LOOP are possible, but LOOP is still approximately true.

■ *High costs.* Suppose *c* is high, say 50%. If the price difference is less than 50%, there will be no arbitrage. There is a wider no–arbitrage band between $1/(1 + c) = (100/150)$ and $1 + c = (150/100)$ in which the market is in equilibrium and no arbitrage is possible. This is shown in Figure 11-1, panel (c). Deviations from LOOP are possible in the range 0.67 to 1.5, and LOOP no longer applies.

This analysis shows that when trade costs or *costs of arbitrage* are higher, arbitrage will not happen for small price deviations, and the possible deviations from LOOP become greater. If the prices of many goods deviated from LOOP, this would imply deviations from PPP. If costs are huge, then arbitrage is practically impossible and the prices of the same good in two locations need not bear any relation to one another and can be very far apart. Under such conditions, goods are almost always nontraded, and LOOP and PPP will not apply.

Trade Costs in Practice These results show that when evaluating LOOP for one good or PPP for a basket of goods, we must take into account trade costs and consider how they affect deviations from price equality. Recent empirical research suggests that trade costs are affected by economic policies, as well as by characteristics of goods and their markets.[1]

An important part of trade costs is costs of transportation. For U.S. imports, for example, estimated freight rates vary from 1% of the good's price (for transport equipment) to 27% (for fertilizer). In many countries with worse transport infrastructure, these costs can be much higher: one estimate suggests that the average landlocked country has transport costs 55% higher than the average coastal country.

A major factor that influences trade costs is a country's trade policy. Average tariffs of 5% (rich countries) or more than 10% (developing countries) constitute an additional cost, and such tariffs vary widely by type of good. Quotas (limits to import quantities) and regulatory barriers (such as health and environmental regulations) also add to trade costs, but the costs they add are difficult to compute. In addition to transport and policy costs, economists have found statistical evidence of other causes of price gaps between markets, including distance between markets, crossing international borders, having different currencies, having floating exchange rates, and so on.

Following is one recent summary of international trade costs for advanced countries.[2] Like the variable c above, these costs are expressed as a percentage markup over the pre-shipment price of the goods. The data are averaged over all types of goods and are based on direct measurements and econometric estimates:[3]

	Transport costs, 21%	Freight costs, 11%
		Transit costs (time), 9%
Total international trade costs, 74%		
	Costs at the border, 44%	Tariffs and nontariff barriers, 8%
		Language barrier, 7%
		Different currencies, 14%
		Security and other costs, 9%

(Note that the subcosts are aggregated by compounding: e.g., a 21% markup on top of a 44% markup on a $1 good in the middle column results in a 74% markup in the left column, because $1.21 \times 1.44 \times \$1 = \$1.74$.)

These data show that trade costs are large—and typically they are even larger outside the advanced countries and create a very wide no-arbitrage band.

Trade costs matter.

NET WORK

Find the price of some of your favorite books or CDs on Amazon.com in the United States. Now find the price of the same items at Amazon.co.uk in the United Kingdom. Are there arbitrage opportunities? What if you ordered 100 or 1,000 items? What are the shipping costs as a fraction of the cost of your order? How would you determine the tariffs and duties you would need to pay? Are there any other barriers to trade?

---

[1] Charles Engel and John H. Rogers, 1996, "How Wide Is the Border?" *American Economic Review*, 86(5), December, 1112–1125; Maurice Obstfeld and Alan M. Taylor, 1997, "Nonlinear Aspects of Goods-Market Arbitrage and Adjustment: Heckscher's Commodity Points Revisited," *Journal of the Japanese and International Economies* 11(4), December, 441–479; David C. Parsley and Shang-Jin Wei, 2001, "Explaining the Border Effect: The Role of Exchange Rate Variability, Shipping Costs, and Geography," *Journal of International Economics* 55(1), October, 87–105; James E. Anderson and Eric van Wincoop, 2004, "Trade Costs," *Journal of Economic Literature*, 42(3), September, 691–751.

[2] From Prabir De, 2006, "Why Trade Costs Matter," Working Papers 706, Asia-Pacific Research and Training Network on Trade (ARTNeT), an initiative of UNESCAP and IDRC, Canada. Based on James E. Anderson and Eric van Wincoop, 2004, "Trade Costs," *Journal of Economic Literature*, 42(3), September, 691–751.

[3] Another important trade cost element is the *intranational* distribution and retail costs that are incurred as a good moves within a country from the sellers/importers to buyers/exporters. Intranational distribution costs may be around 35% to 50% of a good's cost in developed countries, but there is wide variation. In the United States, for example, distribution costs can be as low as 14% (electronic equipment) or as high as 216% (ladies' clothing).

It's Not Just the Burgers That Are Cheap

If real exchange rates can deviate from the PPP-implied value of 1, the next question to ask is, how do they vary, and why? One place to find a clue is in the pattern of deviations from PPP. For example, look at the *Economist* newspaper's Big Mac index by Googling "economist big mac index" (as featured in Chapter 3). If deviations from PPP were random, the deviations might easily be dismissed as an approximation error. However, deviations from PPP in the Big Mac index are not entirely random: burgers tend to be cheaper in poorer countries. In 2004, for example, the *Economist* found that, expressed in U.S. dollars, a Big Mac cost 21% less in Mexico and 53% less in Malaysia than it did in the United States.

It isn't too difficult to think of a reason for this finding—the presence of nontraded goods. A Big Mac is a combination of some traded goods (such as flour, beef, and special sauce) and some nontraded goods (such as cooks and cleaners). The nontraded goods contain a strong element of local labor input, so they tend to cost less in a poor country. The evidence in Figure 11-2, panel (a), supports this logic. This scatter plot shows that the dollar price of the Big Mac is strongly correlated with the local hourly wage in dollars.

Why stop here? The argument shouldn't apply only to burgers, so in 2004 the *Economist* did a parallel experiment and compared the prices of another globally uniform and omnipresent consumer product: the Starbucks tall latte. Similar patterns emerged: in dollar terms, the latte cost 15% less in Mexico and 25% less in Malaysia than the corresponding frothy beverage in the United States.

FIGURE 11-2

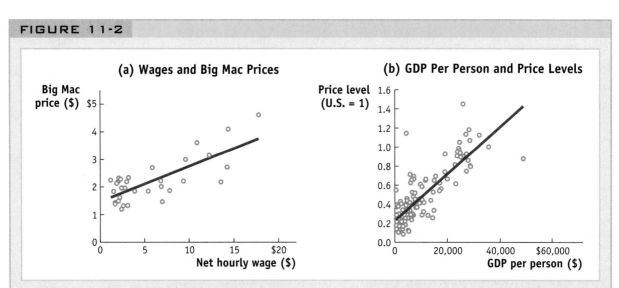

Price Levels in Rich and Poor Countries Panel (a) shows that richer countries (measured by higher wages) tend to have higher Big Mac prices (measured in a common currency). Panel (b) shows that richer countries (measured by higher GDP per person) tend to have higher overall price levels (measured in a common currency).

Source: Michael R. Pakko and Patricia S. Pollard, 2003, "Burgernomics: A Big Mac™ Guide to Purchasing Power Parity," Review, Federal Reserve Bank of St. Louis, November, 9–28.

The argument applies to most goods that are included in calculations of national price levels. Almost all goods have some local, nontraded component—some local value added or some local retail and distribution costs. Thus, the general price level might be expected to vary systematically in the same way, and it does. Figure 11-2, panel (b), shows that a country's price level is strongly correlated with the level of GDP per person. Rich countries have higher price levels; their baskets cost more. In other words, the real exchange rate $q = EP^*/P$ is *not* equal to 1 for all countries—PPP does not hold, even in the long run. The remainder of this section explores this pattern using economic theory and considers what effect the lack of PPP has on the exchange rate models and predictions we derived earlier in the book. ■

Latte disparity: Starbucks in the Forbidden City, Beijing.

Nontraded Goods and the Balassa-Samuelson Model

Trade costs have major implications for international macroeconomics. In fact, we can gain a great deal of insight by simply expanding our analysis from one good that is traded to two goods—one traded and one not traded. In this section, we explore a model of an economy with traded and nontraded goods that can explain price level differences and deviations from PPP.

We assume there are two countries, Home and Foreign (values for Foreign are denoted by an asterisk). Thus, w denotes the Home wage and w^* denotes the Foreign wage, each measured in the respective currencies. The Home exchange rate is E (units of Home currency per unit of Foreign currency). There are two goods. Each good is produced competitively and labor is the only input needed. One is a nontraded, service good (say a haircut), denoted N, and its trade costs are effectively infinite. The other is a costlessly tradable good (say a DVD player), denoted T, that has no trade costs at all. Prices of goods will be denoted p and p^*, each measured in the respective currencies, with subscripts T and N to denote traded and nontraded goods.

A Simple Model The model can be solved in three steps, with assumptions as follows:

1. *The traded good has the same price in both countries.* This is true because trade costs are zero. For simplicity, we assume that the traded good has a price of 1 when measured in Home currency (say, dollars). This is its price in Home and Foreign, so

$$p_T = 1 \qquad Ep_T^* = 1.$$

In our example, the DVD player sells for $1 everywhere.

2. *Productivity in traded goods determines wages.* Suppose that one Home worker can make A units of the traded good (the DVD player) per hour. Then the worker's hourly wage w will be equal to $A because each unit of the good sells for $1 and competition means that the wage will equal the value of the output produced by each hour of

labor input. Similarly, if Foreign workers can make A^* units of the traded good per hour, their dollar wage Ew^* will be equal to $\$A^*$. Thus, wage levels in each country are equal to productivity levels:

$$w = A \qquad Ew^* = A^*.$$

In our example, if Home workers make ten $1 DVD players per hour, their hourly wage is $10 per hour. If Foreign workers make only five per hour, their hourly wage is $5.

3. *Wages determine the prices of nontraded goods.* Crucially, we assume that the level of productivity in nontraded goods is stagnant and the same everywhere and equal to 1. In our example, it always takes one hour to get a haircut in Home and Foreign, but with the wages given previously, this means the cost of a haircut will be equal to exactly one hour of labor. In general, the dollar price of the nontraded good in each country equals the wage, so $p_N = w$ and $Ep_N^* = Ew^*$. Because these wages are given by productivity (as we saw in the second step),

$$p_N = A \qquad Ep_N^* = A^*.$$

To continue our example, if the productivities are ten and five in Home and Foreign, we showed that the hourly wages must be $10 and $5, respectively, and so we now see that Home haircuts will cost $10 and Foreign haircuts $5.

The conclusion from these three assumptions? Countries with higher traded goods productivity will have relatively high wages and hence relatively high prices of nontraded goods. This means they will also have relatively higher overall price levels, depending on how large is the share of nontraded goods in the consumption basket. To see this, suppose the nontraded goods share of consumption is n (so the traded share is $1 - n$).

Changes in Productivity Now suppose Home productivity A increases, with the proportional change given by $\Delta A/A$. What happens to the Home price level? The price of traded goods is unchanged and stays at 1, but the price of nontraded goods is equal to A and it rises. Taking the weighted average, we can compute the (percentage) change in the Home price level as

$$\underbrace{\frac{\Delta P}{P}}_{\substack{\text{Change in}\\\text{Home price level}}} = \underbrace{(1-n)}_{\substack{\text{Share of}\\\text{traded goods}}} \times \underbrace{\left(\frac{\Delta p_T}{p_T}\right)}_{\substack{\text{Change in}\\\text{Home traded}\\\text{goods price}\\= \text{Zero}}} + \underbrace{n}_{\substack{\text{Share of}\\\text{nontraded goods}}} \times \underbrace{\left(\frac{\Delta p_N}{p_N}\right)}_{\substack{\text{Change in}\\\text{Home nontraded}\\\text{goods price}\\= \Delta A/A}} = n\frac{\Delta A}{A}.$$

By the same logic, the same is true for Foreign: a change in its dollar price level will result from a change in foreign productivity:

$$\underbrace{\frac{\Delta(EP^*)}{(EP^*)}}_{\substack{\text{Change in}\\\text{Foreign price level}}} = \underbrace{(1-n)}_{\substack{\text{Share of}\\\text{traded goods}}} \times \underbrace{\left(\frac{\Delta(Ep_T^*)}{(Ep_T^*)}\right)}_{\substack{\text{Change in}\\\text{Foreign traded}\\\text{goods price}\\= \text{Zero}}} + \underbrace{n}_{\substack{\text{Share of}\\\text{nontraded goods}}} \times \underbrace{\frac{\Delta(Ep_N^*)}{(Ep_N^*)}}_{\substack{\text{Change in}\\\text{Foreign nontraded}\\\text{goods price}\\= \Delta A^*/A^*}} = n\frac{\Delta A^*}{A^*}.$$

The last two equations are intuitive. For our example, a 1% rise in Home DVD player productivity A will raise Home wages w by 1%; therefore, Home haircut prices rise 1% and, because these haircuts have a weight $n < 1$ in the overall basket, the overall price index rises by n%.

By putting these last two results together, we can solve for the change in the real exchange rate q. Recall that q is equal to EP^*/P, so the percentage change in q is given by the percentage change in the numerator EP^* minus the percentage change in the denominator P. *But we have just computed those changes in the last two equations.* Hence, subtracting the first equation above from the second, the change in the real exchange rate is given by

$$(11\text{-}1) \qquad \underbrace{\frac{\Delta q}{q}}_{\substack{\text{Change in} \\ \text{real exchange rate} \\ \text{(Foreign price level } EP^* \\ \text{relative to Home } P\text{)}}} = \underbrace{n}_{\substack{\text{Share of} \\ \text{nontraded goods}}} \times \underbrace{\left(\frac{\Delta A^*}{A^*} - \frac{\Delta A}{A} \right)}_{\substack{\text{Change in} \\ \text{Foreign traded productivity} \\ \text{level relative to Home}}}.$$

Thus, relative productivities in the traded goods sector drive relative prices through their effects on wages and prices in the nontraded sector.

Generalizing The choice of DVD players and haircuts was for illustration. The model generalizes, and it embodies the logic of the cheap Big Mac story told earlier. A country has relatively low wages because it has relatively low labor productivity in traded goods. Low productivity and wages hold down the prices of nontraded goods and the nontraded part of the overall price level.

This equation describes an important relationship between productivity and the real exchange rate known as the **Balassa-Samuelson effect,** named for the economists Bela Balassa and Paul Samuelson:

When compared with other countries, a country experiencing an increase in productivity will see wages and incomes rise and will see its real exchange rate appreciate, meaning that its price level will rise.[4]

Overvaluations, Undervaluations, and Productivity Growth: Forecasting Implications for Real and Nominal Exchange Rates

The Balassa-Samuelson model makes a firm prediction that is supported strongly by evidence: price levels are higher in rich countries. The scatter plot in Figure 11-2, panel (b), showed this fact, and we zoom in and examine a part of it in Figure 11-3.

In such a figure, a point on the line of best fit is the predicted **equilibrium real exchange rate** $\tilde{q}$ of the Balassa-Samuelson model. Figure 11-3 plots

---

[4] Note that the traded goods sector is the *only* sector in which productivity can vary, so the only way for a country to get richer is by raising the productivity level in that sector, leading to higher wages and output. Also, in this model, GDP is equal to wages times the supply of labor. Thus, high wages are also synonymous with high output per person.

FIGURE 11-3

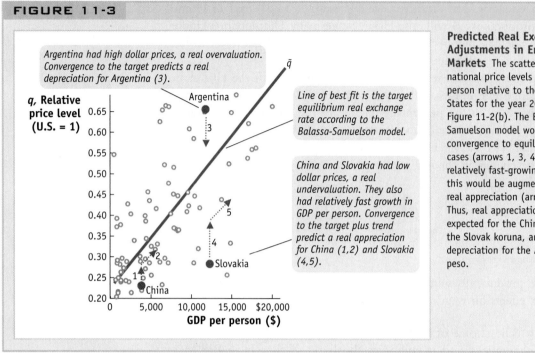

Argentina had high dollar prices, a real overvaluation. Convergence to the target predicts a real depreciation for Argentina (3).

Line of best fit is the target equilibrium real exchange rate according to the Balassa-Samuelson model.

China and Slovakia had low dollar prices, a real undervaluation. They also had relatively fast growth in GDP per person. Convergence to the target plus trend predict a real appreciation for China (1,2) and Slovakia (4,5).

Predicted Real Exchange Rate Adjustments in Emerging Markets The scatter plot shows national price levels and GDP per person relative to the United States for the year 2000, as in Figure 11-2(b). The Balassa-Samuelson model would predict convergence to equilibrium in all cases (arrows 1, 3, 4). In relatively fast-growing countries, this would be augmented by trend real appreciation (arrows 2 and 5). Thus, real appreciations were expected for the Chinese yuan and the Slovak koruna, and a real depreciation for the Argentine peso.

the U.S. real exchange rate against each foreign country—it shows foreign dollar prices EP^* relative to U.S. prices P. So an increase on the vertical axis is a rise in the relative price of foreign goods: it is a U.S. real depreciation, or a foreign real appreciation. The actual data do not sit precisely on the line of best fit. That is, the observed real exchange rate q may differ from its equilibrium value $\tilde{q}$.

As we saw in Chapter 3, the real exchange rate q can experience an overvaluation or undervaluation relative to its equilibrium value $\tilde{q}$. In Chapter 3, however, that equilibrium value was assumed to be 1, as predicted by PPP theory. But here the equilibrium $\tilde{q}$ isn't necessarily 1, given the Balassa-Samuelson theory.

Here, we judge deviations from equilibrium by looking at the distance from the equilibrium, that is, from the line of best fit. For example, if actual q is 10% above predicted $\tilde{q}$, then foreign prices are "too high": we would say that the U.S. real exchange rate is *undervalued* and the foreign real exchange rate *overvalued* relative to the equilibrium level $\tilde{q}$.

We can now begin to see how the Balassa-Samuelson theory can improve our theory of exchange rates in the long run and the forecasts that depend on such a theory.

Forecasting the Real Exchange Rate By comparing actual exchange rates with their predicted equilibrium values, forecasting the real exchange rate can be broken down into two problems: (i) how quickly q will return toward its equilibrium value $\tilde{q}$ and (ii) how quickly the equilibrium value $\tilde{q}$ will change over time as a result of productivity changes. In other words, q may be heading toward a target level $\tilde{q}$, but our model tells us that it might be a moving target that is moving along a trend. This means that real exchange rate prediction must be broken down into two parts.

For example, suppose q is currently 0.5 but the Balassa-Samuelson model says the equilibrium value of $\tilde{q}$ is 0.6. Clearly, q is predicted to rise by 0.1, or by 20%, to return to equilibrium (0.1/0.5 = 20%). How long will this take?

Convergence The first step is to figure out the speed of convergence to equilibrium. In Chapter 3, we discussed empirical estimates that real exchange rate deviations from equilibrium might decay slowly: *the consensus "half life" of deviations from PPP was reported to be five years.* For illustration, we adopt this *rule of thumb* estimate in the rest of this section. Thus, in our example, if half of the 20% gap is likely to be closed over five years, then over five years, q would rise by approximately 10% from 0.5 to 0.55, an increase of about 2% per year.

Trend The second step is to figure out whether $\tilde{q}$ is a moving target and forecast what its trend rate of growth will be. The Balassa-Samuelson theory shows how. In our example, suppose that the home country is expected to grow rapidly, with GDP per capita and wages rising; then $\tilde{q}$ could be much higher than 0.6 in five years' time. For example, if the nontraded share is 0.4, then Equation (11-1) says that a country's $\tilde{q}$ will rise 0.4% for every 1% of real GDP per capita growth in excess of the U.S. growth rate. So if a country is growing at, say, 8% per year faster than the United States, then $\tilde{q}$ should be rising by 0.4 × 8%, or 3.2% per year.

Convergence + Trend For this numerical example, we would conclude that the observed real exchange rate q is likely to increase at 2% per year toward its equilibrium and to increase at a further 3.2% a year due to the upward drift of that equilibrium, resulting in a predicted real appreciation for the foreign country at a rate of about 2 + 3.2 = 5.2% per year. (Note that adding growth rates in this way is only an approximation.)

Forecasting the Nominal Exchange Rate This kind of real exchange rate forecast can then help us predict nominal exchange rates, an essential component in the asset approach to exchange rates. How?

By definition, the real exchange rate is $q = EP^*/P$; by rearranging we find $E = qP/P^*$, and we have an expression for the nominal exchange rate. When PPP holds, this equation becomes $E = P/P^*$, as we saw in Chapter 3: under PPP, the real exchange rate q equals 1, and the exchange rate is equal to the ratio of national price levels.

When PPP *doesn't hold,* however, we have to worry about possible changes in q. Since $E = qP/P^*$, then taking rates of change we find

(11-2)
$$ \underbrace{\frac{\Delta E}{E}}_{\substack{\text{Rate of} \\ \text{nominal depreciation}}} = \underbrace{\frac{\Delta q}{q}}_{\substack{\text{Rate of} \\ \text{real depreciation}}} + \underbrace{\left(\frac{\Delta P}{P} - \frac{\Delta P^*}{P^*} \right)}_{\substack{\text{Inflation differential} \\ \text{(home minus foreign)}}}. $$

In Chapter 3, we saw a simpler version of this expression: PPP forced q to be constant and equal to 1, and the first term on the right vanished. We were left with a result, known as *relative PPP*, which said that changes in nominal exchange rates depended on inflation differentials alone. Taken literally, forecasters could then focus just on inflation forecasts.

When the Balassa-Samuelson effect is present, PPP fails, but we can still forecast future exchange rate changes using Equation (11-2). In using this equation, however, we not only have to forecast inflation, we have to forecast changes in the real exchange rate, too. Thus, in real-world financial markets, foreign exchange traders have to pay attention to many macroeconomic forecasts before forming an expectation about how E is likely to evolve over time.

Adjustment to Equilibrium Finally, we note that the Balassa-Samuelson model does not tell us how the real exchange rate will adjust. Suppose we have forecast a 1% real appreciation (−1% change in q). In Equation (11-2), this could imply either a 1% nominal appreciation (−1% on the left) or an extra 1% of home inflation over and above foreign inflation (+1% on the right), or some combination of the two.

Thus:

■ *If the model says there is currently a real undervaluation, either home goods prices have to rise or the value of the home currency has to rise—there is no other way to make home goods more expensive.*

■ *If the model says there is currently a real overvaluation, either home goods prices have to fall or the value of the home currency has to fall—there is no other way to make home goods less expensive.*

APPLICATION

Real Exchange Rates in Emerging Markets

To see how these ideas can be put to work to make forecasts of real and nominal exchange rates, we examine three cases in Figure 11-3 that were recently in the news. The data are for the year 2000, which allows us to look back to see how well the predictions of the model turned out.

China: Yuan Undervaluation? The Balassa-Samuelson model predictions: In 2000 the real exchange rate with China was $q = 0.231$, well below (0.088 below) the predicted equilibrium level of $\tilde{q} = 0.319$. The yuan was undervalued according to the model and would have to experience a 38% real appreciation (0.088/0.231) against the U.S. dollar to close the gap. Using our old rule of thumb, half of this gap or 19% would be eliminated in five years, implying an approximate 3.5% annual increase in q due to convergence.

However, in addition, China was a fast-growing economy at this time and its GDP per capita was growing about 6% per annum faster than U.S. GDP per capita. So the real exchange rate would have to appreciate *even more* due to Balassa-Samuelson effects. Figure 11-3 suggests that every 1% gain in GDP per capita is associated with an approximate 0.4% real appreciation (as expected if the nontraded share were 0.4). So a 6% differential growth rate per year (China minus United States) would imply a further $0.4 \times 6 = 2.4\%$ per year real appreciation in the yuan due to the trend of the moving target.[5]

What actually happened: Adding up both effects, the model predicts a real yuan appreciation of $3.5 + 2.4 = 5.9\%$ per year. As noted previously, this would imply either a nominal appreciation of the yuan against the dollar, or higher inflation in China. Inflation did start to rise in China, up to as much as 4.1% in 2004, although the data are not considered terribly accurate. This was not that much higher than U.S. inflation. Until mid-2005, China pegged the yuan to the dollar but then decided to switch to an unofficial crawling peg, allowing the yuan to appreciate gradually against the dollar, but very slowly. Many commentators saw this as a response to protectionist pressure in the United States, where cheap Chinese imports were raising hackles. But the Chinese had reasons of their own to let the yuan rise: to keep domestic inflation at a reasonable level.

Argentina: Was the Peso Overvalued? The Balassa-Samuelson model predictions: Figure 11-3 clearly shows that Argentina's currency was overvalued in 2000: Argentina's price level was 0.656, but the predicted equilibrium level of $\tilde{q}$ was 0.512. For a country at that level of GDP per capita, Argentina's dollar prices would have had to fall by 22% to reach that equilibrium. Argentina's growth had slowed after 1998, so, unlike in the China case, very little rise in the equilibrium $\tilde{q}$ could have been expected (which would have mitigated the need for a fall in actual q).

What actually happened: Argentina was pegging the peso to the dollar at 1:1, so adjustment had to come through a fall in Argentine prices relative to U.S. prices. With U.S. inflation at only 2%, this would happen slowly unless Argentine prices actually dropped. Unfortunately, this deflation process was slow and politically painful, involving wage and price cuts in an economy that was far from liberalized and competitive. The overvalued exchange rate was also hurting the demand for Argentine goods. Although the peg held for a long time, the country was driven into crisis by fiscal and financial sector problems. In the crisis of 2001–2002, the peso depreciated to three per dollar: the overvaluation was eliminated, and then some.

Slovakia: Obeying the Rules? The Balassa-Samuelson model predictions: Figure 11-3 also shows Slovakia. Like China, Slovakia was a fast-growing country, part of a group of countries in Eastern Europe lined up to join the EU and ultimately the Eurozone. Slovakia's real exchange rate was $q = 0.282$ in 2000 and undervalued relative to the predicted equilibrium $\tilde{q} = 0.534$. Here q needed to rise by 89% to reach equilibrium. Using our rule of thumb, half of this gap, or 45%, would be closed in five years, implying a real appreciation of about 7.5% per year. In addition, fast GDP per capita growth relative to the EU probably added another 1% to 2% on top of that, as in the China case, as

---

[5] Jeffrey A. Frankel, "The Balassa-Samuelson Relationship and the Renminbi," Harvard University, December 2006.

NET WORK

According to the adjoining Application and the Headlines box, the EU accession countries faced appreciation and/or inflation pressure. In March 2007, a step was taken to resolve these problems in the case of the Slovak koruna. The EU gave permission for Slovakia to "bend the rules" a bit. Which one of the Maastricht criteria was relaxed? Use the Internet to find out (hint: Google "Slovak koruna"). What does this say about the importance that the EU authorities attach to low inflation? Suppose Slovakia was still relatively poor but in the Eurozone. The Balassa-Samuelson effect would still be present even with a common currency, so how would inflation rates differ in the rich and poor parts of Europe? Why could that be a problem for ECB policy makers?

a result of the moving target. Thus, the expected real appreciation would have been 8% to 10% per year.

What actually happened: Slovakia notched up high rates of real appreciation of between 5% and 10% per annum from 1992 to 2004, as did many other countries in Eastern Europe.[6] The situation was like that in China: it required some combination of nominal appreciation and inflation. But Slovakia (and many of its neighbors) also wanted to join the euro. As we saw in Chapter 10, the Maastricht criteria would require Slovakia to peg to the euro (no appreciation) and keep its inflation within limits (within 2% of the "best" in the EU). Our model suggests this would be impossible: the koruna would have to appreciate or Slovakia's inflation would have to accelerate! As an exercise, you may wish to explore in more detail what actually happened. (See the **Net Work** box and **Headlines: Eastern Europe and the Euro.**) ■

Conclusions

In general, PPP does not hold. Goods prices are not the same in all countries. Arbitrage fails, most likely because of trade costs. The Balassa-Samuelson theory can explain how prices vary when goods are not traded and why rich countries have higher price levels. As countries get richer, their wages rise, driving up the prices of their nontraded goods (which use local labor as an input). This will drive up the overall price index and will cause the real exchange rate to fall—that is, a real appreciation. The theory finds strong empirical support and can be used to make better models of real and (hence) nominal exchange rates, with improved predictions, in situations in which an assumption of PPP is inappropriate.

2 Exchange Rates in the Short Run: Deviations from Uncovered Interest Parity

In Chapter 2, we examined interest arbitrage in the forex market and introduced uncovered interest parity (UIP), the fundamental condition for forex market equilibrium. Recall that UIP states that the expected return on foreign deposits should equal the return on domestic deposits when both are expressed in domestic currency.

For such an important foundation of exchange rate theory, however, UIP remains subject to considerable debate among international macroeconomists. The topic is important because any failure of UIP would affect our theories about exchange rates and the wider economy. For that reason, in this section we further explore the UIP debate to better understand the mechanism of arbitrage in the forex market.

[6] Balázs Égert, Kirsten Lommatzsch, and Amina Lahrèche-Révil, 2006, "Real Exchange Rates in Small Open OECD and Transition Economies: Comparing Apples with Oranges?" *Journal of Banking and Finance,* 30(12), December, 3393–3406.

HEADLINES

Eastern Europe and the Euro

The ERM rules were originally devised for a group of mostly rich Western European countries, where similarities in GDP per capita meant that Balassa-Samuelson effects were weak. Nobody adjusted the rules when a very different group of poorer countries arrived on the threshold of the Eurozone.

Estonia, Lithuania, Slovenia, Latvia and Slovakia have joined the exchange rate mechanism of the European monetary union and are candidates for near-term eurozone membership. . . . [Note: Slovenia did join in January 2007.]

All candidate countries easily meet most of the Maastricht criteria for eurozone membership. They satisfy the exchange rate and interest rate criteria and only Slovakia narrowly misses one of the two fiscal criteria. This is in contrast to Belgium, Germany, France, Italy and Greece, which, if they were not already eurozone members, would not be able to join today, as they do not meet the fiscal criteria. However, according to the European Central Bank and the European Commission, only Slovenia satisfies the inflation criterion, which specifies that annual inflation cannot exceed the average of "the three best performing EU member countries in terms of price stability" by more than 1.5 percentage points in the year prior to the examination.

Forcing candidate countries to meet both an exchange rate criterion and an inflation criterion makes no economic sense. Neither the ECB nor the Bank of England attempts the impossible: to control both inflation and their ex-change rate. Opting for stable exchange rates, the Baltic candidate countries have seen their inflation rates rise with energy price increases and impressive productivity gains in their traded sectors. The latter factor, which occurs as the candidate countries rapidly catch up with the eurozone, means that the relative price of non-traded goods rises faster than in the eurozone and is known as the Balassa-Samuelson effect. A conservative estimate of its contribution to the candidate countries' inflation is 1.5 per cent per year. . . .

The ECB's egregious misinterpretation of the term "best performing" further compounds the injustice. In March 2006 (the most recent month for which we have data), the three lowest inflation rates belonged to Sweden, Finland and either Poland or the Netherlands. These countries, two of which are not eurozone members, had an average inflation of 1.2 per cent. Adding 1.5 points to this rate yields an inflation criterion of 2.7 per cent. Slovenia meets this benchmark and Lithuania, with inflation of 2.7 per cent, scrapes by. Estonia, Slovakia and Latvia do not.

Defining "best performing" as having the lowest (positive) inflation rate contradicts the ECB's own formulation of price stability for the eurozone. The ECB defines price stability as inflation below, but close to, 2 per cent. By its own definition, inflation in Sweden, Finland, Poland and the Netherlands is far too low. The ECB itself has not managed to maintain inflation in the eurozone as a whole below 2 per cent. If we accept the ECB's own definition of what price stability means, then the target, achieved by several EU countries, should be about 1.8 per cent, putting the benchmark at 3.3 per cent. Slovenia, Lithuania and Slovakia satisfy this criterion but Estonia and Latvia do not. We maintain that sound economics would increase the benchmark by 1.5 points to allow for the Balassa-Samuelson effect, allowing Estonia to pass the test.

All that stands between Estonia, Lithuania and Slovakia and near-term eurozone membership is a rigid application of an inconsistent interpretation of a flawed inflation criterion. What should be done when "the law is an ass"? Failure to enforce a law weakens the rule of law and respect for rule-bound behaviour, but so does enforcing a harmful and senseless rule.

Source: Extract from Willem Buiter and Anne Sibert, "Europe Must Relax Its Inflation Test for Euro Entrants," Financial Times, May 3, 2006.

APPLICATION

The Carry Trade

As we saw in Chapter 2, UIP implies that the home interest rate should equal the foreign interest rate plus the rate of depreciation of the home currency. If UIP holds, it would seem to rule out the naive strategy of borrowing in a low interest rate currency and investing in a high interest rate currency, an investment referred to as a **carry trade.** In other words, UIP implies that the expected profit from such a trade is zero:

$$(11\text{-}3) \quad \text{Expected profit} = \underbrace{i_F}_{\substack{\text{Interest rate} \\ \text{on foreign currency}}} + \underbrace{\frac{\Delta E^e_{H/F}}{E_{H/F}}}_{\substack{\text{Expected rate of depreciation} \\ \text{of the home currency}}} - \underbrace{i_H}_{\substack{\text{Interest rate} \\ \text{on home currency} \\ \text{Cost of carry}}}.$$

Expected home currency rate of return on foreign deposits

From the home perspective, the return to an investment in the foreign currency (the foreign return) consists of the first two terms on the right-hand side of the preceding equation. Let's suppose the foreign currency (Australia, say) has a high interest rate of 6%. Now suppose the home country (Japan, say) has a low interest rate of 1%. The final term in the preceding equation is the cost of borrowing funds in local currency (Japanese yen) or, in financial jargon, the *cost of carry.* The interest rate differential, 5%, would be the profit on the carry trade *if the exchange rate remained unchanged.* If UIP is true, however, it would be pointless to engage in such arbitrage because the low-yield currency (the yen) would be expected to appreciate by 5% against the high-yield currency (the Australian dollar). The exchange rate term would be −5%, leaving zero expected profit.

The Long and Short of It In recent years, the predominant low interest rate currencies in the world economy have been the Japanese yen and the Swiss franc, and carry traders have often borrowed ("gone short") in these currencies and made an investment ("gone long") in higher interest rate major currencies such as the U.S. dollar, pound sterling, euro, Canadian dollar, Australian dollar, and New Zealand dollar. The profits from these trades have been very handsome. Has UIP failed?

To grasp how a carry trade functions, Figure 11-4, panel (a), shows actual monthly profits (in percent per month) from a carry trade based on borrowing low-interest yen in the Japanese money market and investing the proceeds in a high-interest Australian dollar money market account for one month. Also shown are the cumulative profits (in yen) that would have accrued from a ¥100 carry trade initiated on January 1, 1992. Panel (b) shows the underlying data used to calculate these returns. We see that over this entire period, the annual Australian dollar interest rate exceeded the Japanese yen interest rate, often by 5 or 6 percentage points. Thus, returns would be positive for this strategy if the yen depreciated or even appreciated only slightly against the Australian dollar. But if the yen appreciated more than slightly in any month, returns would be negative, and losses would result.

Panel (a) shows that in many months the high interest being paid on the Australian dollar was not offset by yen appreciation, and the carry trade resulted in a profit; this pattern was seen frequently in the period from 1995 to 1996, for example. There were other periods, however, when a sharp yen appreciation far exceeded the interest differential, and the carry trade resulted in a loss; this pattern occurred quite a bit in late 1998. In each of three months, in fact—August, October, and December 1998—the Australian dollar lost about 10% in value, wiping out the profits from *two years' worth of inter-*

FIGURE 11-4

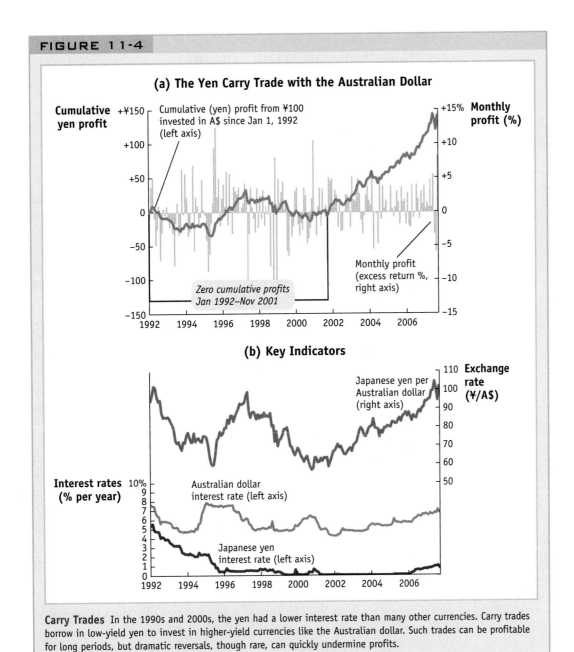

(a) The Yen Carry Trade with the Australian Dollar

Cumulative yen profit

Cumulative (yen) profit from ¥100 invested in A$ since Jan 1, 1992 (left axis)

Monthly profit (%)

Monthly profit (excess return %, right axis)

Zero cumulative profits Jan 1992–Nov 2001

(b) Key Indicators

Exchange rate (¥/A$)

Japanese yen per Australian dollar (right axis)

Interest rates (% per year)

Australian dollar interest rate (left axis)

Japanese yen interest rate (left axis)

Carry Trades In the 1990s and 2000s, the yen had a lower interest rate than many other currencies. Carry trades borrow in low-yield yen to invest in higher-yield currencies like the Australian dollar. Such trades can be profitable for long periods, but dramatic reversals, though rare, can quickly undermine profits.

Source: econstats.com.

est differentials in all three cases. Overall, we see that the periods of positive and negative returns were driven not by the fairly stable interest differential seen in panel (b), but by the long and volatile swings in the exchange rate.

To sum up, the carry trade strategy was subject to a good deal of volatility, and over the decade from the start of 1992 to the end of 2001, the highs and lows canceled each other out in the long run. On November 1, 2001, for example, the average return on this carry trade was virtually zero. Cumulative interest since 1992 on the two currencies expressed in yen was virtually the same, about 13%. Over that period, 100 yen placed in either currency at the start would have been worth 113 yen by the end.

What happened after that date? Subsequent trends again caused the value of Australian investment to pull ahead, as can be seen in panel (a) by the mostly positive returns registered month after month from 2002 to 2006. By June 2007, cumulative profits were well over ¥100. The reason? As panel (b) shows, the yen persistently weakened against the Australian dollar over this five-year period (by about 6% to 7% per year), reinforcing the interest differential (about 6% to 7% also) rather than offsetting it. Adding up, from 2002 to 2006 the cumulative return on the carry trade was about 15% per year! Would that trend continue or was there to be another sudden swing resulting from yen appreciation? This question brings us to a consideration of the role of risk in the forex market.

Investors face very real risks in this market. Suppose you put up $1,000 of your own capital and borrow $19,000 in yen from a bank. You now have 20 times your capital, a ratio, or *leverage,* of 20 (not uncommon). Then you play the carry trade, investing the $20,000 in the Australian dollar. It takes only a 5% loss on this trade to wipe you out: 5% of $20,000 eats all your capital. And without that *margin* to back you up, the bank bids you goodbye. As we have seen, losing 5% in a month is quite possible, as is losing 10% or even 15%.

For policy makers and market participants, the broader fear is that while big losses for households would be bad enough, big losses at large, high-leverage financial institutions could have damaging spillover effects in the global macroeconomy. For example, in June 2007, Jim O'Neill, Goldman Sachs chief global economist, said investment firms had been caught on the wrong side of huge bets against the Japanese yen: "There has been an amazing amount of leverage on currency markets that has nothing to do with real economic activity. I think there are going to be dead bodies around when this is over. The yen carry trade has reached 5% of Japan's GDP. This is enormous and highly risky, as we are now seeing."[7] Days later Steven Pearson, HBOS chief currency strategist, said, "A sizeable reversal at some point is highly likely, but the problem with that statement is the 'at some point' bit, because carry trades make money steadily over long periods of time."[8]

In the carry trade, as history shows, a big reversal can always happen as everyone rushes to exit the carry trades and they all "unwind" their positions at the same time. The answer to the dangling question above is yes, a big reversal did come along for the trade in question: after rising another 10% against the yen from January to July 2007, the Australian dollar then fell by 15% in the space of a month, eating up about three years' worth of interest differential for anyone unlucky enough to buy in at the peak. Many hedge funds and individual investors who made ill-timed or excessively leveraged bets lost a bundle (see **Headlines: Mrs. Watanabe's Hedge Fund**).

---

[7] Ambrose Evans-Pritchard, "Goldman Sachs Warns of 'Dead Bodies' after Market Turmoil," telegraph.co.uk, June 3, 2007.
[8] Veronica Brown, "Carry Trade Devotees Keep Faith in Testing Times," Reuters, June 12, 2007.

HEADLINES

Mrs. Watanabe's Hedge Fund

The OECD estimated the total yen carry trade at $4 trillion in 2006. This trade involves not just large financial institutions but increasing numbers of Japanese individual investors, who place money in high-yielding foreign currency deposits or uridashi *bonds.*

"FX Beauties" founder, Mayumi Torii

TOKYO—Since the credit crisis started shaking the world financial markets this summer, many professional traders have taken big losses. Another, less likely group of investors has, too: middle-class Japanese homemakers who moonlight as amateur currency speculators.

Ms. Itoh is one of them. Ms. Itoh, a homemaker in the central city of Nagoya, did not want her full name used because her husband still does not know. After cleaning the dinner dishes, she would spend her evenings buying and selling British pounds and Australian dollars.

When the turmoil struck the currency markets last month, Ms. Itoh spent a sleepless week as market losses wiped out her holdings. She lost nearly all her family's $100,000 in savings.

"I wanted to add to our savings, but instead I got in over my head," Ms. Itoh, 36, said.

Tens of thousands of married Japanese women ventured into online currency trading in the last year and a half, playing the markets between household chores or after tucking the children into bed. While the overwhelmingly male world of traders and investors here mocked them as kimono-clad "Mrs. Watanabes," these women collectively emerged as a powerful force, using Japan's vast wealth to sway prices and confound economists. . . .

Now Japan's homemaker-traders may become yet another casualty of the shakeout hitting the debt, credit and stock markets worldwide.... Most analysts estimate that Japanese online investors lost $2.5 billion trading currency last month. . . .

Some of the women used their own money, some used their husband's, and some used a combination of both. But by trading, they challenged deeply held social prohibitions in Japan against money, which is often seen here as dirty, especially when earned through market speculation.

"There are strict taboos against money that isn't earned with sweat from the brow," said Mayumi Torii, a 41-year-old mother of one who said she earned $150,000 since she started margin trading in currencies early last year.

Ms. Torii is one of Japan's most famous housewife-traders. She has written a book on her investing strategies and founded a support group for home traders, the FX Beauties Club, which now has 40 members. (FX is financial shorthand for "foreign exchange.") . . .

One reason Japan's homemakers can move markets is that they hold the purse strings of the nation's $12.5 trillion in household savings. For more than a decade, that money languished in banks here at low interest rates. But as the rapid aging of Japan's population has brought anxiety about the future, households are starting to move more of it overseas in search of higher returns.

A tiny fraction of this has flowed into risky investments like online currency accounts. Most of these accounts involve margin trading, in which investors place a cash deposit with a brokerage that allows them to borrow up to 20 or even 100 times their holdings for trading.

The practice has been popular not only because it vastly raises the level of potential profits, but also because it allowed wives to trade at home, said

Hiroshi Takao, chief operating officer of TokyoForex, an online trading firm.

The housewife-traders were so secretive that many market analysts did not realize how widespread the trend had become until this summer, when the police arrested a Tokyo housewife accused of failing to pay $1.1 million in taxes on her foreign exchange earnings. . . .

For a time, margin trading seemed like a surefire way to make money, as the yen moved only downward against the dollar and other currencies. But last month, in the midst of the credit turmoil, the yen soared as hedge funds and traders panicked.

Ms. Itoh recalled that she had wanted to cry as she watched the yen jump as much as 5 percent in value in a single day, Aug. 16.

"But I had to keep a poker face, because my husband was sitting behind me," Ms. Itoh said.

She did not sell her position, thinking the yen would fall again. But by the next morning, only $1,000 remained in her account, she said. . . .

[M]ost of the half dozen homemaker-traders interviewed for this article said they were already trading again, and the rest said they soon would be—including Ms. Itoh, who said she would probably invest her remaining $1,000 in savings.

"There's no other way to make money so quickly," she said.

Source: Excerpted from Martin Fackler, "Japanese Housewives Sweat in Secret as Markets Reel," New York Times, September 16, 2007.

Still, given the persistence of profits, anyone predicting such reversals may appear to be crying wolf. Money managers often face incentives to follow the herd and the market's momentum keeps the profits flowing—until they stop. All this ensures high levels of stress and uncertainty for anyone in the forex trading world and for some of the households engaged in this kind of risky arbitrage.

Carry Trade Summary Our study of the carry trade focuses our attention on several facts. First, even if expected returns from arbitrage are zero, actual realized returns are often not zero. Second, such returns appear to be persistent. Third, the returns are also very volatile, or risky. All of these issues need to be addressed as we judge the success or failure of UIP. ■

APPLICATION

Peso Problems

The example of carry trades between the Japanese yen and the Australian dollar shows how actual returns from interest arbitrage may be nonzero (but risky) for a pair of currencies that are floating. But the same can be true for two currencies that are fixed. To illustrate this case, we turn to recent data involving the U.S. dollar pegs of two emerging market countries, Hong Kong and Argentina.

As we saw in Chapter 9, in the case of a credibly fixed peg with no risk of a depreciation or any other risks (no currency premium and no default risk premium), the UIP condition states that the home interest rate should equal the foreign interest rate because investors treat domestic and foreign currency as perfect substitutes that always have been and always will be interchangeable at a fixed rate. Thus, the interest differential between the two currencies should be zero. Again, if true, this outcome would seem to rule out any desire on the part of investors to engage in arbitrage (e.g., via the carry trade). But there is an important exception: when pegs are not credible, risk premiums can cause large interest differentials—and cause investors to smell a profit.

Figure 11-5, panel (a), shows data for Hong Kong from 1990 to 2000, including the crucial period in 1997 when many Asian countries were in crisis and their exchange rate pegs were breaking. Most of the time, the interest differential between the Hong Kong dollar and the U.S. dollar was zero, as one would expect for what was perceived to be a credible peg. Hong Kong was operating a quasi-currency board with reserves of approximately 300% of the base money supply. Short of dollarization, this was considered about the most bulletproof peg around.

Nonetheless, in late 1997 investors started to fear that Hong Kong might suffer the same fate as the other Asian economies. Expecting a future depreciation of the Hong Kong dollar, they started to demand a currency premium. At its peak, the Hong Kong interest rate rose almost 20% per year above the U.S. interest rate. However, *the expected depreciation never happened.* The Hong Kong dollar's peg to the U.S. dollar survived. Investors may have been reasonable to fear a crisis and demand a premium beforehand (ex ante), but after the fact (ex post), these unrealized expectations became

FIGURE 11-5

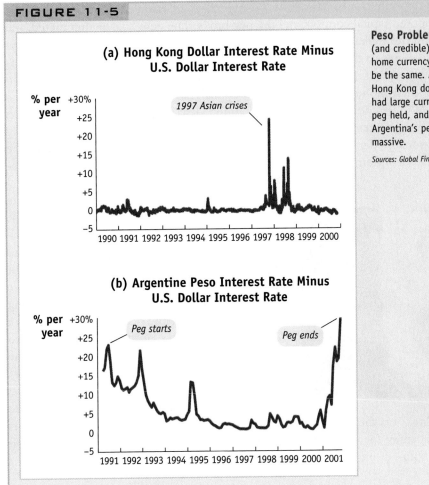

(a) Hong Kong Dollar Interest Rate Minus U.S. Dollar Interest Rate

1997 Asian crises

% per year

+30%, +25, +20, +15, +10, +5, 0, −5

1990 1991 1992 1993 1994 1995 1996 1997 1998 1999 2000

(b) Argentine Peso Interest Rate Minus U.S. Dollar Interest Rate

% per year

Peg starts

Peg ends

+30%, +25, +20, +15, +10, +5, 0, −5

1991 1992 1993 1994 1995 1996 1997 1998 1999 2000 2001

Peso Problems If exchange rates are fixed (and credible), then the interest rate on the home currency and the base currency should be the same. As seen here, however, the Hong Kong dollar and Argentina peso often had large currency premiums. Hong Kong's peg held, and carry trade profits were made. Argentina's peg broke, and losses were massive.

Sources: Global Financial Data; econstats.com.

realized profits. As a result, there was handsome money to be made from the carry trade for those willing to park their money in Hong Kong dollars during all the fuss.

Should you always bet on a peg to hold in a crisis? No. Figure 11-5, panel (b), shows data for Argentina from 1991 to 2001. This includes the period of looming crisis for the Argentine economy in 2001, as the likelihood of default and depreciation grew. The country was in fiscal trouble with an ailing banking sector. It no longer had the ability to borrow in world capital markets and was about to be cut off from International Monetary Fund (IMF) assistance. A recession was deepening. All of this was raising the pressure on the government to use monetary policy for purposes other than maintaining the peg. Investors began to demand a huge currency-plus-default premium on Argentine peso deposits to compensate them for the risk of a possible depreciation and/or banking crisis. Peso interest rates at one point were more than 25% above the U.S. interest rate. But in this case, investors' fears were justified:

in December to January 2001 the Argentine government froze bank deposits, imposed capital controls, and the peg broke. The peso's value plummeted, and soon the exchange rate exceeded three pesos to the dollar, erasing more than two-thirds of the U.S. dollar value of peso deposits. In retrospect, the precrisis interest differentials had been too small: the carry traders who gambled and left their money in peso deposits eventually lost their shirts.

We can now see how expectations may not be realized, even when exchange rates are fixed. Fixed exchange rates often break, and investors may reasonably demand currency premiums at certain times. However, after the fact, such premiums may lead to returns from interest arbitrage that are positive (when pegs hold, as in the Hong Kong case) or negative (when pegs break, as in the Argentine case).

International economists refer to this phenomenon as the **peso problem** (given its common occurrence in a certain region of the world). But again, it is far from clear that the profits seen are a sign that UIP fails or that investors are acting irrationally. The collapse of a peg can be seen as a rare event, an extreme occurrence that is hard to predict but that will lead to large changes in the values of assets. This situation is not unlike, say, fire or earthquake insurance: every year that you pay the premium and nothing happens, you make a "loss" on the insurance arrangement, a pattern that could go on for years (hopefully, for your entire life), but you know that the insurance will pay off to your advantage in a big way if disaster strikes. ■

Peso problems: a man hammers on the door of a bank in a protest over frozen accounts, Buenos Aires, June 2002.

The Efficient Markets Hypothesis

Do carry trade profits disprove UIP? To explore this question further, let us rewrite Equation (11-3), which calculates expected profits, by replacing *expected* or *ex ante* values of the exchange rate with *actual* or *ex post* realized values.

$$(11\text{-}4) \quad \text{Actual profit} = \underbrace{i_F}_{\substack{\text{Interest rate} \\ \text{on foreign currency}}} + \underbrace{\frac{\Delta E_{H/F}}{E_{H/F}}}_{\substack{\text{Actual rate of depreciation} \\ \text{of the home currency}}} - \underbrace{i_H}_{\substack{\text{Interest rate} \\ \text{on home currency} \\ \text{Cost of carry}}}.$$

Actual home currency rate of return on foreign deposits

Note the one subtle difference: the disappearance of the superscript "*e*," which denoted expectations of future exchange rate depreciation. This expression can be computed only after the fact: although interest rates are known in advance, the future exchange rate is not. We know actual profits only after the investment strategy has run its course.

Thus, the sole difference between actual and expected profits is a **forecast error** that corresponds to the difference between actual depreciation and expected depreciation. (Again the importance of exchange rate forecasts is revealed!) This forecast error is the difference between Equation (11-3) and Equation (11-4), that is,

$$(11\text{-}5) \quad \text{Forecast error} = \begin{pmatrix} \text{Actual} \\ \text{profit} \end{pmatrix} - \begin{pmatrix} \text{Expected} \\ \text{profit} \end{pmatrix} = \frac{\Delta E_{H/F}}{E_{H/F}} - \frac{\Delta E_{H/F}^e}{E_{H/F}}.$$

Armed with this way of understanding *unexpected* profits, we can now confront an important and controversial puzzle in international macroeconomics: What can the behavior of this forecast error tell us about UIP and the workings of the forex market? One way to attack that question is to study expected and actual profits side by side to see the size of the forecast error and its pattern of behavior.

Expected Profits On the one hand, strictly speaking, UIP itself says nothing about the forecast error. It says only that before that fact, or *ex ante,* expected profits should be zero. Expectations are not directly observable in markets, but we can recall the evidence from Chapter 2 based on surveys of traders' expectations for major currencies in the period from 1988 to 1993. As a recap, Figure 11-6, panel (a), presents this evidence again. The figure plots the expected depreciation against the interest differential for several major currencies.[9]

On the 45-degree line, these two terms are equal, and expected profits will be zero, according to Equation (11-3). As in several studies of this sort, on average the data line up close to, but not exactly on, the 45-degree line, so they are not wildly inconsistent with UIP. The slope is close to 1. But the survey data are probably prone to error and cover only some (but not all) of the traders in the market. Even using formal statistical tests, it is difficult to reject UIP based on shaky evidence of this sort. The hypothesis that UIP holds can typically survive this kind of test.

Actual Profits On the other hand, we know that actual profits are made. It is enlightening to see exactly how they are made by replacing the expected depreciation in panel (a) with actual depreciation, after the fact, or *ex post.* This change is made in panel (b), which, to be consistent, shows actual profits for the same currencies over the same period.

The change is dramatic. There are plenty of observations not on the 45-degree line, indicating that profits and losses were made in some periods. Even more striking, the line of best fit has a slope of about 0.2. This means that for every 1% of interest differential in favor of the foreign currency, we would expect only a 0.2% appreciation of the home currency, on average, leaving a profit of 0.8%. At larger interest differentials, the line of best fit means even larger profits. (Some studies find zero, or even negative slopes, implying even bigger profits!)

The UIP Puzzle A finding that profits can be made needs careful handling. On its own this need not imply a violation of UIP: the realization of a random variable need not be the same as its expectation, due to variation about

---

[9] Recall that given *covered* interest parity, which does hold, the interest differential also equals the forward premium.

FIGURE 11-6

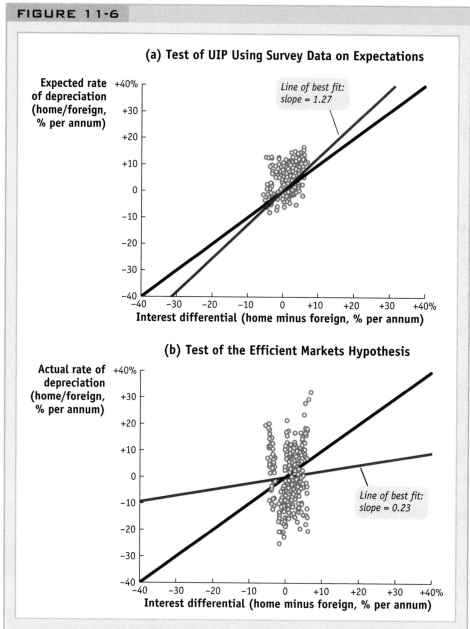

(a) Test of UIP Using Survey Data on Expectations

Expected rate of depreciation (home/foreign, % per annum)

Line of best fit: slope = 1.27

Interest differential (home minus foreign, % per annum)

(b) Test of the Efficient Markets Hypothesis

Actual rate of depreciation (home/foreign, % per annum)

Line of best fit: slope = 0.23

Interest differential (home minus foreign, % per annum)

UIP and the Efficient Markets Hypothesis Each dot represents an actual 12-month period for a given currency versus the U.S. dollar. According to trader surveys, expected depreciations were *on average* more or less in line with UIP, as seen in panel (a), where the slope is not far from 1. But panel (b) shows that, after the fact, these forecasts were not very good, and systematically wrong, in this sample. Actual depreciations were far out of line with expectations: the slope is only 0.23. On average, high-yield currencies systematically depreciated only 23% as much as the interest differential would have forecast under UIP.

Notes: Line of best fit is through the origin. Data shown are monthly for the German mark, Swiss franc, Japanese yen, British pound, and Canadian dollar against the U.S. dollar from February 1988 to October 1993.

Source: From Menzie Chinn and Jeffrey A. Frankel, "Survey Data on Exchange Rate Expectations: More Currencies, More Horizons, More Tests," in W. Allen and D. Dickinson, eds., 2002, Monetary Policy, Capital Flows and Financial Market Developments in the Era of Financial Globalisation: Essays in Honour of Max Fry, *London: Routledge, pp. 145–167.*

the mean. However, looking at actual profits, the pattern of the deviations from the 45-degree line is systematic. The slope of the best-fit line is well below 1, indicating, for example, that when the interest differential is high, actual depreciation is typically less than expected and less than the interest differential. In other words, *on average* the carry trade (borrowing in the low-yield currency to invest in the high-yield currency) is profitable. Actual profits are risky, but they appear to be forecastable. Forecastable profits are like a grail to economists: mythical, sought after, and a cause of division in the court.

This finding is widely considered to be a puzzle or anomaly. If such profits are forecastable, then the forex market would be violating some of the fundamental tenets of the modern theory of finance. The **rational expectations hypothesis** argues that on average all investors should make forecasts about the future that are without *bias*: on average, actual and expected values should correspond. But, as we just saw, the difference between actual and expected exchange rates reveals a clear bias.

In addition, the **efficient markets hypothesis,** developed by economist Eugene Fama, asserts that financial markets are "informationally efficient" in that all prices reflect all known information at any given time. Hence, such information should not be useful in forecasting future profits: that is, one should not be able to systematically beat the market.

Ultimately then, the UIP puzzle isn't just about UIP. The expectations data (the best that we have) suggest that UIP does hold. The real UIP puzzle is why *UIP combined with the rational expectations and efficient markets hypotheses* fails to hold. Yet these hypotheses seemingly do fail. This appears to be an **inefficient market** instead. Why are those big forecastable profits lying around?

Limits to Arbitrage

Economists have proposed a number of ways to resolve these puzzles, and at some level all of these can be described as explanations based on a **limits to arbitrage** argument. What does this mean? In the first section of this chapter, we argued that there were limits to arbitrage, in the form of trade costs, that can help explain the PPP puzzle: purchasing power parity will not hold if there are frictions such as transport costs, tariffs, and so on that hamper arbitrage in goods markets.

Limits to arbitrage arguments can also be applied in the world of finance. But how? And can they help explain the UIP puzzle?

Trade Costs Are Small It is tempting but ultimately not fruitful to look for the same kinds of frictions that we saw in goods markets. Conventional trade costs in financial markets are simply too small to have an effect that is large enough to explain the puzzle. There are bid-ask spreads between currencies, and there may be other technical trading costs, for example, associated with when a forex trade is placed during the day and which financial markets are open. But none of these frictions provides a sufficient explanation for the forecastable profits and the market's inefficiency.

There is also the problem that if one wishes to make a very large transaction, especially in a less liquid currency, the act of trading itself may have an adverse impact on the exchange rate and curtail profitable trades. For example, an order for $1 billion of more liquid yen is more easily digested by the market than an order for $1 billion of less liquid New Zealand dollars. But again, this possibility is not likely to explain the UIP puzzle because investors can avert such a situation by breaking their trades up into small pieces and spreading them out over time. So even though these trading costs are real, they may not be large enough to offset the very substantial profits we have seen.

If trading costs are the sole limit to arbitrage, there is still a puzzle. We must look elsewhere.

Risk versus Reward A recent and promising approach to the puzzle examines traders' alternative investment strategies, draws on other puzzles in finance, is based less on introspection and more on observations of actual trading strategies, and connects with the frontiers of the emerging field of behavioral economics.

To approach this research and to make the investment problem facing the trader a little clearer, we can reconsider the data shown in Figure 11-6. In panel (b) we saw that the slope was only 0.23, meaning that for every 1% of interest differential, we would predict only 0.23% of offsetting depreciation, leaving a seemingly predictable profit of 0.77%. Suppose we followed a carry trade strategy of borrowing in the low interest rate currency and investing in the high interest currency. If the interest differential were 1% then we would expect to net a profit of 0.77%; if the interest differential were 2% we would expect to double that profit to 1.54%; a differential of 3% would yield 2.31% profit, and so on, if we simply extrapolate that straight line.

This strategy would have delivered profits. However, there are two problems with it. First, profits do not, in fact, grow linearly with the interest differential. The straight line model is a poor fit. At high interest differentials there are times when profits are very good, and other times when the carry trade suffers a reversal, and large losses accrue, as we have seen. The second problem is a related one. At all levels of the interest differential, Figure 11-6 clearly shows the extreme volatility or riskiness of these returns due to the extreme and unpredictable volatility of the exchange rate. Actual rates of depreciation can easily range between plus or minus 10% per year, and up to plus or minus 30% in some cases.

One measure of the volatility of returns used by economists is the the standard deviation, which we can now put to use to explore why these positive but risky profits are left unexploited.

The Sharpe Ratio and Puzzles in Finance Carry trade profits are the difference between a risky foreign return and a safe domestic interest rate. This kind of return difference is called an **excess return,** and to analyze it further we can draw on one of the standard tools of financial economics.

The **Sharpe ratio** is the ratio of an asset's average annualized excess return to the annualized standard deviation of its return:

$$\text{Sharpe ratio} = \frac{\text{Mean (annual excess return)}}{\text{Standard deviation (annual excess return)}}.$$

The ratio was invented by William Forsyth Sharpe, a Nobel laureate in economics. As a ratio of "rewards to variability," the Sharpe ratio tells us how much the returns on an asset compensate investors for the risks they take when investing in it.

Figure 11-7 displays data on returns to the simple carry trade strategy for several major currencies against the British pound for the period 1976 to 2005. For each pair of currencies, it is assumed that each month a trader would have borrowed in the low interest rate currency and invested in the high interest rate currency. Details on the returns to a portfolio of all such trades (equally weighted) are also shown.

In panel (a) we see that the returns to these strategies were positive for all currencies (they were also statistically significant), and on average they were about 4% per year. However, the volatility of the returns was even larger in all cases, as measured by the standard deviation. On average, this was about 10%

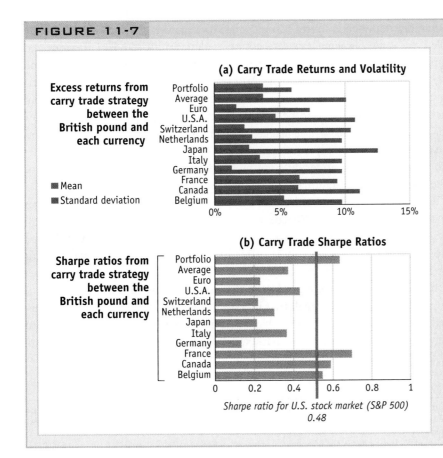

FIGURE 11-7

(a) Carry Trade Returns and Volatility

Excess returns from carry trade strategy between the British pound and each currency

- Mean
- Standard deviation

(b) Carry Trade Sharpe Ratios

Sharpe ratios from carry trade strategy between the British pound and each currency

Sharpe ratio for U.S. stock market (S&P 500)
0.48

Risk versus Reward in the Carry Trade This chart shows details of returns for carry trades between the British pound and selected foreign currencies (and an equally weighted portfolio of all such trades). The strategy supposes that each month an investor borrowed in the low interest rate currency and invested in the high interest rate currency, and transaction costs are assumed to be negligible. Panel (a) shows that there have been predictable excess returns to the carry trade based on data from 1976 to 2005, on average about 4% per year. However, the standard deviation of these returns has been substantial, at about 10% per year. Thus, the average Sharpe ratio for this strategy has been about 0.4, as shown in panel (b). The diversified portfolio does a little better with a Sharpe ratio of 0.6.

Source: Craig Burnside et al., 2006, "The Returns to Currency Speculation," NBER Working Papers 12489. Monthly means, standard deviations, and Sharpe ratios have been annualized.

on an annual basis, although falling to 6% for the portfolio (due to gains from diversification). In panel (b) the corresponding Sharpe ratios are shown, and we can see that they fall below 1 in all cases. The average for all currencies is 0.4 and thanks to a reduction in volatility due to diversification the equally weighted portfolio has a modestly higher Sharpe ratio of 0.6.

We now must ask: should Sharpe ratios of around 0.5 be considered "big" or "small"? Do they signal that investors are missing a profit opportunity? Should people be rushing to take profits in investments that offer this mix of risk and reward? If this can be judged to be a "big" Sharpe ratio then we have a puzzle as the market would seem to be failing in terms of efficiency.

It turns out that many investors in the forex market would consider that 0.5 is a pretty small Sharpe ratio. To see why, and to understand how this approach may "solve" the UIP puzzle, we note that historically, as shown in panel (b), the annual Sharpe ratio for the U.S. stock market has been about 0.48, based on the excess returns of the broad S&P 500 index over and above risk-free U.S. Treasury bonds. This reference level of 0.48 might be thought of as a hurdle that competing investment strategies must beat if they are to attract additional investment. But we can see from panel (b) that forex carry trades either fall below this bar, or just barely surmount it.

There are indeed excess returns in the stock market, but investors are not rushing to borrow money to buy stocks to push that Sharpe ratio any lower. Admittedly, many economists consider the stock market finding to be a puzzle (called the *equity premium puzzle*) because under various standard theories and assumptions about risk aversion, it is hard to understand why investors sit back and leave such excess returns on the table. And yet they do, a fact that leads other economists to postulate that some very nonstandard assumptions, some drawn from psychology, may now need to be included in models to properly explain investor behavior. Research in *behavioral finance*, a branch of behavioral economics, attempts to explain such seemingly irrational market outcomes using various principles such as rational action under different preferences (e.g., strong aversion to loss) or more limited forms of rationality (e.g., models with slow or costly learning).

To sum up, there are now theories that might explain why nobody arbitrages the stock market when its Sharpe ratio is 0.48. That just isn't a high enough reward-risk ratio to attract investors. But in our forex market data, the Sharpe ratio is about the same, and most other studies find carry trade Sharpe ratios that are little larger than the stock market's 0.48.[10] So we may have an answer to the question why arbitrage does not erase all excess returns. The ratio of rewards to risk is so very small that investors in the market are simply uninterested. Indeed, surveys of trader behavior in major firms by economist Richard Lyons suggest that, in the forex market, if the predicted Sharpe ratio of a strategy falls below even 1 then this is enough to discourage investor interest.[11]

---

[10] Furthermore, in illiquid markets, traders may be concerned that the act of trading itself will cause adverse price movements, eliminating profits. In that case, observed Sharpe ratios may overstate the size of unexploited profits.

[11] Richard K. Lyons, 2001, *The Microstructure Approach to Exchange Rates,* Cambridge, Mass.: MIT Press. Lyons also found carry trade Sharpe ratios of about 0.4 using a historical sample of currencies.

Predictability and Nonlinearity Can we do better than a straight-line or linear predictions of returns and crude carry trade strategies? More complex and diversified forex trading strategies may be able to jack up the Sharpe ratio a little, but not too much. As an alternative way of describing the data, for example, we can use nonlinear models which fit the data quite well.[12]

Nonlinear models show that at low interest differentials (say 0% to 2%), profits are inherently low, and nobody has been much interested in arbitrage given the risks; conversely, at high differentials (say 5% or more), the rewards have often vanished as investors have rushed in, bid up the high-yield currency to its maximum value, causing a reversal that wipes out carry trade profits. At the extremes, arbitrage has tended to work when it should (or shouldn't). Only in the middle do moderate, positive Sharpe ratios emerge, it seems, for investors willing to take some risks. Thus our "small" average Sharpe ratios are a mix of these low and high returns, suggesting more sophisticated strategies should ensure that the investment decision depends on the size of the expected return. But the rewards relative to risk are still quite meager and Sharpe ratios are still pretty low even when arbitrage looks most promising.

Conclusions

The main lesson here is that risky arbitrage is fundamentally different from riskless arbitrage. Based on this sort of standard financial analysis, many economists conclude that although there may be excess returns, even *predictable* excess returns, in the forex market, the risk-reward ratio is typically too low to attract additional investors.[13] In that sense, there is no puzzle left and arbitrage has not failed—it has just gone as far as might be reasonably expected, at least given investor behavior in equity markets and elsewhere. In forex market research, nobody has yet proved that there are large amounts of low-risk money lying on the table (though if they did, they might not publish the result).

What are the implications? Here there is common ground between the UIP and PPP puzzles. In the case of the PPP puzzle studied earlier in the chapter, limits to arbitrage in the goods market (mainly due to transaction costs) may create a band of inaction allowing for deviations from parity in purchasing prices. In the case of the UIP puzzle, limits to arbitrage in the forex market (mainly due to risk) may allow for deviations from interest parity in some situations.

NET WORK

Imagine you are a carry trader. Go to the ft.com site and locate the "Market data" part of the site. Find one-month LIBOR interest rates for some major currencies: U.S. dollar, pound, euro, Japanese yen, Swiss franc, Canadian dollar (hint: Google "ft.com money rates"). Find the lowest-yield currency, and call it X. How much interest would you pay in X units after borrowing 100X for one month? (Hint: the raw data are annualized rates.) Compute the exchange rate between X and every other higher-yield currency Y (hint: Google "ft.com cross rates"). For each Y, compute how much 100X would be worth in Y units today, and then in a month's time with Y-currency interest added. Revisit this question in a month's time, find the spot rates at that moment, and compute the resulting profit from each carry trade. Did all your imaginary trades pay off? Any of them?

---

[12] Jerry Coakley and Ana-Maria Fuertes, 2001, "A Non-Linear Analysis of Excess Foreign Exchange Returns," *Manchester School,* 69(6), December, 623–642; Lucio Sarno, Giorgio Valente, and Hyginus Leon, 2006, "Nonlinearity in Deviations from Uncovered Interest Parity: An Explanation of the Forward Bias Puzzle," *Review of Finance,* 10(3), September, 443–482.

[13] There may be a few exceptions to this general statement, and indeed some currency hedge funds and other large firms with deep pockets and an appetite for risk may be able to eke out worthwhile profits through complex trading strategies, but only time will tell whether these players can whittle the Sharpe ratio down any further.

3 Global Imbalances

In recent years, large and persistent imbalances in the current accounts of certain regions and countries around the world have emerged, with some areas in surplus and others in deficit. These trends have become a focus of intense concern among policy makers and the subject of a great deal of research due to fears that such imbalances may be unsustainable and that they will eventually lead to serious global economic instability. In this section, we survey this topical issue.

Facts about Emerging Global Imbalances

NET WORK

Go to the latest IMF World Economic Outlook Database (navigate from imf.org or Google "world economic outlook databases"). Calculate the current accounts for the latest year for all of the regions shown in Figure 11-8. Collect these data in U.S. dollars. Do global imbalances still persist? Are they growing?

We first examine some facts. Figure 11-8 shows that the imbalances in certain countries and regions have grown very large. Almost all regions have some deficit countries but are in surplus overall. The exception is the United States where, by 2007, a deficit of approximately $800 billion was being offset by surplus in all the other groups of countries, with almost two-thirds of the surplus coming from just two countries: China (around $300 billion to $350 billion) and Japan (approximately $150 billion). Also notable were the $350 billion surplus in major emerging markets of Asia (Hong Kong, Singapore, Korea, Taiwan plus India, Malaysia, Philippines, and Thailand) and the $150 billion surplus from the oil-producing economies of the Middle East region. In light of these trends, economists and policy makers are asking what is causing these imbalances. Will they persist? And why should we care about them?

A Model of Saving and Investment in the World Economy

To begin to answer these questions, we need to understand why global imbalances have emerged, and to understand this, we need a simple model of the

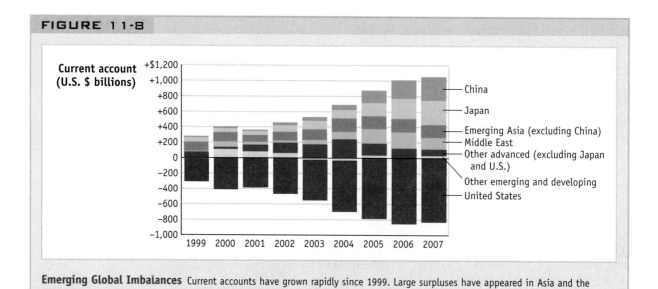

FIGURE 11-8

Emerging Global Imbalances Current accounts have grown rapidly since 1999. Large surpluses have appeared in Asia and the Middle East. Deficits grew in several countries, dominated by the United States.

Source: IMF, World Economic Outlook, April 2007.

current account for use in the medium to long term. Recall from the current account identity of Chapter 5 that the current account is, by definition, the difference between saving and investment, $CA = S - I$. If we can develop a model that explains how saving and investment are determined, then we can model the current account.

Let's start building this model with some familiar assumptions:

1. For two identical countries, Home and Foreign, all quantities are real and prices are flexible. Foreign variables carry an asterisk.

2. Both countries can borrow or lend at the world real interest rate r^W.

3. Saving S in Home (and similarly in Foreign) is insensitive to the real interest rate and is fixed. Saving depends on income minus consumption (including public consumption), and although consumption may be sensitive to income and wealth (and other factors such as taxes and government spending), we treat those factors as fixed, unless noted otherwise.

4. Investment $I(r^W)$ in Home (and similarly in Foreign) falls as the real interest rate r^W rises (as in the short-run IS-LM model in Chapter 7). Because the current account is the difference between S (fixed) and I (which falls as r^W rises), this assumption implies that the current account increases as the real interest rate rises:

$$CA(r^W) = S - I(r^W).$$

Home and Foreign Economies When Closed and Open Home's current account is shown in Figure 11-9. The vertical axis shows the real interest rate r^W, and the horizontal axis shows the quantities of saving and investment. Because we have assumed that saving is fixed, Home saving is unaffected by the real interest rate and the saving supply line S is a vertical line. Home

---

FIGURE 11-9

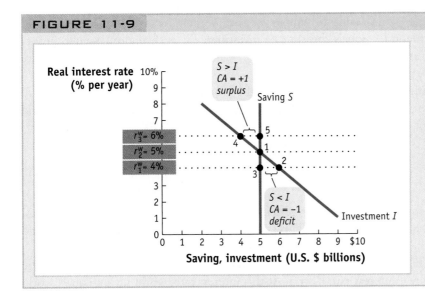

Saving and Investment Home's closed economy equilibrium is at point 1, where saving supply S and investment demand I are equal. Saving is assumed fixed. At lower real interest rates, investment (point 2) exceeds saving (point 3) and there is a current account deficit. At higher real interest rates, investment (point 4) is less than saving (point 5) and there is a current account surplus.

investment decreases as the real interest rate increases, so the investment demand curve I slopes downward. The Home current account is the difference between saving and investment.

To illustrate, we can attach some numbers to this figure. The real interest rates run from 0% to 10% per year. Saving and investment run from 0 to $10 billion. As shown here, when the world real interest rate is at $r_1^W = 5\%$, saving and investment are equal at $5 billion and the current account is 0.

Note that point 1 is where the Home economy would be in equilibrium if it were a closed economy and r^W were the Home real interest rate. If Home is disconnected from the rest of the world, its isolation forces the current account to be zero. The Home capital market would be in equilibrium at point 1 with a Home real interest rate of 5%.

In an open economy, however, saving and investment need not be equal—countries can borrow from and lend to each other and can have current account imbalances. For example, suppose the world real interest rate were 1 percentage point lower at $r_2^W = 4\%$. At this lower real interest rate, Home investment would rise by $1 billion to $6 billion (point 2), but Home saving is unchanged at $5 billion (point 3). Saving minus investment is the current account $CA = -\$1$ billion, a deficit. Conversely, if the world real interest rate were 1 percentage point higher at $r_3^W = 6\%$, then Home investment would fall by $1 billion to $4 billion (point 4) and Home saving would stay at $5 billion (point 5). Saving minus investment is +$1 billion, and the current account is in surplus.

The World Real Interest Rate Up to now, we have taken the world interest rate r^W as given. This may be reasonable for a small open economy. But at the global level, this is inappropriate and we must consider the market forces that determine r^W.

For simplicity, let us imagine a world consisting of two countries or regions, Home and Foreign. Their saving, investment, and current account quantities are shown in Figure 11-10, panel (a) for Home and panel (b) for Foreign. World saving S^W equals the sum of saving in each region, and world investment I^W equals the sum of investment in each region. Saving, investment, and the current account in the world as a whole are shown in Figure 11-10, panel (c).

With this setup, we can see how the world real interest rate is determined. Because the world as a whole is a closed economy, we know that the world current account CA^W must add up to zero:

$$0 = \underbrace{CA(r^W) + CA^*(r^W)}_{\substack{CA^W \\ \text{World current account}}} = \underbrace{(S + S^*)}_{\substack{S^W \\ \text{World saving}}} - \underbrace{\left(I(r^W) + I^*(r^W)\right)}_{\substack{I^W \\ \text{World investment}}}.$$

This equation imposes the restriction that world saving supply must equal world investment demand. This equilibrium can be achieved only if the world real interest rate adjusts until saving supply equals investment demand.

In Figure 11-10, world capital market equilibrium is attained only at the world real interest rate $r_1^W = 5$. At this interest rate, world saving equals world

FIGURE 11-10

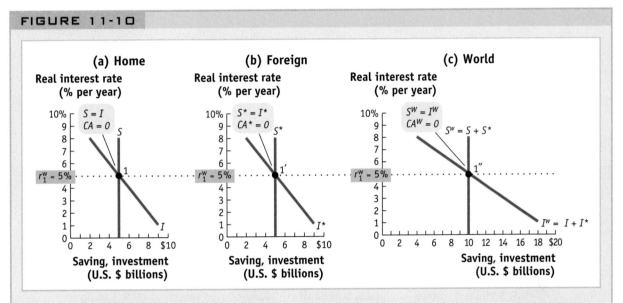

Saving and Investment in a Two-Country Model At the world real interest rate $r_1^W = 5\%$, saving equals investment and the current account is zero in Home, as shown in panel (a), point 1; in Foreign, as shown in panel (b), point 1′; and, hence, in the world as a whole, as shown in panel (c), point 1″.

investment in panel (c), at point 1″. Because we began with the assumption that Home and Foreign were identical, this also means that saving equals investment in Home and Foreign, so both regions' current accounts are zero, at point 1 in panel (a) and point 1′ in panel (b). In this initial setup, there are no global imbalances.

The model tells us how regional saving and investment determine the global equilibrium real interest rate. With this model in hand, we can now show how current account imbalances emerge when there are shocks to saving and investment.

Regional Saving Shocks Suppose Foreign experiences an exogenous increase in saving. This increase may be due to an increase in private saving (households desire to save more, say, due to a temporary income windfall) or government saving (say, due to a temporary budget surplus). What happens in the world capital market in response to Foreign's saving shock?

The countries start out in initial equilibrium at point 1 for Home, shown in panel (a) in Figure 11-11, and 1′ for Foreign, shown in panel (b). Suppose the Foreign saving supply increases by \$2 billion. In panel (b), the Foreign saving supply S^* curve shifts out, causing the world saving supply curve S^W to shift out by the same amount in panel (c). As a result, there is an excess of world saving supply over world investment demand at the initial world real interest rate $r_1^W = 5\%$. To restore equilibrium in the world capital market, the world real interest rate must fall to $r_2^W = 4\%$, increasing the quantity of investment in both countries as we move down each country's investment demand curve.

FIGURE 11-11

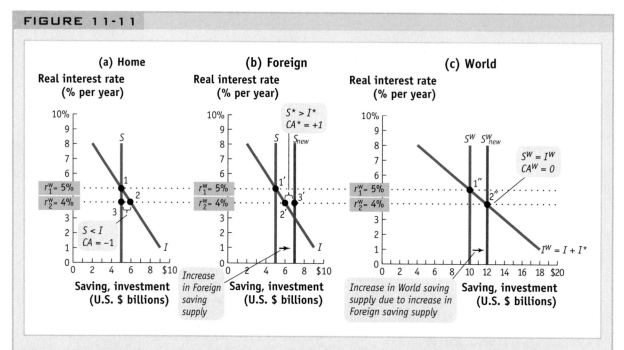

Increase in Foreign Savings From the initial equilibrium at points 1, 1', and 1", Foreign's saving increases to $7 billion in panel (b). World saving supply increases in panel (c) and the world real interest falls until once again world saving equals world investment (point 2"). At the lower real interest rate, Home's level of investment increases to point 2, shown in panel (a). Saving is unchanged at point 3, so the Home current account goes into deficit. Meanwhile, panel (b) shows that at the lower interest rate, Foreign saving (point 3') is now greater than the level of investment (point 2'), and it has an offsetting current account surplus. For the world as a whole, the current account balance is zero.

At the new, lower real interest rate, Home will have an excess of investment demand (point 2) over saving supply (point 3), and Home will run a current account deficit of −$1 billion, as shown in panel (a). With its excess of saving supply (point 3') over investment demand (point 2'), Foreign will run an equal and opposite current account surplus of +$1 billion, as shown in panel (b). In panel (c), the world current account is in balance (point 2"), but each country has an imbalance.

To sum up, Foreign's extra saving supply bids down the world real interest rate. This boosts investment in Home and Foreign. Foreign's extra saving is channeled not only into extra investment in Foreign but also into extra investment in Home, generating current account imbalances.

Regional Investment Shocks Now we return to Figure 11-10 and suppose Home experiences an exogenous shift out (increase) in investment demand. This may be the result of a sudden emergence of profitable investment opportunities, say, due to technological change leading to an increase in productivity. What happens in the world capital market?

Once again, let's start our analysis (shown in Figure 11-12) with the countries in initial equilibrium, Home at point 1 in panel (a) and Foreign at point 1' in panel (b). If Home investment demand increases by $2 billion at each level of the real interest rate, the Home investment demand curve I shifts out as shown in panel (a). This increase causes world investment demand curve I^W to shift out by the same amount as shown in panel (c). As a result, there is an excess of world investment demand (point 2") over world saving supply at the initial world real interest rate $r_1^W = 5\%$ (point 1"). To restore equilibrium in the world capital market, the world real interest rate must rise to $r_2^W = 6\%$.

At this new, higher real interest rate, Home has an excess of investment demand (point 2) over saving supply (point 3) and runs a current account deficit of −$1 billion, shown in panel (a). Foreign has an excess of saving supply (point 3') over investment demand (point 2') and runs an equal and opposite current account surplus of +$1 billion, as shown in panel (b). In panel (c), the world current account is in balance (point 2").

To sum up, Home's extra investment demand bids up the world real interest rate. This crowds out investment in Home and Foreign. The surplus Foreign saving is channeled into extra investment at Home, generating current account imbalances.

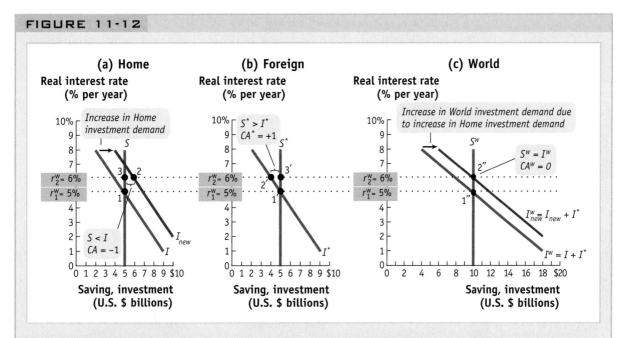

FIGURE 11-12

Increase in Home Investment When Home investment demand shifts out as shown in panel (a), world investment demand shifts out in panel (c), causing the world real interest to rise until once again world saving equals world investment (point 2"). At the higher real interest rate, Home investment (point 2) is higher than saving (point 3), and the Home current account goes into deficit. Foreign's investment, shown at point 2' in panel (b), is now greater than its saving (point 3'), so it has an offsetting current account surplus. The world current account is zero.

APPLICATION

The Savings Glut

Our simple current account model can explain how, in the short run, positive shocks to saving supply and investment demand can generate current account imbalances. (The examples can also be reversed to look at the impact of negative shocks.)

We can now see that Home will experience a current account deficit (its saving will be less than its investment), and the foreign country will experience an offsetting surplus (its saving will be greater than its investment) under the following circumstances:

1. There is a positive shock to Home investment demand.
2. There is a negative shock to Home saving supply.
3. There is a negative shock to Foreign investment demand.
4. There is a positive shock to Foreign saving supply.

This basic analysis allows us to more accurately characterize recent trends in the global economy. In cases 1 and 2, world investment demand rises relative to world saving supply and the world real interest rate rises. In cases 3 and 4, world investment demand falls relative to world saving supply and the world real interest rate falls.

Which of these descriptions best fits the world economy in recent years? Figure 11-13 provides an answer. Since the 1980s, two trends coincide. There has been a steady downward trend in the level of world saving and investment

FIGURE 11-13

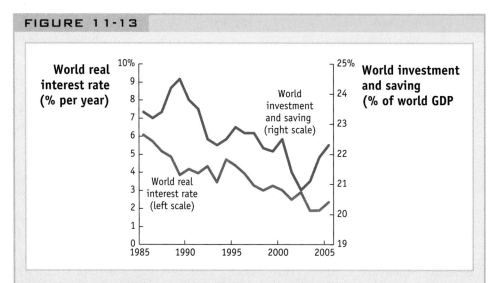

Savings Glut Since the 1980s, world saving and investment have fallen as a share of world GDP. If this decline had been primarily due to negative shocks to world savings supply, the world real interest rate would have risen. That the world real interest rate has instead fallen indicates that the decline in world saving and investment has been the result, primarily, of negative shocks to world investment demand.

Sources: IMF, World Economic Outlook, Martin Wolf, "Fixing Global Finance," SAIS Lectures, March 2006.

(which are equal, notwithstanding statistical discrepancies). And there has been a steady downward trend in the world real interest rate.

Our discussion tells us that the trend of declining real interest rates may be the result of two kinds of shocks. World saving supply could have shifted out, or world investment demand could have shifted in, or some combination of the two events could have occurred. Can we say more?

Yes. In Figure 11-13, the steady decline in the quantities of total world investment and total world saving tells us that in the long run the world must have seen large inward shifts in investment demand over the past two decades, relative to any outward shifts in saving supply. (If outward saving supply shifts had dominated, quantities would have gone up as real interest rate fell, but that wasn't the case.)

This state of affairs—an abundance of saving after a fall in investment causing real interest rates to drop—has come to be known as a **savings glut,** a term that came to prominence after it was used by Federal Reserve Chair Ben Bernanke to describe these trends in global capital markets. ■

Looking Backward: How We Got Here

Although the savings glut hypothesis describes the world capital market as a whole, particular regions have diverged from the global average and experienced imbalances. Some areas have seen investment booms, whereas others have suffered worse-than-average investment collapses. Some areas have seen saving supply rise, others have seen it fall. Some explanations for the most notable areas with imbalances are as follows, the first a group of deficit countries, the next three all groups of surplus countries.

- *Fast-growth advanced countries in deficit.* These include the United States and other countries in the so-called Anglosphere (United Kingdom, Canada, Australia, New Zealand), plus fast-growing EU countries like Ireland, Spain, and Portugal. All have seen investment booms, and some have also seen declines in saving. In the United States, temporary increases in wartime government spending have also required additional borrowing. Current accounts have turned large and negative, as financing flowed in from the rest of the world. Because of its sheer size, the United States dominates this group of deficit countries.

- *Slow-growth advanced countries in surplus.* The notable examples here are Japan and Switzerland. Both have experienced ten or more years of very slow growth with little investment. Saving has remained high. Current accounts have turned large and positive, as financing flowed from these countries to the rest of the world. Several other countries in Continental "Old Europe" also fit this pattern.

- *Oil exporters in surplus.* High oil prices may be only a temporary phenomenon, so countries specialized in oil production, mostly in the Middle East, tend to treat oil booms as temporary positive shocks to output that should be "saved for a rainy day" (see Chapter 6). Thus, the oil exporters have been using export revenue to acquire not foreign goods but foreign assets, and running very large current account surpluses. These assets can be sold later to permit consumption smoothing, a pattern seen in previous oil boom episodes. Typically, most of this saving is done by the government agencies that handle the oil revenues.

■ *Emerging Asia in surplus.* This group of countries has experienced fast growth, with accompanying high rates of investment. However, saving rates have been higher still, leading to net current account surpluses. At some level, this outcome appears to be a puzzle because one might expect such countries to want to finance some increase in current consumption out of higher future incomes. The high levels of saving in these countries are partly due to high levels of private saving, but a large part takes the form of official reserve purchases financed out of government saving (see **Side Bar: Reserves and Global Imbalances**).

Looking Forward: What Next?

A current account imbalance must be financed, and, as we saw in Chapter 5, the balance of payments identity tells us how a current account deficit (surplus) is offset by a financial account surplus (deficit), which in turn leads to a change in a country's external wealth. If current account imbalances persist, then a surplus region would build up an ever-larger credit position (external wealth exploding in a positive direction), and a deficit region would build up an ever-larger debit position (external wealth exploding in a negative direction). This is exactly what has been happening recently, with external wealth declining in deficit regions such as the United States and rising in

SIDE BAR

Reserves and Global Imbalances

The governments in many Middle East oil exporters and many emerging market Asian countries have been engaging in large purchases of foreign exchange reserves. These official purchases have been so large that they have dwarfed the inward private capital flows to the region. Without the reserve buildup, all else equal, these regions would have been running current account deficits and financial account surpluses, the opposite of the pattern we actually see.

This point is clear when we examine the breakdown of the financial account trends shown in Figure 11-14. All of these regions were experiencing net inflows of capital on the private nonofficial part of the financial account (that is, the *nonreserve financial account*). The inflows mean that they were net exporters of assets in private transactions, net private borrowers from the rest of the world. But all that bor-

rowing and all those private inflows were more than offset by massive net outflows of capital on the government part of the financial account (that is, the *official settlements balance*). These massive outflows mean that these regions were net importers of assets in official transactions, net official lenders to the rest of the world.

The central banks of these countries have ensured that their official reserve purchases do not expand the local money supply and thus cause their exchange rates to depart from their pegs to the U.S. dollar. How? Any purchases of reserves in excess of the quantity consistent with the money supply needed to maintain the peg have been *sterilized* by simultaneous, offsetting sales of domestic assets by the central bank. As we saw in Chapter 9, sterilizations of this kind imply a contraction of domestic credit, and all else equal, this decline in public debt

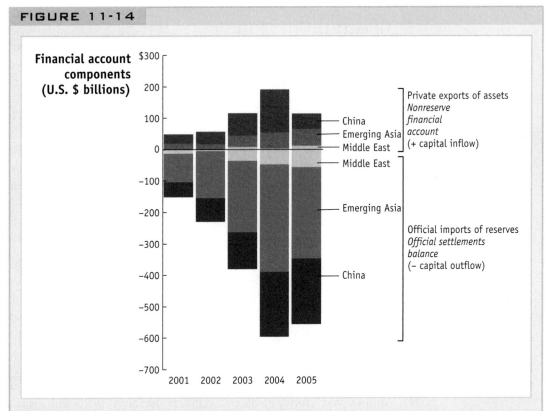

FIGURE 11-14

Reserve Accumulation and Global Imbalances The current account surpluses in emerging Asia and the Middle East (see Figure 11-8) generate financial account deficits. These are mostly driven by reserve flows, a nonmarket phenomenon: capital outflows due to the official purchases of foreign assets by these countries' central banks (deficits in the official settlements balance). These are so large that they overwhelm private capital inflows (surpluses in the nonreserve financial account). Private capital is flowing to these countries, but even more official capital is flowing out.

Sources: IMF; Martin Wolf, "Fixing Global Finance," SAIS Lectures, March 2006.

held by the central bank has to imply higher public saving, a smaller government deficit, or a larger surplus.

In the case of the oil exporters, the reserve hoards may be the temporary but inevitable result of the fact that most oil revenues accrue to government-owned entities, with the saving being handled by various state financial agencies. These state agencies have always largely invested perceived temporary oil windfalls in safe assets such as U.S. Treasury debt.

The emerging Asian countries are in a different situation. Their rise in incomes isn't seen as a transitory resource windfall but a permanent trend in growth. Why aren't they consuming more out of future income and borrowing as necessary as we might expect? In this view, favored by many economists

and policy makers, the Asian accumulation of reserves has been a case of excessive saving.

But as we noted in Chapter 9, others disagree, noting that emerging Asia is largely a bloc of countries that peg to the U.S. dollar and that have suffered devastating exchange rate crises as recently as 1997. The Asian countries have reacted by building up huge war chests of reserves to try to prevent any recurrence of such crises in the future. The rationale for a sovereign policy choice of a fixed exchange rate regime can be quite strong in emerging markets, as we saw in Chapter 8; and with that regime comes the equally sovereign right to choose a satisfactory level of reserves. Apparently, for emerging Asia, the level it considers prudent is very high indeed—but that choice has global consequences.*

* See, for example, Martin Wolf, "The Lessons Asians Learnt from Their Financial Crisis," Financial Times, *May 23, 2007; Chris Giles, "Wrong Lessons from Asia's Crisis,"* Financial Times, *July 2, 2007.*

surplus regions such as emerging Asia and the oil exporters, as shown in Figure 11-15.

As we learned in Chapter 6, persistent imbalances (which lead to diverging levels of external wealth) are incompatible with the *long-run budget constraint*. A country cannot borrow and go deeper into debt forever; sooner or later it must run surpluses and repay. If the imbalances can't last forever, then how long can they persist and what will happen when they reverse? These issues have worried some economists and policy makers. Predicting the turning point is difficult, as is any macroeconomic forecasting exercise. But we can draw on economic theory for some guidance to assess what will happen when the imbalances eventually unwind, and that is the subject of the remainder of this section.

Debtors, Creditors, and the Long-Run Budget Constraint

A closer look at the long-run budget constraint illustrates the limits to global imbalances. The following example assumes the same conditions as the examples studied in Chapter 6. A country initially has external wealth in period 0 (today) of W_0, and the world real interest rate is r^W. We ask, what stable or *steady-state* level of the trade balance must this country adopt to satisfy the long-run budget constraint?

To answer this question, we have to look at the dynamics of external wealth and ensure that external wealth does not explode. To simplify our analysis, we assume that capital gains and transfers are zero. With this assumption, we

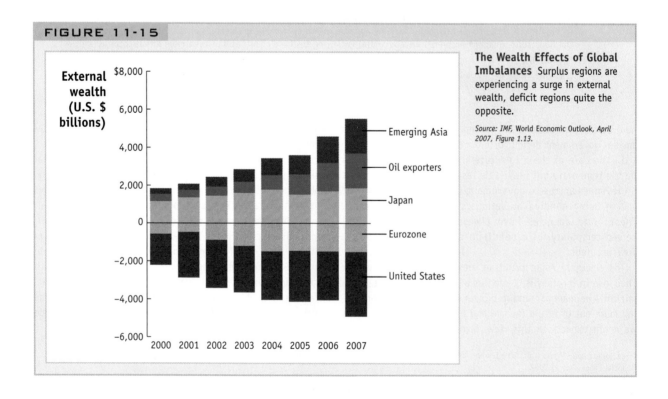

FIGURE 11-15

The Wealth Effects of Global Imbalances Surplus regions are experiencing a surge in external wealth, deficit regions quite the opposite.

Source: IMF, World Economic Outlook, April 2007, Figure 1.13.

showed in Chapter 6 that the change in wealth in any period equals the current account, which equals the trade balance TB plus net factor income from abroad $NFIA$. Net factor income equals $r^W W$, the interest on external wealth earned if W is positive and the country is a creditor nation. If the country is a debtor nation and W is negative, then $r^W W$ is the interest the country pays on its debt.

As we saw in Chapter 6, to satisfy the long-run budget constraint, the country must not let its external wealth explode (in either direction). So if its trade balance is steady, its level of trade surplus (or deficit) must exactly offset its interest due (or received)—this way no new net borrowing is needed, and the country keeps its net indebtedness constant while paying the interest due. That is, the country must choose a level of the trade balance in all periods, or in the steady state, given by

$$TB = - r^W W$$

Why is this so? Remember that the current account in every period is $CA = TB + r^W W = 0$ and so the condition given here ensures that the change in wealth (which equals the current account, given our assumptions) is zero every period. No other choice is feasible. If the country chose a lower trade balance, then in the first period the current account would be in deficit, and the country could not pay the interest on its debt in full; the country would need to borrow more to pay the interest. The same would happen in the second period but on an even larger debt. Persistent current account deficits would mean borrowing every period to pay accrued interest owed, and this would cause the level of debt to explode. Conversely, a trade balance higher than $r^W W$ would create persistent current account surpluses and *external wealth* would eventually grow at the rate of interest toward infinity. The long-run budget constraint rules out such explosive paths for wealth.

This is a crucial condition that tells us that in the future, a creditor country with $W_0 > 0$ will run a trade deficit with $TB = - r^W W_0 < 0$ forever. Conversely, in a debtor country with $W_0 < 0$, the country will run a trade surplus with $TB = - r^W W_0 > 0$ forever.

What does this imply? Recall that, by definition, the trade balance is the difference between what is produced and what is spent in a country, $TB = GDP - GNE$. Creditors live off their wealth by spending more than they produce, and debtors produce more than they spend to pay off their debts.

Real Exchange Rates and Global Imbalances: Two Views

We know that current account imbalances shift external wealth: they cause it to rise in the surplus nation and fall in the deficit nation. But as we have seen, such imbalances eventually require long-run changes in the trade balance to ensure the long-run budget constraint is met. How will that adjustment be achieved?

This is one of the oldest questions in international macroeconomics, known as the **transfer problem,** and it has occupied great thinkers like Mill, Keynes, Ohlin, and Samuelson. Even now that the theory is well understood, however, there is still great disagreement among economists about the strength of the predicted economic responses to changes in external wealth.

The main dispute centers on whether the required change in the trade balance will necessitate large changes in real and nominal exchange rates. If such changes are needed, the concern is that they may prove disruptive to individual economies and the world economy as a whole, either due to the real costs of adjustment or to the potential for disorder in financial markets. The two opposing views in this debate rest on different models of spending behavior and international trade.

Identical Economies, Purchasing Power Parity, and the "Immaculate Transfer" The more benign view of the adjustment process starts off with a two-country model of Home and Foreign economies and a string of assumptions. Both countries are identical and all goods are traded costlessly. In addition, either all goods are identical in Home and Foreign, or they are different but both countries have identical spending patterns.

Now suppose $1 of wealth is transferred from Home to Foreign. What will happen to the demand for Home and Foreign goods in the long run? Under the stated assumptions, nothing. The extra wealth in Foreign will generate increased income and spending in Foreign. The reduced wealth in Home will generate decreased income and spending in Home. The effects will cancel out, and demand for Home goods and Foreign goods will be unchanged.

Now consider the impact of the wealth transfer on the real exchange rate $q = EP^*/P$, the ratio of Foreign prices to Home prices. Even if Home and Foreign goods are different, demand for each type of good does not change and the prices of each type of good do not change. If Home and Foreign prices do not change when expressed in the same currency, then relative PPP holds and the real exchange rate holds steady. When the goods are identical, the point is almost moot: absolute PPP holds and prices are the same everywhere expressed in a common currency so the real exchange rate doesn't move.

For this special case, we can plot the trade balance TB against the real exchange rate q in Figure 11-16, panel (a). The PPP view of the relationship of the trade balance to the real exchange rate says that the relationship is a vertical line with q equal to a constant q_1 regardless of the level of the trade balance and external wealth. The real exchange rate is fixed, relative PPP holds (and in the case of absolute PPP, q is fixed at 1).

In this world, the changes in wealth require no change in the real exchange rate. Suppose Home sees its external wealth fall from W_1 to W_2, perhaps due to a series of current account deficits (perhaps driven by tax cuts or an expensive war) or some other shock that transfers wealth from Home to Foreign. When Home's level of external wealth falls, then the steady-state trade balance required to satisfy the long-run budget constraint rises from $TB_1 = -r^W W_1$ to $TB_2 = -r^W W_2$.

This trade balance adjustment will result from Home's loss of wealth (which will crimp consumption and boost saving). But here we know that such a consumption adjustment will not differentially affect spending patterns on Home and Foreign goods. So Home can achieve the increase in the trade

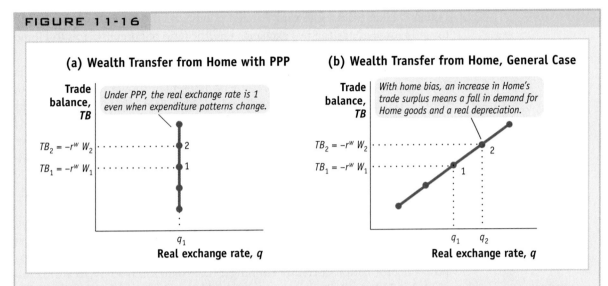

FIGURE 11-16

(a) Wealth Transfer from Home with PPP

Trade balance, *TB*

Under PPP, the real exchange rate is 1 even when expenditure patterns change.

$TB_2 = -r^w W_2$ 2

$TB_1 = -r^w W_1$ 1

q_1

Real exchange rate, *q*

(b) Wealth Transfer from Home, General Case

Trade balance, *TB*

With home bias, an increase in Home's trade surplus means a fall in demand for Home goods and a real depreciation.

$TB_2 = -r^w W_2$ 2

$TB_1 = -r^w W_1$ 1

q_1 q_2

Real exchange rate, *q*

Real Exchange Rates and the Trade Balance Panel (a) shows the relationship between the trade balance and real exchange rates when PPP holds and Home and Foreign have identical spending patterns: a wealth transfer from Home to Foreign increases the Home trade surplus from TB_1 to TB_2 but has no impact on the real exchange rate. Panel (b) shows that under more realistic assumptions, including a home bias in expenditure patterns, a transfer of wealth from Home to Foreign increases the Home trade surplus from TB_1 to TB_2, but expenditure switching has to be induced by a real depreciation in the home country from q_1 to q_2.

balance with the real exchange rate holding steady at q_1. Adjustment to the wealth transfer occurs smoothly and without any impact on real exchange rates. The pleasing absence of potentially disruptive disturbances to exchange rates (given enough assumptions) had led this scenario to be dubbed the "immaculate transfer" by some skeptical economists.

Differentiated Goods, Home Bias, and the Real Exchange Rate The alternative and less benign view of the adjustment process starts with the assumption that goods are differentiated but that Home and Foreign do *not* have the same spending patterns. Specifically, they do not have an equal propensity to spend on Home goods. Instead, Home prefers to spend on Home goods and Foreign prefers to spend on Foreign goods. This pattern is referred to as *home bias* in consumption spending (each country wants to spend more on its own goods).

Under this view, $1 of wealth transferred from Home to Foreign will increase Foreign spending on Home goods by less than the decrease in Home spending on Home goods; and it will increase Foreign spending on Foreign goods by more than the decrease in Home spending on Foreign goods. The net result is that the demand for Foreign goods will rise and demand for Home goods will fall. As in the previous case, the shifts in wealth induce shifts in consumption in each country, but the net impact on the demand for the two types of goods is no longer neutral.

Under standard assumptions about supply, these demand shifts will bid up the price of Foreign goods and bid down the price of Home goods. Because the

Foreign basket is biased toward Foreign goods, and the Home basket is biased toward Home goods, the real exchange rate, the ratio of Foreign prices to Home prices, $q = EP^*/P$, will rise and Home will experience a real depreciation.

When spending patterns show a home bias, the relation between the trade balance and the real exchange rate is very different as shown in Figure 11-16, panel (b). If a country's level of external wealth falls from W_1 to W_2, then its required steady-state trade balance rises from $TB_1 = -r^W W_1$ to $TB_2 = -r^W W_2$. To achieve the increase in the trade balance, the real exchange rate q will have to depreciate from q_1 to q_2. Patterns of demand for home and foreign goods need to change, and when there is home bias in consumption, it is only through a real depreciation that such expenditure switching can be induced.

Real and Nominal Exchange Rates during Adjustment If the resolution of global imbalances requires large changes in real exchange rates, then it might also imply large changes in nominal exchange rates. For example, suppose a debtor nation currently running a trade deficit can adjust to a situation of trade surplus only by having its real exchange rate depreciate by 30%. This means $q = EP^*/P$ has to rise by 30%.

This real depreciation could be achieved without any change in nominal exchange rates *if* all of the change were absorbed by prices, with P^*/P rising by 30%. But in many cases, this type of adjustment is unlikely. If both countries have similar inflation targets, for example, then the authorities are unlikely to allow a 30% differential in price levels to develop, at least in the short run, because that price difference would imply very large inflation differentials. This kind of constraint on price movements leads many economists and policy makers to conclude that as global imbalances unwind, the biggest part of any necessary shift in real exchange rates will be accomplished largely by corresponding changes in nominal exchange rates.

Conclusions

The preceding analysis explained how changes in the level of a nation's external wealth today can have implications for future macroeconomic outcomes. All else equal, an increase in home debt means that the home country must run larger trade surpluses in the future, so as to satisfy the long-run budget constraint. If home and foreign goods are imperfect substitutes and countries' spending patterns are biased toward their own goods, then this process will require an eventual real depreciation of the home currency. If home and foreign inflation rates are similar, this real depreciation also implies an eventual nominal depreciation.

These findings help us understand some of the concerns about global imbalances in the world today, and in particular the worries about the large external debt and deficit position in the United States (and some other major deficit regions). In 2006, according to the Bureau of Economic Analysis, the U.S. trade deficit was $759 billion, or almost 6% of GDP. The U.S. level of external wealth was −$2,539 billion or −19% of GDP. A continued trade deficit of 6% forever is likely to be impossible to sustain.

However, although most economists can agree on these qualitative implications, there is great uncertainty about the size and timing of the needed adjustments. To greatly simplify, these positions can be divided into two camps:

- *Pessimists* argue that the size of the needed adjustment is large and that the exchange rate adjustments will be large and very disruptive. For example, if the trade deficit is 6% of GDP and external debt is 20% of GDP, then debt service requirements in the long run for a normal country might require a trade surplus of at least 0.5% of GDP (a 2.5% world real interest rate times a 20% debt level.) In the April 2007 *World Economic Outlook,* for example, the International Monetary Fund (IMF) presented an upper estimate that a change in the U.S. trade balance of even just +1% of GDP would require a massive 27% real devaluation of the U.S. dollar. Repeating that six or more times to turn a 6% deficit into a 0.5% surplus would imply a spectacular collapse in the U.S. real exchange rate, and by extension, a risk of a large nominal depreciation too. This adjustment could be spread out over time, and take the form of a slow and steady dollar depreciation. In the interim, the United States would continue to borrow, albeit at a declining rate—assuming foreigners continued to be willing to lend.

  A serious macroeconomic risk arises if markets expect such a depreciation to occur quickly, which might be necessary if foreigners became unwilling to keep lending to the United States in the near term. In that case, a rapid expected depreciation would cause great pain in the U.S. economy: the country would need to cope with a rapid shift in the pattern of consumption and production dictated by price changes; J-curve effects might delay and exacerbate adjustment problems; and in the U.S. FX market the foreign return would shift out and uncovered interest parity would bid up U.S. interest rates to high levels. These shocks would likely result in recession and unemployment. This is often called the hard landing scenario for the dollar.

- *Optimists* tend not to dispute the above theory, but instead take issue with the magnitudes involved—they believe that some additional factors will mitigate the adjustment problems. For example, the same IMF report noted above used different econometric techniques and found that a change in the U.S. trade balance of +1% of GDP might require only a 7% real devaluation of the U.S. dollar (versus the 27% mentioned above). With that kind of responsiveness, a large trade deficit could be turned around with much more modest real and nominal depreciations. However, other economists believe that such a large turnaround may not be needed in the United States for a variety of reasons. First, as noted in Chapter 6, the United States has received higher interest payments on its foreign assets than it has paid on its foreign liabilities, and this flow of perhaps 1%–2% of GDP per year could (*if it continues*) support a trade deficit indefinitely. Second, as discussed in Chapter 5, a large nominal devaluation would cause large valuation effects favoring the United States, because almost all U.S.

external liabilities are in U.S. dollars but most external assets are in foreign currencies, and the same forces would tend to boost the dollar value of net interest payments received too. Third, many economists point out that the United States has been historically one of the best credit risks and that the ratio of U.S. external debt to GDP is still low compared to many other countries. Both of these characteristics suggest that an external debt limit will not bind anytime soon. All of these mitigating factors are of disputed magnitude, but taken together these counterarguments suggest a much smaller dollar depreciation, and a more benign macroeconomic outcome, a so-called soft landing for the dollar.[14]

4 Debt and Default

As we saw in Chapter 6, when global capital markets work well, they can deliver gains in the form of consumption smoothing and investment efficiency. Yet international financial relations are often disrupted by **sovereign default,** which occurs when a sovereign government (i.e., one that is autonomous or independent) fails to meet its legal obligations to make payments on debt held by foreigners.

Sovereign default has a long history. Perhaps the first recorded default was in the fourth century BC, when Greek municipalities defaulted on loans from the Delos Temple.[15] Many of today's advanced countries have defaulted in the past. In 1343 a war-weary Edward III of England defaulted on short-term loans, consigning the major merchant banks of Florence to ruin. In 1557 Phillip II of Spain defaulted on short-term loans principally from South German bankers.[16] Spain defaulted 6 more times before 1800 and another 7 times in the nineteenth century. France defaulted 8 times between 1558 and the Revolution in 1789. A group of German states, Portugal, Austria, and Greece defaulted at least 4 times each in the 1800s, and across Europe as a whole there were at least 46 sovereign defaults between 1501 and 1900.[17] The United States has maintained a clean sheet during its brief existence, although several U.S. states defaulted when they were emerging markets in the 1800s.[18]

[14] For a discussion of these risks and their policy implications see Timothy F. Geithner, "Policy Implications of Global Imbalances," remarks by the President and Chief Executive Officer of the Federal Reserve Bank of New York, at the Financial Imbalances Conference at Chatham House, London, January 23, 2006.
[15] Federico Sturzenegger and Jeromin Zettelmeyer, 2007, *Debt Defaults and Lessons from a Decade of Crises,* Cambridge, Mass.: MIT Press, Chapter 1.
[16] Meir G. Kohn, "Merchant Banking in the Medieval and Early Modern Economy," February 1999, Dartmouth College, Department of Economics Working Paper No. 99-05.
[17] Carmen M. Reinhart, Kenneth S. Rogoff, and Miguel A. Savastano, 2003, "Debt Intolerance," *Brookings Papers on Economic Activity,* 1, 1–74.
[18] For example, see section 258 of the Mississippi state constitution. The American colonies did default, for example, on the paper bills known as *continentals,* issued from 1775 to 1779 to finance the Revolutionary War. However, in an attempt to make good, the colonies' bad debts were assumed by the United States in 1790 on the urging of the first U.S. secretary of the Treasury, Alexander Hamilton, a statesman with an acute understanding of the importance of good credit.

The advanced countries of today do not default, but as we noted in Chapter 1, default has been, and remains, a recurring problem in emerging markets and developing countries. One count shows that countries such as Argentina, Brazil, Mexico, Turkey, and Venezuela have defaulted between five and nine times since 1824 (and at least once since 1980) and have spent 30% of the time failing to meet their financial obligations. Another count lists 48 sovereign defaults in the period from 1976 to 1989, many in Latin America but others dotted throughout the world, and 16 more in the period from 1998 to 2002, including headline crises in Russia (1998) and Argentina (2002).[19]

One of the most puzzling aspects of the default problem is that emerging markets and developing countries often get into default trouble at much lower levels of debt than advanced countries. Yet default is a serious macroeconomic and financial problem for these countries. Because they attract so few financial flows of other kinds, government debt constitutes a large share (more than 30%) of these nations' external liabilities.[20]

To understand the workings of sovereign debt and defaults, we must first look at some of the peculiar characteristics of this form of borrowing.

A Few Peculiar Facts about Sovereign Debt

The first important fact about sovereign debt is that debtors are almost never forced to pay. Military responses, always costly, are certainly out of fashion. Legal responses are also largely futile: when developing country debt is issued in a foreign jurisdiction (e.g., in London or New York) there is practically no legal way to enforce a claim against a sovereign nation, and the recent increase in sovereign default litigation has done very little to change this state of affairs.[21]

The repayment of a sovereign debt is thus a matter of choice for the borrowing government. Economists are therefore inclined to look for a rational explanation in which default is triggered by economic conditions. A key question is, then, how painful does repayment have to get before default occurs?

To answer this question, we must evaluate the costs and benefits of default. The benefits are clear: no repayment means the country gets to keep all that money. Are there costs? While not as apparent as the benefits, there must be costs to default—if there were no costs, countries would never pay their debt, and, as a result, no lending would happen in the first place! Thus economists,

---

[19] Carmen M. Reinhart, Kenneth S. Rogoff, and Miguel A. Savastano, 2003, "Debt Intolerance," *Brookings Papers on Economic Activity,* 1, 1–74; Federico Sturzenegger and Jeromin Zettelmeyer, 2007, *Debt Defaults and Lessons from a Decade of Crises,* Cambridge, Mass.: MIT Press, Chapter 1.

[20] About 50% of the external liabilities of these countries consist of debt, and of that, approximately 75% is government debt. Data from 2004 from the World Bank; Global Development Finance database; and Gian Maria Milesi-Ferretti and Philip R. Lane, 2006, "The External Wealth of Nations Mark II: Revised and Extended Estimates of Foreign Assets and Liabilities, 1970–2004," IMF Working Paper No. 06/69.

[21] On litigation, see Federico Sturzenegger and Jeromin Zettelmeyer, "Has the Legal Threat to Sovereign Debt Restructuring Become Real?" CIF Working Paper, Universidad Torcuato Di Tella, April 2006. In theory, foreign assets of defaulters can be legally seized, but defaulting nations naturally avoid this by repatriating such assets shortly before going into default. In contrast, advanced country debt is usually issued at home, in the country's own jurisdiction, where creditors (domestic and foreign) have stronger legal claims against the sovereign.

discounting more sentimental motives for repayment such as honor and honesty, have focused on two types of costs that act as a "punishment" for defaulters and provide the incentive for nations to repay their debts.[22]

- *Financial market penalties.* Empirical evidence shows that debtors are usually excluded from credit markets for some period of time after a default. This could expose them to greater consumption risk and other disadvantages. However, economic theory casts doubt on whether these costs alone are sufficient to ensure the possibility of repayment if the exclusion period is short or when borrowers have other ways to smooth consumption (such as investing previously borrowed wealth, purchasing insurance, or going to a different set of financial intermediaries).

- *Broader macroeconomic costs.* These could include lost investment, lost trade, or lost output arising from adverse financial conditions in the wake of a default. These adverse conditions include higher risk premiums, credit contractions, exchange rate crises, and banking crises. If these costs are high enough, they can encourage nations to repay, even if financial market costs are insufficient.

The Granger Collection

Old style punishment: In response to a default, the French invaded and occupied Mexico in 1862, suffering only one major defeat at the Battle of Puebla (now commemorated by the Mexican holiday Cinco de Mayo).

Summary Sovereign debt is a **contingent claim** on a nation's assets: governments will repay depending on whether it is more beneficial to repay than to default. With a simple model of how a country makes the decision to default, we can better understand why borrowers default some of the time and repay some of the time; what ultimately causes these contingent outcomes; why some borrowers get into default trouble even at low levels of debt, while others do not; and how lenders respond to this state of affairs and why they continue to lend to defaulting countries. The model we develop is simple, but it provides useful insights on all of these questions.[23]

A Model of Default, Part One: The Probability of Default

In this section, we present a static, one-period model of sovereign debt and default. The first part of the model focuses on default as a contingent claim that will be paid only under certain conditions.

Assumptions The model focuses on the desire of borrowers to default in hard times, when output is relatively low, so that they may smooth their consumption. Thus, for now we ignore any investment motives for borrowing and concentrate on the consumption-smoothing or "insurance" benefits that a

[22] Jonathan Eaton and Mark Gersovitz, 1981, "Debt with Potential Repudiation: Theoretical and Empirical Analysis," *Review of Economic Studies,* 48(2), April, 289–309; Jeremy Bulow and Kenneth Rogoff, 1989, "A Constant Recontracting Model of Sovereign Debt," *Journal of Political Economy,* 97(1), February, 155–178; Kenneth M. Kletzer and Brian D. Wright, 2000, "Sovereign Debt as Intertemporal Barter," *American Economic Review,* 90(3), June, 621–639; Laura Alfaro and Fabio Kanczuk, 2005, "Sovereign Debt as a Contingent Claim: A Quantitative Approach," *Journal of International Economics,* 65(2), March, 297–314.
[23] The model is based on Luis Catão and Sandeep Kapur, 2006, "Volatility and the Debt-Intolerance Paradox," *IMF Staff Papers,* 53(2), 195–218.

country derives from having the option to default on its debt and consume more than it otherwise would.

If repayment is to be contingent in our model, what will it be contingent on? To introduce some exogenous fluctuations, we assume, realistically, that a borrowing country has a fluctuating level of output Y. Specifically, Y is equally likely to take any value between a minimum $\overline{Y} - V$ and a maximum $\overline{Y}$. The difference between the minimum and maximum is a measure of the volatility of output, V. Although the level of output Y is not known in advance, we assume that everyone understands the level of V and the probability of different output levels Y. We suppose the government is the sole borrower and it takes out a one-period loan in the previous period, before the level of output is known. The debt will be denoted L for loan (or liability, which it is) and carries an interest rate r_L, which we call the *lending rate*. We suppose this loan is supplied by one or more competitive foreign creditors who have access to funds from the world capital market at a risk-free interest rate r, which we assume is a constant.

We suppose the loan is due to be paid off after the country finds out what output Y is in the current period. The problem we have is as follows: to figure out the lending terms (the debt level and lending rate) and to understand what the country chooses to do when the loan comes due (default versus repayment). As in many problems in economics, we must "solve backward" to allow for expectations.

The Borrower Chooses Default versus Repayment We assume the sovereign borrower faces some "punishment" or cost for defaulting. There are debates about what forms these costs could take, and we discuss this later in this section. For now we do not take a stand on exactly what these costs are but assume that if the government defaults, then it faces a cost equivalent to a fraction c of its output: that is, cY is lost, leaving only $(1 - c)Y$ for national consumption. Note that these costs are unlike debt payments: they are just losses for the debtor with no corresponding gains for the creditors.

Now that we have established some costs of defaulting, the choice facing the country becomes clearer. For simplicity, we assume two possible courses of action: repay or default.[24] If the government repays the debt, the country will be able to consume only output Y minus the principal and interest on the loan $(1 + r_L)L$. If the government defaults, the country can consume output Y minus the punishment cY. Thus, the government will act as follows:

$$\text{Repay if} \quad \underbrace{Y - (1 + r_L)L}_{\substack{\text{Consumption after repayment} \\ \text{(line RR)}}} \quad > \quad \underbrace{Y - cY}_{\substack{\text{Consumption after nonrepayment} \\ \text{and default (line NN)}}}$$

Figure 11-17 plots both sides of this inequality against Y for the case in which both repayment and default will occur within the range of possible output levels between maximum output $\overline{Y}$ and minimum output $\overline{Y} - V$. At some

---

[24] Intermediate cases of partial default are possible in theory and in reality, as is renegotiation, but we focus on a binary default versus repayment choice for simplicity.

FIGURE 11-17

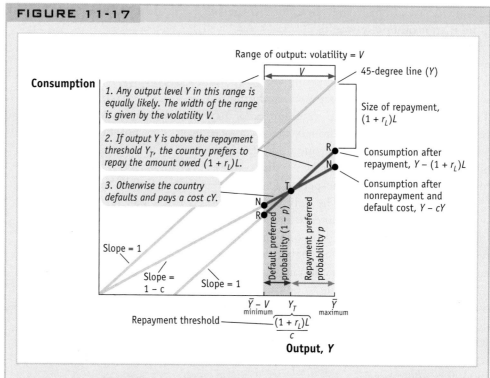

Range of output: volatility = V

Consumption

1. Any output level Y in this range is equally likely. The width of the range is given by the volatility V.

2. If output Y is above the repayment threshold Y_T, the country prefers to repay the amount owed $(1 + r_L)L$.

3. Otherwise the country defaults and pays a cost cY.

Slope = 1

Slope = 1 − c

Slope = 1

45-degree line (Y)

Size of repayment, $(1 + r_L)L$

Consumption after repayment, $Y − (1 + r_L)L$

Consumption after nonrepayment and default cost, $Y − cY$

Default preferred probability $(1 − p)$

Repayment preferred probability p

$\overline{Y} − V$
minimum

Y_T

$\overline{Y}$
maximum

Repayment threshold ——— $\dfrac{(1 + r_L)L}{c}$

Output, Y

Repayment versus Default When output is high, the country repays its debt with probability p (yellow region) because the cost of defaulting is greater than the cost of repayment. In this region, consumption after repayment (shown by line RR) is greater than consumption after defaulting (line NN). When output is low, the country defaults with probability $1 − p$ (orange region). In this region, the cost of defaulting is less than the cost of repayment because line NN is above line RR. The switch from default to repayment occurs at point T, where the critical level of output reaches the repayment threshold Y_T.

critical level of output, called the **repayment threshold,** the government will switch from repayment to default. At this critical level, the two sides of the preceding inequality have to be equal; that is, the debt payoff amount $(1 + r_L)L$ must equal the punishment cost cY. By rearranging the preceding inequality, we can find the level of Y at the repayment threshold Y_T and can restate the government's choice as

$$\text{Repay if} \quad Y \geq \underbrace{\frac{(1 + r_L)L}{c}}_{\substack{\text{Repayment threshold} \\ = \\ \overline{\overline{Y}}_T}}$$

For the case shown in Figure 11-17, we assume that this repayment threshold $Y_T = (1 + r_L)L/c$ is within the range of possible outputs between the minimum $\overline{Y} - V$ and the maximum $\overline{Y}$.

The value of consumption after repayment, $Y - (1 + r_L)L$, is shown by the repayment line RR, which has a slope of 1: every extra \$1 of output goes toward consumption, net of debt repayments. The value of consumption after nonrepayment and default, $Y - cY$, is shown by the nonrepayment line NN, which has a slope of $(1 - c)$, which is less than 1: when a country has decided to default, from every extra $1 of output gained by not repaying the country's debts, only $(1 − c) goes toward consumption, allowing for the net punishment cost.

The lines RR and NN intersect at the critical point T, and the corresponding level of output Y_T is the repayment threshold. Given that the slope of NN is less than the slope of RR, we can see that the country will choose to repay when output is above the repayment threshold Y_T (i.e., to the right of T) and will choose to default when output is below the repayment threshold Y_T (i.e., to the left of T).

Note that the size of the repayment region relative to the default region tells us how likely repayment is to occur relative to default. Let the probability of repayment be p. The key piece of the puzzle is to figure out what determines p. We now show how it depends on two things: how volatile output is and how burdensome the debt repayment is.

An Increase in the Debt Burden The first variation on the model in Figure 11-17 that we consider is an exogenous increase in the level of debt payments, which we suppose increase from the original level $(1 + r_L)L$ to a new higher level $(1 + r_L')L'$. This increase could be due to a change in the debt level, a change in the lending rate, or some combination of the two. This case is shown in Figure 11-18.

FIGURE 11-18

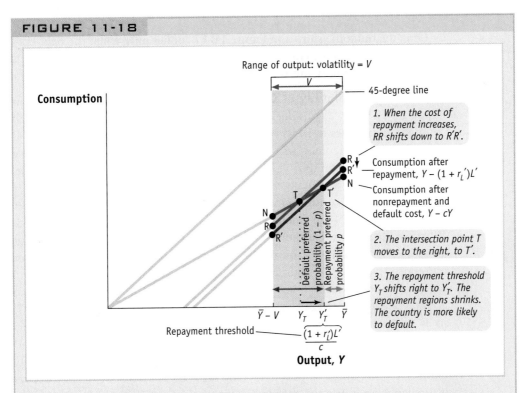

An Increase in the Debt Burden An increase in the level of debt or the lending rate raises the repayment sum and so reduces consumption after repayment at all levels of Y, causing RR to shift down. This shift makes repayment less likely (the yellow region gets smaller) and default more likely (the orange region gets larger). The probability of repayment p falls. The switch from default to repayment occurs at a higher critical level of output at T′, the new repayment threshold Y_T'.

The value of consumption after repayment, $Y - (1 + r_L)L$, must fall as $(1 + r_L)L$ rises, so line RR will shift down to $R'R'$. The costs of repayment are higher, and the country will find it beneficial to default more often. We can see this in the figure because after the RR curve shifts down, a greater part of the line NN will now sit above the line $R'R'$, and the new critical intersection point T will move to the right at T', corresponding to the new higher repayment threshold $Y'_T = (1 + r'_L)L'/c$.

What does this mean for the probability of repayment? It must fall. The repayment region on the right is now smaller, and the default region on the left is larger. With all output levels in the two regions equally likely, the probability p that output is in the repayment region must now be lower.

We have considered only a small change in the debt burden, so the repayment region hasn't vanished. But if the debt burden increases sufficiently, RR will shift down so far that the critical point T will shift all the way to the right, to the maximum level of output, the repayment region will disappear, and the probability of repayment will be zero (or 0%). If the debt burden is high enough, the country is always better off taking the punishment.

Conversely, if the debt burden *decreases* sufficiently, RR will shift up so far that the critical point T will shift all the way to the left, to the minimum level of output, the default region will disappear, and the probability of repayment will be 1 (or 100%). If the debt burden is low enough, the country will always repay.

Thus, the outcome shown in Figure 11-17 applies only when the debt burden is at some intermediate level such that the repayment threshold is between the minimum and maximum levels of output.

An Increase in Volatility of Output The second variation on the model in Figure 11-17 that we consider is an increase in the volatility of output, which we suppose increases from its original level V to a new higher level V'. This case is shown in Figure 11-19. There could be many reasons why a country is subject to higher output volatility: weather shocks to agricultural output, political instability, fluctuations in the prices of its exports, and so on.

In this case, the consumption levels after repayment on line RR and after default on line NN are unchanged because the debt burden is unchanged. What has changed is that there is now a much wider range of possible output levels. Higher volatility V means that output can now fall to an even lower minimum level, $\overline{Y} - V'$, but can only attain the same maximum $\overline{Y}$.

Thus, an increase in V makes default more likely. In Figure 11-17, the country wanted to default whenever output fell below the critical level T, so it will certainly want to default in the wider range of low outputs brought into play by higher volatility. The default region gets larger and now includes all these new possible levels of output to the left of T. Conversely, the range of outputs to the right of T where repayment occurs is unchanged because the repayment threshold $Y_T = (1 + r_L)L/c$ is unaffected by a change in V. Hence, the probability p that output is in the repayment region must fall because the repayment region is now smaller relative to the default region.

FIGURE 11-19

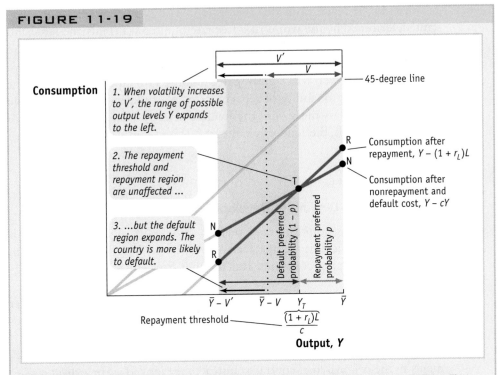

Consumption

1. When volatility increases to V', the range of possible output levels Y expands to the left.

2. The repayment threshold and repayment region are unaffected ...

3. ...but the default region expands. The country is more likely to default.

45-degree line

R — Consumption after repayment, $Y - (1 + r_L)L$

N — Consumption after nonrepayment and default cost, $Y - cY$

Default preferred probability $(1 - p)$

Repayment preferred probability p

Repayment threshold — $\dfrac{(1 + r_L)L}{c}$

$\bar{Y} - V'$ $\bar{Y} - V$ Y_T $\bar{Y}$

Output, Y

An Increase in Volatility An increase in volatility expands the range of low output possibilities. The repayment threshold Y_T stays the same because it is unrelated to V and depends only on the cost of defaulting and the size of the repayment burden. Even though the repayment region (yellow) remains the same size, the increased volatility makes default more likely because the default region (orange) is now relatively larger. The probability of repayment p falls.

To sum up, a rise in volatility lowers the level of debt L at which default becomes a possibility and after that point makes default more likely at any given level of L, up to the point at which default occurs with probability 100%.

The Lender Chooses the Lending Rate All of the preceding results assume a given interest rate on the loan. But now that we know how the likely probability of repayment p is determined, we can calculate the interest rate that a competitive lender must charge. Competition will mean that lenders can only just break even and make zero expected profit. Thus, the lender will set its lending rate so that the expected revenues from each dollar lent, given by the probability of repayment p times the amount repaid $(1 + r_L)$, equal the lender's cost for each dollar lent, which is given by $(1 + r)$, the principal plus the risk-free interest rate at which the lender can obtain funds.

Break-even condition for lender: $\quad p \quad \times \quad (1 + r_L) \quad = \quad (1 + r).$

Probability of repayment

Lender's revenue if repaid

Lender's costs

Lender's expected revenue

What do we learn from this expression? The right-hand side is a constant, determined by the world risk-free rate of interest r. Thus, the left-hand side must be constant, too. If p were 1 (100% probability of repayment), the solution would be straightforward: with no risk of default, and competitive lenders, the borrower will rightly get a lending rate equal to the risk-free rate r. But as the probability of repayment p falls, to keep the left-hand side constant, the lenders must raise the lending rate r_L. That is, to compensate for the default risk, the lenders charge a risk premium so that they still just break even.

APPLICATION

Is There Profit in Lending to Developing Countries?

Our breakeven assumption may seem a little odd. A popular belief is that rich country creditors, like loan sharks, are making huge profits from lending to developing countries. But the long-run empirical evidence suggests otherwise.

Economists Christoph Klingen, Beatrice Weder, and Jeromin Zettelmeyer looked at how lenders fared in emerging markets from the 1970s to the 2000s by computing the returns on government debt in 22 borrower countries.[25] They did not look at the *ex ante returns* that consisted of the promised repayments in the original loan contracts. Instead, they looked at the *ex post returns,* the realized rates of interest actually paid on the loans, allowing for any defaults, suspensions of payments, reschedulings, or other deviations from the contractual terms.

The results were striking, as shown by Figure 11-20. The average returns on emerging market bonds in this period were 9.1% per year. This was barely above the three-year U.S. government bond returns of 8.6% over the same period and below returns on ten-year U.S. government bonds (9.2%) and U.S. corporate bonds (10.5%). This is not because the borrowers were charged low interest rates beforehand. They were charged typical risk premiums. But if the loans had been paid off *according to those terms* we would have expected that lenders would have reaped much larger returns ex post. For example, based on the typical risk premiums seen in emerging markets in the period 1998 to 2007, an extra 2.8% return would have been demanded as a risk premium ex ante, pushing ex post returns up to around 12%–13%. But such high ex post returns were not seen, as Figure 11-20 shows: defaults ate up the risk premiums and the lenders barely broke even.

Considering the highly risky nature of emerging market debt, as compared with U.S. corporate debt, this finding is remarkable and it suggests that the breakeven assumption of our simple model is not far wrong. Admittedly, there were periods when emerging market bonds paid off handsomely. In the early 1990s, there were few defaults and lenders were repaid at high interest rates.

---

[25] Christoph Klingen, Jeromin Zettelmeyer, and Beatrice Weder, 2004, "How Private Creditors Fared in Emerging Debt Markets, 1970–2000," IMF Working Paper No. 04/13.

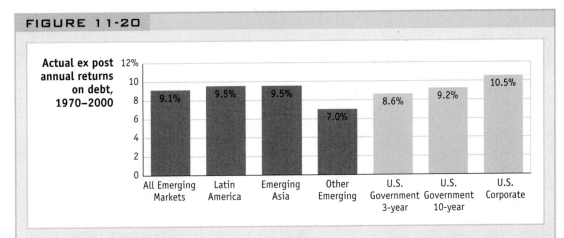

FIGURE 11-20

Returns on Emerging Market Debt, 1970s–2000s The ex post realized returns on emerging market debt have been 9.1% on average, as high as 9.5% in Latin America and Asia, but as low as 7% elsewhere (columns 1–4). Given their riskiness, these returns compare unfavorably with returns on safe U.S. government debt and U.S. corporate debt (columns 5–7). Whatever ex ante risk premiums were charged to emerging markets, defaults ate them all up and lenders only just broke even.

Sources: Ex post returns from Christoph Klingen, Jeromin Zettelmeyer, and Beatrice Weder, 2004, "How Private Creditors Fared in Emerging Debt Markets, 1970–2000," IMF Working Paper No. 04/13.

But there were also periods with massive defaults, like the early 1980s, in which repeated postponements and restructurings meant that creditors got back only pennies on each dollar they had lent to the defaulting countries. Defaults are rare but cataclysmic events for creditors, so only a long-run sample can be informative. But judging from the data in Figure 11-20, lenders to emerging markets have only just broken even, if that. ■

A Model of Default, Part Two: Loan Supply and Demand

The first steps we took in constructing the model were to understand the problem from the lender's standpoint. Knowing the probability p that borrowers will default when output is low, lenders adjust the lending rate r_L they charge depending on the volatility of output V and the level of debt L. Knowing the lending rate and the debt amount determines the loan supply curve for a country, which, combined with an understanding of loan demand, will allow us to determine equilibrium in the loan market.

Loan Supply Suppose output volatility is at some low level V. The probability of repayment is shown in Figure 11-21, panel (a). The loan supply curve $LS(V)$ is shown in panel (b).

At low levels of debt, as we saw, the probability of repayment is 100%, so a loan of size L in this range will be made at a lending rate r_L that equals the risk-free rate. In this debt range, the loan supply curve is flat between points 1 and 2. Then, as debt rises above some loan size L_V that depends on the volatility of the borrowing country's output, the probability of repayment starts to fall below 1 (100%), and the breakeven condition tells us that lenders

FIGURE 11-21

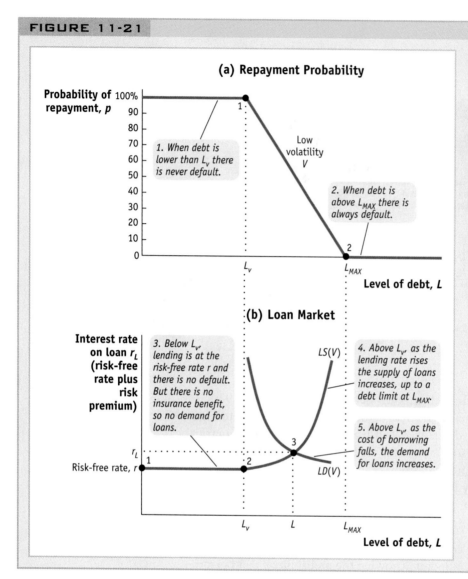

(a) Repayment Probability

Probability of repayment, p — 100%, 90, 80, 70, 60, 50, 40, 30, 20, 10, 0

1. When debt is lower than L_V, there is never default.

Low volatility V

2. When debt is above L_{MAX} there is always default.

1

2

L_V L_{MAX}

Level of debt, L

(b) Loan Market

Interest rate on loan r_L (risk-free rate plus risk premium)

3. Below L_V, lending is at the risk-free rate r and there is no default. But there is no insurance benefit, so no demand for loans.

$LS(V)$

4. Above L_V, as the lending rate rises the supply of loans increases, up to a debt limit at L_{MAX}.

5. Above L_V, as the cost of borrowing falls, the demand for loans increases.

r_L

Risk-free rate, r

1   2   3

$LD(V)$

L_V L L_{MAX}

Level of debt, L

Loan Market Equilibrium When Volatility Is Low A higher level of debt means the probability of repayment falls (and the probability of default increases) between points 1 and 2 in panel (a), starting at L_V. As the probability of repayment falls, lenders increase the lending rate as the quantity of debt increases, so the loan supply curve LS slopes up in panel (b). As the lending rate falls, more debt is demanded by the country as insurance against consumption risk, so the loan demand curve LD slopes down. The equilibrium is at point 3 where demand and supply intersect.

will have to start increasing the lending rate so they don't lose their shirts. At point 2 (the point at which the probability of repayment falls below 100%), the supply curve starts to slope up. For any given increase in loan size L, lenders must decide how much to increase the lending rate r_L to ensure that the breakeven condition is met. In making this decision, the lenders must take into account that any increases in L and/or r_L will adversely affect the repayment probability p (as we saw earlier). Finally, as the loan size approaches its maximum L_{MAX}, the rising repayment burden (higher L and higher r_L) will cause the probability of repayment to approach zero. The lending rate will have to approach infinity to ensure that the loan will break even, so the loan supply curve becomes vertical as the debt limit L_{MAX} is reached. No loans are supplied above this level of debt.

Loan Demand The equilibrium market outcome must be somewhere on the lender's loan supply curve. But it must also be on the borrower's loan demand curve. How is that determined? The formal derivation of borrowing demand depends on the country's consumption preferences, including its aversion to risk; this is mathematically complex, but we can sum up the results intuitively by drawing a loan demand curve $LD(V)$ that depends on two factors: the lending rate charged, r_L, and the volatility of output, V. We restrict our attention to the normal case in which the demand curve slopes down so that an increase in the interest cost of the loan (a rise in r_L) causes a decrease in the size of loan demanded (a fall in L).

We can now finish our graphical representation of the loan market equilibrium, and in Figure 11-21, panel (b), equilibrium is at point 3, where loan supply LS and loan demand LD intersect. Note that this intersection will be, as shown, between L_V and L_{MAX}. Why? Below debt level L_V, the country never defaults and so debt provides no consumption smoothing insurance in this range and the country will want to borrow more and move up and to the right along the loan supply curve. As the cost of borrowing rises, however, the country must consider the trade-off between the amount of insurance it obtains from the debt and the rising cost of that insurance. At some point, this trade-off evens out and we reach the loan quantity the country desires. In Figure 11-21 the quantity of loans supplied and demanded will be equal at equilibrium point 3 with debt level L and lending rate r_L.

An Increase in Volatility What happens if the country has a higher level of volatility V'? We now show how the loan supply and demand curves will shift to $LS(V')$ and $LD(V')$ as shown in Figure 11-22.

In panel (a), higher volatility means that default starts to become a possibility at a low level of debt compared with the low volatility case, as we saw previously. Once above that level of debt, repayment is less likely than when volatility is low. This means that the lending rate rises more quickly to ensure the lenders break even, and the probability of repayment reaches zero at a lower level of debt. The debt ceiling falls to a lower level, L'_{MAX}, because higher interest rates mean that the repayment burden will rise more quickly in this case as debt increases.

Consequently, in panel (b), the interest rate is higher at every debt level, and debt hits a ceiling at a lower level of debt. That is, we have shown that the loan supply curve shifts left and up. The lending rate starts to rise at point 4, at a lower debt level L'_V because higher volatility can lead to the possibility of defaults at lower levels of debt. Second, at higher debt levels, higher volatility always means a higher probability of default, so higher interest rates are imposed by lenders, all the way up to the ceiling at L'_{MAX}.

What about loan demand? When volatility rises, the loan demand curve also shifts. With typical preferences (which include risk aversion), higher volatility means that the country will want more insurance, or more consumption smoothing, all else equal. In this model, defaultable debt is the only form of insurance a country can get, so, at any given lending rate, it will want to have more debt. The loan demand curve shifts right to $LD(V')$.

FIGURE 11-22

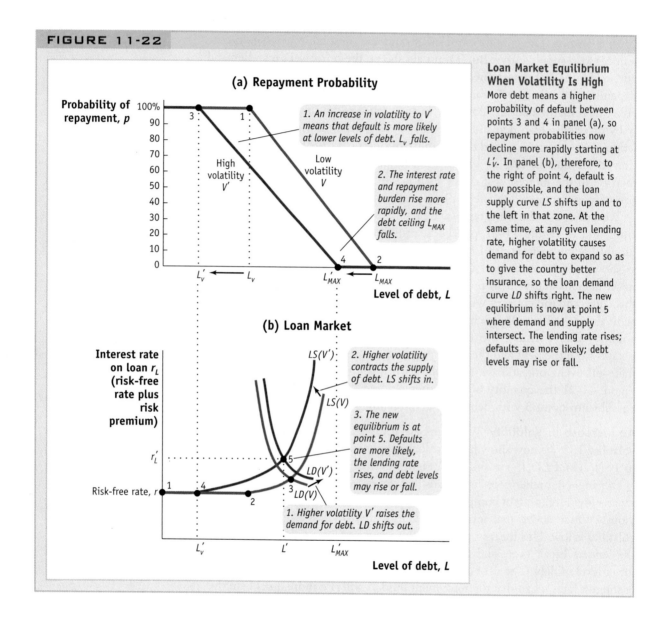

(a) Repayment Probability

Probability of repayment, p

1. An increase in volatility to V' means that default is more likely at lower levels of debt. L_V falls.

2. The interest rate and repayment burden rise more rapidly, and the debt ceiling L_{MAX} falls.

High volatility V'

Low volatility V

Level of debt, L

(b) Loan Market

Interest rate on loan r_L (risk-free rate plus risk premium)

$LS(V')$

2. Higher volatility contracts the supply of debt. LS shifts in.

$LS(V)$

3. The new equilibrium is at point 5. Defaults are more likely, the lending rate rises, and debt levels may rise or fall.

$LD(V')$

$LD(V)$

1. Higher volatility V' raises the demand for debt. LD shifts out.

Risk-free rate, r

Level of debt, L

Loan Market Equilibrium When Volatility Is High More debt means a higher probability of default between points 3 and 4 in panel (a), so repayment probabilities now decline more rapidly starting at L_V'. In panel (b), therefore, to the right of point 4, default is now possible, and the loan supply curve LS shifts up and to the left in that zone. At the same time, at any given lending rate, higher volatility causes demand for debt to expand so as to give the country better insurance, so the loan demand curve LD shifts right. The new equilibrium is now at point 5 where demand and supply intersect. The lending rate rises; defaults are more likely; debt levels may rise or fall.

The net result of the shifts in loan supply and demand is a new equilibrium at point 5. If loan supply moves left/up and loan demand moves right, the lending rate will definitely increase. The net effect on the amount of debt is ambiguous, however, and depends on whether the demand shift is larger than the supply shift. If the supply effect dominates, the country will end up with less debt, higher risk premiums, and more frequent defaults—the very characteristics we see in emerging markets as compared with the advanced countries.

APPLICATION

The Costs of Default

Our model of default, like many others, relies on punishment costs to give debtors an incentive to repay. Is this realistic? How big are the costs?

Defaulters do not get away scot-free, and to see why, we consider evidence from a recent Bank of England study and other research.[26]

Financial Market Penalties First, defaulters are excluded from further borrowing until the default is resolved through negotiations with the creditors. These exclusion periods may vary. The Bank of England study found that in the 1980s defaulters were denied market access for an average of four and a half years; however, in the easy credit atmosphere of the 1990s and 2000s, that figure dropped to an average of three and a half months. Exclusion from credit markets can create future consumption costs when the cushion of borrowing is no longer there to smooth consumption. Exclusion may impair investment, too.

Second, default is associated with a significant downgrade in credit ratings and corresponding increases in risk premiums.[27] The Bank of England study found that 7 out of 8 nondefaulters had credit ratings of BBB+ or better (the exception was India); but 12 out of 13 past defaulters were ranked BB+ or worse (the one exception was Chile). These results applied to countries with a variety of income per capita and debt-to-GDP levels. This kind of penalty has a long history: in the first wave of globalization before 1914, defaulters on average paid an extra 1% per year in interest rate risk premiums, controlling for other factors.[28]

Finally, defaulters may face another major inconvenience when borrowing: an inability to borrow in their own currency. The Bank of England study found that nondefaulting countries, including India, China, Korea, Czech Republic, Malaysia, and Hungary, were able to issue between 70% and 100% of their debt in domestic currency; in contrast, a group of past defaulters, including Brazil, Mexico, Philippines, Chile, and Venezuela, only issued between 40% and 70% of their debt in their own currency. As we saw in Chapter 8, the disadvantage of liability dollarization is that depreciations increase the costs of debt principal and interest in domestic currency terms. These changes can lead to destabilizing wealth effects because these impacts amplify debt burdens on the balance sheets of households, firms, and governments.

Broader Macroeconomic Costs and the Risk of Banking and Exchange Rate Crises The financial penalties are not the only cost that would-be defaulters must weigh. Default may trigger additional output costs, including the serious threats of twin or triple crises.

A default can do extensive damage to the domestic financial system because domestic banks typically hold a great deal of government debt—and they may have been coerced to hold even more such debt in the period right before a

---

[26] This application is based on Bianca De Paoli, Glenn Hoggarth, and Victoria Saporta, 2006 "Costs of Sovereign Default," *Bank of England Quarterly Bulletin,* Fall.
[27] Carmen M. Reinhart, Kenneth S. Rogoff, and Miguel A. Savastano, 2003, "Debt Intolerance," *Brookings Papers on Economic Activity,* 1, 1–74.
[28] Maurice Obstfeld and Alan M. Taylor, 2003, "Sovereign Risk, Credibility and the Gold Standard: 1870–1913 versus 1925–31," *Economic Journal,* 113(487), 241–275.

default.[29] The banks will likely call for help, putting further fiscal strain on the government. But the government usually has no resources to bail out the banks at a time like this (often, it has been trying to persuade the banks to help out the government). A default crisis can then easily spawn a banking crisis. At best, if the banks survive, prudent management requires the banks to contract domestic lending to rebuild their capital and reduce their risk exposure. At worst, the banks fail. The disappearance of their financial intermediation services will then impair investment activity, and negative wealth effects will squeeze the consumption demand of depositors who lose their access to their money, temporarily or permanently, in a bank that is closed or restructured. The result is lower demand and lower output in the short run and hence more risk for banks because debtors find it harder to pay back their bank loans in recessions. Financial disruption to the real economy also disrupts a nation's international trade. Default can disrupt the short-term credit (provided by domestic and foreign lenders) that is used to finance international trade, and there is some evidence that large and persistent trade contractions follow a default.[30]

In addition to a banking crisis, a default can trigger an exchange rate crisis if the country (like many emerging markets) is trying to preserve a fixed exchange rate. An increase in risk premiums on long-term loans to the government may be matched by a similar increase in risk premiums on bank deposits, especially if a banking crisis is feared. A risk premium shock of this sort, as we saw in Chapter 9, contracts money demand and causes a drain of foreign exchange reserves at the central bank as the peg is defended. At the same time, if the pleading of banks for fiscal help is ignored, the central bank will be under pressure to do a sterilized sale of reserves to allow it to act as a lender of last resort and expand domestic credit. But such activity will cause reserve levels to fall even further. The reserve drain may be large enough to break the peg, or at least damage the peg's credibility. Expected depreciation will then enlarge the risk premium further, compounding the reserve drain. In the meantime, interest rate increases further dampen investment in the home economy, lowering output and making it harder for debts to be serviced, which hurts the banks again, lowers output again, and compounds all of the problems just outlined.

Lower output and higher risk premiums can be expected during a default crisis, but they can also trigger banking crises and exchange rate crises. As we saw in Chapter 9, low output and high interest rates can break a contingent commitment to a peg; as we have seen in this chapter, they can generate a greater incentive to default; and we also know they can only worsen domestic financial conditions by making it harder for everyone to service their debt to banks and by damaging bank balance sheets.

---

[29] While some governments, notably Argentina in 2002, can show great cunning in trying to honor debt held by domestic creditors while defaulting on foreigners, this kind of discrimination strategy may be difficult to execute legally and technically. Anna Gelpern and Brad Setser, 2004, "Domestic and External Debt: The Doomed Quest for Equal Treatment," *Georgetown Journal of International Law,* 35, Summer, 795.

[30] Andrew K. Rose, 2005, "One Reason Countries Pay Their Debts: Renegotiation and International Trade," *Journal of Development Economics,* 77(1), June, 189–206.

From all these circuitous descriptions, presented schematically in Figure 11-23, the potential for a "vicious circle" of interactions should now be clear, explaining why so often the three types of crises are observed together.

The consequences of default are therefore not pleasant. As Table 11-1 shows, when default crises occur *on their own,* there appear to be no costs; unfortunately, that applies in only 4 out of 45 cases, less than 10% of all defaults in the sample. In every other case, there is either a twin default/exchange rate crisis (13 cases), a twin default/banking crisis (7 cases), or a triple default/exchange rate/banking crisis (21 cases). In all these other

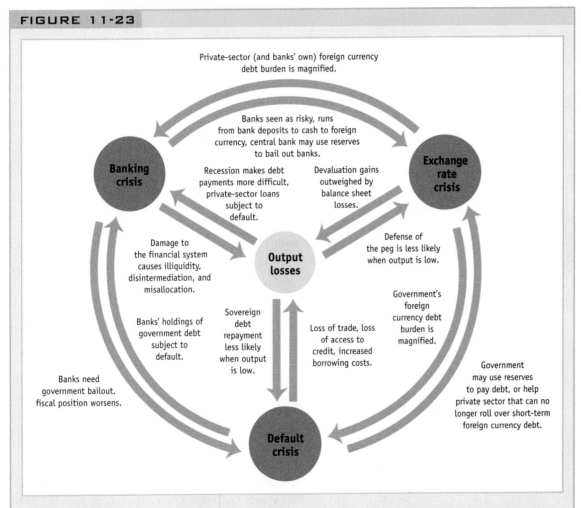

FIGURE 11-23

Vicious Circles in Twin and Triple Crises The chart shows that in developing countries and emerging markets there are complex feedback linkages between banking crises, default crises, and exchange rate crises. A depreciation magnifies foreign currency debt burdens, weakening the financial position of the government, private sector, and banks. A default weakens banks and cuts off foreign credit, leaving reserves as the only remaining buffer. A banking crisis can lead to costly bailouts, undermining either the government's fiscal position or the central bank's reserve. All three types of crises can have serious output costs, which exacerbate the problem.

Source: Based on Bianca De Paoli, Glenn Hoggarth, and Victoria Saporta, 2006 "Costs of Sovereign Default," Bank of England Quarterly Bulletin, Fall.

TABLE 11-1

Costs of Sovereign Defaults, 1970–2000 Output losses can be very large after a default, as measured by deviation from trends. While a default-only crisis may be short and not costly, the more common twin and triple crises last much longer and have very high costs.

Type of Crisis	Number of Crises	Average Length (years)	Mean Cost per Year (% of GDP)
Default only	4	3	–1.0
Default and exchange rate crisis	13	5	10.3
Default and banking crisis	7	8	13.2
Triple crisis	21	10	21.7
All crises	45	8	15.1

Source: Bianca De Paoli, Glenn Hoggarth, and Victoria Saporta, "Costs of Sovereign Default," Bank of England Quarterly Bulletin, *Fall 2006.*

cases (more than 90% of defaults), the output losses associated with the crisis are significant, measured by deviation from trend output growth: on average around 15% of GDP per year for eight years. That is a large cost, even if comparisons with normal trends may be misleading, because it is hard to estimate the costs that the countries would have faced had they not defaulted.[31]

To sum up, if financial penalties and legal action provide insufficient motives for repayment, there is reason to believe that there are many other costs of default that provide enough incentive for contingent debt repayment. ■

Conclusions

We have developed a simple model in which sovereign debt is a contingent claim that will not be paid in hard times. In equilibrium borrowers obtain consumption-smoothing via debt (a form of insurance against volatile consumption levels) at a price—the risk premium—that compensates lenders for default risk. The model is too simple to capture all aspects of the default problem, such as the tendency of borrowing to move in volatile cycles, and the scope for contagion and "animal spirits" in this asset market as in any other.

Nonetheless, the model provides valuable insights and leads us to deeper questions. For example, the model assumes that output volatility is the root cause of default, and we know that output volatility is high in poorer countries. But what is behind that? In some developing countries, it could be a result

---

[31] That is to say, output may have fallen anyway because of the economic shocks that preceded the observed default. Obtaining more precise estimates of default costs remains a goal of ongoing research. See Eduardo Levy-Yeyati and Ugo Panizza, "The Elusive Costs of Sovereign Defaults," Research Department Working Paper 581, Inter-American Development Bank, November 2006.

of commodity specialization, terms-of-trade shocks, climate, and other economic disturbances. Yet an alternative explanation might be the poor institutional framework in these countries, which is correlated with both low incomes and high volatility, as we saw in Chapter 1. Thus, the default problem may be, deep down, a reflection of poor institutions. Poor institutions may also be generating default at lower debt levels through nonvolatility channels: they may obscure financial transparency, generate weak property rights, prevent credit monitoring, encourage corruption and bribery, allow for the misuse of loans, lead politicians to focus on the short term (with risky overborrowing), and so on—all of which add to the risk premium, all else equal.

How did advanced countries eventually find a way to avoid these outcomes? Our model suggests that all countries want to default at some debt level, but for advanced countries, that level might be very high. Why? The model says it must be that the costs of default in such countries are much higher. There may be truth to this on two dimensions: economic and political. Economically, a sovereign default in an advanced country would wreck a highly developed financial system, whereas in poorer countries the very lack of financial sophistication probably keeps such costs lower. In addition, the political costs bite harder in advanced countries, in that a large, democratically empowered, and wealth-holding middle class is likely to punish governments that take such actions; in poorer countries, the political costs may be smaller if the losers are fewer or political accountability is weaker.

Every few years, in a tranquil time, some expert predicts that there will not be any more sovereign defaults. They can't be taken very seriously. History does suggest that many of the deep and intertwined underlying political-economy problems can be solved; but it may take an awfully long time for countries to overcome these impediments and emerge from the serial default club.[32]

APPLICATION

The Argentina Crisis of 2001–02

In this section we focused on the problem of default. But we also emphasized (as in Figure 11-23) the feedback mechanisms at work in twin and triple crisis situations in which default crises, exchange rate crises, and banking crises may simultaneously occur. Just as in the case of self-fulfilling exchange rate crises (Chapter 9) these "vicious circles" may lead to self-fulfilling twin and triple crises where, as the economist Guillermo Calvo puts it, "if investors deem you unworthy, no funds will be forthcoming and, thus, unworthy you will be." In general, theory and empirical work suggest that bad fundamentals only make the problem of self-fulfilling crises worse, and disentangling the two causes can be difficult, leading to ongoing controversy over who or what

---

[32] Philip T. Hoffman, Gilles Postel-Vinay, and Jean-Laurent Rosenthal, 2007, *Surviving Large Losses: Financial Crises, the Middle Class, and the Development of Capital Markets,* Cambridge, Mass.: Harvard University Press.

is to blame for any given crisis. The Argentina crisis of 2001–02 dramatically illustrates these problems.[33]

Background Argentina successfully ended a hyperinflation in 1991 with the adoption of a rigidly fixed exchange rate system called the Convertibility Plan, and a 1-to-1 peg of the peso to the U.S. dollar. As we noted in Chapter 9, this system operated with high reserve backing ratios and (in theory) strict limits on central bank use of sterilization policy. The Convertibility Plan was a quasi currency board.

With a firm nominal anchor, the Argentine economy grew rapidly up to 1998, apart from a brief slowdown after the Mexican (Tequila) crisis in 1994. The country was able to borrow large amounts at low interest rates in the global capital market. The only troubling sign at this point was that despite boom conditions the government ran persistent deficits every year, increasing the public debt to GDP ratio. Most of this debt was held by foreigners, which increased Argentina's net external debt relative to GDP. Given the long-run budget constraints (for the government and for the country) these deficits were unsustainable.

In 1997 crises in Asia were followed by increases in emerging market risk premiums, and these shocks were magnified by crises in 1998 in Russia and Brazil. The Brazil crisis also led to a slowdown and depreciation in one of Argentina's major trading partners. At the same time, the U.S. dollar started to appreciate, dragging the Argentina peso into a stronger position against all currencies. Higher interest rates, lower demand abroad, and an appreciated exchange rate put the Argentine economy into a recession.

Dive With these changes in external conditions, Argentina's macroeconomic regime started to unravel. The recession worsened an already bad fiscal situation. Because no surpluses had been run in the good times, there was no cushion in the government accounts, and the red ink grew. Public debt, which had been 41% of GDP in 1998, grew to 64% of GDP in 2001. Foreign creditors began to view these debt dynamics as possibly explosive and inconsistent with the long-run budget constraint, implying a risk of default. The creditors demanded higher interest rates for new loans and refinancings, which only increased the rate of debt explosion. Risk premiums on long-term government debt blew up, from 3% to 4% in late 1997 to 7%–8% in late 2000.

The fiscal situation thus damaged the economy and the banking sector, as higher interest rates depressed aggregate demand in the short run, and caused a deterioration of banks' balance sheets (as loans went bad and other assets declined in value). This deterioration in turn made the fiscal situation worse,

---

[33] For further reading about the Argentine crisis see: Michael Mussa, 2002, *Argentina and the Fund: From Triumph to Tragedy,* Washington, D.C.: Institute for International Economics; Gerardo della Paolera and Alan Taylor, 2003, "Gaucho Banking Redux," *Economía,* 3(2), 1–42; Andrew Powell, 2003, "Argentina's Avoidable Crisis: Bad Luck, Bad Economics, Bad Politics, Bad Advice," in Susan M. Collins and Dani Rodrik eds., *Brookings Trade Forum 2002,* Washington, D.C.: The Brookings Institution, 1–58; Paul Blustein, 2005, *And the Money Kept Rolling In (and Out): Wall Street, the IMF, and the Bankrupting of Argentina.* New York: Public Affairs.

because in a recession tax revenues tend to fall and government social expenditures tend to rise. The government needed to borrow more, even as the lenders started to withdraw.

In addition, the situation posed a threat to the monetary regime and the Convertibility Plan, for reasons noted in Chapter 9. People were worried that if the government accounts worsened further, then all public credit would be turned off and if the government were then unwilling to impose the austerity of spending cuts in mid-recession, it would have had to finance the deficit using the inflation tax. Finally, even if the government did not use inflationary finance, it still might want to use temporary monetary policy autonomy to relieve the recession through a devaluation and lower interest rates, both of which would make the peg not credible. Either or both of these threats would expose the peg to the risk of a speculative attack.

In addition, people knew that if the banks got into trouble they would need to call on the central bank to act as a lender of last resort, as they had in 1994 (when reserves had plummeted and a crisis was averted only by a last minute lifeline from the IMF). If people felt that their deposits would be safer in Miami or Montevideo, there would be a massive run from deposits to peso cash to dollars, overwhelming even the substantial foreign exchange reserves at the central bank.

Crash In 2001, all of these forces gathered in a perfect storm. Politically, fiscal compromise proved impossible between the two main political forces (the weak President Fernando de la Rúa of the Radical Party and the powerful Peronist provincial governors). The provinces collected and spent large amounts of national tax revenue and were not willing to make sacrifices to help an opponent. They gambled, correctly, that a crisis would bring them to power (even at the cost of destroying the country).

By mid-2001 private creditors had almost walked away from Argentina and the last gasp effort involved a swap of short-term high interest rate debt for long-term *very high* interest rate debt, with an annual yield near 15%. Markets were unimpressed—this scheme bought a few months of breathing space on principal payments, but left Argentina with an even worse debt service problem down the road. Private lending dried up and despite a (noncredible) announcement of a zero deficit rule in July, the risk premium on government debt exploded, from 10% in June to 15% in August, and approached 20% in October. As the debt burden grew and the economy sank, we know from this chapter that default would be increasingly likely.

There was only one lender left now, the IMF. But they were increasingly as unimpressed with Argentina's policy shenanigans as everyone else. In a move that it doubted at the time and regretted soon after, the IMF made one last big loan to Argentina in August 2001. The money was poured into the government's coffers and into the Central Bank's dwindling pot of reserves, but it didn't last very long.

The banks were in a parlous state. Economic conditions were raising the number of nonperforming loans anyway. But banks had also been coerced or persuaded that it would be a good idea for them to buy large amounts of the government's debt in 2001. This dollar debt carried a high interest rate, but was also risky because of the possibility of default and/or exchange rate depreciation after a crisis. Depositors knew this and they knew that banks would probably fail if the central bank and the government could not protect them.

The End The three crises were all now shaping up to happen, encouraged by output contractions, consistent with the "vicious circle" dynamics shown in Figure 11-23. The final act came in November. The IMF concluded that the economy was not being turned around by any of the policies in place and that further loans were therefore a waste of time unless Argentina made radical adjustments, including considering the possibilities of devaluing, defaulting, and even dollarizing. The government would have none of it, and when the IMF announced no more credit, the public knew the game was up and, seeking to put their assets in a safe haven, they started a massive run on the banks. To stem the flow the government imposed capital controls (*corralito*) to stop them, and also froze the majority of bank deposits.

This triggered a political explosion, violence, and unrest, and within days de la Rúa was history, airlifted from the Casa Rosada by helicopter. His numerous successors over the following weeks initiated a default on the public debt (the world's biggest ever default at the time) and allowed the exchange rate to float (it fell to 4 pesos to the dollar very quickly). The private sector was awash with unserviceable dollar liabilities, so the government "pesified" them, causing utter chaos in the courts and grave economic uncertainty. The banks were barely functional for several months, and the savings of many Argentines vanished. Taxes were raised and government spending cut. The economy went from a bad recession to total meltdown, amid scenes of previously unimaginable poverty and deprivation.

Argentina's policies were inconsistent. When the government chose a fixed exchange rate, it had to accept its pros and cons, including the risk of larger recessions when external conditions were unfavorable. But they also had to accept that a fixed exchange rate also ruled out the inflation tax and placed limits on the lender of last resort capacity of a central bank faced with capital flight. Such concerns would not have been as important if the country had kept its fiscal policy in check and maintained access to credit, but in 2001 the country simply had no more room for maneuver.

Postscript As of 2007 there had been no major crisis since 2001, world economic conditions had been fairly benign, and many countries had built up large exchange reserves. This led many observers to call into question the need for the IMF, given its perceived failings in the 1997–2001 crises, and the small size of its lending capabilities in the face of growing private sector financial flows. On the other hand, international economic crises have been around for a very long time, so it may be a little premature to dismantle the only emergency service we have (see **Headlines: Is the IMF Pathetic?**). ■

HEADLINES

Is the IMF "Pathetic"?

The IMF is the closest thing to a global lender of last resort. When times are calm, it may be tempting to think of abolishing the institution.

Meral Karasulu did what any seasoned International Monetary Fund staffer would do: She grinned and, for the umpteenth time, listened to suggestions that the institution was to blame for the 1997 Asian financial crisis.

"Thank you for your question," she replied to an audience member at a May 14 EuroMoney conference in Seoul. Then, she launched into a defense of the IMF's actions.

As the IMF's representative in South Korea, Karasulu is used to the drill. After all, many Koreans routinely refer to the "IMF crisis." It's a reminder that a decade after Asia's turmoil, the IMF is still explaining itself wherever it goes.

Three weeks after the Seoul conference, there was similar griping at an event I attended in Buenos Aires. The mood had barely changed since March 2005, when President Nestor Kirchner scored points with many of Argentina's 40 million people by calling the IMF "pathetic." He has been demanding that the institution stop criticizing the Latin American country.

Korea and Argentina have little in common. Yet Korea is among the nations stockpiling currency reserves to avoid having to go to the IMF for a bailout ever again. Argentina, meanwhile, continues to tout the end of its IMF-backed program last year as an economic victory.

This column isn't a defense of the IMF's actions during the Asian crisis or Argentina's in the early 2000s. The Washington-based fund has a small army of well-compensated people to do that. And the IMF has had its fair share of blunders, including telling Asian countries to tighten fiscal policy during a crisis.

Yet all this talk of IMF irrelevance is overdone. What's more, the chatter suggests the creation of a new bubble called complacency.

"It's ironic to my mind that people say the fund isn't needed anymore because nothing in the global financial system is broken at the moment," John Lipsky, the IMF's first deputy managing director, said in an interview last month in Tokyo. "It strikes me we are trying to anticipate and prepare for when things may go wrong again". . . .

Sure, Asia has insulated itself from markets with trillions of dollars of currency reserves. The IMF's phones may be ringing off the hook if China's economy hits a wall, the U.S. dollar plunges, the so-called yen-carry trade blows up, a major terrorist attack occurs, oil prices approach $100 a barrel or some unexpected event roils world markets.

The thing is, the IMF and its Bretton Woods sister institution, the World Bank, have scarcely been more necessary. How efficient and cost-effective they are is debatable; what's not is that today's global economy needs the buffering role that both of them play. . . .

The IMF was never set up to play the role it did during crises in Mexico, Asia and Russia in the 1990s and turmoil in Latin America since then. Even so, it will be called upon the instant a crisis in one country spreads to another. As imperfect as the IMF is, the world needs the economic equivalent of a fire brigade when markets plunge.

There's much chatter about how global prosperity is reducing the need for billion-dollar IMF bailouts. As of March, IMF lending had shriveled to $11.8 billion from a peak of $81 billion in 2004. A single nation, Turkey, accounted for about 75 percent of the IMF's portfolio.

Isn't that a good thing? The IMF is like a paramedic: You hope you won't need one, but it's great that one is just a phone call away. Plenty of things could still go awry and necessitate a call to the IMF. . . .

Complacency looms large in today's world. All too many investors think the good times are here to stay and all too many governments are ignoring their imbalances for similar reasons. For all the bellyaching about global imbalances—including U.S. deficits, an undervalued Chinese currency, ultra-low Japanese interest rates—no one is doing anything to fix them.

All this means that, far from being irrelevant, the IMF may be in for a very busy couple of years.

Source: Extract from William Pesek, "Is IMF 'Pathetic' or Just Awaiting Next Crisis?" bloomberg.net, June 12, 2007.

KEY POINTS

1. Purchasing Power Parity does not hold between rich and poor countries, in either relative or absolute form. Prices of goods are systematically higher in rich countries. As countries become relatively richer we can therefore expect their price levels to rise and, hence, their real exchange rates to appreciate. Exchange rate forecasts (real and nominal) need to be adjusted accordingly, as do judgments as to whether a country's exchange rate is under- or overvalued.

2. The Balassa-Samuelson theory explains price differences across countries as a result of differences in the wage (labor) costs embodied in non-traded goods. It assumes that nontraded goods have zero (or small) productivity differences. Under those assumptions, large differences in traded goods productivity are associated with large differences in income per capita, wages, and the prices of nontraded goods.

3. Uncovered Interest Parity appears to hold when market expectations are measured directly using data from surveys of traders. But the joint hypothesis of UIP and rational expectations (the efficient markets hypothesis) appears to be invalid because exchange rate forecasts seem to be systematically and predictably wrong.

4. On average, exchange rate movements have been smaller than predicted by UIP, so a carry trade strategy of borrowing in the low-yield currency and investing in the high-yield currency delivers profits or excess returns. However, these excess returns are risky, with a Sharpe ratio well below 1, and typically close to 0.4–0.5. As with the stock market, few investors are willing to devote speculative capital to such risky investments.

5. Global imbalances result from differences in saving and investment in different countries and regions around the world. Globally, investment demand has fallen more than saving supply in recent decades. This has caused a "savings glut" (low real interest rates). Capital has flowed in to (out of) countries with above (below) average investment and/or below (above) average saving, such as the United States and Britain (Japan and Switzerland), causing these countries to see a marked decrease (increase) in external wealth.

6. In the long run, countries that experience a decrease in external wealth must service the incremental debt by increasing their trade balance (in the steady state). In a world of PPP (or no home bias) this may be achieved without any adjustment of the real exchange rate. However, in most cases significant real depreciation may be necessary to divert demand from foreign goods to home goods.

7. Default is as old as capital markets. Sovereign defaults on international lending have been widely documented for several centuries. In the modern era defaults are associated with economic downturns, and a good deal of this pain seems to be a result of default. This "punishment" for the defaulter creates one important benefit—it makes lending possible in the first place, since sovereigns otherwise face no incentive to repay.

8. A simple model of default can explain why countries default in bad times. They need to insure against really painful outcomes and default allows them to do this. The price of this insurance is the risk premium they must pay on top of the risk-free rate when they borrow, so that the lender breaks even. This kind of model explains the existence of default as an equilibrium outcome. Nonetheless, many other factors can precipitate default crises, including complex feedback between default, banking crises, and exchange rate crises.

KEY TERMS

trade cost, p. 481
no-arbitrage band, p. 482
Balassa-Samuelson effect, p. 487
equilibrium real exchange rate, p. 487

carry trade, p. 494
peso problem, p. 500
forecast error, p. 500
rational expectations hypothesis, p. 503

efficient markets hypothesis, p. 503
inefficient market, p. 503
limits to arbitrage, p. 503
excess return, p. 504
Sharpe ratio, pp. 504–505

PROBLEMS

1. (PPP) Richland and Poorland each have two industries, traded TVs and nontraded house maintenance. The world price of TVs is R$100 (R$ = Richland dollar). Assume for now that the exchange rate is R$1 = 1 PP (PP = Poorland peso) and that prices are flexible. It takes 1 day for a worker in each country to visit and maintain 1 house. It takes 1 day for a Richland worker to make a TV, and 4 days for a Poorland worker.

   a. What is the Richland wage in R$ per day? What is the Poorland wage in PP per day? In R$ per day? What is the ratio of Poorland to Richland wages in a common currency?

   b. What is the price of a house maintenance visit in each country?

   c. Assume people in each country spend half their income on TVs and half on house maintenance. Compute the CPI (consumer price index) for each country given by the square root of (TV price) times (gardening price).

   d. Compute the standard of living in each country by dividing local currency wages by the CPI from part c. Is Poorland really as poor as suggested by the last answer in part a?

   e. Productivity now doubles in the Poorland TV industry, all else equal. How many days does it now take for Poorland workers to make a TV? What happens to the wage in Poorland? The price of haircuts? The CPI?

   f. If the central bank of Poorland wants to avoid inflation in this situation, how would it like to adjust the exchange rate?

2. (PPP) "Some fast-growing poorer countries face a conflict between wanting to maintain a fixed exchange rate with a rich country and wanting to keep inflation low." Explain the logic behind this statement. Use the examples of Slovakia and China to illustrate your argument.

3. (UIP) What is a peso problem? In the case of fixed exchange rates, explain how peso prob-

lems can account for persistent interest rate differentials. Study the U.S.–Britain short-term end-of-the-month nominal interest rate differentials shown below for the year 1896 (NBER series 13034). Both countries were on the gold standard at a fixed exchange rate of $4.86 throughout this year. Did the U.S. have a peso problem? When did it get really big? When did it go away? (Extra credit: do some research on the Web and discover the political reasons for the timing of this peso problem.)

Jan 1896	3.84%
Feb 1896	2.94%
Mar 1896	2.76%
Apr 1896	2.40%
May 1896	1.63%
Jun 1896	1.20%
Jul 1896	1.43%
Aug 1896	3.77%
Sep 1896	3.70%
Oct 1896	8.51%
Nov 1896	2.60%
Dec 1896	−1.39%

4. (UIP) You are in discussion with a forex trader.

   a. She reveals that she made a 10% annual rate of return last year. Based on these data, can we say that the forex market in question violates the efficient markets hypothesis (EMH)?

   b. She reveals that she can make predictable 10% annual rates of return on forex trades for a pair of currencies, with a standard deviation of 25%, and has been doing so for a long time. Calculate the Sharpe ratio for these trades. Based on these data, does the forex market in question satisfy the efficient markets hypothesis (EMH)?

   c. Can her predictable profits be explained by trading frictions? By risk aversion?

5. (Global Imbalances) What is the "savings glut" hypothesis advanced by Ben Bernanke? Is it explicable more in terms of a long-term rise in

global savings supply or a fall in global investment demand? Explain your answer.

6. (Global Imbalances) A country has an external (net) debt of 50% of GDP and the world real interest rate is 4%. The country currently has a trade deficit of 2% of GDP, but must run surpluses from now on to service the debt, since no further loans are possible. Each 1 percentage point increase in the trade deficit will require a 5% real depreciation.

   a. What is the required trade surplus as a percentage of GDP?
   b. What is the real depreciation required to achieve this adjustment?

7. (Default) "Poor countries are exploited when they borrow in global capital markets, because they are charged an extortionate rate of interest." Explain how empirical evidence and theoretical arguments might counter this assertion.

8. (Default) The Republic of Delinquia has a non-disaster output level of $100 each year.

With 10% probability each year output falls to a disaster level of $80, and the country will feel so much pain that it will default and pay neither principal nor interest on its debts. The country decides to borrow $20 at the start of the year, and keep the money under the mattress. It will default and keep the money in the event that output is low, but this will entail sacrificing $4 in punishment costs. Otherwise it pays back principal and interest due. Lenders are competitive and understand these risks fully.

   a. What is the probability of default?
   b. The interest rate on safe loans is 8% per annum, so a safe loan has to pay off 1.08 times $20. What is the lending rate charged by competitive lenders on the risky loan to Delinquia?
   c. What does Delinquia consume in disaster years? In non-disaster years?
   d. Repeat part c for the case where Delinquia cannot borrow. Is Delinquia better off with or without borrowing?

Index

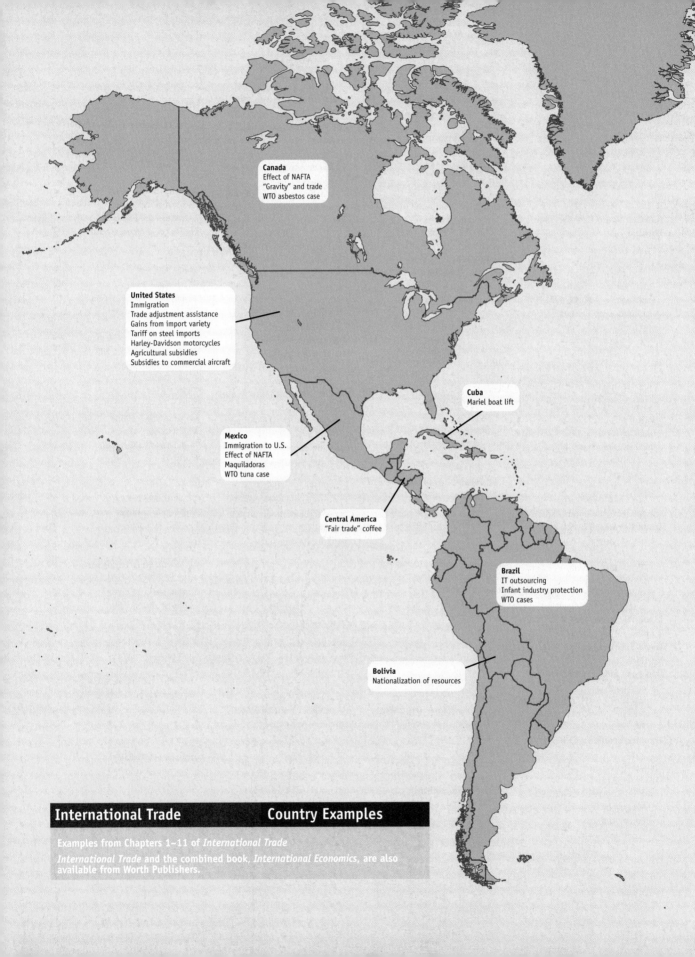

Canada
Effect of NAFTA
"Gravity" and trade
WTO asbestos case

United States
Immigration
Trade adjustment assistance
Gains from import variety
Tariff on steel imports
Harley-Davidson motorcycles
Agricultural subsidies
Subsidies to commercial aircraft

Cuba
Mariel boat lift

Mexico
Immigration to U.S.
Effect of NAFTA
Maquiladoras
WTO tuna case

Central America
"Fair trade" coffee

Brazil
IT outsourcing
Infant industry protection
WTO cases

Bolivia
Nationalization of resources

International Trade   Country Examples

Examples from Chapters 1–11 of *International Trade*

International Trade and the combined book, *International Economics*, are also
available from Worth Publishers.